*Computerized Monitoring
and Online Privacy*

ALSO BY THOMAS A. PETERS

The Online Catalog:
A Critical Examination of Public Use
(McFarland, 1991)

Computerized Monitoring and Online Privacy

by
THOMAS A. PETERS

McFarland & Company, Inc., Publishers
Jefferson, North Carolina, and London

Library of Congress Cataloguing-in-Publication Data

Peters, Thomas A., 1957–
    Computerized monitoring and online privacy / by Thomas A.
Peters.
      p.   cm.
    Includes bibliographical references and index.
    ISBN 0-7864-0706-9 (library binding : 50# alkaline paper) ∞
    1. Privacy, Right of— United States.   2. Human-computer
interaction — United States.   I. Title.
JC596.2.U5P45   1999
323.44'83'0973 — dc21

                                99-32116
                                  CIP

British Library Cataloguing-in-Publication data are available

Manufactured in the United States of America

McFarland & Company, Inc., Publishers
  Box 611, Jefferson, North Carolina 28640
   www.mcfarlandpub.com

To my parents

Acknowledgments

I wish to thank the University Libraries of Northern Illinois University for granting me a part-time research leave during the 1996–97 academic year to work on this book. The staff of the interlibrary loan department at Founders Memorial Library was very helpful and efficient in locating and retrieving needed background reading. Martin Kurth from the University of Wisconsin at Milwaukee and Amos Lakos at the University of Waterloo in Canada provided helpful comments and suggestions regarding an earlier draft. Finally, I thank my wife, Vicki, for her patience and support, and our two cats, Tess and Yma, for reminding me frequently that human-feline interactions are important, too.

Table of Contents

List of Abbreviations

AI Artificial Intelligence
AWT Average Work Time
CGI Common Gateway Interface
CLF Common Log Format
CMC Computer-Mediated Communication
CMI Computer Managed Instruction
CPM Computerized Performance Monitoring
CPMCS Computerized Performance Monitoring and Control System
CSCW Computer-Supported Collaborative Work
CWPMS Computerized Work Performance Monitoring System
DAT Digital Audio Tape
DNS Domain Name System
EDI Electronic Data Interchange
EPM Electronic Performance Monitoring (see Carayon 1993)
EU European Union
FAQ Frequently Asked Questions
FTP File Transfer Protocol
GMT Greenwich Mean Time

GUI Graphical User Interface
HCI Human-Computer Interaction
HHI Human-Human Interaction
HTML HyperText Mark-up Language
HTTP HyperText Transfer Protocol
IA Intelligence Amplification
IMC Internet Mail Consortium
IP Internet Protocol
IRC Internet Relay Chat
ISP Internet Service Provider
IT Information Technology
LAN Local Area Network
LIS Library and Information Science
LISR Library and Information Science Research
MHTML Marketing HyperText Mark-up Language
MOO MUD Object-Oriented
MUD Multi-User Dimension or Domain, originally Multi-User Dungeon
NNTP Network News Transfer Protocol

xi

OPAC Online Public Access Catalog

OPS Open Profiling Standard

P3 Platform for Privacy Preferences

PC Personal Computer

PICS Platform for Internet Content Selection

RFC Request for Comments

TGI Transaction Generated Information

TLA Transaction Log Analysis

URL Uniform Resource Locator

VDT Video Display Terminal

VRML Virtual Reality Modeling Language

W3C World Wide Web Consortium

WAN Wide Area Network

WCLA Web Client Log Analysis

WLA Web Log Analysis

WSLA Web Server Log Analysis

WWW World Wide Web

Preface

Increasingly, computers are being woven into human experience. Human-computer interaction (HCI) has become an everyday aspect of many people's lives. We use computers to accomplish a variety of quintessentially human activities, including working, learning in a formal way, shopping, and structured information seeking. One could argue that computerization has forever changed these fundamental human activities. We have begun to perform them in cyberspace — a sense of place without physical space created when human beings interact with a computer system. At the dawn of a new century and millennium, it appears that an increasing part of human existence will be realized in online environments.

Computers have not only enabled new ways to achieve and understand these basic human tasks; they also have been programmed to monitor and analyze in various ways the interaction between people and computers. This book argues that there is an ongoing but scattered and disorganized human project to use computers to monitor and analyze HCI. Projects to use computers for this purpose were born in the 1960s and spread quickly into diverse environments. The rapid development of the World Wide Web in the 1990s gave new life, direction, and urgency to the amorphous movement.

Human-computer interaction in four distinct contexts will be examined: information-seeking environments, such as online library catalogs and computer databases; formal learning environments, such as educational software; workplace computerized performance monitoring; and Internet monitoring, especially the Web, which comprehends all of the other three domains, and includes computerized monitoring of shopping behavior as well, from the display of advertisements through the consummation of the purchase.

A book-length exploration of the myriad ways computers are used to monitor HCI is necessary. I know of no earlier comprehensive overview of the topic.

Despite over 30 years of development and use in a variety of contexts, the movement to use computers to monitor HCI remains a fragmented, primitive discipline.

To better understand the threats posed by computerized monitoring, we need to grasp the potential of the practice. Unfortunately, even those who practice computerized monitoring often fail to fully comprehend and articulate its potential. This book may help readers see the similarities and enduring challenges (despite the disparate environments) related to the use of computers for this purpose. It also may encourage readers to reexamine the basic nature of HCI, and the present and future roles of computers in monitoring, analyzing, and reacting to that interaction.

Because computerized monitoring often is understood and denigrated as an insidious new form of personal privacy invasion, I explore at length the conceptual issue of human privacy in online environments. Although various computerized monitoring software tools and techniques are enumerated, my intent is to focus on the broader social, conceptual, ethical, and legal implications of the grand, generally unrecognized project to use computers to monitor HCI.

On a more practical level, this book is needed for a variety of reasons. The explosive development of the World Wide Web has led to a relatively broadly held, fairly describable notion of cyberspace. Cyberspace may develop into a viable parallel universe alongside the real world, where people can behave in the fullness of human diversity. The image of one's virtual self that emerges from computerized monitoring of one's interactions with computers may become as important as the image of the real self one projects as one walks down the street, shops in real stores, and works in a tangible, mundane environment.

Although the techniques of computerized monitoring have been advancing for over 30 years, the diffusion of Web browsing and commerce in the last three years has resulted in a phenomenal growth and rapid sophistication of computerized monitoring software and methodologies. Methods for monitoring human behavior in cyberspace are developing rapidly, as is our very sense of the basic characteristics of cyberspace. Is cyberspace more like outer space (vast, inhospitable, and noticeably empty), or, following the philosophy of Martin Heidegger, more like the ontological space that is a clearing in which Being reveals itself?

Commercial interests now are driving the development of software tools to support monitoring activities of human interactions with computers in cyberspace, particularly the World Wide Web. Although most of the computer programmers who are scrambling to meet the incredible need for Web server log analysis software seem unaware of the diverse, rich history of using computers to monitor HCI, monitoring such interaction on the Web has antecedents in mainframe, minicomputer, and stand-alone microcomputer environments. The nature of the vast hypertext that is the Web, coupled with the sophisticated front-end software tools called browsers, creates some unique challenges for people who want to monitor HCI in this environment.

Potential reasons for the noticeably slow rate of cohesion and maturation in computerized monitoring need to be explored. Those responsible for computerized monitoring projects, despite persistent criticism that the method in general demeans people and invades their privacy, remain curiously oblivious to the depth and breadth of this amorphous movement. Educators, librarians, and corporate managers by and large seem uninterested in the use of computerized monitoring in other domains. Webmasters, of course, are not sure that anything existed before the Web. Because computer monitoring is a tool — a data collection and analysis device — users of the tool often fail to step back and think about the history and potential of the tool itself. It remains to be seen if the diverse ways of monitoring HCI with computers contain enough commonality and mass to form an identifiable field of endeavor and knowledge.

I shall argue that there is an identifiable overall project to use computers to monitor HCI. Our unwillingness or inability to recognize the broader project — to see the forest for the trees — has led to some serious misunderstandings about both the positive potential and the dangers of using computers to monitor and analyze human behavior in cyberspace.

For one thing, the ethical aspects of such monitoring have never been fully articulated and explored. For many people, the notion of using computers to monitor HCI causes uneasiness. Sometimes they feel that this is an unwarranted, unregulated invasion of an individual's privacy. It somehow seems to imply a fundamental denial of our humanity. Computerized monitoring seems to treat humans as if they were automatons. It is too brutally honest. Computerized monitoring of HCI often reveals the outstanding inefficiencies of human behavior, such as trial-and-error learning. It bothers us, however, that the computer as monitor and supervisor cannot acknowledge and appreciate that, despite the inherent inefficiencies, trial-and-error learning is a significant form of human learning, perhaps especially in cyberspace, that seems to meet additional, intangible human needs.

For others who disparage computerized monitoring, the whole subject conjures images of an omniscient Big Brother watching our every move, at least to the extent that our moves involve using computers — as increasingly they do. Governments and large corporations are interested in how people behave in cyberspace, not only to detect slackers, hackers, criminals, and malefactors, but also to learn the characteristics of "normal" human behavior in that realm. That way, as the population moves increasingly online, governments can continue to govern, and corporations can continue to organize work and continue to conduct commercial activity.

As we shall explore in a later chapter, the question of privacy and computerized monitoring is complex and emotionally charged. See Kurth (1993) for an overview of some basic arguments about the ethical and legal aspects of transaction log analysis, a particular form of computerized monitoring. He argues, for example, that the online searching behavior of users of online public access catalogs should be as confidential and protected as their borrowing behavior (Kurth 1993, 102).

We need to clarify our collective mental model and sense of moral purpose concerning the use of computers to monitor HCI. Computerized monitoring is a very contentious issue. When informed about the general nature and techniques of computerized monitoring, many people tend to have immediate, strong, negative reactions. Many of the books, articles, and Web sites cited in the bibliography at the end of this book focus on the most egregious or outlandish instances of computerized monitoring. In particular, the literature on computerized monitoring in work environments is particularly susceptible to strong, semi-reflective reactions. External motives often are suggested for these extreme cases of monitoring. The government is out to get us, or some large corporation wants to turn us into brain-dead shopping zombies. One important question is how the application of computerized monitoring data affects our reaction to the entire movement.

The reassuring fact, at least for the overexcitable, is that most computerized monitoring appears to be benign. It appears that most monitoring projects are undertaken by researchers, librarians, small businesses, and webmasters, not by big corporations, the police, or the FBI. Often a computerized monitoring project begins with only a vague notion of how the results will be interpreted and applied. What motivates the mundane majority of computerized monitoring activity? Rather than techno-politico-economic plots, the primary cause may be nothing other than a will to monitor. People are inherently fascinated by the behavior of others, and computer monitoring provides a cheap, effective method for gathering information about HCI, a fascinating new type of human behavior. Add to the mix the fact that people are just beginning to understand what it means to be human in cyberspace and assorted online environments, and one has a recipe for great interest in (and anxiety about) the use of computers to monitor and analyze human-computer interaction.

The alleged dark motives behind some computerized monitoring projects, however, cannot be dismissed as unfounded and outlandish. If monitoring (including computerized monitoring) is somehow related to the need to control and garner power, the will to monitor may be a particular manifestation of the more general will to power that Nietzsche (1901) explored and articulated. Perhaps in some fundamental way these interesting little controversies (e.g., over cookie files) at the dawn of the age of online environments represent basic struggles for control over the contours of cyberspace.

Finally, although computerized monitoring has been used historically to study human behavior, the most recent developments in online environments and computerized monitoring software enable the collection of data akin to demographic data. Web server logs can record users' IP addresses, where they were immediately before visiting the Web server being monitored, and where they went immediately after visiting the Web server. This is a new type of demographic data, but it is demographic data nonetheless. The potential uses of cyber-demographic data also will be explored in this book.

My general argument is that, rather than denounce computerized monitoring of HCI as an invasion of individual privacy, we should examine it as a fundamental environmental factor in emerging online environments. For the purposes of this examination, any HCI defines an online environment. Any human-computer interaction, even simple word processing, creates a sense of cyberspace, however muted and inchoate it may be. Of course, the virtual environment created by the use of an elementary word processing program is not as complex as that created by an environment produced through the use of a cluster of VRML files, but all HCI creates in the human mind some sense of an online environment. It is a sense of space and relationships among objects, events, and entities that is different from the spatial configuration we all know in the real world.

In one sense this book also contains the confessions of a monitor — of a person who has been an instigator of computerized monitoring projects. I have been interested and involved in computerized monitoring for approximately a decade. My interest began with a fascination in how users interacted with online public access catalogs in libraries — a particular type of system in a particular type of information-seeking environment. My interest in computerized monitoring spread when I learned that Web server logs could monitor HCI in the newly emerged Web environment. As I undertook preliminary investigations that led to the writing of this book, I learned about the vast literature on computerized monitoring in work environments, as well as the smaller body of literature on the use of computerized monitoring and analysis in formal learning environments, especially the virtual environments created by computer-assisted instruction software. Despite years of interest and study, I was basically unaware of the field of computerized monitoring as a whole. My experience and reading has led me to conclude that people engaged in computerized monitoring are not amoral monsters without conscience and the basic feelings of a civilized human being. Rather, they are keenly interested in how people behave (in a descriptive, rather than normative, sense) in online environments. This book investigates many aspects of human-computer interaction, but it is at heart an exploration of possible reasons for fascination with computerized monitoring.

Tom Peters
Colchester, Illinois
Spring 1999

1

Computerized Monitoring: An Introduction

Increasingly, software itself is becoming intelligent enough to adapt to a user's preferences and habits (Copeland 1997).

When I compare how much money is invested in the technology itself versus that spent on understanding social dynamics — how human behavior evolves in these environments — it's a hugely baffling imbalance. And yet so much hinges on understanding the latter (John Hagel, quoted in Kelly 1997, 86).

It sounds simple enough. If a person wants to understand how people interact with computers, there appears to be a no more objective, efficient way to gain that understanding than to have the computer itself collect the data. The alternatives are to have the human subject self-report what is being experienced, or to have a second person gather the information, either in an unmediated fashion (e.g., staring over the user's shoulder), or a mediated one (e.g., videotaping someone using a computer). Although self-reporting could yield some interesting phenomenological insights into the human experience of interacting with computers, it is not a particularly good method for gathering objective behavioral data. Observation by another person can generate a broad spectrum of behavioral data (including both verbal and nonverbal), but it yields a data set that is difficult to quantify and analyze. If one wants to understand the dynamics of HCI, one should let the computer collect the data to be analyzed.

Perhaps the delight people take in observing human behavior is second only to the joy of naming things. The opportunity to name things (mountains, rivers, constellations, inventions), however, presents itself with some infrequency, and the rate of the emergence of namable things in the real world is in a marked decline.

Naming children is the exception that proves the rule. On the other hand, opportunities for observing human behavior are nearly limitless. The rapid diffusion of computers and computer networks into the workplace, schools, libraries, and shopping places has resulted in an explosion in the quantity and diversity of human interactions with computers.

Although practiced and refined for approximately 30 years, the use of computers to monitor HCI has not yet reached its revolutionary period. We continue to misunderstand and toy with the method. The overwhelming condition that will affect all future computerized monitoring is that, with the emergence of virtual environments, it now is easier and more efficient to alter the environment to match observed human behavior than to teach people how to survive and flourish in an essentially intractable real environment. Until now, every school was a school of hard knocks, in that the basic goal was to teach people how to adapt their behavior to the real world.

The age of the anti–Hobbes may be upon us. Human life in online environments need not be nasty, brutish, and short. Schools now are on the verge of being replaced by soft warehouses where the environment is modified to match the implied needs of the user, based on the computer's observation and analysis of the user's behavior in the virtual environment. Eventually, as computerized monitoring becomes more mature, effective, and widespread, a person in an online environment may no longer need to negotiate and compromise with that environment. The onus of learning passes from the person to the environment. When computers assume responsibility for the entire enterprise of monitoring and analyzing HCI, then modifying the computer system (and thus the resultant online environment) based on observed activity, the whole system of human education, both formal and informal, will need to be rethought and revamped. If experience is defined as the outcome of a human being interacting with an environment (which may, of course, include other human beings), in the emerging virtual world where computers are used extensively to monitor HCI, it will be the computer that gains and uses the experience, more than the human actor in that environment. The basically intractable environments of the real world will be replaced by the malleable, mutable environments of the virtual world. This is a sobering prospect.

Recently I purchased a 26-cent carpet tack-down strip at a local do-it-yourself home improvement store. Before I paid for my purchase, the check-out clerk asked for my zip code. Although she joked that it was silly to imagine I had driven very far to make such a small purchase, I sensed she had been instructed always to ask for this information. It appeared that the store was gathering some basic demographic information about its customers to link home location with the amount, time-of-day, day-of-week, and product category of purchase.

As I drove home I thought about how that brief moment of data gathering, although jovial, had been a minor intrusion into an otherwise forgettable trip to a home improvement store. What if retailers could perform such data gathering and analysis without having to intrude into the consciousness of the consumer— without interrupting one's unfettered buying behavior? This scenario already is occurring on the World Wide Web. The unobtrusive computerized observation of human behavior in online environments is a major aspect of the overall topic of this book.

That topic is easy to state and difficult to comprehend: the use of computers to monitor human-computer interaction. It is difficult to comprehend for several reasons. Definitions and boundaries of "computer," "monitoring," and "human-computer interaction" are difficult to establish and perhaps inherently mutable, with technological development acting as at least one type of change agent. The horizon of the topic also is difficult to establish. What is within the ken of this topic, and what is beyond the pale? If a bank uses a video camera containing a microprocessor and the capability of producing digital images to monitor customers' use of an automated teller machine, is that part of our topic? When I talk on a telephone or drive a new car, I am engaging in human-computer interaction, although I may be less aware that I am than when I use a microcomputer at work or at home. Computers can be as unobtrusive as unobtrusive monitoring itself. Computers have become so ubiquitous that the era fast approaches when many people (at least in certain classes of industrialized countries) will be interacting with computers to some degree most of their waking hours. Finally, the meaning of "use" needs to be explored and clarified. The vernacular question "What's the use?" that succinctly gets at the ultimate purpose of some form of human behavior is part of the challenge of comprehending this topic.

When we attempt to examine computerized monitoring of HCI in its entirety, we may be looking at a still-nascent discipline. Although computerized monitoring has been practiced for at least 30 years, it has not emerged as a recognizable technique, method, or field. Even the human monitors themselves seem unaware of the overall amorphous movement to use computers to study HCI. The teacher in the classroom, the librarian in the library, and the manager in the workplace all are engaged in computerized monitoring, but they seem unaware or uninterested in how their colleagues in other fields have tailored the movement to meet their specific purposes.

This book provides an overview of major, continuing situations in which computers monitor HCI. We need to try to obtain an overall view of the entire project of using computers for monitoring purposes. Even people deeply involved in this amorphous movement are unwilling or unable to obtain and articulate an overall view of it. Such an overview may shed some light on the ethical issues, impact, underlying motives, and potential applications of computerized monitoring. People interact with computers in learning, information-seeking, commercial, and recreational situations. We interact with computers and computer networks at school, at work, in libraries, at ATM machines, and in the brave new world called cyberspace. I shall endeavor to take a complete look at the overall growth and development of these related activities.

Universe, Galaxy, Solar System, and Planet   The subject at hand can be placed into a hierarchical context, analogous to the nested concepts of universe, galaxy, solar system, and planet. The universe we are dealing with encompasses all types of activity (including, but certainly not limited to, human behavior) and all methods of monitoring it. The universe includes both the use of computers to study other types of activity, such as traffic patterns on a stretch of road, as well as other ways of studying human behavior, such as videotaping and direct observation with the eyes. It is a big universe.

The galaxy we are dealing with encompasses all instances of human behavior, and all methods of monitoring it. The solar system of interest to us here is HCI. Although it seems to be gaining "market share" rapidly, HCI remains a small subset of all human behavior, and computerized data collection is just one of many data collection methods. In the grand scheme of things, therefore, the topic of this book is fairly focused. Nevertheless, the diversity of computerized monitoring of HCI is notable. Business organizations are using computers to monitor the job performance of employees. Library and information science researchers have used transaction logs to better understand how people look for and use information in computerized environments. Advertisers, Web site developers, and marketers are using World Wide Web server logs to better understand how people explore and use that vast hypertext. Both parents and employers have begun to use Web client logs to monitor and filter access to specific types of content. Educators use computers to collect data about student learning through the methods of computer-assisted instruction. Although these spheres of activity all involve the use of computers to monitor HCI, they seem to be more disparate than similar in their goals, methods, and outcomes. This book examines the range of uses of computerized data collection methods to study HCI.*

There are other solar systems in the galaxy of human behavior where computers are used to monitor human behavior. Electronic monitoring of human fetal development and the home detention of convicted criminals—via computerized ankle bands—are other popular uses of electronic monitoring to study human behavior, location, and development. They are beyond the scope of this book, because, although computers are being used to monitor the activities of fetuses and persons convicted of crimes, the fetuses and convicted criminals are not engaged in human-computer interaction. Another parallel development that is beyond the scope of this book (at least until the broadcast television and computer information networks begin to merge) is the development of two-way communication in cable television systems. This development will enable cable companies to engage in real-time monitoring of what is being displayed in every subscriber's household. Whether what is being displayed on the TV screen actually is being watched by someone is another matter. In many households the television has achieved the dubious status of background noise.

As we shall explore in depth, computerized monitoring raises some serious, complex privacy issues. Electronic monitoring in general does not necessarily

---

* For more general examinations of the use of computers to monitor all types of human behavior, see Lyon (1994).

involve an invasion of privacy. In some instances, electronic monitoring actually is less intrusive than direct human monitoring. For example, electronic monitoring of luggage at airports eliminates the need for direct searches of luggage and persons. The use of electromagnetic anti-theft devices on library books and consumer goods also makes costly and intrusive personal physical searches unnecessary (Marx and Sherizen 1989, 404).

Computerized monitoring has been used to study real-world behavior that is tangentially related to the human behavior of primary interest to us in the context of the topic of this book. Atlas, Little, and Purcell (1998) used transaction log analysis to study the use of a real-world online catalog flip chart at the University of Louisville Libraries. The researchers hypothesized that flip charts at the OPAC workstations would decrease the number of online zero-hit searches. They found that the physical flip charts had little effect on users' choice of search options within the online catalog (author, title, subject, etc.). In this instance, transaction log analysis was used to study human–flip chart interaction, rather than the usual HCI. It is close to our topic of interest, but not really part of it.

Now that we have situated ourselves in a universe, galaxy, and solar system, we need to explore our planet a little. The planet we will inhabit throughout this book is the use of computers to monitor HCI. The focus will be on how and what this monitoring activity reveals about human behavior and human being. If we believe in parallel universes, it would be easy to imagine another planet in that parallel universe where some computer is writing a book about the use of people to monitor computer-human interaction. If a human being is interacting with a computer, and if a computer (either the same computer involved in the human interaction or another one) is being used to monitor that interaction, we are on the planet that comprehends the subject of this book.

It can be difficult, however, to determine when a person is interacting with a computer. When I make a long distance call to a friend, computers switch and route my voice from one location to another, but it would be a strange assertion to claim that both my friend and I were interacting with a computer during our telephone conversation. If my friend and I exchange e-mail instead of engaging in a phone conversation, and if my e-mail writing, receiving, and reading were monitored by computer, we could safely say that a computer has been used to monitor a specific type of HCI. One basic prerequisite of inclusion, therefore, would appear to be direct input into a computer by at least one person involved in the HCI being monitored. Input devices, however, can range from the more familiar keyboard and mouse to the less familiar input device known as the accelerator on a motor vehicle.

Another problem with defining the boundaries of our planet is that the beginning, end, and duration of a human-computer interactive event or session can be difficult to define and identify. The vantage point is a critical component of the definition. When I browse the Web I visit many sites and file servers. As we shall explore in depth in a later chapter, the conception and perception of HCI on the Web can be radically different, depending on where the monitoring computer is.

If the server computer is functioning as the monitor, my interaction with it often is very brief and fragmented. I grab files from the server in a pattern that seems haphazard, almost illogical. If on the other hand my client computer is serving as the monitor, my interaction with it is much more smooth and logical, because it can see how my visit to one Web server site is but one component of a larger Web browsing session involving visits to many Web servers.

Proliferation of Software and Methods for Monitoring Human-Computer Interaction

Although using computers to monitor HCI began to be practiced over 30 years ago, in this decade alone the technique seems to have achieved the critical mass necessary to set off an explosion of interest. The rapid growth of the Web was the spark that set it off. Cyberspace, especially the huge space created by the growth of the vast hypertext known as the World Wide Web, is coming to be perceived as a space where human activity can be (and should be) monitored. Although users of standalone microcomputers often have remarked how their perception of the passage of time becomes both accelerated and (paradoxically) lengthened when they are "on" a computer, the widespread development of a sense in individual human beings of virtual space did not occur until many people began to use the Web. We have begun to colonize cyberspace. Communities have sprung up. Landmarks are beginning to be recognized and named. Writers and thinkers like Howard Rheingold (1993) and Stacy Horn (1998) are beginning to explore the nature, meaning, and future of online communities.

The Promise of Computerized Monitoring

Computerized monitoring of HCI holds promise both as a data collection method and as a facilitator of desired outcomes. For reasons that need to be explored, the promise of computerized monitoring rarely is fully articulated. One low-level promise of such monitoring concerns clean, reliable, objective data. Many people assume that data gathered by a computer are completely objective, assuming the computer does not malfunction. They believe that if the data are gathered unobtrusively and without the informed consent of the people involved in the HCI, neither the analysts nor the subjects can sway the type of data gathered. Swaying and prejudice at the analysis stage is another matter. At the moment of data collection, however, the data are pure, if purity is a state in which the information intended to be captured is indeed captured in a systematic way.

Computerized monitoring is important not because it represents the apotheosis of surveillance, but because it opens new possibilities regarding the ways people apply environmental information to serve their needs and interests. In real-world environments, environmental information has to be discovered — from the laws of nature on down — then translated and articulated into human knowledge before it can be of much use to us. For example, the environmental conditions and environmental knowledge that causes birds to migrate already is there in nature. If it were not there, the birds would not migrate. People, however, cannot make good use of this untranslated environmental data. Larsson (1997, 70) notes that, within the artificial context of online environments, computerized monitoring collects data in a "natural" way. We need to discover it. What we call discovery could be more properly described as a translation into human terms of data, patterns, and knowledge already there in the real world so that an uncovering of the meaning can happen for people. Human being in the real world is one long translation project. It is both natural and understandable for people to want to translate the reality of online activity into reports and glimpses that are understandable to others. One of the most fascinating aspects of the Web server log analysis software craze of the last few years is that much of the creative energy has gone into the report writing and presentation aspect of the overall movement to use computers to monitor HCI. Online human behavior is cerebral, unknown, murky, and furtive. Monitors want to shed light on the darkness virtual.

This translation process is so fundamental to our real-world being that we assume that we will continue this project in cyberspace. We assume that cyberspace will be like nature — an encrypted puzzle that needs to be decoded before it can be truly useful to us. We often read and hear that cyberspace is a lawless frontier that needs to be explored and settled, and we often accept this basic externally oriented exploration metaphor. The promise of computerized monitoring in virtual environments is that ambient environmental information will be able to be made truly useful for human beings without being translated into human terms. In cyberspace, computers are nature, and they can make sense of what is happening in virtual environments without translating it into terms comprehensible to people. Digital environments demand (or at least encourage) a new relationship between human beings and online environments. Computerized monitoring of HCI eventually will force this issue. Ultimately, computerized monitoring is an online environmental issue, not primarily a social, legal, moral, or ethical issue. By using computers to monitor HCI, we will not learn that human nature has changed, but that individual human and social responses to environmental conditions in digital environments need to change.

All of our fears about computerized monitoring rest on the assumption that the collected data will be translated into humanly knowable information that will be perusable by anyone and everyone. What we have failed to recognize is that, in its raw state, human behavioral information in cyberspace is not the same as data that has been imported into cyberspace, such as our medical, financial, educational, and legal records. Concerns about the digitization and importation of real-world information about ourselves into online environments are perhaps well-founded, but that particular data privacy issue is not the primary focus of this book. Human "behavioral residue" — the crumbs that are created, not dropped, as we work, play, and wander in online environments — has to be converted or translated to make sense to us. Even though we experience things in cyberspace, the behavioral residue of those experiences is as unintelligible to us as a chaotic crime scene in the real world. The ultimate challenge of the movement to use computers to monitor HCI is not to figure out ways to translate the data into human terms — to satisfy inquiring minds that want to know — but to figure out ways to make it useful to us without translating it into humanly intelligible form. In cyber-space, making data humanly intelligible is not a prerequisite for making it useful to humanity. This is the ultimate promise of computerized monitoring.

That is a vision for a bright, useful future for computerized monitoring, but we also need to cast a discerning eye at the history and current practices feeding the movement. Computerized monitoring can be much more than an efficient, sneaky way to gather or infer demographic information. In this fundamental way, the application of computerized monitoring data has lacked imagination, and despite the new vigor Web log analysis has introduced into the movement, the application of Web server log data may be the most unimaginative of all.

This is why it is a little misleading to call the space created by HCI a virtual environment. Cyberspace does not aspire to be like the real world. It is human beings who want to understand cyberspace as more or less familiar virtual envi-ronments, in the same way that we first wanted to understand the railroad as an iron horse and the automobile as a horseless carriage. Online environments are completely different. As soon as we realize this, we will be able to tap the sub-stantial potential of computerized monitoring.

Basic Criticisms of Computerized Monitoring   As we shall see through-out this book, many criticisms of and arguments against computerized monitor-ing have been raised. Four basic criticisms will serve as a counterpoint to the promise of computerized monitoring. First, some people have argued that col-lecting data in this manner is an invasion of privacy, and thus should not be prac-ticed, especially without the informed consent of those being monitored. The emergence of cyberspace has made personal privacy a hot topic. Second, although computerized monitoring portrays and describes online behavior in a very precise if limited way, it reveals little or nothing about human needs, satisfaction levels, and outcomes, which ultimately are more important and useful than knowledge of online user behavior. Computerized monitoring is very good and efficient at what it does, but it does not do the right thing. There is a huge chasm to leap between observed online behavior and the intentions or motives behind the observed behavior. By itself, computerized monitoring can do little or nothing to help the analyst bridge that chasm.

Third, although computerized monitoring is relatively cheap to perform, especially at the data collection phase of an analysis project, historically the out-comes and application of computerized monitoring have been very disappoint-ing. Despite the efficiencies of gathering and analyzing data, when judged on outcomes and impact, computerized monitoring as an overall grand development has not yet been worth the effort. The returns on the investment of time and tal-ent have been slow to materialize. The processes of transforming the knowledge gained with computerized monitoring into better online environments and expe-riences are far from being perfected. Finally, in spite of the insights gained into the way people interact with computers, computerized monitoring has not resulted in reliable predictive models of future human behavior during HCI. The project of the last 30 years to use computers to monitor HCI has not produced outstanding results, and it always seems to ignore the fundamental ethical issues raised by its critics.

Gains from Using Computers to Monitor Human-Computer Interaction

Although such monitoring appears to be here to stay (at least for the foreseeable future), that question is hotly debated.* It can be subdivided into two distinct questions.

We could begin by asking the broad, general question: What is to be gained by monitoring and analyzing HCI? Another cause of unease and trepidation concerning computer monitoring is ignorance about what is at stake. There seems to be a lot of vigorous activity underway, especially in the Web log analysis sphere, but the nature of the prize remains in doubt. The frantic gesticulations in the pit of the Chicago Board of Trade make sense (assuming that one accepts the world view of the traders), but the purpose and goal of computer monitoring seems less clear, at least to the average educated person, and perhaps even to the heated participants. Viewed from a distance, the frantic writing and deployment of Web server log analysis software in the last three years appears to be crazy compared to the tangible, useful outcomes to date from all that activity. The application of this newfound knowledge source is a general cause of concern.

To understand the human will to monitor, we need to ponder why we want to continuously monitor large groups of people in cyberspace when such monitoring projects rarely if ever are attempted in real-world environments. For example, it would seem silly for anyone to want to continuously track the foot paths of users of Grand Central Station in New York City. Of what possible use is it to know how many pedestrians head for track 9, rather than track 8 or track 10? One way to answer the question concerning the propensity to engage in continuous computerized monitoring is, because it is possible to do it. Computerization enables an essentially suspect human inclination to snoop. Another way to answer is because, after the knowledge is gained, it is possible to alter and individualize the very environment in which the online behavior occurred. Grand Central Station would be difficult and expensive to modify and renovate. Web sites are relatively easy. Computerized monitoring is of interest because of the basic mutability of online environments, not because of an increasing interest in human behavior, or because of a resurgence in the human will to monitor.

Another way to approach the question is to assume that the broad question noted above has been resolved, at least temporarily, in a judgment that this monitoring does achieve desirable gains. The question then becomes: Assuming that monitoring HCI is good or worthwhile, how can computers do it better or more efficiently than people? One often unstated assumption behind the disjointed computerized monitoring movement is that using computers to monitor HCI is more

---

* Some critics of computerized monitoring would rather rephrase the question as, not what is gained, but rather what is to be lost.

efficient than purely human-based monitoring, or that it produces more reliable data, because it avoids the biases and perceptual errors to which people notoriously are prone, or it produces a richer, more sophisticated data set. Computerized monitoring of HCI is more efficient, effective, and reliable than human monitoring of HCI. Stated bluntly, computer technology makes mass surveillance efficient (Linowes 1993).

Furthermore, using people to monitor HCI somehow does not make sense. When my wife observes me writing this book on our home computer, she certainly can see me typing on the keyboard, clicking on the mouse, and staring at the monitor, but, paradoxically enough, by directly observing me she has little or no pathway into the psychic, virtual space I am inhabiting while I am writing this book. She sees my activity, and perhaps with a clipboard and a quick eye she could record my digital behavior (i.e., the movement of my digits), but she really is not with me in cyberspace. Our home computer itself, however, is with me in cyberspace, precisely because it is the HCI that creates a sense of cyberspace in me. The computer is a necessary, but not sufficient, aspect of cyberspace. Computers are much better situated than humans to monitor the digital behavior of human beings in cyberspace, and are much more proficient at it. Whether or not computers can comprehend the riches and depths of the human sense of cyberspace is a related but different question that we will need to explore later.

At present, we need to mention some of the unexamined assumptions about computerized monitoring itself. Computerized monitoring often is perceived as a very quantified method of study. The process seems to be very simple. The basic units of measurement are defined, the computer software is written to capture and count the units, and the rest is a breeze. For many commentators about the overall computerized monitoring project, computerized monitoring is little more than electronic bean counting. Critics contend that, in its limited sphere of meaning, computerized monitoring can be viciously, embarrassingly accurate, but its sphere of potential meaning and influence is very small, and ultimately of not much use for improving HCI or the human condition in general. Computerized monitoring seems to be so cold, efficient, and unblinking that it demeans the humanity of those engaged in HCI. Because they look at HCI in an unfeeling way, computerized monitoring projects attempt to normalize the description of a rich, diverse, inherently inefficient and human set of events. In short, any non-human means of monitoring human behavior (in the real world or a virtual world) is bound to misinterpret and misrepresent the human activity it alleges to monitor.

Imagine a dance floor's sense of a dance. If we had the dance floor collect data about the dance, a complex human social event would be reduced by the monitoring device to so much clomping and weight distribution changes. Although what the dance floor captured about the dance would be undeniably accurate, we still could argue that, although one cannot have a dance without a dance floor, the dance floor as monitor misses the point about the real, human importance of the dance.* We could conclude, therefore, that, although computers are in a much better position than people to monitor HCI, computers are fundamentally incapable of capturing and revealing the real truth about human behavior in cyberspace. This is a serious criticism that needs to be addressed.

Computerized monitoring also can be thought of as a way to archive a series of online events for future study and analysis. Although in the early years of the movement writers such as Treu (1972) were conceptualizing about the possibilities for real-time computerized monitoring, the vast majority of computerized monitoring projects have collected and stored the data for later analysis and interpretation. Markoff (1997a) argues that, unlike archival strategies for most paper-based libraries, a complete archive of the Web would keep track of not only the content but also who has used that content. The ideal Web archive would enable future researchers to follow the paths of millions of Web surfers, noting their likes, dislikes, and communication with other netizens.

How Does Computerized Monitoring Relate to Three Broad Subjects?
An overview of the myriad ways people use computers to monitor HCI (and of the myriad issues that this sphere of human endeavor points to) must situate computerized monitoring into a context involving three established, broader topics: privacy, electronic surveillance in all forms, and the philosophy of technology.

The creation and colonization of virtual environments often is interpreted as a serious threat to accepted notions of personal privacy. The threats posed by cyberspace, however, usually focus on two areas other than computerized monitoring of HCI. Cavazos and Morin (1996, 367), for example, identify two major ways that cyberspace threatens personal privacy: through the increased possibility of illicit interception of private communication (e.g., e-mail), and through the accumulation and aggregation of increasingly accessible private data about individuals. The use of computerized monitoring to study how individuals behave in cyberspace, as opposed to what they traditionally do in real environments, such as seek medical attention, seek loans, etc., and what they deliberately communicate to others, sometimes is not even considered by privacy advocates as a major threat to individual privacy.

Computerized monitoring tends to gather data about unintentional communication, rather than intentional utterances. If two people have a conversation while walking on a wet beach, and if computerized monitoring were capable of gathering data in such a pleasant, real environment, the monitoring facility probably would focus on their footprints (patterns, directions, splaying of feet, pigeon-toed walking, implied weight, etc.) rather than on the substance of the conversation. Barmann (1997) alludes to the analogy when he states that when a person visits a Web site, he or she leaves electronic footprints. Watchdogs of traditional privacy threats tend to concentrate on protecting intentional utterances

---

* *Teenagers at a high school dance probably would add here that even the adult human monitors at the spring prom also miss the point and importance of the dance — perhaps to a degree equal to or greater than our hypothetical floor monitor.*

and intentionally revealed and gathered personal information, such as financial, medical, and educational records. One could argue, however, that in the future the more pressing issue concerning personal privacy in online environments will center on our non-verbal behavior, rather than on either our online utterances or our offline life-records.

Most computer monitoring occurs in uncontrolled settings, and those who contribute to the human–computer interactions being monitored often are unaware that their behavior is under scrutiny. The will to monitor often seems at odds with the right to privacy. The will to monitor may seek to fulfill some social need (or the needs of social groups such as governments and corporations), while the right to privacy often is understood primarily as a right held by individuals.

We need to examine briefly the idea of privacy in the context of computerized monitoring. Because such monitoring deals with the behavior of our virtual selves in cyberspace (assuming that cyberspace is defined as the sense of location — perhaps but not necessarily including a sense of spatial location — that emerges as a consequence of interacting with a computer system, particularly a network of computers), and because the idea of personal privacy developed in the real world of real selves, we need to examine what privacy may mean in cyberspace. The notion of virtual personal privacy may be in a similar stage of formation as that of cyberspace.

Privacy issues have comprised a major portion of the negative reaction to and criticism of computerized monitoring in the workplace, in libraries, in formal learning situations, and on the Web. Is it possible that this stern focus on the issue of privacy has blinded us to other potential negative outcomes of computerized monitoring? Perhaps we should understand and react to computerized monitoring more as an environmental hazard capable of tainting major portions of cyberspace, rather than as a discrete (not to mention discreet) action that violates an individual's right to personal privacy.

Computerized monitoring also needs to be placed in a broader context of electronic surveillance as a whole. The human will to monitor has resulted in a full quiver of surveillance tools. The simplest tools are our own senses. When I was young and playing kick the can with the neighborhood children in the street, and the elderly Mr. Gustafson used to monitor us from behind the curtains in his living room, to ensure that we did not tread on his lawn, he was using his eyes to monitor our young behavior, and his attempt at unobtrusive monitoring was half-hearted and ineffective. We knew we were being watched, and at times it affected our behavior, both for good and ill. The human will to monitor did not begin with the development of the electronic computer, and surveillance techniques became robust and sophisticated long before computerized monitoring emerged in the 1960s.

Because the human senses are limited and unreliable in a number of ways, people have developed surveillance tools in an attempt to satisfy this will to monitor. These tools essentially remove the human monitor from the scene of action. Many of the tools are electronic. Surveillance programs use all sorts of electronic devices (including, but not limited to, computers) to monitor many types of human activities (again including, but not limited to, HCI). Jeremy Bentham and George

Orwell did not envision another form of surveillance, perhaps more intrusive than physical surveillance of the real world. The new form of surveillance is from the inside — little brother-lurking in the digital world of computers and networks (Cavoukian and Tapscott 1995, 49). In our examination of this topic we need to explore and articulate possible distinctions between monitoring and surveillance.

In the twentieth century the power of surveillance has come to be often associated with the state. Rheingold (1993, 289–290) understands surveillance as a powerful tool, usually wielded by the state over its citizens, to confuse, coerce, and control. Electronic surveillance is invisible and unverifiable, proceeding almost automatically, yet requiring the participation of the monitored, who leave ubiquitous traces of transactional information (Lyon 1991a, 609).

The philosophy of technology is a third broad field that could serve to situate the topic of computerized monitoring. A robust subfield of philosophy has developed that addresses the philosophical issues surrounding technology. Much of the literature on the philosophy of technology deals with applied problems, such as ethics, but some of it deals with the meaning of technology in relation to fundamental philosophical problems, such as ontology. Martin Heidegger (1954), for example, sees a connection between twentieth century understanding of technology and our basic way of revealing the world. An examination of the key insights of philosophers of technology may be helpful as we try to comprehend HCI and the use of computers to study that interaction. For example, Bentham's idea of a panopticon, whereby one person, using the power of the mere possibility of unobtrusive observation, is able to control the behavior of many people, seems crucial to understanding the amorphous movement to use computers to monitor HCI. In the twentieth century Foucault (1977, 191) traced the springs of the "modern play of coercion over bodies, gestures and behaviour." Our present focus is more about the postmodern play of coercion over human behavior in online environments. What better way to exercise coercion than to modify the environment? It is much more efficient and effective than direct attempts at mind control. Virtual environments are much more malleable than real ones.

Four Basic Human Activities Amenable to Computerized Monitoring
Despite the diversity of situations and behaviors in which computerized monitoring is used, the amorphous movement has coalesced around four basic human activities: learning, working, information seeking, and Web browsing — itself a curious amalgam of seeking, learning, shopping, recreating, and sometimes working. Although these activities are not mutually exclusive, the literature on computerized monitoring certainly has developed in quadruplicate, with each literature only vaguely aware at best of the other three.

The literature about computerized monitoring on the World Wide Web has exploded in the last three years; the literature on computerized monitoring in the workplace is vast. Direct monitoring of one's work activities involves the immediate computer-assisted surveillance of what one is doing. Detailed statistics and records of an individual's computer-mediated activity produced through direct surveillance often are pieced together to provide elaborate portraits or profiles of her or his work-related behavior (Oravec 1996, 69). Electronic monitoring technologies have been seen as extensions of the traditional management prerogative to observe and evaluate the job performances of workers (Levy 1995, 12). Although it always has been the responsibility of supervisors to monitor worker performance, prior to computerization work performance monitoring was essentially personal. Individual human supervisors conducted the monitoring, and the workers were likely to know when their job performance was being observed (Marx and Sherizen 1989). Management by walking around was the norm. The key issue concerning electronic surveillance in work environments is that the nature of at least some computerized surveillance technologies permits a more extensive and (more importantly) intensive (i.e., directed to a single area or person) degree of information gathering than was possible or practical before the invention and diffusion of computers (Bryant 1995, 507).

Computerized monitoring in the workplace has been upset by the changing understanding of what a workplace is or could be in online environments. It is becoming increasingly difficult to differentiate working behavior from other human behavior, and the notion of an identifiable workplace is evaporating. The diurnal rhythms of human life no longer predict reliably when a person is "at work." In online environments, neither time nor place provide clues to the existence of human labor. Rather than refer to an identifiable workplace, perhaps we should examine work environments in general. Virtual work environments can occur wherever someone interacts with a computer for work-related purposes.

Because identifiable workplaces are being replaced by online work environments, it is becoming increasingly difficult for employers to distinguish between when an employee is on or off the job. Some employers have used the blurring of this distinction to engage in more monitoring of off-the-job employee behavior. Critics of computerized monitoring in the workplace often express fears that a perhaps legitimate management need to monitor the performance of job responsibilities has been subtly transformed into a new way to monitor the online proclivities "in toto" of employees. "As technological methods of surveillance become more powerful and less expensive, and as the social climate becomes more receptive, increased emphasis is being placed on monitoring workers, even when they are away from work, and the distinction between on and off-duty behavior is narrowed" (Marx 1987).

The published literature about computerized monitoring in libraries is substantial. Seeking information may be simply a specialized form of learning, or, conversely, learning may be just a specialized form of seeking information. The use of computerized monitoring to study the information seeking behavior of people as they interact with computerized information systems (especially online public access catalogs) goes back at least 30 years (Peters 1993, 41). The application of the findings of these studies has been difficult, perhaps in part because, compared to work and formal learning situations, the expected behavioral outcomes of information seeking are not well defined. Information seeking may be inherently inefficient and heavily reliant on trial and error techniques. The unforgiving, quantified methods of computerized monitoring may not be the best way for people to understand their own information-seeking behavior in computerized information environments. Transaction log analysis (an early, specialized form of computerized monitoring) of human information-seeking behavior has been used much more often to study command-driven, focused information-seeking behavior than the more loosely structured online human browsing behaviors that the newer online information environments seem to encourage. A fundamental criticism of computerized monitoring of information-seeking behavior is that counting keystrokes and the time between keystrokes cannot possibly capture and portray the complex, subtle decisions and behaviors of someone browsing online for information. Many seekers of information are more interested in learning and being intellectually stimulated than in finding and retrieving information as quickly and as efficiently as possible.

Computerized monitoring also can be used in formal learning situations, especially when the learning is occurring as the result of computer-assisted instruction (CAI). Computerized monitoring of HCI is a form of surveillance, and surveillance is essential to any type of formal learning process that involves teaching. "A relation of surveillance, defined and regulated, is inscribed at the heart of the practice of teaching, not as an additional or adjacent part, but as a mechanism that is inherent to it and which increases its efficiency" (Foucault 1977, 176). Because students in formal learning situations expect to be observed, monitored, tested, and evaluated, the addition of computerized monitoring modules in CAI applications does not appear to have caused widespread concern. Of the four major environments in which computerized monitoring has been extensively applied, the formal learning environment seems to have caused the least interest and controversy. Rather than be dismissively reassured by this, we should contemplate it when we examine the more controversial applications of computerized monitoring of HCI, such as monitoring employees or tracing the behavior of online shoppers.

The general history of the amorphous movement to use computerized monitoring to study HCI has been long on data collection and short on analysis and interpretation of the data, followed by a thoughtful application of the findings. The use of computerized monitoring in formal educational settings may be unique in that historically the initial goal appears to have been to use computers to analyze data. Only later was computerized monitoring implemented to collect the data. Fuchs, Fuchs, and Hamlett (1993) suggest that computerized monitoring could be used to make curriculum-based assessment part of typical practice in special education. Assessment activities would be integrated into the ongoing educational process. Beginning with preliminary tests in the late 1980s, teachers were very satisfied with curriculum-based measurement systems that used computers to both collect and analyze the data. The age of computerized proctors had arrived.

The literature on computerized monitoring in formal educational settings may be relatively small and placid because the application of the movement to this area has been so benign and in concert with earlier, pre-computer principles and practices. Fuchs, Fuchs, and Hamlett (1993) found that when computerized monitoring was used to gather data, manage it, and analyze the skills of the students being monitored, teachers could design more specific program adjustments to assist individual students experiencing difficulties. The program adjustments caused reliably greater achievement among the students than did program adjustments generated by a control group of teachers who used computers only to collect and manage the data. At least in this instance of special education, it appeared that the more computers became involved in the educational process, the better and more effective the process became. Fuchs, Fuchs, and Hamlett also found that the use of computerized monitoring and expert systems improved not only the performance of the learners in this virtual environment, but also helped the teachers (i.e., the persons involved in the analysis program) to break out from their standard instructional routines — to identify alternative teaching methods to assist students having trouble learning. One lesson of computerized monitoring projects in formal educational settings is that the human monitors also can be transformed by such a project. Computerized monitoring helped not only the actors, but also the observers. In fact, in general the benefits of computerized monitoring may have reached the analysts before they substantially reached the analyzed. They helped the analyst to see more clearly.

Browsing and shopping on the World Wide Web has become a relatively major activity in the last three years, and Internet marketers and advertisers are eager to develop computerized monitoring software to unobtrusively observe the behavior of visitors to Web sites. The development of these mechanisms, such as Web server log analysis tools and cookies files, has raised major privacy concerns. Betts (1995) warned of the concerns of privacy advocates that the Internet's culture of commercial-free, anonymous, free-wheeling net surfing was fading fast. For better or worse, the issue of privacy in cyberspace has become entwined with the commercial aspect of the Web and proprietary virtual spaces, such as America Online. The market for software capable of analyzing HCI in Web environments is large and growing. The International Data Corporation estimated that in 1997 owners of Web sites would spend $47 million on analysis software (Kirsner 1997a).

Financial and consumer behavior has gone online aggressively, and the amorphous movement to use computerized monitoring has found a huge, lucrative field of endeavor. Rochlin (1997, 75) argues that financial, stock, and commodity trading has been the first major activity to move to the edge of cyberspace. Getting and spending, we will become virtual. Browsing behavior is common to both information seeking and shopping tasks. The use of an automated teller machine (ATM) served as a prelude to future shopping activities.

Computerized monitoring of behavior in Internet environments — especially the Web — may represent the confluence of all four strains of computerized monitoring activity. On the Web it is possible to work, browse, shop, communicate, seek information, and learn. Web log analysis has the potential to provide insight into all aspects of human behavior in this particular online environment. For some mysterious reason, Web browser software, a creation of the last decade, facilitates the unobtrusive gathering of information. Why have we created these weapons of mass observation? The World Wide Web appears to be a very diverse, robust environment for online activity. As an online environment, the Web is not defined functionally. It truly, effortlessly allows people to mix business with pleasure. Harmon (1997) described it as a looking-glass world just behind the monitor screen into which employees fall with great regularity. People work, learn, seek information, browse, shop, and pursue recreational interests on the Web, often during the same online session or cyberspace experience. Some activity on the Web clearly is shopping behavior. Phil Gibbons of Bell Labs likens Web browsing to walking through a shopping mall while wearing a name tag (Levine 1997). It is no mere coincidence that the group of retailers that is striving to gain acceptance of the Web as a shopping environment is the same group that has fueled the movement to create sophisticated software programs for analyzing Web server logs to learn more about the online shopping behavior and preferences of netizens. The World Wide Web is rapidly emerging as a major browsing and shopping venue. The mouse clicks and keystrokes (collectively known as clickstreams) we make as we traverse the Web are not as ephemeral as they seem. Commercial databases transform the raw data about our online behavior into useful information that is stored for future analysis, application, sale, or barter (Eisenberg 1996).

What do these four basic activities have in common? All four of the fundamental activities are acquisitive. Those involved in them are trying to use computers to achieve or acquire something, whether knowledge, goods, or services. The four activities are not mutually exclusive. The history of computerized monitoring in work environments often is closely tied to projects to monitor and analyze the browsing and shopping behavior of consumers. Although it may be necessary and appropriate to consider workplace and consumer computerized monitoring as separate issues, the complementarity between the two deserves attention (Bryant 1995). The close link between worker and consumer certainly predates the computer revolution, at least back to the development of the assembly line, wage structure, and product pricing structure developed by the Ford Motor Company. Historically we may be witnessing a gradual shift in the attention of corporate bodies away from monitoring employees toward monitoring customers. Outputs and outcomes are becoming more vital to the health and future of corporations than the cost and efficient use of inputs, such as human labor. Rather than focus on input measures (e.g., Are they getting the most from their investment in human labor?), companies are focusing more on output and outcome measures (e.g., Are people interested in and satisfied with our goods and services? Are they finding their way to the company's Web site, and, once they enter it, are they lingering and finding what they need?). The increased degree of electronic surveillance taking place during the production process (where the thing being produced may be a product or a service) may be related to the increasingly detailed surveillance of the marketplace as a whole, and of the individual customers who collectively comprise the marketplace (Bryant 1995, 511).

The distinctions between the work environment and the home environment also are becoming blurred. As the move toward virtual business organizations continues apace, it will become more difficult to delineate the dividing line between work and home, and to determine when an employee's privacy has been violated (Barner 1996).

The study of browsing also provides some bridges across these boundaries. People browse when they shop, but some forms of browsing also are often used when they seek information and learn more about their environment. Online browsing is a fruitful area of study. Kurth and Peters (1995) provide an annotated bibliography of browsing in a variety of environments, including library shelves, retail stores, online library catalogs, hypermedia environments, and browsing among images and sounds.

One could also argue that the goal and purpose of computerized monitoring differs between formal learning and work environments on the one hand, and shopping and information-seeking environments on the other. In formal learning and work environments, the major rewards, such as passing grades and pay raises, are external to the zone of computerized monitoring per se. Computerized monitoring often serves as one method to determine the distribution of these external, real-world rewards. In information-seeking and shopping environments, on the other hand, the major rewards — information, goods, and services — are intrinsic to the computerized monitoring zone. The people behind computerized monitoring projects in information-seeking and shopping environments want the monitored subjects to behave correctly (whatever that may mean in context) because it is difficult or impossible to deliver the rewards if users do not behave correctly. Although we all know people who have received good grades and substantial pay increases despite lackluster performance on the job or in the classroom, it is difficult to imagine someone possessing lots of useful information who is a mediocre seeker of information. Beginner's luck is rare, and even more difficult to sustain. In shopping and information seeking environments the behavior and the reward are inextricably linked, and the goal of computerized monitoring is to strengthen and optimize that essential link, not to parcel out or withhold external rewards such as money and grades.

One problem with human behavior in cyberspace is that it is a relatively new phenomenon. We are not yet sure what normal behavior is in cyberspace. It is natural to try to understand observed online behavior as a cognate to more established behaviors in the real world. The early indications, however, tend to be disappointing, reminding us that we are human, all-too-human. Computerized monitoring appears to reveal human frailty, concerning both behavior methods and attempts at interaction. Flaherty (1993), for example, contains an interesting thumbnail analysis of the computer user's penchant to produce online graffiti.

People who collect and analyze computerized monitoring data appear to be on a quest to discover the tendencies, patterns, and immutable laws of human behavior in online environments. Could there actually be immutable laws about human-computer interaction lurking in these data that have not yet been discovered? The potential for data mining in this field could be very great. Conversely, we must entertain the possibility that there are no immutable laws at work here (other than the absolute limits of the people and computers involved), perhaps just a few shifting, discernible patterns. In a later chapter we will explore the possibility that, if computers assume the majority of tasks related to the collection, analysis, and application of data about HCI, the need to discern patterns and immutable laws may become moot. Computers do not necessarily need to discern patterns and laws to make sense of and use a data set. Computerized monitoring need not present its findings in a manner that is comprehensible by human beings. Although much computerized monitoring of HCI now results in some form of output or report that people interpret so that they can make some decisions about future modifications to the system, in the near future the computer may be free to complete the process of drawing conclusions and acting accordingly on its own. The computer monitoring software will not need to "translate" the results into something intelligible by people. Bailey (1996) argues that Kepler's haphazard method of inquiry was much closer to how a computer would address a problem on its own than to how a traditionally rational human being would address a problem. Now that computers have matured and diffused, Kepler's method of "mere guessing" may be more useful than orderly thought as a way to progress toward a knowledge of universals (Bailey 1996, 81). When we examine the issue of individual online privacy in relation to the movement to use computers to monitor HCI, we must entertain the notion that in the future the interaction data collected by computers may never be touched by human hands or seen by human eyes. Can a sentient online environment invade the privacy of an individual human being in that environment?

Although computerized monitoring focuses on HCI, we tend to concentrate on the behavior of the people, rather than on the behavior of the computers. Like people, computers can act both in the real and virtual worlds. Computer behavior in the real world involves such phenomena as the radiation and heat they give off and the changes in the plastic parts over time. As people in online environments, we are interested in the computer's behavior during the HCI only if there is an error, malfunction, or slowdown. Perhaps computerized monitoring as an amorphous movement should pay more attention to the computer's behavior and its capacity to behave.

In the case of computerized monitoring of HCI, we have a clear, coherent field of human endeavor that, for whatever combination of historical, psychological, and ethical reasons, is not yet self-aware. After over 30 years of activity, it remains a phantom or stealth discipline. There is a dual ignorance to be explored here. First, we need to get inside the mind of the monitor and understand why so many practitioners of computerized monitoring are unaware of the larger, amorphous movement to monitor HCI via computers. Why is this a continuously self-forgetful discipline? Second, the monitored and potentially monitored need to have their awareness raised. What is the driving idea behind the project to use computers to monitor such interaction? Perhaps this is just another high-tech outlet to our seemingly innate penchant for being snoopy about the affairs of others.

People always have wanted to obtain information about others but are reluctant to divulge it about themselves (DeCew 1997, 153). The privacy issue reveals more than one conflict between the individual and society. Both society and the individual need information to flourish, but often the desire to acquire information seems stronger than the desire to relinquish it. Perhaps the movement of computerized monitoring has not become adequately cohesive and self-aware precisely because the monitor is reluctant to have an inquisitive gaze focused on monitoring behavior itself.

Computer monitoring has achieved a state in which the same basic project — using computers to monitor HCI — is used in a variety of environments for a variety of purposes. The complexities and diversity of contemporary practices led Lyon (1994) to call this the "era of disorganized surveillance." Both the techniques and the technology have become diffused. Websters all over the world now are able to watch the online behavior of visitors to their Web sites. An omniscient, intrusive government surveillance program is not really the major threat or trend in computerized monitoring. Technological developments have enabled a relaxing of centralized, bureaucratic management, supervision, and monitoring. Computerized monitoring is not being used primarily to detect illegal activity, but to learn about normal, everyday use of computer systems. Eventually, computerized monitoring of the interaction between a person and a computer or computer network will be used to create and modify an individualized, virtual everyday environment for that specific person. We need to engage in a dispassionate examination of all computerized monitoring activity. It is not as simple as it first appears.

2

Definitions, Distinctions, Boundaries, and Horizons

There is no such thing as computer-based monitoring. Instead, there are several different practices, arranged along a continuum from less to more onerous, from less to more obnoxious (George 1996, 475).

This chapter defines some keywords, makes some necessary distinctions, and establishes boundaries and horizons.

Keyword Cluster: Monitoring, Surveillance, Intrusion   The first keyword cluster we need to examine includes the ideas of monitoring, surveillance, and intrusion. What are the different connotations and denotations of these three words? Monitoring and surveillance often are unobtrusive. Does this imply that they therefore cannot be intrusive? Is it possible to unobtrusively intrude on someone's privacy? Monitoring has a more neutral set of connotations than does surveillance.

Surveillance is often understood as sinister. One concern about the widespread practice of surveillance is that it tends to propagate more surveillance (Botan 1996, 298). The idea and practice of the surveillance of others has existed for some time, but the idea of a society or environment saturated with surveillance is of a relatively recent origin. "Surveillance society" as a phrase was first coined in 1985 by Gary T. Marx (Lyon 1994, 3). The distinction is important because it transforms our understanding of surveillance from isolated, discrete acts to a general ambiance or mood that permeates an environment. Concerns about surveillance focus not only on aspects of individual surveillance activities, but also on the general social milieu that a series of surveillance practices fosters. The social impact of surveillance activities can remain rather localized (e.g., surveillance practices can make a particular work environment feel stifling), or an entire society can be affected by widespread surveillance practices and fears.

Surveillance also has entered the public realm of everyday lives. Whereas surveillance activities used to be limited to espionage and intelligence programs, ordinary people now find themselves under surveillance in their daily routines (Lyon 1994, 4). Increasingly, everyday citizens have the wherewithal to undertake surveillance projects. In certain areas of the real world, the police often encourage citizens to engage in semi-structured surveillance projects such as neighborhood watch programs. Computerized monitoring and surveillance have little to do with intelligence work designed to catch spies and criminals. Computerized monitoring projects are more akin to neighborhood snoops, private security firms, and sanctioned neighborhood watch groups than to national intelligence gathering. Many computerized monitoring projects are small potatoes.

The mainstreaming of surveillance may be closely tied to the emergence of cyberspace. Gandy suggests that surveillance becomes legitimate and diffuses itself in a unique manner: "Surveillance works through its ability to maintain the internalization of the rules. Legislation that protects against occasional 'abuses' of the surveillance merely provides a social justification for its extension in this 'improved' form" (Gandy 1989, 73, quoted in Levy 1993).

Another important aspect of surveillance is that it relates to social order and social control. Surveillance is strongly bound up with citizens' compliance with the current social order, and it can be a means of social control (Lyon 1994, 4). Surveillance is not merely a reflex to capitalism. It is a mode of power mediation which, although displaying traits that seem to make it capable of being analyzed in accord with Karl Marx's sense of class conflict, Adorno's administered society, and Michel Foucault's disciplinary society, it cannot be reduced to any one schema (Lyon 1994, 121). The social aspect of surveillance is not entirely bad. It has a positive social function. Modern surveillance has two faces: it simultaneously serves as a means of social control and as a guarantee of the right of social participation (Lyon 1994, 33).

Rule, McAdam, Stearns, and Uglow (1980, 47) define surveillance (a neutral term) as the systematic monitoring of personal data. This definition raises a crucial question for understanding computerized monitoring as a type of surveillance: Is one's behavior part of one's personal data? The purpose of surveillance is social control. Social control entails any attempt by a person, organization, or society to render another person's or group's behavior more acceptable, predictable, or normal. The longstanding desire to be able to predict the behavior of others may have suffered a serious setback with the emergence of online behavior, perhaps not because online behavior is more complex, but rather because it is impossible to predict online behavior. Even if it were possible to predict online behavior, it may be easier to simply modify the online environment to match the behavior, rather than attempt to mold the behavior to match the environment. Online environments, as opposed to real environments, are easily changed. This simple fact presents a profound challenge to our ways of educating people.

Data surveillance — a particular form of surveillance — is the monitoring of people through their data. It provides an economically efficient method of exercising control over the behavior of individuals and societies (Clarke 1994). The data collected may be of any variety, and it may address the demographic or behavioral characteristics of either the real or virtual person. Data collected through computerized monitoring of HCI could function as a database for a data surveillance program. As defined for the purposes of this book, computerized monitoring could be conceived as a specific form of surveillance.

Monitoring is a more neutral term than surveillance. People monitor their environments and other people to detect any changes that may require corrective action. We monitor something to learn how it changes or behaves over time. If something does not change or act, there is no need to monitor it. It may be more correct to say that what we monitor is the behavior, rather than things and people themselves. For present purposes, the phrase "computerized monitoring" has been adopted so that the neutrality of the movement to use computers to monitor HCI can be maintained until many of the issues and ramifications have been explored.

The notion of intrusion has a complex relationship with the related ideas of monitoring and surveillance. One could argue that the best, most effective monitoring and surveillance is non-intrusive, if we accept as a prerequisite of intrusion that the monitored person must be cognizant of being monitored for an instance of intrusion to have occurred. Often the people who are unwitting participants in computerized monitoring activities do not even know that they are being monitored, especially in Web and computerized information-rich environments.

The very concept of intrusion is grounded in accepted social norms. If the accepted social norm in a given situation dictates that it is permissible to intrude, intrusion is impossible. A permitted intrusion is an oxymoron. A permitted intrusion is more like an act of interruption. Although the technical capabilities of surveillance technologies and their actual uses may differ, without privacy protection features built into emerging virtual social systems, intrusiveness may one day be the accepted norm (Cavoukian and Tapscott 1995, 125). One of the disconcerting long-term possibilities for all of the computerized monitoring activities described here is that computerized monitoring will become so pervasive in online environments that it will become socially acceptable.

We also need to at least question the apparent assumption by many people that most loss of personal privacy is the result of deliberate intrusion. It could be that most (or at least a significant portion) of loss of privacy and private information is the result of accidental situations. For example, on more than one occasion in my life, evidently through some malfunctioning of the telephone system, I have suddenly found myself listening to a conversation between two other, unknown people. Although the privacy of their conversation was clearly lost, I did not intentionally intrude. Not all intrusive acts, in either the online or real worlds, are premeditated and intentional. For the purposes of defining the concept of computerized monitoring and establishing boundaries, however, we should concede that only deliberate, premeditated monitoring is true computerized monitoring.

Computerized Monitoring Systems   Computerized monitoring software systems are not entirely new to the computer age, without precedent in earlier real-world environments. Just as the term "computer" used to refer to a human being rather than to a machine, so too were the tasks currently performed via computerized monitoring performed by human beings. Santos (1995, 33) briefly reviews the literature on the use of annotation by experienced transcribers as a form of "humanized monitoring," the precursor of computerized monitoring. Harris and Maurer (1994) define a computerized monitoring system as a system which automatically monitors usage of an activity or set of activities and gathers statistics based on what has been observed.

One reason computerized monitoring systems are rare is the ratio between the scope of the monitor (i.e., the types of applications from which information can be collected) and the level of information capable of being collected. As the scope of a computerized monitoring system broadens, the level of behavioral information capable of being collected diminishes, thus decreasing the value of analyzing the data. Although theoretically the most useful computerized monitoring system would be integrated with the operating system itself, the level of generalized behavioral information capable of being collected at the operating system level would be quite low (Harris and Maurer 1994).

Transaction Log Analysis   Transaction log analysis (TLA) is a three-word phrase crucial to understanding the development of the amorphous movement of computerized monitoring. The concept and practice of TLA can be broken down into at least three constituent questions: What is a transaction? What is a transaction log? What does it mean to analyze transactions or logs of transactions? Computerized monitoring of HCI is much more than a highly efficient data collection method. The intentions and techniques of analyzing the data remain human.

Transactions between people and computers are the raw material of computerized monitoring of HCI. A transaction is the event of associating a bit of data (such as a keystroke) with a precise time (Lund 1989, 15). In the realm of HCI, a transaction usually is thought of as a paired couple consisting of an action by a person followed by a reaction or response from a computer. As I depress a letter on the keyboard, the computer running a word processing program responds by displaying that letter on the screen. I type, the computer responds, and a series of transactions unfolds over time.

The history of computerized monitoring is grounded in command and response forms of HCI, with a relatively small basic unit of measurement.* As online environments become less Spartan, the computer becomes less passively responsive during HCI. Increasingly, the computer may overtly or covertly prompt

---

* See Chapter 8 on methodology for an examination of the potential basic units of measurement.

the user to perform some action. The user is reacting to a stimulus created by the computer. Command lines are being phased out of online environments. The maturation and sophistication of online environments is creating new challenges for the ongoing project to use computers to monitor HCI.

The World Wide Web has its own way of facilitating human-computer transactions. In client-server environments, the old mainframe notion of transactions does not make much sense. The client computer, in response primarily to pointing and clicking behavior by the user of the client software, is accessing files contained on the server computer. In the Web environment, an HTTP transaction is a conversation between a Web browser (the client) and the host computer (the server). It consists of an HTTP request sent by the browser, followed by an HTTP response made by the server (Stout 1997, 54). In Chapters 11 and 12 we will examine the types of computerized monitoring projects that have been undertaken using information contained in the HTTP header that is transmitted with requests and responses. Nearly all HTTP requests contain header information, even though only the request line is required. No fixed number of header lines must be included (Stout 1997, 76–77). The response from the server always contains a status line, a variable number of optional additional lines called response headers, and a variable number of lines known as entity headers. Response headers relate to any matter not directly pertaining to the requested entity (Stout 1997, 78).

There are other ways to conceptualize transactions. Computerized monitoring focuses on human-computer interactions or transactions in which information functions as the currency of the transaction. People and computers are sharing information back and forth, often in sequences of commands (or questions) and responses. Other types of transactions, such as financial transactions, exist in both the real and online worlds. Cooley, Mobasher, and Srivastava (1997) define a transaction as a semantic unit that is a grouping of individual Web page accesses. They present a general model for identifying transactions for data mining from Web log data. Goldhaber (1997) suggests that human attention will become the precious commodity of virtual environments, rather than information, cash, or anything tangible. He argues that "attention transactions" between people in cyberspace will replace monetary transactions as the basic event unit of the new economy. Although computerized monitoring traditionally has focused on the transactions among people and computer systems, perhaps in the future we should focus more on HHI (human-human interaction) in online environments.

Transactional data can be understood as a subset of all behavioral data involving people interacting with computers. One potential shortcoming with focusing on transactions is that we tend to pay more attention to the activity (and the characteristics of that activity) than to the content of the activity. Transaction analysts tend to become wildlife photographers huddled in tree blinds over salt licks, waiting to photograph animals that come to ingest the precious salt. We tend to downplay questions about where those animals came from, and where they went after they had their fill of salt. Although the behavior of animals around a salt lick is interesting in itself, often we want to place these trips to the salt lick into the broader lives of individual animals and species. Computerized monitoring projects tend to focus on online sessions as relatively self-contained happenings. It is difficult to use computerized monitoring data alone to study real-world human behavior before and after the online session.

Computerized Performance Monitoring   When computerized monitoring is undertaken in work environments, it often is referred to as computerized performance monitoring (CPM). The Office of Technology Assessment of the United States Congress defined electronic work monitoring as "the computerized collection, storage, analysis, and reporting of information about employees' productive activities" (United States Office of Technology Assessment 1987, 27). One shortcoming of this definition is that it does not encompass the study of nonproductive or inappropriate employee activities, which has been a major focus of many computerized monitoring activities in work environments. It is a prescriptive definition, rather than a descriptive one. George (1996, 460) defines CPM as "the use of computerized systems to automatically collect information about how an employee is performing his or her job."

The type of performance being monitored typically is a workplace-related performance, usually involving some sort of HCI. Grant prefers to call this activity CPMCS: computerized performance monitoring and control system. "Silicon supervisors" are computerized systems intended to track work and worker performance (Grant 1990, 1). CPMCS is a "system using computer-generated data on individual or group work for performance evaluation or planning" (Grant 1990, 6). Computerized performance monitoring systems can be designed to execute a variety or range of tasks. Some pure logging software merely collects raw performance data. Analysis of the data requires either a person or another hardware/software configuration. Other CPM systems can perform some analysis of the collected data, ranging from calculating simple sums and percentages to executing extremely complex analyses. The most advanced (or degenerate) CPM systems not only collect workplace performance data and analyze it, but also use the analysis to regulate the type and level of flow of subsequent computer-related tasks to the worker or group of workers being monitored. The use of computerized monitoring in the context of employer-employee relationships is explored at length in Chapter 9.

Aspects of Electronic Monitoring Not Covered by This Book   Several aspects and technologies of the broad electronic monitoring movement are not directly related to the topic of this book. These include videotaping or audiotaping HCI sessions, wiretapping phone conversations, telephone service monitoring, computer matching, the use of active badges, the interception or examination of employee e-mail by employers, and cable television service polling. To exclude videotaping completely from this discussion may be artificially hampering. Gibbs and Baldwin (1996), for example, have used split-screen videotaping to learn much about the way people behave during Web sessions. One half of the video screen captures the expressions, movements, and vocalizations of people as they use a graphical Web browser, such as Netscape Navigator or Microsoft Internet Explorer. The other half of the screen captures the corresponding screen and mouse pointer activity. In other words, one half of the videotape captures the real-world behavior of the user, while the other half peers into the online environment. Although this technique need not involve computers in the monitoring process itself, it may be one of the best ways to understand HCI in the realm of cyberspace known as the World Wide Web.

Wiretapping of telephone conversations usually does not involve computers in either the interaction or the monitoring activities, and it usually is used to discover some sort of illegal activity, rather than to discover how people use telephone systems.

Telephone service monitoring also is of only tangential interest to us. Electronic performance monitoring can be subdivided into two distinct but related components. Computerized performance monitoring systems are computer programs which detect any measurable employee-computer interaction. The data collected can range from the very simple (e.g., number of keystrokes made) to complex, sophisticated interpretations (e.g., informing a worker how her performance compares with the group for that hour). Service observation, on the other hand, refers to a supervisory activity of monitoring telephone transactions between employees and customers. In the service industry it is common to combine service observation and CPM (Miezio 1992, 3). Computerized work performance monitoring is continuous, while service observation is employed on a more random basis, and tends not to be mechanized at all, let alone computerized (Lund 1989, 4).

Computer matching is the practice, often undertaken by agencies of the federal government, of matching unrelated computerized files containing information about individuals to identify suspected violators of the law. Although computers are used for the analysis, we cannot claim that this is an instance in which computers are being used to monitor and analyze HCI. Computer matching is used primarily to match specific individuals to disparate real-world facts or traits (e.g., deadbeat dads who file for income tax refunds).

Active badges contain small computers that permit one person to locate another. They often are used in business and research settings. Although active badges are an application of the use of the computers to monitor human activity (or at least whereabouts), they do not concentrate on HCI activities. Active badges can be used as a form of CPM (e.g., to determine if the night watchman is making his rounds as outlined in the job description and procedures), but generally they are used to locate people in the real world, not the online world.

Cable television service polling is another tangential topic. Wicklein (1981, 18, cited in Mendes 1985, 18) describes how a two-way cable service would poll each subscriber's terminal every six seconds to determine whether the set is in use, the channel selected, and the last response button touched. Nash and Smith (1981, 45, cited in Mendes 1985, 76, note 86) claim that two-way cable service polling is conducted once every 20 seconds. If and when cable television service and online information and entertainment services meld, television service polling may become a viable component of the amorphous movement to use computers to monitor HCI.

One goal of this book is to identify all "amorphous movement" that heretofore has not been self-evident, not even to the alleged practitioners. Such goal begs several questions: Do the boundaries of the subject of this book make sense? Do the types of activities within the boundaries contain enough commonly-held characteristics to warrant looking at them as a group? Do the types of monitoring activities outside the boundaries have enough unique characteristics to warrant excluding them from the examination?

Capture Projects   Already it has been suggested that computerized monitoring of HCI is a subset of the broader electronic surveillance movement of the late twentieth century. Computerized monitoring projects also can be understood as a specific type of capture project. Agre (1994) sees a broader movement in capture projects in the twentieth century, enabled by the diffusion of computing technologies in companies and other work environments. Although Agre's notion of capture is broader than mere computerized monitoring, encompassing such things as tracking systems for parcels and other non-human objects, and active badges to locate and track human bodies in physical space, his articulation of the springs of computerized monitoring certainly warrants careful consideration and reflection. Agre sees the will to capture and analyze data as endemic to the culture of computer system design, rather than as an outlandish way of thinking imposed by big government and big business. Computerized monitoring software is a natural outcome of the early culture of computer programming. Unlike Tang and nuclear energy, it is not the windfall byproduct of big defense and aerospace projects. Agre writes:

> To summarize, the phenomenon of capture is deeply ingrained in the practice of computer system design through a metaphor of human activity as a kind of language. Within this practice, a computer system is made to capture an ongoing activity through the imposition of a grammar of action that has been articulated through a project of empirical and ontological inquiry. Advances in computer science have thus gone hand-in-hand with ontological advances. Furthermore, the phenomenon of capture also underlies the tracking systems discussed earlier. Tracking is impossible without a grammar of states and state changes and the technical means to detect the states (or the state changes) when they occur. Except in the simplest cases, this will require that the grammar be imposed through one means or another: location tracking devices, paperwork, identity cards, and so forth. The resulting technology of tracking is not a simple matter of machinery; it also includes the empirical project of analysis, the ontological project of articulation, and the social project of imposition (113).

What are the Boundaries of Human-Computer Interaction?   Because HCI is becoming such a large part of the totality of human behavior (at least among certain economic classes in industrialized countries), what are the logical boundaries of HCI covered by this book? When the phrase "human-computer interaction" is mentioned, most people probably think of a person sitting in front of a typical microcomputer, with a CPU, screen, keyboard, and mouse. Other types of HCI, however, are becoming more common. Take driving an automobile as an example. Most new cars and trucks contain numerous computers on-board. A car's driver interacts with a variety of computers. The gas pedal, steering wheel, and brake pedal serve as input devices, on a par with the keyboard and mouse during "normal" HCI. Yet it is possible to use computerized monitoring to observe such HCI. For example, freight haulers often use computers to monitor the speed, fuel consumption, engine idle time, and length of stops of commercial drivers (Levy 1995, 9).*

What are the characteristics of HCI in general? Is it like a pair of dance partners? Does someone need to lead, and is the computer user always the leading dancer? In the early days of mainframe computers and batch jobs, the computer was the faithful servant or jobber, waiting for intelligible commands from the user. Computerized monitoring, with the prospect on the horizon for smart online environments that tailor themselves for individual users, not only via up-front stated preferences but also from the computerized observation of the user's online behavior and inferred needs and desires, may be part of the general trend in the evolution of the computer revolution toward a more proactive involvement of the computer in the HCI.

Can interest in HCI become too intense? What if the truth about this interaction — assuming that there is a general truth to be revealed — needs to be cajoled, rather than crunched? The search for the characteristics of HCI can lead to a belief that there is a key characteristic of this interaction. If we could find and identify that characteristic, all HCI would make sense. We must be wary of this belief. Trying to understand HCI probably is not the same as finding the key to all mythologies. Any interaction involving human beings (either human–human interaction or human–computer interaction) is indeterminate. In trying to understand all aspects of HCI, are we really trying to rob it of its chief, perhaps redeeming, quality — its indeterminateness? Do human monitors involved in computerized monitoring projects really want to control the interaction, rather than merely facilitate it or enrich it?

Another characteristic of HCI is that the truly important activity is cerebral. The interesting activity occurs in the mind of the involved individual, not in the CPU of the computer (too predictable) or at the ends of the finger tips (too digital). Computerized monitoring cannot reveal in any definitive way whether or not the person involved in an HCI is paying attention. Both attention and intention are difficult to detect, study, and assess via computerized monitoring. This shortcoming of such monitoring is becoming more important as we diversify human input beyond alpha-numeric input via a keyboard. Whether intended or not, typographical errors usually are relatively easy to spot and correct. Mis-clicks on a mouse are much more difficult to detect, because the analyst does not have a firm grasp of the user's intent.

Despite the decades-long effort to develop graphical user interfaces and to

---

* See also Piller (1993a).

make software as user-friendly as possible, the basic rules of HCI are the same as in the early days of the ENIAC computer. Users must engage in an explicit, machine-oriented dialogue with the computer, rather than interact with the computer as they do with other people (Cooperstock, Fels, Buxton, and Smith 1997).

Why Do We Think of Human-Computer Interaction?   Authors on computer topics often state another basic concern about this way of thinking about people interacting with computers: Why do we think of human-computer interaction? When I talk on a telephone, I do not think of human-phone interaction. In the same way, when I read a book I do not often concentrate on my interaction with the book as a book (i.e., as a physical object or a text-bearing device). Rather, I try to concentrate on the contents of the book — the text itself. Although books have been used extensively for over 500 years, evidently there never has been an amorphous movement to study human-book interaction. For example, I do not keep track of how often I flip backwards (rather than forwards), examine the table of contents, or consult the subject index in the back. As the techniques for computerized monitoring of human behavior in online environments mature, it may be worthwhile to consider applying some of these new data collection and analysis techniques to corresponding human behavior (e.g., learning, shopping, and seeking information) in real environments. It may be informative to study how, in the course of reading it, a user interacts with the book as a physical object.

What Is an Online Environment?   What is an online (or computerized) environment, and what are the salient characteristics of these environments? Different real environments are easily recognized and distinguished: city and country, commercial environments and residential environments, the workplace and home. Perhaps because they are such new developments on the total human landscape, online environments are more difficult to recognize and differentiate. A comprehensive definition of a virtual environment would state that any HCI creates a virtual environment. Computer users often notice after an interactive session that they felt as if they were in a completely different environment. Time often flies by, or at the very least time is perceived differently by people online than it is in real environments.

The concept of online environment used in this book is very broad and inclusive. Any and all interaction between a computer and a human being creates an online environment. A person using a word processing program creates a rudimentary virtual space. As virtual spaces go, it is limited and denuded, but nevertheless it is a virtual space. Can a virtual environment exist prior to HCI? The tentative conclusion offered here is that the virtual environment comes into existence only when a person interacts with a computer or computer network. When the HCI ends, the virtual environment reverts to pure potentiality.

This tentative definition of online environments creates a solipsistic problem. How can more than one person exist in, perceive, and act in an online environment? When people engage in online group activities in shared online environments, such as MUDs and MOOs, they sense that the environmental features and events are shared and perceivable by all. For many online environments, however, such as online public access library catalogs, the resources are being shared (in a real-world sense) by multiple simultaneous users, but any one of the simultaneous users does not bump into or share experiences or information with other users in the online environment itself.

One crucial difference between real and online worlds is that, whereas people find themselves thrust into the real world unasked (without informed consent), they all choose at some level of consciousness to enter an online environment. The choice to enter essentially causes the online environment to come into existence for an individual. In this sense, existence in online environments is more akin to an engrossed reading of a novel than living in the real world.

Cyberspace is to the online environments as the universe is to real-world environments. The notion of cyberspace encompasses all human sense of virtual reality, and every sense of space during HCI contributes to the collective understanding of cyberspace. Although the universe contains everything, in general it is not a very useful space. The same may apply to cyberspace. Somehow we need to make cyberspace useful. Human-computer interaction may not be so much the act of exploring cyberspace as an effort to figure out how to make it inhabitable.

Rheingold (1993, 5) defines cyberspace as the conceptual space where words, human relationships, data, wealth, and power are manifested by people using computer-mediated communications. Foster (1997, 24) defines cyberspace as the conceptual space in which communication occurs. Biocca (1992) describes virtual reality as a computer-generated environment in which the user feels present. Benedikt's (1991) definition of cyberspace is appropriately enthralling:

> A world in which the global traffic of knowledge, secrets, measurements, indicators, entertainments, and alter-human agency takes on form.... A place, one place, limitless; entered equally from a basement in Vancouver, a boat in Port-au-Prince, a cab in New York.... From vast databases that constitute the culture's deposited wealth, every document is available, every recording is playable, and every picture is viewable.... The realm of pure information, filling like a lake, siphoning the jangle of messages transfiguring the physical world, decontaminating the natural and urban landscapes, redeeming them ... from all the inefficiencies, pollutions (chemical and informational), and corruptions attendant to the process of moving information attached to things.

To exist in cyberspace (or, to will cyberspace into a state of existence) implies a tacit withdrawal or rejection from the real world. Although we may not be alone in cyberspace, the act of crossing the threshold into cyberspace represents a momentary cybernetic rejection of the real world. The human being puts the real world on the back burner. The user turns his or her attention to the online environment, even though the body (especially the hands and fingers) remains actively in the attendant real-world environment. Obviously, a person in cyberspace does not leave the real world, but is mentally somewhere else, with a mind not fully focused on the real-world environment. Anyone operating in the real world who observes a person thoroughly engrossed in some form of HCI (e.g., Web browsing, word processing, or playing a computer game) can attest to the fact that, for all intents and purposes, that person is lost to the real world.

Cyberspace also poses problems for the modern idea of the state. The sheer expanse, complexity, and diversity of cyberspace — once colonized (if I may use this modern state term to describe a postmodern process) — may entirely swamp the idea of a state. This fact, if it is indeed a fact, would thwart most or all current efforts to control the use of computers to monitor HCI. As Lyman (1996) observes, cyberspace is cosmopolitan in scale, and in some respects it may transcend the direct regulative powers of any particular real-world state. Lyman (1996, 14) suggests that we should be more interested in the social origins of cyberspace than in the technological. The emergence of cyberspace cannot be understood in technological terms alone. It is a technology originally designed to use people using information as a means of asserting social control.

Cyberspace may be the first active mass medium: "Thus, cyberspace is both an intimate and a mass medium, without the intermediary institutions that might link private expression to public concerns, create intellectual continuity by preserving the collective memory or literature of a group, or create the intellectual quality that public criticism and debate might provide" (Lyman 1996, 20).

Cyberspace sounds like something out of science fiction. Imagine a human environment in which our natural notions of space and time are all confused. In this environment we definitely have a sense of place, but it does not conform to our three-dimensional space. Hypertext links have shredded that old sense of space where a straight line is the shortest distance between two points. In fact, the entire ordinal classification scheme for space — two, three, four dimensions — cannot comprehend this new sense of cyberspace.

The human sense of space in cyberspace is unusual and a little unsettling. In traditional, real-world communities and environments, people have a strong shared mental model of the sense of place, the building or village or city where human interactions occur. In virtual space, however, the sense of place requires an individual act of imagination (Rheingold 1993, 63). Virtual environments are more like trances than vacation destinations. Cyberspace is something that overcomes the individual — like sleep or a coma — rather than something that we enter and explore. Other commentators have suggested that the spatial aspects of cyberspace are overblown, unnecessary, and limiting. For example, Bailey (1996, 37) asserts that computer scientists are attempting to recycle an old fiction — the ancient fiction of space — in order to help themselves and potential users feel oriented when using the Internet.

Some thoughts and theories about the human sense of real space and place may be pertinent here. Tuan (1977) sees a psychological tension between place and space. In the real world, our human sense of place provides comfort, security, and groundedness, yet we long for space (cited in Healy 1997, 56–57).

The human comprehension of time in cyberspace also can be very disorienting and disconcerting. What is perceived as a few moments spent in cyberspace can translate into several hours in the real world. Conversely, seconds online can seem like hours, especially when one is waiting for all the files necessary to build a Web page to download. Sometimes everything in cyberspace seems to move in slow motion. Computers, on the other hand, are very adept at time-stamping. While our sense of the passage of time becomes very unreal and unpredictable during HCI, the computers are on top of it, as if this virtual town were not big enough for two entities to have a precise sense of time. Time-stamping enables a very precise reconstruction of the sequencing of online events. One of the perceived strengths of computerized monitoring is the accurate time stamping, that subsequently enables a fairly accurate reconstruction of the sequence of events.

We also need to ponder the sense of self in online environments. Wilbur (1997, 11) expresses some interesting thoughts about the sense of self in cyberspace. Many computer users seem to experience the movement into (or invocation of) cyberspace as an unshackling from the constraints of the real world — as a form of transcendence. Wilbur wonders if what we call virtual communities are cultures of compatible consumption. In cyberspace consumption is an odd sort, however, not based on finite consumable resources.* The sheep look up, and are not fed.

Being a self in the online world requires a lot of attention. Although being in cyberspace itself may be some sort of out-of-body experience, one cannot daydream or doze off in the traditional sense when in cyberspace. The girders of cyberspace are held up by human attention and cognitive load, not only at the development and programming stages, but also at the realization-through-use stage. The virtual environment will clamor or cajole for the attention of the individual. Yet in other ways, entering cyberspace is similar to falling asleep. It entails a passively willful letting go of at least a portion of one's self. Entering cyberspace is a self-induced trance.

When I am in cyberspace, I often feel either that I am anonymous, or that I can assume a false identity if I choose. I can be myself in a crowd that does not know who I am, or I can pretend to be someone (or even something) else in a crowd that still does not know who I really am. Online environments facilitate dissembling, much to the chagrin of online marketers, who attempt to use computerized monitoring to infer real-world demographic information about the visitors at a Web site. Virtual anonymity in cyberspace has been perceived by many observers as a positive social advance, compared to the real world, because we can choose not to reveal basic information about ourselves (e.g., sex, age, and race) that is difficult or impossible to conceal in the real world of real communities. The unfortunate social barriers that exist in the real world because of race, sex, age, and national origin become virtually transparent in the virtual world of cyberspace, unless and until one chooses to reveal these basic demographic characteristics to the cybercommunity. Even then, it is much more difficult in cyberspace than in the real world to verify these self-declared demographic traits.

Healy (1997) cautions, however, that we should not conclude that virtual anonymity necessarily results in diversity in social relations. Even though in

---

* *The competition for bandwidth, however, is a struggle to use finite resources.*

cyberspace individuals have greater control than in real life over the disclosure of personal details, virtual communities can be just as homogenous and exclusionary as the most upscale suburb, if not more so. The emergence of human colonies in cyberspace seems to have made the demographic ties that bind more mysterious and troubling.

To the extent that computerized monitoring of HCI is able to identify or infer the demographic characteristics of individuals, or, going a step further, to specify the identity of particular individuals, computerized monitoring seems to thwart virtual anonymity. Lockard (1997, 222) asserts that an "illusory ontogeny" prevails, whereby it appears that the explorer of cyber-regions rides alone — solitary even within unperceived electronic crowds. Existence in cyberspace is a pipeline crush, yet the individual often experiences it as a blissful, directionless solitude.

The MUDs appear to be designed specifically to facilitate anonymous online group behavior. Curtis (1997) argues that anonymity is the most significant social factor in MUDs. One could counter-argue, however, that MUDs do not really afford anonymity. True anonymity can happen only if true disclosure is possible, and if the environment (including societal aspects of the environment) allows one to be anonymous. Players of MUDs are not truly disclosing themselves. Rather, because they are playing at a self-selected otherness, they cannot attain true anonymity.

Personally Identifiable Information   A distinction needs to be made between information that identifies a person as an individual human being, as opposed to a non-human entity or a group of human beings, and information that enables its holder to personally identify a specific person. Many computerized monitoring projects merely want to distinguish the behavior of a single, unidentified individual from the welter of accumulated data. Most computerized monitoring data fall short of the threshold of constituting personally identifiable information. This fact is more common in computerized monitoring programs used in information seeking and use environments and Web environments than in workplace and formal learning situations.

Conscious Virtual Selves   One of the reasons the idea of computerized monitoring of one's online behavior can be unsettling is that such monitoring reveals aspects of the cyber-self that one may not care to see, and over which one certainly does not consciously control. Computerized monitoring does to cyber-selves what mirrors in clothing stores do to real bodies. Despite all of the chat rooms, MUDs, and MOOs, where the real-life being controls the disclosure and presentation of ideal virtual selves, computerized monitoring seems unavoidably to reveal aspects of the real self in virtual environments. Even in cyberspace, which in its own way has revived the notion of the perfectibility of human being, beneath the plasticity of virtual selves the base self lurks, manifesting itself through HCI in a way detectable only by computerized monitoring. Because most computerized monitoring data is not revealed to the actors, it does not force the real self to confront the base virtual self beneath the patina of various virtual personae we choose to create, but as an idea it does remind us that it is there, ready to be mined and analyzed.

Specific Identity   In cyberspace, the true identity of specific individuals often is not important. Often for computerized monitoring, it is not necessary to know the name and Social Security number of the individuals being monitored. All that needs to be differentiated is one individual from another.

Computerized monitoring that intends to identify named individuals (and is able to do so) has been perceived as a threat to personal identity. Critics of computerized monitoring who understand it as an invasion of a person's identity that leaves one's identity stripped and denuded see a fundamental relationship between loss of anonymity in cyberspace and loss of (or at least a threat to) one's identity.

Sense of Other Selves   One problem with understanding all of cyberspace as a public, communal area is that unless one communicates with another individual or group, one feels alone. The superficial, gut experience of cyberspace is not one of publicity and community, but of solitude.

Virtual communities are groups of people with common interests and needs who come together in virtual environments to interact in some way (Hagel and Armstrong 1997). Most netizens (i.e., citizens of online, networked communities) are drawn by the opportunity to share a sense of community with like-minded strangers, regardless of where they are physically. The physical location of those who form virtual communities appears to have little influence on membership in the community. The fascination with and widespread participation in virtual communities may stem in part from the perceived decline in the last 30 years of real communities. There may be an inverse relationship between the health of real and virtual communities.

Virtual communities can be more than just a social phenomenon. They also are economic entities. They quickly can become involved in some of the core human activities that hold the attention of computerized monitoring projects, such as formal and informal learning, seeking and sharing information, and shopping. What starts as a group drawn together by common interests ends as a group with a critical mass of purchasing power, partly thanks to the fact that virtual communities allow members to exchange information on such things as a product's price and quality (Hagel and Armstrong 1997). Hagel and Armstrong suggest that the key to exploiting virtual communities as new market opportunities is through combining content and communication. They believe that large companies can build and facilitate virtual communities in cyberspace. This new type of virtual community, however, may be little more than a rehashed company town. Nevertheless, Hagel and Armstrong focus from an economic perspective on the basic principles of successful community development.

Poster (1997, 205) notes that the Internet is more like a social space than a thing or entity. Chat rooms, MUDs, and MOOs usually are communities of real-life strangers. The sense of a common virtual society is created by the group interacting with software that simulates places and situations. Participants in collaborative digital environments experience the interactions as genuine social relationships. People who may never have met in real life experience an intense sense of community, friendship, or dislike (Lyman 1996, 18–19).

The "residents" of virtual communities are voluntary members. Unlike real communities, no one is fated to remain in a virtual community against one's will because of the facts of one's birth, economic status, family obligations, or other real-world constraints. Although such constraints may affect one's opportunity to experience the virtual life, once in cyberspace, the opportunities for community involvement and affiliation are almost limitless and primarily controlled by the individual. One consequence of the voluntary nature of virtual associations among human beings is that the associations tend to be more homogenous than heterogeneous (Healy 1997, 61).

The right of assembly takes on some interesting twists and possibilities in cyberspace. The right of virtual assembly may be one of the chief concerns of the state about the emergence of the virtual world as a parallel universe for the real world of real politics:

> No longer limited by geographical happenstance to the interaction that might develop in a town or neighborhood or workplace, individuals can free themselves from the accidents of physical location to create their own virtual places. The right of assembly, which has always been a legal guarantee, becomes more consequential as the constraints of localization give way to the unfettered opportunities of virtual association (Healy 1997, 60).

Sense of Non-Human Features   When we are in virtual environments, do we ever sense the presence of higher order features and creatures? In the real world human beings have recognized (or developed, depending on one's beliefs and perspective) a host of higher-order features and creatures that inhabit the real world along with human beings. For some, Nature is a higher order creature. For others, God, gods, goddesses, and other higher-order creatures co-inhabit the real world.

The development of cyberspace may be such that eventually it will become a fantastic, sentient environment. The environment itself would know when humans were present, remember and presently observe the behavior of both individuals and groups, then modify itself to better fit human behavior and needs. The analysis of trial and error behavior now would be done by the environment, as well as by the people involved.

Virtual environments are not planned communities. They are not wound-up clocks, playing out their predetermined destinies with a methodical series of ticks. Virtual environments are pure potentiality. They can become anything, depending on how and why we call them into being, as well as how we behave in them. Although computerized monitoring may serve as an important variable in setting the overall look and feel of an online environment (assuming the netizens of that environment are aware that a computerized monitoring system is collecting data), it is doubtful that computerized monitoring is deployed specifically to create a particular online ambiance.

What Is a Human Being?   Although at first it sounds like a silly, self-evident exercise, we need to be clear about what we mean by a human being when we think about HCI. In the names used to describe agents in online environments, often it is difficult to distinguish the human from the non-human. They often go by the same names, such as browsers, servers, and clients. A human being must be a distinct individual, but need not be identifiable. "Unidentified individual" is the term we should use to describe the entities of interest to most computerized monitoring projects. We know (or strongly suspect) that the entity is an individual person, but we do not know specific identity. Although human identity is not like an incandescent light bulb that is either on or off, we generally have a working knowledge of whether an individual involved in some behavior has been identified or remains unidentified. For our purposes, a human being occupies the middle ground between non-individualizable human behavior and the specific behavior of an identifiable, specific person. An example of non-individualizable human behavior would be the trampled, littered ground left after an outdoor music concert. Although it is obvious that people have been there, it is nearly or completely impossible to trace the actions and activities of any specific person in the crowd. An example of the behavior of an identifiable, specific person is that of a known criminal is clearly captured on videotape robbing a bank. Not only are we certain that we are witnessing the actions of an individual; we also are able to identify a specific individual. In most cases, the use of computers to monitor HCI occupies the middle ground between these two extremes. Often we can identify and study individual behavior, as opposed to group behavior, but we cannot positively identify a known individual — by name, e-mail address, fingerprint, dental records or other means.

Some information about individuals creates a situation in which an individual can be specified. Social Security numbers and the names of parents are examples. Other information about individuals indicates that we are monitoring the behavior of an individual, but the information does not enable a positive identification of a specific person. We know we are watching an individual, we know not whom. Most computerized monitoring systems and projects were designed to study the online behavior of individual human beings. Knowing the names and Social Security numbers of those observed is superfluous and does not aid and advance the analysis of the data collected via computerized monitoring. Most computerized monitoring systems do not want or need to know that I am Tom Peters (not the really famous Tom Peters — just one of the other ones), only that I am a cohesive individual who, for example, just surfed the Web for 45 minutes.

It is important to keep these distinctions in mind as we examine the issue of online privacy. Too often the ability to identify an individual as an individual is conflated with the ability to specify who that individual is. The EPIC study of privacy on the Web (Electronic Privacy Information Center 1997) labeled the most specific individual information as Personally Identifiable Information (PII), such as name or address, directly from the user. The researchers even counted e-mail addresses as PII, even though it is possible to have false e-mail addresses and it is not always clear to whom an e-mail address refers.

The question concerning humanity in cyberspace is becoming quite muddled. Not only can real people willingly assume multiple personalities in cyberspace, but human-like intelligent agents and bots have begun to populate cyberspace. A real person in cyberspace may think that she is interacting with another person, but in fact she may be interacting with a piece of software capable of acting like and presenting itself as human, at least to people. The use of intelligent agents may be a special manifestation of the movement to use computers to monitor HCI. An intelligent agent could observe how someone surfs the Web (or, in general, interacts with a computer), regarding both style and content, then go forward into a network to mimic the online behavior of the observed person, then report on the good stuff found and the good deeds performed. Intelligent agents may be a rudimentary way of cloning the actualized self in cyberspace.

Human-Computer Interaction as Lived Experience   Computerized monitoring generally views HCI from the vantage point of the computer. The interaction is portrayed as a series of discrete, time-stamped events. For the person involved in an interactive session with a computer, learning, seeking information, shopping, and (perhaps to a lesser extent) working are amorphous activities. As lived experience, the online behavior that computerized monitoring seeks to capture and dissect is very fluid and mercurial. The process of dissection tends to be disdainful of the value of the complete, whole thing. The HCI becomes most interesting and informative when one forgets that one is interacting with a computer. When an online environment manifests itself as a result of a person interacting with a computer or computer system, self-forgetfulness and self-absorption become one and the same. Total immersion in cyberspace is not unlike human sleep in the real world. It occurs only at the individual level, and only when the individual lets go of his or her hold on the real world of sensation and action.

Perhaps another way of expressing this is to observe that during at least some types of intense HCI, the person and the computer system seem to meld into one thing. They have momentarily ceased to be a distinct individual and a distinct computer that happen to be interacting. The interaction itself swallows or sublimates their separate beings. The interaction, when it becomes very intense or deep, becomes the dominant component of HCI. This situation can be very disconcerting for people. They become mesmerized or automatons. For example, George Larter (1984), an employee at Bell Canada, asserted that computerized performance monitoring systems have become nothing less than tools of harassment to make employees become the mechanical extension of the equipment.

Computerized monitoring often captures new data and generates new knowledge that is not obtainable with a direct appeal to the people who have interacted with a computer. Computerized monitoring does not wrest or divulge information that is already known by the participants. Often they do not know how many typographical errors they have made or how many Web sites they have surfed. The fact that computerized monitoring generates new knowledge (or at least reveals patterns in events that were heretofore undetectable) has important implications for computerized monitoring and personal privacy. Computerized monitoring usually does not reveal information that the individual already knows and controls by knowing and withholding further dissemination. Both the human analyst and the person involved in the HCI are equally surprised by the results of a computerized monitoring analysis of a set of online behaviors.

Motivation, Behavior, and Satisfaction Many critics of computerized monitoring point out that, although the technique is a wickedly accurate method for capturing and studying human behavior, it reveals little or nothing tangible concerning either the motivation for the observed behavior or subsequent satisfaction or dissatisfaction. Although this may be true, it still is imperative to keep the notions of motivation, behavior, and satisfaction separate and distinct. Randall (1997c), for example, erroneously conflates motivation and behavior when he asserts that because Web log files can offer no indication of the reasons behind a user's actions, they provide little useful information about the behavior of a visitor to a Web site.

New Methods for Pursuing an Old Goal Some authors suggest that the impulse of one person to monitor the work of another is ancient. People like to peer over the shoulders of their fellows and watch what they are doing. Cave artists probably had audiences. The monitoring of work has always been part of the responsibilities of supervisors. Certain human activities (oddly enough, the digging of holes in the earth comes to mind as an example) always seem to attract attention from others. Computerized performance monitoring merely makes the pursuit of the old impulse very efficient. Computerized work performance monitoring systems use computer hardware, peripheral devices, and software to perform functions normally handled by time study analysts, job tickets, timekeepers, and human supervisors (Lund 1989, 13).*

Westin (1988) also maintains that we are witnessing the use of new technology to pursue an old impulse. He observes that

> supervision of the quantity and quality of work is as old as organized work itself. Counting units produced or transactions and listening in on telephone workers' courtesy to customers and procedures being followed was widespread long before VDTs [video display terminals] and telecommunications technology arrived. Using the software capacity of VDTs to obtain transactional data provides the most objective and well-recorded basis possible for making fair evaluative decisions about the employee's performance…. To outlaw monitoring or impose a beep tone requirement would make it impossible to get performance data without intervention (Westin 1988, 5–6; quoted in Lund 1989, 21).

---

* *See also Marx and Sherizen (1986a).*

Even keystroke counting predates computerization. Early in the twentieth century mechanical keystroke counters (called cyclometers) for typewriters had been developed, along with various methods for measuring the productivity of a typist. Telephone operators have had their work aurally monitored since the 1920s (Levy 1995, 8). What makes electronic and computerized monitoring unique is, first, the sheer scale of such monitoring activities today, and, second, the extent to which the monitoring activities can be unobtrusive (Levy 1995, 8).

Basic Questions in Sequential Order   To learn more about this amorphous movement to use computers to monitor HCI, we need to ask and answer the following basic questions in a sequential order:

1. What types of computerized monitoring of human-computer interaction are occurring? Related question: what not-yet-occurring types are possible?

2. Why (i.e., for what purpose) is this monitoring occurring? What are the anticipated outcomes and applications? What are the realized outcomes and applications?

Perhaps one reason why many people are wary of (or openly against) using computers to monitor HCI is that the demonstrable benefits of this activity fall far short of the risks and trade-offs. During the first 30 years of the overall project, computerized monitoring of HCI has not produced significant, consistent outcomes.

3. Is this monitoring activity essentially good or bad? Is such a summary evaluation feasible and worthwhile? If so, whose vantage point should serve as the point of reference for this summative evaluation?

Computerized monitoring often is the only efficient way to capture these unique data about how people and computers interact. Real-world observations of such behavior simply cannot capture the same type of data. It pays to be inside the monitor. As we shall see in the next chapter, computerized monitoring has captured the attention of teachers, librarians, employers, business people of all types, and websters.

3

Participants and Interested Parties

Webmasters and their employers are interested in where people go online, how long people stay on the site or page, and what software they are using. Advertisers at the site may also be interested in demographic data on people accessing the site (Lynch 1997, 1).

Computerized monitoring of HCI probably is generally perceived as a tool of big government and big corporations. George Orwell's 1949 novel, *Nineteen Eighty-Four*, framed both the question and the literature on this topic. We must entertain the possibility, however, that Orwell made radical miscalculations. Big corporations certainly are interested (for the wrong real-world reasons, I contend) in computerized monitoring, but big government does not seem to be a major player. Big government has a penchant for (and a fairly good record of) collecting data, but its performances in successful analysis and application are infrequent. Computerized monitoring, however, may be more of a grassroots movement. It is difficult to think of your friendly teacher, librarian, webmaster, and online shop owner as providing the human motivation behind computerized monitoring, but that often is the case. Several groups have been involved in the development and implementation of computer monitoring software programs and projects. What groups have been involved, and what are the social relations among these groups? Are new groups, such as Web marketers, getting into this field? Some groups, for a variety of reasons, have abandoned this field of study. By studying the formation of these groups and the relationships among them, we may generate a better understanding of computerized monitoring. By studying the groups involved, we may be able to better understand the moral and ethical training and inclinations of the researchers, organizational administrators, network administrators, marketers, and other groups involved in such monitoring. We should bear in mind, nevertheless, that it may be unproductive and misleading to think of groups of people involved in computerized monitoring. Although the individuals involved can be sorted into professional groupings, perhaps most of the activity is being done by relatively isolated individuals and small teams. It may be erroneous to portray the development of computerized monitoring techniques as a group movement.

Computer System Designers and Operators   Historically, computer system designers and operators were the first group interested in computerized monitoring. As systems were developed that enabled HCI, and thus the human experience of cyberspace, the designers became interested in monitoring this online activity. Their focus of attention, however, was (and is) on the performance of the hardware, software, and networks, not on the human side of HCI. This group of players has an almost pure interest in the efficient, safe, and secure operation of the computer system.

Web site operators are the latter-day systems operators. They have a natural interest in understanding how the Web exists, not as a static infrastructure, but as a dynamic organism. They are the truck farmers of the vast fertile plains of cyberspace. Their vision tends to be site-centric. They really want to know how many visits their site experienced, who visited the site, where the visitors came from, and where they spent the most time at the site (Wagner 1996a). The prospect of the customization of virtual environments transforms netizens in the eyes of Web site operators from anonymous desktops into specific persons with well-defined and well-known habits and interests (Gallant 1997). Web site operators have much to gain, both in knowledge and potentially in money, from knowing as much as possible about visitors to their sites. They have combined their talents and energy with the online industry to generate the recent explosion of software and services for monitoring HCI in Web environments.

Librarians   Oddly enough, librarians may have been the second major group on the computerized monitoring scene. Librarians are interested in computerized monitoring because it helps reveal the online behavior of people as they seek and interact with information in virtual environments. Online public access library catalogs were an early form of public access computer system, long before the Internet and the Web burst onto the scene. A subset of the library community developed an ongoing research interest in the use of transaction logs to study HCI in online catalogs.

Because seeking and using information remains primarily a solitary pursuit, computerized monitoring projects in libraries tend to focus on how individual users react to (and make decisions in) information-rich and complex online environments. The social interaction between two or more users, or between users and librarians, is of much lower interest. Neither the nature of these virtual environments nor the design of computerized monitoring modules facilitates the study of group information seeking, if it exists (or will emerge in the near future) in any significant way.

Because most libraries operate as not-for-profit organizations, sometimes business applications of computer monitoring are attractive and useful to librarians. Libraries employ people whose job performances need to be evaluated. Libraries also have patrons (also known as clients or users), who share some of the needs and expectations of customers in overt business settings. Libraries also are places where people learn, so the attractions of computer monitoring in formal educational learning environments also can be useful to librarians.

Librarians have become involved in attempts to define and adopt standards for the collection, analysis, and reporting of Web usage statistics. The Web Statistics Task Force, formed early in 1997 at the first JSTOR Users Group meeting in Washington, D.C., has been working on a core set of useful data elements and mechanisms for measuring and evaluating the use of Web-based information resources (Web Statistics Task Force 1998). An organizational sponsor of the task force, JSTOR (Journal Storage) is a project to archive electronically and provide Web access to the full content of complete backruns of core scholarly journals. The task force has focused on server-side analysis of the use of content. The task force sent an early draft of its suggestions to major content suppliers of online academic information, including Encyclopaedia Britannica, SilverPlatter, Project Muse from Johns Hopkins University Press, IDEAL from Academic Press, Ovid, and JSTOR.

Publishers and Content Creators   Publishers and other content creators also have a stake in the overall project of using computers to monitor HCI involved in creating information environments. Publishers sell information content to individuals, so they want to know who is purchasing and using their content (Peek 1998). For example, Borghuis (1997) examines the shared interests of librarians and publishers in transaction log analysis. Borghuis suggests that historically, while authors and publishers have relied on hard feedback (e.g., an article is rejected or a serial subscription is canceled), libraries have tended to work with soft feedback. Feedback from the user potentially could be useful to everyone else in the information chain: librarian, publisher, and author:

> The more successfully that feedback from end users can be brought into the decision-making process of what to publish and what therefore to acquire, the higher the value of the journals produced will be and the better the library collection will be. Thus, when journals are provided in electronic form, monitoring "real-time" usage by end users will contribute to a considerable improvement of the collection development process by libraries (Borghuis 1997, 373).

Borghuis suggests that when full-text electronic journals become widely available, and when computerized monitoring of HCI within these electronic journal environments becomes widely implemented, we may experience a power shift in the information chain away from authors and publishers and toward the evaluating end users. Rather than indicating their approval or disapproval with overt thumbs-up or thumbs-down signs, they will unwittingly evaluate the information environment merely by pointing and clicking within it.

Educators   Educators adopted computerized monitoring as a new way to pursue a timeless aspect of their profession — monitoring the formal learning processes of students. Educators have a natural professional interest in monitoring, because not only are they required to teach, but also to assess student learning. Computerized monitoring can be used to facilitate various aspects or views of student learning, including mastery of content, progress of skills, and the manner and inner processes of learning.

The formal educational environment may be the least controversial one in which the movement to use computers to monitor HCI has been deployed. Students in such an environment fully expect to be monitored and tested. It is part of the milieu, part of the local social contract. The emotional highs and lows of the current academic year, punctuated by test dates, mid-terms, and final examinations, may soon be replaced by a steady state of continual computerized testing. In formal educational environments, the use of computerized monitoring may reduce the need for testing, because the computer always will monitor the learning of the individual students. Even the content, sequencing, and pacing of the learning experience in the virtual realm may be controlled by computerized analysis of learner-computer interaction.

Businesses and Business People   "A key assumption of many of these business models [about Web commerce] is the ability to capture information about users. If that information starts to be systematically abused, we will see a huge backlash around privacy, and we will see policies implemented that will make it very difficult to unleash commercial opportunities" (John Hagel, quoted in Kelly 1997).

Like educators concerned about their students, business people have an abiding interest in monitoring the performance of their employees. Unlike educators, who progress from known individuals (students) toward understanding their behavior, cognitive processes, and learning activities, business people often go from known behavior, cognitive processes, and preferences to understanding more about the individuals and groups that engaged in the known behavior and processes.

The most prolific expansion of surveillance monitoring in recent years has been undertaken not by the government, but by private sector businesses and corporations (Olson 1996, 12). Businesses were interested in such monitoring long before the advent of computer technology. Before 1913 there were mechanical keystroke counters ("cyclometers") for typewriters, and assorted methods for measuring the productivity of typists. Telephone operators have had their calls aurally monitored and their speed measured since the 1920s (Attewell 1987, cited by Levy 1993). Computerized monitoring differs from other traditional supervisory monitoring schemes in that older efforts focus on longer time periods and are not continuous (Ottensmeyer and Heroux 1991). The growth and development of the Internet and the Web, however, have spawned a cottage industry of firms that monitor Web usage, combing through personal profiles created when one visits a site, and then selling these data to marketers (Rothfeder 1997).

Much contemporary surveillance activity is commercial (Lyon 1994, 12). Computerized monitoring has been widely used in businesses employing data-entry clerks, reservation agents, insurance claims processors, and customer service agents (Betts 1991). Two primary uses of computer monitoring in business environments are performance appraisals of employees and customer tracking. Information about customers is a vital competitive asset for businesses.

Despite growing evidence that workers dislike computerized monitoring, that the anticipated productivity gains are not forthcoming, and that legislative bodies are interested in regulating computerized monitoring and other forms of workplace surveillance, electronic monitoring appears to be on the rise, compelled by forces in the workplace (Ottensmeyer and Heroux 1991). Computerized work performance monitoring is attractive particularly to the service industry in which labor is intensive and direct supervision often difficult (Grant and Higgins 1996, 213). Employers have begun to define and keep track of how employees use their personal computers, including which Internet sites they visit, for three basic reasons: productivity, liability, and politics (Rigney 1997, NE1).

Halpern (1992) estimates that more than 25 million people are electronically monitored at work. Anyone who works on a computer, an electronic telephone set, laser-scanner cash register, or other computer-based equipment is potentially subject to constant monitoring (Boss is watching 1993). In work environments, computer-based monitoring automatically records statistics about the work of an employee using a computer. Use of such monitoring is particularly prevalent among data-entry operators, because it allows the employer to count the gross number of keystrokes, the number of minutes on the machine, gross keystrokes per hour, stroke rate for each job, the number of jobs, and the number of corrections of errors (Danaan 1990, 18; cited by Levy 1993).

Susser defines electronic monitoring in the workplace as "the collection, storage, and analysis of information on employee performance using computer and/or telecommunication technology" (Susser 1988, 576; quoted in Ottensmeyer and Heroux 1991, 520). Computer-aided personnel management involves the use of computers to electronically monitor, supervise, and evaluate employee performance (Angel 1989). More generally, electronic monitoring in all of its manifestations is used to collect, store, and analyze data about a worker or group of workers (Levy 1995).

The use of computerized monitoring becomes more prevalent as tasks are broken into discrete quantifiable units that can be performed by relatively unskilled labor. The emphasis on productivity and "average work time" in areas such as telephone services represents a "deskilling" of the job, reduced autonomy and work control (Levy 1993).

Not all business people are enthusiastic about the use of computerized monitoring to learn more about employees, customers, and potential customers. Even the management ranks contain critics of the entire project to use this monitoring to observe and supervise employees. "The monitoring of employee behavior in this manner is just a lazy method for avoiding dealing with more relevant issues, such as employee empowerment and professionalism" (Taylor, Dave 1996b). Traditional negative views of electronic surveillance often express the need to regulate managerial excess. Nevertheless, most business managers and supervisors are intrigued by the prospect of computerized monitoring as a type of automated supervisory system. "The theory and practice of electronic monitoring are rooted in an ideological system which still has many adherents in management circles" (Magney 1996, 207–208). Allen (1994) asserts that the demands for greater monitoring and control come from all directions in organizations.

Business managers have discovered that computers and computer networks are double-edged swords. While computers make business organizations more efficient and nimble, they also can be abused by employees who waste time playing computer games, transmit confidential information outside the organization, or use computer networks in other inappropriate ways (Gibbs 1995). Managers now can monitor workflow and group processes in ways that ensure that even the smallest deviation from the norm or lapse in performance can be identified instantaneously by the computerized monitoring system (Gibbs 1995).

Executives and managers also are interested in use of corporate Web sites by customers and potential customers. Like any business expenditure, the resources devoted to the creation and improvement of a corporate Web site need to be justified, and Web log analysis can provide support for justifying the investment (Sheets 1998). The interest of many business people in computerized monitoring may be shifting from its potential as a way to help assess the performance of employees toward its potential to assist in a better understanding and assessment of the needs, preferences, and behavior of shoppers.* Information previously thought trivial, such as the behavior and preferences of shoppers, now has a high market value and is eagerly sought by businesses desiring a competitive edge over the competition (Lyon 1994, 45). Computerized monitoring of people shopping via computer greatly facilitates the study of shopping behavior. Only rare individuals, such as political dissidents or particularly unlucky criminals, find themselves the targets of electronic surveillance by governmental bodies, but the average individual is subject to intense electronic scrutiny by business (Brook and Boal 1995).

For the marketing segment of the business community, computerized monitoring has the aura and appeal of cold fusion. Many people in marketing perceive the Web as an excellent resource for fast, inexpensive, accurate market research (Testerman, Kuegler, and Dowling 1996, 402). Web usage analysis software is just another tool for pursuing the common business practice of tracking and measur-

---

* "Shoppers" probably is a more descriptive word than "consumers." For instance, people who browse and buy on the Web don't really consume much (other than their credit), and, for consumable purchases, we cannot be certain that the people who shop are the people who ultimately consume.

ing the effects of marketing efforts (Sheets 1998). The interactive nature of the Web makes possible new approaches to target marketing (Brodwin, O'Connell, and Valdmanis 1997). Hagel and Sacconaghi (1996) provide a concise, thoughtful overview of how and why marketing in virtual environments will be so much more precise, productive, and rewarding than the real-world marketing that both consumers and marketers love to hate.

Roth (1998) addresses the prospect of customized online environments from the perspective of the marketing industry. He wonders how marketing firms operating in online environments can draw the line between the quest for customization and invasions of privacy. At the conclusion of the second round of FTC hearings into Internet privacy in June 1997, an editorial in *The Washington Post* noted a growing realization of the enormous financial incentive pushing companies in cyberspace to exploit as much as possible these new sources of personal information (Privacy fears 1997). A Web site manager, for example, can link answers to a questionnaire to the observed behavior of the respondent, and e-mail provides an instant path back to the potential customer (Wildstrom 1996a). Marketing types need to know demographic information about individuals: age, sex, income, education, occupation, etc. (Musciano 1996a). They want to know this demographic information because there is a strong correlation between it and the way individuals shop for and consume goods and services.

For some people the Web appears to be the ultimate environment for targeting specific advertisements to specific people. Behavior reveals interests, and analysis of behavior could lead to better targeting of subsequent ad exposure. The advertising component of the virtual environment may be the first one to tailor itself to the observed behavior of specific users. Companies seeking to collect subject-oriented lists of e-mail addresses often track the postings to subject-oriented Usenet groups (Mann 1997). The Online Agency, a New York City company that creates Web sites for organizations, also operates its own site, Web Digest for Marketers, which provides a weekly summary of Web content (Jaffee 1996).

Some Web site administrators, however, think that the Web has been overblown as the perfect marketing medium. They complain that the Web is not perfect because it contains no efficient way to gather information about visitors to a site (Wagner 1997b). Ultimately, marketers want to obtain real-world information about people, not just data about their online behavior. For marketers, computerized monitoring is no more than a means to a real-world end. As the technology available to measure behavior and activity on the Web becomes more sophisticated, a balance will need to be achieved between a marketer's desire to learn the demographic and psychographic profiles of a target market and an individual's reasonable expectation to travel unobserved through cyberspace (Cooper, Lane 1996b).

Without common knowledge or consent, marketing companies have been using cookies for several years to compile minutely detailed information about the way individuals use the Internet, including the search terms typed into Web search engines, Web sites visited, Web pages viewed, and computer files downloaded

(Pfaffenberger 1997, 7). Savvy cyberspace catalogers have been using session analysis to identify new markets and customers and to determine where to focus future marketing efforts (Oberndorf 1996).

Marketing research has its own tradition and methods. Like other research fronts, however, the prospect of computerized monitoring of online human behavior is both exciting and sobering. Hagel and Armstrong (1997) state the situation and prospects well:

> In the online world, the market researcher must follow a middle path, taking advantage of the depth of information available through [virtual] communities while at the same time bringing focus to the process of data collection and analysis. On line, a plethora of data can be gathered on users' demographics: the sites they have visited; the ads they have clicked on; and, in some cases, every keystroke they have typed (on line, that is). Marketers must work with researchers to try to identify the important questions that a community alone can answer. (For example, what events or changes in product features trigger certain types of purchase? What products are traded off against one another before a purchase decision is reached?) They must then focus market research efforts on gathering and interpreting that information. If successful, the marketer will gain an advantage in its online markets that can be applied in its offline markets as well (Hagel and Armstrong 1997).

By analyzing data about the browser software, files served, modem types and speed, and the domain location of every visitor to a Web site, companies can develop profiles of virtual visitors, predict when an online shopper is likely to purchase products offered by the company sponsoring the Web site, and restructure their content, products, and online marketing plans to better capture sales in the future (Koprowski 1997).

The development of online commerce and computerized monitoring of online commercial activity has fueled the marketing dream of creating widespread one-to-one marketing. Marketers want to communicate with people on an individual basis. They want to develop markets of one, also known as one-to-one marketing. In the real world, this is virtually impossible, but in virtual environments it really is possible. Karpinski (1997) notes that the power and allure of one-to-one Web content and marketing have been obvious to marketing professionals since the Web first burst onto the scene. One-to-one marketing is a sales technique that uses information (keystrokes, destinations, and frequency of visits) users leave behind as they surf the Internet (Stahlman 1996).

Advertisers are keenly interested in computerized monitoring of HCI. They want hard, quantified information about potential customers using an advertising medium. Although random questionnaires may give a Web site manager some sense of where a Web page works and where it does not, a general visitor accounting system also is important, especially if the Web site managers hope to solicit advertisers and generate greater amounts of advertising revenue. Schweitzer (1996) contends that a Web site is valuable to an advertiser only to the extent that the site is visited and used. "For an ad-driven commercial Web site such as ours, advertisers need to know how many people saw their ad and how many people clicked on it," says Kevin Wendle, president of C|Net TV, a San Francisco company that produces technology-oriented television programs (Strom 1996c). Web sites capable of capturing information about unique visitors and presenting it in a credible way will be well-positioned to compete for online advertising revenue (Kirsner 1997a).

Like newspapers, radio, and television, the development of cyberspace largely revolves around the issue of how much money providers can and should charge advertisers for letting them promote and sell goods and services at Web sites (Jaffee 1996). Advertisers realize that with the development and emergence of the Web, they now have an advertising medium with which they can do something they have always wanted, but never been able, to do: directly measure the effectiveness of an advertisement. Because it is easy to measure ad banner click-throughs, advertisers would like to shift the normal advertising industry payment structures from impressions (i.e., the number of people who see the ad) to click-throughs from the ad banner to the advertiser's own Web site (Stout 1997, 191). This shift in focus and capabilities is the driving force behind the software frenzy to analyze how Web surfers interact with Web servers.

Advertisers are very keen on the Web, and the prospect of computerized monitoring of the online behavior of consumers has them salivating. For advertisers, the Web and other virtual browsing and shopping environments have the potential to become the best of all possible worlds. The lure of computerized monitoring of HCI for marketers and advertisers is that it rekindles the desire for perfection. "Never before have advertisers been able to interact directly with consumers, create such strong long-term relationships, exchange information and retain comprehensive consumer data — we must now make it easier for them to do these things more quickly, with the precision and depth of reporting information this new medium can provide" (Schmetterer 1997).

In the mundane world of radio, television, newspaper, and billboard advertisements, the annoyance of marketing and advertising campaigns stems from their imperfection. If a person is annoyed by an ad, the ad has missed its target — the right person at the right time with the right amount of disposable income. Of course, one could argue that the appearance of an ad at a particular time and place in an environment in itself is the annoyance, regardless of whether it is on or off target. Even in cyberspace, or especially in cyberspace, where marketers and advertisers will be able to target ads to the needs and behavior of individuals, restraint will be necessary. If computerized monitoring of HCI is able to make advertising more effective, the amount of advertising bombarding individuals may decline.

At the very least, the purpose of advertisements in Web sites and other virtual environments is to generate information about potential customers: who they are and how interested they appear to be in the product line, judging by how deeply they explore the site and how long they dwell in that virtual commercial space (Hagel and Armstrong 1997). Computerized monitoring is quickly becoming an essential aspect of online advertising campaigns.

Randall (1998a), however, questions whether the advertising industry can survive its own quest for the perfectly defined audience. He points out that the rapid growth of the U.S. advertising industry since the mid–1980s was grounded in the "knowability paradox": the less we have known about how advertising and media work, the more advertising and media there have been, and the more advertising and media have shaped and saturated American culture. The Net/Web matrix represents both the apotheosis and the death-knell for big advertising and mass media.

Monitoring of online behavior could be the apotheosis of advertising, because advertising messages could become so focused to the target audience that recipients would actually appreciate receiving advertising messages — beyond the entertainment appeal of much of today's mass media advertising. The basic foundational assumption of all of today's advertising campaigns — that identifying the demographic characteristics of individuals, then placing them in the proper group, thus targeting the advertisement to the entire demographic group — would be superceded by the ability of computerized monitoring software to watch individual users and tailor the entire online environment (including advertisements) to the individual without ever making demographic inferences.

The Web is the platonic ideal of direct marketing, and computerized monitoring is the light in the cave. Computerized monitoring will become the unacknowledged legislator of entertainment, culture, the economy, perhaps the entire kit and caboodle of online environments.

Credit bureaus are more interested in real-world information than in data about HCI. Their networks store, retrieve, and transmit this real-world credit information. Equifax of Atlanta, a leading U.S. credit bureau, hired a privacy expert from Columbia University to review its privacy protections (DeCew 1997, 151).

Perhaps the most elusive business group involved in the amorphous movement to use computers to monitor HCI has been the information aggregators, database vendors, and Internet service providers. Although published reports are extremely rare, it is easy to imagine that the online database provider DIALOG has been studying how people use and interact with their databases for years. Penniman and Dominick (1980, 23) reported years ago that none of the major commercial online service vendors (at the time, they were BRS, SDC, and Lockheed) reported the capability or utilization of computerized monitoring software to automatically determine user behavior or problems. The two authors reported that the reason given by the major database vendors for not engaging in detailed computerized monitoring (beyond usage information required for billing) was their fear of loss of customers if the customers learned that they were searching a monitored system. It is unclear if Internet service providers are governed by the same or similar fears.

Internet Service Providers (ISPs) enjoy a privileged channel in the clickstream because they have specific information, such as the names and addresses of their subscribers, as well as information about where subscribers go when using the Internet. Web site managers and ISPs could work together to deliver highly targeted demographic information to advertisers and direct marketers, providing ISPs with much-needed revenue from new lines of businesses related to this consumer information (Brodwin, O'Connell, and Valdmanis 1997).

Hagel and Sacconaghi (1996) have suggested that the proprietary virtual environment created by America Online (AOL) and other major ISPs has embedded in it rich information-capture technology platforms. It is not commonly known if AOL is capturing, analyzing, and applying this detailed usage information. Raskin (1996) speculates that although the major online services still use variable IP addressing, they soon may switch over to fixed IP addressing to facilitate the use of computerized monitoring as an online marketing tool. Bucholtz (1997) also sees great potential in computerized monitoring for ISPs. Computerized monitoring data could become for ISPs what call record analysis is for telecommunications companies. Some of the ISPs may see such data as confidential, not so much for individual customers as for the company as a whole. America Online has declined to share information about traffic within its own system (Cohen 1997a).

Visitors to Web sites carry certain demographic information into the site with them. Their IP addresses indicate where they are coming from, both geographic and domain locations (COM, ORG, EDU, MIL, etc.). An analogy would be a case in which visitors to a store in a shopping mall unknowingly have their automobile license plates sewn into the clothing on their backs, so that the sales people know where the shoppers are from without having to ask them and impede or interrupt their unfettered shopping and browsing.

Businesses as organizations and maintainers of online environments also are stakeholders in the use of computerized monitoring. Not only are they interested in using computerized monitoring to learn more about their employees, customers, and potential customers; they also need to consider computerized monitoring by other unauthorized parties as a threat to their own business operations and virtual environments.

Agre (1994, 119) suggests that the larger toolbox of capture technologies may prove suitable for less structured work as well. When the less qualitative structure of workplace interactions has been successfully submitted to automatic tracking and enforcement, it should cost less to coordinate all of these activities.

Magid (1996a) looks at the issue of computerized monitoring, not from the perspective of an invasion of individual privacy rights, but from an interest in how computerized monitoring of employees in workplace environments can lead to problems for the virtual office system.

John Hagel suggests that, if thoughtfully done, commerce in real and virtual environments can reinforce a community and extend value to the members of that community. Community and commerce are not intrinsically at odds, and the emergence of commercial activity on the Web need not be a threat to virtual communities (Kelly 1997).

For several reasons, business persons have a vested, rather than casual, interest in the movement to use computers to monitor HCI. Computerized monitoring of employees and customers has presented a fundamental challenge — ethical, technological, and economic — to the business community. Agre (1994, 121) states the situation in the broadest economic terms: the practice of data capture, of which computerized monitoring is an increasingly significant part, is instrumental to a process by which people in an economic system reduce their transaction costs, thereby transforming productive activities toward an increasingly detailed reliance upon (or subjection to) market relations, as opposed to the hierarchical relations historically common in work environments. Traditional business models may be much too constrained and conservative about exploiting the potential of computerized monitoring and other data concerning online behavior. Hagel and Sacconaghi (1996) warn that the already large gap between the amount of information captured or readily available to be captured and the actual use of that information to create economic value will grow much wider as computerized monitoring becomes widely implemented in online markets. Businesses will be trapped in a quagmire of unanalyzed data.

The Users Themselves   The users themselves are the final essential group involved in the amorphous movement to use computers to monitor HCI. Monitoring of individuals knows no age limits. Monitoring prenatal, neonatal, and infant human behavior is commonly practiced and generally accepted, as is home monitoring of convicted criminals, the sick and infirm, and the elderly. Monitoring the behavior of children and adults causes more concern. The focus of this book is on monitoring the "normal" online behavior of adults. In online information environments, most transaction log analyzers of online public access catalogs tend to see users as public users. Usually, no attempts are made to identify the users individually, or to sell them anything.

Shopping may soon be dominated by virtual environments. In online shopping environments, the users are understood as browsers, shoppers, potential customers, customers, or consumers. The use of Web server log analyses and ATM analyses tends to see users as customers or potential customers. Kevin O'Connor, the president and CEO of DoubleClick, thinks that consumers will love the pinpoint accuracy of targeted marketing on the Web. "We'll be able to get right to the individual consumer, and the individual consumer will control it and love it, because it will be private and control the cost of their products" (quoted in Williamson 1996c, 44).

In online work environments, the monitored users usually are employees. Attewell and Rule (1984) suggest that work environments where jobs already have undergone a considerable amount of de-skilling may be preferred sites for managerial systems emphasizing the electronic monitoring of behavior (cited in Magney 1996, 204). The types of jobs best suited to current electronic monitoring techniques are short-cycle production jobs involving work of a routine nature, divisible into discrete and measurable units, in which workers generally require little training, for which there is an ample supply of labor, and that make data collection straightforward and economical. Computerized monitoring of work performance is moving into higher-level jobs whose output is partly quantifiable, such as those of computer programmers, stockbrokers, and financial loan officers (Levy 1995, 10).

Organizations of all types have used computers to monitor and evaluate the work performance of employees. Computer monitoring also has been used to identify and study unproductive, prohibited, or even illegal employee behavior. Many workers and union officials consider computer monitoring to be a watchdog procedure, intended to observe a worker's activities at all times (Angel 1989).

The role of the user in computerized monitoring of online work environments remains in doubt. One question yet to be systematically explored through studies of electronic surveillance is how much input employees have in the process that leads to a decision to adopt and implement an electronic surveillance system into the workplace (Kidwell and Kidwell 1996, 12). Should employees have access to their performance data as generated by a computerized monitoring system? Should they be able to challenge the data? Hawk (1994) suggests that providing access to CPM data may significantly reduce the stress and health problems associated with CPM. Employee access also could foster a sense of fairness in performance evaluation (Hawk 1994, 955).

One possible reason why the technologies of electronic surveillance often appear to be received by employees with relative passivity is that surveillance is not experienced unambiguously by individual employees (Bryant 1995, 511). Electronic surveillance, particularly the seeming objectivity of computerized monitoring, can be both a comfort as well as a threat. The technologies that monitor the performance of employees also may provide security in an isolated part of the work area, recognition, verification, and rewards for excellent behavior or productivity, or proof that someone else is primarily responsible for problems or mistakes (Zuboff 1988, cited by Bryant 1995, 512). It all depends on how the electronic surveillance is analyzed, interpreted, and applied.

Some users are subjects in controlled experiments. Such computerized monitoring usually involves the explicit, informed consent of the users. Although many researchers prefer to use computer monitoring to study "natural" human-computer interactions in uncontrolled environments, some researchers insist that the users they study be subjects of controlled experiments who have provided informed consent to being studied in this manner.

Beyond the implicit admonition to go about one's business, the role of the observed in the amorphous movement to use computers to monitor HCI is unclear. The terms of the tacit social contract are vague. Willingly or reluctantly, wittingly or unwittingly, users collude with surveillance systems. If they object, they are unsure of the grounds for objecting (Lyon 1994, 18). If users understand that their interactions with the computer are being monitored by the computer, and if they are not offended, is their complacence caused by a judgment that such monitoring is innocuous, or do they perceive potential benefits to being monitored?

Despite the fascination with MUDs, MOOs, and chat rooms, users in online environments continue to interact more with computers than with other people. The formation of online groups and communities can be difficult, and perhaps even more difficult to sustain over a period of time. Many a listserv discussion group has withered on the vine. Most HCI can be understood as an interaction between an individual and a computer. Computers seem to be leading the way in collaboration, based on client-server architecture. Truly human collaboration in cyberspace lags. Would there be any advantage to cohesive group behavior in cyberspace? As an amorphous movement, computerized monitoring needs to do a better job of studying and facilitating group processes in online environments.

Relatively little research has been conducted on the advantages and disadvantages of enabling the monitored themselves to view their own behavior as captured and analyzed by a computerized monitoring software program. Cockburn and Jones (1996) found in their usability study of Web browsers that users often were surprised by the representation of their own behavior captured in their own history list. As a representation of their own recently-lived online experiences, it appeared alien to them. They could not predict how the history list worked (Tauscher and Greenberg 1997, 130).

The remainder of this chapter examines the various Greek choruses of the amorphous movement to use computerized monitoring to monitor HCI. These groups do not actively engage in computerized monitoring. They merely comment on the action.

Organizations, Associations, and Unions   The major clusters of parties interested in computerized monitoring and online privacy include organizations generally aligned with management and advertising interests, those generally aligned with workers and organized labor, real-world watchdog groups that have become interested in cyberspace issues, cyberspace watchdog groups that came into existence since the beginning of the computer revolution, and professional organizations, research centers, and institutes. Although this impromptu classification scheme is not exhaustive, and although some groups could be logically placed in more than one classification, the scheme can help us to make some sense of all of the interested parties.

Organizations Generally Aligned with Management   Some business organizations see attempts to control computerized performance monitoring as a threat to the vitality of American business in the online age. Lawrence Fineran, representing the National Association of Manufacturers, has said that the proposed Privacy for Workers and Consumers Act "goes to the very heart of operating a modern office, and will pretty much destroy the operation of that modern office" (quoted in Graham 1993). In his opposition to that, Fineran regarded the legislation as interfering "with the ability of modern and future equipment that can assist domestic companies in their fight to remain competitive ... otherwise the United States may as well let the information age pass it by" (Piller 1993b, 123). A representative of the National Retail Federation was reported to have described electronic monitoring as a few anecdotal horror stories (Bewayo 1996, 198, note 2).

Management groups and groups generally aligned with labor share an interest in understanding the scope of the use of computerized monitoring in work environments. Early in 1997 the American Management Association conducted a survey of major American companies to learn about their electronic monitoring practices. Approximately 15 percent reported that they review the e-mail and computer files of employees (Harmon 1997). Joanne Capritti, director at the American Management Association, sees the question concerning the monitoring of HCI in work environments as part of the evolution in the perception concerning ownership and control of personal computers in those environments (Harmon 1997).

The Computer and Business Equipment Manufacturers Association (CBEMA), based in Washington, D.C., has developed guidelines for the fair and judicious use of computerized monitoring. According to Charlotte LeGates, director of communications for CBEMA in the late 1980s, computerized monitoring reveals nothing about the quality of the activities being counted (Englander 1987). She recommended that computerized monitoring programs begin with a control or benchmarking period to establish normal levels of employee activity. The benchmark enables supervisors to study the effects of feedback, training, or productivity programs (Englander 1987). Productivity goals should be set over as long a time as possible, to allow for the usual ebb and flow of energy and production (Englander 1987).

In June 1986 CBEMA published a statement about the use of computerized performance measurement in the workplace. "CBEMA believes strongly that the measurement of work by computer is a legitimate management tool that should be used wisely" (CBEMA 1986, quoted in Lund 1989, 22). "Used appropriately, monitoring and related techniques, such as incentive pay or promotion based on productivity, can increase both an organization's effectiveness and the employee's ability to advance" (quoted in Levy 1995, 10). The CBEMA guidelines encourage employers to tell workers why and when they are being monitored by a computer. Employees should receive regular, supportive feedback and ready access to the computerized logs and reports based on their individual activity, so that the employees can spot errors (Englander 1987). Early detection of problems is one of the real advantages of statistics based on computerized monitoring. CBEMA recommends that computerized monitoring statistics not be used to raise production goals, either drastically or incrementally. They also recommend against using computerized monitoring data to heighten competition in the workplace. Production incentives can encourage reward-obsessed employees to sit too long and work too hard in front of a computer terminal, leading to an increase in illness, workers' compensation claims, and long-term production declines (Englander 1987).

Management and labor groups have been sharply divided on the effects of CPM on monitored employees and the online work environment in general. The American Society for Industrial Security (ASIS) disputes the claim that electronic monitoring in the workplace is a major cause of stress (Bewayo 1996, 194). The Society opposed federal legislation proposed by former U.S. Senator Paul Simon of Illinois that would have required employers to inform employees that they are being monitored (Halpern 1992).

Even the venerable U.S. Chamber of Commerce has issued statements on computerized performance monitoring in work environments. Peter Eide, the manager of human resources, law, and policy for that organization, has been quoted as saying that employers should have the right and responsibility to monitor the use of workplace equipment to ensure that it is not misused or used for unlawful purposes. Eide argues that employers do not purchase equipment for the free and unfettered use by employees, but rather to further the business of the company (quoted in Olson 1996, 13).

Advertising and Marketing Groups and Organizations   Advertising groups have been interested in establishing strict definitions for basic units of measurement and established procedures for reporting the use of a Web site. Early in the era of Web-based advertising the Magazine Publishers of America (MPA) pushed for a standardized method of gauging activity on the Internet. The notion of a hit is not very useful to publishers and advertisers, because it does not reveal who the users are, how long they stay at the Web site, or which part of the site they read or download (Gatusso 1995). The MPA developed a set of proposed standards for measuring the visibility of Internet ads, including these principles (Gatusso 1995):

• Ultimately, it is people, usage, and visits that matter.
• Internet sites are the most appropriate vehicles to collect such information.
• The role of any third party is to audit and validate the numbers released.
• All Internet sites selling advertising should adhere to a common standard, if they desire to be audited or validated.
• The development of methods for comparing Internet media with other media are not inherently necessary for the development of the Internet media and will not be part of this standards process.

The Advertising Research Foundation and the Coalition for Advertising Supported Information and Entertainment (CASIE) met with representatives of the new Web media industry in 1997 to attempt to settle on standards for measuring Web activity, and to help Web advertisers make real comparisons (Rich 1997a). Richard Foan, deputy chief executive of ABC and co-chair of the International Federation of Audit Bureaux of Circulations (IFABC) standards committee, has stated that he hopes the new standards of minimal measurement of Web site activity will create an international trademark and a worldwide currency that will unlock all of the wealth hidden in Web site usage statistics (Smith 1996). In mid–1997 BPA, one of the established third-party Web site auditing firms, presented the Advertising Research Foundation with an analysis of ways Web site traffic can be misreported through such things as "spider" activity, internal customer-initiated site work, and log inventory problems caused by multiple servers (Lamons 1997).

Late in 1996 the 32-member IFABC established a working committee to strive toward standardized measurement and auditing of Web site traffic (Move toward global Web audits 1996). Early in 1997 the Federation agreed to the page impression as the standard for measuring such traffic (Demery 1997). The development of this international standard probably will help advertising on the Web more than it will help computerized monitoring as a field. The commercial sector was, however, much quicker than the educational, workplace, and information provision sectors to recognize the need for standard measures and act to meet that perceived need.

In 1997 the Internet Advertising Bureau established a Media Measurement

Task Force to develop standards to enable Internet advertising firms to provide their clients with pertinent data regarding online advertisements (Schmetterer 1997).

Advertising organizations also have been trying to establish privacy policies for online commercial activity. Tob Seven from the Internet Advertising Association is a defender of the advertising and commercial applications of cookies (Kalfatovic 1997). The Coalition for Advertising Supported Information and Entertainment, formed by the Association of National Advertisers and the American Association of Advertising Agencies, is a group whose purpose was to prepare possible guidelines for measuring consumer use of the Web and other potential interactive media. It released a report in 1995 which raised as many questions as it answered. The report, *Guiding Principles of Interactive Media Audience Measurement*, featured extremely broad guidelines (Krantz 1995c). In October 1995 CASIE proposed guidelines for the measurement of Web-based advertising. The CASIE wanted the standard for multimedia measurement to be applicable across all interactive media services, non-intrusive to users, protective of individual privacy, and compliant with the basic principles of research validity (Mandese 1995). Here is one instance in which a measurement standard was developed that intended, perhaps schizophrenically, to be both non-intrusive and privacy friendly.

In 1996 the Association of Accredited Advertising Agencies released its privacy goals for electronic commerce (Beatty 1996). The goals do not appear to address the issue of the privacy of behavioral data.

The Direct Marketing Association (DMA) has created draft principles for online marketing. The principles focus on the idea of letting customers opt out (Bresnahan 1997, 71). Metromail is one of the leading members of DMA. Marc Rotenberg from the Electronic Privacy Information Center has been highly critical of DMA's Mail Preference Service, the voluntary opt-out program intended to protect the personal privacy of consumers. Late in 1995 or early in 1996 Rotenberg wrote a strongly worded letter to Christine Varney, at that time an FTC commissioner, calling for an investigation into the misuse of personal information, especially concerning minors, by the direct marketing industry (Privacy group 1996). Early in 1998, after leaving the FTC to return to the private sector, Varney concluded that, although the DMA guidelines for data protection practices are admirable, they lack a reliable enforcement mechanism, recourse for persons who believe that data about them has been collected or used without their consent, and an unqualified prohibition on the collection of data about young children (Varney 1998).

At the 1996 annual meeting of the Information Industry Association (IIA), Varney warned online businesses that if they do not restrict the collection of data from customers, especially from children, the federal government will (Wildstrom 1996a). The IIA, based in Washington, D.C., has published guidelines for fair information practices that call for the protection of "personally identifiable information" (Wreden 1997).

The online business, marketing, and advertising industry in general would rather protect the privacy of individuals in cyberspace through industry self-regulation and open standards, than through state, national, and international privacy legislation and commissions. The Information Technology Association of America (ITAA) supports a solution to the challenge of protecting privacy on the Internet that is based on technology and open standards, rather than on legislation and government regulation (Netscape, Firefly, and VeriSign 1997). The Interactive Services Association, a trade group of online companies, has created a list of voluntary guidelines for electronic direct marketing. The proposed rules are intended to keep users informed of data collecting techniques, and to give them the right to opt out of mailing lists (Rothfeder 1997). The FTC had asked the ISA to draft a privacy policy (Munro 1997).

Organizations Generally Aligned with Labor   Although labor unions eventually came to accept time and motion studies emanating from Frederick Taylor's principles of scientific management (see Chapter 4), they have taken a more critical stance toward CPM mainly because of the greatly-expanded scope of the new systems. Unlike the older, non-computerized systems of performance measurement, which typically used samples of worker behavior and productivity, the newer CPM systems enable the continuous collection of performance and behavioral data on all workers (Magney 1996, 206).

The American Federation of Labor, Congress on Industrial Organization (AFL-CIO) has focused on three objectionable aspects of the use of electronic surveillance in work environments. An AFL-CIO policy resolution passed in 1987 maintains that electronic surveillance invades workers' privacy, undermines their sense of dignity, and frustrates their efforts to perform high quality work. Because of its intrusive nature, computerized monitoring is an invasion of workers' privacy. Electronic surveillance places a single-minded emphasis on speed and other quantitative measures. Computerized monitoring also is normative. It forces individual instances of behavior toward a mean, even if the mean has been established based on an individual worker's previous performance. Workers may have bad hair days, but if they have days marked by poor performance, computerized monitoring will detect them. The AFL-CIO adopted an objective to eliminate monitoring abuses, including a total ban on secret audio monitoring (AFL-CIO 1987; quoted in Lund 1989, 36).

The Communications Workers of America (CWA) has been one of the most vocal opponents of electronic surveillance of workers (Kidwell and Kidwell 1996, 11). The CWA worked with the ACLU and 9 to 5: The National Association of Working Women to introduce legislation on CPM in four states and the U.S. Congress (Reynolds 1991, 19, cited in Baarda 1994, 13). Lund (1989) reports that grievances based on the computer system used to monitor the work of telephone operators often are made to the CWA. The CWA sponsored a research project by the University of Wisconsin to study the effects of electronic surveillance on monitored employees; it revealed that monitored workers were approximately 20 percent more likely to report severe exhaustion and fatigue, and 15 percent more likely to report severe anxiety than were workers in environments without electronic monitoring (Halpern 1992, 20). The study also suggested a correlation between constant electronic surveillance and repetitive-motion injuries, loss of control of one's job, and higher risk for coronary heart disease.

The United Food and Commercial Workers (UFCW) cautions that the same kind of computer technology that enables an employer to keep track of background information about employees also permits employers to quantify and monitor work performance (Boss is watching 1993, 135). William J. Olwell, executive vice president of the UFCW, has been quoted as stating, "Electronic monitoring plays into the age-old tendency of management to use machines as a false substitute for good supervision" (Boss is watching 1993, 135). According to Gandy (1995, 37), the International Labor Organization also has released a study about computerized monitoring.

Canadian labor unions have been very vocal in their opposition to CPM in work environments. On appeal, the Canadian Auto Workers achieved a ruling in favor of paying benefits to an employee of Air Canada airlines who had missed work because of a stress-related illness caused by supervisory involving electronic monitoring (Historic judgment 1992, cited in Baarda 1994, 13–14). Clement and McDermott (1991) described the Canadian Union of Postal Workers (CUPW) as a militant, successful union on the issue of CPM. This union has been able to restrict the measurement of postal clerks to groups of no less than ten workers. The CUPW negotiated the elimination of individual monitoring of full-time employees (Baarda 1994, 12). The CUPW has been one of the most successful unions at protecting its members from individual surveillance. Their collective bargaining agreement states that electronic surveillance can be used only to measure the productivity of a group, section, or office. Electronic surveillance cannot be used to measure individual performance (Bryant 1995, 514).

Newer organizations generally aligned with labor have come into being during the era of computerization of office work. The Coalition on New Office Technology (CNOT) is a not-for-profit Massachusetts-based organization whose purpose is to help prevent the problems and make the most of the opportunities created by computer technologies (Ottensmeyer and Heroux 1991, 521). The Coalition's newsletter is *Automated Times*.

Perhaps the most prominent new labor-oriented organization on the issue of CPM has been 9 to 5: The National Association of Working Women. In the late 1980s the group had 20 chapters and approximately 14,000 members (Kleiman 1989). This organization believes that if electronic monitoring is used, it should be used to upgrade skills, not to humiliate or brow-beat employees (Nussbaum 1992). Karen Nussbaum, executive director of 9 to 5, likens CPM to spying, which is bad management and bad labor relations (Kleiman 1989). According to Nussbaum, workers feel frustrated with CPM because they cannot explain to a computer printout what they really were doing during monitoring (Kleiman 1989).

The 9 to 5 organization (1985) identified at least six major abuses that CPM visits upon monitored workers. It invades privacy, such as bathroom breaks and personal time during the normal working day; performance evaluations based upon

CPM data are unfair to workers, primarily because the data upon which the evaluations are based often are not made available to workers; it can lead to production speed ups; it reduces worker control (because after the introduction of computerized monitoring, managers realize an increased span of control) and human contact. Computerized monitoring also increases worker stress and is a bad management practice. Computerized monitoring tends to Taylorize the office workplace environment.(See Chapter 4 for a discussion of Taylorism.)

Real-World Watchdog Groups   Several watchdog groups that came into existence over real-world issues have since become interested in the issue of civil rights of individuals in cyberspace. The American Civil Liberties Union (http://www. aclu.org) has been most interested in computerized work performance measurement. In general, the ACLU opposes computerized monitoring in work environments (Ottensmeyer and Heroux 1991). In 1993 Lewis Maltby was the director of the ACLU's national workplace rights office (Graham 1993). In the mid–90s he was the director of the ACLU task force on civil liberties in the workplace. Although Maltby admits that in today's highly-computerized workplace, some form of computerized monitoring is necessary, the question of civil liberties arises in how an organization undertakes a monitoring project or system. Maltby says that the ACLU encourages employers to be open and honest with employees regarding performance monitoring systems and practices (Burger 1995). The ACLU has a Project on Privacy and Technology. See also Goldman (1991) for an essay articulating the ACLU's position on individual privacy.

The Center for Media Education (CME) (http://www.cme.org/) is a nonprofit group dedicated to improving electronic media, especially when HCI involves children. Kathryn Montgomery, president of CME at the time of this writing, has asked the Federal Trade Commission to require Web sites designed for children to obtain verifiable consent from parents before collecting information, to disclose to adults what data are being gathered, how they will be used, and who will have access to them (Eckhouse 1997).

The Privacy Rights Clearinghouse and the U.S. Privacy Council (Koning 1996) also have been active on this issue. The Privacy Rights Clearinghouse is located in San Diego (Bresnahan 1997, 72).

Cyberspace Watchdog Groups   Some computer watchdog groups have come into being during the online era. They tend to focus almost exclusively on social, legal, and ethical issues related to the computerization of society and social relationships.

Computer Professionals for Social Responsibility (CPSR) (http://www.cpsr. org/cpsr) is located in Palo Alto. According to executive director Audrie Krause, Internet monitoring software is different from other ways of using computers to monitor employee activities because most users of the Internet are professionals. The CPSR is formulating suggestions for socially responsible ways for organizations to regulate the Internet activities of their employees (Abate 1996). Computer Professionals for Social Responsibility has produced a five-page white paper, "Electronic Privacy Guidelines," available at the group's Web site (http://www.cpsr.org/ home.html) (Titus 1996).

The debate about CPM does have a class component. Traditionally, workers who were routinely subjected to it were on the lower end of the wage, education, and class structure. Often they worked less than full-time. Now that CPM is spreading up the class ladder, concerns are increasing.

The Center for Democracy and Technology (CDT) (www.cdt.org) is an active supporter of the proposed Communications Privacy and Consumer Empowerment Act, introduced by Congressman Ed Markey, a Democrat from Massachusetts, in June 1996. In a press release, the CDT affirmed its belief that

> the development and implementation of technologies that empower users of inter-active communications media [e.g., the Web] to affirmatively control personal information can fundamentally shift the balance of power between the individual and those seeking information. CDT believes this technological shift is possible and necessary, and offers us an unprecedented opportunity to advance individual privacy (CDT press release 1996a).

A major software development driven by altruism, however, is unlikely.

The CDT supports the development of individual control technologies, such as the Platform for Internet Content Selection, Cyber Patrol, and SurfWatch, to enable individuals to control information about themselves during interaction with online sites (CDT press release 1996a). The CDT Web site also contains a privacy demonstration page that reveals to visitors how computers can be used to unobtrusively monitor human-computer interaction in the Web environment (Eckhouse 1997).

Jerry Berman, the executive director of the Center for Democracy and Technology in Washington, D.C., notes that the Net is a self-correcting social environment (Weber 1996). The prospect raised in this book involves the use of computerized monitoring data as a basis for a technologically self-modifying virtual environment. If this comes to pass, will this new virtual environment preclude and replace the self-correcting work of any social environment, real or virtual? Computerized monitoring could be used to create a virtual environment that would appear to assume some of the functions of the human body, the body politic, and social bodies.

The Electronic Frontier Foundation (EFF) (www.eff.org), based in San Francisco, has been very active in discussions concerning online privacy in general and computerized monitoring in particular. Privacy proponents such as EFF and EPIC maintain that corporate tracking of the online activities of shoppers is an invasion of their privacy that can reveal sensitive information, such as visits to sex-related sites or AIDS information pages (Munro 1997). Electronic Frontier Canada is a nonprofit group that lobbies for the right to privacy on the Internet (Beiser 1997).

Electronic Transaction Ratings Using Secure Technology (eTRUST) was formed in October 1996 by CommerceNet (www.commerce.net) and the Electronic Frontier Foundation.* The group's mandate was to promote electronic commerce

---

* *See also Garber (1997), Privacy Police (1997), Dyson (1997b), Anonymous (1997), Radcliff (1997), and Comaford (1996).*

by addressing the privacy concerns of netizens (Bruner 1997d). Although eTRUST was a program initiated by the Electronic Frontier Foundation, a not-for-profit organization, eTRUST itself has now been spun off as a separate, for-profit organization based in Palo Alto (Weise 1997a). The EFF and CommerceNet, a consortium of businesses to promote Internet commerce, began testing the system originally called eTRUST — now TRUSTe — that displays standard symbols informing online shoppers whether their transactions will be anonymous, customer-to-merchant only, or shared with others (O'Malley 1997). In essence, the intent of the system is to rate the privacy policies and practices of various Web sites (Wildstrom 1996b). It would function as a virtual *Good Housekeeping* "Seal of Approval" for cyberspace, in which the purity of the interaction, rather than the purity and wholesomeness of the consumable product, is approved by an allegedly disinterested third party.

The TRUSTe group (www.etrust.org) is affiliated with the electronic commerce community. This group is attempting to establish guidelines for industry self-regulation regarding informed consent and privacy standards (Mosley-Matchett 1997). Approximately 50 firms, including America Online and CNA Financial Corporation, took part in the eTRUST pilot program during the first half of 1997 (Bray 1997). Companies will pay $500–$5,000 per year to be certified by eTRUST (Bray 1997).

Seymour (1997) praises the idea behind the TRUSTe program. It is a set of standards to which online vendors voluntarily subscribe. If an online vendor chooses to abide, the vendor is audited by a national accounting firm, which examines in detail how the vendor handles customer information. TRUSTe validates its licensees through interviews, questionnaires, and signed contracts (Dyson 1997a). The result of the audit and validation is one of three possible TRUSTe ratings: third-party exchange, one-to-one exchange, or no-exchange warranty, which verifies that the online vendor agrees not to capture, keep, or analyze information about customers' use of the Web site or any transactional data, except as required for billing and system management. To achieve the highest rating, an online vendor also must agree not to monitor or capture online chat, and not to capture, analyze, or use behavioral information about customers as they use the site. Coopers & Lybrand is the largest accounting firm backing the TRUSTe initiative (Seymour 1997). Another accounting firm, KPMG, is helping to design the program and validate the privacy claims of Web sites (Dyson 1997b, 204).

The TRUSTe sites must allow users to correct, update, and delete personally identifiable information. They also are restricted from monitoring personal communications among customers (Privacy police 1997). The TRUSTe-approved vendor then is free to display the rating on the Web site. The highest rating in the TRUSTe program also is reminiscent of the way most libraries handle circulation information. When the book or other library item is checked out, the item record perforce is linked to the patron record, in case the book becomes overdue, lost, or damaged. Once the book is returned, all links between the item record and the patron record are broken. This practice helps maintain patron confidentiality after the item's use. The analogy (with differences) between a surfer's usage trail on the Web and a library patron's book circulation records has been made before. Wilson (1995) noted: "Unlike library records that show which books a person checked out, Internet records can, in effect, show which pages of those books the individual has looked at." Web server log data are more fine grained than library book circulation records, and there certainly is no established tradition of deleting the records once the interaction is complete.

> Techniques to provide users with more information about privacy practices, such as eTRUST and other similar branding techniques, should be encouraged. These services should provide clear and meaningful designations for privacy practices. They should also be backed up with regular auditing. We also have doubts about proposed techniques, such as P3 [Platform for Privacy Preferences], that require users to disclose privacy preferences. We think that good privacy policies should provide meaningful information for users about web site practices and not require users to disclose personal information. Many users are also likely to consider their privacy preferences to be, well, private (Electronic Privacy Information Center 1997).

In 1997 TRUSTe commissioned the Boston Consulting Group to conduct an Internet privacy study. Over 9,000 people responded to the online survey. Over 70 percent of the respondents indicated that they were more concerned about privacy on the Internet than they were about telephone or paper mail information transfer, and 27 percent admitted to providing false personal information on registration forms at Web sites (Straeel 1997).

When a Web site fails to comply with its terms of the contract with TRUSTe, punitive steps include canceling the right to use the TRUSTe logos and posting the site on a list of sites that failed to comply (Dyson 1997b, 205).

Not everyone is convinced that TRUSTe is a good idea. Because the TRUSTe system accredits Internet-based companies according to both the security of their virtual commercial transactions with buyers and their willingness to protect the personal information of customers, TRUSTe is a system grounded in confidentiality as well as trust, but not particularly privacy. TRUSTe was a hotly-debated topic at the Seventh Conference on Computers, Freedom, and Privacy, held in Burlingame, California in March 1997 (Bielski 1997). The initial industry response to eTrust has been lukewarm at best. In the first three months after the pilot project began in November 1996, only approximately 50 sites signed up to be tested and audited for their privacy policies and practices (Bielski 1997).

In 1996 eTRUST formed the Privacy Assured Consortium, a pilot program whose objective is to establish privacy rating for online transaction in order to encourage public confidence in commerce in virtual environments (Fleming 1996). One of the program's standards of conduct is to release only aggregated, anonymous usage statistics (Fleming 1996).

The Electronic Privacy Information Center (EPIC) (www.epic.org), located in Washington, D.C., is one of the major organizations involved in the battle for online privacy. Marc Rotenberg, the director of EPIC, is outspoken and frequently quoted in the press. He has been quoted as stating that anonymity is the de facto way privacy is protected (Internet firms 1997). Rotenberg has been a strong, out-spoken advocate for government safeguards of an individual's privacy, especially in online environments. In Rotenberg's opinion, privacy should be protected by law, not by corporate policies, industry standards, software compliance monitors, or implied informal agreements.

Early in 1997 EPIC, a non-profit consumer group, released the results of a survey of the 100 most popular Web sites. The survey found that only 17 of the sites even mention privacy, and most of the 17 fell far short of what EPIC defines as adequate disclosure: explaining why the information is being collected, how it will be applied, and what steps are being taken to avoid or limit improper use of the collected data (Internet firms 1997).

Privacy advocate groups such as EPIC and Internet groups like cypherpunks (cypherpunks-request@toad.com) believe in the value of untraceable, anonymous communications and in the technology needed to achieve it (Eisenberg 1996). Tim May has been one of the most visible cypherpunks (Lang 1994).

David Sobel from EPIC has asserted that the vast majority of people want access to the Internet primarily for information-seeking activities, not for commerce. The Internet should be primarily a place for people to communicate with one another, not primarily a vast digital marketplace (Weise 1997a).

The Electronic Privacy Information Center is one of the principal supporters of the Internet Engineering Task Force proposal that would give users of the Web more control over the creation, content, and use of cookie files. Rotenberg has stated that EPIC is not against the concept of cookies in general, but the surreptitious way in which they currently are deployed. They want users to be aware of, and in control of, activities involving cookies (Nerney 1997a). More information about the proposal can be found at www.epic.org/privacy/internet/cookies/ (Gallant 1997).

The Internet Privacy Working Group (IPWG) is a consortium of corporations and advocacy organizations. The group is working to develop language for defining individual privacy preferences (Machlis 1997d). The consortium is led by the Center for Democracy and Technology, headed by Jerry Berman, the former executive director of the Electronic Frontier Foundation (Dyson 1997b, 207). The IPWG has been working with the World Wide Web Consortium (W3C) on the Platform for Privacy Preferences.

There are other cyberspace watchdog groups, such as the Internet Privacy Coalition (Weiss 1997). The unofficial encryption flagship on the Internet is a program called Pretty Good Privacy (PGP) (http://www.pgp.com) developed by Phil Zimmermann, a computer security expert (Rothfeder 1997). The purpose of Privacy International is to gather data on surveillance data protection from a variety of countries (Lyon 1994, 13). The group formed in 1990, but really did not get started until March 1992 when an inaugural general meeting was held in Washington, D.C. The organization is a non-profit, non-partisan advocacy group. The group has organized campaigns related to privacy issues in the United States, Canada, Northern Ireland, New Zealand, Thailand, Hungary, and the Philippines (Davies 1992, 142). Private Citizen (www.ctct.com) is an advocacy group against junk e-mail (Bresnahan 1997).

Not all cyberspace watchdog groups defend the rights of the individual netizen against corporations and government. Lauren Weinstein, monitor of the Vortex Internet privacy forum (www.vortex.com/privacy), defends the right of companies to use computers to monitor the behavior of employees in work environments. Because companies can face lawsuits if employees download or send pornography, they must protect themselves (Machlis 1997c). Weinstein also claims to know of many individuals who have been burned by the lack of privacy in virtual environments, but, because they feel so violated, they refuse to talk about it to the media (Eckhouse 1997). Weinstein sees computerized monitoring of work environments as a morale issue for employees subjected to it. The issue is over workplace control. Computerized monitoring in work environments as a means to closely control computer use can be seen as a step toward breaking down skilled, autonomous tasks into their component parts (Harmon 1997). Computerized monitoring facilitates the reduction of laborious tasks to very small components, such as mouse clicks.

Professional Organizations, Research Centers, and Institutes Several professional organizations have become involved in the issues regarding individual privacy, computerized monitoring, and ethical conduct in online environments. The Association for Computing Machinery (ACM) has been active in the development of guidelines for ethical conduct of computing professionals. In late 1992 ACM adopted a new code of ethics and professional conduct that could affect the behavior of those behind projects to use computers to monitor HCI (Association for Computing Machinery 1993). Section 1.7 of the code of ethics of the ACM addresses the need to respect the privacy of others (Olson 1996, 24).

Professional organizations are interested in standardizing definitions and units of measurement for the movement to use computers to monitor HCI. The Institute for the Future is located in Menlo Park, California. Paul Saffo, a contact person, has observed, "The moment you put things in digital form, you can automate the analysis and do real interesting things with the information. There will be lots of products coming out that will allow people to monitor Internet access, and they will raise difficult privacy issues" (Abate 1996). Concerning online information systems, the Federal-State Cooperative System for Public Library Data (FSCS), a combined project of the National Center for Education Statistics and the U.S. National Commission on Libraries and Information Science, has been trying to formulate and agree upon a national set of input and output measures for electronic resources available in or through public libraries (Smith and Rowland 1997). Their work has led them into the realm of basic units of measurement during computerized monitoring of HCI, a topic examined in more detail in Chapter 8. In 1994 the FSCS Steering Committee rejected the concept of hits as a national standard output measure for virtual library services because a hit count does not provide meaningful detail about what one accessing a network server actually used, or about what one found valuable. They recommended instead that the number of Internet sessions would be the most meaningful and collectible output measure. Their recommendation failed to receive the approval of a majority of states, so it has not yet become a national standard (Smith and Rowland 1997, 169).

The more recent cookies controversy also has attracted the attention of professional organizations. Bruner (1997a) reports that the Internet Engineering Task Force is examining a proposed revised standard for cookies that would place more restrictions on their creation, transfer, and use. The IETF's Platform for Privacy Preferences Project will focus on the issue of how to give users control over the distribution of personal information collected while using the Web (Netscape, Firefly and VeriSign 1997).

The Association of Online Professionals (AOP) is concerned about the IETF actions. Dave McClure, the AOP executive director, worries about the impact of the proposed Open Profiling Standard (Wagner 1997b). The AOP also believes that the IETF is proposing standards for cookies that are too restrictive, and that would necessitate major reprogramming of Internet sites (Nerney 1997a). The AOP has formally urged the IETF not to alter the default setting for cookies files in browser software (Welz 1997). The AOP does not see cookies as a valid threat to personal privacy, but sees a greater threat in allowing vague fears to dictate Web technology and the growth of the online industry. McClure insists that this is not a cartoonish war between greedy capitalists and privacy-rights advocates (Bray 1997).

When it comes to computerized monitoring of Web environments, perhaps the most influential organization is the World Wide Web Consortium (W3C). The first technical meeting of the W3C was held in Cambridge, Massachusetts in June 1997. The main discussion topic was privacy on the Web (Machlis 1997d). Proponents of privacy at W3C have been working with industry officials to develop privacy software that allows netizens to articulate their privacy preferences into their Web browser software (Munro 1997). If this happens, privacy preferences could be in danger of becoming nothing but another lifestyle choice. Messmer (1997) sees the W3C consortium as a mediator or arbitrator between Web site operators, with their need to collect information about visitors, and the visitors themselves, with their right to privacy.

In 1997 the Internet Privacy Working Group, part of the World Wide Web Consortium, proposed the Platform for Privacy Preferences (P3) as a way to protect the privacy of Web surfers. The proposed standard would create a language whereby Web sites and Web users could exchange information using the Platform for Internet Content Selection (PICS), a standard already in existence.* The P3

---

* The PICS was designed to block access to Web sites based on content ratings, but it also can block access to sites based on their privacy and information-use practices (Web spies 1997). The Platform was originally intended as a system that would allow users to avoid or block online pornography (Weber 1996). As the proposed standard developed, privacy experts realized that it also could be used as a virtual wall between Web surfers and commercial busybodies. In the real world, privacy often is protected by the erection of real walls, with the dictum concerning one's home as one's castle as the apotheosis of that idea. In the online world, PICS could serve as a virtual wall that moves through cyberspace with the individual. Late in 1997 the World Wide Web Consortium members voted via e-mail to adopt the PICS standard (Harmon 1998).

standard would enable users to define the types and levels of information they are willing to allow to be collected about them as they visit Web sites. If the software detects that a specific site has gathered more information about users than they chose to provide, a pop-up menu would alert users and give them a chance either to accept the higher level of data gathering in this instance, or to revert to the default level of privacy.

Both Microsoft and the Center for Democracy and Technology initially backed the proposed standard (Weise 1997a). The W3C demonstrated a P3 prototype during the FTC Internet privacy hearings held in June 1997 (Machlis 1997d). Consortium officials envision P3 as one piece of an overall plan and goal to help individual netizens implement their own privacy policies as they explore and use virtual environments (Machlis 1997d). The intent of P3 is to define a common format for letting a user view the privacy policy of a Web site before the user's browser releases information about the user to the site server (Messmer 1997).

One positive aspect of the proposed P3 standard is that it continues to situate the power and control over personal privacy in the hands of the individuals themselves. A possible negative aspect is that it seems to downplay and not handle well the situational aspects of privacy decisions, such as environmental conditions (e.g., an open forum or a private chat room), the nature of the information being considered for disclosure (e.g., one's favorite ice cream or secret fantasies), and the other people or systems receiving this information (e.g., one's colleagues or an online marketing system). Another major problem with the P3 proposal is that it focuses on articulated information, rather than on unarticulated behavioral information. It focuses on alphanumeric information (names, addresses, control numbers such as Social Security and credit card numbers), rather than on behavioral information.

Critics of P3 point out that the technical foundation for P3 is the Open Profiling Specification (OPS), which focuses on how to transfer user data efficiently, not keep it private. King (1997) asserts that the OPS standard is not as tight as P3. In turn, OPS is based on Passport, a client-server technology developed by Firefly, a company based in Cambridge, Massachusetts (Messmer 1997).

The assumptions behind P3 and OPS contain at least two challenges. The first is that the overwhelming majority of users will be aware of—and willing to husband—their privacy preferences. The second is that the socio-economic structure of most virtual environments will make it realistically unfeasible for many people to withhold personally private information.

National and International Governmental Bodies   Federal, state, and international governmental bodies have shown some interest in the computerized monitoring movement. Over ten years ago the interest of the U.S. government in computerized monitoring of HCI focused on online work environments. In the mid–1980s the U.S. Office of Technology Assessment (OTA) conducted a major study of CPM, one of the most heavily-cited publications on the topic in work environments. The OTA is now defunct. More recently, the U.S. Office of

Management and Budget (OMB) has been working on a report about government involvement in protecting privacy (Munro 1997).

The U.S. Federal Trade Commission has been very involved in the issue of online privacy for consumers. In the mid–1990s the FTC undertook a privacy initiative to study the protection of consumer privacy in virtual environments. After multi-day workshops during 1995, 1996, and 1997, in December 1997 FTC chairman Robert Pitofsky announced that the FTC would rely on voluntary regulation and restraint on the part of online database producers, rather than push for more federal laws and regulations to protect personal privacy. Fourteen companies, constituting approximately 90 percent of the information broker industry, agreed to submit to third-party audits (Markoff 1997b). By June of 1998, however, the FTC was reporting to Congress that the Web contains many sites that gather personal information about visitors without explaining how the information will be used. The FTC asked Congress to require online companies to put restrictions on the collection of personal information from children (James 1998). The change of heart by the FTC could influence the report that the Commerce Department was slated to submit to President Clinton by July 1998 on the privacy of online commercial transactions (James 1998).

In June 1997 the FTC held four days of hearings about various aspects of personal privacy on the Internet. A set of hearings with a similar format was held a year earlier in mid–1996. The FTC has been one of the most active federal bodies on the issue of privacy in cyberspace. Christine Varney was one of the outspoken commissioners when these hearings were being held.

Early in 1998 the FTC began an audit of U.S. privacy policies (Varney 1998). In March of 1998 the FTC conducted a survey of 1,400 Web sites to determine what the private online industry had done to protect consumer privacy on the Internet for both children and adults (James 1998).

The U.S. government also has been involved in studies of the effects of workplace monitoring on employee stress. A study by the U.S. National Institute of Occupational Safety and Health found that heavily monitored clerical workers showed a greater degree of stress than the unmonitored control group (Kleiman 1989).

International organizations also have become involved in online privacy and online monitoring. In February 1998 the Organization for Economic Cooperation and Development (OECD) sponsored a two-day workshop on privacy protection in a global networked society, involving representatives from various governments, the private sector, user and consumer groups, and data protection authorities from OECD member countries (OECD 1998).

The European Union (EU) is perhaps the most active and involved international body on this topic. It is working on a privacy policy for the Web (Wildstrom 1996a). On October 24, 1995, the Council of the European Union issued the *Directive on the Protection of Individual with Regard to the Processing of Personal Data and on the Free Movement of Such Data* (95/46/ED) (Dorney 1997, 656). The EU directive introduces the government as a third-party supervisory agent in the bilateral process of HCI. When the EU directive took effect in October 1998, the EU imposed strict international rules governing the collection, use, and exchange of personal information about European citizens (Varney 1998).

The potential impact of the EU privacy directive on current U.S. online privacy policies and practices has caused concern among many of the groups identified in this chapter. Privacy & American Business, located in the U.S., is a national, nonprofit publication and business information service (Global privacy 1996). In October 1996 it sponsored a conference held in Washington, D.C., that examined the issues surrounding privacy in cyberspace and across national borders. Specifically, the conference investigated the potential impact of the *Data Protection Directive* of the European Union requiring all nations that operate across European borders to comply with their rules (Global privacy 1996).

In general, governments are not particularly active in using computers to monitor HCI. They are involved primarily as potential legislators and regulators, not as active participants in using computers to monitor HCI. This fact is counterintuitive because, as Poster (1997) observes, the Internet as a matrix of unmonitorable conversations appears to threaten the state. Stratton (1997) also presents a persuasive argument about why the generally interactive Internet threatens the democratic nation-state. While the general argument in this book is that our fears about computerized monitoring as a new form of Big Brotherism are a postmodern failure of the imagination to move beyond a modern notion, the fear may prove to be prescient, rather than outdated. The wheels of government turn slowly. If cyberia is a threat to real governments, in the near future they may begin to use computerized monitoring as a way to better understand, control, and probably tax the behavior of netizens.

Similarities Among the Groups   Some similarities exist among these groups. Web server log analysis seems to signal the intrusion of marketers into the world of HCI as a sequence of events. The analysts of Web server logs often want to understand how people browse in Web environments so that they can make the virtual environment more conducive to online browsing and purchasing behavior. Web client log analysis, on the other hand, appears to signal an intrusion of supervisors into the world of Web browsing. Analysts of Web client logs often want to ensure that browsers are not using time and other resources to engage in non-work-related activities.

Of all the groups normally interested in surveillance in real society, it is odd that computerized monitoring has been implemented among penumbral groups (e.g., teachers, shopkeepers, and librarians), while being largely ignored by the core groups historically interested in social surveillance in the real world — the police and parents. In the case of the police, computerized monitoring of HCI rarely is used to detect crimes and to capture evildoers.* In the case of the parent-

---

* There have been calls, however, for police to team up with employers to catch employees engaged in criminal activity in cyberspace while allegedly at work. For instance, Bob Matthews, a detective staff-sergeant for the Pornography Crime Unit of the Ontario Provincial Police, argues that employers should install Web usage monitoring programs to monitor what employees are doing in cyberspace (Enright 1997).

child relationship, perhaps the dynamic between the watched and the watchers is somehow unique in a way that makes computerized monitoring less attractive. Another class of software has emerged that simply blocks access to certain Web sites, applications, and other material before actual use. Parents know what they don't want their children to see and experience in both the virtual and the real world. Computerized monitoring in most of its applications is used to better understand how people interact with computers and the virtual worlds created by that interaction. Parents as a group seem to be insufficiently interested in how their children legitimately interact with computers to foster the development of software that captures and analyzes HCI that would inform and improve the parent-child relationship. If computerized monitoring of HCI does become a somewhat major social force in the development of cyberspace, certain social relationships (e.g., teacher-student, librarian-information seeker, shopper-shopkeeper, employer-employee) may have the jump on other social relationships (e.g., parent-child, policeman-criminal) that historically have been more privileged in the real world.

Although many groups are involved in computerized monitoring, no single group has asserted or claimed ownership of the technique. Web marketers may be the group closest to developing a sense of ownership. The moral suspicions surrounding computerized monitoring may be one reason why groups have not overtly pledged allegiance to and ownership of the technique.

4

Theoretical Aspects of
Computerized Monitoring

Postmodern people seem inclined to surveillance. Activity on Main Street 30 years ago was subject only to minimal, disorganized surveillance. Today, every corner of a shopping mall is monitored in a very panoptic manner: the locus of surveillance activity is very centralized and out of sight, and shoppers rarely if ever are entirely certain that they are being watched at any given moment. Mall security operations generally use unobtrusive observation, rather than overt presence (e.g., a cop on a beat), to maintain security and control.

Why are we investing all of this time, money, and development energy into developing sophisticated computer monitoring tools and systems? Wouldn't it be easier to ask people what they want, what they find interesting, where they are coming from, and where they are going? Other methods of monitoring HCI have their own sets of problems and limitations.

Some Aspects of Human-Computer Interaction We should begin by enumerating some of the basic characteristics of HCI. Perhaps the most obvious characteristic is the fact that two dissimilar entities are interacting with one another. Computers are fundamentally different from people in that they can record much larger quantities of information than people can memorize, they can process information in parallel (as opposed to sequentially), and they can easily "forget" information (i.e., erase it from RAM) (Bailey 1996). People, however, appear to be more creative, adaptable, and able to recognize complex patterns and similarities. They often engage in trial-and-error learning to look for workable causal behavior.

Most people do not interact with computers primarily or solely for the sake of the interaction. Most HCI is part of a more encompassing project. Is it still true in all cases to state that people do not interact with computers for the sheer joy of the interaction itself?

Although computers and people are different, increasingly the distinctly bilateral negotiations between the two is giving way to a seamless experience of online environments, in which the person and the computer become one in some sense of a shared clearing. "As human activities become intertwined with the mechanisms of computerized tracking, the notion of human interactions with a 'computer' — understood as a discrete, physically localized entity — begins to lose its force" (Agre 1994, 105).

Using a computer or computer network is a little different from using an ordinary tool, such as a hammer. The computer is both an information storage device and a communication device. There is an open-endedness to the use of a computer that distinguishes it from other types of devices. Winner (1991) suggests that "technologies are not merely tools that one picks up and uses. They can be seen as 'forms of life' in which human and inanimate objects are linked in various kinds of relationships."

The human understanding of the virtual self (or selves) is in flux. "We have to decide what human beings are in the electronic age. Are we just going to be chattel for commerce?" (Evan Hendricks, quoted in Broder 1997a). Oravec (1996, 47) defines a virtual individual as a selection or compilation of various traces, records, imprints, photographs, profiles, and statistical information that pertain to an individual, or at least could be reasonably claimed to pertain to an individual. The compilation also includes writing done, images produced, sounds associated with, and impressions managed by the individual. The resulting amalgamation is associated with the individual in the context of particular genres and artifacts. Oravec's definition focuses on the sense of a virtual self as perceived by someone else, rather than on the sense of virtual selfhood as experienced by the real human being behind the mask of selfhood.

In online environments, the real individual probably has little control over the virtual self (or selves) associated with that individual. Some virtual individuals may be constructed by others without concern for correctness or consistency, or the real individual's knowledge or consent. Even if one takes great pains to keep track of one's virtual selves, perhaps to tailor them to certain situations or to create certain effects, the virtual individuals one is associated with may become distorted in a variety of ways. They may not appear to others the way one believes or intends that they appear (Oravec 1996, 48).

Our understanding of virtual groups is even murkier. Using computers to monitor HCI at the group level does not have as strong a history as that of studying the behavior of isolated individuals.

> Virtual groups are composed of transmissions of group interaction (technology-mediated and unmediated), records of group interaction (tape recordings, transcripts, and minutes), decisions and products associated with the group, articulated impressions and imagery associated with the group, and statistics linked with levels of group performance (Oravec 1996, 48).

The ability to study the group behavior of virtual groups, however, is improving. The WebTrends Web server log analysis software, for example, has an intranet management feature that lets administrators track site usage by groups, by individuals, or both, rather than by IP addresses and domain names alone (Rapoza 1997a).

Command and response, the early mode of interaction between people and computers, may be a variation on the master-slave relationship. The user issues a command, and the computer responds. A session involving HCI can be perceived and mapped as a sequential series of commands and responses. Is it possible and, if so, worthwhile to perceive HCI as a sequential series of commands and responses? Are there other components of the interaction that are more salient? For example, perhaps what happens in the human mind before the start of the interaction is more important. Is it true of all HCI that both the human being and the computer are in some sense aware that a human-computer interaction is underway?

Using computers to monitor HCI is part of a larger project to understand the "truth" about the subject. The truth we humans are trying to discover is a human truth. Essentially, we are using computers to help discover the human truth about HCI. Nevertheless, we must at least entertain the idea that a different, computer truth about HCI may exist. If computers could discover that truth (perhaps they already have), and if they could act and adapt based on that learned truth, there would be little or no need to "translate" it into something understandable to people.

In the past, HCI tended to be characterized by a sense of absorbed aloneness, not unlike the solitude of human-book interaction. A person reading a book in a crowd is somehow, fundamentally alone. Several critics, such as Dyrli (1997), however, point out that in many online environments this sense of anonymity and privacy is basically illusory. Nevertheless, when we are on the Internet, even when it appears to be crowded, we never actually "see" the crowd.

Jeremy Bentham's Panopticon and Computerized Surveillance The English Utilitarian philosopher Jeremy Bentham developed the idea of the panopticon in the late eighteenth century. Derived from the Greek word for all-seeing, the panopticon was originally conceived as an architectural design for a prison that would allow prisoners to be potentially observed at all times, while the observer remains invisible to the observed (Levy 1993). In a panoptic human-human relationship the prisoners are vulnerable and have little power because their activities are visible at all times, and their vulnerability is magnified by the invisibility of the observer (Botan 1996, 298). Although the original idea and design of the panopticon was for a prison, Bentham makes clear on the title page its applicability to other situations in which "inspection" is required:

"Panopticon; or, The Inspection House: containing the idea of a new principle of construction applicable to any sort of establishment, in which persons of any description are to be kept under inspection; and in particular to Penitentiary-Houses, Prisons, Poor Houses, Lazarettos, Houses of Industry, Manufactories,

Hospitals, Work-Houses, Mad-Houses, and Schools" (Bentham 1838–1843). In fact, Lyon (1991a, 606) claims that Bentham originally received his inspiration for the panopticon from his knowledge of his brother Samuel's workshop at Critchoff in Tsarist Russia. Perhaps both the deepest roots and the loftiest fruit of the panoptic idea are to be found in work environments, not prisons.

Jeremy Bentham introduced the notion of the panopticon, Michel Foucault (1979) appropriated it as a metaphor for modern social conditions and power structures, and Lyon (1991a and 1994), among others, explored its aptness for making sense of the postmodern situation of electronic surveillance in online environments. The idea of the panopticon originally was developed as a way to reform British prisons, notorious for filth, corruption, brutality, and general bedlam. It builds on the power of uncertainty and inequality in one-way surveillance. For Lyon (1991a, 599), Bentham's truly original contribution to the history of ideas was to make informational subordination rest on uncertainty. In a prison environment, a single guard located in the middle of a circularly constructed array of prison cells should be able to guard and control a large number of prisoners, because the use of backlighting and blinds enables the guard to see the prisoners without the prisoners being able to see the guard. Because the power of surveillance is enabled by this architectural scheme only in one direction (from guard to prisoners), an individual prisoner never is certain at any given moment of being watched. The notion of exploiting uncertainty as a means of controlling a population has obvious resonance with the use of electronic technologies for unobtrusive monitoring, in which the user often is unsure of being monitored (Lyon 1994, 62). The possibility of being observed, rather than one's having full knowledge of being observed, supposedly acts as a behavioral governor and general agent of social control in an environment of incarceration.

Although the panoptic idea has been realized in a variety of prison settings, for our purposes it may be most important in virtual work environments. From the vantage point of employees, electronic surveillance is an attempt to create new power relationships based on an electronic version of Bentham's panopticon (Botan 1996).

The panopticon also overcomes to a certain extent one of the enduring limitations of human attention: At any given moment, a person can pay full attention to only one thing. At any given moment the guard can look only in one direction. Thus Bentham was attuned to one of the real limitations of human surveillance by people: It is very labor intensive and expensive. Both proponents of the current U.S. expansion of the number of state and federal prisons and opponents of computerized monitoring seem to have forgotten the simple fact that both logistically and economically it is extremely difficult to monitor the behavior of a relatively large number of people for an extended time.

For a panopticon to work, all of the nooks and crannies of a defined space need to be observable. The importance to Bentham of the spatial totality of the observation is central to the concept of the panopticon (Levy 1993). Any unobserved space will encourage unregulated behavior:

Cells, communications, outlets, approaches, there ought not anywhere to be a single foot square, on which man or boy shall be able to plant himself— no not for a moment — under any assurance of not being observed. Leave but a single spot thus unguarded, that spot will be sure to be a lurking-place for the most reprobate of the prisoners, and the scene of all sorts of forbidden practices. (Bentham 1838–1843)

The major effect of the panopticon was to induce in the prison inmate a state of conscious and permanent visibility that assures the automatic functioning
of the power of the observer over the observed (Foucault 1977, 201). Bentham invented a technology of power designed to solve the modern problem of surveillance in prisons, schools, factories, and hospitals (Foucault 1980, 148). In a sense, Bentham converted the problem of social control in prison environments into an architectural problem to overcome the limitations of human attention on the part of the observer, rather than on the social deviance of the incarcerated and the observed. Bentham created the idea for a real-world environment in which the force of informed yet unobtrusive observation could manifest itself completely. Bentham's idea as a solution to the British prison problem could point the way toward a new understanding of computerized monitoring of HCI. We need to get inside the monitor, rather than inside the monitored. Bentham believed he had the best possible solution to the prison problem because he focused on the behavior and behavioral limitations of the guards, rather than on the behavior of the guarded.

Just as computerized monitoring of HCI appears to flourish in four basic environments (work, formal learning, information-seeking, and shopping), the panoptic idea appeared to be ideally suited for use in prisons, schools, factories, and hospitals. The notion of a panopticon is premised on the power and limitations of visibility and vision. The image of a prison as a dark, dank place is replaced by one in which every corner of the defined space is visible from one centralized tower. Bentham conceived of visibility as organized entirely around a dominating, overseeing, centralized gaze (Foucault 1980, 152). The idea of a panopticon created a space of "exact legibility" (Foucault 1980, 154).

Computerized monitoring in general, and specifically computerized monitoring of HCI, could be thought of as a sightless visibility. Analysts of computerized monitoring data examine the residue of HCI without ever seeing the person at the terminal. Lang (1994) refers to behavioral impressions as "electronic traces" of a person's passage through cyberspace. These traces are post-hoc indicators of indigenous online human behavior.

The panopticon as originally conceived by Bentham appears to have three salient features for our investigations. The first is one-way vision. The guard can see the prisoner, but the prisoner cannot see the guard, resulting in an uneven, one-way flow of information from the observed to the observer. The same situation exists for the monitor and the monitored. Second, the possibility of being watched at any given moment is intentionally made known to every prisoner. Without an informed group of human beings, the panopticon would not be effective. Every prisoner needs to know that, at any given moment, being watched is possible. Third, actual instances of surveillance are not made known to the prisoner before or during the surveillance. Although every prisoner needs to be aware of the possibility of surveillance as a pure potentiality, instances of surveillance need not be made known to individual prisoners. The system probably works better if surveyed prisoners are not aware of specific surveillance activities.

Another key feature of the panopticon is that it made prison surveillance more impersonal, automatic, and distant. The guards were removed in a central tower, not strolling among the prisoners and prison cells. The sense of distance and impersonality between the monitor and the monitored during computerized monitoring also is pertinent.

The panopticon is also an individualized observation of known, classified persons. The individuals have been arrested, tried, convicted, numbered, classified, and segregated into cells before the moment of observation. The panoptic approach does not do a good job of facilitating the observation and control of interactive group behavior.

As a prison plan, the panopticon did not receive official approval. Millbank Penitentiary in London, the penitentiary in Mettray, France, Kingston Penitentiary in Ontario, Canada, and Stateville Prison near Joliet, Illinois all built (and were built) on the principles of the panopticon outlined by Bentham.

Over the decades the idea of the panopticon evolved into the notion of the panoptic sort. The panoptic sort is a discriminatory use of technology whereby people are assigned to groups based on countless bits of personal information that have been collected, stored, processed, and shared through an intelligent network (Gandy 1995, 36). Some of the information may include not only buying habits in real shopping environments, but also browsing behavior in virtual shopping malls. Mark Poster (1990) called the world of consumer surveillance a Superpanopticon, because the panoptic view now has no technical limitations. The shopping population participates in it own self-construction as subjects under the normalizing gaze of the decentralized Superpanopticon (Poster 1990, 97).

Zuboff (1988) introduces the idea of an "information panopticon" in twentieth century organizations (Bryant 1995, 509). The information panopticon differs from Bentham's idea of prison surveillance and control in that in some applications of electronic surveillance in work environments the gaze is not merely an unverifiable possibility but a constant and continuous certainty (Bryant 1995, 510). For the panoptic effect to work, however, the monitored employees need to be aware that they may be unobtrusively monitored at any time. Botan correctly notes that "there can be surveillance without employees being aware of it, but not a panoptic effect" (Botan 1996, 300).

The notion of a panopticon has made a successful transition to the virtual environment on the Web. See Hibbard (1996) for examples of how corporations are using virtual panopticons to monitor use of the Web by employees. For hyperrealists, hyper-reality is the logical conclusion to the pursuit of the perfect panopticon. A hyper-real environment is the result of the evolution of the panopticon to the point that it recedes from the realm of perception and thought. Everyone becomes convinced that the panopticon no longer exists. People continue to believe that they are free in cyberspace, although their power has disappeared as they become unaware of the panopticon. As online environments awaken and become self-correcting, the need for human intelligence will shift gears. By definition, unobtrusive computerized monitoring is not directly experienced by the monitored. Although one may suspect or have a hunch that one is being monitored online, one has no experiential reason to sense or conclude that one is indeed being monitored. In this sense a virtual panopticon exists, with computerized monitoring as the engine. The online individual never can be certain that one's location in cyberspace, virtual movements, and online behavior are being monitored. If it becomes ubiquitous in online environments, the vague sense of the computerized monitor will simply become an accepted aspect of the environment, like air pressure in the real world. The human emotional need to experience "panopticonical dread" will fall away.

The idea of a panopticon also may apply to a virtual environment where computerized monitoring is fully implemented. The subject, however, may be aware of his or her absolute visibility in a different way than in a real panopticon, such as the prison in Stateville, Illinois, or even when walking down a real street. A virtual environment where computerized monitoring is implemented is an absolutely visible environment in the guise of an individualized, secluded environment.

Computerized monitoring is a unique strain of surveillance that has been liberated (or could be liberated, if we only would allow it) from the need to normalize the behavior to make sense of what is being surveyed. Normalization during both the analysis stage and the application stage no longer are necessary. When we finally comprehend this possibility and allow it to happen, the effects on formal educational practices, information seeking, the performance of work, shopping behavior, and many other social relationships and tensions will change.

The panoptic ideal began as a modern notion, premised on the scarcity of resources (particularly that of the attentional focus of the guards) and designed to be realized in the real world. The panoptic mechanisms of modern and postmodern life are categorically different from the mechanisms of power in the ancient and medieval worlds. The panopticon represents strategies of power rather than any identifiable locus of power. It is a web without a devouring spider (Lyon 1991a, 607). In prison environments, it was impractical and uneconomical to guard every prisoner all of the time. In the online world of computerized monitoring, however, the economics of surveillance have changed completely. Now it is not only thinkable, but realizable, to monitor everyone all of the time.

Taylorism and Fordism   A faint but continuous line of development can be traced from Bentham's panopticon to the automobile assembly lines of Henry Ford and the principles and practices of scientific management of Frederick Winslow Taylor (Lyon 1991a, 606). Taylor (1911) developed principles of scientific management that involved measuring specific tasks in an attempt to increase productivity through increased efficiency and direct supervision. Efficiency of production and increased control over the production process were the twin goals. Based on outcomes of experiments conducted in the steel industry in the late nineteenth century to increase worker productivity, Taylor's core insight was that physical labor could be made more efficient by breaking up a task into its component parts, eliminating the unnecessary or wasteful motions or steps, and then using measurements of the restructured physical activity to establish job performance standards (Magney 1996, 202). Taylor focused on physical activity—people performing manual labor in the real world. With the ascendancy in the latter half of the twentieth century of knowledge workers and the emergence (or creation) of cyberspace, we should not assume that Taylor's work no longer is pertinent. Despite all of the talk about knowledge workers, human interaction with computers still relies heavily on physical activity—not backbreaking labor, but physical activity nonetheless.

Taylorism was applied at the early Ford automobile manufacturing plants, where assembly line production techniques were introduced. Taylor's views on the importance of managerial control, as opposed to worker control, was perhaps implemented to its fullest by the Ford Motor Company (Magney 1996, 203). Fordism is an attempt to ensure certainty in production processes through surveillance (Baarda 1994). Locus of control in the managerial class of a company is a central tenet of Taylor's theory of scientific management. The control structure embedded in computerized monitoring systems is very similar to the control structure of the old assembly line industries (Magney 1996, 203).

In 1912 Taylor was called to testify before a Congressional committee formed to determine whether workers should be subjected to the rule of the clock (Kanigel 1997). Some companies and corporations found Taylor's scientific management methods too crude and cumbersome. The computerization of work opened fresh pastures for the application of Taylor's ideas of managerial control over the production process. Rather than go around with a stopwatch timing employees at work, it is neater and more elegant to resort to electronic monitoring. Rather than bark at employees, managers can send subliminal messages to them through their computer monitors (Bewayo 1996, 189).

Lyon (1994) argues that the post–Fordian electronic monitoring of production processes may be more complex than electronic Taylorism (Bryant 1995, 510). Applying Taylorism to the electronic workplace presents several challenges. First, Taylor's principles of scientific management grew out of an industry that relied more heavily on physical labor than do most current businesses, corporations, and industries. Performance monitors continue to be keenly interested in the human body, its place in the work environment, and its activities. One of the interesting ironies of the entire computerized monitoring movement is that the practitioners seem more interested in the physical residue of HCI (such as keystrokes and mouse clicks) than in fully understanding how the mind interacts with computers. Keyboarding activity has received much more attention than mental activity. Many transaction log analysis projects have revealed that hand-eye coordination often is flawed, but we still know very little about how the mind reacts and behaves in an information-rich setting, be it a shopping, work, formal educational, or library environment. Those who employ computerized monitoring have yet to relinquish their fascination with the human body and its movements. Although cyberspace is a sense of place without the trappings of physical space, monitoring analysts continue to examine the movements of the human body as the primary entry into the hidden workings of the human mind.

Agre (1994) cautions that the age of the "capture mode" has some fundamental differences from the age of Taylorism. Whereas Taylorism treats efficiency and control as inseparable goals, the capture mode permits efficiency and control to be treated separately, so that people engaged in a heavily monitored computer work activity have a certain kind of freedom and decision burden not experienced or enjoyed by people engaged in Taylorized work in the real world (Agre 1994, 117). Interacting with computers and computer networks is not a very linear process, and is apparently becoming rapidly less so. Cyberspace (especially the Web) is a landscape cluttered with forks in the road, decision points, jumping-off points, and opportunities to back up.

Taylorism is not passé. Along with Bentham's idea of the panopticon, Taylor's methods for measuring the productivity and efficiency of human behavior in real-world, industrial work environments continues to serve as a formal aspect of our way of understanding human behavior in online environments. Even Web monitoring software providers invoke the history of time and motion studies. For example, the WinWhatWhere software can be used to perform time and motion studies, so that software designers can quantify and minimize mouse mileage and keystrokes (Rubenking 1997).

Foucault   The French thinker Michel Foucault also makes some theoretical contributions to the amorphous movement to use computers to monitor HCI. Foucault studied how the social manifestation of punishment shifted from the torture of the body to mental reprimands and attempts at rehabilitation. Although Foucault was examining the birth of prisons and regimented army camps, not Web sites and online information systems, some of his thoughts about discipline, observation, control, and surveillance apply to these emerging online environments.

Foucault (1979) adopted the notion of the panopticon as a metaphor for the operation of power in social relations (Bryant 1995). Foucault (1979, 173) also examined the role of the design of prisons, schools, hospitals, and other social institutions in the progressive objectification and the ever more subtle partitioning of individual behavior. He argues that individuals become the bearers of their own surveillance (Bryant 1995, 511). Perhaps the ultimate objectification of individual human behavior ceases to place any value on identifying specific individuals.

Foucault regards the problem of economic changes in the eighteenth century as making it "necessary to ensure the circulation of effects of power through progressively finer channels, gaining access to individuals themselves, to their bodies, their gestures and all their daily actions" (Foucault 1980, 151–152, quoted in Levy 1993). In the late twentieth century the hyper-sophisticated methods of electronic monitoring of workers is viewed as a further refinement of the circulation of power. The use of the panoptic power of surveillance allows the observer access to the most intimate aspect of the individual (Levy 1993).

A computer network may replace Foucault's (1979, 304) carceral network. Because a computer network, unlike a human neural network, does not need to normalize its perceptions to survive and react to events, the "universal reign of the normative" may shortly come to an end. The normalizing power that Foucault says emerged in the late eighteenth century with the birth of modern prisons, hospitals, and schools, may deflate in the early twenty first century as people colonize virtual worlds where the need to normalize is much less pressing.

Philosophies of Technology   Other aspects of the broad field of the philosophy of technology are pertinent to this examination. Kipnis (1991) argues that, because of the close relationship between technology and social behavior, technology should be included as an explanatory variable in social psychology's construction of behavior.

Rather than (or in addition to) questioning authority, we will need to question reality. Are only two types of reality possible, the real and the virtual? What is the relationship between real reality and virtual reality? Is there a generational or sexual tension between these two realities? Do they, like Ford and Chevy, Pepsi and Coke, struggle for market share of an essentially finite pie — human attention or human being? Has the development of the possibility of human being in cyberspace somehow lessened, diminished, or denuded the reality of human being in the real world? Cyberspace begins with a ruse and a willful forgetfulness of reality. Our being in the real world never disappears. Rather, when we are enthralled in cyberspace, we just choose to ignore the real world. The two realities are vying for our attentional focus, and the real world has an established, finite set of wiles.

The prospect of a personalized cyberspace based on one's own previous and present behavior has its antecedents in the use of mass media in the real world. Debord (1988, 27–28) observes:

> At the technological level, when images chosen and constructed by someone else have everywhere become the individual's principal connection to the world he formerly observed for himself, it has certainly not been forgotten that these images can tolerate anything and everything; because within the same image all things can be juxtaposed without contradiction. The flow of images carries everything before it, and it is similarly someone else who controls at will this simplified summary of the sensible world; who decides where the flow will lead as well as the rhythm of what should be shown, like some perpetual, arbitrary surprise, leaving no time for reflection, and entirely independent of what the spectator might understand or think of it.

It is no coincidence that in the late age of the monopoly of reality mass media images have reached the pinnacle of control and suggestiveness. Watching the real world go by from the front porch has been overcome by a more controlled parade of images on the television screen. Like an aging beauty, reality has even retouched itself for controlled mass consumption.

The coming revolution (it would be equally apt to call it an awakening) will witness a radical shift from the controlled dogmatic slumber induced by spectacular mass media images with the fearful responsibility of personalized online environments that depend on the specific behaviors and decisions of the individual. As the late age of monopolistic reality gives way to a new era of competition between reality and virtuality, the role of the individual will shift from that of a passive couch potato to that of responsible mouse potato. Granted, the horizon of possible virtual worlds will continue to be defined by the limits of technology at the moment and the initial programming work performed to create the computerized monitoring modules that collect, analyze, and apply behavioral data to create better virtual environments and experiences, but the final responsibility for the look and feel of the virtual environment will rest with the individual. In this sense, relatively simple word processing programs are better understood as precursors of future virtual worlds than are the early virtual reality prototypes. Although the limits of language and the word processing program itself establish the limits of the possible, it is up to the individual to create something good.

Guy Debord probably would understand virtual environments as an advanced form of integrated spectacle. "For the final sense of the integrated spectacle is this — that it has integrated itself into reality to the same extent as it was describing it, and that it was reconstructing it as it was describing it. As a result, this reality no longer confronts the integrated spectacle as something alien" (Debord 1988, 9). It is difficult to imagine, however, why an integration of real and virtual worlds would be in anyone's best interest. Cyberspace may become better off and more viable if it strives to differentiate itself from the real world. In this sense, it may be unproductive to think of human experiences in cyberspace as virtual reality, as if the ultimate goal of online human experience is merely to approximate the real world.

Spatial Qualities of Cyberspace   Cyberspace has emerged in the last decade as a major new space for human activity. Some historians trace the origins of cyberspace back into the nineteenth century. Stratton (1997, 254) argues that the idea of cyberspace began as a way to overcome circulation time, one of the challenges of capitalism. Davies (1992, 85) observes:

> It is difficult for many members of the old generations to comprehend what has been spawned by the computer revolution of the past decade. We often admire how much faster, or bigger, or smarter information technology has become. But more significant in privacy issues and harder to grasp is the quantum shift in human attitudes and values that this technology engenders. Millions of youngsters around the world nowadays live in a different life matrix, a sort of computer network reality, a virtual reality where tangibility is confirmed through prompts, flags, and program instructions. An entire generation of young people sees reality and change in terms of networks and network communications. Older people might complain that video is keeping their kids indoors. Well, computer networks are achieving the effect of confining young people to a terminal, but they also liberate their movements in time and space. These youngsters have inherited a new dimension known as "cyberspace." In the US

they call it "living on the net." This new lifestyle pushes forward an electronic frontier no less impressive than the old pioneer frontiers of the eighteenth century.

What are the characteristics of cyberspace environments? The creation of a sense of cyberspace is not just a natural (or virtual) act of creation. It carries other social and cultural ramifications. "Anchorage in a space is an economic-political form which needs to be studied in detail" (Foucault 1980, 149). Every space has norms of behavior and expectations. Every space promotes certain activities and inhibits others. What norms regarding surveillance and privacy are being developed for cyberspace? The amorphous movement to use computers to monitor HCI may have some immediate impact on the look and feel of cyberspace, but the long-term, subtle effects on online societies and cultures may be more pronounced. How do norms and accepted boundaries emerge and develop? What do people have a right to expect as they behave in cyberspace?

When one is alone in a private space, one expects to have one's privacy respected. In cyberspace one usually feels alone, unless one is in a MUD or chat room. Because one often feels alone in cyberspace (but also, paradoxically, with others, in some strange, Leibnitzian, monadic way), one assumes that cyberspace is (or should be) a private place, like one's home.* In this respect, the palpable but ultimately erroneous sense of aloneness in many online environments affects the individual's expectations regarding individual privacy in those online environments. "As private a pastime as surfing the Internet might seem, it's not" (Mann 1997, 42). The Internet is not about an escape into isolation, but rather an ongoing, outgoing exercise in connectedness (Healy 1997, 57). "The computer user is no more isolated than is the book reader, although the computer is a far different kind of knowledge artifact. Digital texts evoke a different kind of sociability and sense of public space" (Lyman 1996, 6).

That strange sense of anonymity or liberation from our mundane sense of self is another problematic sensation for the individual in online environments. "The danger of the Internet is the illusion of anonymity," says Janlori Goldman, an attorney at the Center for Democracy and Technology in Washington, D.C. Although people may feel they are incognito online, actually they are highly visible (Rothfeder 1997). It's just an otherworldly type of visibility. Goldman notes, "People think they're invisible and secure when they go online. They're anything but" (quoted in Rothfeder 1997, 226).

The question of ownership of an individual's behavior also becomes confounded in online environments. Is personal behavior in cyberspace owned by the person? What if a set of aggregated behavior is analyzed and presented as a research report? Unless a person is an actor or an exhibitionist, behavioral information never is disclosed by a person for a specified purpose. At least in the real world, behavioral information just happens as a result of behavior. Although I may give the circulation clerk at the library my Social Security number only to check out a

---

The philosopher Gottfried Wilhelm Leibnitz (1646–1716) developed the idea of monads as extensionless entities, capable of appetites and perceptions, but self-sufficient and developing without relation to other monads.

book, the behavioral information I disclose as I walk down the street (e.g., I favor my left foot because of a nagging corn) is not disclosed for any purpose. It simply has to be disclosed to anyone who observes me, if I want to walk down the street, despite my nagging corn. In the real world, I do not walk down the street to disclose my personal walking style, but to go someplace or to get some exercise, or both. If I walk on the wet sand on a beach, the laws of physics dictate that I am going to leave footprints as a form of behavioral information about my behavior — at least until the next high tide wipes the slate clean. In online environments, however, the relationship between behavior and behavioral information may not be as self-evident and real-worldish. Virtual behavior in cyberspace is not like footprints in the sand. It is not necessarily observable by others, and it does not have to be recorded by the environment. It is the intentional recording of behavioral data, coupled with value-adding information like time stamps and IP addresses that is different from merely watching someone walk down the street or observing footprints in the sand and surmising that someone else has walked there since the last high tide. Computerized monitoring subtly challenges us to reconstitute human being in relation to the mundane and the everyday — to basal environmental conditions that we heretofore have take for granted. As we move about the real world, we do not think about smart sidewalks and smart sand on the beach, capable of detecting our mass and responding accordingly.

Even in the smartest online environment, in which computerized monitoring is used to modify environmental conditions, experiences, and options based on observed human behavior as an indicator and predictor of one's needs, desires, and preferences, one is not in a state of complete freedom. It is a dance between the original programmer and the behaving individual, in a ballroom defined by the current technological and human limits of the possible. Because we tend to designate readers and viewers of digital documents as users, that appellation reminds us that the computerized reader does not have perfect freedom, because all choices given to the user are made possible by the technical structures designed by the programmer (Lyman 1996, 7).

The question concerning the sense and meaning of cyberspace is very pertinent to our understanding of the importance of the general movement to use computers to monitor HCI. To many people, the goal of the development of virtual space is to use computer systems to move beyond the capacity and characteristics of real, physical human beings in the real world, and to move beyond simple representations of human space and into a wide variety of virtual, large-scale social activities (Rochlin 1997, 214).

Contracts, Content, and Ownership   What is the implicit social contract, if any, between the person who acts in an environment and the creator, owner, or maintainer of the environment? We have to assume that the person who acts has permission to behave in the environment. A related question: What is the implicit social contract behind computerized monitoring? As a user, I will let you observe my behavioral traces not to place me in a demographic group or class of users, but

to ultimately improve the human-computer interface and the online environment in general, either for me individually or for all future users of the system as
a group.

Businesses and organizations often claim that because they own the hardware
and software that makes cyberspace possible, they own the content of cyberspace,
in the form of e-mail messages, computer files, and Web pages (Halpern 1992, 19).
Computerized monitoring collects behavioral residue, and there is some question
about who owns that residue. We also need to distinguish between "naturally
occurring" residue in cyberspace and residue that is specifically generated for the
purposes of monitoring HCI.

Power and Control in Online Environments   An underlying thesis of this
book is that behind the will to monitor is the will to control. Inside the monitor
lurks a strong desire to control. Shein (1996a) quotes Brian Burba, an analyst with
International Data Corporation in Framingham, Massachusetts: "The [need] for
these types of technologies [i.e., Web server and client monitoring software] is
significant and growing rapidly. You need to have some level of control and a monitoring capability for use of the Internet from corporate desktops in order to
influence individual behavior."

People always seem to regard what they have made as something they can control (Rochlin 1997, 5). In cyberspace control has no locus. Rather, it permeates
the entire system as a lived, experienced space. Foucault (1980, 156) observed that,
in contrast to the era of monarchical control, power no longer is substantially
invested in and identified with an individual who possesses it or exercises it by
right of birth. Power has become a machinery that no one owns. It's simply there,
an intangible part of the environment. This new reality of power describes particularly well the power generated through the computerized monitoring of HCI.
Through such monitoring a tremendous amount of behavioral information flows
from the user and the environment to the computerized monitoring software module. The software module may translate and report that information to the per-
son(s) behind the monitoring project, or it may interpret the information to modify
the online environment. The information rarely returns to the individual user,
except in the form of an improved, perhaps individualized, online environment.
Rochlin (1997, 7) observes how the rapid growth of computer networks is fundamentally a non-revolution: "What makes the process so elusive to characterize and
difficult to analyze is that the conquest of human decision processes and procedures is taking place through the transformation of the means and representation
of interaction rather than through the more direct and potentially adversarial
processes of displacement of authority or assertion of control." In some very fundamental ways, such as the definition of basic discrete units of online human behavior (see Chapter 8), computerized monitoring programs control the representation
of interaction. Computerized monitoring projects also can be a prime mover in
transforming the means and tenor of HCI in online environments. In contrast,
the human, phenoenological representation of HCI is a poor cousin, because it is

difficult to define, measure, and describe, and because once defined, measured, and described, it is more difficult to apply to some useful purpose.

The modern state may have served as the middle way in this transformation of the locus of control from powerful individuals (e.g., kings) to the mutable online environment itself. Brzezinski understood increased surveillance as a tool or weapon by which the state would assert social and political control over individual citizens. "It will soon be possible to assert almost continuous surveillance over every citizen and to maintain up-to-date, complete files, containing even the most personal information about the health or personal behavior of the citizen in addition to more customary data. These files will be subject to instantaneous retrieval by the authorities" (Brzezinski 1971, 163, quoted in Kiesler 1997, 210). Brzezinski was referring to the real world. In online environments, computerized monitoring projects do not require the power of the state to create, maintain, and apply up-to-date, complete behavioral files on individual netizens.

As critics of computerized monitoring, we mentally continue to centralize our perceptions and fears. Centralized use of disparate information is still a conditioned fear, just as the Russian, I have heard, continues to fear the Mongolians, hundreds of years after Ghengis Khan. Modernity has conditioned us to fear the centralization of information and control, yet this conditioned fear may be causing us to fundamentally misunderstand what is happening in the amorphous movement toward sophisticated computerized monitoring. Centralization of online behavioral information into huge databases is not only unnecessary, but also inefficient. The mutual control model may or may not be vital to actual instances of control in online environments. According to the mutual control model, increasing pressures for tighter monitoring and control come from mutual access to and dependence on shared electronic information that can be linked to the behavior of identifiable individuals and groups (Allen 1994). Computerized monitoring data need not even be translated into humanly intelligible form. We almost seem to be oblivious to computerized monitoring as a decentralized threat. Despite the main lesson of the Internet — that great and grand things can come from a totally decentralized system — decentralization has yet to become part of our fundamental world outlook. There is almost something comforting about our conditioned fear of centralization. It is something to fall back on.

David Brin (1998), a popular science fiction author, has argued that the only way to avoid a state of Big Brother is to give the birdlike power of surveillance to everyone. If everyone has the power to survey a scene, surveillance will not lead to centralized power, control, and knowledge. Privacy will become as extinct as the dodo bird. For Brin, mutually enabled and enforced accountability is the key to running a complex society. Solipsism is a rising passion (Teitelbaum 1996). Meeks (1997), however, criticizes Brin for not addressing the psychological stress of living in a no-privacy world. Some people may become completely docile, resigned to having their every move recorded. Others will react in extreme, emotional opposition.

The interpretive challenge concerning the struggle for control that permeates the use of computers to monitor HCI is that this struggle does not seem to fit into the usual classification scheme for power struggles. This struggle for control seems almost without volition. Evidently, no one is making an intentional power play. It is merely happening. It is truly an amorphous movement. Class struggle does not describe the situation well, nor does this seem to be a case of the state versus the citizenry. In fact, the state in general seems to be having a particularly difficult time discovering or creating its role in cyberspace. Of all the potential types of control that could be at stake here — political, economic, social, and psychological — what we are witnessing may be basically a struggle for environmental control. The landscape created by people interacting with computers and computer systems, however, is a new type of environment, resulting in a new type of environmental control. Green parties do not seem to be part of it, and we are not facing the prospect of one nation invading or annexing the territory of another. Rather, the goal of this struggle seems to be for control of the substrata, givens, or basic mood of cyberspace. Are we creating a space in which computerized surveillance is expected, accepted, and commonly practiced, or are we creating a space in which people feel that most or all of their behavior is private?

Baudrillard (1988) saw a form of closure of the mind when everyone sees oneself promoted to the controls of a hypothetical machine. With computerized monitoring, however, the machine works best and molds the best of all possible online environments when the user acts in the environment, without seriously thinking about manning the controls and worrying about the consequences of one's actions. For example, if I click on that hotlink, will the software misinterpret or overestimate my interest in the site and the subject? Computerized monitoring may be most effective when the online actors are not self-conscious of the fact that their behavior is being monitored.

Control Applied   Clement and McDermott (1991) boldly claim that the essence of computing technology is control, and that CPM is the most dramatic illustration of this general truth. Is it merely a coincidence that the methods of controlling through computerized monitoring of HCI developed and merged as remote access to libraries, self-directed computer-assisted instruction, online shopping, and decentralized work environments became truly possible? This new method of control emerged just as there were serious threats to established control in formal learning, work, shopping, and library environments. As social interest in the need to control human behavior in real-world environments began to decline, computerized monitoring developed to fill the control gap in online environments.

Among the online actors themselves, there is a strong sense — yet perhaps only an illusion — of control among shoppers, browsers, and information seekers. Generally, students and workers do not have such a strong sense of autonomous control. Syllabi, work assignments, and deadlines constantly remind the student and worker that, unless they freely choose to drop out or quit, they willingly relinquish some control over their schedules and activities in these two environments.

In general, computerized monitoring is perceived by the monitored — especially people in work environments — as a technique for decreasing the autonomous control of the monitored.

What does it mean to be in control during a human-computer (or, more generally, a human-machine) interaction? When one drives an automobile, one controls it in a very real, immediate way. Failure to maintain control of a moving automobile is a punishable offense. But the driver does not exert much individual control over the design of the automobile, and has not contributed much to the fact that the automobile has come to dominate ground transportation in the late twentieth century. Paradoxically, the driver of the automobile is both in control (with social expectations to maintain control of the vehicle), yet, in another understanding of control, powerless and out of control. Analogously, simply by behaving in cyberspace one controls one's online environment, but does not contribute much to the design of the computerized monitoring system that converts observed human behavior into environmental changes, and does not control (in a political or social sense) the fact that cyberspace quickly is becoming an environment subject to online surveillance.

Now that virtual environments have emerged, control means the ability to exert power over and through the technological means of communication (Tabbi 1997, 237). Perhaps virtual environmental control will be the next frontier. By acting in cyberspace, individually we will control how cyberspace looks and feels to us. But the software programmers who create the code that collects, analyzes, and translates our actions into environmental modifications also will continue to exert control. These two forms of environmental control — one as pure potentiality and the other as pure online actuality — will need to find a symbiotic relationship. The struggle for control in online environments will be very different from the struggle for control in real-world environments.

The issue of control is particularly self-evident in work environments, much more so than in learning, information-seeking, and shopping environments. The introduction of the factory system in the eighteenth and nineteenth centuries constituted an important change in the degree of social control capable of being exercised over workers, primarily because of new possibilities for visual supervision (Bryant 1995). The introduction of computers and computer networks into work environments seems to have caused an increased management interest in control. Nussbaum (1989, quoted in Oravec 1996, 68) notes that "there's a resurgence of management control today — almost a fetish — with managers attributing the need for it to rising competition and falling productivity."

Levy (1993) asserts that electronic monitoring is the newest means by which employers can inexpensively assert their control in the workplace, and still allow a measure of participation and employee input. Although increased productivity and improved customer service may be the professed goals of employers, the unstated objective is to reassert their traditional prerogatives in the workplace to control and establish the basic mood of the work environment. Questions of control of the workplace and whether electronic monitoring should even be introduced rarely are open to debate. This confines the issue to what is the most effective means of implementation from the perspective of the employer, rather than fundamental questions of worker control (Levy 1993). Most workers wish to retain some control and discretion over the work environment and the means of production.

The Office of Technology Assessment report (1987) also touches on this issue of workplace control: "When jobs are redesigned to facilitate computerized monitoring of work performance, they are also reshaped in ways that increase the degree to which management directs both the place and the method of work. This lack of personal control, in turn, places workers at significantly greater risk of ill health" (OTA 1987, 54–55; quoted in Levy 1993) . Although employers may justify various workplace surveillance tactics as necessary to protect against theft, to boost productivity, to increase safety, or to hold costs down, the underlying agenda always concerns control (Boss is watching 1993).

The control we are facing with computerized monitoring of HCI is decentralized, individualized, and based on our own behavior. Finally, as online environments become more mature, we will literally receive the government we deserve. The prospect of fully automated computerized monitoring — from data collection to the application of the findings — puts a new twist on William Blake's fear of mind-forged manacles. As computerized monitoring increasingly is deployed to create individualized environments based on the observed online behavior of individuals, to a certain extent the online environment itself becomes mind-forged, at least to the extent that the mind controls human behavior.

Normalization is the complement to surveillance. People survey an environment to draw inferences and to mentally normalize their perceptions into something that can be understood, and that can be translated into action. In formal education environments, in the modern period the normal was established as a principle of coercion by introducing standardized education, standardized textbooks, and normal schools for the training of future teachers — beadles of the normal. "Like surveillance and with it, normalization becomes one of the great instruments of power at the end of the classical age" (Foucault 1977, 184). In online environments controlled by computerized monitoring, however, normalization as an instrument of power begins to lose its edge. Computerized monitoring of HCI lowers the threshold of describing individuality to absolute zero, but individuality no longer need be used to define some norm to which we all must strive to conform (or deviate from). The need to normalize human behavior to conform to essentially intractable environmental conditions no longer exists in online environments. The impact of this sea change on shared human experiences may be profound.

The inhabitant of cyberspace has a new type of authority — control over the environment. The software and the person interact at a non-conscious level to construct and configure the virtual environment (Lyman 1996). Many people, especially those who use the Internet as employees or consumers, fear loss of control and privacy during electronic communication (Kiesler 1997, xi).

Control in online environments may be a seductive lullaby, rather than a hobnailed boot. Perhaps the appropriate literary metaphor for the late twentieth century experience of electronic surveillance, particularly computerized monitoring, is more the seduction portrayed in Huxley's *Brave New World* than the heavy-handed control predicted in Orwell's *Nineteen Eighty-Four* (Bryant 1995, 516). Gary Marx (Westin, Marx, Zahorik, and Ware 1992) suggests that computerized monitoring in work environments often focuses on engineering behavior, prevention, or soft control.

Discipline Discipline may be the manifestation of control. "'Discipline' may be identified neither with an institution nor with an apparatus; it is a type of power, a modality for its exercise, comprising a whole set of instruments, techniques, procedures, levels of application, targets; it is a 'physics' or an 'anatomy' of power, a technology" (Foucault 1977, 215). If computerized monitoring of HCI is a form of control, how are the individuals and computers disciplined? On the other hand, we do not want to invest computerized monitoring of HCI with a sinister intent that may be nothing more than a figment of our imagination. As a discipline, computerized monitoring is remarkably disorganized. Its practitioners also are not very aware of computerized monitoring as an encompassing method. To get into a position to be able to discipline, the disciplinary force needs to acquire and refine the power of observation. "The exercise of discipline presupposes a mechanism that coerces by means of observation; an apparatus in which the techniques that make it possible to see induce effects of power, and in which, conversely, the means of coercion make those on whom they are applied clearly visible" (Foucault 1977, 170–171).

Cash Nexus Many critics of computerized monitoring of HCI, particularly in work environments, have long suspected that the method is being used to ensure the extraction of more human labor for the amount of money invested in human resources. At one level, computerized monitoring has been used to systematically detect underperformers. At another, perhaps more insidious level, it has been used to implement computer pacing, in which the software gradually raises the benchmark of acceptable levels of productivity. Perceived in this light, computerized monitoring of HCI is no more than a high-tech gadget for pursuing an age-old struggle between management and labor. Computerized monitoring, however, may have emerged from a more subtle type of cash nexus. Because the use of information itself is becoming a major source of wealth, the goal of computerized monitoring may be to monitor the processes of the creation of this new type of wealth. Zuboff (1988), for example, identifies the new origin of wealth as the ability of workers to use information in a skilled way (cited in Lyman 1996, 25).

The Will to Monitor What is the final cause or purpose of all of this computerized monitoring of HCI? Why do we pursue this line of action with such ardor? Several possible explanations can be posited as primary causes of the amorphous movement to use computers to monitor HCI. It may be a manifestation of some unconscious group will. If left to their own devices, people tend to create environments and tools in which others can be watched and observed. Main streets, shopping malls, and commercial Web sites are the historically linear progression of this trend. Compared to main streets and malls, however, a major panoptic shift in perspective with Web sites is that the right and power to observe is strictly controlled. There are no park benches in this virtual town square. If this explanation for the human will to monitor is plausible, why then does the will to monitor seem so ferocious at the data collection stage, yet often wane during the data analysis, interpretation, and application stages?

Conspiracy theories form another class of possible explanation. Conspiracy theories tend to understand the entire movement to use computers to monitor HCI as a deliberate attempt to create environments in which computers provide unprecedented knowledge of, and control over, human behavior. One problem with the conspiracy theory is that much computerized monitoring activity is cheerfully open, rather than furtive and clandestine. Another problem with this theory is that the application of computerized monitoring systems has been very diverse, evidently from the beginning of the movement. It is difficult to imagine that educators, librarians, websters, and employers are in cahoots.

One possible function of new technology is to permit a split between surveillance and bureaucratic management methods. Capitalism may retain its salience and its reliance on new technology, but within a flexible, post-production line framework, geared primarily not to production but to consumption (Lyon 1994, 128). The will to monitor becomes redirected from the production process to the consumption process. The amazing drive during the last few years to develop software tools and techniques for observing and measuring Web use can be understood as this redirection of the will to monitor into its natural growth channel for the foreseeable future. Monitoring employees, students, and library users is child's play compared to the immense wen that has developed to study the online habits of consumers.

How Does Computerized Monitoring Conceptualize Human Beings and Human Being?   How does computerized monitoring reflect a way of thinking about human beings? The focus of most monitoring projects is on human behavior as a series of discrete actions. The emotional component of human being is not of much interest, and the cognitive component can only be inferred. Computerized monitoring tries to use factual observation of human behavior to infer probable future behavior, or to infer past, present, and future cognitive activity that caused or resulted from the observed behavior.

When computerized monitoring is used in shopping environments, people may be perceived as a commodity. If HCI can be used to infer the demographic characteristics of the people involved, and if demographic characteristics are a good predictor of future spending and consuming, those behind the computerized monitoring project could sell this information to advertisers and other business interests. In this context, computerized monitoring is being used to generate demographic knowledge that can be resold.

Computerized monitoring of HCI has had a difficult time understanding the emergence of people in online environments as virtual social animals. There is a strong and growing body of research that suggests that the primary purpose of human colonization of cyberspace is not to get information and spend money, but to connect with others. Survey research conducted by Bickson and Panis (1997) supports the thesis that computerized networks are social technologies that serve the need for such affiliation. Many commentators are looking beyond the interface and the basic interaction between an individual and a computer to better understand the future of human being in cyberspace. "The defining interaction of Internet culture lies not in the interface between the user and the computer, but rather in that between the user and the collective imagination of the vast virtual audience to whom one submits an endless succession of enticing, exasperating, evocative figments of one's being" (Porter 1997, xiii).

Most computerized monitoring projects are perfectly content to operate at the level of anonymous individuals. Once the online behavior of individual A can be distinguished from that of individual B, there is little need, for the purposes of analysis of the behavior, to know the identities of these individuals. This situation may occur more often in library (information seeking) and Web (and other online shopping) environments than in formal learning and work environments. In most instances, the identities of students and employees needs to be known.

How Does Computerized Monitoring Conceptualize Computers?   As a field of research, computerized monitoring of HCI postures itself toward the computers and computer networks that comprise a portion of the field of study. Why are we more interested in human behavior than computer behavior during HCI? Partly because the researchers are human, and partly because, unless computers are malfunctioning, they are much more predictable than people. The computer or computer network almost serves as the substratum or given during studies of HCI. A hidden assumption here may be that the behavior of a computer is relatively slow to change, despite the acceleration of releases of software upgrades. As computers become more adept at analyzing computerized monitoring data in real time in the midst of an HCI, then modifying its behavior to better accommodate the emerging human behavior, studying the behavior of computers may become as interesting and informative as studying the behavior of people during HCI.

What Do We Really Want to Know?   To make computerized monitoring of HCI truly useful and worthy of status as an organized discipline, we must ask ourselves what we really want to know, and then whether or not (or how) computerized monitoring assists in the pursuit of that knowledge. One problem with some of the human activities we want to know more about, such as learning and information seeking, is that the main activity appears to occur neither in the physical world of human action nor in online environments. What we really want to know more about is human cognitive processes, and we study physical and online behavior only because we believe it provides clues into some cognitive processes or progress that we cannot observe directly. In the case of work and shopping perhaps the focus on cognitive activities is not as strong. Nevertheless, even a virtual manual labor activity, such as telemarketing, has its cognitive aspects, and the decision processes underlying shopping activities are neither insignificant nor completely known.

In online library environments the goals of evaluation are shifting from product to process (Borgman, Hirsh, and Hiller 1996). Shute and Smith (1993) suggest that computerized monitoring data are a useful way to trace and study the exploration and decision processes during HCI. This general shift toward an emphasis on knowledge of process can be seen in a variety of applications of computerized monitoring in diverse online environments. Even online marketers are becoming very interested in the processes by which online browsers become online buyers. High-level process analysis could become a major component of computerized monitoring. Although the push toward finer granularity in data seems to be at odds with this trend toward high-level process analysis, as the tools and techniques of analyzing the data continue to develop, there is no reason why a fruitful high-level analysis of fine-grained data would be impossible.

Human behavior in real environments has been extensively studied. Human behavior in virtual environments, however, is a new field of study because virtual environments have emerged within the past 50 years for humanity as a whole, and the past 10–15 years for most of us. Naturally we are interested in how people will act in these new virtual environments. We turn to computerized monitoring to collect and analyze data because the development of computers made the emergence of virtual environments possible. Computerized monitoring is built on human fascination with human behavior in online environments. Because we realize that human behavior in this new venue is complex, or at least capable of complex analyses, we turn to computers for help. "Behavior emerges in ways that thought cannot grasp" (Bailey 1996, 7).

Bailey's argument could extend to the conclusion that the computer's knowledge of the HCI ultimately will be much more important than human knowledge of the interaction, either by the human participant or by others studying HCI. The evolutionary make-up of our mental processes does not leave us well-suited for this analysis, in which there are vast amounts of data and the goal (perhaps) is not to find eternal patterns and immutable laws, but to immediately improve or enhance a specific individual's experience or functionality within a specific online environment or situation. Bailey notes that "what we learn in math class has a powerful effect on which alternative views of the world we are able to listen to and which we cannot even hear. In particular, the old equational maths can make us tone deaf to behaviors that work simultaneously in parallel and to behavior for which history matters" (Bailey 1996, 220).

Computerized Monitoring as Idea and Reality   For critics and proponents alike, computerized monitoring is encountered more often as an abstract idea than as a perceived component of a lived experience. We think about computerized monitoring, rather than feel it. Computerized monitoring as an object of study is most interesting and instructive when it is examined as an idea to the monitored, rather than as an idea to those who developed and championed it, or as an actual set of realized manifestations. The idea of computerized monitoring has flourished in the minds of the potentially monitored, especially employees and Web surfers. In contrast, for example, the nineteenth century idea of manifest destiny is an example of an idea most interesting as an idea to those who lived by it, rather than to those who suffered and died by it. Despite its massive size, the literature on computerized monitoring contains very few lengthy, glowing visualizations of the promise and potential of the idea of such monitoring. Examinations by practitioners of the anticipated benefits of computerized monitoring often are dry, sober, and short. The prospect of this monitoring evidently does not inspire the literary muse. The writings of Siegfried Treu are the exception that prove the general rule.

The idea of using computers to monitor HCI clearly is unsettling. Perhaps the primary cause of our wariness is not so much the sense of intrusion and loss of privacy, but rather that the mundane, incontrovertible evidence captured and presented by computerized monitoring bursts the fantasy bubble about the dreamy world of cyberspace. Computerized monitoring may reveal human activity in online environments in too harsh a light. It leaves us feeling human and vulnerable. Rheingold (1993, 11) speculates that the Internet might become the next great escape medium, in the grand tradition of serial radio programs, Saturday afternoon movie matinees, and television soap operas. Computerized monitoring, with its time stamps and small units of measurement, grates against this collective will to escape. The data collected via computerized monitoring are at odds with the dreamy lived experience of being online.

Another potential cause of uneasiness about computerized monitoring is the way it focuses on discrete individuals. The methodologies of computerized monitoring tend to isolate the individual. The behavior of individuals may be aggregated in the course of the analysis of the data, but the tendency of many computerized monitoring projects is to view HCI as one person interacting with one computer or computer system. If computerized monitoring becomes the basis upon which online environments are created and customized, the isolation of the individual in cyberspace will intensify. Computerized monitoring does not seem particularly well suited for the study of the collective behavior of computer-mediated work teams, collaborative learning groups, and virtual communities. Regardless of its role and complicity in the generally-perceived decline in privacy, computerized monitoring may be a threat to human community.

Another cause for concern is the growing realization that more and more of our private behavior is migrating from more-or-less private places in the real world (e.g., the privacy of the home) to more-or-less public, monitored places in the virtual world of cyberspace. What is the human role in this fearful new world of pervasive surveillance, sentient online environments, and perpetual flux and mutability? Are we relegated to the role of dumber primates pounding away on keyboards? In the real world of relatively static objects, people had a near monopoly on the bringing forth of new things into creation. They were responsible for the creation of man-made artifacts. As Heidegger (1977, 9) notes, "The principal characteristic of being responsible is this starting something on its way into arrival. It is in the sense of such a starting something on its way into arrival that being responsible is an occasioning or an inducing to go forward." However, virtual worlds evolving from the computerized monitoring of HCI never will arrive into full being and stasis, and the people and the monitoring software will share the responsibility for starting the virtual environment on its way and modifying it as time passes.

5

Ethical and Moral Issues

The fundamental problem of electronic monitoring is that it is used almost invariably as a means to reinforce prior social relations of subordination Clement and McDermott 1991, 195).

Computerized monitoring of HCI is an act (or series of acts) of acquiring, analyzing, and applying data. The ethical and moral implications of the act focus on the boundaries of acceptable use of behavioral information about people as they interact, singly or in groups, with computers or computer networks. Like most things in both the real and virtual worlds, computerized monitoring can be misused. As a society, what are the methods available to us to prevent or mitigate the misuse of this monitoring? When we examine the value and propriety of computerized monitoring projects, we can focus on the acts, on the resultant data, or on the application of the analysis of the data in the form of subsequent acts. For the activities of both the user and the analyst of the user's behavior, how can good and bad behavior in this environment be differentiated? What are the principles of moral and ethical behavior in the study of human behavior in online environments?

In computerized monitoring in work environments, an ethical controversy exists over the use of computer systems to continuously gather a stream of data on employee performance. Labor unions and a substantial portion of the general public think computerized monitoring systems are inherently unethical, but the business community and the managerial class maintain that management has an inherent right to deploy and use these systems. This claim to a right is not currently restricted by any state or federal laws (Magney 1996, 207). The topic of computerized monitoring often elicits strong emotions and opinions. For the purposes of this book, there may be some value in attempting to temporarily suppress or bracket the natural, understandable impulse to express righteous indignation.

Strong, Persistent, Negative Reactions to Computerized Monitoring   It seems impossible to be disinterested about the issue of computerized monitoring. The issue has a polarizing effect on people. Rheingold (1993, 280) succinctly states the basic concern: "When people use the convenience of electronic communication or transaction, we leave invisible digital trails; now that technologies for tracking those trails are maturing, there is cause to worry." Although the sense of foreboding permeates all four environments in which computerized monitoring is used, the feeling appears to be strongest in the world of work, where computerized monitoring is used (at least ostensibly) as a performance appraisal tool. George (1996) notes that much of the popular literature on computerized performance monitoring stresses the negative effects of monitoring on workers, no matter how or where it is implemented. The work and Web environments, rather than the formal learning and library environments, seem to elicit the most vehement responses to computerized monitoring.

People not directly involved in computerized monitoring often exhibit a negative response to it. Often when I speak about computerized monitoring of HCI at conferences, workshops, and in private conversations, someone will question, often in a very indignant tone of voice, the moral and ethical aspects of this practice. The complaint often suggests that this data collection and analysis method may violate accepted ethical norms observed when conducting research on human subjects. One's gut reaction to computerized monitoring is that it constitutes a clear violation of a person's privacy. Computerized monitoring focuses on the most minute aspects of our virtual existence. The data are so fine-grained that often one involved in the online behavior would not recognize one's own behavior as articulated on the logs. Although we do not complain about public records of the major events in our lives (birth, marriage, real estate transfers, and death), the systematic collection of data about the daily minutiae of our digital lives riles us, even if we are not specifically identified.

Why do many people become concerned and possibly indignant when they learn about the use of computers to monitor HCI? Perhaps it is the idea of computer monitoring, rather than self-conscious experiences with it, that causes the unease. Something in the very notion of using computers to monitor HCI offends many people. Laws, ethical principles, policies, and procedures governing the conduct of research projects involving human subjects do not seem to be much help here, perhaps because the sense of violation is general, rather than specific.

Perhaps the most vexing aspect of these recent technological developments is that they were not designed with malicious intent. Computerized monitoring programs and projects are not second cousins twice removed from projects to develop weapons of death and destruction. The designers and developers of these technologies look more like the kid next door than the evil figures in spy movies. None of the perceived privacy threats are the product of malevolence. The designers of EZPass (that facilitates the electronic collection of tolls on tollroads) have developed a system that efficiently speeds the collection process; the creation of cookies files and the capturing of demographic information from visitors to Web sites provides advertisers with information that will have a positive impact on the intelligent solicitation of consumers; a uniform citizen identification system could have a great positive impact on processing benefits and preventing fraud; and the FBI and National Security Agency have legitimate interests in protecting U.S. citizens from enemies, both foreign and domestic (McMullen 1997). These technological developments, however, could lead to unintended, unanticipated consequences. They almost force us to accept the potentially bad with the good.

Large groups of people seem to have a predilection for disliking computerized monitoring. For example, Chalykoff and Kochan (1989) found that employees who were predisposed to oppose monitoring could not be swayed by positive implementation strategies (George 1996, 462). Some observers have suggested that strong resistance to computerized monitoring by employees in work environments is not centered so much in the monitoring activity itself, or in the application of the analysis of the data, but rather in the non-participatory nature of the design and implementation of these systems. A particularly controversial element surrounding electronic monitoring is the means of implementation. When employers unilaterally introduce electronic monitoring with little or no participation by the workforce, often there is resentment, increased levels of stress and perhaps little increase in productivity. Some commentators suggest that these effects can be avoided or reduced if the employer involves the employee in the design and implementation of the monitoring system (OTA 1987; Westin 1992, cited in Levy 1993).

Online shoppers as a group also are wary of computerized monitoring of their interactions with computer systems. Gandy (1995) contends that as high as 93 percent of consumers agree that there ought to be legal requirements reflecting the moral responsibility of marketers to seek permission from individuals before they share personal information derived from transactions, including transactions that involve HCI.

People do not like to feel trapped. They like to have the sense that there is something on the other side of the fence, and that the grass may be greener there. Many critics argue that productivity surveillance as it has been practiced by many businesses for the past 15 years is bad not only because it often is covert, but also because it is ubiquitous, inescapable, constant, and measured in real time (Halpern 1992, 20). Gibbs (1995) suggests that achieving a workable level of trust in a work environment is one of the most profound management challenges. The use of CPM, however, extends the level of mistrust down to that of every keystroke and every byte of data sent and received.

One of the major complaints about CPM is that the computer systems are inflexible and cannot consider, unlike a human supervisor, the context in which performance occurs (Grant and Higgins 1996, 213). It is seen as a dehumanized, inhuman way of capturing and revealing the "truth" about how people use computers. Often when considering the amorphous movement to use computers to monitor HCI we get the vague feeling that computerized monitoring does not conceptualize human being and human activity in the best of all possible ways. Computerized monitoring is premised on a desire to see people as typing, clicking creatures — as the source of clickstreams. It seems to fail as a robust world view. Most critics of computerized monitoring do not argue that the data as collected is inaccurate because of some system failure. Rather, the truth (or, more objectively, the vision) of human behavior as we interact with computers that is revealed through computerized monitoring has a brutal brilliance that is unsettling. It can be a very cold, analytic view of human behavior. If computerized monitoring can ever predict human behavior at the individual level, the predictive power may be as welcome as actuarial tables.

When computerized monitoring is used to study online behavior, the results often are not flattering insights on the human condition. The occasional glimmers of perseverance are outweighed by evidence of incompetence, impatience, laziness, poor training, and poor basic skills. Analysis of computerized monitoring data often concludes that human learning and behavior apparently are quite inefficient. In the game of repetitive accurate actions people are bound to lose against computers. Electronic circuits are good at meticulously noting details about the world around them and then carefully recording the details (Bailey 1996, 4). People tend to learn more through trial and error. One could argue that computerized monitoring is an unfair and ultimately unproductive way to observe and measure trial-and-error learning.

Computerized monitoring also has a patina of objectivity that can gall. Although this monitoring seems to be completely, undeniably objective, often people may misuse or misinterpret the objectively collected data. Although the computer collects the data, usually someone has to analyze it, or at the very least interpret and implement a computer-assisted analysis. The problem with computerized monitoring is that the raw data do not in themselves provide a complete picture of human behavior. Computerized monitoring may be fair and objective, if fairness means that everyone is measured in the same increments on the same scale by a non-human measuring device, but the entire measurement contains no mechanism for measuring actual human factors that may truly reflect how well someone is performing a job or behaving in another environment typically subjected to computerized monitoring (Halpern 1992). Numerous social scientists have argued that the very process of imposing numbers onto life events causes the analysts to misread the events, corrupt or truncate the meaning of the events, or to see things not actually there (Bailey 1996, 8).

Computerized monitoring also has radically altered the economics of collecting, analyzing, and applying behavioral data about others. Because surveillance techniques in cyberspace are so sophisticated and cheap, people worry that virtual environments will be saturated by monitoring and surveillance.

Inappropriate, unfair, or incorrect applications of computerized monitoring data also cause concern. Usually computer monitoring is not used solely to understand and improve HCI. Many people have concerns about using computers to monitor human-computer interaction because the goal of the monitoring is assumed to go beyond merely understanding and improving that interaction. People mistrust the assumed motives behind computer monitoring.

Commentators are divided over the overall impact of computerization on human labor and workplace environments. Some critics see computerization as the logical extension of Taylor's theory of scientific management. Employees in a computerized work environment are made more productive by having their job routines de-skilled and increasingly circumscribed via computerization. Furthermore, their job performances are monitored and guided by various forms of computerized surveillance (Magney 1996, 200). When the computer becomes the job performance monitor, only the job activities that fall within the perceptual ken of the monitoring program really matter.

Other commentators, on the other hand, perceive computing technology as having a democratizing, empowering impact on the worker in the work environment. Because of computerization, workers have developed new skills and become more involved in workplace decisions (Magney 1996, 200). Computerized performance monitoring has freed many workers from the vague practices of partial human managers. One vision of the overall impact of computerization on work places it on the control and surveillance axis, while the other places it on the democratization and empowerment axis. Although CPM would enable an increased span of control for supervisors, because it automates much of the work involved in collecting and summarizing performance data, CPM should not be implemented so extensively that supervisors have little time or incentive to understand in other ways the performance of employees (Hawk 1994, 955). Although CPM opponents accept the need for electronic monitoring, they seek to curb its excesses and ensure a more equitable balance of power between employer and employee (Levy 1993).

Computerized monitoring also is a concern because of the possibility of negative consequences on the biological real-world health of those subject to frequent monitoring activities. The results of a study conducted by Hawk led him to conclude that health problems and job stress occurred to a greater extent when computerized performance monitors measured a large number of behaviors (Hawk 1994, 953).

Most Computerized Monitoring Is Not Consciously Nefarious The openness and cheekiness with which most computerized monitoring is done may be very unsettling to some observers. Computerized monitoring never was dominated by spies, government intelligence, cloaks and daggers. Computerized monitoring may be part of a larger historical process that has made machine-assisted surveillance a mainstreamed, everyday activity. "The power to snoop has become democratized" (Rheingold 1993, 292).

Some Moral Theories Before delving deeper into the ethical aspects of computerized monitoring of HCI, perhaps we should briefly review two important moral theories. Utilitarians claim that the morality of an act can be judged by its consequences. If an act produces the greatest good for the greatest number of people, it is morally good. Utilitarians could argue that business owners, employees, customers, and society in general benefit from CPM. Most critics of CPM argue that although owners, customers, and society in general benefit from CPM, employees suffer to such an extent that it is reasonable to conclude that, on balance, CPM is morally bad behavior, from a utilitarian point of view (Hawk 1994, 950).

Kantian moralists believe that the inherent features of an act make it right or wrong, regardless of consequences. If, for example, a Kantian believes that individual privacy, human dignity, and human autonomy are good things, and if the Kantian believes that CPM invades an individual's privacy, undermines human dignity, and violates human autonomy, then CPM is a morally bad act, regardless of any positive outcomes for employees, owners, customers, and society in general (Hawk 1994, 950–951).

The ethical and moral issues surrounding the large, diverse aspects of using computers to monitor HCI are so complex that a deliberate strategy for investigating the issues is needed. Hawk (1994) suggests that it would be more useful to examine the ethical considerations surrounding the detailed, specific design decisions related to CPM, rather than attempt to understand the ethical ramifications of CPM in general.

Computerized monitoring basically is a way to collect data. Data collection can be unethical in at least three broad ways. First, the data themselves generally can be accepted as private (or at least confidential) information, so that collecting them represents an invasion of privacy. Second, although the data themselves may not be private information, the method used to collect the data may be unethical. The procedure itself, which in the twentieth century often has included the use of some technology, is an unethical practice. Third, although the data themselves and the collection method may be ethical, the application of the data may be unethical. For example, reselling consumer purchasing behavior to a third party may be considered unethical, even though one's behavior in a shopping mall is not considered private information, and the data were collected at the point of sale with the full knowledge and consent of the purchaser. As we shall see in Chapter 9, the applications of the findings of computerized monitoring of HCI are varied and complex, and often play a crucial role in the determination of the ethical value of the entire activity. Many critics of computerized monitoring focus their concerns on the unethical application of analyzed data. For example, Keizer (1997) adopts the stance that, while collecting data about Web surfing behavior may not be evil in itself, the potential for inappropriate and abusive application and analysis of these data abound, because of the speed and efficiency with which the data can be collected, analyzed, sold, reused, and combined with other data. Computerized monitoring (at the feedback stage, rather than at the data collection stage) could be used to sway an individual's sense of need, desire, and, ultimately, one's sense of self.

Research Ethics and Human Subjects in Online Environments   The ethics of conducting research on human subjects in online environments is a thorny problem. Waskul and Douglass (1996) provide an overview of the ethics of conducting such research. A first step in any research project involving computerized monitoring is to collect or obtain the data. Often the raw data already are being collected; they merely need to be obtained from the administrators of the computer system. Some critics of the movement to use computers to monitor HCI argue that computer system administrators are too cavalier about releasing transaction logs and other data sets to researchers (Wilson 1995). The researchers often are not questioned about their methods of analysis, the steps they will take to protect individual human subjects, how they will disseminate the results of the analysis, and whether or not they will redistribute the raw data to other researchers or other third parties. All criteria for ethical research apply to the process of conducting Internet research. However, Internet researchers face some issues of particular concern: invasion of privacy of unknowing subjects while collecting data, lack of professional credentialing, and rushing to publish incomplete or unreviewed work (Duncan 1996).

Other Ethical Concerns   Many people believe that the protection of individual privacy is the dominant ethical issue regarding computerized monitoring of HCI. The seriousness and complexity of the privacy issue obscures other ethical questions to the point that the privacy issue may be a red herring. Most of the ethical eyebrows raised over computerized monitoring have focused on invasion or violation of individual privacy. Perhaps we should focus instead on the environmental degradation (especially in cyberspace) caused by persistent, pervasive monitoring. The issue of computerized monitoring as a contributing cause of environmental degradation is more important in the work and Web environments than in the learning and information seeking environments.

The question of sexual equity also arises when the topic of computerized monitoring is examined. The 9 to 5 organization has been a leader in exploring and expressing how computerized monitoring, especially in work situations, is a women's issue. It may not be a coincidence that computerized monitoring has flourished in environments where predominantly male supervisors, managers, and administrators oversee a workforce that is primarily female, including schools, libraries, and jobs involving clerical, telephone, and data entry tasks.

Identified Individualism   There may be movements in corners of the computerized monitoring field toward obtaining behavioral information about identifiable individual users. For perhaps obvious reasons, the CPM movement in work environments settled on the individual level almost immediately. The use of CPM to identify and catch virtual criminals (i.e., those attempting to commit crimes in virtual, computerized, networked environments, as opposed to those who commit crimes in real environments) also needs to achieve identifiable individualism. In other corners of the computerized monitoring field, the need to get to the level of identifiable individuals often is neither necessary nor desirable, and the need to be able to identify individuals by name is almost non-existent. Although critics of computerized monitoring rarely note it, there is great diversity across the field of computerized monitoring concerning the need to identify the individuals being monitored.

Virtual Selves, Digital Personae, and Data Images   The goal of many computer monitoring projects is to reveal group behavior, rather than unique, individual behavior. Is this interest in group behavior in cyberspace threatening to the individual's sense of self and self-worth? Sherry Turkle has been quoted as saying that at the end of the twentieth century we find ourselves with very unstable notions about the boundaries of the individual (Quittner 1997b). Real personae, digital personae, and fictitious personae vie for prominence in a schizophrenic dance. Clarke (1994) defines a digital persona as a virtual model of a real human being established through the collection, storage, and analysis of data about that real person. Fictitious personae can exist in both real and virtual environments. For example, although one could argue that MUD and MOO humunculi reveal something about the real people who project them, they are fictitious personae. A data image, on the other hand, is a cobbled concatenation of known real-world and online facts about a real person. "The 'data-image' circulating within and between organizational databases both requires our participation and has increasing impact on our life-chances, but as [sic] the same time is less visible and accessible to us" (Lyon 1994, 55).

Justice and Fairness

> Questions of justice and fairness must be raised when people's everyday activities are monitored and their habits, commitments and preferences classified by the would-be omniscient organization. Such classification is both an outcome not only of social differences but of advantage and disadvantage, and often serves to reinforce inequalities of life-changes. And while it undoubtedly enables us to participate in society in numerous important ways, it also constrains us and encourages us to comply with the social order (Lyon 1994, 19).

The Will to Monitor   The human will to monitor seems to have increased during the past decade. What is the relationship between the will to monitor and the ability to monitor? Was the will there before the ability to engage in computerized monitoring had been developed, or did the ability create the will? The will to monitor has gone mainstream, no longer confined to wiretapping covert, clandestine, and illegal activities. Computerized monitoring of HCI (as well as other types of human activity) may be fueling this increased manifestation of the human will to monitor both by making it easier and cheaper to collect and analyze data, and by threatening to wrest control of the monitoring process from human beings. "The will to mastery becomes all the more urgent the more technology threatens to slip from human control" (Heidegger 1977, 5). Frantic attempts to control HCI through computerized monitoring may be a response to a sense of loss of human control at another level. This may be especially true in work and formal learning environments, where one of the implicit duties of managers and teachers is to maintain some sort of control over productive, learning processes.

Arguments in Favor of Computerized Monitoring of Human-Computer Interaction Ethical concerns about computerized monitoring are not unanimously negative. There are some arguments that computerized monitoring is morally and ethically beneficial to the human condition. One strong argument in favor of such monitoring is the widely held belief that data it collects is objective and unbiased. "The information collected through electronic monitoring is also totally objective. The video camera, the listening device and the computer cannot on their own be selective in what they pick up" (Bewayo 1996, 189).

The surface objectivity of computerized monitoring causes the most unease in work environments. In formal learning environments, the anticipated outcomes, as well as the means of measuring those outcomes, usually are known by all in advance. Although formal learning environments are complex environments for socialization, primarily because they often are populated by young people, as formal learning environments they are relatively straightforward. Information seeking and shopping environments are complex, but the participants in these environments tend not to worry that the objective measurement of their activity will negatively affect the rewards they receive from the pursuit of that activity. Work environments, however, are much more complex, and the social aspects are more closely intertwined with the principal activities. People's livelihoods depend on their performance in work environments.

Rothwell studied the introduction and acceptance of computerized monitoring in the United Kingdom. She found that "while the potential use of information technology for monitoring worker effort and errors is resented by trade unions … workers appear to be less resentful of errors unambiguously attributable to them than being blamed for omissions that were largely the responsibility of others" (Rothwell 1984, 23, quoted in Long 1989, 329).

One also can argue that computerized monitoring is a professional necessity in the age of online environments. Educators, librarians and computer science professionals, personnel professionals, and professional business people need the information obtainable via computer monitoring to pursue their professional responsibilities. As long as they act responsibly and maintain professional confidentiality, professionals who use computer monitoring are acting ethically. The situation is analogous to physicians' relationships with their patients. Doctors often must ask embarrassing questions of patients to accurately diagnose their patients' ills.

The right of the employer to use computers to monitor employee-computer interaction can be defended by pointing to the analogous precedent of the employer's right to scrutinize itemized phone bills. Employers invest in both phone systems and computer systems to facilitate the production of goods and services, and they have a right to analyze and assess the use of those systems. Brian Burba (Shein 1996a) argues that employer monitoring of employee Internet activity is no different from monitoring a company's phone bill. No one questions the employer's right to examine the corporate phone bill and question employees, if necessary, about unusually long phone calls or phone calls to phone numbers that appear to be unrelated to work tasks.

The weakness of this defense of computerized monitoring is that, whereas a phone conversation is an impromptu communication between two or more persons, the content of which is open to change until it actually occurs, a visit to an online catalog, Web site, or piece of educational software is an interaction with more-or-less static texts. If management knows that an employee visited a Web site, the sphere of available content is then known. If all of the available content is known to be outside of work-related information, then, based solely on knowledge of where the user went, conclusions can be drawn about the appropriateness of that information gathering.

Proposed Code of Ethical Conduct for Individual Monitors   Given all of these arguments and concerns about the ethical aspects of computerized monitoring, it may be worthwhile to propose a few tentative planks for an ethical code of conduct for individuals who undertake projects involving the use of computers to monitor HCI.

First, the human monitor should never interfere with the HCI under study. If we accept the idea that the unobtrusive collection of data concerning HCI is ethical, that must be a first principle of ethical conduct within this system. "The presence of a monitoring activity should in no way interfere with the interaction. It should not change the behavior of the system, and it should not introduce apparent delays in processing or system response times" (Santos 1995, 166). This principle can be very difficult to achieve in practical situations. Interfering or retarding the progress of a search session can be very subtle and difficult to avoid. For example, some Web server logging software that converts on-the-fly numerical IP addresses to alphabetic Domain Naming System names can slow down the server's response (Udell 1996). Hildreth (1997) reported that the transaction logging software on an online catalog apparently caused slower system response time. Unless the transaction log analyst has detailed knowledge of how the logs are generated, the analyst may be unaware that the creation of the logs is noticeably slowing down the response for all users of the system. Although the principle of "first, do no harm" for the monitor (i.e., do not allow monitoring activities to impair the pace or form of the HCI being monitored) would appear to ensure pristine data, end-user efforts to thwart privacy compromises also can sully the data. For example, Pitkow (1997a) explains how cookie-crunching software can result in a potential overestimate of the number of unique visitors to a Web site.

A second potential plank for a code of ethical conduct for the human monitors is to maintain confidentiality. Never reveal how an identified individual has interacted with a computer system, unless that individual has consented to the revelation.

A code of ethical conduct must be made manifest in practice. What are the ethical decision points during the capture, analysis, and application of computerized monitoring data? Because it is a subset of all human behavior, ethical behavior manifests itself over time through action. Human behavior is a series of decisions. The time when a decision is or must be made is a decision point. Because the development, deployment, and use of computerized monitoring systems is a complex process, involving many decision points, we can identify and analyze the primary ethical decision points during and after the acquisition of computerized monitoring data. Bellotti and Sellen (1993) articulate four classes of concern that parallel the flow of information in a computerized monitoring environment: capture, construction, accessibility, and purpose.

1. Capture: What information is being captured?
2. Construction: What will happen to the information?
3. Accessibility: Who will have access to the information? A crucial decision here is whether or not the people being monitored should have such access. This decision should not be confused with whether or not those being informed should be notified that their behavior in a particular computerized environment is subject to computerized monitoring. Informed consent is possible without releasing the data gathered as a result of informed consent. Martin (1997) has suggested that nearly all computerized monitoring should be undertaken only if the prior consent of the users of the system during the proposed period of data collection has been obtained.
4. Purpose: How will the information be used?

Does there need to be a separate code of conduct specifically for computerized monitoring of online behavior in the workplace? Ottensmeyer and Heroux (1991, 524, quoted in Hawk 1994, 956) identify one reason why ethical considerations often are absent from discussions leading to decisions regarding the adoption and use of computerized job performance monitoring systems: Often there is an absence of ethical analysis from the manager's world. Susser suggests that business organizations adopt a code of conduct specifically related to the use of CPM systems. For example, measurements of work should be averaged over periods no shorter than one week, and employers should measure only behaviors that are essential for meeting organizational goals (Susser 1988, 594; quoted in Hawk 1994, 956).

Henriques outlines four basic guidelines for the ethical use of computer monitoring during work performance monitoring and appraisal. First, output standards must be reasonable and attainable, with monitoring periods of sufficient length to allow for short-term variations in an employee's performance. Second, only relevant work tasks should be included in the computer monitoring purview. Third, evaluation intervals should be fair and timely. Continuous monitoring rarely provides significant additional information. Finally, employees should have access to their work performance data generated by computer monitoring (Henriques 1986a).*

Proposed Conduct Code for Organizations Engaged in Computerized Monitoring As we have seen, different types of organizations are involved in computerized monitoring: for-profit corporations, not-for-profit research organizations,

---

* *See the guidelines published by Marx and Sherizen (1986a).*

and governmental bodies. In recent years the greatest pressure has been placed on the for-profit sector to create a common code of ethical conduct in online environments. "Online commerce will succeed only if it can foster trust by ensuring security and privacy through an enforceable code of electronic ethics" (Markey 1997).

The first task of an organization involved in generating and analyzing Web server logs is to articulate who has initial, direct control of these log files. It may be the person or department tasked with the care and feeding of the server itself. What are their rights and responsibilities regarding data contained in the log files? Critics of computerized monitoring in general may argue that these front-line keepers of the logs are much too cavalier about providing access to the data. Proponents of computerized monitoring could argue that systems people and departments have been insufficiently conscientious about informing other people and units in organizations about the potentially valuable data contained in these logs.

Shein (1996a) articulates four basic planks for a code of ethical conduct for organizations involved in (or even contemplating) a CPM program:

1. Create a formal Internet access policy that specifies whether monitoring tools will be used.

Willis Ware makes a very forceful plea for corporate policies to govern and control computerized monitoring in specific corporations. "Technology facilitates a lot of actions and a lot of events, but it is not the central issue. The central issue is information use — information use in the context of what society will tolerate in the use and exploitation of information on our people, or what the individual will tolerate in the workplace, or outside the workplace" (Westin, Marx, Zahorik, and Ware 1992).

2. Define who in the organizational hierarchy has access to specific systems and resources.

3. Provide reasons for policy provisions.

Some policies may be driven by economics, such as the cost of providing Internet access. Other policy provisions may be driven primarily by technological limitations, such as limited bandwidth and slow responses during periods of peak demand.

4. Monitor usage of the network by application or department, rather than by individual users.

Shein effectively argues that, for most organizations, aggregated usage patterns and needs have much more impact on policy decisions than the minutely detailed clickstreams of individuals within the organization.

Social Aspects of Computerized Monitoring   Although computerized monitoring clearly has some social components, it tends to emphasize the information seeking aspect of online behavior, rather than the socialization aspects. Most computerized monitoring projects assume that people interact with computers primarily to find or create information, rather than to interact with other human beings. Online behavior is interpreted primarily as information-seeking behavior. Librarians in particular have been chastised for understanding the Web primarily as an asynchronous document delivery medium, rather than as a synchronous communication medium. In his remarks during a panel discussion reported in Westin, Marx, Zahorik, and Ware (1992), Gary Marx saw computerized monitoring in work environments as part of broader social changes that are altering the boundaries between the public and the private — between the self and society. While Marx's comments were neutral on the topic of the relationship between computerized monitoring and society, Edward Markey (1997) clearly sees computerized monitoring as something that debases society and weakens the social fabric. Markey contends that the Web

> makes it possible to track where people are going on the Net and what they're doing there — to sneak corporate hands into a "cookie jar" of personal information to compile profiles of hobbies, buying habits, financial status, health, and who they associate with online. In short, that wondrous wire may allow digital desperadoes to roam the electronic frontier unchecked by any high-tech sheriff or adherence to any code of electronic ethics.

While Markey uses inflammatory language to describe the situation and reinforces the cognitive and emotional link between the American frontier myth and the emerging myth of a digital frontier, this statement is more important in that it appears to contain factual errors (e.g., cookies by themselves cannot reveal who people associate with online) and it ties computerized monitoring or surveillance with corporations and criminals.

We should not underestimate the long-term social effects of the manifestation of the will to monitor in the form of computerized monitoring. Rochlin (1997, 97) makes the general observation that

> the creation and expansion of new technical capabilities, even those as narrowly defined as better ways of moving bits of data between computers, may cause long-term and indirect effects that strongly alter the way in which people visualize and interpret their status and role in society, both in regard to relationships with governmental actors and with regard to other forms of social interaction.

Conclusion   It can be stated in broad, undefined terms that both good and bad uses have been made of computerized monitoring technology. If the bad uses (however defined) predominate, does that lead to the conclusion that computerized monitoring itself is bad and should be restricted, redirected, or abandoned? As we shall see in the Chapter 7, although there are nagging moral and ethical misgivings about computerized monitoring, the misgivings have not led to much legislation and regulatory action in the United States.

Most individuals and groups involved in computerized monitoring are not aware of the entire field, nor of its historical development. If the field exists as an identifiable whole, it is severely polarized by the disparate environments in which computerized monitoring is undertaken. Even though the same basic techniques are being used across the field, the researchers in library, learning, and work environments are but vaguely aware of their counterparts in the other environments.

6

Computerized Monitoring
and Privacy

In the electronic era, the whole concept of privacy has changed. We've learned that we cannot participate in this brave new world as consumers without forgoing at least some of what we have traditionally thought of as our privacy rights. We give our names, addresses, telephone numbers, and credit card information to complete strangers — an act not fundamentally different from giving your Visa card to a waiter who then disappears for 10 minutes, but often perceived as riskier (Seymour 1997, 93).

The commercial use of transaction generated personal information in networked computer environments represents the latest and most significant challenge to personal privacy in the United States (Sessler 1997).

During the computer age the issue of personal privacy has been hotly debated. It is a topic that elicits extremely emotional responses from many people. For instance, Raskin (1996) warns that commercial activity on the Internet puts people on the brink of the biggest invasion of privacy to date. Privacy in cyberspace is an immense, emerging issue that causes much uneasiness.

The general population in the United States, if not that of the entire world, appears to be extremely sensitive to digital privacy. The relationship between personal privacy and the use of computers to monitor HCI appears to be one in which two large issues have significant areas of overlap. Neither issue, however, entirely comprehends the other. The issue concerning personal privacy in cyberspace appears to be the more volatile of the two — recently receiving much attention from the popular press, the federal government, and privacy watchdog groups. Lyon (1994, 60) contends that the significance and challenge of electronic surveillance is missed if it is reduced to a concern merely with privacy.

The relationship between the two issues also can be tentatively described as inverse. In other words, it appears that as the ability to use computers to monitor HCI increases, becomes more sophisticated, and diffuses throughout the realm of human endeavor, the ability to establish and maintain one's privacy correspondingly shrinks. "Indeed, as the free-flowing exchange and exploitation of information is being celebrated as the main engine of economic prosperity into the next century, individual privacy is looking more and more like an endangered natural resource" (Bernstein 1997, A1). The value of personal privacy for the well-being of any society, perhaps especially a democratic society, seems heretofore to have remained largely unarticulated and taken for granted, and now needs further reflection and articulation, especially as more people devote more of their time to pursuing their social and personal lives in cyberspace.

In both law and ethics, privacy serves as an umbrella term for a variety of meanings and interests (DeCew 1997, 1). Everyone seems to possess a basic intuition that what is private is that which is nobody else's business (DeCew 1997, 56). When privacy is compromised the "business" of the other person seems to have at least two main components: Some previously private information about someone is known by another, and that other uses or acts on the basis of the formerly private information. Knowledge and action are the two basic components. Sometimes it bothers me to know that someone else knows some private information about me (although some of that sense of bother may be fear that the other will act on knowledge of my private information), and other times what offends is not so much that someone simply knows some private information about me, but that this person has acted on the information in a way that seems inappropriate (e.g., by revealing it to a third party).

In turn, the knowledge component of a privacy invasion can be broken down into at least two parts. First, someone needs to find out some private information about me. Second, I need to learn that someone else has found out this information. Both the offender and the offended need to know. A purist would argue that, just as a tree that falls in the forest with no creature within hearing distance still makes a sound, if someone learns some private information about an individual, yet does not act in any way on that knowledge, and the intruded person does not know of the breach of privacy, an invasion of privacy does nevertheless occur.

The affect of computerization on personal privacy involves at least a perception of increased vulnerability. In the United States the issues of personal privacy and technological advance always have been closely linked. DeCew (1997, 13) suggests that technological advance in the nineteenth century was a major impetus for the codification of privacy protection via written laws. The changes in information technology have increased the probability that at least some privacy violations will occur (Mendes 1985, 2). The argument can be made that computerized monitoring represents a type of privacy violation.

Although the possibility of computerized monitoring as an invasion of privacy was raised early in the computer revolution, most of the early concerns about privacy invasions centered on computers as storage, aggregation, and analysis devices for other types of sensitive individual information — information that had little or nothing to do with the way people interact with computers and computer networks. With the arrival of the computer revolution and postindustrial economies, the notion of personal privacy needs to be reexamined. The networking of the post-industrial state will require a reconceptualization of the dynamic relationship between organizational practices and information technology, and a more comprehensive appreciation of the privacy problem (Bennett 1991).

The main question for the present discussion concerning privacy is whether or not unobtrusive, uninformed computerized monitoring of individuals as they interact with computers and computer networks constitutes an invasion of privacy.

Why Is Privacy Valuable?   How can we articulate, either in some quantified or qualified way, the value of privacy to individuals and societies? What does privacy protect? Or perhaps privacy is a good in itself. Some philosophers and legal scholars have argued that privacy is an intrinsic good — fundamental and irreducible (Spinello 1995). Others contend that privacy is an instrumental good. The right to privacy is derived from other rights such as the right to hold property, the right to a secure person, and the right to freedom (Spinello 1995). Scanlon (1975) suggests there is something unique and of special value in privacy (cited in DeCew 1997, 3). Galkin (1996), however, observes that most private information has no value if retained by the individual, and only a negative value if released to others. He seems to suggest that the only reason a person wants to maintain the privacy of information is to prevent it acquiring a negative, damaging value if released to the public. The value of private information, as opposed to privacy itself, is either zero or a negative value.

Rachels (1975) wonders why people are interested in maintaining their privacy. Most people seem to have an intense, almost innate interest in protecting their privacy. What is the value of privacy in normal, ordinary situations? Rachels argues that an individual's sense of privacy cannot be adequately explained merely regarding the fear of being embarrassed or disadvantaged by an invasion of privacy. He argues that the value of one's privacy rests primarily on the close connection between one's ability to control who has access to one (and, by extension, to information about one), and one's ability to create and maintain different types of social relationships with different people. Privacy protects the diversity and complexity of an individual's relationships with others. If everything is public (or at least not private), human relationships will become homogeneous and bland. Perolle (1996) suggests that in computerized monitoring environments the damage done to the fragile dynamics of group processes (including collaborative work) may be more significant than the reduction in personal privacy.

Cate (1997), following Westin, identifies four primary benefits served by or derived from privacy: autonomy; release from public roles; self-evaluation and decision-making; and limited and protected communication. One could argue that, by the inherently inhuman way computerized monitoring collects and analyzes data about human behavior, it is an affront to human dignity. "Privacy is an essential component of individual autonomy and dignity. Our sense of liberty is partly defined by the ability to control our own lives — whether this be the kind of work we undertake, whom we choose to associate with, where we live, the kind of religious and political beliefs we hold, or the information we wish to divulge about ourselves" (Marx and Sherizen 1989, 398–399).

In the real world privacy protects individuals from undue pressures to conform to social norms and group behavior. If, however, computerized monitoring leads to truly individualized environments, insisting on privacy in cyberspace may actually make self-differentiation and self-actualization more difficult.

Another perceived value of privacy is its role as a necessary condition for the existence of freedom. A shield of privacy is absolutely essential if an individual is to pursue freely personal projects or cultivate intimate social relationships (Spinello 1995). Without personal privacy, the concept of democracy based on individual choice makes little sense (Laudon 1996).

Brin (1998), however, questions the notion that privacy is a necessary condition for the existence of freedom and democracy. He suggests that in a wired world, we will need to decide between privacy and freedom. He argues that rather than attempt to save individual privacy, we should strive to create an online society that is more transparent and more exposed. For Brin, freedom ultimately is more important and savable than privacy.

Other observers of the transformation of the idea of privacy in the online age worry that privacy is becoming increasingly a commodity to be sold, bartered, and hoarded. They fear that if privacy takes on the trappings of a commodity, the right to privacy will become a relative class issue, in which the wealthy classes are able to maintain more privacy than the poorer classes. This trend may already have been established in the modern, real world.

Perhaps individual consumers are leading the way in the commodification of privacy. They are learning that releasing private information can have a positive value for the individual, as well as the more traditional sense of a negative value attached to loss of privacy. Often it depends on the situation and who is in control. Bernstein (1997) suggests that the conflict over privacy is growing and escalating because people are learning how little control they exercise over the use of personal information — an increasingly valuable marketing and corporate asset. The issue concerning personal information privacy is in danger of becoming commodified. Rheingold (1993, 291) argues that improvements in information networks have been turning privacy into a commodity for years. Frye (1997), however, suggests that personal information does not reveal or compromise personhood in any meaningful way.

We should clarify this notion of the commodification of privacy a little by noting that privacy itself cannot become a commodity, because privacy is a state of being in which certain personal information has not been divulged to certain persons or the public in general. One in control of one's personal information may elect to sell (or give away) that information to certain persons, entities, or the public in general, or another person or party may intentionally or unintentionally acquire that private information. What we really mean by the concept of the commodification of privacy is the commodification of certain personal information that could result in a state of being that we conveniently, generically call private.

The commodification of privacy is growing out of the convergence of computers and communications — the same convergence that makes virtual communities possible. Within the ethereal zone of human being known as cyberspace, information is capable of being mixed, matched, sold, and resold to other potential users or consumers of that information — users who frequently view information about private lives as public commodities (Hausman 1994). Munro (1997) also explores the concept of commodifying data about the online activities and real-world commercial and health information, then letting individuals control their own data by hoarding, trading, or selling it. Bresnahan (1997, 74) reports that CyberGold in Berkeley, California, monetarily compensates readers of Web ads. This could be an early instance of the commidification of private information in cyberspace. Scanning advertisements was a private activity in the real world. In online environments, manifestations of viewer interest in certain advertisements (e.g., banner ads on Web pages) have become non-private information that can be appropriated or acquired through purchase or barter by second and third parties (the viewer is understood as the first party).

Several writers have suggested that personal information, both demographic and behavioral, should be something the individual can stockpile or sell, depending on one's preferences, beliefs, and socioeconomic status, not unlike the way some people regularly sell blood to blood banks. For example, Gattiker et al. (1996) state that our current understanding of privacy and the environments in which it can exist requires that we treat personal data and information as if it were cash, because privacy represents something of value to many parties with diverse, perhaps conflicting, interests. Treating information as a commodity is a lucrative business, and financial incentives have prevailed over the recognition and defense of privacy rights (Spinello 1995). Laudon (1996) makes a long argument that to protect individual privacy into the next millennium, we should consider market-based mechanisms grounded in the notion of individual ownership of personal information and a National Information Market in which individuals can receive fair compensation for the use of information about themselves. Laudon does not explain why these personal information markets should be national, rather than international.

Privacy Lost: Aspects of Invasion and Loss   Why is privacy valuable to an individual? Loss of privacy often opens one up to other unwanted intrusions. A single instance of loss of privacy can produce a domino effect. For example, if the bank sells my name and address to credit card companies, I will be deluged with unwanted credit card offers. My responses to those credit offers may alter my credit history forever, ultimately affecting my life chances.

Rule, McAdam, Stearns, and Uglow (1980) distinguish between aesthetic and strategic considerations of privacy. An aesthetic invasion of privacy occurs when things or information are exposed which the offended person believes are inappropriate to reveal to others. The privacy invasion is embarrassing to the invaded person, but it has little additional impact. A strategic invasion of privacy occurs when the invasive act compromises the interests of the offended person (summarized in Bellotti 1996, 244). Loss of privacy can be either an unaesthetic, ugly event, an event that hampers the future life chances of an individual or group, or both. Loss of privacy also can result in lost opportunities. Tracing the loss of these opportunities to an earlier invasion of privacy often can be difficult or impossible. Persons who violate our private space by acquiring confidential information without permission may use it to control our activities (Spinello 1995).

Privacy Regained   While many people focus on the invasion and loss of privacy, few examine how privacy is regained. In some cases, simply shooing the intruder out of the previously private space (e.g., a room) is sufficient to regain one's privacy. However, regaining information disclosed during a breach of privacy can be difficult or impossible. Many information scientists have noted the unique qualities of information as a commodity, compared to more tangible commodities, such as orange juice, precious metals, and pork bellies. Information can be given away, yet retained. The rarely mentioned corollary that is pertinent to invasions of privacy is that once exclusive, private knowledge has been shared, it is difficult or impossible to regain that exclusivity. For example, if my wife ever discovers my taste for melancholic poetry, although I will retain my own knowledge of this inclination, I will not retain the exclusivity of that knowledge.

Simply put, privacy protects private life. Without privacy, a rich, sustained private life is not possible. It would not be a reasonable expectation of a rational human being. The question concerning individual privacy in the age of online environments concerns who or what is capable of violating an individual's privacy. This is one of the vital questions regarding personal privacy in the present age, yet most privacy commentators, rather than becoming fully engaged with this question, quietly assume that big government and big business continue to be the two main threats to the privacy of the individual. Can the online environment itself invade an individual's privacy?

Another challenge of thinking about privacy in cyberspace is that in cyberspace, unlike in the real world, the distinction between thought and action is less apparent. The action that occurs in cyberspace is more akin to the action portrayed in literary works of fiction. Nothing observable happens (other than a little eye and hand movement), but, because of the power of human imagination, entire virtual environments spring into action. Although computerized monitoring measures human input (via keystrokes, mouse clicks, and other means), the interest of nearly all computerized monitoring projects is not in the actions themselves (e.g., the force of the clicks), but in what the real actions reveal about what the human being understands about (and intends to do in) the imaginary spaces we collectively call cyberspace.

How to Frame the Privacy Issue?   The privacy issue often is pre-reflectively framed in such a way that what is uttered about individual privacy is an offshoot of the largely unexamined framing. Agre (1994) attempts to bring this prerequisite framing of the issue into the light of reflection by comparing and contrasting two models of privacy issues. The more familiar and dominant surveillance model employs visual metaphors (e.g., Big Brother is watching) and derives from historical experiences with police surveillance. Agre correctly notes that the majority of existing literature on computers and privacy uses the surveillance model without critically analyzing it or considering possible alternative models. Vague visual images of totalitarian states — real or imagined — often are conjured up as references to the surveillance model.

Related to the visual metaphor of personal privacy is the tendency of persons who believe that their privacy is threatened to individualize (but not specifically identify) the suspected intruders and to specifically individualize the suspected instance that they are being targeted for a privacy intrusion attempt. For example, if I fear that the federal government is spying on me, I tend to visualize the governmental spying by imagining one or more individuals who have been assigned to my case (even though I do not know who they are or what they look like), and I imagine that they must be invading my own privacy because I have been specifically identified as someone who needs to be kept under surveillance. I individualize and humanize the suspected intrusion and see myself as an identified, particularized victim. I imagine that some federal employee has been assigned to spy on me because Thomas A. Peters (not just some individual selected at random) is under suspicion. For the intruded upon, their first impulse is not to imagine that some computer selected them at random for computerized monitoring, not as a specific, known individual, but as an anonymous individual. We tend to imagine that human eyes are examining us, our movements, and data about us as specific, known individuals. When it comes to imagining privacy intrusions, the eyes have it.

The less familiar capture model employs linguistic metaphors for human activities, assimilating them to the constructs of a computer system's method of representing some situation or process. The capture model has its roots in the practices of applied computing. The driving aims of the capture model are philosophical rather than political. Human activity is reconstructed through assimilation into a transcendent order of mathematical formalism (Agre 1994, 107). One conclusion we can draw from Agre's analysis is that our thinking about the issue of privacy versus computerized monitoring in virtual environments has been misframed by many in the surveillance model. Agre suggests that computerized monitoring somehow evolved almost naturally from the dominant culture of computing, rather than from modern state politics. In the early culture of computing, it was natural to want to monitor the interaction between person and computer. The original impulse to monitor this interaction may have sprung from an interest in monitoring, or need to monitor, the performance of the computer, rather than from innate snoopiness or the will to monitor.

Definitions of Privacy   Bellotti (1996) differentiates between normative and operational definitions of privacy. Normative definitions usually rely on the idea that there are some immutable categories of a person's nature and activity that are inherently private and should not be revealed to anyone. Operational definitions of privacy concentrate on privacy as a capability, rather than as a set of norms. Bellotti refers to the capability to exercise or experience privacy as access control.

Huebert (1997) provides an interesting examination of the early history of the meaning of privacy in Western society. Thomas More in his *Utopia* envisions a society in which private property and privacy no longer were necessary. The society as a whole achieved full collective surveillance. In his poem, "The Garden," Andrew Marvell articulates privacy as a sense of solitude and repose. Privacy enables the speaker in the poem to gain access to an interior landscape of even greater pleasure than anything in the sensory world (Huebert 1997). The entire world — all that is made — gets annihilated and replaced by a green thought in a green shade. Marvell's sense of solitude presages the potential virtual monadology that complete computerized monitoring of human behavior in online environments may bring about. The treatment of privacy in Marvell's poetry implies that the private self is the authentic person — the self that must be deposed to create the public self (Huebert 1997).

Huebert suggests that the difference between More's disdain for any type of privacy or private property and Marvell's suggestions that privacy is the state in which the true self reveals itself to itself reflects not only the differences between the two authors but also a cultural change in conceptions of personal privacy between the early sixteenth century and the mid–seventeenth century. The widespread use of the words privacy and private from the sixteenth century onward indicates a substantial change in meaning. During the Renaissance privacy was emerging as a category of experience in its own right. No longer merely an attribute attached to certain kinds of behavior, the concept of privacy was beginning to become robust, requiring a vocabulary of its own (Huebert 1997). Just as public life preceded the emergence of private life, so too has real human experience as a whole preceded virtual human experience. At present they are commingled. Our challenge is a neo-renaissance challenge of sorts — to liberate and differentiate the experience of human being in online environments from the older, richer, more established sense of human being in real environments. Computerized monitoring of HCI may help or hinder the pressing human need to meet this challenge, depending on how we use it.

During the Renaissance privacy also carried a sense of interiority of the inner self. When the uses of "privacy" and "private" in the early modern period are arranged in chronological order, in general a progression in meaning can be detected from suspicion of or hostility toward privacy in the earlier texts to acceptance of and even a cherishing of privacy in the later ones (Huebert 1997).

Warren and Brandeis (1890) differentiated the right to privacy from other legal rights, defining it as the right to be let alone — the right to some measure of solitude in one's life (Spinello 1995). In the 1928 U.S. Supreme Court decision in the case of *Olmstead v United States* (277 U.S. 438, 478) the notion of the right to privacy as the right to be let alone was reaffirmed (Galkin 1996). Warren and Brandeis stress that privacy is increasingly necessary as a way to provide sanctuary or retreat from the growing complexity and intensity of life, with its accelerating rate of technological advance (DeCew 1997, 16).

This centenary argument may not apply well to the question concerning privacy in cyberspace, because virtual environments are part and parcel — the leading edge — of this dizzying technological advance. It may be more difficult to define what it means to be let alone in online environments than in the real world. There is no state of nature in cyberspace. It is completely artificial. In online environments, furthermore, it may be much more difficult to draw the line between being let alone and otherwise. If information about one's online behavior has been collected and analyzed (by a person, a computer, or both) to facilitate or improve one's future interaction with that computer or computer system (and the resulting online sense of space), yet one was not made aware of this activity before, during, or after the data collection and analysis, has one been "let alone" or not? The Warren and Brandeis idea of individual privacy is alive and well in the digital age. Junkbusters (www.junkbusters.com) is a Web site developed to enforce the Web surfer's right to be let alone (Brown 1998).

"Privacy is perhaps the most fundamental of all liberties. It's the right to be left undisturbed. The right to live and work without being constantly and unnecessarily monitored. The right not to have one's personal information exploited without consent" (Pfaffenberger 1997, 8).

Spinello (1995) briefly distinguishes between psychological, communicative, and informational privacy, then concentrates on informational privacy — the right to have access to information about one's self. DeCew (1997) also sees informational privacy as just one type of privacy. DeCew (1997, 73–80) articulates three aspects of privacy: informational, accessibility, and expressive.

During the second half of the twentieth century, the definition of privacy has turned toward the concept of a desire (or right) to control one's own self-disclosure. Thus privacy involves a struggle to control information. Personal privacy is one's desire, right, or ability to control, withhold and reveal at will information about one's person and activities. Westin (1967, 7) defines privacy as a desire by individuals to choose freely under what circumstances and to what extent they will expose themselves, their attitudes, and their behavior to others (cited in Davies 1996, 23). Branscomb (1994) understands privacy as that which maintains boundaries around areas over which we can presume to maintain exclusive personal control (cited in Nideffer 1995, 283).

Parent (1983b, 269) defines privacy as "the condition of not having undocumented personal information [knowledge] about oneself known [possessed] by others" (quoted in DeCew 1997, 28). Cate (1997, 22) accepts Westin's basic definition of privacy as a claim to determine the communication of information about the self to others. Cate sees information privacy as a social value, but not itself a legal right. These definitions of privacy concentrate on informational privacy.

The definitions claim and proclaim the right of individuals to control what information about themselves is disclosed to whom. One could argue that these definitions of privacy place it on a course to become a commodity, originally owned by the individual.

Information can be described as private, and an individual or a group can achieve a state of privacy. A distinction needs to be made between private information (including human behavior, a subset of all information) and a state of privacy. It is entirely possible for private information about a person to be revealed without compromising that person's state of privacy. For example, if a homosexual is "outed" (without the person's consent), some private information about that person has been made public. However, that person's state of privacy (e.g., the privacy of the home) has not necessarily been compromised. Although invasions of privacy may necessarily imply that a person's state of privacy has been compromised, it seems that the phrase "privacy invasion" often is used when what has happened is an unauthorized release of private information.

Privacy encompasses more than alphanumeric data. Perhaps part of the problem with our conception of privacy is that we tend to associate it with records — medical, financial, political, religious, and so on. These data and databases are important aspects of the realm of personal privacy, but they are not the entire domain. Privacy over behavioral events is a part of the equation that has received much less attention. In the emerging realm of human behavior in cyberspace, however, privacy in relation to behavioral events may become much more important than privacy in relation to alphanumeric records and real-world events.

Privacy and Confidentiality Differentiated   Privacy and confidentiality are related but distinct concepts. At least one (and often only one) person is needed to keep something private, but it takes at least two to hold something in confidence. Confidentiality often is a professional issue, when information expressed or entrusted to a professional (e.g., physician, lawyer, librarian, or psychiatrist) is held in confidence as part of a professional relationship. Privacy, on the other hand, tends to be a moral, ethical, and legal issue. Cavoukian and Tapscott (1995, 30) also differentiate between privacy and confidentiality. The two notions occasionally are conflated. DeCew (1997, 1), for example, wonders if threats against another's life, when made in confidence to a lawyer or psychiatrist, should be protected in the name of privacy. It appears that this hypothetical situation has more to do with professional attitudes toward confidentiality than with privacy.

In the 1975 decision in *White v Davis* (13 Cal. 3d, 757), the California Supreme Court stated:

> The right of privacy is the right to be left alone. It is a fundamental and compelling interest. It protects our homes, our families, our thoughts, our emotions, our expressions, our personalities, our freedom of communion and our freedom to associate with whom we choose. It prevents government and business interests from collecting and stockpiling unnecessary information about us, and from misusing information gathered for one purpose in order to serve other purposes or embarrass us....

The proliferation of government and business records over which we have no control limits our ability to control our personal lives (quoted in Davies 1992, 2).

"[C]onfidentiality — and the perception of confidentiality — are as necessary for the soul of mankind as bread is for the body" (Diffie and Landau 1998, 150).

The Office of Technology Assessment of the U.S. Congress defined confidentiality as referring to how data collected for approved purposes will be maintained by the organization that collected them, what further uses will or may be made of the data, and situations when individuals will be required to express consent to such uses of the data (United States. Congress. Office of Technology Assessment 1993). The OTA agreed with the position articulated by Allen (1988) that a state of confidentiality has been achieved when designated information is not disseminated beyond a community of authorized knowers. Often that community of authorized knowers is a subset of a profession, perhaps even an individual professional. Confidentiality often is best understood within a context of the mores or code of ethical conduct within a profession.

As noted above, Westin (1967, 7) defines privacy as the desire of people to choose freely under what circumstances and to what extent they will expose themselves, their attitudes, and their behavior to others. "Privacy is the claim of individuals, groups or institutions to determine for themselves when, how, and to what extent information about them is communicated to others" (Westin 1967, quoted in Mendes 1985, 13).

Mendes (1985, 14) points out that individuals constantly are unintentionally communicating about themselves to others. It would be unrealistic to claim, as Westin's definition appears to do, that individuals and groups can have and should have complete control over the information they communicate to others. Mendes suggests that the notion of privacy should apply only to personal and confidential information. Loss of privacy occurs only when personal and confidential information is disclosed without the subject's authorization. Mendes defines personal and confidential information as information about oneself that one would not want disclosed without one's prior consent. Thus Mendes (1985, 15) defines privacy as a "condition in which individuals, groups or institutions can determine for themselves, when, how and to what extent private information about them is communicated to others."

Privacy allows us to achieve other values that our society considers important (Mendes 1985, 5). The Office of Technology Assessment defined privacy in this social way as a balance struck between the society and the individuals comprising it whereby the individual's right to keep information confidential and the societal benefit derived from knowing and sharing this information are kept in equilibrium. This balance and equilibrium are codified by legislation giving individuals the right to control information about themselves (United States. Congress. Office of Technology Assessment 1993).

The two concepts of privacy and confidentiality can be resolved in the following manner:

Privacy is the question of what personal information should be collected or stored at all for a given social function. It involves issues concerning the legitimacy and legality of organizational demands for disclosure from individuals and groups, and setting of balances between the individual's control over the disclosure of personal information and the needs of society for the data on which to base decisions about individual situations and formulate public policies. Confidentiality is the question of how personal data collection for approved social purposes shall be held and used by the organization that originally collected it, what other secondary or further uses may be made of it, and when consent by the individual will be required for such uses (quoted in United States. Congress. Office of Technology Assessment 1993, but perhaps first written by Westin in *Computers, Health Records, and Citizen Rights*).

Gathering data and disclosing it are two separate issues. If an analyst of data gathered via computer monitoring has no intention of ever trying to correlate the observed behavior of individuals with specific people, is it an invasion of privacy to gather this data? Perhaps the generalization can be made that the question concerning privacy encompasses both issues, but confidentiality tends to protect against unwarranted and unnecessary disclosure of private or sensitive information about an individual.

Professional observers and confidants (e.g., doctors, lawyers, librarians, journalists) often have professional obligations to maintain the confidentiality of what they learn from their patients, clients, patrons, and sources. This responsibility to maintain confidentiality does not prohibit the professional from acting appropriately, based on the professional's knowledge of confidential information. It merely means that the observer should not divulge confidential information in an inappropriate manner or setting.

Privacy and Anonymity   Privacy and anonymity are another pair of concepts.* Rotenberg (1993, 62) suggested that the right to anonymity is an important aspect of privacy protection (Olson 1996, 17). Computerized monitoring of HCI, however, often is not focused on the specific identities of individuals. Many computerized monitoring projects may involve an invasion of individual privacy without upsetting anonymity. Throughout the 1990s Marc Rotenberg has continued to support the idea of anonymity as a good move toward a higher form of privacy. The EPIC report (Electronic Privacy Information Center 1997), of which Rotenberg was the director, recommended that sites continue to support anonymity while developing policies and practices to protect information privacy.

Anonymity during browsing also has been defended as a type of privacy that encourages information seeking and shopping. The EPIC study of the most popular Web sites in mid–1997 concluded that the widespread practice among Web sites of allowing anonymous browsing, even on the most popular Web sites, was an important indicator of how privacy is protected on the Internet. By avoiding the collection of personal information, Web sites encourage users to visit them. In the physical world, very few stores require the collection of personal information

---

* *Dyson (1997b) contains two good chapters on privacy and anonymity.*

before allowing a shopper to enter (Electronic Privacy Information Center 1997). This rosy optimism concerning anonymous online browsing, however, did not include an examination of the collection of individualized information and behavior via Web server log analysis. It focused on the overt collection of personally identifying information through questionnaires, forms, and other means.

Is Privacy a Right, a Claim, or an Interest?   In what sense is privacy a right? Is privacy a right, a claim, or an interest? Thomson (1975) argued that there is no unified right to privacy (DeCew 1997, 3). Prosser (1960) identified four distinct interests in privacy. DeCew (1997, 27) defined an interest as something it would be good to have. The question concerning how extensively an interest ought to be protected remains open. For example, Huff (1980) defines tort privacy as an interest (as opposed to a right) in being free of the potential for certain unwarranted evaluations (DeCew 1997, 38). A claim is an argument that someone deserves something. For example, Laudon (1996) articulates privacy as the moral claim of individuals to be left alone and to control the flow of information about themselves. A right is a justified claim. In turn, a right can be differentiated as either legal or moral. A legal right is a claim that has been justified by legislation, judicial decisions, or a combination of both. A moral right is a claim justified on moral principles. If we are going to argue that privacy is a right, then we need to specify what it claims (e.g., to be let alone), how it is justified (i.e., legally, morally, or both), and other characteristics of the right to privacy. If privacy must be balanced with other interests and claims, and if computerized monitoring is in some sense an invasion of privacy, what are the competing interests and claims of the computerized invaders? What are they trying to accomplish? The amorphous movement to use computers to monitor HCI must be self-aware, so that it can better articulate its interests, claims, and promise.

Privacy as a Realized State of Being   In addition to being a concept (e.g., an interest, claim, or right), privacy also is a realizable state of being that most people experience at least once in a lifetime. It is not, however, an all-encompassing state of being. For example, the privacy of one's medical records may be invaded while the privacy of one's financial life remains private and under one's control. If the privacy of one's medical records is temporarily or permanently lost, one would not conclude that any and all private states of being have therefore been forbidden to one. Nevertheless, Laudon (1996) correctly observes that the behavioral, phenomenological reality of privacy can be differentiated from privacy as a moral claim, political statement, or a right that is constitutionally or legally protected. That is one of the nagging aspects of the human sense of online environments. The individual often experiences these online environments as private places where the individual seems to be alone.

Is Privacy an Absolute or Relative Right?   One of the fundamental debates among privacy advocates involves whether privacy is an absolute or a relative value.

An absolute right is not contingent on any situational or environmental factors. If privacy is an absolute right, that right would apply to both the real and online worlds, equally to employees, students, library users, browsers, and consumers. Most organizations adopt the stance that there are trade-offs between personal privacy and public interests. The individual must surrender some privacy for the common good and social advancement (Davies 1992, 9). Claims to privacy cannot be protected absolutely because of changes in facts, conflicts between the needs of individuals and society, changes of circumstances or developments which may give rise to new claims, and failure to assert certain claims (Mendes 1985, 13).

Does privacy adhere to the basic task being undertaken, rather than to the individual? Is the right to privacy during formal learning situations somehow less defensible than the right to privacy in formal work situations? If we adopt this stance, an individual's right to privacy waxes and wanes based on what one is doing. One problem with this stance is that distinctions between the basic tasks of learning, seeking information, working, and browsing may never have been very strong, and they certainly are becoming weaker as the pursuit of these tasks goes online.

Is Privacy a Passive or an Active Right?   Some rights, such as life and liberty, usually are passive rights, in the sense that most people do not need to spend much time, if any, protecting them. Of course, there are times when life and liberty are in peril, and the individual must fight to protect them. Other rights, such as the pursuit of happiness, are active rights, in that they require most people to pursue them with persistence and fervor.

Environmental changes may be transforming privacy from an essentially passive right to an essentially active one. Implicit in the notion of privacy as the right to be left alone is the idea that the individual should not need to do much to protect this right. It is a right that ought to be socially accepted and respected. If the right to privacy is generally accepted and respected, it falls to the individual like manna from heaven. What we may be facing with cyberspace, however, is a totally different technological and social environment in which privacy is not generally accepted and respected. The individual who wants to achieve and maintain some semblance of personal privacy, therefore, will need to pursue it aggressively and persistently. Privacy will become more like happiness — an ideal goal which we have a right to pursue.

Gattiker et al. (1996, 84) succinctly state this need for an aggressive protection of privacy: "We can no longer be passive about the privacy issue, relying on the law to adequately protect our right to privacy. Instead, our legislated rights must be augmented by aggressive action, to maintain and protect an individual's right to privacy." Bellotti (1996) also explores the idea that privacy is becoming something that needs to be managed, not by governments and policy makers, but rather by individual online users and online collaborative workgroups. Computer supported collaborative work and computer-mediated communication systems in general should be designed to support the management of privacy and privacy-related decisions by individual and group inhabitants of an online environment.

Constitutional, Legislative, and Judicial Aspects of Privacy   People who care about their privacy are a powerful political and consumer constituency, and numerous companies and trade associations are actively supporting federal legislation as a good way to assure the public that their personal information and privacy in general are safe. One's right to decide what people know about one lies at the heart of the U.S. constitutional values of liberty, autonomy, and freedom (Goldman 1991). DeCew (1997, 7) suggests that "reasonable federal regulations" would be able to protect privacy while allowing new technologies to flourish and be fully exploited.

Warren and Brandeis (1890) wrote the seminal article on the recognizable right to privacy as the right to be let alone. Although their article was motivated by a series of then-current technological developments, including the telephone, microphone, audio recorder, and portable camera, the concept of the right to privacy generally has not been subsequently expanded or refined to deal with more modern technologies (Mendes 1985, 8).

The legal development of the concept of privacy has been peculiar and complex, involving both tort and constitutional law (DeCew 1997, 2). Whereas tort rights generally are held by individuals against other individuals or businesses, the rights of individuals against governmental intrusion are protected by the Constitution (DeCew 1997, 18). Some of the early privacy legal cases did not deal with the question of governmental invasions of privacy, but rather with civil tort actions brought by one individual against another (Tuerkheimer 1993, 69).

The stated goal of the Clinton administration's privacy policy, announced on December 17, 1997, is to protect personal privacy in the Internet age without creating new laws and regulations (Markoff 1997b). The policy seems to be at odds with the impending European Union Data Protection Directive. Whereas the Europeans are relying primarily on legislation to protect individual privacy, the U.S. is arguing that data industry agreements and self-regulation will meet the data protection standards of the European directive. Canada, on the other hand, has a relatively strong network of governmental commissioners of privacy. In May 1997 Ann Cavoukian was named Acting Information/Privacy Commissioner of Ontario, and Bruce Phillips was serving as the Canadian Privacy Commissioner (Hendricks 1997).

Although the U.S. Constitution does not explicitly mention or protect the right to privacy, the U.S. Supreme Court has recognized an unwritten right to privacy, essentially limiting this right to one's reasonable expectation of privacy (Bernstein 1997). In his dissenting opinion to the 1928 Supreme Court case of *Olmstead v United States* (277 US 438), Justice Brandeis wrote that the makers of the U.S. Constitution conferred on individual citizens, as against the government, the right to be let alone, the most comprehensive of rights and the one most valued by civilized people (DeCew 1997, 19).

Numerous laws enacted by the U.S. Congress have been designed to protect the right to privacy in specific situations, usually involving specific types of parties (e.g., federal agencies), specific types of information (e.g., financial information), and specific types of technologies (e.g., the telephone). This patchwork of laws includes the *Fair Credit Reporting Act of 1971*, the *Right to Financial Privacy Act of 1978*, and the landmark 1974 *Privacy Act*, which addresses the protection of privacy during the use or distribution of government records. The 1974 *Privacy Act* gives individuals the right to access and correct their personal records. It also prevents information from being used for other purposes without the individual's consent. The law, however, applies only to U.S. federal agencies (Spinello 1995).

Olmstead v United States clarified that the Fourth Amendment did not apply to telephone communication, thus making wiretapping constitutional (Tuerkheimer 1993, 69–70). Justice Brandeis dissented and shifted his defense of privacy from his earlier statements about the right to be let alone to the idea of communications privacy.

Thirty-nine years later another Supreme Court decision overruled the earlier Olmstead decision. The 1967 decision stated that what a person seeks to preserve as private, even in an area accessible to the public, may be protected by the Constitution (Tuerkheimer 1993, 70). In *Katz v United States* (389 US 347, 352–353) Justice Harlan stated a two-stage test to determine whether an individual has a right to privacy. First, the person must have exhibited an actual expectation of privacy. Second, the expectation of privacy must be one that society is prepared to recognize as reasonable (Mendes 1985, 67, note 11). If a reasonable demonstration of privacy is evident, the Fourth Amendment applies.

Most people who interact with computers and computer networks seem to assume that privacy in this environment is a reasonable expectation. The intimate nature of their messages and the files they access or download probably would serve as an exhibition of an actual expectation of privacy, thus passing Justice Harlan's first qualifying test. Passing the second test, however, is more difficult. On the World Wide Web, which society (real or virtual) is authorized to declare a recognition that the expectation of privacy is reasonable? The Web transcends most real-world social boundaries, or creates its own social infrastructure.

Privacy rights arising from tort law usually govern the conduct of private parties (Dorney 1997, 639). The tort law tradition of protecting privacy often is described succinctly as the right to control information about oneself (DeCew 1997, 14). There is the potential for action under the common law tort of invasion of privacy, which has four distinct torts: intrusion upon one's seclusion, the public disclosure of private facts, publicity that places one in a false light, and misappropriation of one's name and likeness for commercial purposes (Dorney 1997, 639).

The first and third categories could conceivably apply to computerized monitoring of HCI. False light invasions of privacy, however, generally apply only if the publicity that places an individual in a false light is disseminated to the general public. Very little computerized monitoring data is disseminated to the general public. Usually the data are analyzed and shared among specific individuals and parties. Also, although computerized monitoring may paint an incomplete picture, what it represents is not false. We can agree with Sessler's conclusion (1997,

669) that "the tort of false light publicity would not generally be the basis for a viable TGI [transaction generated interaction] action." Sessler (1997, 671) argues that the fourth tort (misappropriation of likeness) implies a deprivation of dignity and economic loss. It seems to specifically address the harm done by computerized monitoring of HCI, because the personality profiles extracted from computerized transaction logs can be interpreted as a new type of image of a specific, individual person.

The right of seclusion is a particular aspect of the more general right to privacy. The right of seclusion protects individuals against the unauthorized gathering of personal information. To qualify as intrusion, the conduct in question must be highly offensive to a reasonable person, and the personal information must not be voluntarily disclosed to the public (Dorney 1997, 640). The chief question for us, as we examine privacy in the context of computerized monitoring of HCI, is whether or not the right of seclusion pertains to life in virtual environments. The answer may depend in part on whether a reasonable person understands the virtual environment in question as a public or private space. It probably does not make sense to assert that all of cyberspace is public or private, any more than it would to make a similar claim about the real world. A significant difference between the real world and virtual environments is that, in the real world, a public space generally feels like a public space, and a private space generally feels like a private space to anyone inhabiting that space. There is little or no disagreement between the feel of the space to the inhabitants and the abstract expectations of a reasonable person. It is reasonable to expect in the abstract that one's home is private, and in reality it feels that way. This congruence between abstract expectation and actual experience is missing in most online environments. Most online environments are experienced as private spaces, even when a reasonable expectation would posit that they are not.

In a particular case of employee reasonable expectations and rights, the case law surrounding the concept of "intrusion into seclusion" indicates that the employee must prove a reasonable expectation of privacy, and that the intrusion must be into a matter in which the employee has a right of privacy. The latter burden of proof is problematic in an employer-employee relationship. The public nature of the work environment mitigates against this, as does the nature of the monitoring system, because it is applied to many as opposed to a single person (Addressing the new hazards 1991, cited in Levy 1993). Finally, implicit or explicit consent to monitoring would vitiate employee claims (Levy 1993).

Dorney (1997, 640) speculates that the increasing ability to gather, use, and disclose information in the electronic world may result in the recognition of new privacy rights based on traditional tort theories and principles developed in the real world.

Privacy also can be understood as a property right held by individuals. Chlapowski (1991) traces the idea of privacy as a personal property right back to John Locke's argument that every man possesses property in the form of his own person (cited in Cate 1997, 21). Miller (1969) suggested that the easiest way to safeguard privacy is to understand the ability to control personal information as a property right. Sessler (1997, 629) refers to the type of data collected via computerized monitoring as transaction generated information (TGI). Sessler (1997, 674) goes further to suggest that such information about persons could be protected as a type of trade secret. Sessler argues for increased government restrictions on the collection and use of TGI, and for a broadening of the basis for privacy law.

Some commentators on privacy, particularly from the legal standpoint, suggest that the privacy issue has become completely muddled. Wacks (1980) separates at least eight other categories that have become entangled with privacy: autonomy; other liberties, including freedom from unreasonable search, freedom of association, and freedom of expression; confidentiality; secrecy; defamation; property; computers; and privilege (Mendes 1985, 71, note 59).

Who Are the Potential Violators of Privacy?   In the traditional privacy debate, and perhaps also in the popular imagination, potential violators of personal privacy usually are perceived as the federal government or private corporations, with state government perhaps running a distant third. Meeks (1997), for example, asserts that the assault on personal privacy is being led by corporate America in concert with local, state, and federal governments. Most privacy laws in the United States are designed to prevent the intrusion of personal privacy by government, rather than by corporations or other individuals. One of the ironies of our modern sense of privacy in a postmodern, online world is that intrusions in a person's privacy often are believed to be done for secret, nefarious reasons. The old medieval equation of privacy with the sinister now has been recalculated so that the invaders of privacy are presumed to have sinister intents until proven otherwise.

It is possible that an individual's right to privacy in online environments could be expanded to include the right to be let alone by the environment itself. Being let alone would include not only the right not to be constantly subject to computerized monitoring, but also the right not to have the online environment constantly correcting and tailoring itself based on an individual's behavior and decisions. Even the Windows 95 operating system — a presumably crude precursor of software to come — makes decisions without conscious input from the individual. If one has some input into the decision-making process, one may question or avoid certain decisions.

Spatial Aspects of the Privacy Issue   The privacy issue also contains some fundamentally spatial components. The words used to describe invasions of privacy, such as "eavesdropping," have strong spatial orientations and are grounded in the real world. Human behavior must play itself out in some sort of space — real or virtual. Mere presence itself is a form of behavior. To sit perfectly still does not mean that one has temporarily suspended one's behavior. Just being somewhere (as opposed to all other possible places) is the basic component of human behavior.

If I am in a public place (e.g., walking down the sidewalk, sitting on a public park bench, or attending a sporting event), I should expect to be observed, and not be offended if I learn that I am being observed.* My behavior in public places is public behavior. In turn, the observer of my public behavior could be located either in a public place or in a private place. In the example of walking down the sidewalk, the person who observes me could be a fellow walker, or someone peering out a window of a private residence. If I am in a private place (e.g., my home), I have a right to expect not to be monitored, and to be offended if someone intentionally observes my behavior. However, if I am in a private place that I do not own (e.g., a friend's house, or a retail shop), does the owner have the right to monitor my behavior when I am on the owner's premises?

Another example of privacy being thought of as something with place-like qualities is the opinion written by Justice William O. Douglas in the 1965 Supreme Court decision in *Griswold v Connecticut*. Justice Douglas wrote about a zone of privacy, a penumbral right emanating from the U.S. Constitution and its amendments (DeCew 1997, 22). This harkens to the 1886 Supreme Court decision in *Boyd v U.S.*, which suggested that privacy protects places likes homes, not people themselves. Laudon (1996) suggests, however, that a gradual shift in thinking about privacy from place-based views to reasonable expectations of privacy began with the 1967 U.S. Supreme Court decision in *Katz v U.S.* (389 US 347).

The challenge with the issue of privacy in cyberspace is that, traditionally in the real world, we have tried to defend privacy by defining (or socially agreeing to) geographic spaces where privacy needs to be protected. The home, the physician's office, and the confessional room are examples of geographic spaces where privacy is honored. People literally have learned to protect privacy by erecting walls. Outside observers sometimes are hesitant and furtive when either a wind storm or an estate auction enables the outside public to peer into the contents of a house. Expectations of privacy based on defined geographic spaces have become an unfortunate habit as people venture from the real world to colonize and socialize cyberspace. The very way we talk about privacy reveals this geographic proclivity. We often say that someone's privacy has been invaded, as if privacy were a geographic place or realm. Our expectations regarding personal privacy in online environments develop out of the time-honored spatial aspects of real-world privacy expectations and practices. Bill Mann (1997) contends that the individual deserves a level of online privacy that is at least as good as, if not better than, the privacy the individual has walking down the street.

The act of invading someone else's privacy often is couched in terms that imply a spatial metaphor. Privacy often is portrayed as a space (or perhaps a part of the body) that someone else violates. Mendes explores the extent to which personal privacy may be violated by computer technology as a result of aggregation, unauthorized access, intrusion, misuse, and piracy (Mendes 1985, 2). Intrusion is defined

---

* However, Meeks (1997) maintains that an individual has some expectation of privacy even in a public park.

as "repeated or continuous monitoring or surveillance of a user's terminal for purposes other than billing or checking system integrity" (Mendes 1985, 107).

We must entertain the notion that not all loss of privacy is the result of unwanted invasions. It is possible for persons to willingly give up part or all of their privacy. Situations could arise in both the real and the virtual worlds in which some or most people would freely relinquish parts or types of their personal privacy, if the advantages of doing so outweighed the disadvantages. Such a scenario assumes, perhaps erroneously, that most people are (or even can be) fully cognizant of the advantages and disadvantages of surrendering one's privacy. The willing release of private information could be seen as a subtle form of counter control that preempts the more blatant invasions of privacy.

Privacy in Our Four Basic Virtual Environments   Steve Steinberg (1996) has written: "People seem to have very different concerns about privacy in the virtual world than in the real one. A new contract between advertisers and consumers is needed that clarifies what are reasonable expectations of privacy and anonymity on the Web." In cyberspace we need to figure out some non-geographic way to protect privacy. We need a new non-spatial dimension upon which to base our expectations concerning privacy. The notion of space in cyberspace is so unusual, compared to our notions of place and space in the real world, that it would be difficult or impossible to simply move our ideas about privacy from the real to the virtual world. It may be possible, but not practical and truly realizing the potential of cyberspace, to erect virtual privacy fences and walls in cyberspace to create private places in the old-fashioned, real way.

The idea of individual privacy in online environments takes on different shades, depending on which of our four basic monitored activities (working, learning, information seeking, or shopping) is being pursued at the time.* It is ironic that, although human learning is arguably one of the most private, mysterious processes, very few attempts are made to assert and defend the privacy of the learner in a formal learning environment. Learners constantly are asked to declare, display, and make manifest the outcomes of their learning activity.

For a private employee there are minimal constitutional protections of privacy. The principle of state action in the Fourteenth Amendment gives limited constitutional privacy rights to those in the private sector. Even for public employees and those states that have explicit privacy provisions in their state constitutions, the difficulty in claiming an invasion of privacy revolves around the test of a "reasonable expectation of privacy" in the workplace. While the Fourth Amendment provision against unreasonable search and seizure is applicable to persons and not just property, there are two elements to the protection: the subject's reasonable expectation of privacy, and, if this is satisfied, whether the search itself was objectively reasonable and therefore permissible (Barker 1992, 1117, cited in Levy 1993).

James-Catalano (1997) provides a good overview of sources for more information on this topic.

Duvall-Early and Benedict (1992) discuss the importance of privacy in work environments. "One of the difficulties with conceptualizing workplace monitoring as a privacy issue is that it frames individuals as having an assumed set of rights as participants in a free and equal contract arrangement, and does not account for the power relations implied in the labour contract" (Bryant 1995, 515).

Bellotti (1996, 242) argues that the debate concerning privacy and the design of computer systems has been too constrained around the two issues of system security and legislation that creates a virtual zone of permissibility. A third area of debate on computer systems and privacy should center on the need for sophisticated, flexible means by which netizens can control how accessible they are and how much information they want to share with others.

Morris-Lee (1996) sees three potential areas for privacy abuse on the Internet and the Web: the increasing ease of monitoring people, the increasing ease of merging and reusing information contained in databases, and the decreasing cost of direct solicitation. In traditional marketing in the real world, it was not possible to record efficiently what individuals purchased until the advent of barcode scanners and the ubiquitous use of credit cards. In cyberspace, where by definition everything must be mediated by computers, it is practically impossible for human activity not to be logged (Morris-Lee 1996).

> The one tradition on the Internet that must be respected more than any other is regard for an individual's privacy. Internet users point to loads of junk mail that fill their real-world mailboxes and swear that they will never let that happen in the virtual world. Therefore, if you are collecting information about users directly or via a software mechanism such as cookies, be wary of selling this information to others. Using it discreetly for your own purposes is fine, but selling it to others, resulting in unwanted direct mail, will anger your users (Yesil 1996, 124).

What is interesting about the rapid development of Web monitoring tools and techniques in the last few years is not that the privacy of individuals is being invaded (personal privacy is invaded every day in many ways), but that many Web users do not seem to be concerned about this monitoring.

> Why so much concern about privacy and security in the online world? Because it's a new, barely regulated frontier, and the same virtues that make the Internet so appealing — interactivity, customizability, addressing conventions, versatile messaging, and so on — also make it an ideal medium for others to keep tabs on us without tipping us off to the intrusion. If other mass media had these virtues, they would be vulnerable as well. Yet the Internet is too valuable to do without (Lemmons 1997).

Glen Roberts, a computer consultant whose hobby is exploring the opportunities for database misuse, has a Web site (ironically named "Stalker's Home Page") that has become the definitive source for information about how privacy can be violated online (Quittner 1997a).

Privacy, Secrecy, and Control   Bok (1983, 11, quoted in Mendes 1985, 66, note 8) argues that personal control over secrecy is related to the personal right to privacy, because the purpose of both privacy and secrecy is to become "less vulnerable, more in control." Personal control over secrecy protects four values: identity, plans, action, and property. DeCew (1997, 53) counter-argues that it is much too broad a definition to characterize a privacy interest as an ability to control. Reiman (1995) also argues that privacy must be a condition independent of the issue of control. We should not jump to the conclusion that online environments are an inevitable threat to individual privacy. The forces of privacy in virtual environments are at least as strong as the forces of surveillance and disclosure. The forces referred to here are not the political, economic, or technological forces of the adherents and combatants, but rather the forces inherent in the technologies of computerized networks themselves.

Private Information and Private Behavior   Perhaps we need to differentiate between private information and private behavior. Although behavior has the potential to become information (e.g., if some mechanism such as a computerized monitoring module translates and distills behavior into a set of data), invasions of privacy are very situational. At the moment of invasion, some breaches of privacy involve the discovery of private information (e.g., when a boy reads his sister's diary), while other invasions result in the disclosure of private behavior (e.g., when an elected official is video-recorded in a hotel room snorting cocaine). Although much of the rhetoric concerning privacy on the Internet and in cyberspace in general focuses on the disclosure, trafficking, and aggregating of private information without the consent of the individual, computerized monitoring, if it is indeed an invasion of privacy, is the unauthorized observation of private behavior. We need to distinguish between information about one's person and information about one's behavior. Some computerized monitoring projects, particularly Web server log analyses conducted by advertisers, attempt to use observed information about online behavior to make inferences about a person. DeCew views this way of thinking about privacy as entirely different: "This is an alternative approach to privacy, a broad conception encompassing both tort and constitutional privacy claims, where privacy is a property of types of information and activity viewed by a reasonable person in normal circumstances as beyond the legitimate concern of others" (DeCew 1997, 60).

Who Owns the Property Rights to Behavioral Residue?   A major aspect of the privacy issue involves reaching a consensus on what constitutes public information. Such a consensus seems a long way off—and retreating. "I think public information should be widely disseminated on the Internet, but the difficult question is, what should be public information and what should be private?" asks Marc Rotenberg, director of the Electronic Privacy Information Center. "When people began storing public records in town halls, no one imagined that you'd be able to sit down at a computer and access it all" (O'Malley 1997). Although what it means to have access to information appears to becoming very complex very quickly, overall trends seem to indicate that the accessibility of information is increasing (if not diffusing throughout the population) rapidly.

All human behavior, including mere presence, leaves a trace or residue of one's presence. Footprints, sales receipts, dander, and keystrokes and mouse clicks are examples of residual confirmation of the fact that one came, behaved, and left. Some of this behavioral residue (e.g., bodily waste and trash) we readily throw away, in essence declaring that it no longer has any value for us, and, if someone else can find or add value to it, they are free to do so. The question then arises: Does one own any or all of the residue of one's behavior? If this is an ownership question, who decides the question? Does the individual hold first rights to ownership of this stuff, exercisable upon some sort of declaration? Postrel (1998) basically rejects the premise that an individual retains a fundamental right to control what information is available to others.

Bernstein (1997) also likens this behavioral residue to a dander-like substance, noting that most people have no idea about what happens to the steady stream of personal data they shed by living in the modern world of increasingly complex computerized systems. If someone can take this dispersed, raw residual material, process or combine it in some way that increases its value, who owns and profits from the resulting products and sales? Nelson Thall, the research director at the Marshall McLuhan Center for Media Sciences in Toronto, worries that most people do not even realize that every time they enter cyberspace and move about, they leave a trail of data that others can follow and collect (Betts 1995).

The argument that the exertion of energy (often in the form of work) creates at least a claim to ownership does not shed much light on the question of ownership of behavioral residue. Clearly, one expended energy in creating one's behavior, even if it was only the basal metabolic energy required to be. But computer monitoring systems and analysts also exerted energy to gather and analyze one's behavioral residue. Because behavioral residue in cyberspace is not naturally occurring (in fact, nothing in cyberspace is naturally occurring, except the flow of electrons), the existence of behavioral residue relies not only on the actor, but also on someone else who willed that behavioral residue should exist and be capturable. Both the individual actor and the subsequent analyst have invested time, energy, and other resources into the resulting product. The question becomes particularly troublesome when the clearing for one's behavior is a virtual space created by the existence of a computer network. As one browses through the vast hypertext called the World Wide Web, does one own one's behavioral residue? If one does not explicitly assert and declare ownership over it, does one automatically relinquish all rights and claims to its future use?

Dern (1997) uses the metaphor of eddies in flowing liquids to describe this residue. When we move around in cyberspace, we leave little eddies — virtual footprints and fingerprints other people can find and use to learn about our virtual selves and our virtual lives. Currently, the metaphor of an eddy is not very apt, because an eddy itself is an action event, with a beginning, a middle, and an end. At present, traces of our online behavior are more like fingerprints — a thin, almost undetectable film that requires some expertise and analysis to determine that a person was there. The problem, in turn, with the fingerprint metaphor is that fingerprints usually are sought to confirm that a specific, named individual committed a crime. As computerized monitoring becomes more automated throughout the cycle of gathering, analyzing, and applying data, the metaphor of the eddy may become more descriptive of what is happening as we move through cyberspace. In the near future this movement of virtual selves through an imagined space may routinely set off little eddies of programs that analyze the movement and adjust aspects of the environment accordingly. Applets may behave like eddies.

It may be both possible and necessary to differentiate between natural behavioral residue and artificial, contrived behavioral residue. This distinction probably has nothing to do with the reality or virtuality of the environment in which the behavior occurs. If one walks across soft earth, because one has mass one can expect to leave footprints. The footprints could be classified as the natural behavioral residue of walking across the soft earth. This behavioral information is not intentionally disclosed by individuals for any purpose. It is part of behaving in the real world of gravity, beyond the control of the individual engaged in the behavior. Uttered information usually is controllable by the individual, but behavioral information is not as easily controlled or concealed, especially in public places. This natural behavioral residue can be exported from the real world and imported into cyberspace in online data sets. Although data about strolls on the beach may be interesting in themselves, it is the more high-powered natural behavioral residue, such as records of the medical, financial, and legal aspects of our real lives, that make people uneasy when these data are introduced into online environments.

It is a debatable point whether anything like natural behavioral residue exists in cyberspace. As packets of information are shunted about the Internet and other computer networks at the speed of light, there seems to be no uneradicable residue left behind. On the other hand, it is entirely possible to create artificial, contrived behavioral residue in cyberspace. Little software programs that place time stamps on events in cyberspace are simple examples of the intentional human creation of behavioral residue. One type of artificial behavioral residue may be intentionally generated to monitor use. One challenge to understanding the nature of cyberspace is that, unlike our imaginary barefoot walker on a wet beach who, because of the nature of gravity, mass, and wet sand, must leave footprints, in cyberspace there may be no naturally occurring behavioral residue. It's all artificial. Every attempt to use computers to collect behavioral residue in cyberspace is intentional. The manifestation of the intent to create behavioral residue may be far-removed from the actual capture, analysis, and use of behavioral residue. Nevertheless, the very existence of behavioral residue in online environments is intentional and deliberate. That does not make it good or bad. It is simply a characteristic of behavioral residue in cyberspace that we need to acknowledge.

Throughout the debate about the future of privacy in cyberspace and the value or threat of computerized monitoring of HCI, it is important to maintain this differentiation between imported, natural behavioral residue and environmentally integrated, artificially induced behavioral residue. Health records online and a transaction log of clickstreams are categorically distinct things. This does not mean, however, that natural, real-world behavioral residue and contrived, virtual-world behavioral residue cannot be related. Broder (1997b), for example, sees a great potential for abuse when data about the Web browsing habits of users are combined with data about the real-world lives of those users.

Commercial (Cash Nexus) Privacy   The issue of individual privacy in online environments seems to be in the process of being distilled down to a question concerning privacy during our behavior as economic beings. Often the issue of privacy in cyberspace gets reduced to that of privacy on the Internet, then reduced again to privacy rights during electronic commerce. Getting and spending, we force the issue of privacy.

The privacy of consumers and commercial transactions in virtual environments has grabbed the main spotlight. When associated with consumer behavior in online commercial environments, privacy usually refers to personal information, and invasions of privacy in this context usually are interpreted as the unauthorized collection, disclosure, or other use of personal information as a result of electronic commercial transactions (Wang, Lee, and Wang 1998, 64). Both industry and consumer groups are exploring ways to achieve an equitable balance between the privacy interests of individuals and the desire by companies to use personal information to promote and enhance electronic commerce (Dorney 1997, 650). Dyson (1997b, 203) asserts that commercial consumer privacy is a simple moral issue: Customers have a right to choose what information to reveal about themselves and how it may be used, although they may have to relinquish some privileges to assert and maintain that right.

What seems to upset some online consumers are situations in which personal information is captured without their knowledge, and when they appear to receive nothing in return for unwittingly relinquishing their personal behavioral information. Yet real-world commercial environments such as markets, bazaars, and stores traditionally have been understood as public places. If one is in a space where things and services are bought and sold, one should expect to be monitored by the owner of the goods and services for sale.

During the latter half of the 1990s the U.S. Federal Trade Commission has been very interested and involved in the debates concerning individual consumer privacy in online environments. Bushey (1996) provides a brief recap of the June 1996 workshop, "Consumer Privacy on the Global Information Infrastructure," held by the Bureau of Consumer Protection within the FTC. The workshop was part of a continuing effort by the FTC to encourage Internet businesses to address the consumer privacy issues exposed by the emerging use of cyberspace to conduct business. The workshop focused on whether or not to require disclosure to consumers of the planned use of data gathered at Web sites. For Web sites geared toward children, workshop participants discussed the merits of limiting information that could be gathered, analyzed, and sold without parental knowledge and consent (Teinowitz 1997a).

In 1996 Christine Varney, one of the FTC commissioners at that time, threatened the Internet industry that unless it made substantial progress toward setting and complying with industry privacy standards, federal regulation or legislation would be imminent (Weise 1997a). During 1996 FTC hearings on electronic consumer privacy, Marc Rotenberg, director of EPIC, suggested that privacy will be to the emerging information economy what consumer protection and product safety were to the mature phase of the industrial age in the late nineteenth and early twentieth centuries (Bernstein 1997).

On June 10–13, 1997, the FTC held another round of hearings on privacy in cyberspace. The hearings responded to complaints made by privacy advocates such as EPIC that personal information was being gathered and used by online vendors without users' knowledge or consent (Internet firms 1997). The three major participating groups in these hearings were database industry representatives, privacy advocates, and government officials (James 1997a). During a speech at the CATO Institute before the four-day workshop, Commissioner Varney stated that "although privacy is important, the marketplace should be the proper paradigm to determine how information-collecting practices are utilized" (Farnet 1997). Karpinski (1997) surmised from this and other statements that the unstated mandate emerging from the 1997 FTC workshop on consumer privacy was that unless the Internet industry regulates itself regarding this matter, Congress will consider federal legislation to protect consumer privacy on the Web.

Marc Rotenberg attended, as did Evan Hendricks, editor of a newsletter that monitors computer privacy issues. Hendricks advocates greater government oversight of computerized data collection services (Broder 1997a). The basic question looming behind the FTC hearings, according to Broder, was whether there is a need for federal supervision of the rapidly growing and largely unregulated industry of collecting, analyzing, buying, and selling computerized information about individuals. Broder saw these hearings as an unusual examination of some profound questions about the role of individuals in a technological, computerized society. If privacy in cyberspace is endangered, the FTC hearings also point to some fundamental choices that need to be made about the preferred solution. Industry standards, government legislation and regulation, technological fixes, and the Internet itself as a social system all have been discussed as ideal solutions (Broder 1997a).

In commenting on the FTC hearings of June 1997, Dyson (1997a) notes that both options of government regulation and industry self-regulation have serious potential shortcomings. The FTC is considering two tools that may represent a third viable way to protect the online privacy of Internet users: eTRUST and the Open Profiling Standard (OPS). On December 17, 1997 the FTC released its report, *Individual Reference Services: A Report to Congress*. The EPIC criticized the report because the FTC guidelines lacked an enforcement mechanism and provided no recourse for aggrieved parties (Peek 1998).

International organizations also have an interest in protecting the privacy of individuals in online commercial environments. In February 1998 the OECD held a workshop on privacy protection in a global networked society. The workshop focused on protecting consumer privacy during online commercial transactions. "The growth of electronic commerce requires increased consumer confidence in privacy protection, including access to information and choice" (Organization for Economic Cooperation and Development 1998). The workshop participants reaffirmed that the 1980 OECD *Privacy Guidelines* continue to provide a common set of fundamental privacy principles. They noted that there basically are four types of instruments for safeguarding privacy in cyberspace: legal sanctions; industry and individual self-regulation; contractual agreements between sellers and buyers; and technological safeguards (Organization for Economic Cooperation and Development 1998). The delegates to the workshop called for a study of ways to provide seamless privacy protection across national boundaries and jurisdictions.

The online database industry has made some attempts at self-regulation. On June 10, 1997, on the first day of FTC hearings about personal privacy on the Internet, eight database companies as a group announced plans to reassure users that steps are being taken to protect personal privacy in cyberspace (James 1997a). The eight companies participating in the agreement included Metromail, Reed Elsevier's LEXIS-NEXIS unit, Experian, Choicepoint, Database Technologies, Information America, First Data InfoSource, and IRSC, Inc. (Chandrasekaran 1997b). The proposed guidelines also reaffirmed the right of database producers to gather and distribute data gleaned from public sources, such as telephone directories, land sales, court records, and licensing records (James 1997a).

On June 11, 1997, the McGraw-Hill Companies announced their own self-policing policy. They planned to separate information gathered about individuals into two basic categories: personally identifiable information (PII) and sensitive data. The PII, such as birth dates, addresses, and employment histories, would be collected and sold only with prior consent from individuals. Sensitive information, such as Social Security numbers, salaries, and credit histories, never would be distributed outside of McGraw-Hill (Broder 1997a).

The data gathered through computerized monitoring is valuable, especially when it has been thoughtfully analyzed and applied. Although Web site designers and owners have a legitimate interest in collecting aggregate statistical information about how Web site visitors navigate through the server, trafficking in information about the personal preferences or habits of Web users is an invasion of privacy (Moore 1995). Environmental conditions may soon develop, however, in which Web sites will pay visitors to access their personal information. An OPS (Open Profiling Standard) personal profile may become a new form of currency or password to be used to gain access to Web sites. If one is willing to release one's personal profile information, the Web site will allow access, perhaps including some monetary remuneration. People will be able to sell their privacy, just as in the real world people in different desperate situations have been known to sell such possessions as their blood or their virtue. Privacy advocates may be dumbfounded to learn how many people are willing to sell portions of their privacy to acquire virtual experiences, goods, services, and information.

Some commentators have suggested that all privacy exists for the individual in the context of a barter economy. We retain or release private information or exhibit or conceal private behavior (assuming that one's privacy has not been invaded and thus unwillingly revealed) based on a complex economy of perceived advantages and disadvantages in doing so. Alper Caglayan, president of Open Sesame, a software vendor in Cambridge, Massachusetts, sees the privacy issue as a cost-to-benefit formula in the individual's eyes (Wilder and Dalton 1997). The tacit promise from online disclosure of personal information of better-targeted advertising is not a sufficiently enticing benefit for most individuals to motivate them to disclose much of that information.

The Economics of Privacy and the Surrender of Privacy   The economics of maintaining, invading, and surrendering privacy appears to be changing. The relative freedom to buy and sell information about consumer activity on computerized networks will in all likelihood profoundly influence the realization of the vast potential for value creation from this potentially vast amount of raw data (Hagel and Sacconaghi 1996). It has been noted above that the cost of collecting data about HCI has dropped significantly. The cost of analyzing and applying these massive amounts of data seems to be plummeting as well. Along similar, perhaps related, lines, Laudon (1996) suggests that the technological cost of invading personal privacy has fallen well below its true social cost. As a result of the imbalance, the use of personal information is wasteful and inefficient, while personal privacy is expensive and dear.

The emergence of the Web has redefined our understanding of privacy in the postmodern digital age. Our understanding of privacy seems to be shifting from seeing it as an inalienable right to seeing it as an assignable right. Dyson (1997b, 210) observes:

> Some people object in principle to the concept of privacy as an assignable right — one that can be sold or bargained away. They'd rather see it as an inalienable right, one the poor can enjoy as fully as the rich. But I believe that people should decide for themselves how to value their data. Since privacy is not an absolute, and since individuals' preferences vary, it seems foolish to insist on an absolute approach.

Does one have the right to relinquish one's privacy? At the individual level, the answer would appear to be yes. Because privacy relies, however, on general social acceptance and respect, one who voluntarily relinquishes one's privacy may endanger the privacy of others, in the sense that one's actions indicate either that, in this particular situation, protecting one's personal privacy is not worth it, or that, in general, one does not have a high regard for the privacy of individuals.

Personal information one voluntarily discloses is not in itself a privacy issue, but it can become one when the information is used in ways not intended by the individual discloser, or when it combines with other information obtained involuntarily to generate new, different information (Mann 1997, 42). It can be very difficult or impossible for the obtainer of voluntarily disclosed information to learn and understand the parameters of its acceptable use as understood by the person who revealed it. The individual discloser may have only a vague or incomplete notion of parameters of acceptable use for this information. For example, if one fills out a warranty registration card for a newly purchased appliance, then later learns that the manufacturer of the appliance has used this information to attempt to sell one other appliances, one may or may not feel that this is unacceptable use of the information one provided.

The concept of information liquidity addresses the issue of whether or not an online vendor can sell or distribute in any way this information to third parties. One possible outcome of the current debate over privacy on the Internet could be tighter restrictions on information liquidity, rather than on information capture itself— a necessarily prior but completely different activity (Hagel and Sacconaghi 1996).

Gandy (1989, 66) also discusses the economics of privacy and loss of privacy. Because the surrender of each isolated bit of information about an individual has such a seemingly small privacy cost, and because the cost to the individual of monitoring how a bureaucracy uses that information would be high, individuals are incapable of acting in their own interests in this matter (Bryant 1995, 512). If additional monetary or access rewards are applied to the voluntary surrender of private information, many individuals may choose the immediate value to be gained, even if ultimately the immediate value is significantly less than the long-term value, both for the individual and society, of maintaining privacy. Hagel and Sacconaghi (1996) speculate that "customers themselves may become competitors (with online companies) for information about themselves."

Privacy in Cyberspace   The issue of personal privacy in online environments also has environmental aspects. Some of the privacy challenges on the Internet flow directly from the peculiar nature of cyberspace — for example, the ease of tracking communications, which makes it difficult to engage in otherwise protected expression, such as anonymous political argument (Privacy and the cookie pushers 1997). The Internet is both a social milieu and a virtual environment. Whereas Shoeman (1992) focused on the social dimensions of privacy, in this situation it may be useful to examine briefly the environmental dimensions. The environmental prospect we face is that, as computerized monitoring in cyberspace develops as a method for the virtual environment itself to monitor human behavior in that environment, the environment may be able to invade an individual's privacy. As computers become more involved in HCI, the role of human and non-human elements in invasions of privacy comes into question. Is it possible to invade someone's privacy if no one ever sees the collected information?

In the real world privacy has served as a form of protection from other forms of social control. As such, privacy is part of a system of social checks and balances. In cyberspace, where computerized monitoring quickly is becoming an expected feature of the virtual environment, we need environmental protection from other forms of environmental control. In this age of early exploration of cyberspace, we need anti-environmentalists. If real-world environmentalists can be loosely described as those who seek to protect the environment from human excess and imbalance, in cyberspace we will need anti-environmentalists to protect people from the potential excesses and imbalances of an infinitely mutable, individualizable environment. We often understand real-world environments as passive, fragile, suffering entities. Through the use of computerized monitoring, online environments may become aggressive and mutable — far different from their real-world cousins.

At least in theory, cyberspace is capable of supporting both private and public virtual environments. The dominant tenor of cyberspace as a whole, however, appears to be still emerging. On the one hand, authors such as Raskin (1996) assume that to be on the Internet involves being studied and subject to demographic research. On the other hand, much e-mail correspondence assumes the tone and tenor of private conversation. Whatever our reasonable expectations turn out to be regarding individual privacy in virtual environments, enforcing social compliance with those reasonable expectations probably will involve a mixture of technological fixes, industry standards for ethical conduct, and federal legislation.

The Anonymizer (http://www.anonymizer.com) is a Web site that acts as an intermediary between a browser and other Web sites. It prevents the managers of the sites visited from learning anything about the visitor (Mann 1997). Basically, the concept behind the Anonymizer is to protect an individual's privacy in cyberspace by introducing a middle agent into the HCI. One misgiving I have about proposed solutions such as the Anonymizer to the challenge of preserving personal privacy in online environments is that, rather than protect privacy, these proposed solutions merely make virtual public actions anonymous. A real-world analogy would be hooded Ku Klux Klan members. Their social actions continue to be public and frequently observed, but they are anonymous. Anonymous actions in public spaces are not the same as private actions.

Privacy Policies   Although there are many types of privacy policies, all good policies share certain common characteristics: They explain the responsibilities of the organization or individual that is collecting personal information, as well as the rights of the individual who provided the personal information. Typically, this entails explaining why information and data are being collected, how the data will be analyzed, combined, and applied, and what steps will be taken to limit improper disclosure or sale to other individuals or organizations. A good privacy policy also enables individuals to obtain their own data and make corrections, if necessary (Electronic Privacy Information Center 1997). Privacy policies for virtual environments, transactions, and behavior probably will evolve in a way that requires treating computerized monitoring and other forms of information capture as options to be consciously chosen and enabled by the users themselves.

The Privacy of the Human Monitor   An interesting but rarely mentioned aspect of the relationship between the human monitor and the monitored individual or group is that the monitor has at least as much interest as the monitored in maintaining his or her privacy and anonymity. Like the Wizard of Oz behind the screen, the person behind the monitoring project does not want to be in turn observed and found out. The rapid growth in computerized monitoring software may be a result of not so much a shift in the economics of monitoring or an escalating social paranoia, but of a fortification of the ability of the monitoring individual to remain private and undetected during the monitoring project. Computerized monitoring enables those behind the monitoring to recede further into the shadows.

Individualized Invaders of Privacy   One other aspect of the privacy issue needs to be noted in this context. When I imagine someone invading my privacy, often my imagination individualizes the invasion process. Although specific individuals do not come to mind, I imagine the invasion as being undertaken by an individual, even if the individual is a big government goon or a low-level supervisor for a large corporation. Invasions of privacy as imagined events often involve a bilateral interaction between two individuals. The imagined act of some other individual examining private information about me causes me great unease.

Privacy As a Social and Cultural Value   Although privacy often is conceptualized as a right of individual persons, it also exists as a social and cultural value. Shoeman (1992) argues that privacy is important and has a positive value because it facilitates associations and relational ties among human beings, not because it liberates or withdraws an individual from the crowd. Viewed in this way, privacy is a foundation of society, not an anti-social retreat. Privacy, then, can be understood as a social value, rather than (or in addition to) an individual prerogative. If so, is protecting privacy basically a personal or social responsibility? Privacy has a strong social value, but little basis as a legal right. "We're a culture that has a high regard for privacy," notes Marc Rotenberg, director of EPIC. "To most people, [computerized] list gatherers like these, while they may not be doing anything illegal, are doing something unethical and intrusive" (quoted in Rothfeder 1997, 227). Ideas about privacy are cultural phenomena, shaped through historical experience (Agre 1994, 101).

Based on Justice Harlan's concurring opinion in the 1967 case of *Katz v U.S.* (DeCew 1997, 20), the question concerning privacy in cyberspace boils down to whether or not society is willing to recognize the expectation of privacy in online environments as reasonable. This raises another fundamental question concerning privacy in cyberspace: What real or virtual society holds sway here? DeCew (1997, 52) notes that "once it is settled that something is a private matter, it is a separate issue to decide whether or not, in some social context, an invasion of it can be justified."

Privacy and Publicity   Often the notion of privacy is discussed and understood in the context of its value relative to other equally nebulous rights, such as the public's right to know (Hausman 1994). In the real world, privacy and publicity appear to be pure, antagonistic opposites. Poster (1997), for example, provides a nice thumbnail sketch of the evolving tension of meanings between the public and the private. Stratton (1997, 266) suggests that the modern idea of a real public sphere depends on a distinction between public and private life. Just as the real and the virtual seem to comprehend the entirety of human consciousness, the public and the private encompass all information. Many commentators on the plight of personal privacy in the postmodern world suggest or argue that, just as the virtual appears to be overtaking the real, public information is squeezing out the private.

In cyberspace, however, the relationship between privacy and publicity appears to be more unsettled, and perhaps permanently more complex. The development and diffusion of computers and computer networks has unleashed a data storm that is eroding the traditional boundaries between public and private information (Hausman 1994). Quittner (1997b) notes that by the mere act of browsing the Web, which connotes something passive, leisurely, and solitary, we "go public" in a way that was unimaginable as little as a decade ago. Whether regarded primarily as a psychological, social, political, economic, or environmental problem, the struggle concerning privacy in cyberspace, with computerized monitoring as a major threat, is not primarily between privacy and publicity. The alleged invasions of privacy caused by most computerized monitoring do not result in public knowledge of private behavior. Computerized monitoring rarely if ever results in tabloid exposes. Often, other private individuals find out about the online behavior of private individuals. If the analyst of computerized monitoring data is a professional, the issue becomes one of confidentiality.

People simultaneously dwell in both the real world and cyberspace. When one's consciousness enters an online environment, one's body does not leave the real world. One is simply distracted or enthralled by some other type of reality. The experience is similar to the way one feels and acts in the real world when engrossed in a novel, mesmerized by a television show, or sleepwalking. One continues to exist in the real world, but one's mind is not primarily focused on it. How well do people make the transition from real-life levels of privacy to virtual publicity? For example, if one moves into an online public space from the privacy of one's home, does one have more transitional discontinuities than if entering from a public access terminal in a library?

The value of private information or private behavior changes when it becomes public. "Once privacy has gone public, so to speak, it runs the double risk of not quite living up to the standards of the public domain, on the one hand, or of ceasing to be private on the other" (Huebert 1997).

Virtual privacy really is a concern of virtual communities, not only of virtual selves. In the real world, privacy certainly is more of a concern in cities and towns than it is in the country. On frontiers and in rural areas, loneliness is a bigger issue than privacy. It is in cities and towns where public and private life are demarcated. Although many commentators have noted that the issue of online commerce may be lurking behind the heated debate about online privacy, another lurking concern may center on the viability of virtual communities. Virtual communities require both private and public behavior and communication. If virtual privacy can be made an issue, that must mean that some form of virtual community exists.

In spite of the raging debate about ways to protect individual privacy on the Internet and other computer networks, it may be publicity, rather than privacy, that ultimately is in danger of diminution during human colonization of cyberspace. Foster (1997, 29) suggests that the transformation of social space brought on by computer-mediated communication facilitates the intrusiveness of the private upon the public, not vice versa. Ironically, although the Web appears to be headed toward a status in which nothing is private, in the end it may become completely personalized. A personalized publicity is difficult to imagine in the real world, but entirely possible, if not probable, in the virtual world.

Privacy and Personal Identity   Westin (1984) concentrates on the biological springs of privacy. Individuals lay claim to private places to promote individual well-being and small-group intimacy. The problem with applying this biological notion of privacy to cyberspace is that, despite all of the sex talk, cyberspace has no direct biological links. We need to articulate some other way that privacy promotes individual well-being.

"People are losing control of their identities," U.S. Senator Diane Feinstein has said. "Our private lives are becoming commodities with tremendous value in the marketplace" (quoted in Quittner 1997a, 65). DeCew (1997, 65) also asserts that in the real world privacy protects both peace of mind and bodily integrity. In cyberspace, however, there is no body, and it could be argued that if peace of mind is the goal, computerized monitoring in the long term has a chance of delivering (in the form of amazingly personalized environments) a peace that passes all human understanding.

Privacy and Personal Autonomy   Both Henkin (1974) and Gross (1971) attempt to differentiate privacy from autonomy and liberty (DeCew 1997, 35). For Henkin, autonomy is freedom from official regulation, while privacy is freedom from official intrusion (DeCew 1997, 36). DeCew (1997, 168, note 56) also thinks there has been confusion over the relationship between privacy and autonomy. She argues that it is intuitive to think that liberty, privacy, and autonomy are distinct concepts that overlap in their extensions. DeCew goes on to argue that privacy interests derive from a need for independence that is broader than information, autonomy, property, or intimacy — the bases of narrower theories of privacy — allow.

Two questions remain: Is privacy possible in virtual environments that appear to be gravitating toward becoming public spaces in some postmodern sense, and, if so, is privacy even needed? In the real world, privacy enables the individual to realize a personal lifestyle and sense of integrity in a world that is essentially intractable. Privacy is one of the consolation prizes for a real life that is nasty, brutish, and short. Most virtual worlds, however, are eminently tractable, and they seem to be becoming more so, which opens up new ways to realize a lifestyle and to develop a sense of integrity. If this is true, perhaps privacy will lose some of its value and utility.

Autonomy manifests itself through decision-making and action. DeCew (1997, 41) asserts that many privacy issues, such as protection from unwarranted electronic surveillance, have nothing to do with an individual's right to autonomous decision-making. I disagree. If computerized monitoring leads to automatic customization of an individual's virtual environment, this scenario restricts or precludes the individual's decision-making opportunities. In essence, the computerized monitoring facility, after analyzing the observed behavior of the person, makes certain decisions. On the other hand, individual human beings (Ozymandias excepted) never have been able to make such decisions about the configuration of real environments, so the loss of opportunities to make them in virtual environments is not tangible or noticeable.

Personalize and Privatize   It is ironic that, although computerized monitoring often is understood as a major threat to personal privacy, as the technology develops and human intervenors are removed from the loop of collecting data about HCI, analyzing it, then applying the results, computerized monitoring will greatly increase people's ability to pre-reflectively personalize their virtual environments. A trivial example illustrates: To personalize the background of one's Windows 95 desktop, one needs to either choose from one of the available customization patterns or design one's own truly personalized pattern. The process involves time, thought, and conscious intention. In the future, as computerized monitoring becomes more vertically computerized, the background will become personalized simply as a result of one's indigenous online behavior, without one's having to expressly intend to change it.

Uninformed Monitoring and Informed Consent   In many situations in which computers are used to monitor HCI, the users are not informed that their interactions with the computer system are being monitored. Do users of computers and computer systems have a right, grounded in ethical reasoning and norms of moral action, to expect to be informed? Amy Bruckman, an assistant professor of computer science at the Georgia Institute of Technology, asserts that it is unethical for researchers to study the online behavior of Web users without their informed consent (Kiernan 1998). Lewis Maltby of the ACLU sees the arguments surrounding informed consent during computerized monitoring as part of broader philosophical arguments about the nature of human beings — arguments that go back at least as far as Rousseau and Hobbes (Burger 1995). Is it unethical to obtain personal information about someone without consent? We do it every day when we meet face to face. Usually someone's race, age, and sex are self-evident. Why should we chastise people for trying to make remote interactions at least as revealing as face to face interactions? The problem with human activity in online environments is that these data are not ambient, as it is in real environments. The information has to be coaxed out of the interaction. It is not self-evident.

During computer monitoring activities in operational, deployed computer systems, privacy issues can be addressed by posting notices of monitoring activities, allowing users a choice about having their actions captured, stripping all personal identification from the captured data, or other means that meet guidelines for the fair treatment of human subjects (Borgman, Hirsh, and Hiller 1996, 572).

The explosive use of Web server log data and information stored in cookies files has added fuel to the debate over uninformed monitoring and informed consent. Privacy activists have never liked the fact that many Web sites use cookies on hard disks to store behavioral information about the owners or users of the hard disks, without obtaining informed consent from the users or giving them any control of the collection and use of this behavioral data. Stanton McCandlish from the Electronic Frontier Foundation sees this primarily as an issue about informed consent (Abate 1997). "We are very concerned about sites that don't inform users. It's important that people know what's being collected and for what purpose," says Lori Fena, executive director of the foundation (Moukheiber 1996, 343).

Informed consent can be implemented through either the "opt-in" approach, which requires participating individuals to give explicit approval for secondary uses of their personal information, or the "opt-out" approach which entails notifying all potentially participating individuals that their personal data will be used for secondary purposes unless they disapprove and notify the vendor before a specified deadline (Spinello 1995).

Informing users about the possibility or presence of computerized gathering of data about HCI contains risks as well. Perhaps the greatest risk is the Hawthorne Effect. The Hawthorne Effect essentially posits that one changes what one measure by measuring it. It follows, then, that any attempt to metaphorically or really look over shoulders at the users of company computers is destined to fail. It automatically alters what would have been done if the users had remained uninformed (Sellers 1997).

Many commentators have argued that informing users that they are (or even may be) subject to computerized monitoring is basic fairness. The EPIC study of popular Web sites concluded that it is a matter of such fairness to inform Web users when personal information is being collected and how it will be used (Electronic Privacy Information Center 1997). The meaning of personal information, however, is not clearly defined and is open to various interpretations.

Do employees in online work environments have a right to be informed that they are being monitored by computer? Several attempts to control CPM with legislation have focused on the need to inform the employee that CPM is used in a particular workplace (Baarda 1994, 17). The most pervasive questions with proposed federal legislation concern the need to tell employees exactly when they will be monitored and the generality of terms used, such as "electronic monitoring" and "the workplace" (Anderson 1993).

Unobtrusive Monitoring   Most computerized monitoring is unobtrusive. Unobtrusive monitoring simply is monitoring that does not obtrude. It does not announce or reveal itself when it occurs. On the positive side, unobtrusive monitoring does not distract the person monitored, nor does it interrupt the natural flow of the HCI. If the goal of a computerized monitoring project is to observe people as they act "naturally" in admittedly artificial, computer-enabled online environments, the value of unobtrusiveness is great, simply because many people act differently when they know or sense that they are being observed. The sense of being watched often is unsettling and disruptive to the behavior of the individual being observed. From a research standpoint, informed consent is not necessarily the best of all possible worlds. Even in real-world environments, seeing a surveillance camera in a public place or a store is slightly unnerving. There may be reasons for making computerized monitoring as unobtrusive as possible.

Nearly all, if not all, computerized monitoring projects are intended to observe people interacting with computer systems, not with the computerized monitoring module itself. Although the human ingenuity reported by Clement and McDermott (1991), whereby data entry operators tried to outwit the CPM program, is interesting in itself, to the project of computerized monitoring it represents troublesome noise or artificial data.

Obtrusive data collection methods, on the other hand, are used primarily to obtain feedback from users regarding their preferences and opinions (Lancaster and Sandore 1997, 207). Obtrusive data collection methods usually focus on opinions and value judgments, while unobtrusive data collection methods usually focus on observable behavior. The three basic unobtrusive methods for studying HCI are transaction logs, direct human observations of people using computer workstations, and video or audio taping of user behavior (Lancaster and Sandore 1997, 207). The goal of unobtrusive data collection is to obtain more objective observations of human behavior as people interact with computers. Human cognitive processes and patterns only can be inferred from an analysis of computer-monitored behavior. If the goal is to understand why people do what they do in online environments, computerized monitoring will not provide irrefutable answers.

Unobtrusive monitoring can be either good or bad, depending on the situation. For example, intrusive methods of measuring the impact of advertising have troubled the industry for years. Some see the potential of unobtrusive computerized monitoring of reactions to advertising in Web environments as a very advantageous development (Dreze and Zufryden 1997a). Because computerized monitoring as a form of surveillance often is unobtrusive, it does not confuse, upset, or alter the behavior of the user.

Although uninformed and unobtrusive monitoring often occur together, they need not be conjoined. It is possible to create environmental conditions in which users are informed of the potential of having their interactions with a computer system monitored, yet any actual monitoring is unobtrusive. For example, in research conducted by Tauscher and Greenberg (1997), they used informed, yet unobtrusive, observation coupled with a pledge of confidentiality. The U.S. federal *Cable Communications Policy Act of 1984* provides an interesting annual disclosure model that could be applied to some Internet privacy concerns. The act requires cable television companies to provide annual notification to subscribers about the purposes for which personal information is gathered and how that information is used and disclosed to others. Informed prior notification of the possibility of computerized monitoring would be preferable to obtrusive monitoring at the time of data capture — at least from the perspective of the people involved in the computerized monitoring project.

The power of the panopticon resides in such informed, yet uncertain, unobtrusiveness. The model of undetected surveillance keeps the watched in a subordinate role through uncertainty: The watched never know for certain if or when they are being watched (Lyon 1994, 60). Such monitoring has power, however, only when the monitored suspect that they are being monitored. Purely unobtrusive monitoring (i.e., monitoring of uninformed subjects) may create other ethical problems, but it does not disrupt the behavior of the monitored.

Uninformed and unobtrusive computerized monitoring may be less unsettling to the user population. Quittner (1997b) asserts that we are "hurtling toward an even more intrusive world." The CASIE–proposed principles of Web measurement also saw the value of non-intrusiveness: "Non-Intrusiveness (Measurement methods which are least visible to consumers, and require the least effort on their part, are preferable to methods which are more visible to consumers and/or which require more effort)" (Krantz 1995c, 28). We are moving toward the habitation-through-creation of online environments in which uninformed, unobtrusive computerized monitoring is dominant, because the needs to intrude have declined. Scare tactics are a form of informed dissent, the opposite of informed consent along the consent continuum, but at the same end of the informed continuum.

Some critics have claimed that unobtrusive computerized monitoring of HCI violates the generally accepted norms of ethical research practices involving human subjects. Regulations governing the use of human subjects requires consent and encourages researchers to share their findings with experimental subjects (Martin 1977). "The extent to which such unobtrusive observations constitute ethically objectionable invasions of privacy depends on the context in which the observations are made. The clearest violation occurs when persons are secretly observed in a situation that, for good reason, they assumed to be private" (Kelman 1977, 181). Martin (1977) states this argument most forcefully and succinctly:

> Monitoring is a practice that, unless done openly and within well-defined limits, is likely to lead to temptations, fear, and righteous anger. Managers have a right (if not an obligation) to protect their systems from illegal or damaging usage, and to gather data necessary for improving service or reducing costs. In all other cases, monitoring should not be done without prior consent. For example, researchers wanting unobtrusive traces of naturally-occurring behavior should obtain permission from each subject to be monitored beforehand.

For public access systems, however, such as online library catalogs and Web servers, it would be difficult or impossible to obtain prior consent from each subject to be monitored. It would slow down users' sessions, and force them to forsake their anonymity to specify their consent or withholding of consent.

Karpinski (1997) believes that the unobtrusive nature by which information is gathered on the Internet is the root of the problem of personal privacy in cyberspace. For Karpinski, the key to ensuring Internet privacy is to bring efforts to collect personal data out into the open.

If computerized monitoring remains both unobtrusive and unknown to the general monitored population, the causes of certain conditions of online environments will remain mysterious. The actors will be the unwitting authors of the warp and woof of cyberspace. If they do not like certain aspects of their virtual environments, they will not be able to determine whether to modify their behavior or the computerized monitoring software to most easily effect the desired environmental change. Online environments will not be open books, either in the sense that all human actions are known to all, or in the sense that environmental causal changes will be self-evident to the human inhabitants. Online environments may remain fundamentally more mysterious and inscrutable than real environments. The laws of cyberspace, unlike the laws of nature, are not silent and immutable, waiting to be discovered and harnessed by human beings.

Response Avenues to the Privacy Issue   There are several response "avenues"—not necessarily diverging—to the privacy issue in the online age. One is through governmental legislation. Legislation has a fairly good track record of affecting group behavior. The majority of the U.S. adult population, moreover, appears to want more government intervention to protect personal privacy in cyberspace. Nearly two-thirds of the respondents to the 1996 Equifax/Harris consumer privacy survey agreed that the government needs to scan Internet messages to prevent online fraud (Heubusch 1997). Another avenue entails industry self-regulation on the part of companies and people who collect, analyze, apply, and perhaps resell potentially private information. The FTC workshops in 1996 and 1997 focused on these first two avenues of action. Another avenue is lined with technological fixes, like so many fast-food restaurants and ten-minute oil-change shops. The avenue of technological privacy protections could lead to something akin to an arms race, in which the protectors and invaders engage in an endless round of minor technological advances that provides one camp or another a temporary advantage. Another avenue is to commodify privacy and establish a more equitable economy for the sale, barter, and exchange of private information. A fifth avenue, perhaps the least explored in Jeffersonian democracies and elsewhere, is to educate the citizenry and netizenry about the subtleties of privacy issues and invasions in a computerized information society. An informed citizenry could develop its own system of checks and balances.

> If the general public is aggressively enlightened in the ways and means of information technology, then it follows that perhaps we can expect the general population to be more discriminating when it comes to privacy protection. Just as we speak of a green consumer culture, so too we might encourage the beginning of a privacy culture (Lutz 1997).

Although the concept of privacy is a vague, complex idea, and although it apparently emerged as a major ideal only in the modern era, privacy will continue to have some value in the postmodern world where real and online environments vie for our attention and participation. Privacy is about the control of the dissemination of information and the attempt to define and control private spaces and places. It is not primarily about the protection of essentially private behavior. Computerized monitoring is more about the generation, collection, analysis, interpretation, and application of behavioral information in online environments, where natural behavioral residue, such as footprints in the wet sand in the real world, does not occur. The behavioral traces have to be manufactured. DeCew (1997, 63) observes that although the concept of privacy may be popular, mysterious, and elusive, we cannot conclude that privacy is worthless or too vague to serve as a meaningful idea. In the near future the Net and the Web may become overall much more private, and the variations in levels of privacy may become much more diverse. Eventually in cyberspace people will spend much of their time within relatively closed spaces, much as they do now in real life (Dyson 1997b, 217). Some parts of the Web will become completely private, while others will become hyperpublic, more public than the most public places in the real world.

Privacy is very situational and occasional. It depends on environmental conditions, including the primary human activity pursued in that environment, such as learning, working, and shopping, as well as on the reasonable expectations of the people in the environment. In the final analysis, our expectations concerning privacy and publicity in cyberspace will carry the day, driving policy, rules, legislation, and possibly even software development.

One irony of the debate over privacy in cyberspace is that while people involved in computerized monitoring are trying to depersonalize the process to personalize virtual spaces, defenders of privacy are trying to personalize the process of computerized monitoring to generate resentment toward it.

Perhaps the most unsettling aspect of privacy invasions is not so much that they happen, nor what we reveal about ourselves because of the invasion, but rather that privacy invasions force us to confront the fact that often we are nearly powerless to protect this right we sense is fundamental to our being.

7

Legislative Efforts
and Legal Implications

Legislative efforts to control computerized monitoring of HCI have been spotty. Most have focused on acceptable interaction between the government (federal, state, and municipal) and individual citizens. In the past decade, interest in protecting the online rights of workers and consumers has increased. In online work environments, new monitoring technologies generally have been seen as extensions of traditional management prerogatives, leaving workers the opportunity to organize and collectively bargain over work environment issues (Levy 1993). The result has been that "Employees currently have few legal tools available to combat electronic monitoring. Policy makers have left the issue to the free market, which is only partially encumbered by unions. Consequently, employers are free to implement monitoring systems in virtually any manner" (Addressing the new hazards 1991,1904, quoted in Levy 1993).

Constitutional Rights and Protections   Generally, constitutional protections of privacy treat the national government and individual citizens as the principal parties. Although not explicitly guaranteed, the privacy rights implied in the U.S. Constitution and the Bill of Rights protect individual citizens against impositions by the government (Dorney 1997, 639). In Canada there is no explicit constitutional right to privacy (Baarda 1994, 15). In their state constitutions, a few U.S. states expressly protect the privacy of the individual. For example, the California State Constitution identifies the right to privacy as one of the inalienable rights of all people (Dorney 1997, 649). Federal and state constitutions have not comprehensively addressed the right to privacy in online environments.

U.S. Federal Legislative Initiatives   Human-computer interaction is a type of social interaction. Legislation is a form of social control. Computerized monitoring of HCI is a way for second and potentially third parties to monitor the viewing and other behavior of people in cyberspace. Just as the *Cable Communications Policy Act of 1984* forbids cable operators and third parties from monitoring the viewing habits of subscribers (Sessler 1997, 663), it has been argued that federal legislation should be enacted to prohibit system operators, Internet service providers, and other online individuals and industries from monitoring the online habits of netizens. This may be a classic situation of the general fear concerning computer technology in which the pace of technological advances far outpaces the speed of social control mechanisms, including legislation. The inability of legislation to keep up sends us back to the general observations coming from philosophers of technology about the relationship between technological advances and social change.

Westin (1986), Susser (1988), and Schroeder (1988) review the case law pertaining to workplace monitoring. Schroeder holds out little hope under the present law for non-unionized workers for redress of monitoring-related adverse actions (Lund 1989, 47). Kiesler (1997, xii) asserts that the 1973 *Code of Fair Information Practices* now serves as the basis for U.S. privacy legislation.

The United States Congress has not passed an omnibus privacy law governing the private sector's collection, analysis, and use of personal information (Dorney 1997, 642). Rather, federal legislation has focused on pieces of the entire privacy puzzle. Dorney (1997) summarized six federal statutes addressing the privacy of individuals during the use of communications, computers and computer networks, and video equipment and networks. Any federal legislative limits on online tracking of human behavior probably will focus first on children (Wildstrom 1996a).

Federal employees were afforded some privacy protection through the *Privacy Act of 1974* (Levy 1995, 12). Sessler (1997) notes that during the debates and discussions preceding passage of that act, there was some talk of extending the scope of the act to cover the private sector and establish a Federal Privacy Board.

The *Electronic Communications Privacy Act of 1986* requires the federal government to obtain a court order before intercepting most forms of electronic communications, broadly defined (Tuerkheimer 1993, 71). The act establishes the boundaries of monitoring. The act presumes that an employer can control and monitor the use of any electronic tool furnished by the employer for employees' use (Abate 1996). The act articulates no specific restrictions against the collection of personal information gathered from transaction logs, nor are any restrictions placed on the duration of storage of such transactional data (Sessler 1997, 664, note 190).

The proposed Privacy for Consumers and Workers Act was first introduced in 1988 (Lund 1989, 49). It would have required employers to provide prior written notice concerning what kinds of monitoring are to be used, what information will be collected, how the information will be analyzed and used, and the extent to which performance appraisals and disciplinary actions will be linked to data gathered by electronic monitoring. The bill further stipulated that employers can use monitoring to collect only work-related information. Individual employees would have been allowed access to their records (CWA legislative Update Staff Memorandum of 5/11/89; quoted in Lund 1989, 50).

The Privacy for Consumers and Workers Act was reintroduced in the 1990s as HR 1900. This legislation aimed to prevent abuses of electronic monitoring in the workplace (Levy 1995, 8). Note that the emphasis of the goal of the legislation is on the application of the findings and conclusions of electronic monitoring, not on the gathering of the data. Note also that the proposed legislation seems to assume that the meaning of a "workplace" is self-evident.

This bill was introduced during the 103rd U.S. Congress (George 1996, 459). On April 28, 1993 Rep. Pat Williams (Dem.–Mont.), Chairman of the House Subcommittee on Labor-management Relations, introduced HR 1900, a revised version of HR 1218 (the Privacy for Consumers and Workers Act) that had been approved by the full Education and Labor Committee in July 1992 (Adler 1993). HR 1900 was nearly identical to HR 1218. The bill defined electronic monitoring as the "collection, storage, analysis, or reporting of information concerning an employee's activities by means of a computer, electronic observation and supervision, telephone service observation, telephone call accounting, or other form of visual, auditory or computer-based technology which is conducted by any method other than direct observation by another person" (quoted in Adler 1993). Telephone service observation is the practice of listening to or recording telephone calls involving an employee to monitor and assess the quality of service being provided by the employee (Adler 1993).

The proposed bill would require that each employee to be electronically monitored receive prior written notice of the data to be collected and the times when electronic monitoring would occur (Adler 1993). The proposed bill generally would prohibit employers from engaging in electronic monitoring on a periodic or random basis, unless the employee has worked for the company less than 60 days. If an employee has a cumulative employment period of at least five years with the employer, electronic monitoring is not allowed at all, even if the focus of an electronic monitoring program is on a work group, rather than on an individual employee.

According to Adler, the proposed bill also specified that employers may not use quantitative data obtained with electronic monitoring as the sole basis for employee performance evaluations, nor to set production quotas, unless the employee works outside the employer's facilities and this data collection method is the only quantitative basis available to the employer. Adler reports that both the Senate and House have held hearings on proposed federal legislation (i.e., S 984 and HR 1900) that would control electronic monitoring in work environments (Adler 1993).

In May 1993 Sen. Paul Simon (Dem.–Ill.) introduced S 984 (HR 1218), the Privacy for Consumers and Workers Act. Simon chaired the Senate Subcommittee on Employment and Productivity. The subcommittee held hearings in late

June of 1993 (Anderson 1993). In an attempt to limit the potential abuses of electronic monitoring, the bill would have allowed employers to electronically monitor employees only if they complied with guidelines regarding notification, tenure, review of data obtained by electronic monitoring, employee access to data, use of data, and employee privacy.

HR 1900 is the companion bill to S 984. As introduced, both bills would require employers to notify staff and customers when monitoring will occur and the type of electronic monitoring to be used. However, if an employee has been employed less than 60 days, the employer may be monitored randomly and without notice. Someone employed with the same company more than five years would be protected from all forms of electronic monitoring. Third-party monitoring also is covered by the proposed legislation (Anderson 1993).

Supporters of S 984 claim that electronic monitoring invades consumer and worker privacy, increases employee stress, hinders Total Quality Management efforts, constitutes a form of de facto discrimination and sexual harassment, and is antithetical to the management culture of empowerment (De Tienne and Alder 1995, 7). Critics of the bill argue that several of the arguments against performance monitoring are unfounded; monitoring can be useful and beneficial; because of the growing risk of negligent hiring and vicarious liability suits, employers must monitor; requiring a monitoring program to provide advance notice to potentially monitored employees would reduce or eliminate many of the benefits of monitoring, and using tenure on the job to restrict monitoring is irrational. Critics contend that the bill is unnecessary, overly broad and administratively complex, and that it contains ambiguous definitions and questionable interpretations, leaving several issues unaddressed (De Tienne and Alder 1995, 11–12).

Westin, Marx, Zahorik, and Ware (1992) review the major points of the Privacy for Consumers and Workers Act. This unenacted U.S. federal legislation would require organizations to provide written notice of their electronic monitoring practices to current and prospective employees, and to provide affected workers who are intermittently monitored with a signal when monitoring is taking place. Aiello asserts that both of these requirements invariably would increase the salience of computerized monitoring (Aiello 1993).

On June 20, 1996, proposed legislation commonly known as the Communications Privacy and Consumer Empowerment Act was introduced into the U.S. House of Representatives by Ed Markey (Dem.–Mass.).* Markey was the ranking Democrat on the House Commerce Committee's Subcommittee on Telecommunications, Trade, and Consumer Protection.† Markey himself (Markey 1997) has described the proposed legislation as a privacy bill of rights. The bill was designed to address citizen's concerns over the online collection and use of personal information. Weber (1996) notes that the proposed legislation would force companies to disclose what types of information they collect about and from visitors to their

---

* *House Resolution 3685, 104th Congress, 2nd Session (Sessler 1997, 660, note 171).*
† *For an overview of Markey's views on the topic of privacy in cyberspace, see Markey (1997).*

Web sites. In situations and areas where online privacy protections need to be created or upgraded, the proposed legislation would empower the Federal Trade Commission and the Federal Communications Commission to develop rules that would ensure the protection of individuals' privacy in online environments.

The bill contains arguments that there are three fundamental privacy rules that give people control over the use of personal information: People must know that information is being collected about them; the collectors of the personal information must provide adequate and conspicuous notification that they intend to reuse or sell the information gathered; and individuals must have the opportunity to refuse permission for further use or resale of personal information (Center for Democracy and Technology 1996a). The proposed legislation also includes a proposal to establish a federal Privacy Protection Committee (Sessler 1997, 660). The proposed legislation would force companies on the Web to disclose what types of information they collect about and from visitors to their Web sites (Weber 1996).

Like much of the debate about privacy in cyberspace, the proposed legislation appears to focus primarily on real-world demographic information (e.g., legal, financial, and health information) that has been transported into online environments. The focus of this book is on the indigenous information of cyberspace, especially human behavior in virtual environments such as the World Wide Web. Although the proposed legislation affirms the idea of individual control over dissemination and use of information about oneself, it does not specify if behavioral residue in virtual environments is personal information, and thus subject to the proposed legislation.

On January 7, 1997, Rep. Bruce Vento (Dem.–Minn.) introduced proposed legislation commonly known as the Consumer Internet Privacy Protection Act of 1997.* The proposed legislation would require prior written consent from an individual before a computer service provider could disclose personal information about the individual to a third party. The bill was referred to the Committee on Commerce (Electronic Frontier Foundation 1997). Consumers also would have the right and opportunity to see and correct errors in personal information stored by an online database (Eckhouse 1997).

The proposed act would prevent the disclosure only of personally identifiable information (Dorney 1997, 655). If passed, the bill would grant investigative and enforcement authority to the Federal Trade Commission (Sessler 1997, 662). Again, the proposed legislation does not articulate whether captured behavioral residue from online activity is considered personal information, and it concentrates on potential uses and abuses by third parties, rather than articulating acceptable use of this information by the party of the second part, usually Internet providers. Sessler (1997, 662), however, interprets the proposed legislation as "a clear warning to Internet service providers and system administrators that even transactional information belongs to their customers and should be handled securely."

---

* *House Resolution 98, 105th Congress, 1st Session (Sessler 1997, 661, note 175).*

In May 1997 U.S. senators Dianne Feinstein and Charles Grassley introduced the *Personal Information Privacy Act of 1997*. The proposed legislation would make it more difficult for businesses to sell Social Security numbers, unlisted phone numbers, and other kinds of personal data (Quittner 1997a).

U.S. State Legislative Initiatives   Legislating individual privacy at the state level has been about as successful as attempts over the years to enact explicit omnibus federal legislation on this topic. According to Westin (1986), proposed legislation to regulate computerized monitoring in the workplace has been introduced without success in Ohio, Minnesota, Massachusetts, Pennsylvania, California, Illinois, and New Jersey (Lund 1989, 48). The Connecticut legislature authorized two studies of VDT health and safety (Westin 1986, 107; cited in Lund 1989, 48).

In the 1990s state legislatures have become more active on the privacy front. Sessler (1997) reports that ten states explicitly define personal privacy as a fundamental, protected right. Minnesota's legislature recently has been debating an online privacy bill, which would make that state the first in the nation to broadly regulate the use of "personally identifiable information" via online services (O'Malley 1997). The New York *Civil Rights Law* established various categories of privacy rights (Dorney 1997, 649).

Other Federal and International Legislation and Conventions   The Europeans have pursued legislative initiatives with much more success and comprehensiveness than the Americans. Dorney (1997, 637) notes that European nations have more organized, comprehensive, and restrictive approaches to privacy issues than does the United States.

In 1973 Sweden was the first nation to pass a national privacy law (DeCew 1997, 152). As a legislative response to worker concerns about the physical and emotional stress that may accompany computerized monitoring in work environments, the Swedish government has enacted legislation that restricts the degree to which Swedish companies can electronically monitor the work performed by individual employees (Kolb and Aiello 1997, 203).

The German government has proposed legislation that would limit the collection of personal data to the extent necessary to perform the requested services, after which the data must be immediately erased (Dorney 1997, 659). A strict interpretation of the proposed legislation would outlaw the retention of data in cookies files after the completion of a visit to a Web site.

In 1981 the Council of Europe passed "Convention 108," the "Convention for the Protection of Individuals with Regards to Automatic Processing of Personal Data." It provides protection for personal data held by either governmental or private organizations. Hong Kong followed the spirit of "Convention 108" and passed legislation protecting the privacy of personal data (Wang, Lee, and Wang 1998, 67).

The New Zealand *Privacy Act* not only mandates that marketers ensure any information collected is relevant and essential for an organization's business purpose, but requires that personal information be collected directly from the individual. They must also actively seek the individual's authorization to collect it (Morris-Lee 1996).

On July 25, 1995, the Council of Ministers of the European Union approved the *European Directive on the Protection of Personal Data*. The purpose of the directive is to narrow the divergence between the national privacy and data protection laws of member nations. The directive is intended to protect the fundamental rights and freedoms of individuals — in particular, their right of privacy with respect to processing of personal data (Morris-Lee 1996).* The directive states that personal data can be used only for the purpose for which it was acquired, unless the person provides the organization explicit permission to reuse it (Gattiker et al. 1996). The principles of fair information practice adopted by the European Union basically assert that personal information belongs to the individual (Bernstein 1997). Post-retrieval processing or reselling of any personal information can be done only with the prior consent of the individual.

General Outcomes of Legislative Initiatives   Legislative forays into the world of computerized monitoring have tended to focus on protecting the rights and well-being of workers and consumers, not learners and information seekers. Despite heavy lobbying efforts undertaken by unions and other special interest groups in the last decade, political pressures thus far have not resulted in U.S. federal legislation that protects workers in the private sector from electronic monitoring (Kidwell and Kidwell 1996, 11). Alan Westin has predicted that, concerning online privacy in general, privacy advocates will not be able to get a federal privacy law passed because of the "naked" political power of the direct marketing and advertising industries (Munro 1997).

Court Rulings   The rulings of U.S. courts on cases involving computerized monitoring have been mixed, if not outright contradictory. In the case of *Ram Avrahami v U.S. News & World Report Inc.*, the court ruled that it is not illegal for companies to collect, analyze, and sell data about their customers (Bresnahan 1997). Nussbaum (1989, 5) cites four important court cases about computerized monitoring in work environments that have yielded mixed verdicts.

Public Policy   Wang, Lee, and Wang (1998, 69) have noted that balancing the beneficial uses of computerized monitoring and other online sources of data with the privacy rights of individuals has become one of the most challenging and important public policy issues of the information age. The problem of how to formulate public policies designed to regulate the use of information technology to

---

* *The full text of the EC directive is located on a Web site maintained by the Data Council of the U.S. Department of Health and Human Services: http://aspe.os.dhhs.gov/datacncl/eudirect.htm (Bennett and Raab 1997).*

protect personal data has been defined in technological, civil libertarian, and bureaucratic terms (Bennett 1991).*

The U.S. Office of Technology Assessment report (1987) identified three public policy options regarding computerized monitoring: Take no federal action at this time, determine whether the alleged stressful effects of computerized monitoring are an occupational health hazard, or consider federal legislation aimed to fill gaps in current laws (Lund 1989, 45–46).

The *Framework for Global Electronic Commerce*, released in mid–1997, was a joint project involving 18 federal agencies in the Clinton administration. Ira Magaziner, a White House advisor of the shelved Clinton health care reform fame, headed the task force. The report rejects new taxes and regulatory initiatives, favoring a market-driven approach (Piller 1997). The report recommended that the online industry be left to draw up its own rules and procedures for protecting the online privacy of individuals (Munro 1997). While stating the essential need to protect personal privacy in virtual environments, the report expresses confidence in the efficacy of industry self-regulation to protect that privacy.

Framework for Global Electronic Commerce is surprisingly laissez faire and market-driven. The policy paper recommends that state and local governments not tax Internet sales transactions. The directive also warns Internet software developers and access providers to police themselves regarding pornographic material, lest the government step in and do it for them (Simons 1997).

Public policy also can be formulated at the community level, even if the community is virtual. Rotenberg (1994) outlines preliminary considerations for a grassroots privacy policy for the Internet community.

Corporate Policies   Corporate policies that attempt to control computerized monitoring and protect individual online privacy have been enacted in the last ten years.† Shein quotes Waverly Deutsch, an analyst at Forrester Research in Cambridge, Massachusetts. Deutsch sees a dark side to the monitoring software tools, especially because many companies using the software have not yet created official Internet policies that inform employees that they are being watched, and what is considered acceptable Internet activity (Shein 1996a). Salt River Project, a water and power utility in Phoenix, Arizona, is developing a corporate policy on the use of the Internet by the company and its employees (Maddox 1996). Some direct marketing firms are trying to use corporate policy as a way to protect individual privacy. For example, CMG Direct Interactive tries to keep its data-collection practices above reproach by never linking the Web usage or preference data of individuals with identifying information (Foley 1996).

Arbitration   Labor union efforts to slow the diffusion and limit the application of computerized work performance monitoring have been constrained by

---

* See also Ottensmeyer and Heroux (1991) for a discussion of the public policy issues.
† For a sample privacy code implemented in various organizations, see http://www.uleth.ca/man/deprtmnt/tech/infohigh.htm (Gattiker et al. 1996).

the fact that arbitrators generally have ruled that the introduction of new technology is a unilateral right of management (Magney 1996, 207). In the mid–1980s the Oregon Employment Division used a "Machine Statistics System" to generate a workplace transaction log of activity for a pool of employees engaged in word processing. The records in the log contained the following fields: an operator identification number, a date and time stamp, an identification number of the document created or modified, the starting and finishing times, the type of activity being performed, and the number of pages created and keystrokes made. The software program was modified to identify which operator was at which word processing terminal. When documents began to disappear, and supervisors, through the use of the software, discovered that all of the missing documents disappeared at a terminal used by one particular employee, the employee was disciplined for allegedly tampering with the computerized productivity statistics. Her employer charged that not only did she attempt to falsify her own keystroke count, but also deleted documents created or modified by co-workers. The employee was discharged, and she took the action to an arbitrator. The arbitrator upheld the termination action on the grounds that the computerized monitoring system provided an unbiased, completely reliable account of the activity (Lund 1989, 42–44).

Collective Bargaining Agreements   Collective bargaining agreements also have addressed these issues. The collective bargaining agreement between the Communications Workers of America and Michigan Bell Telephone Company, Michigan Bell Unit, effective August 10, 1986, contained a letter of understanding that provided specific guidelines for the collection, analysis, and application of computerized performance monitoring (Lund 1989, 62).

Industry Self-Regulation   Industry self-regulation may be the weakest form of legislative initiative to maintain privacy and control computerized monitoring. The FTC hearings of 1996 and 1997 were interpreted by many observers as a challenge from the federal government to the online industry itself to develop and enforce self-regulating systems for protecting the privacy of consumer information. The response from privacy watchdog groups to this implicit federal message has been less than enthusiastic. Even commentators from the business and online marketing industries have been skeptical. Morris-Lee (1996) asserts that enabling the success of U.S. business and fortifying the future of direct response marketing while protecting the privacy rights of individuals — and constraining unwarranted governmental interference — will take more than good intentions or strong encryption technology. It requires the development of better, more universal, self-regulated privacy systems. Sessler (1997) argues that the inherent problem with industry self-regulation is that agreements and practices are not legally binding, that there are few enforcement mechanisms, and that lapses need not be reported.

The basic policy and legislative issue here resolves into the question: Who is monitoring the human monitors? The general population wants some assurance that computerized monitoring adheres to some policy or law, and that, if a monitoring program violates the policy or law or accepted norms of monitoring behavior, the violation will be detected and the violators punished. Historically, however, federal and state governments have not been very involved in computerized monitoring of HCI. When government is involved, it often is as but another institution engaged in monitoring work, learning, information seeking, and shopping behavior, not as a state body. Tuerkheimer (1993, 72) sees a fast-approaching crossroads: Either legislation with teeth will be enacted to protect personal privacy in cyberspace, or technological changes will swallow up privacy rights. Tuerkheimer (1993, 73) predicts that the rate of technological change will render privacy obsolete. Gary Marx (Westin, Marx, Zahorik, and Ware 1992) sees a need for legislation in this area because the proposed laws will compensate for the weaknesses of the social structure, such as the relative weakness of organized labor in the United States.

Legislation probably will be effective only as a way to control real-world unfair applications of the results of computerized monitoring of human behavior in cyberspace. When the collection, analysis, and application of computerized monitoring all occur in the realm of cyberspace, attempts to control it through legislation probably will become very inefficient and ineffectual. Rheingold (1993, 295) agrees with the thesis that laws alone will not be adequate to protect netizens from net-snooping, especially if the profit or power derived from net-snooping proves significant.

The law as it currently stands provides little protection to monitored workers. Proposed legislation, while addressing some important concerns of workers, has not addressed the vital question of power relations in the workplace. The parameters of discussion have been determined by business and continue to revolve primarily around the most efficient means of running the enterprise. Stress, inter-worker competition and performance evaluations are seen as important issues by business because of their ultimately detrimental effect on productivity and the smooth operation of the business. Management is concerned primarily with devising more efficient and less draconian means of implementing and administering monitoring systems (Levy 1993).

8

Data and Methods

Data gathered via computerized monitoring of HCI essentially are data about human behavior. (Persons interested in monitoring the behavior of computers have different ways of doing that.) What is the value of these data? Why are hard data about one's wanderings in cyberspace any more interesting, informative, or valuable than traces of footsteps around a real, physical environment? In the next two chapters we will explore some of the issues surrounding data collection and analysis, as well as ways of applying the findings and conclusions drawn from that activity. Pfaffenberger (1997) calls the information captured or left behind during HCI "digital DNA."

The advocacy literature against computerized monitoring of HCI in work environments generally portrays the method as a uniform practice, always producing the same negative effects wherever it is used (George 1996, 461). The methods of collecting, analyzing, and applying computer-generated data about HCI are, however, quite diverse. Robertson and Hancock-Beaulieu (1992) provide a good overview of the methodological issues pertaining to the study of HCI in online information retrieval environments.

Problems of Other Methods of Monitoring Human-Computer Interaction Computerized monitoring is not the only way to monitor HCI. Each method has its strengths and weaknesses. Winne, Gupta, and Nesbit (1994) note that many contemporary empirical methods for studying learner cognition fail to represent well the temporally unfolding cognitive engagements that constitute a learner's expressions of knowledge, motivation, cognition, metacognition, and self-regulation. Protocol analysis is the method of asking people to think aloud while they use a computer system. Their vocalized thoughts are then recorded (often onto audiotapes), transcribed, coded, and analyzed. Although the "think-aloud" method captures user behavior, thoughts, and emotions while they occur during a learning, information seeking, working, or shopping session, the very act of thinking aloud is not natural for most people.

The focus group technique involves a facilitator who gathers a group of people to ask questions (often open-ended) about how they use a computer system, what they like and dislike about it, and their ideas for ways to improve the system. Focus groups cannot gather human behavior during HCI at the moment of use, but can be used to obtain summative self-reports from users about their online sessions. Like focus groups, questionnaires rely on self-reports of behavior (or intended behavior). "Retrospective questionnaires and stimulated recall protocols about cognition engaged in an earlier setting have potential to represent such patterns, but because they do not gather data as cognition happens, there is the possibility that learners misrepresent cognition and motivation by engaging in reconstructive processes" (Winne, Gupta, and Nesbit 1994, 178).

In Web-based economic environments, where the primary activity is the buying and selling of goods and services, the current main contender against computerized monitoring for gathering information about the preferences, behavior, and intentions of shoppers is the online registration form. In virtual environments marketing researchers must relearn what can and cannot be done to obtain information about customers. There are many mechanisms for capturing information online, and they vary in scope, accuracy, and application. Asking users to register at a Web site, for example, will not by itself help marketing researchers track their activity within the site (Hagel and Armstrong 1997). Roth (1998) observes that overt registration programs at Web sites are failing, due primarily to the lack of response from visitors. Online registration forms in Web environments are used primarily as an intrusive method for gathering real-world demographic information about the subset of users who elect to complete the registration form. Of course, a sub-subset of users who elect to complete the online form also elect to enter erroneous or spurious information.

Gibbs and Baldwin (1996) developed an interesting way to use videotaping to monitor HCI. In some ways it is more elegant than using a computer to monitor HCI. They positioned one video camera to capture the visage (and voice) of the user, and another to capture the activity on the computer screen. The two videotapes were then collated so that a split screen simultaneously revealed both the user's face and the activity on the screen.

Attractive Aspects of Computerized Monitoring   Although computerized monitoring of HCI is not the only method available to researchers, it does have several attractive aspects. First, computerized monitoring can gather large quantities of data at a relatively low cost. Borgman, Hirsh, and Hiller (1996) note that online monitoring is one of the few methods capable of capturing detailed data about the online search process at a reasonable cost. This characteristic of computerized monitoring can be both a blessing and a curse. Analysis of such large quantities of data can be challenging, expensive, and time-consuming.

One direct outcome of the low cost of gathering large quantities of data via computerized monitoring is the possibility of doing away with sampling. Theoretically, everything and all activity can be monitored. Within the limits of the spectral horizon of what can be observed by computerized monitoring software, the totality of the HCI can be included in the data set.* Of course, a researcher on a drunken binge brought on by the extremely low cost of gathering computerized monitoring data often is quickly sobered up by the jolt of the different costs of analyzing and applying all of that cheaply gathered data.

Not all computerized monitoring researchers are convinced that sampling has become unnecessary. Pitkow (1997a) argues that sampling would serve better than hit metering (i.e., gathering all hit data at a Web server). Pitkow questions the assumption made by other researchers that a computerized monitoring project should attempt to collect as much information about all users and usage as possible. When considered in the light of the four existing monitoring environments, however, it appears that random sampling of Web usage would work in libraries and commercial activities (browsing and spending), but it probably would not be too useful in work and formal learning environments.

Computerized monitoring can be an attractive method because it is unobtrusive, provides large volumes of data at a relatively low cost, and because it can be used to build quantitative models, and to assist in qualitative interpretations of quantitative models (Borgman, Hirsh, and Hiller 1996, 569). Computerized monitoring may be most obtrusive in work environments. Obtrusive monitoring may create an entirely different psycho-social structure of expectations and responses than unobtrusive monitoring.

Another attractive aspect of computerized monitoring is the very specific time stamping of events that is possible. Compared to other data collection methods, computerized monitoring provides the most discrete timing data (Borgman, Hirsh, and Hiller 1996, 575). Perfect time stamping has not yet been achieved, especially in the Web server logs of busy Web sites that handle many file requests per second, but compared to human data collection methods the time stamping potential of computerized monitoring data collection programs is impressive. The quest for quantifiable standards seems unstoppable. It is now possible to monitor the productivity of software programmers with a measuring standard called the "function point." This is a weighted total of inputs, outputs, inquiries, files and interfaces (Iadipaolo 1992, cited in Levy 1993). Another attractive aspect of computerized monitoring data is that they enable quantitative analyses, qualitative analyses, or both.

The prospect of being able to provide immediate feedback to the user is theoretically attractive, but it has not been implemented to a great extent. Although immediate feedback is one of the strengths of computerized monitoring, it also could lead to rat-like behavior in people, who receive immediate response (positive or negative) based on the speed and accuracy with which they press certain

---

* *Neal Kaske first brought this possibility to my attention.*

keys on the keyboard. One of the fascinating aspects of the amorphous movement to use computers to monitor HCI is that not much development effort has gone into devising ways of conveying this captured behavioral information to the user in some immediately useful form. If it ever arrives, the payoff of computerized monitoring for the user population has been notoriously slow. As smart, individualized online environments become more pervasive, the feedback to the user may become more immediate and perceptible.

Problems and Shortcomings of Computerized Monitoring   Computerized monitoring in general has several problems and shortcomings. Although transaction log data provide extensive detail on what the user is doing, because the data do not readily reveal why the user is behaving as observed, the technique often is combined with obtrusive evaluation methods such as interviews, verbal protocols, direct observation, or playing back the search so that the user can comment after the event on the search process and results (Borgman, Hirsh, and Hiller 1996, 570).

Despite the large quantities of data, computerized monitoring captures information from a selective range of all possible data. Santos (1995, 35) notes that all computer-based monitoring techniques totally disregard actions and conditions not directly affecting the computer itself. As with all techniques based exclusively on information gathered by the computer, automatic transcribing cannot record aspects of the interaction that are not communicated to and received by the computer, such as user satisfaction levels and environmental conditions or perturbations (Santos 1995, 34).

Another shortcoming of many computerized monitoring projects is that they studied the use of only one system in specific environmental situations. It is difficult to make reliable generalizations about the online behavior of human beings. Grant and Higgins (1996) note that nearly all pertinent research has studied computerized performance monitoring systems as uni-dimensional systems. They claim that only two studies — Grant (1990) and George (1993) — collected data on the features of different computerized monitoring systems and incorporated the data into the findings.

One problem with computerized monitoring is that the user often is treated as a black box. The user begins an initial interaction with the computer, receives a response, somehow processes that response, and follows with another action. The ability of computerized monitoring to portray the activity is vivid and irrefutable, but the user's motives and anticipated or expected outcomes are murky. Evaluation methods designed for use on older query-matching online information retrieval systems tend to compare system inputs and outputs, relegating the user to the black box role (Borgman, Hirsh, and Hiller 1996, 568). Computerized monitoring also tends to emphasize isolated individual behavior, rather than social interaction between or among people. Perhaps computerized monitoring could learn something from social network analysis, as articulated by Wellman (1997, 179).

One limitation of many computerized monitoring projects is that they focus on human use of input devices, primarily the keyboard and, more recently, the mouse. Motor skills are easier to study than cognitive skills. We must remember that most of what computerized monitoring knows and does is based on the behavior of the observed. Furthermore, it is limited to behavior performed with input devices such as keyboard, mouse and joystick. The power of computerized monitoring is enhanced or limited by the power of those input devices. As such devices have become more powerful over the decades, so too has computerized monitoring. For example, a keystroke that underlines a word in a word processing software program is much less powerful than an input device behavior that moves one through a virtual environment. Computerized monitoring can only infer thoughts, desires, and emotions from the observable behavior with input devices. The logical extreme of computerized monitoring as it currently is conceived and practiced is to use past and current observed behavior with input devices to determine the look, feel, and configuration of virtual spaces at the level of the individual. Cyberspace will become my space, your space, his space, and her space — similar in some respects, yet unique to each individual. If a technique ever is developed for translating a person's thoughts and desires directly into an online environment, computerized monitoring as we know it will lose its power and appeal. If voice recognition has arrived, can thought recognition be far behind?

Another problem with computerized monitoring is that it can be difficult to move from one stratum of data or behavior to another. Santos (1995, 34) noted that if the recorded data are based exclusively on system-level actions such as keystrokes, the higher level semantics of the HCI cannot be recorded or inferred. Yet another regrettable aspect of the history of computerized monitoring research is that it has often been preoccupied with the load on and performance of the computer (e.g., the mainframe, the Web server, etc.) rather than with the person involved in the HCI. This was especially true during the early years of the movement to use computers to monitor HCI.

Another difficulty with using computers to monitor HCI is that computers generate unbelievable amounts of data. In this field, the economics of data collection and the economics of interpretation and analysis are vastly different. A moderately busy Web site can be expected to generate an extended format transfer log of approximately 100 megabytes of data per month. A very active site could log that much data in a day (Stout 1997, 178). The log file for an average day's activity at *The Washington Post* Web site contains over 500 megabytes and requires three hours to process and analyze (Kirsner 1997a). The main problem with transaction logs is not extracting the data, but interpreting it (Nicholas 1996, 232). This surfeit of data is a relatively recent development, but it is something we will need to deal with into the foreseeable future. Only in the final decade of the twentieth century has the longstanding shortage of facts about the world turned into a glut.

The entire economics of data has been upended (Bailey 1996, 69). We continue to explore ways to analyze all this data, not to mention how to apply the results of the analysis. Yet in the midst of this glut of data, which now can be gathered and analyzed continuously, we should not lose sight of the fact that the aspects of events captured by computerized monitoring are rather limited. One thing is clear: Computerized monitoring projects are so data intensive that there is no feasible way for people to be actively involved on a continuous basis in the collection, analysis, and application of data resulting from the computerized monitoring of a population of users of any appreciable size. Ultimately, in most instances of computerized monitoring, prying human eyes focusing on the behavior of a known person will not be an effective use of human attention. One way to make such a large amount of data useful is to employ computers more and more to analyze the data. Computerized monitoring began as an efficient and effective way to collect data about HCI. Future developments in computerized monitoring, however, will concentrate on using computers during the analysis and application phases of these projects.

The challenges of such large quantities of data have some bearing on the debate concerning privacy issues and computerized monitoring. Large-scale, long-term human analysis of these data sets simply is impossible and will not happen. If computerized monitoring is perceived as an invasion of an individual's personal information privacy, we will need to imagine it as prying CPUs, rather than prying eyes. Although the cultural imagination concerning the surveillance of people by others is very mature and rich,* our imaginative powers concerning the possibility of the surveillance of human behavior by computers have not yet been awakened and challenged.

Although computerized monitoring exacerbates the problem of too much data to realistically analyze and digest, the problem was not unknown in the realms of real-world human surveillance of others. Debord (1990, 81) notes:

> Surveillance would be much more dangerous had it not been led by its ambition for absolute control of everything to a point where it encountered difficulties created by its own progress. There is a contradiction between the mass of information collected on a growing number of individuals, and the time and intelligence available to analyse it, not to mention its actual interest. The quantity of data demands constant summarising: much of it will be lost, and what remains is still too long to be read. Management of surveillance and manipulation is uncoordinated.

Although Debord is describing real-world surveillance of the kind imagined by Orwell, his comments would describe equally well the current situation with computerized monitoring.

Computerized monitoring, especially at the data collection phase of a project, is burdened by the false sense that computer-collected data must contain

---

*I would argue that video cameras and other technologies for visual surveillance of human behavior really function as surrogates for human eyesight. As such, the prospect of video surveillance does not seriously challenge the imagination concerning surveillance in the postmodern era. In the same vein, wiretapping technologies function as surrogates for human ears in the realm of aural surveillance. Computerized monitoring is not easily matched up and understood as a simple technological surrogate for one or more of the human senses.

irrefutable facts. Gary Marx (Westin, Marx, Zahorik, and Ware 1992) identifies six fallacies of computerized monitoring in work environments, including the fallacy that machine-generated facts speak for themselves, with little or no human interpretation, and thus they are necessarily more valid, reliable, and neutral than human-generated facts. Like any other set of data, computerized monitoring data must be analyzed and interpreted to become meaningful to human beings. As we shall see, however, it is not absolutely necessary to make computerized monitoring data comprehensible to human intelligence for it to be useful, if usefulness is something that adds value or enriches HCI. In recent years computerized monitoring software modules have emerged that gather, analyze, and apply the data without any direct, overt human intervention or interpretation.

A related shortcoming with data gathered with computerized monitoring is that people cannot know for certain that a computer has collected a data set completely and correctly. Computerized monitoring provides a window onto HCI that is difficult or impossible to verify by other means. Computerized monitoring projects involve some trust in the veracity and completeness of the data sets.

One major problem with using computerized monitoring to create tailored online environments is that people have used trial and error to understand their functionality in the world, both in real environments and in early online environments. People try different actions, note which worked better than others to complete a task or achieve a goal, then engage in that better behavior in the future. How can computerized monitoring differentiate between tentative trial and error behavior and trusted, tried, and true behavior? Most computerized monitoring systems treat all human behavior as having equal value. A mouse click is as good as a keystroke to a blind monitor.

Perhaps the best way to use computerized monitoring is to combine it with data obtained with other methods. Evaluating the search process of people looking online for information requires both quantitative data about the HCI and qualitative interpretations of user behavior (Borgman, Hirsh, and Hiller 1996, 568).

A fundamental flaw of the entire computerized monitoring project is that it aspires to observe and understand human behavior in a machine context. If the floors of Grand Central Station could speak, they would tell us of a predictable but inexplicable pattern of stress placed on them by pedestrians. Their tale, told in their idiot context, would reveal little or nothing about the meaning of this mysterious, yet predictable, human behavior. The data would be true and irrefutable, but not of much use. The same may be true for the amorphous movement to use computers to monitor HCI. On the road to enlightenment, computerized monitoring may be a dead-end.

How to Frame Research Questions and Projects   A primary task involves resolving how to frame research questions and projects that propose to use CPM. For example, in the use of computerized monitoring to study HCI in work environments, Grant and Higgins (1996) derived five dimensions of computerized monitor design that are important independent constructs in studying system impact: the sensor (Who or what performs the measurement?); the discriminator (Who performs the comparison?); the feedback (What is the message?); the activity (What is the employee's response?); and the performance (What is measured?).

What Types of Data Can or Should Be Collected?   The first step in any computerized monitoring project is to translate human behavior into a set of data. Because it probably is impossible and certainly is impractical to capture all possible data about an instance of human behavior (e.g., a sneeze), we need to decide which data we want or need to collect from within the horizon of data we can collect. Collecting, storing, and analyzing data cost time and money, even if computers do most or all of the work. Data about HCI are valuable both for people and computers. Agre (1994, 113) correctly notes that, because a computer can process only what it can capture, the less a system can capture, the less potential it has as a system.

> This trade-off [between the cost of capturing data and the value and usefulness of the captured data] is also found in systems for tracking human activities through automatic capture. Simply put, a system can track only what it can capture, and it can capture only information that can be expressed within a grammar of action that has been imposed upon the activity. Numerous systems, including many of the examples cited earlier, reside toward the minimal end of this trade-off, since they track only simple position information. Systems like these are not particularly convincing cases of the capture model, since they do not usually require much imposition beyond the installation of the tracking instruments themselves. But position tracking is frequently a precursor to more qualitatively complex kinds of capture, for example, when positional information is stored along with other events or transactions that might be captured: arrival at a certain destination, crossing a certain boundary, changes in the status of materials or participants, encounters with other participants, and so forth (Agre 1994, 114).

Human-computer interaction is a complex event or series of events. We cannot collect all conceivable data concerning these events. For example, facial expressions and vocalizations made while interacting with computers rarely are collected. Computerized monitoring often focuses on nonverbal behavior, rather than on the content analysis of verbal messages, such as e-mail. One fundamental tension in the entire debate about the basic unit of measurement is between the evidently technological imperative to capture increasingly smaller, more discrete human actions and the need to think about human activity in bigger, more complex, chunks of behavior. For example, most early transaction log analysis projects of first and second generation online library catalog systems chose the single command line as the basic unit of behavior. The relationships between the behavior recorded on the individual command lines, and more broadly, the human behavior before and after the interaction session with the OPAC, was much more difficult to study and understand.

The resultant set of data has a potentially dual role as both an historical representation of an event or series of events and as a product or commodity. Many of the expressed fears of privacy advocates about computerized monitoring tend to focus on the second potential role of these data sets as products or commodities to be traded and reused in an information market. The first role, however, has its own power and limitations, even if it has not received as much attention in the marketplace of popular ideas and fears. Agre (1994, 120) captures these tensions between the dual roles well:

> Regardless of its particular content, captured information is distinguished by its dual relationship — both product and representation — to the human activities upon which particular grammars of action have been imposed. In particular, the capture process makes "visible" a great deal of information-creating activity that had formerly been left implicit in the production of other, historically prior commodities. Moreover, the phenomenon of capture extends market relations not simply through the commodification of the captured information itself (if, in fact, that information is marketed), but also through the movement toward market relations, through a reduction in transaction costs, of the human activities that the information represents.

Through the use of computerized monitoring, suddenly the product of HCI has expanded to include not only the word processing documents, spreadsheets, and the myriad other outputs of HCI, but also the very events that make up the HCI event itself. All netizens are in danger of becoming performance artists.

Trances in the Blast Another challenge of collecting data about HCI is that human pauses may be more important than deliberate action. It is in the trances in the blast where meaning and understanding are made or emerge. The truly interesting things occur between the clicks and keystrokes. For example, Santos (1995) divided the observable stream of HCI into chunks and pauses. Both the chunks and the pauses have equal value in the effort to understand human behavior in virtual environments. Pitkow (1997a) defines "reading time" as the inter-arrival time between the request for a Web page and a subsequent page request from the same IP address. A time-out period of 30 minutes has become the standard used by commercial Web log analysis programs. What this all means is that it is much more difficult, not easier, to identify reliably and track the behavior of an individual (known or unknown) in cyberspace than in the real world.

What Human Behavior Should Be Identified and Studied? We need to distinguish between behavioral information and all other types of information about individuals, such as medical and financial records. The distinction between behavioral and extra-behavioral information is not clean. Medical and financial records are records of life events. Nevertheless, most computerized monitoring projects are concerned primarily in behavioral information, especially real-world human behavior (e.g., mouse clicks and keystrokes) that facilitates a cognitive bridge to cyberspace.

At least four basic activities can be performed with behavioral information. First, it must necessarily be gathered and stored in some format, ranging from the human memory to a Web server log, before any further processing. The most basic method of processing gathered behavioral information is to analyze it — perhaps to look for patterns or in general try to make sense of the data in the set. After the information has been analyzed in some way, it can be used or applied. A variety of applications can be made with an analyzed set of data, and the various applications are not necessarily mutually exclusive. One research team may apply analyzed computerized monitoring data in the form of improvements to the user interface, while another research team may apply the analyzed data in the form of a new theory about HCI. Both applications are potentially valid and useful. Finally, behavioral information can be disclosed or sold to third parties. Revealing computerized monitoring data to third parties is highly offensive to many critics of the movement to use computers to monitor HCI.

One major decision for any computerized monitoring study entails whether normal or anomalous activities will be the primary focus. Of course this assumes that the boundaries and interior terrain of normal activity already have been established. What human behavior should be identified and studied? Overall, more work has been done trying to identify normal human behavior in online environments than trying to identify aberrant, unethical, or criminal behavior. For example, the recent transaction log analysis conducted by Blecic, Bangalore, Dorsch, Henderson, Koenig, and Weller (1997) designed and timed their data collection method so that they would be examining normal use.

We need to distinguish between the online behavior of an individual as an individual and the identification of a specific individual. Most project managers who use computerized monitoring to monitor HCI are interested in separating the behavior of one individual from another, but they may be less interested, to the point of being uninterested, in identifying specific individuals by name. Work and formal learning environments, however, often require attaching specific names to observed behavior.

Another fundamental question surrounding these captured behavioral traces concerns their meaning and value for analysis. How can we place a value on the data collected and analyzed with computerized monitoring? We also need to entertain the possibility that the value of the data will vary over time. The data also may gain value as they are subjected to analysis and other value-adding procedures. The value of the monitored activity itself could be a clue to the value of the data about the activity. Some analyzers see the logs as windows into the souls of users. Bangalore (1997), for instance, observes that the keystrokes captured by transaction logging modules are clues to the preferences and unmet needs of users. If the keystrokes left behind by users and captured by transaction logging modules are valuable clues to the preferences and unmet needs of users of automated library systems, we need a forensic method to interpret these clues. The amount of translation and interpretation required to move from observed behavioral traces to reliable assessments of needs (both the met and unmet varieties) is daunting. Without that methodological system, we are reduced to divination and the reading of entrails.

When our ancestors first saw "automobiles," which in itself is a very vague appellation, they saw horseless carriages rather than cars. To make sense of these new objects in the real world, they had to perceive them in a way that made sense to the world as they had known it up until that moment. Hence they tended to see horse-drawn carriages without the horses. What is reality for an individual is a rather limited and limiting construct of perceptions and notions. Agre (1994, 121) suggests that "grammars of action" play a significant, deceptive, self-effacing role in the human sense of reality. The articulation and imposition of grammars of action usually involve a type of mythologizing about the wellsprings of those grammars. Once the grammar of action has been adopted as a way to construct reality and to understand the observed human behavior within that reality, a mythic notion takes hold that the behavior in question already has been organized in accordance with the grammar of action, and that the scheme for capturing information about that behavior simply reads off in real time a comprehensive representation of this pre-existing formal grammar of action. What this means for computerized monitoring is that, although such monitoring captures only limited information about the rich cognitive, emotional, motor, and social interaction among people and computers, we often assume not only that a computerized monitoring module captures a fairly complete picture of the interaction, but also that those involved in the behavior already have adopted the grammar of action embedded in the computerized monitoring system and are playing to it. Once we focus on one way of thinking about capturing HCI, it is difficult to admit the resultant hazy, barely perceptible phenomena.

Basic Units of Measurement and Analysis Let us turn, then, to the rather complex selection process for basic units of measurement and analysis. Computerized monitoring of HCI is the collection and analysis of a specific set of human motor events. Most computer input devices, such as the keyboard, mouse, and touch-screen, rely on digital (finger-based) actions to initiate virtual events and situations. Through this analysis of digital events, often the analysts hope to gain insight into human cognitive processes during HCI. Observation of motor events is a way to better understand these processes. Is it the best way? Perhaps a phenomenological investigation of HCI would be more revealing and useful.

Human-computer interaction can be understood as a sequence of petty events that cumulate into recognizable human behavior as people interact with a computer or a computer system. These petty events, such as the click of a mouse or a minor computer computation, can be defined and measured in various ways. The researcher's choice of units of measurement and analysis can have profound effects on the conclusions that are drawn, as well as on the acceptance of the research. Sajaniemi and Tossavainen (1996, 386) caution that care must be taken when selecting the basic unit of measurement and interpreting its meaning. A search session containing only one search statement may suggest that the quality of the result was so bad that the user did not consider it worthwhile to proceed. On the other hand, the single statement search session may indicate that the search was so successful that there was no need for further activity.

Parties affected by computerized monitoring also have a stake in the selection and interpretation of basic units of measurement. In the Walton and Vittori study of the use of CPM in a work environment, employees objected specifically to the units of measure used in the monitoring system, rather than to the general use of computerized monitoring, as opposed to other systems of measuring work performance (Grant 1990, 22).

Michael Berger's dissertation (1994) is a pertinent example of the importance of the selection of the basic unit of measurement and analysis. Berger's analysis of human interaction with a library system's OPAC divided user interactions into three levels: individual commands, the search objective (containing one or more search commands in pursuit of a single objective), and the search session (containing one or more search objectives). Berger focused on the search objective as the basic unit of measurement and analysis. He concluded that users of the MELVYL system were more successful than is usually reported in the literature. He also concluded that null set searches pose less of a problem than previously believed. If the search objective is used as the basic unit of analysis, the high frequency of zero-hits searches is not indicative of high failure rates, because a significant number of zero-hits searches are fixed in subsequent search statements, or are valid results because there is nothing in the database for requesters' searches. Berger concluded that the number of search statements retrieving null sets has been a seriously misused indicator of user failure.

This is a very rich and thought-provoking study, worthy of a careful reading. Perhaps the greatest contribution made by this study to the overall mission of using TLA to study OPAC use is the basic finding that the choice of the unit of measurement and analysis is vital to the findings and conclusions capable of being drawn. Using the search objective, rather than individual commands or full search sessions, as the basic unit of analysis may be an advance in the use of TLA as a data analysis method, but Berger never explores how search objectives are made manifest, or how (or how well) a transaction log analyst can come to know the search objectives of OPAC users. He never really explains how the intent of the user was able to be known by the analyzer. The definition of a search objective appears to be user-dependent, as opposed to the session-centered definition of a "search leg" made by Peters and Kurth (1991).

Foucault (1980) has something to contribute to this examination of the best basic unit of measurement for HCI, which is fundamentally a quest to establish the basic event (at least for the purposes of analysis) for HCI. "It's not a matter of locating everything on one level, that of the event, but of realising that there are actually a whole order of levels of different types of events differing in amplitude, chronological breadth, and capacity to produce effects" (Foucault 1980, 114). Agre (1994, 108) suggests that determining the basic event-unit, which usually involves some basic human behavior, such as a keystroke, is part of a larger need in computing design environments to effectively treat human activity as a kind of language, for which a good representation scheme serves as an accurate grammar. The grammar specifies a set of unitary actions.

There is a drive in the general field of computerized monitoring for finer granularity. We want to know exactly where the mouse pointer was on the screen when it was clicked. We want to know what characters were typed in, then deleted before the hitting of the enter key. Borgman, Hirsh, and Hiller (1996, 568) express the need in this field for evaluation methods that support fine-grained analyses of searching behavior. Often, however, a finer granularity translates into a larger set of data, so a simultaneous push is on to have the computers themselves perform more of the analysis of the data.

Articulating and defining units of measurement and analysis is an essential process for the growth and maturation of any discipline or field of inquiry. Even Web server log analysis, which has been on a phenomenal fast track for development, quickly realized the need to standardize measurements. Novak and Hoffman (1996) attempted to provide a comprehensive baseline terminology for the advertising and measurement communities.

Unqualified and Qualified Keystrokes and Mouse Clicks   The following potential basic units of measurement and analysis are listed and examined in rough ascending order, from the most minute unit of measurement to the most expansive. Qualified and unqualified keystrokes and mouse clicks comprise the finest units of measurement. Santos (1995) and his team of researchers developed a computerized monitoring software program capable of recording when alphanumeric keys and mouse buttons are both depressed and released. They called the resultant highly-detailed logs lexical logs.

Counting keystrokes as a unit of measurement in computerized monitoring projects probably is most common in work environments. In some work situations keystrokes are not just an indicator of productivity; they directly measure it. In Clement and McDermott's 1991 summary of McDermott's 1987 study of service workers in Ontario's provincial government, they note that keystroke counting was the major form of computerized monitoring of data entry operators.

Although counting keystrokes has been used with computerized monitoring in work environments, it did not catch hold with transaction log analyzers of users seeking information in online environments. Perhaps because the first generation of computers was the mainframe generation, many transaction log analysis projects wait until the enter key is pressed before saving the character string in a log with a time-stamp. This method of defining a basic event-unit usually cannot detect the use of the backspace key as a way of finding input errors made and self-detected by the user before hitting the enter key.

Individual Commands (Including the Computer Response)   The back-and-forth of user command and system response made sense in the early days of HCI, but today the interaction has become much more complex. "In today's graphical, direct-manipulation systems, the relationship between input and output is more complex: A user may select several options from a dialog box or visit several buttons or windows on a screen before receiving an explicit system response.

Similarly, one user action may generate several actions by the system" (Borgman, Hirsh, and Hiller 1996, 570). Analyses of aggregate distributions of the use of search features, taken out of context of the search sessions in which the features were employed, may be misleading and statistically incorrect (Hirsh 1996).

Raw Hit Count (for Web Sites)   The mass migration to the realm of the Web has created an entire new set of basic units of measurement. In the realm of Web log analysis, Stout (1997) sees three basic building blocks for meaningful Web site statistics: hits, views, and visits. A hit is a separate HTTP transaction. A hit is any type of file transfer request made by a user to a Web site, including HTML, image, sound, and video files (Kirsner 1997a). A hit, also known as an access, is a successful request for and receipt of a file from a server (Pitkow 1997a). In contrast, a view occurs when one person views one page of a Web site. Counting hits focuses on the activity of the server computer, while counting views focuses on the experience of the individual. Of course, a page on a Web site need not adhere to the physical constraints of paper pages. Some Web pages are rather short and contain little content, while others are quite long.

Strom (1996c) defines a hit as "an entry into the log file of a World Wide Web server, generated by every request for information made to that server. The number of hits has no predictable relation to the number of visitors to a Web site." A count of raw hits does not necessarily indicate the entire situation regarding access to and readership of the content of the Web site, nor is it analogous to a Nielsen rating of the enjoyment of content (Nemzow 1997). Note that our notion of hits in virtual environments is changing. In the older environments of mainframe database searching, a hit meant a record retrieved as the result of a search command. We often spoke about and analyzed the number of hits retrieved by a certain search argument. In the newer Web environments, a hit has come to mean more of a user action. Early aggregate Web traffic analysis indicates that the average visit to a Web site contains 13 hits (Yesil 1996, 125, citing information contained at CyberAtlas, the Internet research guide at http://www.cyberatlas.com).

The raw hit count is a tally of every file (including HTML files, images, sound files, CGI programs, etc.) sent from a Web server to a browser. Web-presence providers and webmasters often use raw hit counts to measure the level of traffic at a particular Web site. Although the raw hit count produces the largest (and thus most impressive) usage numbers, it is not a very accurate measure of how many people have visited a Web site (Testerman, Kuegler, and Dowling 1996, 402–403).

Chen (1997), however, takes issue with the definition of a hit as the transfer of a file from a server to a client. He states that, more specifically, a hit is merely a request for a file sent by a client to a server. Each request could result in a successful file transfer, an unsuccessful transfer (recorded as an error), or an aborted file transfer, if the person making the request interrupts the transfer process. Strom (1996c) defines qualified hits as hits that actually deliver information to a user. This measurement of activity excludes such things as error messages and redirects.

The number of qualified hits, however, does not provide an indication of the number of visitors.

The interested hit count is a calculation of the number of pages seen by visitors that were of interest to those visitors. It is an estimate, rather than a true count. The "second click" is the link users select from the first page they view at a particular Web site. One way to estimate the interested hit count is to subtract from the page count all of the first clicks that failed to result in a second click. Isolated first clicks usually indicate that those users saw the site's homepage and did not find it sufficiently interesting to continue browsing around in the site. Next, if we assume that the last clicks at a Web site indicate that some of the visitors were losing interest at that point, we could subtract 50 percent of all last clicks from the page count. Another way to measure bona fide interest is to establish a minimal click threshold (e.g., at least three clicks) as an indication of genuine interest in the content of a Web site (Testerman, Kuegler, and Dowling 1996, 406).

The click count is a measure of the number of times a user clicks on any link at a Web site. The execution of a CGI script is counted only if the user clicked on the link. The click count is useful to Web advertisers because it provides a better indication of how many people visited the Web site. Although the click count may be significantly lower than the raw hit count, it is a more accurate measure of activity at a Web site. It can be difficult, however, to count the number of requests for specific images (Testerman, Kuegler, and Dowling 1996, 403).

Advertisement clicks are a specialized instance of click counting. Strom (1996c) defines the ad click count as the number of times users click on an in-line ad (commonly called a banner ad) within a certain time. The ad click count does not measure the effectiveness of an advertisement. It merely indicates how often visitors to a Web site were sufficiently interested in the "content" of a banner ad (including color, motion, size, placement, and other factors beyond any verbal content) to click on it. Strom (1996c) defines adviews as the "number of times an in-line ad is downloaded by users within a specific period of time. A better measure of an ad's impression than Adclicks, but does not indicate whether a sale resulted from the download." An adclick rate is calculated from the number of adviews and adclicks. Strom (1996c) defines the adclick rate as the number of adclicks as a percentage of adviews, or, stated differently, the number of clicks on an in-line ad as a percentage of the number of times users actually downloaded the ad. A high click rate indicates higher level of user interaction.

The CGI count measures how many times a given CGI program has been executed. The CGI count can be used for billing purposes. The Web-presence provider may charge a Web advertiser a higher rate for CGI programs than for regular Web documents (Testerman, Kuegler, and Dowling 1996, 407).

The page count is second only to the raw hit count as the most popular way to measure the amount of traffic at a Web site. The page count includes every Web document sent to users, including pages generated by a CGI program. The page count never includes images, even if a user specifically requests an image (Testerman,

Kuegler, and Dowling 1996, 403). More specifically, if one or more image files are required to construct a page on the client workstation, all of the files required to build one page are bundled together and counted as one. "Page requests (also called page impressions and page views) attempt to tally only the number of actual pages seen by a user, without including images or other components of a page" (Kirsner 1997, 37a). Kirsner's definition of page views, however, fails to account for the difference between requests and satisfied, successful, completed requests. On the Web, this difference can be substantial.

Counting and examining page hits can help the monitor get into the mental landscape of the user. Yan, Jacobsen, Garcia-Molina, and Dayal (1996) consider each page an interest item, capable of being counted and used as a basic unit of measurement. Bertot, McClure, Moen, and Rubin (1997) defined an access (i.e., a page hit) as an entire page downloaded by a user, regardless of the number of individual file requests needed to create that page on the screen. Dreze and Zufryden (1997) found that the number of pages accessed and time spent during a Web site visit were the two effectiveness measures that were most relevant to what they wanted to study on the Web.

Precise definitions of the basic units of measure for activity in virtual environments has important implications for businesses. In November 1996 the Board of the Audit Bureau of Circulations endorsed standards recommended by two subcommittees. They defined a page impression as "the combination of one or more files presented to a viewer as a single document as a result of a single request received by the server," the decision to count a frame, defined as multiple documents or pages viewed on one screen simultaneously, as one page impression, no matter how many pages are displayed on the same screen; and the definition of a visit as "a series of consecutive qualified page impressions between a user and a Web site" (Step toward 1997).

Many commentators (e.g., Pitkow 1997a) have concluded that the page view measure is a much more useful unit than file hits. Cohen (1997a) reports that all the major Web site auditing companies audit by page views, not hits. The increasing use of frames, however, has put a damper on the acceptance of page views as the standard unit of measurement of Web site activity. A screen containing multiple frames is constructed of separate HTML pages, so it gets counted in the Web server log as multiple page requests (Kirsner 1997a). Nevertheless, page views can be roughly measured by counting hits only for HTML files.

One significant drawback to adopting and using page views as a basic unit of measurement is that Web pages themselves are not of a standard length. The Web page as a unit of measurement or human experience needs further assessment and perhaps refinement. Some Web pages (which are not the same as the concept of the Web site) are quite large, while others contain only one button and a few words. To treat these two experiences as quantifiably equal could lead to erroneous (or at least suspect) analytical conclusions. An analogous situation would be to suggest that motion pictures be adopted as a basic unit of measurement of time or human experience. Most commercial, Hollywood-made motion pictures last approximately 90 minutes, but some are much shorter, and others are much longer. To adopt now the idea of viewing Web pages of variable length and containing various quantities and types of information as a basic unit of measurement may result in inconclusiveness and babel down the road.

BIR, BIT, PIR, PIT (NetCount's Terminology)   Proprietary definitions of basic units of measurement also have begun to emerge. NetCount, one of the leading commercial log analysis firms of the last half of the 1990s, distinguishes between a BIR (Browser Information Request) and a BIT (Browser Information Transfer). They also define a PIR (Page Information Request) and a PIT (Page Information Transfer) (Stout 1997, 95). A BIR is a regular hit or request made to the Web server for such information as HTML pages, graphics, sound objects, and video clips. A BIT is the subset of BIRs that resulted in a successful request. A PIR is a request for an HTML page. PIRs are the subset of BIRs that were requests for HTML files. A PIT is a successful PIR (Stout 1997, 136–137). A BIE (Browser Information Error) is a request from a browser for any object that results in anything less than success (e.g., requests for pages that do not exist or reside on the server, broken links to images, etc.). A BTA (Browser Transfer Abandonment) may be the result of the user clicking on the stop button before the page is completely loaded. A DPO (Distinct Point of Origin) is analogous to a visitor. The DPO is based solely on the domain name or IP address of visitors (Stout 1997, 137).

More generally, and avoiding the three-letter acronyms favored by NetCount, page cancellation counts indicate when the transfer of the files that constitute a page is interrupted. Page cancellations can be caused in several ways. The user can initiate the cancellation, by clicking on a link already identified in the partially downloaded page, by clicking on the stop button, or by clicking on the back arrow button that returns the user to the previous page. Page cancellations also can be caused by network problems. Most Web site analysis software cannot determine with confidence what caused a page download to be canceled (Stout 1997, 95). It also is difficult to measure how long it takes for an entire page to be downloaded to a specific browser.

It also may be useful to count the number of images retrieved from Web sites. Some images are stand-alone: The user clicks on that particular image to retrieve it. Other images are parts of built pages. Users do not specifically request the retrieval of those images; the image files are sent as part of a request for a page at a Web site.

The impression count is the number of times visitors to a Web site have viewed a corporation's hallmark or indication of Web sponsorship. Often a sponsor is billed based on the number of impressions it generates rather than on the amount of time a sponsorship is available on the site (Testerman, Kuegler, and Dowling 1996, 407).

Click-through rates typically serve as a basic unit of measurement for advertising on the Web. In essence, the user clicks through from a banner advertisement on a page at a search engine site, for example, to the site of the company that placed the ad (Nemzow 1997, 91). When a user clicks on an advertisement on a Web page, it may be useful to count these click-throughs as a way to gauge the attractiveness and usefulness of the ad. The company paying the webmaster advertising royalties may want to compensate the webmaster based on click-through rates. The click-through rate is the ratio of click-throughs to the number of times an advertisement was viewed (Kirsner 1997a).

Stout (1997), however, argues that click-through rates are not a good basic unit of measurement for advertising commerce. In any advertising agreement, generally it is the responsibility of the media manager (e.g., a webmaster) to attract impressions and to provide adequate placement for the advertisement. The click-through rate, on the other hand, indicates more about the ad audience and the quality of the ad itself. Although click-through rates may be attractive to companies that advertise, they are not particularly attractive to advertising agencies, because the factors that affect click-through activity are not primarily in the control of the advertising medium.

The Coalition for Advertising Supported Information and Entertainment (CASIE) also has expressed reservations about click-throughs as a basic unit of measurement, especially for determining the impact of advertising. The CASIE's revised guidelines for Web measurement, released late in 1996, dismissed click-throughs as a viable measurement, according to Denman Maroney, director of research at D'Arcy Masius Benton & Bowles, New York, who worked on the study and the revised recommendations. "Click-through only measures final action, " not the pages that carry banners, said Maroney (Rich 1996).

Clickstreams are another way to think about and measure HCI. The original idea for clickstreams was as a measurement tool for the use of interactive media that would count the number of times a user clicks on a TV remote control device or computer mouse while making navigational and content selection decisions (Mandese 1995). With the arrival of the Web, a clickstream has been defined (by Dorney (1997, 636), following the CASIE guiding principles) as a database created by the date-and-time-stamped, coded input events undertaken by users of interactive media controlling computer systems with alphanumeric keyboards, mice, and other input devices. In practice, a clickstream is a concept that refers to the previous and subsequent sites visited (Rich 1997). Both session IDs and cookies files enable the analysis of clickstreams. Chen (1997) defines a clickstream as a sequence of page requests made by any group of visitors. The idea of clickstreams captures the sequential nature of HCI.

Threading is a site-centric concept related to the user-centric idea of clickstreams. Threading is the path a user pursues through a Web site (Bertot, McClure, Moen, and Rubin 1997).

AdView, AdClicks, and AdClick rates are another way to measure the exposure and efficacy of advertising on the Web. AdViews measure the number of times an in-line (or banner) ad is downloaded by end users within a specified time. Because of caching, the number of times end users saw the ad may be slightly higher than the measured AdViews rate. AdClicks measure the number of mouse clicks made by end users on an in-line ad within a specified time. The AdClick rate is a fraction in which the AdClicks are the numerator and the AdViews is the denominator (Yesil 1996, 113). It provides an indication of viewer interest in the ad.

Most of the basic units of measurement mentioned so far have built on the concept of command lines and single, isolated actions. In the good old days when dumb terminals were connected to mainframe computers and users interacted with computers primarily by entering commands after a command prompt, most computerized monitoring studies focused on these commands as discrete events, usually represented in the event log as separate, sequential lines of alphanumeric characters with some meaning, such as time stamp, user input, or terminal location. The meaning of each individual line was relatively easy to ascertain. Discerning the meaning between the lines, however, was much more difficult.

States, Cycles, Legs, Chunks, Objectives, and Action Sequences   The next cluster of measurement units includes those defined as bigger than individual events but smaller than search sessions. The search state was one of the earliest clustered concepts to emerge. Penniman (1975) identified 11 search states oriented toward online information-seeking behavior. These formed a set of mutually exclusive and exhaustive conditions through which a user moved during a session involving HCI. Penniman wanted to analyze the patterns of users' movements through these states to map online user behavior. Of the universe of 11 possible states in 1975, some (e.g., begin session, end session, exit database) continue to be pertinent, some (e.g., offline print) no longer are pertinent, and some new states probably have been added to the original pantheon.

Search states designate a gestalt online situation. The user may be in a beginning state, an ending state, an error state, a reviewing state, or other states. The search state is a tag describing in a general manner the overall current situation of the search session being analyzed. The idea of a search state occupies the middle ground between a purely human cognitive state and the structure of the database being searched.

Qiu (1993) built on Pennimen's earlier work by using the Markov model to study how people browse through a hypertextual environment. Qiu found that the second-order Markov model was the best one for the prediction of human behavior in this particular hypertext environment. In other words, the previous two search states provided the most reliable indication of the current search state. Borgman, Hirsh, and Hiller (1996) also built on Penniman's search state as a basic unit of measurement and analysis. They wanted to identify and analyze search paths.

> By analyzing search paths at multiple levels of detail, we can see trends in the use of system features, errors, and other actions; inspect individual actions and groups of actions suggested by the trends; and identify recurring patterns of behavior. Search path analysis allows us to examine intermediate search outcomes rather than the final search product alone. It also allows us to trace backward from outcomes and analyze the actions taken to reach that point (Borgman, Hirsh, and Hiller 1996, 580).

One problem with the notion of search states is that they become increasingly difficult to define as virtual environments become more complex and robust. Our accepted idea about search states from the early days of mainframe computers is that they may be governed more by the structures, capabilities, and limitations of the computer system than by the desires and aptitudes of system users.

In their study of controlled and uncontrolled vocabulary subject searching in an academic online catalog, Peters and Kurth (1991, 203) defined a search leg as "a portion of a subject search session that began and ended with a vocabulary shift, a logon, or a logoff." They defined a vocabulary shift as the point during a search session when the user decided to switch from controlled vocabulary subject access to uncontrolled, or vice versa. Within the realm of subject searching, the search leg functions as a way to differentiate one type of subject searching from another.

The action sequences that Winne, Gupta, and Nesbit have defined as a basic unit of measurement for online formal learning activities have some relation to Berger's definition of search objectives and Peters' and Kurth's definition of search legs for the online information seeking behavior. Winne, Gupta, and Nesbit (1994, 181) define a transaction log file as the chronological record of events occurring during a single interactive session by one student using the STUDY software. The analyst processes the raw log file by filtering out events that have no relevance to a particular analysis, rewriting the remaining items of interest to a new file, classifying each event as belonging to one of several action types, and designating each action type by a unique symbol. These action sequences serve as the primary units of analysis used to describe the online studying activities of the student.

A chunk is a cluster of user actions that tends to be defined according to temporal boundaries. Pauses in activity between the person and the computer may be good indicators of chunk boundaries (Santos 1995, 43). Santos found that chunk detection alone, not coupled with an analysis of the contents of the chunks, does have some usefulness. Automatic chunk detection is an easy, efficient way to determine chunk size (i.e., the number of events per chunk), chunk duration (i.e., the elapsed time between the first and last event in a chunk), and inter-chunk pauses (i.e., the elapsed time between the last event of the previous chunk and the first event of the next chunk) (Santos 1995, 187). Santos sought to identify users' semantic constructs based on the computerized detection and analysis of users' mental chunks, based in turn on a computerized analysis of lexical and syntactic events and their timing. In essence, Santos was exploring a systematic way, within the context of computerized monitoring, to make reliable inferences about the needs, motives, and desires of people as they interact with computers, based on their observed behavior. The fulcrum of the automatic chunk detection algorithm was the comparison between predicted, estimated pauses and actual, observed, executed pauses. Santos (1995, 186) concluded that uncertainty in chunk identification always will be present, regardless of the data source and chunking method: "Until such time that we can get into the inner structures of the human brain and obtain information directly from the brain cells' activity, we will always have to rely on approximations" (Santos 1995, 186). Santos' research is important to the movement to use computers to monitor HCI because it is an attempt to fully computerize the process, because the analysis moves from human behavior to human goals, and because the analysis builds on predictive models of behavior, chunking, and pausing.

Search Sessions and Site Visits   Search sessions and Web site visits are another way to think about and measure HCI. The challenge and process of linking separate, discrete requests and commands into a sequence of actions and interactions between an individual and a computer system is called session analysis. Advances in the movement to use computers to monitor HCI are making this challenge easier to attain (Robertson 1996, 30). Identifying and analyzing individual search sessions (or, more generally in a behavioral sense, use sessions) has been a goal of computerized monitoring research for many years. The addition of stateless Web environments appears to have not diminished the monitor's ardor to isolate and study search sessions. Tracking visits is vitally important for a deeper analysis of the use of a Web site (Stout 1997, 73). Identifying the individual use session is as vital and as nettlesome as differentiating a single user from the undistinguished mass of HCI events. Borgman, Hirsh, and Hiller (1996, 572) make a strong case for treating the search session as the fundamental unit of measurement and analysis.

As an event, a search session encompasses the time and activity from the moment a user first connects to a computer or computerized network until the activity ends. The length of a search session can be measured by the passage of time, by the number of actions made by the user, or by the amount of data scanned or sifted by the user (Sajaniemi and Tossavainen 1996, 385). From an infrastructure perspective, search sessions make sense as a unit of measurement and analysis, but they may not make much sense from a user-based perspective. Simple command-response analyses assume not only that a fixed goal exists for the search session, but also that each search session can be evaluated independently (Borgman, Hirsh, and Hiller 1996, 571–572).

Yan, Jacobsen, Garcia-Molina, and Dayal (1996) argue that even in Web environments the idea of a user session has utility. It is better to model user interests on a per-session basis than on any smaller unit of measurement. They suggest that it is possible to identify user sessions by encoding session identifiers in URLs. This appears to work, however, only if the user session is confined to one Web site. Stout (1997, 5) also considers the site visit a meaningful, useful unit of measurement and analysis. The biggest problem with trying to summarize all visits to a Web site is not how to present the information, but how to acquire the information in the first place (Stout 1997, 70). Yesil (1996, 115) defines a visit as a series of consecutive file requests made by one user at a given Web site. If such a user makes no requests from that site during a predetermined period, the next hit by that user would constitute the beginning of a new visit. To enable comparability, the industry standard time-out interval for the automatic termination of a visit is 30 minutes (Kirsner 1997a).

The idea of a search session may contain assumptions that no longer apply. If a search session primarily is seen as one person interacting with one computer (perhaps even one software program or database on one computer), reality has veered away from our staid perception. Human-computer interaction no longer is one isolated human being interacting with one computer. If we call this one-on-one interaction a session, defining and isolating search sessions has become a nearly completely artificial way to understand and describe the events occurring in the environment being studied. The human experience of cyberspace has advanced beyond search sessions in which one relatively isolated individual interacts with one relatively isolated computer, software program, database, or Web site. For some reason, people continue to prefer to think of "sessions," even though, for example, a Web browsing session involves interaction with a variety of computers, including the client and several servers.

Buchanan and Lukaszewski (1997, 170) circumvent this problem of the one and the many by defining a session as an individual visit to a Web site, regardless of the number of pages viewed. A session can be calculated as all page views from the same network address occurring within an established session time limit of one another. Buchanan and Lukaszewski (1997, 171) prefer to define session length according the number of pages viewed, rather than according to the passage of time. To calculate the average length of a session, they divide the sum of all page views from all sessions by the total number of sessions, minus the number of sessions containing only one page view.

Strom (1996c) defines a visit as "a sequence of hits made by one user at a site within a set period of time. [It] does not indicate whether visitors are digging into the site's content or just skimming." Chen (1997) defines a session as a series of uninterrupted clicks from a visitor. The period of inactivity that qualifies as a session-ending interruption, however, is arbitrarily established by the analyzing team. Chen (1997) argues that issuing session identification numbers is the best way to estimate the number of sessions at a site during a specified time. Interestingly, Pitkow (1997a) defines session length as the amount of attention spent by visitors at a Web site. Such a definition, however, raises the more difficult challenge of defining and measure human attention.

Dorfman (1996) provides a step-by-step examination of how to use Web server access logs to determine individual use sessions. He concludes that gathering meaningful Web usage statistics is very difficult. The best way to avoid confusion and misinterpretation is to avoid boiling the analysis down to a single number. Rather, one should gather several numbers and report them for what they are.

Standards bodies have attempted to standardize this idea of a visit to a Web site as an online session. Late in 1996 the International Federation of Audit Bureaux of Circulations adopted several standard definitions that distinguish between page impressions and visits, also known as sessions. The Federation defines a visit as a period spent at a Web site, regardless of the number of page impressions the visitor views (Demery 1997). The shortcomings of the site-centric method of measurement are painfully obvious when we try to define and discuss sessions. From the user's point of view, a single browsing session may entail visits to several sites, perhaps including repeat visits to specific sites during the same session.

An interesting sub-field of the movement to use computers to monitor HCI focuses on the conclusions of HCI sessions and the causes of those cessations. Cessation analysis tries to understand what causes people to leave cyberspace and return wholly to the real world. Usually it is the user who breaks off the HCI session, but sometimes it is the computer or computer network. Pitkow (1997a, 1348) defines attrition as a measure of site visitors who stop traversing through the site versus the number of visitors who continue to traverse the hyperlinks emanating from a given page. Attrition can be calculated for an individual or for a group. Cessation analysis can concentrate on human behavior sequences that lead to a session cessation. For example, multiple unproductive or erroneous actions often precede user termination of an HCI session. If cyberspace is a human sense of space sans place, where in the sense of cyberspace do search sessions typically end? Many studies have found that an error state often precedes a cessation. Perhaps the sense of state (e.g., an error state) is another way of thinking about cyberspace. A "cyberstate" may be a more accurate description of the human mode of being that occurs during HCI than cyberspace.

Site navigation is the method by which a user moves around in an information environment. In a bibliographic information environment, the movement among citations, subject headings, abstracts, full text, and images would be a useful way to conceptualize and measure site navigation. A Web environment, on the other hand, may be oriented more in a spatial fashion.

Measuring online group behavior involves other complex challenges. Fundamental measures of the activity in a chat room could include the number of visitors to the room, or the average, minimum, and maximum stay in the room (Buchanan and Lukaszewski 1997, 127).

Visitor Counts (Primarily for Web Sites)   It is possible to be interested in identifying individual users of a computer system without being interested in their demographic characteristics, buying habits, and other personal information. Being able to identify visitors, rather than mere visits, provides a better opportunity to understand how people interact with computer systems. Until we get to the level of lived experience, our computerized monitoring data is alloyed with the system's perspective of the HCI. An alloyed view of the HCI may not be all bad (after all, the HCI itself is alloyed), but it also may be useful to get to the level of the visitor. Buchanan and Lukaszewski (1997, 165) define a person as a single individual visiting a Web site, regardless of the number of sessions involved. The number of persons can be measured either through unique cookies or unique user identifiers. Chen (1997) also defines visitors as the number of unique persons accessing a Web site. Chen asserts that it is impossible to count visitors accurately without requiring them to register. Kirsner (1997a) refers to counts of unique visitors as the Holy Grail of Web measurement. Counting the number of unique IP addresses visiting a Web site over a specified time is the simplest and least accurate way to estimate the number of unique visitors (Chen 1997). Because both online content providers and Internet service providers often spread a limited number of IP addresses among many users, there certainly is not a one-to-one relationship between IP addresses and unique individual visitors. Borghuis (1997) presents a compelling argument that the number and growth of repeat users of an information database is a valid measure of the success of that database.

Client software counts also can serve as an indication of the number of visitors to a Web site. The number of unique cookies is the number of unique browsers (i.e., browser software programs) that have been assigned permanent identifying codes that can be detected by a Web server during subsequent visits (Buchanan and Lukaszewski 1997, 209). It also is possible to count the brands and versions of browser software used by visitors to a Web site. This information can help the site designer tailor the site to match the functionality of the software being used by most of its visitors (Chen 1997).

Attempts to measure "read time" involve trying to figure out what people are doing during the lulls in HCI. An essential, inferred unit of measure is the amount of time a person spends reading information displayed on a screen. Gibbs (1996c) laments that there is not a direct, irrefutable way to determine the amount of time a user spends reading a document after it has been transferred to the client computer.

Beyond Users and Search Sessions: Topical Sessions   A topical session can be understood as a fourth type of basic unit of measurement. Topical sessions potentially transcend both users and search sessions. A topical session may be smaller, the same size, or larger than a given search session. A topical session comprises all searches for information on a topic by a specific individual. Some people search for information on a topic only once, and for a short time, while others may have a lifelong interest in a topic. Although probably rare, self-conscious, semi-coordinated group information-seeking activity for a specific topic would add a new wrinkle to the problem of using topical sessions as basic units of measurement.

One theoretical problem with trying to identify and count topical sessions is that the meaning of a topic is not crystal clear. Another problem is that people have a nasty habit of pursuing topics both in virtual and real environments. A typical user of a postmodern academic library could serve as an example of multi-environmental, yet single-topic, searching. One may begin by logging onto the library's online catalog from one's dorm room. One also may surf the Web in search of additional information on one's topic. Next one may physically enter the library to retrieve the books identified during remote access of the library catalog. While in the library, one may use a standalone CD-ROM database to further pursue the topic. One also may surf the Web again from a terminal in the library. One may return to the online catalog to conduct further online research of the topic. One's trip to the library probably ends with a visit to a photocopier. Finally, one may return to the computer in one's dorm room to begin consolidating the information retrieved from multiple environments in the form of a word processed term paper. All of this activity in multiple real and online environments took place in pursuit of a single topic. Even if computerized monitoring modules were operating on the PC in the dorm room (Web client monitoring), on the online catalog (transaction log analysis), on the standalone CD-ROM workstation (transaction log analysis again), and on each of the Web sites the researcher visited during two separate surfing outings (Web server log analysis), it would be difficult to pull these separate computerized monitoring data sets together and study them as a cluster of human behavior in pursuit of a single topic. Even if that feat were possible, our analysis still would be missing all of the behavior the researcher performed in the real world in pursuit of this single topic. One practical problem with trying to identify and count topical sessions is that it entails identifying and tracking speciic, identified individuals, which most computerized monitoring software is unable to do.

As we have seen, some of the basic units of measurement in computerized monitoring are quite small and fragmented. The movement to use computers to monitor HCI may be part of a general social trend to micro-analyze large, complex phenomena. For example, Mondex USA is a company created in 1996 by a consortium of communications and financial firms such as AT&T, Chase Manhattan, Dean Witter, and Wells Fargo, to undertake a fragmentation of virtual economic activity. Rather than ask a netizen to subscribe to an online journal for a year, Mondex USA will charge by the single article, single viewing of the table of contents, and so on (Hodges 1997). The smallness and discreteness of the basic units of measurement in computerized monitoring seem to be enabling this fragmentation of consumer behavior.

All of these different potential units of measurement reveal that a sequence of observed human activities as people interact with computers can be aggregated at different levels. Winne, Gupta, and Nesbit (1994, 178) differentiate among acts, tactics, strategies, and self-regulatory activities. Santos' research (1995) is pertinent here, because it involved user interface management system (UIMS) transcription facilities, which contained some knowledge of the model of the human-computer interface, thus allowing them to build and record higher-level interaction units. Santos asserted the value of a hierarchical event log, combining in one log file a record of the HCI at multiple levels of abstraction, including a representation of the user's task structure. Santos' research attempts to rehumanize the computerized monitoring agenda. Rather than characterize people as primates pounding away on keyboards and mice, Santos tried to use computerized monitoring to understand their goals as they interacted with computers. The biggest problem with Web traffic counters and auditors is that there are too many ways to count and not enough widely accepted definitive language (Rich 1997a, 24). This situation has plagued the entire brief history of computer-monitored HCI. Useful, accepted, adaptable standard definitions are difficult to assert and maintain.

Equations Founded on These Basic Units   Once the basic units of measurement have been defined, various ratios and equations can be constructed. Only a few can be mentioned here. After defining the meaning of "hits" and "aware surfers" in the context of Web use, Berthon, Pitt, and Prendergast (1997, 7) construct equations for "locatability/attractability," "contact efficiency," and "conversion efficiency." Borghuis (1997) briefly explains how computerized monitoring that focuses on user sessions can be used to calculate conversion rates in databases containing various levels and components of texts, ranging from brief citations to full images. Conversion rates are the percentages of how often a user stays within a certain subdomain of the bibliographic sphere represented by the database, or the rate at which users move from one level (e.g., brief citations) to another level (e.g., abstract). Cooley, Mobasher, and Srivastava (1997) created a maximal forward reference transaction identification module, based on transactions defined as the set of Web pages in the traversal path from the user's first page in a server log up to the page before a backward reference is made. The formula assumes that backing up is a signal of completion or pursuit of a new tack. In 1995 Arbitron NewMedia, ASI Market Research and Next Century Media undertook a joint venture to develop an Interactive Information Index — a research tool designed to enable advertising agencies and marketers to compare usage of various interactive media. The Interactive Information Index was designed to provide summaries of time spent, the degree of interactivity, the depth of exploration of content, and the number of desirable responses during the media's use (Mandese 1995).

Perhaps the library and information science profession needs to develop key digital library ratios analogous to accepted key business ratios. Project Muse is an online full-text database of journal issues maintained by Johns Hopkins University. Project operators collect and distribute quarterly use statistics which indicate how often various elements of the online journals (e.g., tables of contents, images, full-text articles, and explanatory background information) are accessed from a specific IP cluster, such as a college campus. In the Project Muse use statistics, it may be helpful to calculate the number of article hits per search, or the number of article hits per table of contents hit.

Vinge's Notion of an Event Horizon   In this chapter we have been discussing ways of describing and measuring online events, defined as the basic units of interaction between a person and computer. Vinge (1993) developed and explored the related notion of an event horizon, beyond which everything becomes unrecognizable to people. Bailey (1996) also toys with the idea that we may be entering an era when computerized analysis of data and events (including HCI) will reach a level that passes all human understanding. If the computer program can modify itself (and thus the virtual environment) based on this high-level (or at least a different-level — it may be an extra-humanly low-level) analysis, there will be little or no need to translate the results of this analysis into something that people can understand. Just as other creatures can perceive light and sound waves beyond the normal human perceptual range, it is reasonable to expect computers to be able to perceive and analyze data above or below that range. Rather than spend so much time and energy trying to develop artificial human intelligence in computers, perhaps we should try to develop computer systems that are differently intelligent, then let them manifest that intelligence by creating better online environments. We should allow and enable computers to be intelligent and creative in the way that is right for them (assuming that a "natural" computer intelligence can exist), rather than force them into some anthropomorphic Procrustean bed.

How to Measure the Passage of Time?   Any discussion of basic units of measurement also must consider ways of measuring the passage of time. Computerized monitors of HCI tend to time-stamp everything. The timing precision of machine-level computerized monitoring is much greater than can be obtained manually, and no worse than that obtained by a careful and detailed analysis of a videotape (Santos 1995, 166). What role does time play in computerized monitoring? Online monitoring data are most useful when they include time stamps on user actions and system responses. No other monitoring method is easily capable of providing such discrete timing data (Borgman, Hirsh, and Hiller 1996, 575). Accurately measuring time seems to be one thing that computerized monitoring does extremely well. Of course, time online can be measured in accepted real-world units, such as seconds and minutes. The research argument made by Fuller and Graaff (1996) is pertinent here. But time also can be measured according to the frequency of discrete event-units. For example, one user may take 15 minutes to enter five commands, while another user may take only three minutes to enter the same five commands. If measured by standard units of time, the first search session was five times as long as the second. If measured in event-units, the two search sessions were the same length. Some aspects of time are geographically dependent. The hour of the day, for example, depends on where one is on the globe. Environments in cyberspace, however, are not very geographically dependent. In many emerging online environments, the diurnal passage of time has little or no meaning to the observable online behavior.

What Level Within the Computer Environment Is Appropriate?   The appropriate level to monitor usage is an intermediate level below the application level and above the physical I/O level of the page manager (Dearnley and Smith 1995, 661). Much computerized monitoring is summarization and pattern recognition. Bailey (1996) suggests that computers can modify themselves, and thus the virtual environment, by simply analyzing the data at the level of fundamental units. But human prejudice against formulation directly at the level of the data remains strong (Bailey 1996, 144).

Siting and Situating the Data Collection   Siting or situating the collection of data is a fundamental decision. Santos (1995, 166) cautions that, in general, a monitoring program should not be integrated into the software application that the user is executing. Denise Davis of the Division of Library Development and Services at the Maryland Department of Education raises an important and interesting methodological point. The location either in cyberspace or in procedural space of the data collection activity is crucial to what can be collected and analyzed. She conceptualizes a two-dimensional plane, with users and resources ranging from local to remote (Smith and Rowland 1997, 170). In attempts to analyze Web browsing behavior, a fundamental decision involves whether the data will be gathered at the server end, at the client end, or somewhere between.

Bench Marking   Although the predictive capabilities of computerized monitoring remain in doubt, the need for bench marking is beyond question. Ted Boyd, the director of new media technologies at Young & Rubicam, an online marketing firm, notes that to determine the importance and value of a set of online behavior, benchmarks must be established so that the observed behavior can be placed in a basic context of being either typical or atypical. For example, a five percent clickthrough rate on banner ads at a Web site has no inherent meaning until a benchmark has been established (Sangster 1996). The need for bench marking also has been expressed in the online library domain. Hightower, Sih and Tilghman (1998) explore how Web server log analysis can provide academic libraries with benchmarks for normal, low, and high usage Web sites.

What Analysis Methods Are Possible?   Most computerized monitoring studies capture time-stamped, discrete behavioral events. Pitkow (1997a) notes that descriptive statistical analyses of a set of discrete events can yield the frequency, mean, median, mode, minimum, maximum, standard deviations, variance, and range. Statistical analyses of computer monitoring data indicate trends, graphic displays of the data enable close inspection of the actions underlying those trends, and pattern matching enables the analyst to determine the frequency of selected sequences of actions and to extract interesting sequences for closer inspection (Borgman, Hirsh, and Hiller 1996, 577).

Should we focus on the sequential march of events (the "and then, and then") during HCI, or should we try to focus more on the overall environment or state of being (either for the person or the computer)? Analogously, to understand and appreciate a painting, would it be wise to recreate and study the sequence of brushstrokes? Painting, like novel writing and the composition of music, is a sequential process, yet, unlike novels and music, paintings are not experienced sequentially. The activities of interest to us in this book (online working, learning, information seeking, and shopping) historically have been realized as sequential events, but as the computer age settles in they may be becoming less so. Perhaps we should try to understand and appreciate HCI, at least at the individual session level, as a complete thing, rather than as a sequential series of discrete events of varying size and frequency.

Aggregation More Feared Than Analysis   Many users of the Internet fear not so much that behavioral residue will be collected and analyzed, but that disparate bits of personal information will be aggregated in a way that the whole aggregation has more resale value, is more revealing, and perhaps is more erroneous than the sum of the parts. Wreden (1997), for example, worries that the Internet sites a person visits can be aggregated and sold without the person's knowledge or consent. In his concurring opinion in the 1970 case of *Nader v General Motors*, the judge expressed this fundamental fear of aggregation of disparate public acts: "Although acts performed in 'public,' especially if taken singly or in small numbers, may not be confidential, at least arguably a right to privacy may nevertheless be invaded through extensive and exhaustive monitoring and cataloguing of acts normally disconnected and anonymous" (quoted in Sessler 1997, 655). One could counter-argue, however, that the analysis of computerized monitoring data merely attempts to reaggregate and humanize online experiences that computerized monitoring fundamentally disaggregated and atomized at the data collection stage. In the normal human experience of virtual environments, the discrete human actions that computerized monitoring captures and analyzes are not experientially, phenomenologically disconnected. They are so seamless and all of a broader, fluid experience of an online session that the monitored subjects often are amazed and confounded when they see an "objective" analysis of their keystrokes, commands, clickstreams, and wanderings in cyberspace, because their lived experience of what happened online is dissonant with this record of discrete, petty, seemingly disjointed actions.

In this regard, and despite popular tendencies to conflate the two practices, computerized monitoring of HCI differs radically from merging databases containing real-world information about individuals. Computerized monitoring does not artificially or unnaturally fuse information together. Because the basic unit of measurement of a computerized monitoring study often is quite small, much of the analysis effort is an attempt to reconstruct the sequences of events so that meaning can be obtained. Later I will argue that this attempt to humanize computerized monitoring data probably will become less productive in the near future, as the computers that facilely gather data about HCI become more adept at analyzing and applying the data. The need to look for patterns, aggregate discrete events, and to present the analysis in humanly comprehensible terms will diminish.

Attempts to Measure Human Interest Many critics of the movement to use computers to study HCI have noted that while computerized monitoring captures behavior well, in its own way, it reveals little or nothing definite about the opinions and attitudes of persons responsible for this observed online behavior. Some researchers have taken this basic criticism a step further and have suggested that opinions and attitudes do not matter as much as user interest. Is the user interested in the information space? The content, the structure, the medium, and other aspects of the HCI either build or diminish user interest. Measuring this interest improves the quality and delivery of information service to the user by providing tools for the system administrator and the creator of the document space to determine the value of the information they are providing (Fuller and Graaff 1996).

This path to knowledge of quality and value includes two rickety bridges. The first bridge traverses the gorge between the measurement of use and estimations of user interest. Human interest is very fleeting and easily swayed. A user's interest in a Web site may be high before visiting the site, then diminish as the result of the visit. Perhaps we should try to measure the change of interest between the user's first visit to the site and the time when the user finally leaves the site. If the change is positive, we could conclude that the Web site interested that user. The other challenge with human interest is that it can be measured both for individuals and for groups. The second rickety bridge attempts to span the chasm between user interest and estimations of the value of the Web site itself.

Success Versus Satisfaction   In many situations involving computer monitoring, the collectors and analysts of the data want to know not only if people used the computer system successfully, but also whether they were satisfied with the interaction and its results. Using computers to monitor HCI always has been a difficult method for pinpointing positive proof of the existence of the more nebulous states of success and satisfaction. "The number of hits can't be a stand-alone measure of success," says Edwin Hastings, chief technology officer at Online Computer Market in Natick, Massachusetts (Strom 1996c, S36).

Is Computerized Monitoring Absolutely True and Irrefutable?   A view often is expressed or implied that computer monitoring is absolutely true and irrefutable. It is perceived as producing data untouched by human hands and uninfluenced by human biases — intentional or unintentional. In the application of computer monitoring to appraise worker performance, Angel (1989) flatly states that computers do not contain biases, and that computer monitoring mitigates against negative, unfair managerial expectations, such as personal grooming preferences, religious affiliations, and political views. We need to question this common assumption about the nature of data collected by computer monitoring. First, the computer monitoring mechanism is a tool created by human beings. It may be impossible for people to design and construct tools that do not contain assumptions and biases embedded into the very "toolness" of the tools.

Salient Characteristics of Human-Computer Interaction   One of the complaints often raised about using computers to monitor HCI is that it tends to concentrate on how one interacts with the machine or a body of inanimate information, rather than with other human beings. Sproull and Faraj (1997) suggest that the Internet should be studied as a social technology, through which people act as social beings looking for affiliation, support, and affirmation, rather than for information to retrieve and manipulate. Viewing the Internet as fundamentally a technology for providing access to information and information tools is unnecessarily narrow-sighted. Great good places (see Oldenberg 1989) can be found not only in the real world but also in cyberspace, often in the form of electronic groups (Sproull and Faraj 1997, 39). Different online environments are loaded with different behavioral expectations. In a learning environment, individuals are expected to learn. In an information environment, they are expected to seek and retrieve information. On the Web, they are expected to browse, surf, and, increasingly, to shop.

Economics of Collecting, Analyzing, and Applying Computerized Monitoring Data   In the past, the economics of human monitoring by others tended to work against intensive surveillance (Marx and Sherizen 1989, 399). Computerized monitoring radically alters the economics of observing and controlling HCI. Collecting behavioral data during HCI has become relatively cheap — much cheaper than engaging in random inspections by human intermediaries. The costs of analyzing and applying these data have not dropped as quickly as the cost of collecting the data. Borgman, Hirsh and Hiller (1996, 575) note that studying the search paths of users of a computerized information system is very challenging and taxing on the analyst's resources, including time, patience, and computer CPU time. Once people figure out how to change the economics of analyzing and applying the cheaply gathered data, the true revolution promised by computerized monitoring of HCI will begin. The cheapest way to perform the analysis and application of the findings is to remove the human element from these methodological stages and turn the whole show over to the computers.

Diffusion of This Innovation   Diffusion of the methods of using computers to collect, analyze, and apply data about HCI appears to be relatively slow. The technique has been applied to human activity in at least four distinct environments (work, school, libraries, and the Web), but the extent of the diffusion within these four environments has been uneven. The diffusion in work environments may be the most extensive, and the current fastest rate of diffusion appears to be in the Web. There appear to be no published studies of the diffusion of the innovation of computerized monitoring within an environment or field and across environments. If the basic argument of this book (i.e., that there is a recognizable, encompassing movement to use computers to monitor HCI, and that there are reasons and advantages to studying the amorphous movement as a whole) is tentatively accepted, a logical next step would be to undertake studies of the diffusion of this innovation. What causes the diffusion to accelerate (e.g., in Web environments), and what retards the diffusion?

Characteristics of the Resultant Data Sets   Depending on how one understands it, computerized monitoring of HCI either captures or generates data. The result of the data-collection phase of a computerized monitoring project usually is a database contained in a computer file. This database usually is not a "people-base" — one containing information about people listed under the names of specific individuals (Flood 1997). Rather, it usually is a collection of discrete acts involving people and computers, arranged in chronological order.

Computerized Monitoring Used with Other Data Collection and Analysis Methods   Computerized monitoring can be used with other data collection and analysis methods. Most of these other data sets are collected from the real world, not from cyberspace. For example, computerized monitoring analysis of one-time-only and repeat users of an online information database could be followed by qualitative research (e.g., focus groups or questionnaires) to obtain a better understanding of why one-time-only users did not return to the online environment, or why the repeat users keep coming back for more (Borghuis 1997). Wiberley, Daugherty, Allen, and Danowski (1995) used real-world unobtrusive observation to validate user search sessions in an OPAC. The research conducted over several years by Micheline Hancock-Beaulieu has been particularly strong and noteworthy in its methodological multidimensionality.

Multiple data collection methods can yield a more complete picture of an event or series of events. On the Web Amazon relies on server logs, cookie files, and user registration forms to learn more about its customers (Brodwin, O'Connell, and Valdmanis 1997). One of the major third-party Web site analysis companies, I/PRO encourages users of its NetLine service to cross-analyze log file data with visitor-supplied registration files to develop more sophisticated behavior profiles of Web site visitors (Lamons 1997). The general argument in favor of multiple data collection and analysis methods points to the richness of HCI and human behavior in cyberspace. The spectra of most data collection methods are too narrow to yield a good picture of this activity. "Multiple evaluation methods are required to achieve a full characterization of behavioral processes as complex as online searching" (Borgman, Hirsh, and Hiller 1996, 568–569).

All of these methodological issues both reveal and conceal the fact that, despite the frequent inability to identify specific individuals, most computerized monitoring still focuses on the individual. Information about individual behavior may be aggregated during the analysis, but analysts rarely accept the behavior as disassociated from an individual. The stateless nature of the client-server architecture of the Web could provide a different method for thinking about and analyzing human behavior. If we could perceive in a way similar to the way a server "perceives," requests for files and information are coming from all directions, and identifying the individuals (or even the specific client computers) sending those requests is not very important or productive. The virtual directions from which the requests arrive do not make much sense either. Perhaps the methodology of studying HCI has failed to understand the very nature of that interaction. Many computerized monitoring studies seem to be based on the assumption that HCI is like a cryptic telegram transmitted in Morse code, laden with full stops. Human-computer interaction may be more drawn out, almost courtly.

There is a hopeful purity and verity to the method of computerized monitoring that recalls the folk wisdom that urges us not to listen to what people say, but to watch what they do. Also lurking at the conceptual roots of this method is the realization that people have been behaving so long (at least in the real world) that they have become blind to their own behavior. Part of the fascination of unobtrusively watching people act in online environments is that we are seeing ourselves again for the first time. Via computerized monitoring, human being appears fresh again. Either that, or the online environments have become so complex and removed that unmediated observation of human behavior no longer is practical. Computerized monitoring gives us new eyes with which to see. Watching from a real-world vantage point a person engaged in some interaction with cyberspace can also be very limiting (regarding data collection possibilities), misleading, and boring.

Many human events occur in the real world, and many human-computer events occur in cyberspace. Computerized monitoring can capture and analyze a wide variety and massive quantities of these online human events. Although the possibilities are almost limitless, we also need to be realistic and practical. We need to remember that, in real-world environments, lots of event-based information is simply lost, in the sense of never being recorded and analyzed for its human knowledge potential. In our analogy of the stroller on a wet sandy beach, after high tide the footprints left during low tide are washed away — the information forgotten and unanalyzed by the real-world biosystem. In a computerized environment, the computer can retain, analyze, and use much more of this ambient environmental information. This fundamental difference between real-world and online environments raises a policy question: How much of this information do we want our computers to retain and use? Although this question can be understood as concerning individual privacy rights in cyberspace, it may be fruitful to understand it as an environmental question about the basic nature of online environments.

9

Applications
and Outcomes

We are entering the age of the infinite examination and of compulsory objectification (Foucault 1977, 189).

The previous chapter examined some of the important issues and decisions relating to the data collection phase of a computerized monitoring project. Now we need to examine the myriad ways these data can be analyzed and applied. The proof, payoff, and benefit of all this prior activity of designing a computerized monitoring module, collecting data, and analyzing it is the application. After using a computer to monitor HCI, one needs to apply the results of the analysis of the monitoring activity in some way. Computerized monitoring could be used to measure and improve productivity in work environments, or to monitor and control theft or illegal activity in a variety of computerized environments. The application of computerized monitoring of HCI may reveal the motives behind the entire project. Applying this newfound knowledge is the final frontier. A basic, enduring criticism of using computers to monitor HCI is that, in general, the applications of this knowledge have been very haphazard and unsystematic. The secret of success will lie not in ownership of information but in its application (Hagel and Armstrong 1997).

Is Generalized, Absolute, Enduring, Pure Knowledge Possible in This Field? Before turning our attention to the applications and outcomes of specific computerized monitoring projects, and for the field as a whole, we should briefly examine whether or not generalized, absolute, enduring, pure knowledge is possible and attainable in this field. Can we "just know" how people and computers interact in online environments without applying that knowledge?

Much of the long project to use computers to monitor HCI appears to have been misguided about expected outcomes. Often we seem to believe that there exists some overwhelming truth about HCI that, once discovered and known, would shed its light throughout cyberspace, immediately and profoundly improving the quality of graphical user interfaces and the effectiveness of all HCI. What we may be facing, however, is an online future characterized by an endless series of minor — perhaps imperceptible — environmental modifications made for each individual netizen. The challenge for human beings in cyberspace — pattern-recognizing creatures that they are — is to articulate and measure a new sense of progress for the online era.

General Prerequisites for Applicability   To be successfully applied, computer monitoring needs to produce outcomes pertinent to some broader need or goal of the person or group attempting to apply it. Stated bluntly and generally: What is the point, end, final cause, or anticipated outcome of this monitoring activity? Is this knowledge of how people interact with computers good to know in itself, or does it justify the effort required to obtain it only when the real and potential applications are explored? Because we are dealing with online environments created by human beings, we can concentrate on the purpose for the environment. Stout (1997, 92–93), for example, suggests that the three basic objectives of most commercial Web sites are to establish an organizational presence, to sell products and services, or to sell advertising. Within this environmental context, data obtained by computerized monitoring should be applied to advance these goals.

Pure Knowledge Outcomes   In perhaps the purest application of computerized monitoring of HCI, personal identity does not matter. What matters is not so much who did that but what happened. The environment and the computer will be of more interest than the individual involved in HCI, because the computer and the online environment are more tractable and malleable. Although the belief in the perfectibility of humankind may have resulted in all sorts of dire consequences and silliness, the abandonment of the notion could be worse. Computerized monitoring projects may be a threat to human worth, not because of our real-world notions concerning invasion of individual privacy, but because computerized monitoring of HCI in online environments ultimately will make it much easier to change the online environment. The social need to educate and change individual human beings may diminish.

Because the promise of applying the results of computerized monitoring is so essential to the entire project, it is perhaps doubly imperative that we defend the analysis of HCI — of human behavior in cyberspace — as a form of pure knowledge, of inherent value. If cyberspace becomes an entirely new and rich environment in which human being manifests itself, knowledge of the fundamental characteristics of that being (assuming that fundamental characteristics exist) would be worth knowing. The early results on the pure knowledge front indicate that human being in cyberspace may be more environmentally sensitive (i.e., sensitive to environmental conditions) than it is in real life. When in real Rome, we may do what the Romans do. In online environments, we seem to do what Rome itself as an online environment gently encourages us to do. Environmental pressures may overtake peer pressure.

Pure knowledge outcomes of computerized monitoring projects are not worthless. Lee and Heller (1997) point out that perhaps the greatest value of computerized monitoring projects is to raise questions for further study and analysis, not to provide answers. "Perhaps the most significant value of the log file is the identification of open questions ... that have to be addressed by additional studies" (Lee and Heller 1997, 100).

Applications Focusing on People   Applications of computerized monitoring of HCI tend to focus on either legitimate human use of the computer system, or on illegal or unauthorized use. Computerized monitoring systems tend to pay attention either to the valid users or to the hackers. Of course, a study of legitimate use may focus on inefficient or uninformed use of a computer system, but it continues to concentrate on legitimate use and how to maximize output or outcomes from such legitimate use. These systems are categorically different from computerized monitoring systems designed primarily to detect intruders and unauthorized use. It is possible to imagine a computerized monitoring system capable of detecting and analyzing behavior undertaken by both the white and black hats, but most computerized monitoring projects focus on one or the other. Most published reports of computerized monitoring activity are about legitimate use of computer systems. Computerized monitoring of HCI in work and formal learning environments often concerns the behavior of specific, identified individuals, while computerized monitoring of HCI in information seeking and shopping and browsing environments more often focuses on group behavior and the behavior of unspecified, unidentified individuals.

For an odd combination of reasons, the last half of the twentieth century has experienced a rapid increase in the demand for demographic information. Unfortunately, the movement to use computers to monitor HCI has become caught up in that modern quest. Marketers quickly learned that demographic information is a good guide to future purchasing and consumption. More recently, Web marketers have learned that it is possible to infer demographic information from Web server usage logs. Thus there is a strong retrograde pull to develop software tools to facilitate the inference of demographic information from usage logs. Many computerized monitoring projects attempt to translate observations about online behavioral information into demographic information about persons. It is not necessary to identify individuals, and certainly not specified individuals, to perform such analysis, but past individual behavior may be an even better predictor of future behavior than mere demographic information. For example, although demographic information about one may indicate that one is in a socio-economic group primed to purchase a certain make and model of automobile, if one's individual history reveals that one bought another make and model last month, the demographic hunch has little value in this particular case. Computerized monitoring has the potential of easily, cheaply replacing the real-world movement of collecting demographic information and making intelligent guesses from that information with individual monitoring of online behavior.

Numerous transaction log analysis projects have tried to discern or verify demographic information about users of computerized library systems. In a recent example, McGlamery (1997) found that transaction log analysis can answer at least four basic questions about users of a specialized digital library: 1) Who are the users? 2) Where are the users on the IP address map of cyberspace? 3) What are their primary interests? 4) How do they move through the digital library? McGlamery (1997, 507) believes that the answers to these questions are necessary to determine how to provide digital library services. McGlamery found that the "service" pages on the digital library site were often visited and used. Because of transaction log analysis, in some instances librarians are able to know more about virtual users than about real world users.

Judy Black, a senior partner who directs Bozell, Jacobs, Kenyon & Eckhardt's interactive media marketing plans, maintains that advertisers have little interest in or use for hit counts. Advertisers want measurements of visits to a particular site, the number of users visiting the site, and especially the identity of users visiting a site (Fitzgerald 1996). Although advertisers may not need to know the specific identities of Web site visitors, they want to know basic demographic information about each user. Pitkow (1997a) notes that many of the commercially available Web server log file analysis programs contain databases that match domain names with basic demographic information.

Demographic information in online environments has value only as a predictor of other things. In shopping environments, demographic information has proved a good predictor of group purchasing trends. Because the Internet is a collection of small, unique, niche markets, rather than a mass market, retailers on the Internet must be able to identify the correct demographic and psychographic characteristics of potential customers (Yesil 1996, 109).

Psychographic information complements demographic information. "Businesses using subscription/membership services and tracking systems can begin to piece together the psychographics of their visitors, thereby enabling themselves to deliver products and information directly to the user — relative to that user's interests and at competitive prices" (Yesil 1996, 108). Computerized monitoring, also known as session analysis, enables the creation of "Webographic" profiles, the Internet equivalent of psychographics (Oberndorf 1996). Lee and Heller (1997) tried to use transaction log analysis of the usage patterns of a sophisticated interactive multimedia system at the Wexner Learning Center of the U.S. Holocaust Memorial Museum to differentiate search sessions in which the user primarily engaged with the functionality of the online environment versus sessions in which the user seemed to engage primarily with the content.

Monitoring the Workplace Behavior and Performance of Employees   "An employee, by the very nature of the employment relationship, must be subject to some level of monitoring by the employer" (Galkin 1996, 48).

Work environments are a prime example of situations in which computerized monitoring projects are implemented with applications and outcomes focused on human beings. Computerized monitoring of HCI in work environments is widespread. In the early 1990s it was estimated that as many as 26 million workers in the United States were subject to computerized performance monitoring (Baarda 1994). In 1997 *CIO Magazine* surveyed 125 major corporations and found that approximately half reported that they used computerized monitoring software to keep track of employees as they surf the Web. For corporations with over 5,000 employees, approximately 75 percent reported using computerized monitoring programs (Harmon 1997). During a phone survey conducted in May 1997, Martin (1997) found that a third of the companies surveyed currently monitored employee online behavior, and another 11.5 percent of the respondents intended to begin monitoring within the next 12 months. The majority (72.7 percent) of respondents who monitored examined Web sites visited, followed by types of files downloaded, time spent on the Internet, size of files downloaded, and the content of e-mail messages. The survey reported by Martin (1997) revealed that monitoring online work behavior was much more common than instances of blocking access to specific Internet sites.

Computerized monitoring of employee job performance is a type of electronic control system (ECS). Kidwell and Kidwell (1997) suggest that ECS research (including computerized monitoring) can be classified into three broad types of organizational studies: social psychological, structural, and ecological. They note that most ECS research has focused on the social psychological level. Regarding the application of computerized monitoring analysis in work environments, Lund (1991) notes that it is important to distinguish between organizations using computerized performance information as the basis for promotions and pay raises, and those using computerized monitoring information to detect and discipline employees who are not working properly or performing at expected levels.

Computerization in work environments is, in the deepest sense, a reconfiguration of the representation of work (Rochlin 1997, 12). What happens to both the worker and the work in environments where work is monitored by a computer? Advocates of computerized monitoring would claim that supervision (i.e., verification that productive work is being undertaken) will become both more efficient and more reliable than the more traditional methods of management by casual observation and walking around in the real workplace. Critics of CPM claim that work becomes more quantified, routinized, and degraded, and that the worker becomes a set of digits, rather than a sentient, complete human being.

Definitions of computer monitoring in workplace environments run the gamut from the harshly realistic to the ideal. Kallman (1993) defines electronic monitoring as the use of specialized computer software to capture and analyze data to measure the quantity of work being done by employees using computer terminals.

Computer monitoring in workplace environments involves the use of computers to collect and process information and provide feedback about work, with the intent of improving employee performance and development (Griffith 1993a). The monitored employees themselves also attach different meanings to the use of computerized monitoring. Kidwell and Bennett (1994) proposed that variation in perceptions of procedural justice may influence a person's satisfaction with CPM (Aiello and Kolb 1995b, 169). Miezio (1992) sees CPM primarily as a production control tool. A computerized monitoring system gives managers greater control over the production process, even if the product is a service.

The 1987 report by the U.S. Office of Technology Assessment defined CPM as the "computerized collection, storage, analysis and reporting of information about employees' productive activities ... [obtained] ... directly through their use of computer and telecommunication equipment" (p. 27). The three basic forms of electronic monitoring used by employers are service observation, computerized work measurement, and electronic surveillance, such as video monitoring (Jenero and Mapes-Riordan 1992). Computerized performance monitoring can monitor aspects of productivity, errors and problems during productive activities, and non-productive activities or inactivity. Critics have charged that CPM leads to unfair performance evaluations, employee stress, and other employee health problems (Hawk 1994).

Computerized performance monitoring differs from other forms of employee supervision and evaluation. Marx (1985) identified nine attributes of CPM that distinguish it from the more traditional forms of employee supervision. CPM transcends distance, darkness, and physical barriers. It also transcends time, in that monitor data can be easily stored, retrieved, combined, analyzed, and communicated. It is capital intensive, rather than labor intensive. Computerized performance monitoring involves a programmatic shift from targeting a specific employee for intense supervision and surveillance to categorical suspicion of all employees. The major concern of CPM projects and programs is to prevent violations of policies and procedures. It is decentralized and fosters self-policing. Computerized performance monitoring either is invisible or has low visibility. Its reach is deeper than that of more traditional supervisory techniques, in that it is capable of discovering previously inaccessible information about employee behavior. Finally, its scope is broad, and it tends to become more extensive over time. Kolb and Aiello (1997, 190) also note that CPM makes possible real-time management and assessment of employee performance. With computerized monitoring, there is no need to wait for the annual performance appraisal interview to provide performance feedback to an employee. Feedback can be instantaneous.

Computerized monitoring of HCI in work environments has certain attractions for managers and supervisors. Kolb and Aiello (1997) point out that monitoring employee performance is a managerial behavior. Computerized monitoring, which gathers and analyzes data about human behavior during HCI, is itself another type of human behavior, and thus potentially subject to other data gathering and analysis activities. This is what makes the general lack of self-awareness on the part of people "behind" computerized monitoring so fascinating and instructive. Inside the monitor lurks a heart of darkness in the sense that, for some reason or combination of reasons, this cohort of people engaged in computerized monitoring is unable or unwilling to examine or understand completely their own behavior. Ultimately, the behavior of the person engaged in monitoring may be more interesting and informative than the behavior being captured by computerized monitoring of HCI.

As computers permeate the workplace, managers are looking to computers themselves to capture performance data pertaining to computer-mediated tasks (Grant and Higgins 1991a, 116). Nussbaum (1989) argues that while supervisory monitoring of employees is not new, the technologies of computerized monitoring make it qualitatively different from old modes of supervision. Computerized performance monitoring is relatively easy and inexpensive to implement. The costs of managing a company are quite high, so conscientious managers try to hold down the costs of managing itself. Computerization of certain aspects of management practices and responsibilities can be relatively easy and inexpensive to implement.

One could argue that as work has moved into online environments, the existing span of managerial control exercised by the usual methods in the real world has diminished. Recreational Web browsing during work is difficult for a supervisor to detect by simply walking around the office (assuming that the cyberworkers still physically congregate in an office environment). The challenge of the virtual work environment is that, from the real world vantage of supervising by walking around, the difference between one employee intently working on a sales report and another intently pursuing an avocational interest is impossible to detect. Activity in cyberspace — learning, seeking information, shopping, and working — is virtually hidden or withdrawn from the real world. It is withdrawn, furthermore, in such a way that it never can be revealed without special tools such as computerized monitoring devices.

Computerized monitoring in the work environment can be understood as a management effort to regain (and perhaps extend) the span of control of supervisors. But how does computerized monitoring increase the supervisor's control over the employee? Perhaps in defense of management one could note that the supervisor really wants to understand and control the production processes in virtual worlds for goods and services. The focus is on the process, not on the processors. It is the production process, rather than employee behavior, that has spun out of control and become inscrutable as work has gone online. "Engaging in surveillance is a conscious choice those in control of the work situation make to extend control, usually in an attempt to achieve some organizational goal more fully" (Botan 1996, 297). Computerized performance monitoring occurs in all types of companies as an outgrowth of efforts by management to control and rationalize work (Rule and Brantley 1992, 405). It provides management an immediate, continuous, vicarious presence with the employee (Larter 1984).

Computerized performance monitoring may be able to free supervisors from the time-consuming task of observing employee activities, thus freeing the supervisors to spend more time on job coaching, counseling, and employee training and development activities (Lund 1989, 108). By assuming certain management tasks, electronic monitoring makes managers more efficient, because they now can devote more time to other management functions, such as planning (Bewayo 1996, 188).

Computerized monitoring can provide increased feedback (theoretically to both the employee and the supervisor) on employee performance in online work environments and activities. Gorman (1998) suggests that the debate over online privacy in work environments centers on employee productivity in the emerging online service economy. Gorman reports that a recent monitoring project at Black and Decker Corporation revealed that only 23 percent of the computer traffic through the company's Internet connection during regular business hours was work-related. As more work occurs in online environments, employers are facing a control challenge, which translates in practical terms into increased legal liability. Martin (1997) notes that the big problem for companies resulting from inappropriate Internet surfing by employees is such liability.

Computerized performance monitoring also enables remote management and supervision in virtual environments. The manager or supervisor no longer needs to observe directly the workplace behavior of the employee. The significant residue of the behavior can be captured by the networked computer system and accessed by the manager or supervisor in some location perhaps quite distant from where the work was performed. Networked computers facilitate the remote surveillance of workers by capturing and comparing keystrokes, e-mail messages, completed transactions on the system, and even the tone of voice of telemarketers, agents, and inbound claims processors (Gandy 1995).

In her case study of companies using new information technology, Zuboff (1988, 318) gives the example of a computer-monitoring system that assigns daily tasks to a craftsworker. As each task is completed, it is entered into the computer with the time taken and how it alters the rest of the day. The time, or "price," of the task can only be altered by the foreman. The whole system allows evaluation of performance which in turn becomes part of the rubric for determining "prices," assigning workloads and assessing efficiency of the organization (Zuboff 1988, 318). Consequently workers are evaluated and can compete on the basis of these "standards." Clearly, the effect of the monitoring produces a means by which to compare, contrast and place workers into an easily calculated hierarchy (Levy 1993).

The lure of increased productivity may be the driving motivation behind most use of computerized monitoring systems in work environments. Garber (1997) goes so far as to suggest that those who oppose computerized monitoring in work environments are the unproductive types who are fearful of being found out. The goal of deterring theft and preventing espionage probably runs a distant second. The pursuit of increased productivity is the driving force behind management's decision to implement CPM (Baarda 1994, 5). The question whether CPM does in fact lead to improvements in productivity is central to the debate over its value

(Baarda 1994, 19). Early CPM programs and research projects focused on the impact of computerized monitoring on relatively low-level online work tasks. The studies conducted in controlled work-like environments by Aiello's research teams in the early 1990s consistently found that, while monitored subjects outperformed non-monitored subjects on easy tasks, non-monitored subjects outperformed monitored subjects on more difficult tasks (Kolb and Aiello 1997, 193).

The use of CPM could result in increased employee job satisfaction, because it provides direct, meaningful feedback, plus more objective measures of performance, which relate directly to the organization's reward system (Lund 1989, 108).

Employers and managers may view CPM as a way to decrease employee theft and unwanted or unproductive behavior. Support for the use of electronic monitoring as a method of deterring theft has come from the National Association of Convenience Stores, the National Association of Manufacturers, the National Association of Chain Drug Stores, the National Retail Federation, the National Restaurant Association, the American Society for Industrial Security, the American Warehouse Association, and the U.S. Chamber of Commerce (Bewayo 1996, 194). Electronic monitoring also helps improve the distribution of compensation and benefits as a result of work completed (Bewayo 1996, 192). Employee opposition to electronic monitoring may decline considerably if employees perceive its purpose as to achieve a greater degree of fairness in performance evaluation (procedural justice), which in turn leads to equitable compensation (distributive justice) (Bewayo 1996, 193).

Computerized monitoring of HCI in work environments can be used to more efficiently allocate and deploy resources in pursuit of work goals. Efficient staffing levels by time of day and day of week can be achieved in certain organizations, such as telemarketing, through computerized monitoring. Electronic monitoring can help improve personnel systems in organizations, and alleviate some of the problems caused by weak personnel systems (Bewayo 1996, 193).

The literature on CPM in work environments is filled with cautionary tales. When applying computerized monitoring research to workplace situations, managers should be cognizant of the assumptions the researcher has made about organizations in general and their purpose in society. Some computerized monitoring projects rest on an assumption that the organization is a closed system, while others tend to treat it as an open system, thus making CPM a matter of cultural or political activity at the organizational and societal levels. Most previous research on CPM and other methods of electronic surveillance in the workplace has viewed organizations as closed systems, in which computerized monitoring is seen as a new way to assess and enhance control over an eminently controllable set of workplace behaviors (Kidwell and Kidwell 1996, 8).

The interaction between CPM and employee performance is complex. Longitudinal studies are needed. Kolb and Aiello (1997) tentatively conclude that CPM appears to have a beneficial impact on worker productivity, but only when workers are performing simple, well-learned tasks. When making decisions about whether or not to introduce CPM into specific work situations, managers should consider the complexity of the work to be monitored and the degree to which workers have mastered the tasks to be monitored. Botan and McCredie (1989) note that a management policy of surveillance does not exist in a vacuum. It usually is part of an attempt to subdivide and isolate job assignments to facilitate individual control and accountability, consonant with the Taylor-based approach to scientific management.

Possible applications of the collected, analyzed data about HCI during work are diverse. Aiello and Kolb (1995b, 176) articulated four basic uses of CPM for any business organization: to identify training needs, to facilitate goal setting, to make performance evaluations more objective, and to assist in managerial planning. At the first company participating in the George (1996) study, data collected with computerized monitoring were used only for in-house competitions. Clement and McDermott (1991) note that CPM sets up a dynamic in which a piece-work system becomes attractive to management.

At other companies CPM has been used to build and bolster the case for dismissing an employee. Managers who suspect employees are wasting too much time on the Internet are seeking confirmation from Web monitoring logs. According to LAN specialist Peter Williams, Bell Mobility Cellular in Toronto, which uses Purview Internet Manager from On Technology Corporation in Cambridge, Massachusetts, recently fired one employee after issuing several warnings about spending too much time on the Internet (Machlis 1997c). Human-computer interaction can foster certain types of addictive behavior that probably are not advantageous for either the employee or the employer.

The advantages of CPM for the monitored employees themselves are not as obvious as the advantages for managers and supervisors. Nevertheless, CPM is not perceived uniformly by employees as a threatening, bad practice. In the survey research reported by Martin (1997), 65 percent of employees who responded to the survey thought that employers had the right to monitor the online behavior of employees, but 94 percent thought employees should be informed first. Some employees and employee groups perceive some potential positive advantages to the diffusion of computerized monitoring of HCI throughout virtual workplace environments. Griffith (1993b) reported that some computerized monitoring systems were considered both helpful and satisfying by monitored employees (George 1996).

In an interesting justification for monitoring, Ehrlich (1993, 5) states, "the increasing reliance on new technologies in the American workplace has led to a real need for employers to monitor their employee's use of these technologies." Ehrlich continues: "Through the use of electronic technology, American companies are able to guarantee their customers receive a quality good or service in a timely manner. They are also better able to enhance employee safety, protect employer and employee property, improve accounting efficiency, provide perquisites and benefits to employees, enhance employee convenience and prevent fraud" (Ehrlich 1993).

Computerized performance monitoring can diminish the influence of personal biases in the assessment of the work performance of an individual or group. A computer-monitored employee interviewed by Grant and Higgins (1991b) observed that evaluation of performance by computer is much better than by a human supervisor. The computer has no feelings and evaluates only on the basis of performance. A CPM system is not biased racially, sexually, or emotionally, and the data collected and used for the performance appraisal is purely objective (Miezio 1992, 11). The computer is not aware of, or interested in, religious and political affiliations, sexual preferences, and other personal traits that may subtly influence how one person evaluates the performance of another. Most computerized monitoring systems have an almost monomaniacal fixation on performance and outcomes.

Another possible advantage of CPM over human performance measurement is that it can provide immediate, objective feedback (Aiello and Kolb 1995b). The value of open access by the monitored employee to the data is not self-evident. At the fifth company participating in the George (1996, 474) study, employees were able to access their performance statistics on their computers, and compare them with those of other workers. Despite this open access to CPM data, 20 percent of the 77 respondents to a questionnaire indicated that they were either not very satisfied or not at all satisfied with the way work is measured by computer. If feedback is not supplied immediately, it can be provided in a delayed fashion with greater frequency. For example, an employee may wish to check his performance as measured by the computer on a self-selected, regular basis, such as first thing on Monday mornings, just before a break, or during e-mail viewing.

An employee at Toyota defended CPM as a morale boost. In many instances, computer monitoring increases morale and motivates the employee to do the best job possible (Laabs 1992, 102). Other commentators on CPM in work environments have noted that its use can make merit pay increases less capricious. Although in general Marx and Sherizen (1989, 404) are not keen on computerized monitoring, they do acknowledge that "some workers may welcome close monitoring when it is tied to a system of merit pay" (quoted in George 1996, 478).

Computerized performance monitoring can facilitate employee empowerment, if it is used to identify areas or skills of individual employees that need to be enhanced (Burger 1995). "In the long run, electronic monitoring will promote product quality (and workplace safety) only if it is designed in such a way that it feeds back collected data to those employees whose performance is being measured. Used in this way electronic monitoring becomes a form of empowerment" (Bewayo 1996, 196). If safeguards are built into a computer-monitored appraisal process, workers can become both more satisfied and more efficient (Angel 1989). Kidwell and Bennett (1994) found that positive feedback, frequent feedback, the extent of supervisor consideration, and the extent to which employees felt the evaluation process to be fair were all positively associated with employee satisfaction with CPM (George 1996, 462).

Whether imagined or real, the list of possible disadvantages of computerized monitoring for employees is quite long. Research on this issue, however, is relatively sparse, and it tends to rely heavily on the self-reports of monitored employees.

George (1996), for example, focused his study on four issues related to computerized monitoring: employee attitudes, trade-offs between quality and quantity of job performance, stress-related illnesses, and employee perceptions of supervision.

The widespread sense that the use of CPM in work environments increases employee stress is perhaps the most important negative effect of the use of technology for this purpose. The case of Harriet Ternipsede may be the most celebrated instance in which a computerized monitored employee (an airline reservations agent) suffered an emotional breakdown, allegedly because of the monitoring system (George 1996, 463). Researchers have had a difficult time establishing a clear link between CPM and stress, because often many stress producers exist in a work environment (Baarda 1994, 7). In the OTA study (1987, 51), however, many monitored workers reported higher levels of stress because of computerized monitoring. There seems to be some empirical evidence to support the theoretical assumption that electronic monitoring techniques can alter the basic dimensions of the work experience, thus producing or increasing stress (Smith et al. 1992, 17). A survey of 762 telecommunications workers revealed that monitored employees reported feeling significantly more tension, fatigue, anxiety, anger, and depression than employees not subject to computerized monitoring. (Smith et al. 1992, cited in Aiello and Kolb 1995b, 166). The research conducted by George (1996, 477), however, led him to conclude that the relationships between CPM and stress-related illnesses were not simple and causally deterministic.

Throughout the 1980s skeptics of the causal link between computerized monitoring and increased worker stress pointed out that although the belief was widespread that computerized monitoring makes a job more stressful, there still exists no scientifically-substantiated, causal link between computer monitoring and stress (Ottensmeyer and Heroux 1991). Laboratory research conducted in the 1990s, however, has tended to confirm the hypothesis of a causal link. Aiello and Shao (1993) found that computer-monitored participants in a laboratory setting obtained significantly higher scores on Speilberger's State Anxiety Scale (Aiello and Kolb 1995b, 166). Chomiak, Kolb, and Aiello (1993) used a laboratory setting to reveal that even with opportunities for social support, demands for productivity, and perceptions of control held constant, computer-monitored respondents reported feeling more stress than respondents in the control group.

Some commentators have argued that privacy is a reasonable expectation even in work environments. Electronic performance monitoring does not so much invade that workplace privacy; it makes it difficult or impossible to attain. When the computer functions as both work partner and performance monitor, the employee has no sense of privacy. Aiello and Kolb (1995b, 163) note that although employees expect to have their work performance somehow examined and evaluated by their employers, CPM extends the pervasiveness of observation and the degree of concealment used to obtain performance data. Computerized monitoring of work performance, however, is not very pervasive in the sense of a broad range of data being collected. It is more persistent than pervasive. With computerized monitoring of HCI, performance monitoring has been extended into the realm of the non-human. Now the employee needs to worry not only about what one's supervisor and co-workers think of one's performance, but also about how one's computer workstation itself perceives and records one's performance.

Employees and employee groups often are wary of CPM because computer monitoring focuses on quantity rather than quality. Thus service to customers may suffer in monitored environments, along with teamwork and the quality of work life. Through the use of CPM and other techniques, human labor is being increasingly quantified and benchmarked.

Other disparagers of CPM argue that the technique is better for simple tasks than complex ones. Angel (1989) admits that, whereas at present computer monitoring is being used to assess performance of data-entry tasks, in the future, characterized by distributed processing and telecommuters, it will be more difficult to use computer monitoring to assess higher-level computerized work, because many of these tasks are not as well-defined as data-entry work. Although CPM is very accurate in what it measures, it measures a relatively small number of tasks, thus producing, by itself, an incomplete picture of the overall performance and worth of the employee for the evaluation period.

In the George (1996) study of five companies engaged in CPM and phone call monitoring (also known as service observation), in general most respondents to a questionnaire were less dissatisfied with computerized monitoring than they were with phone monitoring. It may be that they saw computerized collection of performance data as less intrusive and upsetting than the lurking knowledge that, periodically or randomly, some human supervisor was listening in on the service telephone calls between an operator and a customer.

The use of computerized monitoring to set and monitor production quotas may result in a decreased sense of the employee's control over the job task and work environment. If employees are expected to work at a uniform rate established and enforced by the computerized monitoring module, they may sense a loss of control over the ability to modify the pace of work depending on other factors (Aiello and Kolb 1995b, 168). Computerized monitoring can be used to homogenize the process of working with computers. The managerial focus of attention can shift from a relatively pure attention to outcomes to a major interest in uniformity of process, not only among workers but also within the working life of an individual.

Computerized performance monitoring also can pit worker against worker. At least one CPM program has been reported to inform lower-productivity workers that they are not working as fast as the persons sitting next to them (Fogel 1987, 13). CPM can lead to an unhealthy, divisive, heightened sense of competition in the workplace. Holton Simon, an airline reservation agent, was quoted as observing that the focus of electronic monitoring is on policing rather than teaching and helping staff. Group computerized monitoring merely replaces the pain of discipline from management with the sting of peer pressure (Papp 1991).

The long-term effects of the introduction of CPM into online work environments are equally troubling. Ccomputerized performance monitoring could lead to a decline in employee morale and job satisfaction for a number of reasons, including unrealistic production standards or goals and an overemphasis on quantity of work performed, coupled with a declining emphasis on quality of service (Lund 1989, 109). Computerized monitoring systems are being used to destroy the individuality, creativity, and spontaneity of workers (Larter 1984). Employees working in a computerized monitoring environment may feel that, overall, the work environment has become less human and more machine-driven and technological. Supervision by another person need not necessarily be perceived by the worker as threatening and stressful. Simply as a form of human contact, it can be warm and reassuring.

Amick and Smith (1992) suggest that computerized monitoring may increase an employee's stress because it reduces the need or opportunity for the employee to receive social support from co-workers (cited in Aiello and Kolb 1995b, 167). Aiello (1993) found that because more workers are learning that most of the information they need to perform their jobs is available through the computer system, they report feeling lonely at work. The very knowledge on the part of employees that a computerized monitoring system has been introduced into their work environment may subtly change their basic sense of that work environment. Aiello and Kolb (1995b, 168) speculate that even though the objective conditions of the work environment do not change, the introduction of computerized monitoring may influence an employee's perceptions of it.

"The biggest drawback of electronic monitoring systems," writes one critic, "is that they can make employees feel helpless, manipulated, and exploited" (Barner 1996, 16–17). Nussbaum (1989) also argues that the basic rights of employees are compromised by computerized monitoring, including the right to know that one's behavior is being monitored, the right to privacy, the right to due process, and the right to health and dignity.

The risk of real-world physical injury could increase after the introduction of CPM systems. After the introduction of laser scanners in check-out lanes in grocery stores and other retail establishments, the rate of repetitive motion disorders increased dramatically, due to the combined factors of pressure to work faster, improper training, and poorly designed equipment (Boss is watching 1993).

The introduction of computerized monitoring into a work environment also can produce a fundamental change for the worse in employees' views of management. Some employees may feel or conclude that, in some fundamental way, management has abdicated its responsibilities to the overall production process. Computerized monitoring makes the vital management function surly and jaded. "Monitoring is the ultimate expression of lack of trust. Supervisors don't trust their workers to do their jobs. Workers don't trust their supervisors to be fair. Upper level management doesn't trust lower level management to handle basic supervision" (Nussbaum 1989, 4). "Surveillance and control now take the place of supervision, commitment, and training" (Nussbaum 1989, 2). George (1996) presents five interesting case studies on this issue. Rick Broadbend, a Canadian author on Internet topics, has said that monitoring the Web activities of employees is not the best way to foster a good, trusting relationship between employees and an employer (Meckbach 1997).

Computerized performance monitoring can have a negative effect on managers as well. Because computerized monitoring can produce large quantities of data, and because, especially with older computerized monitoring software, emphasis goes on data collection rather than data analysis, supervisors may experience increased stress as they sift through this additional data to provide better performance appraisals. Bewayo (1996, 187) argues that excessive electronic monitoring causes more serious problems in small businesses than in large businesses.

Botan (1996, 308–309) found that employees who were subjected to electronic surveillance at work experienced several panoptic effects, including a sense of reduced privacy, increased uncertainty, and reduced communication with supervisors and fellow employees. Production and interaction are two key components of a worker's performance. Although CPM tends to focus on production, the use of a CPM system can affect the interaction component of performance (Grant 1990, 8–9).

Several critics of CPM have pointed out a fundamental flaw in the method: It measures the wrong thing, or it measures in the wrong way. Pounsett (1989) seems to see computerized performance monitoring as the second generation of Taylor's time and motion studies. The electronic interface between the employee operator and the machine allows the employer to capture and analyze precise information about the employee's performance. Pounsett cautions that speed is deceptively easy to measure, while assessment of actual effectiveness on the job is much more difficult. Stuart Millar, a management consultant at Peat Marwick Stevenson and Kellogg, suggests that good managers use computerized monitoring as a tool, not as a whip (Papp 1991).

According to Westin (1992) the difference between Europeans and Americans over monitoring revolves around different attitudes toward individualism: "This difference reflects the more individualistic orientation of American white collar workers (even those that are represented by unions); their concern over supervisor favoritism and subjectivity under purely observational evaluations; and their penchant for individual 'due-process' protections" (Westin 1992, 39). It is interesting and potentially worthwhile to speculate about what may happen to human individuality in the more mature computerized monitoring environments of the future. On the positive side, computerized monitoring may enable the environment itself to treat the individual as unique — or at least as a unique conglomeration and expression of interests and behavior. In a computerized monitoring environment the individual need not be treated as an undifferentiated member of a large group, or even of a demographically homogeneous smaller group. The individual also will play an active role in articulating a personalized online environment. In the real world, we are what we eat (or, more generally, consume). In the online world, we are what we do and where we go in cyberspace.

Other ways of using computers to monitor HCI in work environments are beginning to emerge. Sherman and Judkins (1996) proposed an employment rationing system to be implemented with computerized identity cards that measure a worker's annual allotment of work hours. The cards continuously monitor how many work hours remain in the year for each person. In this HCI in work environments has become a precious commodity, and computers monitor the dispersal of this precious interaction.

The literature on CPM also covers the experiences of specific companies with CPM programs. When Air Canada introduced CPM in 1977, it was presented as a quality of work life improvement initiative (Baarda 1994, 19). In the late 1980s Bell CORE (a division of AT&T, based in New Jersey) was developing an expert system upgrade to their computerized monitoring system to further enhance productivity measurement and employee development (Lund 1989, 65). The system under development was a knowledge-based expert system intended to automate analysis of operator productivity reports, to provide managers another operator evaluation and feedback tool (Lund 1989, 69). Bylinsky (1991) found that when General Electric implemented a customer service monitoring system that emphasized the quality of the performance of operators, while de-emphasizing the quantity of calls handled, the satisfaction of both employees and customers rose (Aiello and Kolb 1995b, 170). Toyota focused its monitoring efforts on the quality of service provided to customers. When the monitoring system was implemented, employee morale rose, and several employees asked to be monitored more frequently (Laabs 1992; cited in Aiello and Kolb 1995b, 170). With the relatively recent release of the Web into online work environments, the 6,000 Internet-using employees at National Semiconductor are monitored randomly to ensure that they are not visiting adult-oriented Web sites while on the job (Martin 1997).

Computer monitoring is not used exclusively to measure the performance of rank and file employees. Although computer monitoring often is associated with production and clerical tasks, Nussbaum found that even in the early 1980s approximately 13 to 15 percent of managers may have been subjected to computer monitoring (Grant and Higgins 1991a, 116). In an organization using computerized monitoring techniques, the supervisor has as little control as the employee being monitored. If the supervisor is rewarded for the productivity of the unit, as measured by CPM, the supervisor is being monitored indirectly (Miezio 1992, 14).

One of the most active groups on the topic of computerized performance monitoring has been 9 to 5: the National Association of Working Women, based in Cleveland, Ohio. Betts (1991) reports on calls to the Computer Spying Hotline, which enables VDT users to complain about supervisors' use of computer software that monitors keystrokes, errors, transactions, and breaks. The National Association of Working Women runs the hotline.

Although the National Association of Working Women appears to be concerned about all instances of computerized monitoring of computerized work environments, there is some evidence that there is a sexual imbalance built into the early decades of CPM. The labor performed by service workers has been an active target of computerized monitoring, and the majority of service workers are women. Silberger (1990) reports that as many as 85 percent of computer-monitored workers are females. Zahorik notes that computerized monitoring in work environments operates as de facto discrimination because primarily women work in the jobs typically subject to such monitoring (Westin, Marx, Zahorik, and Ware 1992).

Computerized performance monitoring also is becoming involved in online collaborative projects and online teamwork in general.

> It is our argument ... that the development and continued refinement of electronic surveillance systems using computer-based technology can provide the means by which management can achieve the benefits that derive from the delegation of responsibility to teams whilst retaining authority and disciplinary control through the ownership of the superstructure of surveillance and the information it collects, retains, and disseminates (Sewell and Wilkinson 1992, 283).

> The analysis of electronic monitoring that is derived from Foucault and Bentham's concept of the Panopticon places power in its rightful place at the center of the debate. The use of surveillance is a fundamental means by which the employer inexpensively and effectively exercises power. The beauty of the electronic Panopticon is the cooption of the worker into the very system that is used to administer control and discipline. Management trends such as "work teams" and "Total Quality Management" are primarily means to more effectively run a capitalist enterprise. Feedback of information gathered from monitoring allows workers to compare themselves to others, to be notified of their place in the hierarchy, to judge their performance against the objective rules and standards determined by the business. This provides for a convenient means to further inculcate the values of the organization into the worker. In contrast, the placing of real power over the direction and principles of the business into the hands of the employee would be a revolutionary act, which would undermine the entire rationale of American business (Levy 1993).

Computerized monitoring need not necessarily focus on the work-related performance of individuals. Analysis of group online behavior may be more useful and less stressful to the individuals involved. Studies by Aiello, DeNisi, Kirkhoff, Shao, Lund, and Chomiak (1991) and by Kolb and Aiello (1993) found that, when the production statistics of work-groups were electronically accumulated and reported, participants felt less stress (Aiello and Kolb 1995b, 170).

There are effective, humane ways to introduce CPM programs into work environments. Baarda (1994) articulates several of them. One should carefully and deliberately choose the tasks to be monitored. Computerized performance monitoring programs that measure the most important and appropriate tasks are likely to be accepted as fair (Aiello and Kolb 1995b, 170). One should also consider the subjects and recipients of CPM; monitor regularly; correctly attribute performance to individuals or groups; supplement the monitoring data with data or observations on the quality of the work performed; place equal importance on quantitative and qualitative performance factors; provide mechanisms for employee participation in designing, testing, implementing, assessing, and improving the CPM program; train supervisors and managers how to interpret and apply CPM data; explicitly demonstrate the role and rationale of the CPM program for the entire organization; and keep electronic monitoring in perspective.

Some utilitarian arguments lurk behind the issue of using computer monitoring in the workplace, especially to monitor the performance of workers. Proponents of such computer monitoring often do not deny that there are some drawbacks to it, but they assert that the benefits outweigh the potential negative consequences. This may be a subtle variation on the basic utilitarian argument: That which produces the greatest good for the greatest number of people is good. Because the client population usually outnumbers by far the worker population for a company using computerized monitoring, the potential negative consequences for the workers do not carry much weight in this construction of the argument in favor of the practice.

Compared to users in other computer monitoring environments (learners, seekers of information, and shoppers), do workers have special rights as users in computer monitoring situations? Few people argue that learners in formal learning environments, users of online public access information systems, and browsers and shoppers on the Web have a right to be party to the design, implementation, and administration of computer monitoring programs. This differs from the assertion of the right to be informed that one's behavior is being monitored by computer. Employees in computer monitoring situations in the workplace, however, may have an unusually strong argument for the right to be included in the development and deployment of the program itself, beyond their obvious role as subjects. Employee involvement in the design, testing, implementation, and continuing adjustment of CPM is crucial (Baarda 1994, executive summary).

The controversy over the use of CPM in the workplace sends us back to fundamental questions about the inalienable, residual rights of both managers and employees. What measures and monitoring methods can a business use to ensure that it receives an honest day's work in return for an honest wage?

The use of computerized monitoring in work environments can improve efficiency (and perhaps lower costs) in at least two ways: by increasing the efficient use of work-time by employees, and by increasing the efficient pursuit of supervision. Perhaps the second gain is the main one. Traditional supervisory techniques are expensive and inefficient. Barner (1996) predicts that over the next ten years there will be a dramatic increase in the use of computerized systems to accelerate employee learning, augment decision making, and monitor performance.

Westin, Marx, Zahorik, and Ware (1992) suggest that it is a dangerous time for new technological applications such as computerized workplace monitoring, because the workplace is a societal area undergoing profound change, value conflicts, and tension among competing interests. The undesirable consequences of computerized monitoring in the workplace may be subtle and long-term. Any healthy social environment is based on a substantial amount of trust, and CPM may lead to a decline of trust in work environments. Botan (1996, 302) observes that electronic surveillance serves as a kind of meta-communication that tells employees that the employer does not trust them. The right to privacy and respect is at the core of the employee monitoring issue (Gorman 1998, 23). "Issues of ethics and privacy are important to consider when looking at ECS [electronic control systems] through the organism perspective because they are non-economic factors which have an impact on satisfying basic needs" (Kidwell and Kidwell 1997, 95). Future research involving computerized monitoring in work environments should determine whether employee opposition to computerized monitoring encompasses all types of monitoring in work environments, or if it is system specific (Kidwell and Kidwell 1997).

Monitoring Consumer Behavior From one perspective, the project to use computers to monitor workplace behavior seems to be doomed to atrophy. Already in the late 1990s we may be witnessing a profound but gradual shift from monitoring employees to monitoring consumers. In the long run, better knowledge of the demand and preferences and coupling of goods and services will be more useful than better knowledge of how to meet that demand efficiently. Using computerized monitoring to study consumer behavior will become much more important than using it to study employee behavior. Business managers and supervisors are not in danger of turning into little generalissimos, at least not because of computerized monitoring, but rather into analysts of systems so large and pervasive that they become full-fledged environments. And eventually these systems and environments will analyze themselves and all that they contain.

Consumer behavior on the Web and other virtual environments remains largely unknown. Koprowski (1997) notes that the behavior of Web surfers is influenced as much by frustration as it is by gratification. The second generation Web analysis software uses sophisticated Java visualization techniques to report on both content requested and network delivery and performance.

It is amazing how much computerized monitoring focuses on the human body. It can reveal where the body is, either really or virtually. It can study what the body is doing. Much of the behavioral data collected concerns hand and finger movement — mouse clicks, keyboarding, and typographical errors. Sophisticated computerized monitoring also may be able to reveal other aspects of the body, including sex and age. Computerized monitoring is the logical progression and refinement of the drive to inspect and regulate that emerged with the Enlightenment. "The meticulousness of the regulations, the fussiness of the inspections, the supervision of the smallest fragment of life and the body will soon provide, in the context of the school, the barracks, the hospital or the workshop, a laicized content, an economic or technical rationality for this mystical calculus of the infinitesimal and the infinite" (Foucault 1977, 140).

Data mining is the practice of creating software programs that autonomously search data, not for information about individuals, but for groups and group patterns (Eisenberg 1996). Data mining algorithms can detect commercially meaningful patterns in extremely large veins of information (Agre 1997, 3). From the vantage point of a data miner, the human behavior on the Internet is the mother lode. Perhaps computerized monitoring is best understood as a form of data mining. Cohen (1997a) notes that data mining is a relatively new term that refers to analyzing audience responses to Web pages or online classified advertisements to identify meaningful trends. A simple example of data mining would be generating a numerical comparison of the click-throughs elicited by two different versions or placements of a banner ad for the same product or service.

Data mining in cyberspace, like mining in the real world, can be a great value-adding venture or a foolish, ugly, destructive blunder, depending on its execution. The metaphor of data as a resource that is like coal always there (at least in the human sense of time) waiting to be mined does not shed much light on what computerized monitoring is all about. Although in the early years of computerized monitoring the data often were collected and stored long before their analysis and application, the future of computerized monitoring points to situations in which the data will be collected, analyzed, and applied almost instantaneously. Mannila, Toivonen, and Verkamo (1995) used data mining techniques on Web server logs to discover frequent episodes. Chen, Park, and Yu (1996) proposed the measurement of maximal forward reference as a way to extract meaningful sequences from user access logs.

Most computer monitoring attempts to better understand the normal behavior of the general user population of the system being studied, be they learners, seekers, workers, or shoppers. There are potential applications, however, that seek to detect extreme deviations of behavior, unauthorized or unlawful intruders, and violators of system security or integrity. These applications go far beyond the detection and analysis of slow learners, inefficient searchers of information, workers with low productivity, and inefficient or illogical shoppers. People who use computer monitoring for these purposes want to detect hackers, lawbreakers, and the pathological.

Computerized performance monitoring programs also have been used to attempt to modify the behavior of the monitored employees. Increasingly, computers set tasks and performances for all levels of worker (Levy 1993). Formal education is perhaps the most recognizable form of behavior modification. Other critics may argue that the primary purpose of formal education is not behavior modification, but the transmission of knowledge, or socialization, or acculturation. Some computerized monitoring software can flash subliminal messages on computer screens informing clerical workers that their work pace has slowed unacceptably (Marx and Sherizen 1986b, cited in Ottensmeyer and Heroux 1991, 519).

Computerized monitoring can also facilitate human learning, not only in obvious, formal situations, but in all instances involving human interaction with computers and computer systems. For example, Santos (1995) attempted to determine how to use computerized monitoring to facilitate user transitionality, defined as the progress users make from novices to experts. Santos hypothesized that the observable behavior of computer users is influenced by their knowledge and the "chunks" they form, with a chunk as the basic unit of information held in one's working memory. The size and contents of chunks, expressed in bursts of activity, indicate the user's expertise at a particular task (Santos 1995, 3). Santos' doctoral research introduces a method for automatically identifying a user's goals and knowledge about a computer system solely by computerized analysis of the user's interaction with the system. Santos is confident he can infer goals and knowledge from the analysis of observed behavior. His emphasis on the facilitation of human learning and transition to higher-level chunks seems to be an attempt to avoid the coming slowdown or even stasis in human learning, when computerized monitoring becomes so sophisticated that it can modify virtual environments to meet the needs (as expressed by behavior) of a user. Santos (1995, 25) is interested in aspects of human behavior that change over time due to learning. We must at least entertain the competing hypothesis that if the user's virtual environment changes over time based on a computerized analysis of the observed behavior, the mutability of the environment will cause the user's behavior and learning to reach a plateau, because the virtual environment validates the behavior to a greater extent than do real environments. In general, the tension between applying the results of computerized monitoring studies to improve the user interface and applying the results in the form of user edcation has been keenly felt in the computerized monitoring field, especially in its application to information-seeking environments. For example, Miller, Kirby, and Templeton (1988) suggested that improvements to the CD-ROM computer system would increase search success far more than improvements in instructional programs for the system users.

A critical question for the entire field of computerized monitoring concerns the role and value of human learning in virtual environments. As the human race enters cyberspace, the value of such learning no longer is self-evident and beyond question. Human learning in real-world environments is valuable primarily because the environments are complex and fundamentally intractable. If people are going to survive and flourish at both individual and social levels in real environments, they need to learn. To survive in nature, humanity has engaged in a long process of learning the laws of nature, and how to mold its actions to maximize the return on behavior in this lawful environment. In cyberspace there are no laws of nature beyond those establishing the horizon of the possible. As increasingly sentient environments, through the use of computerized monitoring and other tools, learn how to learn from experience, the human race is entering a contest to prove which type of learning — human or machine — is more efficacious and thus more valuable. Although I would not bet against the human race in that competition, I am willing to bet that the competition will be keen and the outcome uncertain. Because human dolts in a sentient online environment will not fare as poorly as dolts in real environments, the value of human learning and guile will need to be reasserted and reaffirmed.

Hildreth (1997) has noticed the emergence of a large population of dolts in cyberspace — specifically, in information seeking environments. He worries that the danger of easy-to-use online catalogs that perform implicit Boolean searches is that they are heavily used by many searchers who apparently have little understanding of how these bibliographic retrieval systems process the keyword and Boolean searches submitted to them. We need to build on this observation and ask: What purpose would increased understanding of behind-the-scenes computer processing have in these emerging virtual environments? Although our ingrained real-world sensibilities might scoff at the very posing of this question, in virtual environments, if we shed all of our preconceived notions and expectations carried over from our experiences in real-world environments, this question is vital.

In virtual environments with sophisticated computerized monitoring systems, the monitored themselves may appropriate the monitoring function. The electronic surveillance of today engenders self-discipline and anticipatory conformity, rather than mere external management control (Lyon 1994, 135). Building on the work of Foucault (1979), Levy (1993) notes that the workers, prisoners, soldiers or students in a panoptic environment are not only transformed by observation, but also internalize the values of the overseeing organization and become elements in their own repression. The system of surveillance relies only on an inspecting gaze, under the weight of which everyone surveyed will eventually interiorize to the point that one becomes one's own overseer. Everyone thus exercises surveillance over and against oneself (Foucault 1980, 155).

The visibility of the worker or performer certainly has the power to induce conforming behavior. Psychologically there is the risk of shame and humiliation in the ever visible environment. Zuboff (1988) describes the results as anticipatory conformity: "The behavioral expectations of the observer can be so keenly anticipated by the observed that the foreknowledge of visibility is enough to induce conformity to those normative standards" (Zuboff 1988, 345).

Applications of computerized monitoring of HCI that focus on people themselves often develop a "user model" to make sense of the human role in these new environments. A user model contains explicit assumptions about the relevant characteristics of an individual user, such as preferences and interests, domain knowledge, and physical, sensory, and cognitive abilities. Except for information available a priori, such as information about the real-world environment of a specific terminal, most information in a usage model is collected at the time of use, either directly by monitoring file transfers or indirectly through statistical methods such as regression analysis (Fink, Kobsa, and Schreck 1997, 461).

The applications of computerized monitoring of HCI data that focus on people themselves has a definite Rubicon. Should computerized monitoring be used to examine or infer aspects of human lives that have little or nothing to do with HCI? Marketers and demographers, for example, are interested in Web server log analysis not primarily for what it can tell us about how visitors to a Web site behave, but for what demographic and psychographic profiles can be inferred from the usage data.

Applications Focusing on the Computer System or Network   Another set of applications of computerized monitoring data focuses on the computer system itself. The goal often is to ensure that the system is operating properly, efficiently, and without security compromises. System-centered applications also can yield system modifications and enhancements that are based on known historical patterns of system use, rather than on other criteria. Sometimes the use of computers to monitor the functioning and behavior of a computer system or network becomes so focused on the system that the human behavior becomes almost irrelevant. The proposal made by Chen, Liu, Want, Samalam, Procanik, and Kavouspour (1996) to use computerized monitoring to control ATM networks is an example of a computerized monitoring system with very little interest in the human side of HCI. Some businesses and corporations have begun monitoring employee use of Internet and intranet resources not so much to learn more about or control their half acre of HCI, but to learn more about bandwidth demands placed on the system so they can managed it better.

A frequent conclusion drawn from computerized monitoring studies is that the interface needs to be changed and improved. Often this conclusion is arrived at in a pre-reflective manner, and it seems to be based on the assumption that it is simpler and cheaper to change the computer system and interface than to educate users or modify their behavior. After studying users of an online catalog in an academic library, Hildreth (1997) concluded that improving the design of online catalogs based on design models that more closely reflect information-seeking behavior is more practical and attainable than improving the training and instruction methods and programs for users.

In another example of system-centric computerized monitoring projects, Braun and Claffy (1994) analyzed two days of queries to the NCSA Mosaic server to study the geographic distribution of transaction requests. They argue that the wide geographic diversity of query sources should cause server managers to deploy geographically distributed caching mechanisms to improve server and network efficiency. They conclude that operational geographic analyses of queries to library and archival servers will be fundamental to the effective evolution of the Web.

Even substantial improvements to Web client software have been identified with computerized monitoring. Tauscher and Greenberg (1997, 130) found that the best Web browser history display method evaluated was context-sensitive Web sub-spaces. Using that method, the Web browser software itself, using a set of only ten URLs, was able to predict successfully 53 percent of all URL selections made by the Web browsing subjects.

Computerized monitoring of HCI also can detect intrusion. Intrusion detection finds system security violations by identifying abnormal system usage (Lam, Hui, and Chung 1996). The system monitors users' activities, analyzes the data to recognize users' typical behavior, then looks for deviant behavior. Intrusion detection rests on the assumption that because users of a computer system perform typical activities that cluster into behavioral norms, security violations can be detected on the basis of abnormal system usage (Lam, Hui, and Chung 1996). To pursue intrusion detection in this manner, the systems operator or manager first needs to determine the typical activities evident in normal system use. This involves monitoring all users, or at least a statistically reliable sampling of users and their use. One major challenge of this technique is that general monitoring mechanisms tend to generate massive volumes of monitoring data (Lam, Hui, and Chung 1996). Detecting intruders is akin to grabbing the motes in a wind tunnel. Subjects (i.e., the system users) initiate actions on objects in the monitored system. Activity profiles can be defined for individual subject-object pairs, or for aggregated subjects and objects (Lam, Hui, and Chung 1996).

One interesting aspect of the techniques of intrusion detection is the ability to identify and isolate components of HCI that best characterize user behavior. Determining what activities and statistical measures provide the best discriminating power is challenging (Lam, Hui, and Chung 1996). Another important aspect of intrusion detection is the system operator's desire and ability to develop use profiles for specific, potentially identifiable individuals. Intrusion detection is designed to identify and catch culprits, not merely to determine, for example, that one in a thousand users exhibits hacking behaviors. In one intrusion detection system, once a user's behavior has been identified as a potential intrusion, records of the current session as well as past records of the specific, individual user in the log files can be combined and displayed graphically for inspection by the system operator (Lam, Hui, and Chung 1996). In the real world, this would be like the police calling up files on specific individuals while observing them committing a suspected crime.

Applications Focusing on the Interaction Itself Applications that focus on HCI may be the purest type of application. Interaction-based research concerns primarily the event itself, more so than what the individuals or computer systems bring to (or take away from) the search sessions. Within the movement to use computers to study HCI, we may be witnessing a gradual shift in attention to the interaction itself. A fundamental change in evaluation goals for a computer monitoring project or program is the shift in emphasis from the output or product of the search to emphasis on the process of the search itself (Borgman, Hirsh, and Hiller 1996, 571). At this point, such applications may be only theoretical. They would focus on the event or cluster of events that we describe as HCI. The ability to study online searching behavior in all its complexity requires data collection and analysis methods able to capture the details and intricacies of the search process itself, rather than the product, output, or outcome of an HCI session (Borgman, Hirsh, and Hiller 1996, 580).

This application line raises an interesting philosophical question: What is the relationship between a computer network system and use of the system? Does the system configuration primarily drive and shape the methods and patterns of use? That relationship seems to be the historical precedent. Computer monitoring, however, may be able to reverse the historical conditions that find people more or less molding their behavior to match the system configuration, so that the system self-corrects and improves itself based on one's previous personal behavior. One potential danger with this scenario, however, is that the idea of a present environment that perfectly incorporates one's personal history actually may retard one's future growth and development. The long-term trend of this application line on human development (both individually and in the aggregate) could be deleterious. If we see the present real world as history made manifest, we recognize the present manifestation was driven mainly by others, not by one personally. If monitoring of networked computer environments comes to such fruition, the present as a cluster of historical influences made manifest may become almost solely one's own, not some group's. If online activity becomes a bigger part of all human activity, this change in the way people perceive the present environment could have a profound affect on their attitudes toward and dealings with others.

Vinge (1993) presents intelligence amplification (IA) as an alternative to artificial intelligence (AI). The design and use of information systems (particularly computerized information systems) represents an increase or extension over natural human intelligence. Every time our ability to access information and communicate it to others is enhanced by improvements to computer networks and human-computer interfaces, in some sense we have achieved an increase over natural intelligence (Vinge 1993, 92). IA may allow us to participate in a kind of transcendence (Vinge 1993, 94).

"The notion of ego and self-awareness," writes Vinge, "has been the bedrock of the hardheaded rationalism of the last few centuries.... Intelligence Amplification undercuts our concept of ego.... The post–Singularity world will involve extremely high-bandwidth networking. A central feature of strongly superhuman entities will likely be their ability to communicate at variable bandwidths, including ones far higher than speech or written messages" (Vinge 1993, 95).

In a more practical line of computerized monitoring research that focused on the interaction itself, Siochi's research (1989) used transaction logs to explore the use of the repetition indicator as a way to evaluate the user interface in software programs. Siochi hypothesized that repetitive user actions are important indicators of potential problems with the user interface.

Applications Focusing on the Virtual Environment   The mutability of the virtual environment is the issue. The normalized center will not hold. Rather than mold the individual to fit the common, intractable environment, the environment will be personalized to match the individual and the observed behavior of individuals and groups. The most profound and longest lasting outcome of the entire project to use computers to monitor HCI may be the realization that in cyberspace it is much easier to change the look, feel, and performance of an online environment than to attempt to mold or directly alter human behavior. If the changed environment leads to changes in human behavior, the environment will simply modify itself again. The real danger in this scenario is that the environmental changes themselves may take on a normative intent. The formal educational system has been attempting this for centuries, but the idea that computer systems would appropriate this project makes mere mortals wary.

Computerized monitoring projects that focus on the online environment itself create some interesting conundrums about how we understand such environments. An online environment is any sense of a space-time continuum that HCI creates in the mind. A database could be considered a primitive environment. Computerized monitoring allows analysts to examine in detail how a database (defined provisionally as an organized collection of records or files) is used during HCI. The emergence of Web server logs has given a tremendous boost to applications focusing on databases and environments, rather than on the people, the computers, or the interaction itself as a cluster of behaviors and events. "The process of reflecting on [Web site] traffic statistics and making content and structural changes to your web site based on those statistics is a little bit science, a little bit voodoo, and a whole lot of guesswork. In short, it's highly subjective, nebulous, and even more situational" (Stout 1997, 88).

More than the act of computerized monitoring itself, the sense of being monitored in online environments created by cookie controversies and a widespread use of computerized monitoring affects one's mental model of the hospitality of online environments. Both real-world and online environments are human environments. Neither is necessarily more cold and hostile than the other. Computerized monitoring has a profound effect on the way a human environment is constituted and perceived. With the Web, we seem to have willed an environment in which inhabitants should expect to be openly monitored.

Applications Focusing on the Information Content The information content within an online environment could be thought of as the inert substratum of the environment. An appropriate real-world analogy might be the role books play in a library environment. It is difficult or impossible to have a library without books, but books alone do not constitute a library. In addition to focusing on the people, the computers, the interaction itself, and the resulting online environments involved in HCI, computerized monitoring also can focus specifically on the information content. In essence, computerized monitoring data can serve as a rich, relational form of circulation data. Although a detailed analysis of the shelf-browsing behavior of real library users is very difficult to execute, a variety of Web server log analysis software tools can easily reveal how individual visitors to the Web site browse and maneuver through the site, lingering over certain content files, ignoring individual stimuli or whole sections of the site, or backtracking in a seemingly unnecessarily redundant fashion.

Numerous computerized monitoring studies have focused on the analysis of the information content use within the site. These latent online environments are being designed so that, once they are actualized as true virtual environments through HCI, the computer monitoring system can study users interacting with information content. The digital delivery system between the University of Akron and Case Western Reserve University was designed to include extensive data collection facilities for monitoring user behavior as users interact with digitized periodical backfiles (Neff 1997). Dunn, Chisnell, Szak, and Sittig (1994) used a transaction logging module in a CD-ROM online environment to study at the journal title level the use of journal information content. Cooley, Mobasher, and Srivastava (1997) differentiated between information content Web pages and pages that serve more navigational purposes. They note that this classification scheme for Web content pages also depends on user needs and the situational context of use. What is merely a navigation page for one user may be a content page for another, or for the same user in another context.

Applications Focusing on the Organizations Involved Applications of computerized monitoring can focus on organizations, which in turn can be considered primarily as closed or open systems. The introduction of electronic surveillance can be considered in the framework of a new technology resulting from political processes within the organization (Kidwell and Kidwell 1996, 10). As a new source of information, a computerized monitoring system can contribute to organizational flexibility within turbulent and rapidly changing organizational climates (Kidwell and Kidwell 1996, 12). The challenge for the organization as a whole is how to incorporate computerized monitoring projects and practices into the overall management practices and policies of the real organization. Often this inability or fumbling of the incorporation of computerized monitoring into the overall organization is a major focus of the concerns expressed by critics of such monitoring, especially in work environments. The outcomes of the data analyses are poorly understood and applied by the organization as a whole. The disagreements between organizational management and employees about the value, efficacy, and validity of CPM in the workplace could stem from conflicting view of the role of organizations in society (Kidwell and Kidwell 1996, 8).

Machine pacing serves as an example. The use of computerized monitoring to enforce machine pacing of work-related tasks must be considered an application that focuses on the organization, rather than on the human being, the computer system, or the interaction itself. Machine pacing is not an instance of the computer molding the interface to better meet the needs and capabilities of the user. Because most computers twiddle their thumbs waiting for users to make the next move during an interactive session, it would be in the best interest of the computer to speed up the interaction, but that is not why machine pacing is employed. Machine pacing usually involves an attempt to achieve some organizational objective (e.g., a production or service goal) that is extraneous to the HCI.

The long-term impact of a computerized monitoring program on an organization can be profound. Stanton (1994) cautions organizations to be careful and deliberate in their use of CPM systems:

> Organizations that choose computer monitoring must consider carefully the consequences of various supervisor-subordinate interfaces. The design of a computer monitoring system clearly impacts both psychological states and "hard" measures such as work rate variability and productivity. Systems that give supervisors monitoring flexibility and the "element of surprise" may reduce subordinates' feelings of personal control. This reduction may in turn decrease subordinates' performance and/or cause performance to become more variable (38).

Computer monitoring can involve applications in pursuit of organizational management in business environments. As noted above, computerized monitoring in the workplace may be related to Taylorism and the scientific management movement. Computerized monitoring can complement other forms of employee monitoring. Of course, computerized monitoring in the context of production also has been used to monitor machine-computer interaction, but that topic is beyond the scope of this book. Scientific management involves three processes: controlling and evaluating what employees do from moment to moment so that costs can be accurately counted, integrating this information with a detailed control of production, and planning and monitoring production by means of new central management staff (Lyon 1994, 124). Holding on to the means of surveillance is the only remaining basis of power of managers over their workers (Lyon 1994, 133). Computerized monitoring, when integrated with a self-regulating system, could lead to a decline in the need for human managers to perform certain tasks of work performance monitoring, interpretation, and correction. It may be possible to develop virtual work environments that, based on the results of sophisticated computerized monitoring systems, tailor themselves to the behavioral styles of the workers and the production needs.

A computerized monitoring research perspective focused on organizational learning would attempt to measure and understand the organizational role of a computerized monitoring system as a feedback mechanism, a reducer of uncertainty, a preserver of the integrity of data, and as a challenge to normal procedures (Kidwell and Kidwell 1997). Electronic control systems provide data that, when analyzed and applied, can reduce an organization's uncertainty and enhance organizational performance. If, however, such a system is designed and used only to detect errors, the two salutary outcomes will be limited (Kidwell and Kidwell 1997).

Applications Focusing on Business and Commercial Activity   The primary intended application of other computerized monitoring projects is in the arena of business and commercial activity. Buchanan and Lukaszewski (1997, 87) suggest that to measure the impact of a Web site, data probably will need to be collected from four sources: business measures, existing systems, the Web site itself, and the audience.

From this vantage, increased productivity has been a siren call. Computerization of work environments generally has not resulted in the predicted and anticipated productivity gains. Explanations for this lack of increased productivity are diverse and complex, but one recent theory is that more and more employees are spending more and more time on the job engaged in HCI that is not directly related to the business at hand. When Black & Decker's computerized monitoring showed that only 23 percent of the traffic going across the company's Internet connection was business-related, management sent out general notices urging people to use the Internet for business purposes. "Employee productivity is probably the major issue" in monitoring traffic, said IS manager Stephen Swam (Machlis 1997c). Swam called the Black & Decker case "a shocker."

Computerized monitoring also can lend itself to the business need for financial tracking. Believe it or not, libraries have begun to use computerized monitoring to track the financial aspects of information transfer. Neff (1997) reports that Case Western Reserve University and the University of Akron have formed a consortium to digitize and share scholarly journal articles. They developed a Rights Manager software system that monitors users' online behavior primarily to obtain the necessary permissions and financial information to complete the transfer of scientific journal articles from the server to a client.

Marketing agents argue that better, richer demographic information about consumers could lead to better focused marketing strategies. As marketing campaigns become more focused, either the number of marketing pitches the average person encounters will go down, or the marketing pitches will be so well-tailored to the target audience that the average interest level of individual members of the exposed audience will go up. Junk mail will become treasure mail, because the marketing plan will be so focused, as a result of computer monitoring, that the targeted consumer will truly be interested in the advertised product or service. Computer marketing could become so sophisticated and effective that, if something intrudes on one's consciousness, the system will be reasonably confident, based on one's previous behavior, of one's interest. Computerized monitoring programs this effective may be difficult to realize.

Using transaction information to try to influence consumer behavior is sometimes called social management (Mosco 1989, cited in Lyon 1994, 70). Transaction information can include credit card payments, ATM withdrawals, and browsing and shopping on the Web.

Randall (1997c) argues that the demand by companies that are creating Web sites for accountability and detailed analysis of return on investment is fueling the development of software that analyzes Web activity. Lamons (1997) also attributes the rapid development of Web server log analysis software to this primary cause.

Some businesses have begun to use computerized monitoring to verify compliance with acceptable use policies and practices. The monitored subjects in this application can include both employees and customers. For instance, the Fourll Web site for telephone directory white pages–type information monitors user activity to detect unusual behavior, such as downloading multiple addresses in sequence to create a mailing list (Dyson 1997b, 212).

Applications Intended for the Monitored   Few applications of data gathered with computerized monitoring are intended for those monitored. It is theoretically possible, however, for feedback from a computerized monitoring project to get back to the monitored immediately and individually. In the situation described in Marx and Sherizen (1987, 35), a computer-monitored worker is informed by the system that the next-door worker is working faster. Feedback to the monitored also can be delayed and aggregated. An example of delayed and translated feedback is the use of computerized monitoring to upgrade the user interface in subsequent versions of the interface software. It may stretch the limits of credulity, however, to assume that the monitored will understand an improved interface as feedback from analysis of computerized monitoring data. When computerized monitoring is used in Web environments, Bertot, McClure, Moen, and Rubin (1997) see it as an issue involving the effective, meaningful, and confidential presentation of Web usage statistics via the Web back to the monitored end-users. They understand Web server log file data as user-based measures of Web services. The cross-tabulation of various Web server log files would be both useful and informative to the monitored.

Applications Made by People versus Applications Made by Computers
Another way of examining the applications issue is to concentrate on who is making the application. The first distinction is between applications made by people and applications made by computers. Much of our discontent about the human application of computerized monitoring of HCI may center on the baseness of those applications. It all seems so tawdry and belittling. Collectively, we seem to be using a very powerful and clean data collection and analysis system to pursue very mundane applications. Human applications of the results of a computerized monitoring project often reveal the predispositions of the analysts. One analyst can look at a set of computerized monitoring data and decide that a complete overhaul of the user interface is required, while another may decide with equal rapidity that a major user education program will be needed.

Human analysis of computerized monitoring data often requires the analyst to sublimate the natural human impulse to interpret the world of observed events according to the good, the bad, and the ugly. Value judgments often creep into an analysis project during the application stage. Note the multiple value judgments in the following human analysis of the behavioral traces left by remote users of the MEDLINE database employing the CD Plus search engine: "Analysis of the data indicates that remote users misuse CD Plus in several significant ways. Author only or textword only searches are more the norm than the exception. In addition, searchers browse through too much information without applying appropriate limits" (Chisnell, Dunn, and Sittig 1994). The analysis is loaded with value-laden words, such as misuse, norm, too much, and appropriate. Analysis of transaction logs or other computerized monitoring data often is a consciousness-raising experience for the analysts themselves, as they suddenly confront their own preconceived notions of how HCI should work. In general, it is better to be frustrated by the lack of congruence between the analyst's sense of what should be happening and what the data indicate than to implicitly or explicitly impose the analyst's sense of rightness or normality during the interpretation and application phases of the computerized monitoring project.

Multiple Applications and or Analyses of the Same Data Set Reuse of natural resources in the real world generally is encouraged and applauded, but reuse of online information, including data gathered through computerized monitoring of HCI, generally meets reactions ranging from suspicion to outrage. Online systems developed with good intentions often are used for various unintended purposes, some of which are not socially acceptable. Two examples beyond the narrow scope of this book include automatic, no-stop tollway collection systems for motor vehicles, which critics claim can be used to track the movements of ordinary citizens, and computerized image databases of children as an aid in case of future abduction, which critics suggest could be used against the children as they mature and have dealings with the criminal justice system themselves.

Social Outcomes The introduction and diffusion of computerized monitoring in multiple environments may change the social structures among people.

In work environments alone, this technology could alter not only the balance of power between employers and employees, but also the nature of social relations (Aiello 1993). Many critics of computerized monitoring express admittedly vague fears about the long-term, less-obvious negative consequences of a social environment permeated by computerized monitoring. Whether computerized monitoring systems are used to measure individual performance or aggregate group performance could affect such social phenomena as teamwork, competitiveness and conflict among co-workers, and feelings of social isolation (Aiello 1993).

Cyberspace may become an entirely public space, with little or no possibility for intimacy. Wellman (1997) raises some interesting questions about the social impact of computerized monitoring. As online surveillance becomes more proficient and efficient, netizens may seek other venues and formats to exchange potentially sensitive information. Wellman tends to understand surveillance as agency-driven and focused on message content, rather than on behavior. This mode of understanding could be described as the traditional way of understanding surveillance, conducted primarily by governments, businesses, and clandestine organizations.

An unusual aspect of the rapid growth and diffusion of computerized monitoring in various environments during the last 25 years is that the entire movement seems to have sprung from the convergence of curiosity about the behavior of others and increased technical capabilities for satisfying that curiosity, rather than from any urgent social need. In this sense, computerized monitoring is very unlike, say, the search for the polio vaccine or a cure for AIDS. Society as a whole does not really understand the fundamental intent of computerized monitoring, nor is the project being funded at broad social levels.

Perhaps the two greatest failings of computerized monitoring to date as a general human project are the inability to efficiently analyze the data gathered and the inability (perhaps rooted in the failings of the human imagination) to thoughtfully apply the findings. Many computerized monitoring projects, particularly in the library and Web realms, have resulted in little more than "fun" facts to know and tell. When people came to understand that interesting trivia about human behavior online may be the primary outcome of the movement to use computers to monitor HCI, the concerns about privacy invasions and confidentiality issues increased. Attempts to limit or prevent the misapplication of computerized monitoring data often adopt the procrustean tactic of trying to prohibit all computerized monitoring.

For several reasons, the application of computerized monitoring data is a crucial stage in computerized monitoring projects. First, if the application is done by the computer system, and if no one is privy to the data at the collection, analysis, or application stages of the project, then the issue of personal privacy claims during computerized monitoring projects may be moot, unless the idea of personal privacy is revised so that intrusions by computers are perceived as invasive as intrusions by human eyes, regardless of how those eyes are assisted by technological devices. Second, if the application is done in a professional context (e.g., by a teacher, librarian, researcher, computer professional, or even a direct marketer), then the rules and standards of professional confidentiality apply. Third, if the application is done in a workplace setting, then company policies and any applicable state and federal laws apply. Finally, if the application is done by a governmental body acting as a governmental body (rather than as an employer), then the Constitution and other federal and state laws apply.

Over the first 30 years of its development, computerized monitoring of HCI overall has been a disappointment. The promise has not been articulated well, and the realization of the promise has been spotty and disjointed. Overall, the applications of computerized monitoring have been unimaginative, and many of the applications have caused mistrust and anger. By and large, CPM and Web traffic analyses are pursuing very mundane goals. Those behind these analysis projects are interested in how people interact with computers and computer networks only as a means to make the people more efficient and productive employees and consumers — two expressions of human being that have been on a steep convergence course throughout this century. Educators and librarians would be closer to accepting HCI as it is on its own terms, if they could see beyond the goals of skills development (also known as computer literacy) and lifelong learning skills.

Computerized monitoring of HCI has been unable to predict future user behavior at the individual level, and there are reasons for concluding that it may never be possible to do so. However, this method can describe user behavior fairly well. The strength of the method lies in its descriptive, not predictive, powers. Computerized monitoring can provide a unique perspective on the playing out of HCI.

Computerized monitoring of HCI is one way to examine behavior in an increasingly modifiable environment. Rather than strive to predict human behavior in an immutable environment, perhaps we should turn our attention more toward the challenge of how to create self-evolving virtual environments that complement observed human behavior and predilections. We could create a Web site, then use computerized monitoring to study the behavior and preferences of visitors to that Web site, then modify the Web site environment (both structure and content) either to facilitate the observed behavior or to encourage other behavior. This is social engineering either at its best or worst.

There may be some value in attempting to take a long view of the general anticipated outcome of computerized monitoring. It is becoming evident that, in an information-rich environment like cyberspace, the glut of data can quickly overwhelm an individual. People have not evolved to live and work in such an information-rich environment. Computerized monitoring can be conceived as an essential first step toward good, intelligent filtering of data. If an individual can exist in an environment where a large part of the perceived information is truly useful to the personal projects of that individual, cyberspace would become more friendly and productive.

Agre (1994) reminds us that no matter how thoroughly the capture process is controlled, it is impossible to remove the aspects of interpretation, strategy, and institutional dynamics. Capture projects never are purely technical but always socio-technical in nature. The question, however, remains: How do computerized monitoring projects become infused with these social components? Rather than blindly assume that big government and big business are covertly pushing these projects, we should at least entertain the possibility that the will to monitor is embedded in the basic social structure of human computing as a way of revealing Being, as articulated by Heidegger (1977) and other ontologists. Despite what Borgman, Hirsh, and Hiller (1996) claim, computerized monitoring is more than merely a data collection method. It is more than a research method. It is a way of conceptualizing, articulating, and studying human-computer interaction. Ultimately, it is a way of revealing the role of human being in online environments. We must ask questions about the essence of computerized monitoring, and wonder how we could possibly develop a free relationship with that essence.

10

Research Projects
Involving Computerized
Monitoring

Why and how did the ongoing amorphous movement to use computers to monitor HCI get started, if there was no immediate, pressing need for the data such monitoring could provide? Cate (1997) suggests that software programmers and system developers created this functionality as a side-thought simply because the emerging technology seemed to facilitate the collection of transactional data.

> Computer technologies and services even record what might be characterized as gratuitous data — data that are captured for no immediately apparent reason. Often uses will later develop for such data, but recording each web site a user visits on the Internet or the keystrokes used in a computer session tends to reflect the interest of programmers and designers to record data simply because their equipment and software can do so (Cate 1997, 16).

Research projects involving computerized monitoring of HCI have been around for at least 30 years. Many of the field's pioneers initially were much more interested in the performance of the computers than in the performance of their users, or in the dynamics of the HCI itself. The technique evolved from a prior desire to monitor the performance of the computer systems themselves (Peters 1993, 42). The work of Lucas (1971) is representative of this early focus. Lucas concentrated on system performance, rather than on user performance, to discover the present limitations of the computer system. Once the stability and predictability of computer behavior during HCI was established, the focus of attention of computerized monitoring projects turned to the human aspects of the interaction.

There are three basic types of computing environments in which computers have been used to gather (and perhaps analyze) data about HCI: those of mainframe and mini computers, of standalone microcomputers, and of networked computer systems (e.g., local area networks and the Web). Computerized monitoring began with human-mainframe computer interaction. The user often sat at a dumb terminal and issued commands, using a character-based interface.

Research involving computerized monitoring is very diverse. One of the main theses of this book is that even though a broad general field of computerized monitoring has emerged, even most of the practitioners of such monitoring are not aware of, or have not acknowledged, this overall field. Even though computerized monitoring occurs in a variety of environments, including schools, libraries, businesses, and the Web, the techniques of data collection, definition, analysis, and application are similar. Despite these latent similarities, a distinction needs to be made between two types of research involving computerized monitoring of HCI. The first type of research uses computerized monitoring as a data collection and analysis technique. The second type uses another data collection technique to study the incidence and effects of computerized monitoring, usually on those being monitored. An example of the second type is the survey research conducted by Gallatin (1989) in Massachusetts. The two primary goals of the research project were to provide an empirical description of how electronic monitoring was being used by companies in Massachusetts, and to obtain self-reports from monitored employees about how monitoring affected their productivity, job satisfaction, health, and individual rights. Although Gallatin's research did not directly involve the use of computers to monitor HCI, it clearly is germane to this book.

Much of this second type of research has emerged from studies of employees and workplace environments. Although computerized monitoring is widely practiced by employers in those environments, research projects of the first type (i.e., that use computers to monitor HCI), conducted by disinterested parties, is relatively rare. Miezio (1992, 25) goes so far as to claim that none of the questions regarding the potential negative effects of computerized performance monitoring on monitored employees has been fully answered by substantial research. Many of the potential negative effects have been raised by anecdotal stories told by interest groups who generally are against CPM.

Reviews of the Research Literature   Reviews of the research literature about computerized monitoring are difficult to find. Usually they cover only one of the four primary environments in which this monitoring historically has been practiced. For example, Safayeni, Irving, Purdy, and Higgins (1992) review the early academic literature on CPM in workplace environments (George 1996, 461). Baarda (1994, 8) provides a nice tabular overview of five CPM research projects conducted in the 1980s and 1990s. Aiello and Kolb (1995a) do a good job of summarizing the research involving CPM in work environments in the late 1980s and early 1990s. In his research and literature review article, Lund (1992) notes that a variety of research methods (e.g., case studies, cross-sectional studies, and laboratory designs) have been used to study the effects of electronic performance monitoring in work environments. Peters (1993) provides an overview of the literature on computerized monitoring in online catalogs and other information-seeking environments from the late 1960s through the early 1990s. The use of computerized monitoring in Web environments is very recent, but the literature is maturing rapidly.

Research Agendas Articulated research agendas that explore beyond the scope of particular computerized monitoring projects are as rare as literature reviews. Again, the research agendas that have emerged tend to be limited to one of the four main environments. Ottensmeyer and Heroux (1991) ask four basic questions about computerized monitoring in work environments: 1) How are computers used as monitoring tools? 2) How does the use of computer technology differ from traditional monitoring practices? 3) How widespread is the use of computers as monitoring tools? 4) What impact has computerized monitoring had on the workers and the work they perform? Kidwell and Kidwell (1997, 92) observe that much of the existing research on electronic control systems in work environments is premised on a view of organizations as machines (in contrast to organisms), in which efficient performance is the primary goal.

Regarding libraries and other information-seeking environments, Sandore, Flaherty, Kaske, Kurth, and Peters (1993) wrote a seven-point research manifesto on the future of transaction log analysis. They called for definitions of common terms and concepts, international standards for transaction logging systems, easy access to computerized monitoring data by librarians (as one group of analysts in applied settings), user-centered analysis methods (as opposed to system-centered or site-centered), more communication between analysts and system designers, a lasting and meaningful resolution to the confidentiality and privacy concerns raised by computerized monitoring, and an articulation of the overall mission of transaction log analysis.

Research agendas concerning computerized monitoring in formal learning environments also are rare. One major aim of the research agenda for the use of computerized monitoring in such environments is to capture and analyze data about learner activities during study sessions that will reveal the patterns of cognition and metacognition that develop during those sessions. Studying and learning involve a stream of varied and interacting cognitive activities, including seeking and selecting information, reading, rehearsing, elaborating, and self-testing. Some of these hidden cognitive events can be traced by observable actions the learner performs during study, such as underlining, looking up information, copying it into a notebook, circling a feature in a diagram and drawing a line to link it to a portion of a text, or attempting to answer a test question (Winne, Gupta, and Nesbit 1994, 178).

Although the use of computerized monitoring to study Web environments and other online shopping environments is the fourth and most recent estate, the overall research agenda for this domain may be in the best shape of all. This is because there is money in those Web logs, and advertisers, webmasters, and marketers are eager to prove the existence, whereabouts, and economic extraction methods of the mother lode. Computerized monitoring of HCI in Web environments involves people who have a fairly good sense of a shared research agenda, even if their research is applied. They have a good sense of what they are trying to capture and know. Until an overall research agenda for the entire amorphous movement is articulated, researchers in the other three online environments could learn something from the rapid development of computerized monitoring software, projects, programs, and standards in the commercial Web environment.

Real-Time Monitoring   What group led the start of the computerized monitoring movement? Based on the published evidence, Edwin Parker and William Paisley (1966), two psychologists, were early pioneers. Parker and Paisley were interested in using computers to monitor the information-seeking behavior of their fellow psychologists. They also argued that the criteria for evaluating a computerized information retrieval system should be based on human behavior, not on technology itself.

Computerized monitoring began in earnest in the 1960s. Meister and Sullivan (1967) conducted one of the early transaction log analysis studies. It was also an early attempt to define a successful search, within the context of transaction log analysis. A successful search session was one in which at least one title was viewed. Early ethical perceptions about the use of transaction logs seemed to be very tolerant. Some of the most intrusive proposals concerning computerized monitoring, such as those articulated by Sigfried Treu, seemed to germinate during the 1960s. Treu proposed a form of human-based, unobtrusive, computerized monitoring whereby the human observer of a person using a computer system would, based on the observer's own judgment, be able to intervene in real time during the search. Such computerized monitoring probably approximates the popular understanding of computerized monitoring in the 1990s.

Treu's writings indicate that the possibility of real-time monitoring emerged early in the history of computerized monitoring. The issue continues to intrigue and disturb the software development and research communities. Rigney (1997), for example, recently lamented that WebSense, one of the best Internet-access manager software programs on the market, still was not capable of real-time monitoring and alerting. Cooper (1998, 906) asserts that a "truly dynamic monitoring system can be used in real-time to analyze user behavior, deduce patterns of behavior, compare such patterns to those previously stored, and immediately suggest to the user ways of modifying a search to improve its quality." Real-time observation of work performance has been a major source of consternation to critics of CPM. During his study of five companies that used CPM, George (1996, 470) noted that, while the job-related phone calls were in progress, supervisors and their assistants listened to phone service calls and viewed the same computer screens the operators saw from removed but nearby areas. According to Nachiketa Lolla, an Aquas, Inc. spokesperson, Bazaar Analyzer can be used for real-time monitoring of a Web site (Balderston 1996). In addition to monitoring visitors in real time, while they are in a Web site, alert mechanisms also can be installed to let the web-master know when specific users are visiting the site (Busch 1997). Rapoza (1997a) reports that at least two other Web server log analysis software programs — Aria from Andromedia and WebTrends from e.g. Software — make real-time analysis possible.

Siegfried Treu's ideas concerning "transparent stimulation" during HCI need further examination, because the basic notion continues to crop up in the literature. The purpose of the proposed stimulation feature was to identify and validate human behaviors that should be reinforced by the human-computer interface. Treu proposed that unseen search intermediaries unobtrusively scan and, if warranted, intervene in HCI sessions in real time.

The major advantage of real-time, rather than delayed, computerized monitoring is that it opens the possibility of intervention in the interactive session being monitored. The intervention could be undertaken by a person, such as a work supervisor or teacher in a formal learning environment, or by the computer itself. If the computer undertakes the intervention, it need not be in a threatening manner. Immediate performance feedback can be very helpful to someone interacting with a computer to perform a task or accomplish a goal. For example, the word processor on which I am composing this book automatically spell-checks what I type as I write, then underlines in red words it cannot find immediately in its dictionary. My ability to catch most of my spelling and typographical errors on the fly saves me the onerous task of putting a large text file through the spell-checker after I have finished composing. The major disadvantage of real-time monitoring is that it requires rapid — almost instantaneous — collection, analysis, and assessment of the data. Either the human or computer monitor must be able to draw conclusions quickly (Council on Library Resources).

Research Projects of the 1980s   The use of computers to study HCI developed significantly during the 1980s. This was the decade of big studies in OPAC use (e.g., the CLR study released in 1983) and in computerized performance monitoring (e.g., the OTA study released in 1986 and 1987).

A 1983 study by 9 to 5: The National Association of Working Women surveyed stress in female clerical workers (9 to 5 1985). A quarter of the survey respondents reported that they were monitored by computer. The results indicate that female workers, especially minority women, in clerical occupations are most susceptible to having their workplace behavior monitored (Lund 1989, 74).

Walton and Vittori (1983) studied the impact of a computerized monitoring system installed in an insurance company. They found that the system caused stress by increasing the visibility of individual employees and decreasing the visibility of the supervisors who were observing the performance. Walton and Vittori found that workers did not mind the computerized performance monitoring system (Miezio 1992, 34). Grant (1990, 20) describes this project as exploratory, theory-building research that focuses on identifying significant issues and important constructs. Exploratory research seeks to expose, but not necessarily explain, relationships among variables, and to generate hypotheses. The objective of exploratory research is to comprehend the problem during the early stages of a research effort.

Nussbaum (1984) demonstrated a significant relationship between CPM and stress. A magazine survey asked only one question about whether or not the respondent was monitored at work. Through the use of chi-squared tests a significant relationship was discovered between computerized monitoring and negative health effects (Miezio 1992). Because respondents to the magazine questionnaire were limited to a simple yes or no, it is difficult to determine whether simple, low-level computerized monitoring had the same stressful effect as more sophisticated, pervasive monitoring systems capable of continuously monitoring all aspects of performance and attendance to the human-computer job task (Grant 1990, 22).

In 1985 the Connecticut Union of Telephone Workers surveyed 900 Southern New England Telephone workers who used VDTs. The results indicated a high correlation between reported health complaints and reports of electronic monitoring. Approximately 75 percent of the VDT operators who reported dizziness, headaches, and muscle aches also reported that they were electronically monitored in the workplace. Ironically, the majority of the respondents reported that their workstations had good ergonomic designs. Overall, over 90 percent of the respondents who reported being electronically monitored reported experiencing at least one health complaint that appeared to be stress-related. Slightly more than half of the respondents claimed that data obtained through computerized monitoring was used for disciplinary purposes (Lund 1989, 74–75).

Irving, Higgins, and Safayeri (1986) used a 36-item questionnaire administered during semi-structured interviews to study the effect of CPM on job satisfaction, supervision, and the performance appraisal process. The study team itself did not collect individual performance data because of the sensitive nature of the issue (Lund 1989, 89). They found no significant difference in satisfaction between the monitored and unmonitored employees. Individuals in the monitored group reported a perceived increase in production. They concluded that an overemphasis was placed on quantity of production, and that monitored employees were more closely supervised than unmonitored employees (Miezio 1992, 35).

Smith, Carayon, and Miezio (1986) used interviews with 41 monitored employees in five different work environments to study the effects of CPM on job satisfaction, motivation, supervision, performance, and stress. They found that the problem was not the monitoring system itself but the manner in which information from the monitoring system was used to modify and control employee behavior. Most of the interviewees thought that the monitoring system failed to motivate them, and 83 percent believed it watched them (Miezio 1992, 36).

Eisenman (1986) studied how the type and level of CPM affected the behavior of supervisors. She found that monitored workers did not differ in their perceptions of how closely they were supervised, regardless of the intensity of the monitoring. Eisenman found that supervisors did not fully use the monitoring system, and that they used other factors in their evaluations of employees (Miezio

1992, 35). Miezio, Smith, and Carayon (1987) describe the use of CPM in the medical transcription field. They found a link between monitoring and stress, and that the implementation of CPM affected the social interaction within the unit. Social interaction may function as a stress reducer (Miezio 1992, 37).

DiTecco and Andre (1987) surveyed Bell Canada employees. They concluded that average wait time targets, not electronic monitoring, were the most important influence on work-related stress (Grant and Higgins 1996, 215). McDermott (1987) studied the 55,000 unionized employees of the Ontario provincial government. The study involved 200 structured, in-depth, taped interviews with a representative sample of office workers who spent a significant portion of their working day using VDTs. The data entry operators (mostly female) were most affected by CPM.

Earley (1988) conducted a field experiment to evaluate the relation of computer-generated feedback to an employee's performance of tasks. Sixty male and female magazine-subscription processors worked on assigned goals. Results indicated that the source of feedback (i.e., from the supervisor or the computer) and the specificity of feedback (general versus specific) were linked directly to performance. Earley suggested that computerized monitoring benefits employees by increasing the objectivity of the performance appraisal and by improving feedback to monitored workers (Hawk 1994, 949–950).

Grant, Higgins, and Irving (1988) conducted a study in the group claims processing division of an insurance company to examine how computer monitoring affected the decisions made by service workers when resolving conflicts between service and production. The findings suggested that CPM programs that cannot appropriately measure an important facet of performance tend to promote bureaucratic behavior, that objective measurement of performance is not necessarily perceived as fair, and that monitored workers who internalize the production standards and are intrinsically motivated by the feedback from the computer monitor may function more productively. Grant, Higgins, and Irving argued that the statistics generated by CPM do not comprehensively summarize an employee's performance (Hawk 1994, 951). They found that workers perceived a decline in customer service as a result of the introduction of CPM (Miezio 1992, 37). The objectivity of the CPM was not considered fair by the monitored employees. The researchers also found that some employees internalized the performance monitoring system and were comfortable and productive in this environment.

In 1988 the Massachusetts Center for New Office Technology conducted a study based on data obtained through a survey of close to 700 respondents (Curbs 1989). Most of the respondents received the questionnaire through their union. Of the respondents 63 percent worked in the telecommunications industry, ten percent in the federal government, four percent in utilities, three percent in insurance, and six percent in other sectors, such as state government, finance, and travel. Of the respondents 85 percent reported that they were computer monitored, 81 percent reported that they were monitored through service observation, 18 percent through telephone call accounting, and 69 percent reported that they were monitored both through computerized monitoring and service observation. For the respondents who were computer monitored, the number of tasks completed and time to complete tasks were the two most common units of measurement. The number of keystrokes made, number of errors, and time away from work were other, less-frequently used units of measurement. Nearly two-thirds of all respondents reported that they were not informed before being hired that an electronic monitoring system would monitor their workplace behavior. Only 26 percent of the respondents either agreed or strongly agreed with the statement that electronic monitoring helped them work more productively. According to 81 percent of the respondents, electronic monitoring made their jobs more stressful. The findings of this survey tend to support the claim of union and advocate groups that electronic monitoring increases stress levels and the incidence of stress-related health complaints (Lund 1989, 75–82).

Dumais, Kraut, and Koch (1988) used a multi-method, lagged, time-series design to examine the impact of a computerized record system on the work life of customer service employees at a large utility company. The results indicated that computer technology had mixed effects on productivity and the overall quality of work life. These effects varied depending on the local culture of the organization, the quality of the management, the type of employee, and the detailed work tasks. Chalykoff and Kockan (1989) examined the effects of computerized monitoring on job satisfaction and turnover. The study involved 740 employees of the Internal Revenue Service. The researchers found that the dependent variables of job satisfaction and turnover could be linked to the affective responses of the subjects to computerized monitoring, including their prior beliefs about monitoring.

Grant and Higgins (1989) studied the effects of the design of the computer monitoring system. They interviewed 85 employees and 13 supervisors at a major insurance company, and through a survey of 1,500 employees of 50 Canadian service companies. The findings indicated that using CPM does not automatically increase employee attention to productivity, nor does it necessarily reduce attention to customer service. The findings also suggest that CPM does not improve or replace human supervision, and that less than one-third of service employees are opposed to computerized monitoring.

For computerized monitoring research in information-seeking environments, the 1980s may have been the zenith for pure, disinterested research. The decade began with the major CLR (Council on Library Resources) study of online catalog use, and ended with an increasingly diverse use of computerized monitoring.

One of the major research projects in this field during the decade of the 1980s involved the transitions from one state within a search session to another. For example, how often is one error followed by another? This research issue continues to be significant in the Web environments of the 1990s. The order of page accesses is an important piece of information in the attempt to study how users explore a Web site (Yan, Jacobsen, Garcia-Molina, and Dayal 1996).

Research Projects of the 1990s   In the 1990s the very nature of HCI became more complex and difficult to monitor via computer. Winne, Gupta, and Nesbit

(1994) noted that computer-based adaptive learning systems provide a high degree of learner control during studying, as well as an excellent environment for collecting extensive behavioral data on learner activity. The STUDY system is a computer program for writing and delivering adaptive tutorials. It is a milieu where a student studies and, during a study session, generates traceable cognitive and metacognitive events. The researchers developed a methodology, based on the mathematics of directed graphs, for analyzing the log file data. The directed graph approach reduced study actions to a set of nodes representing action types and a set of links representing a temporal relation. This project's goal was to develop and test analytical techniques for identifying and understanding the cognitive and metacognitive individual differences in the studying of individual students (Winne, Gupta, and Nesbit 1994, 178). The researchers hypothesized that "temporally unfolding actions create tactical and strategic structures, and that such structures may be inter- and intra-individual differences that add important information to theoretical accounts about how achievements are created in the course of studying" (Winne, Gupta, and Nesbit 1994, 181).

Schofield, Davidson, Stocks, and Futoran (1997) have been employing HCI usage statistics to understand how Internet use grows and diffuses through a given K–12 student population.

A few computerized monitoring studies of information seekers in Web environments have been published in the latter half of the 1990s. Yan, Jacobsen, Garcia-Molina, and Dayal (1996) conducted a brief study of how users of the Web site at Stanford University cluster into groups based on the pages they accessed during use sessions. They also studied the amount of time (measured in seconds) visitors spent with a Web page on their screens. They found that approximately half of all sessions at the Web site retrieved only two or three pages. Less than ten percent of all sessions accessed more than nine pages of information from the site. Cousineau, Little, Lane and Coble (1997) studied the use of the Web by patrons within a physical academic library. They wanted to learn if human Web browsers within the library were engaged in legitimate information-seeking behavior, or if their online activity was more recreational in nature. They found that of approximately 7,000 server addresses visited by in-library users, the 100 most frequently visited domain names accounted for 60 percent of the use. Approximately 73 percent of the Web sites visited were academic. The most frequently visited academic site was the online catalog server, and the most frequently visited non-academic site (eighth overall) was that of ESPN.

Smith, Carayon, Sanders, Lim, and LeGrande (1992) surveyed 762 members of the Communications Workers of America. The response rate was only 29 percent. They found that monitored workers differed significantly from unmonitored workers with the same general job description, especially regarding important job demands and characteristics which may be stressors. When working with an electronic monitoring system in place, respondents reported significantly lower feelings of control. The monitored employees reported higher workload, less variation in workload, and greater workload dissatisfaction than the unmonitored employees.

The monitored employees also reported less sense of control over their jobs, less fairness in their work standard, and more frequent interactions with difficult customers. This research is one of the few studies to specifically investigate the health and stress effects of CPM. The researchers found that computerized monitored workers reported more boredom, tension, anxiety, depression, anger, and fatigue than non-monitored employees. The monitored workers also reported more problems with their wrists, arms, shoulders, necks, and backs than non-monitored employees.

Griffith (1993a) found that the electronic presence of CPM enhanced performance of a simple task much as the physical presence of a human supervisor would (Stanton 1994, 2). The results of Griffith's experiments under controlled conditions revealed no significant correlation between monitoring and perceived stress (Grant and Higgins 1996, 214). Nebeker and Tatum (1993) found that accurate feedback from a CPM system enhanced employee performance of relatively simple data-entry tasks. A pure, unmediated feedback system that provides performance data only to the employee seems to enhance performance (Stanton 1994, 2). Grant and Higgins (1996, 215) found little evidence to suggest that monitoring affects stress, and concluded that quotas and rewards, rather than performance data collected by a computer, led to increased employee stress.

Stanton's research (1994) is a rare instance in which computerized monitoring (rather than, say, questionnaires and interviews) was used to learn more about the effects of computerized monitoring on human behavior and performance in workplace environments.

Silverman and Smith (1995) used arousal measures, such as urinary cortisol, heart rate, and a subjective questionnaire, to assess the effects of human and computer monitoring on 40 white female college students. They wanted to determine whether the type of monitor (human or computer) affected the arousal level of a worker to an extent that monitoring could be labeled a stressor.

During the 1990s Web research projects involving computerized monitoring of HCI, the interests of commerce began to assert themselves. Late in 1996 I/PRO and DoubleClick undertook a comprehensive study of advertising banner impressions and click-throughs on the Web. Their report, "The Web in Perspective: A Comprehensive Analysis of Ad Responses," details their findings about the relationships between precise read/frequency and user response to ad banners (Stout 1997, 190). Crovella and Bestavros (1996) modified the Mosaic Web browser software so that it logged all user access to the Web. They recorded the Uniform Resource Locator (URL) of each file accessed, the time the file was accessed, and the time required to transfer the file from its server, if necessary. For completeness, the researchers recorded all URLs accessed, whether recalled from the client software's cache or via a file transfer from a remote host.

Researchers at the HomeNet project in Pittsburgh have been collecting and analyzing "detailed electronic audit trails" to better understand how 150 individuals in 50 families used the Internet, the Web, and Usenet newsgroups in their homes. All of the participants signed consent forms. The field trials began in February 1995 and were expected to run for three years. Early results indicated that the group was not particularly interested in Internet erotica and pornography. Most people browse for information on their established interests (Manning, Scherlis, Kiesler, Kraut, and Mukhopadhyay 1997).*

The United States federal government has enthusiastically adopted the Web in the 1990s as a medium for disseminating public information, and has funded some studies that used Web server log analysis. Bertot, McClure, Moen and Rubin (1997) present the findings of an analysis of 14 days of Web server log files gathered from a Web site maintained by a federal agency. They wrote their own Perl scripts to analyze the Web server log data.

Tauscher and Greenberg (1997) employed a user-centric Web log analysis to try to improve the design of history mechanisms in Web browser software. The history mechanism allows people to select and revisit pages previously viewed. Other ways to revisit Web content include the back button, bookmarks, and HTML files saved locally. Tauscher and Greenberg modified Xmosaic version 2.6 to record a user's browsing. For six weeks, 23 volunteer, experienced subjects used the modified browser. The authors claim that this study is one of only two published client-side computerized monitoring studies of HCI in Web environments. The other known published study was that of Catledge and Pitkow (1995). Tauscher and Greenberg found that people go back in cyberspace much more often than they go forward, and that most commercial Web browser software programs do not provide search engines for the history list itself. This research is interesting because it focuses on how to make computerized monitoring data available in a usable format to the user. Inter-sessional historical maps of where a human browser has been are rare.

General Outcomes of Computer Monitoring Research   Most of the fundamental computer monitoring issues, including those involving morality and ethics, were identified early, but the issues tended to persist throughout the develop of new methods and applications.

The outcomes over the decades of computerized monitoring of HCI in work environments have been mixed and contradictory. Not much of the research into CPM in work environments used computer monitoring to collect the data to be analyzed. Most of the research relies on questionnaires, focus groups, and interviews. Most of the research on CPM in workplace environments has concentrated on health and privacy issues, rather than on controlled research into the effects of CPM on employee role perceptions, performance, or general attitude (Grant 1990, 8). CPM research tends to divide into two basic categories — exploratory research and theory-testing research (Grant 1990, 20).

Human perceptions of the locus and balance of control (among people and machines, and among different groups of people) are crucial to the diffusion and adoption of a CPM system. Much of the early research into the impact of CPM

---

* *More information about the HomeNet research can be found at http://homenet.andrew.cmu.edu.*

systems on organizations suggests that monitoring systems which increase the power of the supervisor at the expense of the worker will be resisted or perceived as detrimental by the employees (Grant 1990, 21–22).

Shortcomings and Limitations of Computerized Monitoring Research Of all potentially interested parties in computer monitoring activities, no one group has made a strong claim for ownership of the process and product. Computer systems managers started the process, but their interest has not grown at the same rate as the process. Organizational managers never have broadly, successfully integrated computer monitoring activities into their overall management duties (Peters 1996). Pure researchers have not widely adopted the method. Web masters (Web site creators and maintainers) are interested in the technique, but have done little about applying the results. Sales people and marketing agents currently seem to be adding the most resources to computer monitoring.

One problem with computerized monitoring as a grand, ongoing project is that it developed in an era of easily identifiable, paired actions between a user and a computer system. Transaction log analysis was relatively simple when the log consisted of a strictly sequential series of human commands and system responses. As computers become more powerful and computer networks more complex, the transactions between people and computers also are becoming more complex. The old days of simple back-and-forth command and response interchanges are rapidly disappearing.

Possible Future Research Projects Within the broad field of computerized monitoring, several possible future research avenues present themselves. Because such a high percentage of computerized monitoring is applied research, it may be worthwhile to examine how well (or how poorly) the employment of computerized monitoring has advanced the software applications and online environments themselves.

The field needs a serious study of all of the extraneous things people input during HCI. Many transaction log analysts have noted that some types of HCI tend to abandon the basic premise of the interaction. Drabenstott and Weller (1996) found that of 1,919 OPAC queries being examined, 203 (10.6 percent) were "nonlegitimate," including gibberish, expletives, explicit sex terms and known-item searches. Flaherty (1993) provided a hint toward a serious study of online graffiti.

Is computerized monitoring a bona fide methodology, or is it no more than an efficient way to collect lots of data? Although computerized monitoring remains fairly new, it does not seem to be drawing the same type of self-reflective attention that, for example, the survey and focus group methodologies have. For some combination of reasons, the movement to use computers to monitor HCI has not become a unified, overt discipline.

Computerized monitoring projects generally focus on the end-users of computer systems. The human monitor, like the system designer, rarely turns his gaze upon himself and his own behavior. "For all the extensive research that has taken place on users and user communities, there has been almost no systematic research done on designers and the community of design" (Rochlin 1997, 33).

11

Web Monitoring Software

We have passed from a form of injunction that measured or punctuated gestures to a web that constrains them or sustains them throughout their entire succession (Foucault 1977, 152).

It is tempting to view the Web as a paradise for easy counting — after all, if an interaction is electronic, then it should be easy and obvious to count it electronically (Berthon, Pitt, and Prendergast 1997).

Within the last quarter century the ability to use computerized information systems to unobtrusively monitor HCI has become a substantial component of the diverse field of library and information science research. Studies of online catalog use that employ transaction logs as a data source now are commonplace. The first generation of mainframe transaction logging software eventually was complemented by transaction logging software for personal computers. Several studies of the use of standalone CD-ROM workstations have used transaction logging software to gather information. Within the past few years a third type of transaction logging software has emerged that enables researchers, administrators, and business people to study how users interact with a hypertextual, graphical, webbed information environment. This chapter explores this emerging Web logging software, the analysis the software supports, and the potential applications of Web log analysis. Web analysis software tools interpret and present the details of the interaction between a Web client (also known as a browser) and a Web server (Randall 1997c).

As we have explored in previous chapters, computers are used in a variety of environments to monitor HCI in the workplace, in formal learning environments where computer-assisted instruction is used, in public access computer systems (such as OPACs), and most recently on the World Wide Web. The development and use of Web access logs, however, has been qualitatively different from previous generations of transaction logging software. During the early stages of the development of Web monitoring software, few attempts were made to be unobtrusive or secretive about monitoring. Many Web sites were proud to announce how many hits they had received since a specified date. Some sites let the visitor know readily that they recognize the brand of browser one is using, as well as one's current operating system. They do not seem to be doing this involuntarily as some form of fair warning or disclaimer of responsibility for any future harm that may befall the site visitor. Rather, the emerging Web culture appears to condone such open, yet unobtrusive, observation of people using computers to find information. The library and information science research community will need to learn how to pursue its own goals within this new social environment.

The Web has become a virtual environment where learning, seeking information, communicating, working, and shopping all are possible. Web tracking software can monitor all of this activity. Weber (1996) correctly notes that before the advent of Web tracking software consumers already divulged substantial information to marketers via price scanners at retail outlets, ATMs, and through credit card purchases. Web site designers and managers have attempted to capitalize on the power of Web server log analysis by promising consumers the ultimate take-out menu and marketers the ultimate focus group (Bayers 1998, 130). At times (perhaps most of the time) the prospects for Web-based computerized monitoring seem too good to be true. Stout (1996) claims that analyzing Web server log files is one of the hottest Web-related topics, because thousands of businesses with Web sites want to measure the effectiveness of those sites. The challenge is to figure out the best way to measure and report Web site readership patterns with the greatest accuracy, depth, and efficiency. Busch (1997, 75) suggests that the phrase "log-file analyzers" is the most accurate way to describe these software utilities that analyze the usage data collected by Web servers.

The growth and development of Web log analysis software has been phenomenal. Jaffee (1996) noted that a cottage industry to measure Web site traffic was born overnight. Software products quickly evolved from simple programs that analyzed the number of hits received by a site to more sophisticated software that detects, for example, how many visitors to a Web site hit the stop button of their browser client software because they did not want to wait any longer for an elaborate home page to download (Niccolai 1997). The development of Web-based computerized monitoring software has been so rapid that the movement threatens to overwhelm itself before it reaches its full potential. Making sense of Web server log files is like trying to read electronic mail by listening to the key clicks as the sender types a message (Wagner 1997a).

Stateless Transactions   Stateless transactions can be understood as both a solution and problem for Web-based HCI. One shortcoming of the client-server concept of computer interaction is that each exchange of information between a browser and a server is independent of every other (Glass 1996). A client-server connection is referred to as "stateless" because at the core of the HTTP protocol there is no facility for continuity from one request to the next (Stout 1997, 80). What the user experiences as a Web search (or surfing) session is perceived by the network as little more than a series of file grabs (also known as hits) in an ocean of file grabs. Requests are coming at the server from a confusing mess of IP addresses. The designers of the HTTP protocol saw no compelling reason to keep track of the sequence of incoming requests, so the server tends to treat each request as a discrete event.

Because HTTP servers were designed for the rapid and efficient delivery of hypertext documents, interactions with HTTP servers are stateless. An HTTP connection has four distinct stages:

1. The client contacts the server at the Internet address specified in the URL. The server responds that it is up and ready to receive the request.

2. The client requests service and delivers information to the server about the capabilities of the browser software.

3. The server sends the state of the transaction and if successful, the data requested. If the server is unsuccessful, it sends a failure code.

4. The connection closes and, in its pure state, the server maintains no memory of the transaction (Lewis 1997). It has moved on to the next request for information.

Despite this limitation of HTTP connections, often it is useful for the server to maintain state information within a browsing session that consists of a series of hits. Information about these browsing sessions is stored at the client end, rather than at the server site (Glass 1996). There are two basic methods for overcoming the stateless nature of HTTP transactions. The first involves using cookies. The second method involves serving all of the content on the Web site dynamically through a CGI program (Stout 1997, 80).

A virtual shopping cart metaphor is used at many Web sites. As users browse through a Web site, they select items for further review and potential purchase, saving, or downloading. The idea of selecting items from a long list for later codification or further processing is fairly common in many online information systems. Online sales catalogs and online library catalogs do have some things in common. Although the Web hypertext environment appears to be ideal for online shopping purposes, HTTP by itself provides no easy way to keep track of the items an online shopper wishes to purchase, nor a method of identifying the shopper. Baron and Weil (1996) examine three ways to transmit state data over the Web: the type-hidden attribute of HTML forms, the Netscape cookie method of storing and transmitting state information, and the use of a database for storing current states on the server.

Differences: Web Server Logs and Web Client Logs   Because Web site logging devices are set up by the creators and maintainers of sites, they are site-centric rather than user-centric. To use an analogy from efforts to study animals in the wild, they pick a likely area (i.e., the Web site), create a blind (i.e., the logging software), then sit patiently and watch which animals (e.g., Web users) visit the site. Web server log analysis is anti–Web, in that it denies the hypertextual power of the Web. The goal of many Web server log analysis projects is to keep the user interested in the site, so that the user does not wander off into cyberspace, and so that eyeballs (i.e., human attention) can be sold to advertisers. A totally different paradigm would be to somehow tag these animals, then watch where they roam. Web sites are nothing more than isolated watering holes and salt licks in the vast hypertextual forest known as the World Wide Web. It would be much more fascinating to study how users freely roam from site to site on the Web. Web server logging devices use the tree-stand method of observation, while Web client logging devices use a virtual tracking device. Rather than deal with and learn about a person's unfettered exploration of cyberspace, site-centric Web server log analysis watches how that person interacts with a specific server — the analyst's half-acre of cyberspace. The site-centric nature of most Web monitoring software hurts the value of the collected data as marketing information.

Web server logs have some inherent limitations. One problem arises when an analyst wants to include log data from other virtual services, such as from FTP servers, to provide a more complete picture of online activity. Not all Web server log analysis software tools can understand and integrate data from logs from other protocols (Gibbs 1996c). Randall (1997c, 263) succinctly articulates the motivation of analysts to get beyond or behind the information typically contained in Web server logs:

> The point of developing analytic solutions that bypass log files is to move the moment of data collection closer to the activities of the actual user. Ultimately, even the network layers aren't low enough to capture those activities accurately. For that, you'd need software on your visitor's machines capturing every mouse click from every session, since even information about attempted TCP/IP connections wouldn't explain why a user might have bypassed a link to your site in the first place. Given the outcry against software that transmits user data over the Internet (by cookies, for example), you're unlikely to be able to tap into a user's machine.

Although Web client logging software probably has greater potential usefulness for the library and information science, educational, and work-related research communities, most of the development dollars and energy appear to be going toward the development of Web server logging software. Some client-side logging software, however, has begun to emerge. Whereas server-side Web logging software is being developed largely in response to the needs of marketers, client-side software seems to respond to the expressed needs of corporate managers to monitor the Web surfing behavior of employees. In the emerging world of Web log analysis, the library science and educational research communities find themselves forced to snuggle with some strange bedfellows: business marketers and corporate managers.

Web client logging software, also known as Internet-usage utilities or Internet-access managers, first appeared on the market during the summer of 1995. Although the software was originally designed to protect children from objectionable Internet content, especially pornography, recently software designers have developed corporate versions of these access controllers that run on dedicated servers, thus avoiding the need to run client software (Rigney 1997, NE4).

There are at least two types of solutions to the problem of how to control access to the Internet by a given population of users: proxy servers such as Smart-Filter, SurfWatch, and WebSense, and network monitors or protocol sniffers such as LittleBrother and ON Guard (Rigney 1997, NE4). Because a proxy server can increase performance by caching frequently visited Internet sites, and because it forces potential Internet surfers and Web browsers to pass through the proxy server to get to the router and onto the Internet, a proxy server is a good place to have monitoring and blocking software (Rigney 1997, NE4). Protocol sniffing software runs on a single PC. Because it monitors every network packet traveling across a LAN, the software product must be installed on every LAN segment (Rigney 1997, NE4).

One troubling aspect of this strain of software development is that it represents and facilitates the convergence of the will to monitor and the desire to block access. Most manifestations of the will to monitor during the first 30 years of the development of this amorphous movement have not involved any overt attempt to block user access to anything. Critics of the entire project to use computers to monitor HCI, however, may suggest that the interweaving of monitoring and blocking is the natural, intended outgrowth of this decades-long slippery slope. Forcibly blocking access to objectionable content is a much more overt method of control that appears to be attractive mainly to employers and parents. "Though some employers may choose only to monitor users, blocking is the most popular method of protecting your company from the dangers of the Internet" (Rigney 1997, NE4). Kathryn Munro (1998) notes that parental filtering software monitors child-computer interaction by observing keyboard activity (mainly for outgoing information, such as credit card numbers), screen displays, winsock packets, or proxy servers at the Internet server provider level.

Monitoring Network Activity   A third way to monitor HCI in client-server environments is to monitor neither the client end nor the server end, but the activity on the network in between. Because the server log files do not tell the entire story of the HCI, developers and users of Web analysis software increasingly are analyzing network activity itself as a way to add depth to the picture of use (Randall 1997c). Accrue Insight developers see a crucial distinction between log files created at the server end of client-server interaction and the ability to analyze what happens at the network level (Taylor, Cathy 1996d). The Mitel Corporation, an Ontario-based communications hardware vendor, uses Net Access Manager 2.0 from Sequel Technology to monitor and control the flow of data over its network (Meckbach 1997).

From Transaction Log Analysis (TLA) to Web Log Analysis (WLA)
Computerized monitoring began with transaction log analysis over a quarter century ago in the environment of mainframe computers, dumb terminals, character

cell interfaces, and command lines. When microcomputer applications emerged, some transaction logging software was written for both DOS and Apple operating systems. The development and diffusion of client-server architectures opened up the possibility for a new generation of computerized monitoring software: Web log analysis. The possibilities for computerized monitoring of HCI in client-server computing environments was not immediately recognized and implemented. Rahmel (1997) notes that client-server database applications written in PowerBuilder, Visual Basic, and many other application development tools have never automatically maintained logs or audit trails that documented what users did inside an application. Web server protocols contained a latent possibility for logging that has been rapidly developed into a new source of information for Web site administrators and developers.

Web server logging projects, nevertheless, continue to pursue some of the long-standing goals of traditional transaction log analysis: how many use the system for a given time (hour, day, week, etc.); where do the users come from; what are some of their basic demographic characteristics; how do they behave when they are in the system or at the site; when are the periods of peak demand; which resources within the site are most popular.

Transaction logs and transaction log analysis began in the 1960s in the world of mainframe computers with dumb terminals as the primary input and output devices. Parker and Paisley (1966, 1068) noted that online computer systems established environments in which information-seeking behavior could be accurately and unobtrusively observed, the success of information searches could be directly and efficiently measured, and experiments of various kinds could be conducted. Although the gist of their observations as generic insights on HCI has not changed in 30 years, the online computer environment certainly has, and possibly online information-seeking behavior as well. The nature of human-computer (and computer-computer) interaction on the Web is fundamentally different from that in mainframe or standalone microcomputer environments. Randall (1996) provides a good, brief explanation of how an HTTP-driven Web transaction between a client and a server works.

The evolution from command lines to graphical user interfaces with pull down menus and clickable hot buttons has affected user behavior in online information environments. The new method of interacting with the environment (e.g., via the Netscape browser in the Web) creates both new challenges and opportunities for computerized monitoring projects and programs. Would studies of typographical errors, a common feature in transaction log analyses of command line systems, make sense in the Web environment? It would be interesting to study error frequencies and patterns when entering URLs. Is there any possible way to study errors during mouse clicking? We all know it is possible to mis-click, but how could a Web server log identify this error? A subsequent action of going back to the previous screen does not necessarily mean that the user mis-clicked. Virtual browsing creates an interesting wrinkle in that, even though a user may mis-click, one may become interested in the content of the originally undesired or unintended page request. Browsing sessions may be fundamentally different from information-seeking sessions based on commands. When one mis-clicks in a browsable hypertext environment, one receives some content that may (or may not) be of some interest, rather than an error message commonly retrieved when a user mis-types in a command-driven online information environment.

Any project to collect and analyze transaction logs still contains four basic steps, regardless of the source environment of the transactions: a mainframe system, a standalone CD-ROM system, or a webbed, client-server system. By definition, the data must be collected by some software embedded in (or with access to) the computerized information system as it is being used. Most HTTP server software, for example, can collect rudimentary data about incoming file transfer requests and the server's responses to those requests.

The analysis of the collected data could be performed entirely off-line and manually by the human analysts, or by the data-collecting software itself, or by some form of HCI. Most contemporary Web server logging software contains not only data collection capabilities, but can also analyze the data and present the results of the analysis in a variety of formats, including tables, graphs, and pie charts. The old first generation mainframe transaction logging software was much more adept at collecting data than in analyzing it. Compared to older mainframe and microcomputer logging programs, Web server log software seems to have struck a much better balance between data collection and data analysis. The older logging software could collect lots of data, but analysis was difficult and tedious.

We need to keep in mind, however, that even at the basic data collection stage, certain assumptions have been made about the goals of subsequent analysis. No computerized monitoring software collects all aspects of the HCI. The author of the data collection software itself must make some basic decisions about what forms of data analysis would be useful and in demand. Decisions made at the software programming stage about the basic unit (or units) of measurement are crucial to all subsequent analyses. Although transaction log analysis manifests an aura of being entirely objective and machine-driven, many subtle human value decisions are embedded in any computerized monitoring project, from the earliest data collection phases right through to the conclusions and recommendations.

The third step involves interpreting and drawing conclusions from the raw data and the analysis of the data. Conclusions made about the quality, efficiency, and effectiveness of the HCI must be made with extreme caution. This is particularly true when analyzing Web browsing or surfing sessions, because analysts may be predisposed to bring principles and assumptions about command-driven HCI to the analysis of these sessions.

The fourth step, optional in pure research projects, is to apply the results of the first three steps. Although the third and fourth steps currently continue as human endeavors, it is not unimaginable to envision a complete data collection, analysis, and application system capable of completing all four stages of the process with little or no direct human interaction (other than by the original human user of the system, of course). There is some early evidence that the development of

Web server logging software tends to be moving toward an interventionless state of environmental evolution, in which the results of continuous Web logging analyses are used to modify the online environment created at the Web site.

Who Is Involved in Creating and Using Web Server Logs?   Free-lance programmers apparently wrote the first Web server logging software. They often gave the fruits of their labors away as shareware. Most of these programs are rather simple. Commercial, for-profit software developers then learned that a Web server logging component was desired, so they started to expand upon the existing freeware and sell it bundled with the main server software.

The interests of the advertising sector in Web log analysis may differ not only from the not-for-profit sector (including most schools and libraries), but also from the portions of the for-profit sector involved in the sale of goods and non-advertising services. Stout (1996) examines how Web site log analysis could affect the marketing and sale of either products and services or advertising, but he detects some unique qualities in the interest of advertisers in Web log analysis. Whereas detailed knowledge of the way a visitor uses a site can contribute to the sale of products and services, the volume of use is important information for the sale of advertising. Aside from the technical problems associated with measuring Web traffic, compounded by the fact that continuing enhancements in graphic technology fuel ongoing Web advertising creativity, measurement of advertising outcomes in Web environments is a unique challenge, because Web advertising has hybrid characteristics combining aspects of print, broadcast, outdoor, and direct response media (Dreze and Zufryden 1997).

The primary market for Web server logging software appears to be the for-profit organizations, primarily corporations, that are creating Web sites for commercial purposes. They want to determine the demographic characteristics of visitors to their Web sites, and they want to learn how people move around in them. Projects to collect and analyze Web server logs appear to be driven mainly by the marketing departments of these organizations, and secondarily by the webmasters and Web administrators, who are looking for ways to improve the Web site itself. According to estimates made by the International Data Corporation in Framingham, Massachusetts, the start-up and annual maintenance costs for a Web site range from $25,000 to $1.25 million. Companies and organizations want hard figures on the use of these sites (Niccolai 1997). For many people involved in Web server log analysis projects, the only reason server traffic analysis is necessary is to track and maximize Web advertising exposure (Stout 1997, xviii).

The not-for-profit sector, including most libraries, also could benefit from projects to collect and analyze Web server logs. Like their for-profit cousins, these organizations are interested in learning the behavior and demographic make-up of their users. The results of this analysis could be used to inform the expansion and refinement of the Web site itself, which can be understood as a virtual library of information content and services.

Many Web site administrators want to know on which page users entered their site, or, perhaps more importantly, from which page users left the site. They also want to know how users navigate through the site so that they can revise the structure and content of their pages to guide users to information more efficiently (Robertson 1996). Although at present designing a Web site is mainly an art, in the future, based on Web server log analysis in controlled or semi-controlled conditions, it may become more of a science.

Many businesses are interested in learning what their employees are reading or viewing and how much time they spend on the Internet. Some companies are concerned primarily about productivity, while others are focused on security issues. Salt River Project (SRP), a water and power utility company based in Phoenix, Arizona, began monitoring employee use of the Internet and prohibiting workers from going to questionable sites. According to Joe McKee, the principal electrical engineer at SRP, the company took these actions "to prevent any embarrassing situations and to maintain control over what SRP is supposed to" (quoted in Maddox 1996, 71). Web sites also are business investments. Businesses that invest in creating and maintaining Web sites are interested in assessing the productivity of these sites and the return on investment.

The library and information science research community also has been a minor party in the development and use of Web logging software. The interests of this research group encompass both applied and pure research projects. Sometimes they want to know how users are exploring a Web site for the sake of the knowledge, without any particular application in mind. At other times they want to analyze traffic to provide an objective measure of the usage of paid access to a Web site containing information.

Types of Logs Capable of Being Generated from Web Servers   Access logs are produced automatically by every Web server (Strom 1996a). Web site statistics are generic measures, appropriate to virtually all sites, even when the sites have very different justification strategies (Buchanan and Lukaszewski 1997, 103). In the early phases of the Web, as in the early stages of computerized monitoring in general, the log files were analyzed manually. It did not take long, however, for programmers to begin designing little programs to analyze the log files and present the results, often in graphical form. In a four-tiered hierarchy of measurements (raw, consolidated, approximate, and impact), Buchanan and Lukaszewski (1997, 80) see Web site measures as raw data.

There are four common types of Web server log files: access, error, referrer, and agent logs (Noonan 1995). NCSA-like HTTP servers generate these four basic log files (Dorfman 1996). Bertot, McClure, Moen, and Rubin (1997) provide good brief explanations of the four basic Web server log files.* Regardless of the operating system on the server (Unix, Macintosh, Windows NT, etc.), every Web server

*I have not been able to verify why there are four basic Web server log files, and who decided on their structure and content, but this basic structure probably emanated from early Web development work undertaken either at CERN (Conseil European pour la Recherche Nucleaire) or NCSA (National Center for Supercomputing Applications).

for every platform records log files in basically the same way (Stout 1997, 7). Nearly all log files are plain text files. They contain no special formatting characters or codes, except for an embedded line feed at the end of each line (Stout 1997, 7). However, Web server log information also can be stored as individual records in a database (Rahmel 1997). Rahmel suggests that this is the more flexible storage solution for saving server log information because it enables indexing and querying of the database. Thus one can search server log data in an ad hoc manner. The downside of logging directly to a database is that it may consume system resources and processor time (Rahmel 1997).

During the early development of Web server log analysis, the access log received the most attention. All Web servers produce access logs that record visits to Web pages. The access log is a file created by Web server software containing every access to a Web site (Musciano 1996a). All access requests received by the server from client software are considered hits, including both successful and failed transfers (Stout 1997). Most early freeware log analysis programs examined only access logs (Noonan 1995). Each line of the access file logs a single request for data from the Web server (Dorfman 1996). Each line of the access log captures the domain name of the machine making the request, the date and time of the access, the request made by the client browser (including the HTTP command and the path component of the URL being accessed, and the name and version of the protocol used to send and receive data with the client), the server response code (e.g., the infamous 404: document not found), and the number of bytes transferred by the client (Musciano 1996a). Although there is an accepted Common Log Format for the access (or transfer) files, no guidelines or rules exist for the format of the other three log files (Stout 1997, 30).

Error logs are the second type of Web server log file. Each line in the error file logs a single error encountered when handling a request for data from the Web server (Dorfman 1996). The error log contains two fields: a time stamp and a description of the error or failure (Stout 1997, 30). The error log originally was designed primarily to be read by people, so it is more verbose than a computer format that would be optimal for a computer program to read (Stout 1997, 33). When an HTTP transaction results in an error or failure status code, generally (but not always) the server logs information about the transaction in both the access log and the error log (Stout 1997, 7). Errors are recorded in the error log not by a three-digit code, as they are in the access log, but by a textual description of the error.

The error messages cluster into four basic types: administrative messages, access failures, lost connections, and time outs (Stout 1997, 31). Administrative messages include informational text logged by the server that have nothing to do with usage of the Web site. Access errors include such things as the non-existence of a requested file, an unauthorized user, or a forbidden directory. Lost connections often are the result of user impatience. Most browser software allows the user to cancel the download of a page by clicking either on the stop button or back arrow button, by clicking on a link in the new page before the entire page and all associated graphics have been completely transferred, or even by closing the Web browser software in the middle of a transfer (Stout 1997, 33–34).

Error logs contain some non-standard data elements. For most server brands, the time stamp in the error log is in a different format than in the access log (Stout 1997, 8). The Netscape servers (i.e., the Enterprise Server and the Fastrack Server) use almost identical formats for the time stamp in the access log and the error log (Stout 1997, 30). One of the most common messages in the error log indicates a lost connection, usually because the user canceled a file transfer before the transfer was complete (Stout 1997, 8).

Referrer logs list the site that a user came from before accessing a particular page. It could be a page on another Web site with a hypertext link to a page at the monitored site, or it could be the URL of a search engine with the search criteria the user entered to find a listing for the monitored Web site (Stout 1997, 27–28). Most of the highly touted commercial Web tracing services and software depend on referrer logs to produce a better picture of user activities (Noonan 1995). The referrer log enables the analyst to identify the Web sites that have hyperlinks into the Web server being examined (Dorfman 1996). The referrer log includes the URL from which the reader came and the page in the present Web site at which the user arrived after following the link (Stout 1997, 9). When a user initially enters a monitored Web site, the referrer log effectively shows where the user was in cyberspace before entering the Web site. Unfortunately, there is no way to tie the entries in the referrer log to specific visitors or hits unless a combined log format is used (Stout 1997, 9).

The existence and use of the referrer log is pertinent to the broader issues of privacy and confidentiality being examined here. The HTTP protocol specification strongly suggests that Web browser software make the sending of referrer information to Web servers an optional, conscious decision in the control of the user of the Web. Most developers of browser software, however, have largely ignored the strong recommendation of the specification (Stout 1997, 39).

Agent logs record the type of browser or client software used to access Web pages on a particular host server (Noonan 1995). Each line of the agent file logs the agent (i.e., the browser software) making a single request (Dorfman 1996). The agent log typically includes the name of the browser software, the version, and the operating system. Sometimes the name and version of a proxy server will be appended to the line in the log (Stout 1997, 45). Agent logs also record the names of robots, including spiders and worms, and search engines (Stout 1997, 9). These software programs traverse the net, following links and exploring domains to catalog pages they find and list them in their databases (Stout 1997, 44). Robots are another threat to the grand plan to use computers to monitor HCI. The increasing surrogacy of software programs for online activities and searching currently performed by people themselves may foreshadow a future whose computer-computer interaction is much more central to human colonization of cyberspace than HCI. Human-computer interaction may eventually be abandoned as too frustrating and inefficient for both parties. My computer will call your computer. The behavior of intelligent agents in cyberspace may be worthy of study itself. In the future, people probably will benefit more from online environments while paradoxically participating less in them.

One major problem with the agent log is the lack of any method to tie the data contained in it to individual transfers in the access log (Stout 1997, 45). Another major concern is the usefulness of these data about software agents. Neither system administrators nor marketing types find this information very helpful. Agent information appears to be useful for two purposes: to identify bugs, errors, or logging anomalies encountered or created by a specific brand of browser or version of a browser, and to identify and eliminate the effect of Web spiders and robots that inflate and distort Web server traffic statistics (Stout 1997, 47).

This basic four-sided logging structure has several problems and shortcomings. The developers of Web servers should turn their attention to cleaning up the deficiencies in the existing logging scheme (Stout 1997, 48). The lack of even a de facto standard for the format of these logs has created many choices for Web server logging software, but many problems for analysts and researchers attempting to obtain meaningful, useful information from the variety of logs. The lack of standards also could have a long-term retarding effect on this overall research agenda. It will be difficult to compare the results from different research studies using logs of a slightly different format, and it will be difficult to replicate important research findings.

Web servers rely on HTTP, a stateless protocol that does not depend on the identities and authentication of users or the hardware and software environment in which it runs (Gibbs 1996c). In 1994 there were only two brands of Web server software: freeware from CERN (Conseil European pour la Recherche Nucleaire) and NCSA (the National Center for Supercomputing Applications in Urbana, Illinois) (Murphy and Lynch 1996). By mid–1996 the number of Web server software products had reached approximately 40 (Murphy and Lynch 1996). All NCSA-derived Web servers, including NCSA's httpd and the Apache server, write a one-line entry to a log file each time someone attempts to access the Web server (Musciano 1996a). For the foreseeable future most Web server software will run on Unix computers (Stout 1997, 176). Murphy and Lynch (1996) provide a good overview for the lay person on the state of Web server software. According to their survey of the server software scene, ten of the 29 major software programs in existence in 1996 provided some built-in log analysis software:

InterWare software from Consensys (http://www.consensys.com).
Webware from Electronic Dimensions (http://www.edime.com.au).
SuperWeb Server from Frontier Technologies (http://www.frontiertech.com).
Internet Information Server from Microsoft (http://www.microsoft.com).
FastTrack Server from Netscape (http://www.netscape.com).
Enterprise Server from Netscape (http://www.netscape.com).
WebServer from Open Market (http://www.openmarket.com).
WebSite from O'Reilly & Associates (http://www.ora.com).

Purveyor from Process Software (http://www.process.com).
WebSTAR 95/NT from Quarterdeck (http://www.qdeck.com).

The first step, then, is to collect some usage data. Each time the Web server software receives a request from a Web browser software installed on someone's Internet-connected PC, the server software records the request into a log file. The transaction between the browser software and the server software on the Web often is referred to as a hit or a page access (Murphy and Lynch 1996). In the world of Web servers the collection of the data has become so routine that most of the Web server log analysis software being developed focuses on the analysis portion of the process.

The raw access (or transfer) log file can be analyzed to produce the following statistics: the total number of requests made to the server; the total bytes transferred in response to those requests; the number of requests for each page, graphic, and file; the most-requested documents; the most-requested files; the top submitted forms and scripts; the most-requested documents by directory; the average number of requests by day or hour; the average bytes transferred by hour or day; the average number of hits on weekdays; and the average number of hits on weekend days (Stout 1997, 73).

One basic function of Web server logging software is to count the number of files retrieved by client browser software, such as Netscape Navigator and Microsoft's Internet Explorer. The first measurement of Web traffic was hits, but even the boastful admit that the measurement is misleading or useless. Transferring one screen of information may be counted as several hits or file transfers by the Web server log (Wagner 1996a). In the long run, especially for most research projects, a file transfer will not serve well as a basic unit of measurement. Although file transfer load and usage is important to the server and the server manager, it does not mean much to the human Web browser, or to anyone who wants to study the behavior of those browsers.

A new standard called page views has emerged to replace the older practice of counting hits (Wagner 1996a). It counts as one unit all of the files that are transferred to create one page on the browser's screen. The number of page views has much greater potential for the research community as a basic unit of activity measurement. It enables an analysis of Web server logs to function at the same perceptual level as experienced by the end user. This enables the analyst to perceive the interaction in a way similar to the user's perception of the event — a boon to any transaction log analysis project.

The term "clickstream" was coined by Next Century Media in 1993 to designate the series of events enacted by users of interactive media who manipulate their systems with remote control channel changers, PC keyboards and mice, keyboards of PDA devices, and voice command media (Conaghan 1995). Advanced Web site analysis programs enable the analysis of clickstreams — the path a visitor takes from page to page within the Web site (Bayne 1996).

Common Log Format (CLF or CLOG)   Busch (1997, 76) reports that more than 30 different formats exist for storing server usage log information. Fortunately, most Web servers support the common log format (CLF), and many support their own extended log formats. The types of extended log formats vary widely and can be modified to meet specific analysis needs (Randall 1997c). The CLF applies to the access (or transfer) logs generated by Web servers. The CLF derives from an early version of the National Center for Supercomputing Applications Web server. It is a proprietary format that captures several types of data (Randall 1998). The CLF contains only the site visitor's host name, the date and time of the request made to the server, the HTTP request to the server (which contains the URL), a return code for the request, and the number of bytes returned (Robertson 1996).

Most of the time, the host field contains the fully qualified domain name of the remote host making the connection to the server and requesting a document. The server software uses the Internet Domain Name System to look up the name of the remote host, based on the IP address. Sometimes, however, this field captures only the IP address of the client making the connection (Stout 1997).

The Identification (RFC [Request for Comments] 931) field almost always contains only a hyphen. It rarely contains meaningful data. This field was to enable the webmaster to know the identity of the person requesting a Web page. To obtain this information, however, the client computer must be running a software program capable of responding to the request for the username and supply it. The biggest obstacle to using the identification field in Web server transfer logs is the relatively small percentage of computers connected to the Internet that run the requisite software. However, requiring identification authentication is becoming more common in the Unix world. In February 1993, RFC 931 was written and renumbered RFC 1413 (Stout 1997, 18).

The authorized user field stores the username (but not the password) that the user enters to gain access to protected files. This field is similar to the identification field, except that the username stored is that for the protected portion of the Web site, not the user's username for the user's client computer (Stout 1997, 20).

The date and time field contains three pieces of information: the date, the time, and the offset from Greenwich Mean Time (Stout 1997, 21). The time stamp indicates the time the request was made to the server, rather than the time when the server completed the transfer of the file (Stout 1997, 62). The time stamp is accurate only to the second, even though a busy Web site can deal with multiple requests within the span of a second (Randall 1997c). This is the time at the server location, not the time at the client's location. Even though diurnal time means more to people than to computers, it is the computer's local time that gets stamped into the server log.

The data in the HTTP request field is surrounded by quotation marks so that the data can include embedded space characters. The field first contains the command (GET, POST, or HEAD). The last part of the HTTP request field contains the name and version of the protocol (Stout 1997, 23).

The status code field contains a code issued by the server describing the success or failure of the transaction. Status code 200 indicates either a successful retrieval of a Web page or a successful interaction with another entity, such as a CGI program (Stout 1997, 24).

The transfer volume field contains an ASCII representation of the number of bytes transferred by the server to the client as a result of an HTTP request (Stout 1997, 27).

One limitation of the common log format is that it does not capture information about post-retrieval processing undertaken by seekers and users of information. Examples of post-retrieval processing include printing, exporting, saving to disk, and e-mailing found information. Because post-retrieval processing takes place at the client end of the client-server network architecture, and the server side often is unaware of this activity, the common log format is not well-suited to provide data for the monitoring and analysis of this aspect of information retrieval in online environments (Borghuis 1997). Another limitation of the CLF is its intended audience. The common log format is oriented toward collecting the data needed by network administrators, not for in-depth site analysis (Robertson 1996). The CLF was designed by network administrators for their colleagues, not specifically for researchers. Pitkow (1997b) examines the limitations of the current Web log standard in more detail.

Extended (or Combined) Log Formats Most extended log formats are locally developed and unique to each site or brand of server software (Robertson 1996). The combined log format, one extended log format, integrates the referrer and agent data into the transfer log (Stout 1997, 28). A cookie field also can be part of an extended log format (Stout 1997, 28). Stout (1997, 41) recommends that it is better and more useful to record data commonly contained in the referrer and agent logs into a combined log format that, in essence, is an extended version of the access log. One advantage of the extended log format, as noted by Bertot, McClure, Moen, and Rubin (1997), is that it allows all log information to be collected into one log file. The only drawback to doing this is that, because adding fields to the access log is a deviation from the Common Log Format, some server log analysis software cannot handle the additional data. Use of a combined log format can waste significant amounts of disk space by capturing redundant information about every single hit of a visit (Stout 1997, 48).

Microsoft IIS log format (i.e., the log files produced by the Microsoft Internet Information Server) adds a few unique wrinkles to the Web server log format scene (Stout 1997, 135). The MIIS log adds extra fields such as the server IP and processing time to determine the efficiency of the server and the connection (Rahmel 1997).

Session-based tracking offers another way to think about capturing information about HCI. Session-based Web tracking opens and closes in real time a relationship between the buyer and the seller. No information about the customer stays on the server after the site visit. Session-based tracking is useful because it encourages spontaneity while providing anonymity to customers. The Open Market site and Time Warner's Pathfinder are two examples of sites that use such tracking (Yesil 1996, 112).

With increasing frequency, many Web browsing sessions contain one or more command-driven uses of search engines embedded within the broader browsing session. Some search engines purport to provide access to most or all of the World Wide Web's contents, while other search engines scour only a specific Web site or cluster of sites. Are logs of the use of a search engine at a Web site possible? If so, these logs would be similar to traditional transaction log analysis of Boolean-based search engines running on mainframes, minis, and microcomputers.

New Capabilities and Possibilities for Web Server Logs   Although information in Web server logs offers new capabilities and possibilities for analysis, it would be prudent to understand the recent explosion of interest in Web server log analysis as the most recent development in the movement to use computers to study HCI. Aptex Software from San Diego uses Cold War concepts and technologies to study the surfing patterns of users (Bayers 1998, 132). Although Web server logs can be understood as a logical third generation of transaction logging software, they also enable new questions to be raised and studied, such as what browsers and operating systems are used to access the site. In older transaction log analysis studies of dial access use of OPACs, an analogous study would have involved knowing which telecommunications package was used to access the site. One major difference, however, is that the browser significantly affects how the end user sees the site. Knowing how a common reader perceives a novel ultimately may be more useful than knowing what the author intended when writing the novel.

A distinction needs to be made between demographic and behavioral information. Demographic information tends to be relatively constant, or it changes in somewhat predictable patterns in such categories as age, sex, nationality, race, income, and education. Behavioral information is tied to specific activities, thus tending to be less constant, stable, or predictable. As it currently exists, Web site monitoring attempts to gather and analyze both demographic and behavioral information, and it may end up doing neither one very well. Business marketers are driving the development of Web server log analysis software. Often they want to extract demographic information from the logs, because demographic groups often exhibit similar shopping and buying behavior.

Odd as it seems at first, cyberspace information such as IP addresses is being used to infer demographic information about people. Worldata's Roy Schwedelson has observed that IP addresses are like ZIP Codes in that one uses them to track activity of individuals as they surf the net site (Internet a big hit 1997). Based on the domain name of the client accessing a Web server, DoubleClick can discern the following demographic information: the site or computer from which the human browser is coming, the frequency of visits by the human browser to the server site, the geographic location of the organization with which the browser is associated, the SIC (Standard Industrial Classification) codes of the organization, the size of the organization, the browser software being used, the operating system being used on the client PC, and the Internet Service Provider, if applicable (Stout 1997, 192–193). Analysis of Web server log data by client subdomain enables analysis by real-world environmental situations, such as the library, classroom, lab, office, dorm room, or satellite campus. For some monitoring projects, knowledge of the real-world places where online behaviors occur may be more useful than knowledge of the specific individuals responsible for the observed behavior. For example, an individual professor engaged in HCI in a variety of campus environments, including classroom, office, lab, and library, may behave quite variously online depending on the place involved.

The future of Web measurement, according to Ariel Poler, founder and president of I/PRO, lies with advertisers who will ask not only how many people a Web site is bringing them, but the quality of people (Cohen 1996a). The rush to gather or infer demographic information about visitors to a Web site, however, may not be very useful to other research communities involved in this amorphous movement. In the long run, access to accurate behavioral information may be much more useful than large quantities of demographic information. Although demographic groups may exhibit similar buying habits, the correlation between demographic characteristics and information-seeking and information-use behaviors may not be as strong.

Nevertheless, the lure of demographic information is very strong in the advertising community. Even Dreze and Zufryden (1997), who conducted a very interesting study on the effects of Web environmental conditions on the unobtrusively observed online behavior of individuals, succumbed to the demographic siren call in their concluding paragraph:

> As tracking measures on the Web become more refined in the future, it is expected that more accurate individual measurements will ultimately be available that will provide not only unique individual user behavior patterns (e.g., the specific click streams of unique site visitors) but also the specific characteristics of the site visitors (e.g., demographics). Thus, it is expected that the Web will eventually come closer to fulfilling its potential and promise as the ultimate medium for market segmentation at the individual consumer level, that is, for targeting unique individual surfers with individually designed promotions, content, products, and services on the Web.

Web server log analysis has the opportunity to revive some dormant aspects of computerized monitoring from the early days of mainframe systems. For example, interest in the question of response time waned as those times improved and stabilized during the 1980s. When Web browsers became the rage in the early 1990s, complaints about slow response resurfaced. Either Web server logs or Web client logging software should be able to measure response time. Response time could have a profound impact on the nature of human-computer use in this online environment.

Advanced Web server logging software opens the opportunity for a sophisticated variation on eyetrack research. This research examines how the human eye moves over an information space, such as a sheet of paper containing both textual and graphical information, or a computer screen with a graphical user interface. Eye movement is a basic form of human behavior, and it may correlate well with higher forms of human behavior and cognition. Howard (1991) studied the extensity, intensity, and motility of the eye movements of subjects as they examined bibliographic citations. Von Keitz (1988) and Drucker (1990) explored how eyetrack research can be used in marketing studies in for-profit situations. Drucker found that in the environment of printed sales catalogs, large photos and other graphics tended to be perceived first, followed by large-type text, then prices, and finally the smaller-type text. Web logging and analysis software could be used to study what areas of the screen, or what objects and their characteristics, such as color, motion, and size tend to be clicked most often. Such analyses would rest on the assumption that the user first notices something with the eye, then clicks on it.

Specific Web Server Log Analysis Programs and Services   "The search for better understanding of web site traffic has led to an explosion of software programs which analyze web server logs and site visits…. [M]ost web site managers are as confused about the differences between these products as they are about the actual data means…. [N]either the trade press nor the vendors of analysis products have done a good job of differentiating their offerings" (Buchanan and Lukaszewski 1997, 177).

Web server log analysis software programs work by converting the standard log files generated by the Web server software into a common database format such as Access or SQL. After the data have been converted into a database, the analysis utility turns the raw numbers into a wide variety of reports about who (i.e., IP addresses) has been visiting the Web site being monitored, how often, and when (Gerding 1997). Web server log analysis software programs focus primarily on analyzing and presenting the raw data. Although the raw data about human behavior on the Web is collected by the server software itself, analysis of the data often is undertaken, enhanced, or extended by additional software programs or third-party analysts. Some of these software analysis tools store data in external relational databases, rather than in internal, flat files. This allows them to manipulate the data and display it in spreadsheets, HTML, text files, or highly graphical tables (Wagner 1997a).*

Buchanan and Lukaszewski (1997, 178–179) classify Web server log analysis tools into three basic types. Local server analysis tools are installed on the same computer as the Web server software itself. They process the Web server log data at specified times and make reports available at a special Web site. Local server analysis tools are relatively inexpensive, and they provide timely reports while maintaining considerable local control. It is easy to backup and restore the log files.

For a more complete and interactive list of Web server logging software and companies, see the list of Web logging software at the Yahoo site. See also NCSA's HTTPD Log Analyzers page at http://union.ncsa.uiuc.edu/ HyperNews/get/www/log-analyzers.html

However, they also place a greater load on the computer that is running the server software, which could affect response time for users of the Web site. Most local server analysis software has been developed for UNIX servers.

Remote server analysis software often is used by third-party service providers. Usually, a small application is installed on the Web server computer that transfers the log files automatically to the analysis computer operated by the service provider. Remote server analysis by a third-party analysis provider is a good way to obtain independently audited traffic statistics, which may be vital for Web sites that are supported by advertising revenues. Although remote server analysis can lower the load on the Web site server, the reports may be less timely. Standalone desktop analysis software is not automatic. Web server log files must be downloaded and transferred from the Web server computer to the desktop computer. If the log is large, it may take a relatively long time for the computer to process the files.

Marketing Hyper Text Markup Language (MHTML) lets marketers watch user behavior across general editorial and marketing content. The language assigns a token to each site visitor. The tokens respond to the visitor's activities with predefined commands from a database (Hodges 1996, 46).

Commercial Web server log analysis software has become a crowded market. Although most such software programs import data into proprietary databases, a few store the data in proprietary flat files (Randall 1998). Third-party analysis services also have made strong gains in recent years. Although I/PRO is perhaps the best known Web traffic measurement service, Interse may be the most widely used, with more than 1,500 customers in late 1996 (Keeping track of the traffic 1996). Waltner (1997) reports that newspaper publishers are divided over the importance of third-party audits of use of online advertising. Some newspapers have found that third-party audits of Web site traffic are essential for generating advertising sales.

Although locally developed analysis software was the first Web server log analysis software to emerge, its market share has dwindled as the market has grown. Amazon.com, the online bookstore located in Seattle, developed its own analysis tools because none of the commercial Web traffic analysis software could digest data about the use of dynamically generated Web pages. In general, the commercial Web server analysis products were not designed to examine data from Web servers that generate pages from data stored in databases, rather than static data files stored in the server's file system (Wagner 1997a).

C|Net of San Francisco seeks to discover insights from Web usage to reinforce use and keep visitors online longer with C|Net. The company is experimenting with a software application that creates a graph that describes the path a user takes through a Web site. By representing individual pages on the vertical axis and the passage of time on the horizontal axis, the software represents the Webpilgrim's progress as a jagged horizontal line (Wagner 1997a). One goal of these C|Net projects is to determine what information about users is most important to monitor.

Although third-party Web server log analysis is perhaps the most expensive analysis, it is conducted by an allegedly disinterested third party, so the results often are accepted as reliable data upon which Web advertising rates are determined. The first third-party Web site audit was completed in June 1996 by BPA Interactive (Cohen 1997a). The online audit of the Lycos Web site by ABVS (http://www.access abvs.com.Lycos) was released in October 1996 in what ABVS President Michael J. Lavery called "a defining moment for Web auditing" (Cohen 1997a). BPA Interactive, ABVS from the Audit Bureau of Circulations, and I/PRO have emerged as the three major players in the fledgling field of Web site usage auditing (Kirsner 1997a). Having Web server logs analyzed by third parties saves time and system resources. Off-site analysis also increases platform independence, because the generated log files are text files (Robertson 1996). Increasingly, advertisers are insisting that Web log analysis be done by third-party service providers. Ian Murphy (1996), for example, advises that marketers would do well to hire third-party Web traffic auditors to establish the veracity of the data collection and analysis. Potential advertisers often require third-party statistical reports and audits before they will seriously contemplate buying the right to have their advertising banner displayed at a particular Web site (Stout 1996).

> The key drawback with auditing services is that they rely on a site's server logs, and thus are subject to all the stickiness associated with trying to get good intelligence from raw data. Most audits, for example, note that their certified tally of page requests does not include material that has been cached by America Online or another service. Most have trouble calculating page requests for sites designed with frames. And not one of the auditors attempts to translate hits and page requests into a number of actual readers who have visited the site — the much sought-after tally of "unique users" (Kirsner 1997a, 38).

As a side note, hits on Web sites are not the only data advertisers and marketers collect in these online environments. They also glean valuable demographic and preference information from questionnaires that users voluntarily complete (Eisenberg 1996). In its long investigation of online personal privacy, the FTC has focused on these online questionnaires (especially geared toward children). Even if behavior rather than demographics is the focus of a Web log analysis project, other data collection methods can provide a more complete picture of the user's intentions, needs, attitudes, and satisfaction. The Internet is the perfect medium for gathering demographic information, because of the two-way communication capabilities of e-mail (Yesil 1996, 110).

Audience tracking methods align themselves into two basic approaches. Active tracking involves voluntary registration by the visitor. Passive tracking involves Web log analysis (Conaghan 1995). Although the focus of this book is on passive tracking, active tracking methods warrant some mention. Two companies involved in such tracking are Newshare and Next Century Media (Conaghan 1995). Dreze and Zufryden (1997) correctly observe, however, that registration of visitors to a Web site can be done only on a voluntary basis. Registration methods, therefore, are inherently biased, because they are neither census-based nor representative, because of their inherent self-selection biases.

Web Client Log Analysis   Although Web server log analysis has received much of the interest and development support, it is possible to engage in Web client log analysis. Such analysis focuses on the client side of the basic client-server architecture. The need to monitor Internet use at the client end has been presented as a bandwidth issue, especially in work environments. For network managers, bandwidth allocation becomes a crucial issue when an entire company needs consistent Internet access (Spangler 1996).

Despite the lack of interest from advertisers and a subsequent lack of research and development money, some Web client log analysis projects have been undertaken. A study conducted at Georgia Tech by Catledge and Pitkow (1995) examined user behavior on the Web by capturing client-side user events on NCSA's XMosaic. The analysis of the transaction logs resulted in several design and usability recommendations for future development of Web pages, sites, and browsers. Chen, Park, and Yu (1996) studied the path traversal patterns in the Web distributed information environment. They filtered out the backward references from the original sequence of client-side log data, and derived two algorithms to determine the frequent traversal patterns.

Tauscher and Greenberg (1997) used client-side computerized monitoring to suggest software design and interface changes. They collected data from late October to early December in 1995. They found that 90 percent of all log statements were requests to navigate to a URL. They identified seven types of Web browsing patterns. Tauscher and Greenberg found that the only history mechanism used with any frequency by Web surfers was the back button. The recurrence rate was approximately 60 percent, defined as the probability that any URL visited repeats a previous visit. Tauscher and Greenberg concluded that Web browsing activity is a recurrent system, defined by Greenberg (1993) as one in which users predominantly repeat activities they have performed before, while continuing to add new actions and behaviors from the many possible actions. On average, of all the Web pages visited by a human browser, 60 percent were visited only once, 19 percent twice, eight percent three times, and four percent four times. Only a handful of Web pages are loaded with high frequency by a single human browser (Tauscher and Greenberg 1997, 118). A key design principle for browser software is to give preferential treatment to the high frequency of repeated actions (Tauscher and Greenberg 1997, 113).

Problems and Shortcomings of Web Server Log Analysis   "Ironically, there's actually far less information available to marketers about consumer activity on the Web than they're able to gather elsewhere, particularly through credit-data companies such as Equifax or TRW" (Bayers 1998, 132).

Web server log analysis, predominantly server log analysis, but also client-side analysis of HCI, has several limitations and shortcomings. One fundamental problem with Web logs is that they contain too much data to economically mine, interpret, and apply. Perhaps the typical Web site contains too many files and receives too many hits to analyze human behavior at that level. Early in 1998 it was estimated that the Excite Web site collects 40 gigabytes of data in its log files every day (Bayers 1998, 132). Bayers also suggests that executives at Amazon.com, the Web-based bookseller, privately admit that the company's growth has out-stripped its ability to store the data it collects, let alone mine it.

Another perceptual problem with Web server log analysis capabilities is a generally inflated sense, particularly among potential purchasers of commercial Web log analysis software, of the accuracy of Web log analysis projects. Morgan Davis, director of operations for CTS Network Services, an independent Internet Service Provider in the San Diego area, believes that far too many people are under the impression that Web server log files are accurate (Stout 1996). This is an endur-ing challenge for the movement to use computers to monitor HCI. Many people overlook the human elements of these projects and assume that computerized mon-itoring is completely accurate and irrefutable.

Another problem with Web server log analysis is that not all browser soft-ware interacts with servers in the same way. Different browser software can have different effects on a server completing and logging an identical transfer of files (Morgan Davis, quoted in Stout 1996).

Another shortcoming of Web server logs is inherent in the fundamentally stateless nature of the interaction between clients and servers. Each time a request is made to a server, it is done out of context of previous requests.* Servers cannot explicitly correlate individual requests from the same user. Session analysis links separate requests into a meaningful, veracious sequence of requests (Robertson 1996). The problem of identifying the boundaries of user search sessions in OPACs and other public access systems has become exacerbated and ingrained in the client-server environment. Session analysis during client-server interactions is much more useful for tracking trends over time than for pinpointing an exact number of users of a Web site (Robertson 1996).

The cache-flow problem is increasingly complex and nettlesome for Web log analysis projects. A cache is information temporarily residing in the RAM mem-ory or hard disk of the computer running the Web client browser software being used by the Web surfer. Because many Web browsers are able to cache files at the client end for use later in the Web browsing session, the user may grab a file only once from the remote server, yet refer to it more than once during the session. The use of caching accelerates the retrieval of information, reduces network traffic, and decreases the load on both the server and the client (Berthon, Pitt, and Prender-gast 1997, 6). As soon as the early 1990s Braun and Claffy (1994) were calling for the deployment of geographically distributed caching systems to improve the efficiency of the server and the network, even though such caching would dimin-ish the usefulness of data gathered in the logs of any one Web server (Larsen 1997, 53). Because Web server logging occurs at the server end of the relationship, server logs potentially under-represent use of files by end-users. Web server logging soft-ware may undercount the number of hits on a document made by the end-user.

---

* See also Randall (1996) for information about how clients and servers interact.

The use of cache systems, either by the Web client software or proxy servers, aims to improve performance, but it also makes it extremely difficult and complicated to determine with confidence the number of times a user views a given Web page. Because local caching has become common practice in browser software, and because users can select and control different cache management practices within their browser software, page view measurement schemes typically are defined to reflect and verify only that the page was viewed at least once (Pitkow 1997a).

An example of the cache-flow problem occurs when a visitor to a Web site uses the back arrow on the client browser software to return to a page viewed previously during the visit. The second and subsequent viewings are completely invisible to the server (Stout 1997, 67). The use of caching can have a big impact on Web server log analysis projects. When the Hollywood Online Web site implemented a method that thwarted caching, traffic on the server increased between 10 and 15 percent (Kirsner 1997a).

Proxy servers also can cause the undesirable consequence of undercounting or misrepresenting hits on a Web site. A proxy server essentially is a shared cache memory for a group of users (Berthon, Pitt, and Prendergast 1997, 6). Use of proxy servers on the Internet seems to be increasing, which diminishes the usefulness of Web server logs as data sources for demographic analyses. One function of the proxy server is to act as a trusted go-between from inside a security firewall to the outside, rough-and-tumble, networked environment. When a proxy server sends a request to another server, the server receiving the request logs the host name or IP address of the proxy server, instead of that of the original requesting client machine (Larsen 1997, 49). If visitors are lurking behind a proxy server, they are not recorded (Strom 1996a). Thus the actions of caching proxy servers are largely immeasurable (Stout 1996). To further complicate the situation, proxy servers can be layered or nested, so that a page retrieved from the original Web server may end up being retrieved by thousands of people, yet counted as only one hit by the Web server log running on the original server (Berthon, Pitt, and Prendergast 1997, 6). Of course, derivative use can and does occur with print-based documents as well. For example, a single copy of *Newsweek* may reach hundreds of patients in a physician's waiting room, yet the publishers and advertisers know for certain that only one copy of the issue was mailed to that address.

The problem (or opportunity) of various uses of the same packet of information by multiple individuals seems to be accelerating as the digital age moves forward. The impact of proxy servers on Web server log data can be substantial. In 1997 MatchLogic, a company which handles banner advertisements for General Motors and other corporations, found that Web sites routinely undercount the number of visitors by an average of 76 percent (Taylor, Catharine 1997).

All Web audit service providers must grapple with the technical and social problems that can skew an analysis. The most important of these are count distortions caused by caching on proxy servers; framesets and splash pages; and server log manipulation and tampering by site managers. One of the biggest impediments to auditing accuracy is America Online's internal procedure of caching: capturing copies of Web pages within AOL's own system to speed up response for AOL customers (Cohen 1997a).

Bruner (1997a) reports that early in 1997 the Internet Engineering Task Force proposed standards for improving the count of cached page views on the Web, which may add up to 40 percent to the previous counts of Web site traffic. The proposed new counting standards would take into consideration the number of pages viewed when proxy servers are used by ISPs.

Web site administrators have developed ways to reduce caching. Cache busting techniques have been developed to prevent the local caching of information originally transmitted over computer networks. Cache busting is another way of altering the pace and flow of HCI in cyberspace to gather more reliable statistics at the server side of the interaction. As such, cache busting violates the proposed code of conduct for human monitors (see Chapter 5). Cache busting is an attempt, often undertaken in the interest of gathering more reliable Web server log data, to alter the normal interaction between a person and a computer functioning as a Web client.

Another problem with Web server analysis is that it measures outgoing information packets. By itself, analysis of a Web server log cannot determine if the outgoing packets reached their destinations. If the file transfer is interrupted, waylaid, or incomplete for some reason (e.g., the impatient user clicked the stop button on the browser client software), the Web server logging software must count interrupted and successful file transfers as an undifferentiated mass of outgoing data (Kirsner 1997a).

Another limitation of pure Web server logs is that they record only HTTP server information. They cannot capture details about the HCI that do not get past the TCP/IP layers and into the HTTP layer. HTTP rides on top of TCP/IP, which in turn rides on the NIC layer. Some important information concerning HCI in Web client-server environments can be collected only at levels below HTTP. User-initiated disconnects and file transfer requests that never reach the server (for whatever reason) never enter the server's log file (Randall 1997c). Because of this shortcoming, server logs often cannot provide a complete picture of a Web surfing session as it was experienced by the surfer.

Yet another shortcoming of Web server log files is that they are by nature historical. They merely are a log of past activity. Because they are compiled and analyzed after the fact, for certain applications they can be hopelessly out of date (Randall 1997c). Experiments in real-time analysis of log file data and application of the findings (usually in the form of modifications to the online environment currently being experienced by an individual user) are underway.

Search engines and robots such as AltaVista and Hotbot that scour the Web looking for new files to index will artificially inflate the number of hits on files at a specific server (Strom 1996a). These online robots that imitate human Internet surfers tend to skew and inflate Web traffic (Taylor, Catharine 1997). Trawler software may lead to the under-reporting of usage of documents on a Web server. Trawler software such as FreeLoader (http://www.freeloader.com) downloads Web documents onto a local hard disk during off-peak hours. Trawler software aims to avoid long waiting periods during document retrieval. Trawler software also may cause inflated usage figures, because the software may update locally-held information more often than it reaches an end-user (Berthon, Pitt, and Prendergast 1997, 7). Although one's trawler software may be configured to download information from a site every weekend, one may look at the information only once a month, or sporadically.

Most Web servers cannot distinguish a single-user computer from a multiuser computer (Stout 1997, 54). Because Web server log analysis software measures computer-computer interaction, rather than HCI, it may be erroneous to assume that hits from a single hostname come from the same person (Stout 1997, 55). Networked computers in classrooms and libraries often are used by many different individuals. Although it is easy to verify this through real-world observation, it is difficult for a computerized monitoring project to detect these differences, short of requiring everyone to logon with a username and ID that can be linked to a specific, identified individual. Domain names in IP addresses really do not convey much demographic information about the users at those IP addresses. When my colleague's middle school aged son used the Web from his father's university workplace on Saturday mornings, an analyst of activity from that IP address could have concluded either that my university has very immature students, or that my colleague's interests become very puerile on the weekends. They may indeed, but Web server log analysis is a very unreliable method for arriving at that knowledge. Some domain names (e.g., ibm.com and aol.com) also do not help the Web log analyst locate the user (Robertson 1996).

Dynamic IP addressing is a way to spread a large user demand for IP addresses across few actual addresses. Dynamic IP addressing often is used to assign a temporary IP address to dial-access users of a service. As a result of repeated use of dynamic IP addressing, an individual user may come from one IP address on one day, and from another IP address on the next. Operating in isolation, the Web server log has no way of knowing that the two access events were made by the same person (Robertson 1996). Many Internet Service Providers (ISPs) use dynamic IP addressing for their clients. The best that analysts of Web server logs can do is determine the name and geographic service area of the ISP that owns and uses the dynamically assigned IP address (Stout 1997, 15).

Unbundling usage information from a variety of Web sites all located on one physical server can be a difficult project. Every Web server can host multiple Web sites on a single computer. This is called virtual hosting, or virtual site hosting. Internet service providers often do this for their customers. They can satisfy the varying log analysis needs of their customers by configuring their Web servers to maintain separate server log files for each of the sites for which they are the virtual host (Stout 1997, 182).

Often a user can pursue the same goal at the server site or within the client browser software. For example, a user one link away from a home page who wants to return to that page can often, in well-designed Web sites, click on a link near the bottom of the page to return to the home page, or in the client browser software can click on the "Back" button. Alternatively, one could click on the "Go" pull-down menu, then click on the URL for the home page. Although all three methods will return one to the home page, the Web server logging software may capture different data, depending on the method chosen.

We also need to remind ourselves that, from a certain perspective, navigating hyperspace is inherently inefficient and redundant. Browsing is different from more focused searching. Moreover, different types of online browsing have been identified and classified. It may be difficult, for example, for a Web log collector and analyst to differentiate between informed, deliberate Web browsing and lost, confused, irrational browsing. Fuller and de Graaff (1996) analyzed the problems of using Web server traffic as an indicator of user interest. One problem with counting the number of times users grab files from a Web site is that hyperlink usability has a path-dependent nature. In a non-indexed hyperspace users must follow paths to clearings of interest (Fuller and Graaff 1996). Until they find files of interest, and perhaps establish bookmarks, users mainly are wandering or browsing. To assume that grabbing a file from a server indicates user interest is to assume that users are as interested in the misses, pathways to desired pages, and dead ends as they are in finding what they seek (Fuller and Graaff 1996). Usually, the user's own full estimation of interest in a file or cluster of files cannot be made until after the file has been retrieved. Interest is fully determined after the Web server logging software's moment of opportunity to count usage.

The second problem with using file grabs as an indication of user interest is that users access Web pages in a variety of ways. There may be inequalities in users' abilities to access content, because of network bottlenecks, user-terminated transfers, excessive delays in downloading, server errors, and other factors (Fuller and Graaff 1996). To count users' file-grabbing activities almost assumes that equal access to files exists at all times. Interrupted transfers (for whatever reason, including user-initiated interruptions) are difficult to track reliably (Stout 1996).

If any images are embedded in a Web page, when that page is accessed by a Web client browser, every file that comprises the page gets logged, including each embedded image. Therefore, one page load may write more than one line to the access log. Most Web log analysts contend that simply counting the number of files accessed inflates the apparent use of the site. Loading images does not really count as use of a Web site. Images get no respect. Musciano (1996a) goes so far as to suggest removing all image references from the access log before true access log analysis begins.

Another challenge with Web site computerized monitoring is how to deal with dynamically generated pages that often are pieced together from the results of a user search of a database. While older forms of computerized monitoring, such as transaction log analysis, focus on human queries to a database, Web server logs originally focused on user retrieval of static HTML pages. Using computerized monitoring software and techniques to study Web access to a database presents special challenges. Rahmel (1997) notes that most Web access to a database occurs through a database connector. Search results in the forms of HTML pages are dynamically built by a piece of middleware (e.g., a CGI application, Perl script, Active Server Page, or custom connector) via an SQL query. The professional edition of Hit List solves this problem by storing the query string of keywords that generated the dynamically generated Web page (Gerding 1997).

As the design and functionality of Web sites becomes more complex, the challenge of measuring activity in those sites becomes a bigger challenge. Two additional aspects of the challenges are framesets and splash pages. Cohen (1997a) describes the problems they can cause for analyzers of Web site traffic:

> Framesets, an element of a Web site structure, can inadvertently cause a single page view to be recorded as multiple page views. The structure usually includes a navigation frame, a large content frame and an advertisement frame on the top or bottom. Although they appear together on a single screen, the server logs them as separate Web browser windows. So, a user viewing one frameset page leaves behind a record of multiple page visits. Splash pages, sort of welcome signs, usually contain little content and sit on top of actual home pages. Users must click through to get to the home page, thereby fattening the traffic count.

Another reason why file-grabbing events do not measure user interest well is that users may be constrained in the ability to view content because the site creators failed to consider the human factors related to navigating the Web (Fuller and Graaff 1996). The structure and content of a document space may be poorly designed.

Positioning a Web site, regarding both cognitive (e.g., an easily remembered URL) and virtual locations (e.g., the ability to have others interested in the same topics link to the site), probably influences the number of people accessing the site (Fuller and Graaff 1996). Even advertising agency executives agree that the site-specificity of much Web usage tracking activity ultimately is not very useful. They still need a way to compare activity across sites (Marx 1996a).

Another problem with this method of monitoring HCI is that the perceptual fog is very thick around a specific Web site. Usually a Web server log can detect only where the user has been immediately before and after the visit. It is impossible to see users off in the distance coming toward a Web site. For the moment, the Web is fog-bound. Recent software developments, however, have improved the situation. Some Web server log analysis software can gather and analyze detailed information about how visitors to a site learned about it. Hit List Professional can trace which search engine was used to locate a site, including the keywords searched to locate the site (Busch 1997).

The reports generated by many Web server log analysis software programs also have their shortcomings and embedded assumptions. Most of this software is so intent on providing easy to understand summary statistics that it does not provide an option to perform more arduous, intensive analyses. For research purposes, therefore, much of this software is too simplistic. Another shortcoming of the current trend in commercial software for analyzing Web server logs is that the reports are designed solely for human consumption. In the long run, it is better to have the computer system itself analyze the data, then apply the findings of the analysis, with human intervention occurring only on an ad hoc basis.

Perhaps the primary shortcoming of the Web server logging movement is that ultimately it only measures grabbing files or creating page views in a networked environment, not the use of the information contained in them. Regardless of the information environment (either real-world or virtual), retrieving information and using it may be two related but different activities. Web server logs record the documents that users fetch, but indicate nothing about how they interact with those documents (Udell 1996). They cannot reveal how the information contained in those files is understood and used by human beings (Lakos 1997). The files tend to cluster into texts, so that it is possible to tell how often a rather artificially defined text is grabbed, but it still tells us little about how a text is used. Thus the computerized monitoring research community continues to dance around perhaps the principal activity that commands our attention — the use of information. In this sense, Web log analysis represents little or no improvement over the more traditional gate counts and circulation transactions that have been employed to measure use of real-world libraries. Use continues to be inferred, rather than verified.

Although Web server log file analysis software in general does a good job of recording and analyzing how visitors use a Web site, this class of software will not notify site administrators if a site has a link problem or has crashed altogether. Site analysis software tools, a related software class, are needed for their link checker features and around-the-clock monitoring capabilities (Rapoza 1997a).

All logging software used in mainframe, mini, standalone micro, and client-server networked environments has problems and shortcomings. The software captures certain behavioral actions with frightening efficiency, but it can be difficult or impossible to infer a user's purpose, attitude, estimation of success, and sense of satisfaction from the user's behavior alone. Web server logs do not collect raw data that directly relate to user preferences, attitudes, comments, or acceptance of the site (Buchanan and Lukaszewski 1997, 110). Cooper (1998), however, maintains that a comprehensive logging system should have some way of recording users' perceptions of the online experience according to their current needs.

The ethical issue of unobtrusively monitoring HCI persists. The breezy openness of Web server log monitoring (e.g., Welcome to this Web site! You are the 7,546th visitor since the beginning of the year. How do you like Netscape 2.0 running in the MS Windows 3.1 environment? How is life at NIU.EDU?) puts a new spin on these ethical qualms. Wittingly or unwittingly we seem to be creating an entire virtual environment where people expect to be unobtrusively monitored. Because using computers to monitor HCI serves a variety of purposes, it is difficult to determine whether computerized monitoring is fundamentally good or bad in itself, or whether ethical judgment depends on the goal and application of each individual analysis project.

Some Web site monitoring software enables real-time monitoring of visitor behavior. According to Nachiketa Lolla, an Aquas, Inc. spokesperson, Bazaar Analyzer can be used for real-time monitoring of a Web site (Balderston 1996). The ethical issues surrounding real-time monitoring go back at least 25 years to the "transparent stimulation" aspect of an information retrieval (IR) system proposed by Siegfried Treu (1972).

For a variety of economic and cultural reasons, site-based analysis of HCI has received much more development attention to date than user-centered analysis. Teachers want to see how well a specific computer-assisted instruction program works, rather than how a specific individual interacts with all available virtual formal learning situations. Librarians want to know how users interact with specific computerized catalogs and databases, not how specific individuals move in and out of all online information environments available to them. Web site managers of all stripes want to know how their particular site is being used, rather than how specific individuals wander over the entire World Wide Web.

Despite its domination of the monitoring field, site-specific analyses have some inherent limitations. Site-based usage analysis is too atomistic. This atomism appears to be influencing the general conception of what the Web is and could become. These analyses tend to take the observed activity out of its broader context. For example, rather than reinforce the concept of the Web as a worldwide hypertext, site-based usage analysis reinforces the notion of the site as a self-contained fiefdom. Ultimately, Web server log analysis may reveal little tangible knowledge of individuals and individual behavior in cyberspace. Raisch (1996) argues that the only bit of information that can be known for certain about a visitor to a Web site is the IP address of the workstation: "There is nothing intrinsic in the Internet technology or the World Wide Web that allows us to uniquely identify a specific user."

Web site usage analysis subtly denies the true nature of the Web as an amorphous hypertext. The goal of much Web site usage analysis is to attract people to a particular Web site, then cajole them into lingering. Web site analysis does not encourage users to roam freely through cyberspace. There are some indications, however, that even serious businesses are becoming interested in how users interact with the Web as a whole, not just with a particular site. Late in 1996 Knight-Ridder Newspapers announced plans to construct an internal traffic system to measure the way people use content and view advertisements on 30 separate Web sites developed by the newspaper chain (Buchanan and Lukaszewski 1997, xvi).

Current and Potential Impact of Web Log Analysis The preceding list of shortcomings and limitations of Web server log analysis does not mean that these projects have no current value or will have no future impact. If these analyses are put into a context, they can help us better understand how people and computers interact. Web server log files can be understood and analyzed as indicators of digital service output (Bertot, McClure, Moen, and Rubin 1997).

At present, development of a Web site is basically higgledy-piggledy. Web server log analysis could turn site development into one long controlled experiment. For example, if a resource at a Web site is not being heavily used, the aspects of the resource could be systematically modified, then monitored to see if each change had any significant impact on use. Web site development could be transformed from its current state as an art (and often bad art, at that) into a science, or, at the least, a combination of art and science. The analysis of the server access logs of the Hasbro Web site revealed that 40 percent of the visitors did not proceed past the home page (report published in *Web Week*, mentioned in Strom 1996a). The webmaster at the London site redesigned the Web pages. As a result, the number of lingerers increased 50 percent.

As often mentioned here, Web usage analysis could lead to the on-the-fly development of truly personal online environments, with the environments personalized based on unobtrusively observed behavior, rather than on stated preferences. Every click one has ever made (including the mistakes) in the past will subtly determine how the Web environment one presently perceives appears. If one knows (or even suspects) that one's online behavior influences one's online environment, what effect would that knowledge have on one's behavior?

Jeffrey Chester, executive director of the Center for Media Education, a nonprofit advocacy group, questions this trend toward customized Web marketing tailored to individuals, including children. The Ad System from StarPoint Software constructs user profiles by combining data from demographic, geographic, psychographic, online behavior, and collaborative filtering.* Specific profiles of individual users of the Internet are automatically assembled as the service analyzes the behavioral residue of users' browsing sessions (Piller 1997). Many online marketers believe that, compared to collaborative filtering software based on the stated preferences of individuals, software products that track online behavior and tailor Web content accordingly have more long-term potential (Wilder and Dalton 1997).

What Is the Research Potential of Web Server Log Data? Even though Web access log data analysis does have some pure research potential, we must keep in mind that marketers and advertisers are driving this software development. In his overview of the development of mathematics, Bailey (1996, 87) observes that the "field of practical navigation was absolutely fundamental to the ascendancy of the new maths and thought processes because it provided clear feedback and the inexorable pressure to improve. Purely academic uses do not provoke the same level of urgency." Perhaps in a similar way the pressure to navigate, buy, and sell on the Web has pushed the development of software tools for collecting and analyzing information about HCI to a feverish pace in the last three years, compared to the snail's pace of the previous 30 years. Strom (1996a) argues that Web server logs provide a simple, low-cost method of developing new customer leads and further cementing relationships with existing customers. Given that, at least to date, Web logging and analysis software has not been developed primarily for the educational and library and information science research communities, we should not let that deter us, but rather explore how existing software can serve our research purposes.

One of the shortcomings (or blessings, depending on how one perceives it) of traditional transaction log analysis is that it indicated little if anything about

---

* See Cleland (1997) for more information about Starpoint Software of Mountain View, Calif.

the demographic aspects of system users. When I was conducting a manual analysis of the transaction logs of an OPAC, it was futile and pointless to try to infer demographic information from the captured HCI. The ability of Web server logs to provide useful demographic data probably is tenuous and declining. Most software advances in this area diminish the reliable links between use of this information environment and demographic aspects of the users. Additionally, the importance of demographic data itself may be declining. Demographic data are useful only as predictors or as explanations of behavior. If middle-aged white, college-educated males do not use the Web environment in the same ways, clustering users into that demographic corral will not be of much use, even to online marketers. As the technological and economic abilities to create "markets of one" advance, the value of demographic information will decline.

If we assume that some Web log analysis research involves interest in how Web users move from server to server (including movement within a single server site), the primary focus of attention is on what traditionally has been called the search session. Perhaps in the Web environment it would be more appropriate to call it a Web browsing session. Unfortunately, the user's (and the analyst's) sense of a continuous session — from the time the user fires up Netscape until closing it down — is virtual. Unlike older mainframe online catalog searches, there is no continuous connection that, for analysis purposes, can serve as a real representation of the user's cognitive sense of a Web browsing session. Moving around on the Web is nothing more than a series of discrete request and response transactions between the browser software and one or more HTTP servers. Normally, neither the client software nor the server maintain any record of the state of the previous, subsequent, or any other connection (Baron and Weil 1996). The server lives for the moment, handling as many file requests as it needs to.

As the third generation of transaction logging software, Web logging software does make some major contributions to the lineage. During the first two generations, transaction log analysis focused either on the individual or the computer. Either the human behavior (such as persistence, typing errors, and logical errors) or the system performance (such as response time, number of hits, and error messages) was studied. Web logging software opens a vast potential field for analysis: use of content.

Because server access logs are written chronologically, the log analyst can trace the access path of a single visitor through the Web site (Musciano 1996a). Web logs enable human monitors to learn more about how people move through an information space. Web server logs also could be used to undertake a more traditional transaction log analysis study of the search terms entered into both inter-site and intra-site Web search engines.

Perhaps the greatest contribution made by emerging Web server log analysis tools to the movement to use computers to monitor HCI is the realization of a third potential focus for studying HCI. Most if not all of first and second generation TLA studies focused either on system performance or on user behavior. Early analysts assumed that in the realm of HCI, the person and the computer would be the two primary objects of our attention. By enabling the study of how files are grabbed from a server site, Web log analysis has made possible a third focus of attention — on use of the database itself. In the first generation OPAC TLA studies, this focus, if it had been possible, would have concentrated on which specific records were retrieved from the database, the situational characteristics surrounding their retrieval (e.g., was the record retrieved in a single item set, or a 3,000 record set), and subsequent pursuit of the item for which the bibliographic record or item record serves as a surrogate. If there is a way to capture the record numbers or file names or record identifiers within retrieved sets, along with the size of each retrieved set, and possibly the ordinal position of the record within the sorted, retrieved set of records, an analyst could study how often a bibliographic record, for example, was retrieved from the database, the sizes of the retrieved sets that contained the record in question, and how often the record was called up for a more complete display of holdings information, location codes, and similar data. In paper-based information environments, the circulation records for books could be matched to the logs of retrieved bibliographic records. The lists of retrieved bibliographic records could be sorted by date, call number, or other categories to reveal how the database is perceived through retrieving subsets from it. Because users never see the entire database, they construct a mental model of it (and its overall value as a database) based on these partial views in the form of retrieved sets. Rather than examine the demands placed on the system as a conglomeration of hardware, software, and network demands, perhaps we should examine the demands placed on the database itself. This analysis could open a whole new field of methodologies and techniques for deciding how to archive records from a database. In this way, the nature of Web log analysis has expanded our understanding of the possibilities of the amorphous movement in general beyond the big two players — the human and the computer. With Web server log analysis the analyst can get an indication of the documents on the server which are attracting the most interest (Musciano 1996a).

The study of successful file transfers from Web sites could be analogous to the study of shelf availability studies of books and other items in real libraries. The rate of successful file or page transfers indicates the degree of success in delivering the information to the user in the intended format and completeness. As a user of a real library first identifies and locates a desired item through the use of indexes, catalogs, and citations in books and journal articles, then attempts to follow these "hot tips" and retrieve the full text, so too a surfer on the Web first identifies a desired item through search engines, hotlinks, and even citations in paper-based media, then attempts to retrieve the full text. In both information environments, there are many possible reasons for an unsuccessful full object retrieval.

"The Web is much more accountable [than other media]. I view that as a strength. But it's a vulnerability to people who think of it as a branding medium. It's a qualitative medium rather than quantitative" (Larry Chase, President of The Online Agency, quoted in Jaffee 1996).

There are two major concerns with the current emphasis on computerized monitoring, in the form of Web server log analysis, to fuel Web advertising campaigns. First, computerized monitoring infers real-world demographic data. Second, the emphasis of the analysis is on exposure to specific Web content, rather than on a pure analysis of human behavior in virtual environments that one tends to see in educational, library, and work settings.

The methods undertaken to measure and analyze the traffic, popularity, and effectiveness of a Web site should be directly related to the purpose, goals, and objectives of the site itself (Stout 1996). Stout (1996) differentiates between Web sites that sell goods and services and sites that sell advertising space.

"The Web's ability to monitor demand in real time connects information providers to their customers in a way that's exhilarating and also a bit scary. There's nowhere to run, nowhere to hide: If you don't understand your audience, it's only because you don't want to" (Udell 1996).

The wide array of statistics capable of being generated from the variety of software packages and third-party auditors on the market contributes to the frustration currently felt by many about the burgeoning field of measuring activity on the Web (Chen 1997).

Although I have suggested that, in the long run, site-centered Web log analyses probably will not serve the computerized monitoring research community as well as user-centered analyses would, the current research and development emphasis on site-centered usage does make the Web site an object for scrutiny and contemplation. How should we think about a Web site: as a book, library, store, terminal, or node of a hypertext? As questions about the basic units of information-seeking behavior are becoming urgent and murky, so too are questions about the fundamental units of online information environments. The old, reliable, nested units of journal issues, journal articles, books, and book chapters have given way to file clusters and dynamic hypertext links. The Web site as a city-state in cyberspace may be, like the Italian city-state of the Renaissance, a brief, brilliant phenomenon.

There is something sad and disappointing about this entire movement to develop, use, and refine Web logging and analysis software. The desire to establish and control a defined space is so great and ingrained that Web server logs are much more popular than Web client logs. We all wish to be bouncers at virtual bars, monitoring and controlling who gains access to our bar, and virtually defenestrating anyone who misbehaves while in our bar. The notion of cyberspace as a wide open space with infinite possibilities for browsing and exploring runs against the comforting notion of defined space. Atkinson's (1996) idea of the control zone on the Internet is both inevitable and intensely sad.

With the emergence of Web server log analysis in the last few years, the lack of a pervasive sense of computerized monitoring as an amorphous movement is glaring. Those who do not know about the rich past of computerized monitoring are doomed to perceive the latest killer app as sui generis. The inability or unwillingness of people involved in computerized monitoring to recognize the general field has resulted in much unnecessary redundancy, confusion, and retarded growth. Much of the controversy about basic units of Web measurement would have benefited from earlier thought about such units when computerized monitoring was explored in mainframe and PC environments. Web log analysis certainly has invigorated the movement to use computers to monitor HCI. Much money and creative energy are being invested in the development and refinement of Web server log monitoring software. Web monitoring is overshadowing and outpacing the other environments where computerized monitoring occurs. Perhaps the greatest contribution of Web server log analysis to the amorphous movement is that analysis and application tools and techniques finally are able to keep up with the flood of data.

12

Cookies, Applets, and Shopping Baskets

The rapid development of the Web as an information, entertainment, and advertising medium has resulted in an equally rapid and sophisticated development of software tools and techniques for monitoring HCI in this virtual environment — perhaps the first to contain significant amounts of advertising, discounting the subscription services such as America Online and Compuserve. In this chapter we will explore some of these new methods for monitoring online behavior. The development and deployment of cookies technology in the last three years has been the most significant — and most controversial.

Cookies   Cookies, officially called "persistent client state HTTP cookies," were conceived and created by Netscape and first released in version 1.1 of Netscape Navigator (Stein 1996). The idea for Netscape cookies to be used in an HTTP client-server environment may have come from UNIX objects called magic cookies — tokens attached to a user or program that change depending on the areas entered by the user or program (Kalfatovic 1997). The term "cookie" derives from the software programmer's concept of magic cookies, which are verifications sent back to the programmer that a piece of software code is running smoothly, and that the entire process is worthwhile (Hannaham 1996). Cookies are a method of capturing and retaining information about HCI in inherently stateless Web environments, which rely on HTTP client-server protocols to enable people and computers to interact. Cookies were designed to overcome some of the limitations and shortcomings of the basic stateless architecture of the Web. Although cookies do not naturally occur in online environments, it has been necessary to invent them, because Web client and browser software cannot retain information from the

retrieval of one Web page to the next (Mosley-Matchett 1997). Cookies were introduced at an early stage of the Web environment to enable certain desirable effects.
Like plants and animals that have been introduced into real environments to produce a desired outcome, however, sometimes long-term unwanted and unintended
consequences develop after it is too late to reverse the process. Although cookies
have many beneficial uses, the enduring impact of their introduction into the Web
environment may be retarding at best, and deleterious at worst. Due to broad negative public reaction to cookies as threats to personal privacy, Netscape was forced
to make the cookie technology an optional feature in later releases of its browser
software (Hagel and Sacconaghi 1996). The default mode, however, continues to
be one in which the cookie feature is enabled.

Cookies are playing an important role in the development of tools for computerized monitoring of HCI. When an analyst needs accurate information about
the use of a Web site, user information, and how the content on the site is being
explored, the analyst builds into the site a complex cookies or CGI tracking mechanism employing identification, passwords, and user authentication (Nemzow 1997,
97).*

A cookie file enables the software running on a Web server to send a piece of
information to a Web browser software application (such as Netscape Navigator or
Microsoft's Internet Explorer) residing on a user's hard disk, then retrieve that information from the hard disk at a later time (Berg 1996). Eric Raymond sees the claim
check one receives when one drops off clothes at the dry cleaners as the perfect real-
world counterpart to cookies. The sole purpose of the claim check is to relate a
subsequent transaction (the picking up of the clean clothes) to the previous one
(Bayers 1998, 134). Cookie files are essentially tokens of information, such as preferences and passwords, collected by a Web server from the clients that access the
server, then stored on the user's hard drive (Barr 1996). Cookies contain only information discernible by the Web server, either because of information deliberately
disclosed and provided by the user (often in the vehicle of Web forms), or because
of information passed back and forth between the client and the server.

The cookie concept, developed by Netscape and MCI, is useful for masters
of Web sites who want to provide a stateful or customized experience for their visitors. Lou Montulli, the Netscape programmer who is generally acknowledged as
the father of the Web cookie, recalls that the need for a shopping cart (a type of
stateful Web interaction) sparked the cookie idea (Bayers 1998, 134). By using
cookies, a host server can tag a visitor at the end of a session with information to
be used during future visits (Yesil 1996, 125). Cookies are a general mechanism
used by server-side connections in client/server applications to both store and
retrieve information on the client side of the connection (Netscape Communications 1996). A cookie can store information (e.g., the user's name, password, shopping list, demographic data, and method-of-payment) for reuse by a server at a

* For more information about cookies and how they work, visit the Web site at www.illuminatus.
com/cookie.fcgi (Wildstrom 1996b).

future time (Staten 1996). A cookie is a magic header that a server (or CGI program) sends to a client browser (Stout 1997, 80).

Cookies have played a role in the evolution of the amorphous movement to use computers to monitor HCI. One way to perform session analysis in client-server environments involves their use. As a client-side feature of the Netscape Navigator software, magic cookies are identifiers that store persistent information about a user's interaction with a Web site over a series of requests to the server. Magic cookies can be handled by CGI scripts or by the Web server itself (Robertson 1996).

When someone uses a browser to visit a Web site, the site server may ask the visitor's browser software to store information about the visitor in the visitor's browser's cookie file — information such as preferred background color, favorite Web sites, or credit card number. On this visitor's next stop at that Web site, the visitor's browser uploads that cookie file to the server (Nemo 1996). Many browsers can capture and regurgitate cookies. Netscape Navigator, Microsoft's Internet Explorer, Netcom's Netcruiser, and Quarterdeck's Mosaic 2.0 all support the HTTP cookie concept (Staten 1996).

In general, cookies allow Web site administrators to tag visitors with unique identifiers so that they can be identified each time they visit (Sessler 1997, 633). Although cookies can be used to gather and retain demographic and psychographic information, our primary interest in cookies involves their use as a way to track an individual's Web wanderings. "Cookies are well-suited for the purpose of session analysis in that the unique identifier for a session is logged each time a client makes a request of the server, thus providing a kind of audit trail in the log" (Larsen 1997, 51). Web site managers can use these data to tailor the structure, content, and presentation of a Web site for specific individuals. The basic purpose of cookies is to enable a Web site to remember certain information about a user as that user moves through a site, or returns to a site for multiple visits (Vandore 1996). Cookies often are used either to streamline or customize an online environment at the level of the individual user. Cookies enhance the default stateless nature of the HTTP protocol by adding enough state to identify and track a Web wanderer from one click to another (Sullivan 1997). Information in cookies files also can be used to modify the mode and outcomes of HCI within a single search session or site visit. Cookies can be understood either as a database containing personal demographic, psychographic, and behavioral information, or as a temporary device for creating a stateful, tailored online environment. These diverging ways of conceptualizing cookies have contributed to the controversy about them.

Cookies represent a thorny privacy issue because they can serve three basic purposes. First, cookies can be used to record user-articulated preferences for future recall and use. This use of cookies appears to be only tangential to individual privacy concerns. If a user takes the time to articulate his or her preferences, it would not seem to be a blatant invasion of privacy to store that information on the user's hard drive for later retrieval. Second, cookies are used to make it easier to make subsequent visits to a Web site. Passwords and other logon information may be stored in a cookies file so that the user need not remember yet another password or string of numbers. Again, in this context cookies do not appear to represent a major threat to personal privacy. They function more or less like an auto redialer on a telephone in that they make it easier to reach an information resource previously visited. Note that the first two of the three basic purposes of cookies merely facilitate articulated information exchanges between the user and the Web site.

The third basic purpose of cookies causes the uproar. Cookies are used to track user behavior within a Web site (or cluster of affiliated Web sites) so that the Web site can identify the visitor as an unspecified individual to learn more about the behavior of that user, and possibly to modify the virtual environment to better meet the inferred needs and interests of that user. In contrast to the first two purposes of cookies, this third purpose represents a form of unobtrusive computerized monitoring of HCI. The third purpose explains our interest in cookies as a manifestation of the primary topic of this book. It also is one reason why the use of cookies has raised privacy concerns.

Cookies typically work in the following way: Either a CGI script or a javascript sends cookie information from a server to a client using a specific "set cookie" syntax (Kalfatovic 1997). Most of the information contained in a cookie file has been encoded as strings of alphanumeric characters, generally lacking meaning without the key (Bott 1997). As the file extension implies, the cookies.txt file is a text file, so the contents can be easily viewed, even if it may not be easy to understand the meaning of the alphanumeric string of characters. The server can use the cookies file for the duration of a Web site visit, or it can store the file on the user's hard drive for a specified time. If during Web browsing the user accesses the server again before the file expires, the server will retrieve the file because it represents a "report" of the previous interaction(s) between that particular IP address and the specific server.

Cookies work by passing data in the HTTP request and response headers between the client and the browser (Baron and Weil 1996). "Whenever your browser communicates with a site for which it has a cookie, the browser sends the contents of the cookie back to the site. The cookie can record which pages you visited, which files you downloaded, and to which ad you've been exposed" (Mann 1997, 44). A server site can retrieve cookie information only if that site issued the original message to collect cookie information. Browser software actively sends cookies only to servers in the appropriate Internet domain (Berg 1996).

Cookies apparently also can be used within a search session at a Web site to track the choices and movement of a person within the site. John Yang, a research assistant in the Geology Department at Florida International University in Miami, reports that it is possible to build a cookie program capable of tracking a user's movement while connected to a particular server (Staten 1996).

Cookies are used to separate one individual Web surfer from the next, but by themselves they cannot be used to identify the differentiated individual by name, Social Security number, or other means. Although a cookie file can tell a Web site that one click came from one user, while another click came from another user, the

Web site cannot determine the names of those users without gathering information in some way beyond unobtrusive observation of online behavior (e.g., by having the user fill out an online registration form) (Sullivan 1997). Most cookies apologists maintain that, like most things in life, during 99 percent of use cookies are safe. A cookie file cannot be larger than 4K in size, and cookies files can be read only by the Web site that sent them (Snell 1997). Although cookies files assign a number to the user's client to identify the user as a discrete individual, the file does not contain personally identifying information, unless one relinquishes that information. Pfaffenberger (1997) cautions, however, that it is technically possible to create a centralized database of clickstreams capable of linking these anonymous numerical IDs with names, e-mail addresses, and other personally identifying information.

Cookie information is not stored exclusively on hard drives. During a surfing session the information also resides in the RAM of the client computer (Hancock 1997). The expiration time of the contents of a cookie can range from a few hours to several years. The first word of every line in a cookie file is the name of the Web server that added that line to the text file (Hancock 1997).

By themselves, cookies cannot find out the identity of a user, nor can they collect any more information than is already available elsewhere, such as from the Web server's access logs. This desire to keep track of an unidentified surfing individual during HCI is not new. Penniman (1981) used recorded ID numbers in a manner similar to the way cookies identify individuals as individuals without discovering specific identities.

Cookies also cannot as a rule track a user's movement from one site to another (Sullivan, E. 1996). Web sites that are clustered in some way can be configured to capture and use a shared pool of cookie files. Recent developments have made the inter-site transfer of cookie information much more feasible. For example, Match-Logic operates an advertisement management service at Preferences.com that relies heavily on cookies to track advertisement views and clickthroughs across a cluster of Web sites (Bayers 1998, 184). Early in 1998 Engage Technologies, a subsidiary of CMG Information Services, announced plans to create and rent access to a large, anonymous database of user profiles called Engage.Knowledge, which will collect data from cookies delivered across multiple sites and make it available for real-time queries (Bayers 1998, 185). McCarthy (1997a) reports that both Focalink and DoubleClick coordinate the display of advertisements over several Web sites. They use cookie files to track which ads have been displayed to individual human browsers within the confederation of Web sites.

Cookie files can count the number of computers that access a Web site, not the number of unique human beings (Kirsner 1997a). Because many computers in university computer labs, libraries, cyber-cafes, and other real-world locations are shared by more than one individual, cookies have some inherent limitations as a method for studying HCI. Cookies study computer-computer interaction at the HTTP level in client-server environments. By themselves, cookies cannot spread computer viruses. Cookies files are simply text files, not little software programs, so it is virtually impossible to catch a computer virus from a cookies file.

One positive limitation of cookies is that because of a strict definition of maximum size, they cannot fill up a user's hard drive at the client end of client-server interaction. The browser software limits the number of cookies it will retain and stores them on a first-in/first-out basis, or until an established expiration date is reached (Cookies might hurt 1996).

The cookie concept is a major breakthrough in the longstanding problem within the computerized monitoring field of how to unobtrusively identify and study the behavior of an individual user across multiple search sessions. This problem goes back to the earliest days of mainframe OPACs. Unlike most workplace and formal educational HCI situations, in which the person usually identifies oneself by logging on, most public access systems do not require any form of logon. Although this is a great way to protect everyone's anonymity, it also makes it very difficult to differentiate the actions and online behavior of one individual from the rest of the collected activity. Cookies can automatically collect basic information about a cluster of search sessions, including the IP address where the search sessions originated, the dates and times of the visits, and the pages viewed.

Cookies also provide an excellent way to focus on use at the user level, rather than on use based on hits or pages retrieved. Cookies are an easy and inexpensive way for Internet content providers to home in on a fairly accurate number of unique IDs visiting a Web site during a given time. This number would be much more meaningful than the number of hits and page requests received by the site (Machrone 1997). Webmasters and marketers argue that cookies are necessary for conducting accurate market research in online environments. Cookies enable them to distinguish (in a non-disruptive manner) 50 hits from 50 different people and 50 hits from one person (Hancock 1997). Cookies files enable a Web site manager to verify that one's aggregated behavior represents a distinct individual user (Weber 1996).

Cookies also are a good way to work around the inherently stateless architecture of the Web. Because cookies are passed in HTTP headers, they can identify individual users, even through a proxy server or firewall (Glass 1996). If a unique cookie identification number is assigned to each visitor to a Web site, the inherently stateless HTTP transactions will gain the continuity or state information that typically is absent in the HTTP protocol itself (Stout 1997, 81).

Cookies are better than the use of hidden-form fields:

> Cookies overcome nearly all the short-comings of the hidden-form field method and are just as easy to implement. They provide superior security because cookies are only sent to URLs matching the cookie's criteria. This reduces the chances of spoofing and inadvertent transmission of sensitive data to the wrong server [i.e., any server other than the one that originally caused the creation of the cookie]. Users do not normally see the cookies, and listing the source of an HTML form will not reveal their contents. Persistence is improved over the hidden-field method since the cookies are stored in a field on the client machine. They will survive any amount of Web surfing and even shutting down the client. The expiration-date parameter provides fine-grain control over how long the cookie is valid and provides automatic deletion when it expires. This can significantly reduce the effort required to track and expire

old data, which is often needed with a system that uses databases to store the state (Baron and Weil 1996, 68).

Because cookie information is stored either in RAM or on the hard drive of the client computer, it is held close to the vest of the person using the client computer, even though the information contained in the cookie file is used to configure the look and feel of some far-off server.

Some columnists and writers actively defend the existence and use of cookies files. Bott (1997) argues that there are dozens of legitimate uses for cookies. They can remember items in a virtual shopping basket prior to checkout. They can store usernames and passwords, so that people do not need to remember them. They enable Internet search engines to remember one's search argument preferences. Last but not least, they can create a profile of an individual's intra-site browsing habits.

Unfortunately, sometimes the arguments of cookie apologists verge on becoming ad hominum. Carlberg paints an unflattering picture of opponents to cookies as privacy freaks intent on ridiculous levels of privacy in cyberspace: "When Cookies first appeared on the scene, the privacy freaks raised quite a flap. These are the people who use the PGP (Pretty Good Privacy) protocol to encode e-mails that say 'How are you? I am fine'" (Carlberg 1997).

Other proponents or defenders of cookies argue that the information in cookies essentially is redundant. Cookies simply are a more efficient and productive way to manage and use information already available in the system. The cookies files do not contain any information not already divulged by the visitor to the site — either deliberately via articulated choices or pre-reflectively by the choices and decisions made by moving through the virtual space. "Cookies are real benign," said Bill Wadley, director of Internet services for Netcom Interactive in Dallas. "They don't know something about you that you haven't already told them" (Rampey 1996).

Some proponents of cookies defend them as a helpful way to enable narrowcasting. In this context, narrowcasting involves situations in which Web content providers channel specific information to a particular audience, based on the previous browsing behavior of that audience (Piven 1996). The logical conclusion to the narrowcasting movement is to narrowcast at the individual level. Each individual visitor to a Web site receives a configuration of content, including advertisements, specifically tailored (more or less) to that visitor. It is easy to envision an online environment where, based on the use of cookies and other computerized monitoring techniques to study the online behavior of individuals, Web content is customized and narrowcast for specific individuals.

Several apologists for cookies also maintain that fears about cookies are overblown, perhaps based on misunderstandings about their power and content. Bott (1997) succinctly states the limitations and controls:

> There are strict security controls over what a Web server can and cannot do with cookies. They can't be used to retrieve information from your hard disk or your

network. Also, a server can retrieve information only from a cookie that it or another server in its domain created. A cookie can track your movements only within a given site — it can't tell a server where you came from or where you're going next. The data in cookies is usually encoded, so it would be useless to a data thief.

Unique forms of anxiety seem to be possible in online environments. A virtual crowd on the Internet quickly can become unruly in ways that are difficult to counteract. Berg (1996) insists that the alarm about cookies is excessive. Cookies contain only information passing to or coming from a Web server. Use of the cookie function is optional for the creators of Web-based applications. Barr (1996) also argues that the cookies do not represent an increased security risk. Even before the introduction of cookies, the browser software already provides the server much information about the individual user, such as the user's IP address and which browser software program the user employs.

Some advocates for cookies argue that they give the user more control of private or confidential information. Jeff Treuhaft, a product manager at Netscape, contends that cookie files give the user more control over profile information, because the cookie files are stored on the user's hard drive, and can be deleted at any time (Wingfield 1996). Dave Morgan, CEO of Real Media, goes so far as to describe cookies as pro-user (Cohen 1997a). Cookies critics counter-argue, however, that this type of control can be realized and used only if users know about cookies and have been trained how to modify, withhold, or delete the contents of a cookie file.

Cookies can make advertisements more relevant, thus furthering a rapprochement between annoying, irrelevant ads and truly useful information. Cookies have been employed extensively during the use of advertisements in Web environments. People have developed negative opinions about advertising perhaps because of the inherently flawed broadcast nature of much advertising in the real world. A roadside billboard is seen by everyone who drives over the road. Weber (1996) notes that Web tracking could be convenient for shoppers, if it filters out advertisements that individuals do not want to see.

Other proponents of cookies emphasize the convenience and efficiencies enabled by cookies. Cookies are convenient, and they can save the user's time. At Web sites such as that of *The New York Times* (www.nytimes.com), once a user has registered initially with the site, a cookie file can replace the need to log-in during subsequent visits. That data is stored in a cookie file (Snell 1997).

Many individuals and groups are concerned for various reasons about the existence and use of cookies. McMullen (1997) suggests that cookies are virus-like in that they gather information concerning the contents and use of the computer. This criticism appears to be based on incorrect understanding of the nature and power of cookies. Whereas most viruses are on missions to seek and destroy files, cookies tend to be on reconnaissance missions. The Center for Democracy and Technology (CDT) operates a Web site (www.cdt.org/privacy) that provides a demonstration of the information about an individual that any Web site can collect through server log analysis and the use of cookies (Carlberg 1996).

Not all browser software programs support cookies. Mosaic, MacWeb, and America Online's browser 2.7 are examples of browsers that do not accommodate cookies (Murdoch 1997). For someone involved in a computerized monitoring project, the decision to use cookies means that one probably will not be studying the behavior of everyone visiting a Web site. In the broader world of social science research, the situation is akin to using a local telephone directory to create a random sample of the population. Although most households are listed in the printed phone directory, not all are, because some households do not contain phones and other households have unlisted numbers.

> A minor shortcoming of cookies is the limited amount of data they can contain: specified as 300 total cookies, 20 cookies per domain, and 4 KB total per cookie (name+data). A more serious shortcoming is the limited set of browsers that support the specification. Although the percentage of users with a cookies-supporting browser is over 80 percent, shopping-cart systems that must support all browsers will have to use a different method until the specification is more universally supported (Baron and Weil 1996, 69).

Cookies concentrate on IP addresses, rather than on individuals. Through the use of cookies we are able to infer things about individuals only because most IP addresses are used by only one person. When this is not true, the efficacy of cookies as a computerized monitoring tool is seriously compromised. A floating Web surfer is defined as anyone who uses the Web from more than one Internet-connected computer. If one uses the Web at work as well as at home, then one is a floating Web surfer. Because cookies are hard disk specific, it is difficult to reconcile the workplace virtual self with the at-home virtual self. Floating Web surfers may develop split virtual personalities. The "same" Web site (i.e., with the same URL) may look rather different to the same individual if that individual accesses the Web site from more than one IP address, if the Web site uses cookies to customize the environment, and if the user behaves quite differently from one IP address to the next.

Shafer (1997) sees cookies as a limited, limiting form of local persistence. Cookies are inadequate for true data storage. To compensate for this limitation, often only a unique identifier is stored on the user's hard drive, which points back to real data stored on the Web server itself.

Many people believe that cookies are an invasion of privacy in online environments.

> Cookies feed some of the more dire privacy scenarios. With them, a Web magazine can see which articles you read; a merchant can tell not only which products you bought, but also which product descriptions you simply viewed. (Imagine a supermarket scanner that monitors every thing you look at in a store.) Similarly, it not only knows which ads work; it also knows which don't (Weber 1996).

Allen Olivo, the senior director of worldwide marketing communications at Apple Computer, thinks that the cookie controversy could be the death blow to the Internet. "I think they're insidious. I realize the need for good, solid tracking information, and I have no problem with that. The problem is that they're hidden, and that's an invasion of electronic privacy" (quoted in Bayers 1998, 184).

Netizens who know about the existence and use of cookies generally are suspicious of them. During an online survey, Pitkow and Kehoe (1996) found that only one in five respondents to the survey thought that identifiers such as cookies that can track a user at a site across sessions ought to be permitted.

When cookies first were used, they arrived on one's hard disk unbidden and often without one's knowledge. The user probably had no awareness that these files were being created and retrieved. A survey of 300 Internet users conducted by CyberDialogue, a market research firm, found that approximately 72 percent of online users never had heard of cookies (Bruner 1997a). Mark Rotenberg and Robert Ellis Smith are two privacy advocates involved in the DoubleClick and Magic Cookie brouhaha. Smith argues: "If people are fully informed about what's going on, there is no invasion of privacy" (Jones 1995). Hertzoff (1996) echoed the call for full disclosure of the nature and purpose of cookies. Nick Grouf, the CEO of Firefly, thinks that cookies represent a way of watching consumers without their informed consent — a fairly frightening phenomenon (Quittner 1997b). Lori Fena, the executive director of the Electronic Frontier Foundation, also sees the lack of a mechanism for informed consent as the biggest issue concerning cookies (Steinberg 1996). Keizer (1997) is concerned not so much about the fact that cookies collect data as by the fact that most cookies collect data surreptitiously. Cookies usually collect information unobtrusively. They were designed and intended to be unobtrusive. Unobtrusive, uninformed monitoring of consumers, however, has been going on in real environments for years. Cookies are not something new under the sun. Marc Rotenberg, director of the Electronic Privacy Information Center, says cookies might be less objectionable if they were more obvious to Web surfers. "Instead of burying the cookie, put it on the top window so the user can see what's going on," he says (Bruno 1996).

Although most people, if informed, would object to having their online decisions monitored without their prior consent, the development of cookies technologies and techniques will be crucial to the management, customization, and improvement of the growing amount of commercial activity on the Web (Dyrli 1997).

A May 1997 editorial in *The Washington Post* suggested that cookies are deceptive "only in that they usually collect more information than just the facts you put in when you register" (Privacy and the cookie pushers 1997). The Web surfing habits of an individual may or may not be trivial information. The editorial seems to suggest that capturing self-declared information from users is permissible, but capturing behavioral information that is not by nature self-articulated and self-declared by individuals is not.

Although cookies do not explicitly reveal an individual's specific identity, they seem to contradict two assumptions widely held by netizens: that exploring the Web is a confidential, anonymous, transitory experience, and that one's hard drive is one's castle. Some Web users are very irate about the unannounced development and deployment of cookies technology. They argue that this is an invasion of privacy, because Web sites potentially could collect information about the browsing behavior of identified, individual users (Vandore 1996). The very notion of some-one from an outside source creating files and storing information on an individ-ual's personal hard drive seems to be a clear invasion of privacy to many netizens and privacy advocates. Piven (1996) carries the argument to the extreme by claim-ing that the controversy surrounding cookies is not only about how they are used, but also about how the cookies files get deposited on a user's hard drive in the first place.

The use of cookies raises privacy issues because it removes some of the tradi-tional anonymity associated with viewing Web sites, and it uses a small portion of the user's hard disk (Yesil 1996, 113). Mosley-Matchett (1997) notes that, due to the spread of computer viruses and electronic fraud, netizens are justifiably con-cerned about the practice of strange computers depositing files on their hard dri-ves. Some computer owners think that the use of cookies is a violation of their own resources. They are being forced to store information on their computers for the benefit of remote sites (Stout 1997, 85). They believe that creating a cookie file is a flagrant violation of privacy, because the file is created on the user's own hard disk. What one's home is to the real world, one's hard disk is to the virtual world — an inviolable sanctuary. Users' concerns about cookie files on the hard disk is reminiscent of the Stage.DAT file that users of the Prodigy online service had to have installed on their hard drives in order to access the service. Some users were fearful that Prodigy might be able to read or retrieve private information from personal computers from a distance (Rheingold 1993, 277).

Carlberg (1996) presents an interesting variation on the argument that because a person's hard disk is a private place, placing a cookies file there represents an invasion of privacy. Carlberg argues that the hard disk is not only a private place, it also is an owned place. The person who owns the hard disk should be informed about any use of that space. It is common courtesy, akin to asking permission from a landowner to fish or hunt on his or her land. The informed hard disk owner would have the option of charging rent for the use of the space. Carlberg's argu-ment is an interesting twist on the commodification of personal information and individual privacy.

The knowledge gained through cookies could be used to bother users. For example, students who use the Web to perform online research on controversial, politically charged topics could find themselves pestered by special-interest groups who use cookies to identify people exploring their particular special interest (Dyrli 1997).

Cookies have dual uses. They can gather and store demographic information and behavioral data. Some critics of cookies see them as a sloppy substitute for true demographic information. Raisch (1996) understands cookies in most appli-cations as nothing more than an inexpensive, lazy way by which marketers avoid the admittedly arduous and expensive task of gathering information voluntarily offered by consumers. Cookies files could be aggregated, sold, and reused. Privacy advocates worry that Internet businesses could trade cookie information and use the aggregate to track most or all of the Web browsing of an individual (Kleiner

1997). The manager of a Web site could use cookies to track the pages one downloads and presumably reads, the advertisements one appears interested in because one lingers over them, and the products one purchases, then analyze that data, package it, and sell the reports to other companies (Eckhouse 1997).

Cookies could be used for unintended purposes. The security issue lies not in the cookie itself, but rather in executable code extensions like Java, JavaScript, and ActiveX — HTTP extensions that allow Web client browser software to download and execute programs on the user's computer (Stout 1997, 84). Cookie files are not very secure, so the contents could be used for unintentional purposes, perhaps by hackers looking for identification numbers, passwords, credit card numbers, and personal information, such as waistline size (Berg 1996). Security First Network Bank, which established a financial presence on the Internet in 1995, has reported that some unscrupulous websters have attempted to forge identification numbers contained in the cookies files of other bona fide bank customers (Machlis 1997a).

The widespread use of cookies files could threaten not only the personal privacy of individuals, but also the security of the Web as a computerized information system. Information in the cookie files that get Internet privacy advocates up in arms also can threaten World Wide Web site security if site administrators do not use it carefully (Machlis 1997b).

The cookie concept was first conceived and developed as a strictly bilateral interaction between one server computer and one client computer. If lines in a cookie file on one's hard drive were created by Web server A, only Web server A could access and use the information contained in that line. All other Web servers would be blocked from accessing that line of alphanumeric, coded information. The growth of Web advertising networks, however, has begun to advance the use of cookies beyond bilateral interactions to the multilateral. Hinton (1997) reports that advertising networks such as DoubleClick's enable an affiliated group of Web servers and sites to share and use cookie information. This enables the use of cookies to track the inter-site wanderings of a Web surfer. For the moment, use of cookies in this expanded way is limited to affiliated groups of Web sites, not the entire Internet. It may, however, represent a first step onto a slippery slope. Although this information, if used professionally and ethically, ultimately is more valuable and useful than information about intra-site user movement (because the Web after all is a massive hypertext of linked sites, not a stew of discrete, disjointed sites), it nevertheless represents a major extension of the use of cookies — an extension that increases the threat of misuse involving invasions of privacy.

The debate over cookies never has been purely philosophical. It always has had political and economic ramifications. Kevin O'Connor, president of Double-Click, has suggested that proposals to limit the use of cookies are being driven by opponents of advertising on the Internet (Kleiner 1997).

Cookies are being used by both Web site managers and advertisers — two different groups in the field of computerized monitoring. Focalink and DoubleClick use cookies extensively because they coordinate the display of advertisements over several sites. Cookies are used to keep track of who has seen which ads, so that new advertising graphics can be rotated into sites frequently visited by that particular user. Of the 100 popular Web sites studied by the Electronic Privacy Information Center (1997), 24 were positively identified as creating and using cookies files. The cookies feature often is used for registration and password storing, but may also be used to create logs of user interests (inferred from observed behavior) and preferences. A list of well-known Web sites that use cookies can be found at http://www.geocities.com/Solto/4535/cookie.html. Federal government agencies also have been found using cookies. In 1997 a study of 70 federal Web sites conducted by OMB Watch, a private research organization, found that three federal agencies (the Department of Veterans Affairs, the Federal Emergency Management Agency, and the National Science Foundation) were using cookie files without informing visitors (Doherty 1997).

Some critics contend that cookies are used primarily as marketing tools. They let Web site owners gauge how often a user visits a Web site and what the user does there. A site manager can combine these data with user registration information, then create a demographic database of users to sell to marketers (Rothfeder 1997).

The Web site for *The New York Times* requires a new user to register, then assigns a username and password so that the site manager can track usage of the site. The user, however, need not memorize or jot down the username and password, because during the registration the Web site software creates a cookies file on the user's hard disk. The file contains the user's username and password. When the user visits the Web site of *The New York Times* again, the browser software on the user's hard disk automatically sends the authentication information contained in the cookie file so that the user automatically is identified as a registered user (Berg 1996). Computerized monitoring can generate substantial data, but user registration procedures also can bring an automated system to its knees. The registration program at *The New York Times* Web site created a new database record for each new registered user. When the Web site was announced, the computer managing the registration database crashed, forcing the newspaper to disable its sophisticated registration system (Kirsner 1997a).

Cookie files can be used for online browsing and shopping. An online shopper browsing through a sales catalog can add selected items to a virtual shopping cart. Each time an item is selected, the server software adds that information to the recently created cookie file on the shopper's hard disk. When the user decides to check out, pay for his selections, and leave the Web site, a server-based script reads the data stored in the cookie file and totals up the complete order (Berg 1996). For example, marketplaceMCI uses cookies to store items a user has selected for ordering while the user continues to browse through other pages at the Web site. The use of cookies avoids requiring the online shopper to order on each page individually (Wingfield 1996).

Cookie files also can be used by Web server software at a Web site to remember one's personal preferences from one visit to subsequent visits. These preferences can be articulated verbally, or they can be inferred from the way one behaves at a given Web site. Netscape's Personal Workspace page (http://home.netscape.com/custom) enables Web surfers to create their own personalized Web work spaces. Although such personalized workspaces appear to be located at the Netscape server site, the sense of space is based on information stored in a cookie file on one's hard disk (Berg 1996). Unwitting personalization can occur if the Web server determines that a specific individual has been there before and what the visitor has seen and retrieved. If so, then the Web server can personalize the environment (Wildstrom 1996b).

Cookies also can be used to conduct an unobtrusive, personalized, interest survey. After one has visited a Web site that uses cookies, a cookie file can be employed by the Web software to automatically direct one (or draw one's attention) to areas of the site in which one probably will be interested, based on what one did during previous visits to the site (Kleiner 1997).

Some individual Web sites and clusters of sites that offer advertising are using persistent cookies to lessen the chance that a specific user will become burned out by repeated appearances of the same advertisement. Although normally only the Web server that originally stored a persistent cookie can retrieve information from it, affiliated companies that want to avoid bombarding visitors with the same ads have started to share access to cookie data to provide visitors with some advertising variety (Mosley-Matchett 1997). Schweitzer (1996) reports that cookies are being used by the Internet Link Exchange to create a more robust relationship between individuals and the ads they see and indicate some interest in.

Advertisers also are interested in using cookies because they verify the financial cost of placing an advertisement on a Web site. Hinton (1997) correctly observes that because any money currently being made on the Web usually is made through the sale of advertising space, information leading to effective ads currently is considered very valuable. Cookies are a very effective, cost-efficient way to gather such information.

Many people find both the idea and use of cookies offensive. Programmers have started to develop ways to combat the use of cookies. The timeless struggle between the buyer and the seller has been transplanted to the Internet. Cookie management software gives the user a modicum of control over this by-default unobtrusive computerized monitoring. Randall (1997b) notes that three types of software packages have emerged. The first simply blocks all cookies, refusing them without asking the user. The second allows them to enter the client computer, then gives the user the option to wipe out all cookies information. The third allows the user such options as blocking cookies from specific sites or during specific times of the day. Desmarais (1998) articulates a similar three-part classification scheme for cookie crunching software programs.

Another way to avoid the intrusiveness of cookies is to take a hint from the MOO crowd and assume multiple personalities. The Lucent Personalized Web Assistant (LPWA) from Lucent Technologies is a proxy system that transparently filters the flow of information from the user to a Web site. LPWA uses cryptographic functions to create a separate identity for a user for each Web site visited (Levine 1997). It sounds like a case of endless virtual multiple personalities. Eventually the Web may be inhabited by many more personalities than actual people.

Although popular browsers such as Netscape Navigator and Microsoft Internet Explorer contain options that enable a person to block incoming cookies, Randall (1997b) suggests that it is more practical to use a dedicated cookie management software utility. Browser software can alert a user of an incoming cookie, but it cannot indicate the intent or eventual use of the data placed in the cookie file.

Although the development and diffusion of cookies have made unobtrusive computerized monitoring a popular topic, they do not really add much to the amorphous movement of using computers to monitor HCI. Cookies are not data-generating or gathering devices, nor do they analyze or apply the data. In essence, cookies are little more than a distributed, temporary storage protocol for both demographic and behavioral information. Their main contribution is to overcome the primal stateless nature of client-server environments using the HTTP transfer protocol.

Mayer-Schonberger (1997) argues that the creation and retrieval of cookies could lead to the disclosure of personal information about unsuspecting Web users at an unimaginable rate, thus violating a number of national and international legal norms and principles designed to protect personal data. At least one recent lawsuit has been filed based on the idea that cookie files housed on the computers of government employees are public documents. In 1997 Geoffrey Davidian, the publisher of *The Putnam Pit*,* an alternative monthly newspaper in Cookeville, Tennessee, filed a suit in the Tennessee Chancery Court (later moved to the Federal District Court in Nashville) seeking to generally establish that cookie files are public records that should be archived, maintained, and made available for public inspection (Noack 1997). The case of *Geoffrey Davidian v T. Michael O'Mara* has gone to the U.S. Middle District Court of Appeals in Tennessee (Evans 1998).

Plans to standardize the cookie concept are underway. Lori Fena, president of the Electronic Freedom Foundation, suggests that we should look to the Web industry to create a set of acceptable information practices that would be as socially accepted as general accounting principles and practices (Hinton 1997). Jeff Treuhaft, product manager for Netscape, reports that the Internet Engineering Task Force (IETF) has seen the value of the cookie feature and is planning to standardize similar functionality under the phrase "state-info" (Mills 1996).

Bruner (1997a) reports that the IETF is examining a proposed revised standard for cookies that would place more restrictions on their creation, transfer, and use. A committee of Internet users and technologists released details of the proposed new standard in February 1997. The proposal encourages Web site managers to make the creation and transfer of cookies more apparent to users (Bruner

---

* *The Putnam Pit also is available online at http://www.putnampit.com (Noack 1997).*

1997a).* One section of the recommended standards seeks to limit circumstances in which a user visiting one site can be sent a cookie from a different domain (Bruner 1997a). This point concerns members of the nascent Web advertising community. Bruner (1997a) concludes that the IETF proposal is an attempt to wrest control of cookies away from Web site managers and marketers, who use the technology to learn about the behavior of users, and increase the control users have over the creation, content, and distribution of cookies.

On May 27, 1997, Netscape Communications Corp., Firefly Network, Veri-Sign, and more than 60 other companies and corporations announced their support for the proposed Open Profiling Standard (OPS), which the proposers claim would enable the personalization of Internet services while protecting the privacy of individuals. The idea behind OPS is to allow computer users to create electronic passports that identify them to online companies and marketers without revealing their real names (Quittner 1997b). At the behest of Microsoft, the OPS specification was submitted to the World Wide Web Consortium (W3C) for consideration as a plank of their Platform for Privacy Preferences (P3) (Karpinski 1997).

Marc Andreessen, the senior vice president of technology at Netscape, has been quoted as stating, "OPS is an important standard that will enable users to enjoy personalized services on the Internet while preserving their privacy." (Netscape, Firefly and VeriSign 1997). If we were back at the dawn of the industrial revolution in the real world, the personalized information space would be the desired, intended outcome of the industrial production process, and loss of privacy would be the unwanted, unintended tailings that need to be minimized or avoided. OPS allegedly will allow us to achieve the intended outcome (electronic commerce) without suffering the unwanted consequences (a diminution of privacy).

The Open Profiling Standard is a set of programming interfaces designed to allow software developers to write applications that add the digital equivalent of business cards to Web browser software (Wagner 1997b). Users of computerized networks will be able to exercise control over the distribution of personal profile information stored on their local hard disks (Sliwa 1997). At first glance, it appears that OPS is little more than a cookie file controlled by the consumer.

According to Netscape, Firefly, and VeriSign (1997), the OPS standard would give users control over their personal profiles. They would retain the ability to manage the disclosure of personal information. Information contained in the profile can be withheld from specific Internet sites. The press release asserts that the functionality of OPS would provide a framework for informed consent. Through the use of OPS and Personal Profiles, users enter personal information into a file which resides on their hard drives. Users then decide with which Internet sites they wish to provide this information.

The OPS is based on two accepted technologies, VCard and digital certifi-

---

* *The text of the proposal can be found at http://ds/internic.net/rfc/rfc2109.txt.*

cates. VCard is a proposed specification managed by the Internet Mail Consortium. These electronic business cards are used to exchange personal information. VCard has been submitted as a proposed Internet standard to the Internet Engineering Task Force. Digitial certificates already has been adopted as a standard by the PKIX working group within the IETF (Netscape, Firefly and VeriSign 1997).

The OPS initiative seems to be focused on demographic and other real-world information about individuals, including self-declared preferences. It does not appear to address the need for, and advantages of, gathering and analyzing online behavior. King (1997), however, reports that an OPS profile could be used by a Web site to store its own data, such as what a user did while at the site. If this is indeed possible, use of OPS could be more intrusive than the more traditional forms of computerized monitoring. Whereas most computerized monitoring projects are satisfied to identify individual behavior without knowing the exact identities of the individuals involved in that behavior, OPS would be able to link specific behavior in Web sites and other virtual environments with known, specific individuals. The proposed OPS standard also contains secure transmission features. When an individual's profile information is transferred from one computer to another, digital certificate technology and Secure Socket Layer encryption will guard the data (King 1997).

Not everyone is enthused about the proposed standard. Web site administrators are concerned that OPS would prove too expensive to implement broadly (Wagner 1997b). David Sobel from EPIC predicts that the proposed standard will not eliminate the need for legislative and legal recourse, in situations in which personal information allegedly has been misused (Wagner 1997b). Sullivan (1997) notes that although OPS has performed a useful service by making the levels of privacy available on the Internet easier to understand, the standard adds nothing of substance to Internet privacy. The OPS is being misunderstood as the solution to the cookies controversy.

Compared to hidden, unintelligible cookies, the virtue of OPS is that, because consumers can understand data created through the OPS, they can control it (Dyson 1997a).

One concern about all of the hubbub over cookies and the alternatives is that sometimes it seems that individual privacy has been boiled down and equated with consumer privacy. Although the privacy of personal information about demographic characteristics, financial data, medical records, and legal proceedings is an enduring concern, it is not the only threat to privacy in virtual environments. Most of the proposed standards and software fixes focus on these older privacy concerns, rather than resulting from reflectively thinking through the entire consort of issues related to privacy in cyberspace.

McCarthy (1997a) suggests that only in early 1997 did the functionality of cookies rise to the point at which many webmasters realized that they could use them to track usage and modify site displays and content. Frank Chen, the security product manager at Netscape, said that newer versions of Netscape will restrict the creation and retrieval of HTTP cookie information to make it more secure. The Internet Engineering Task Force is trying to make the cookie specification more secure (Staten 1996). The cookie method has been adopted by the IETF as a draft specification for maintaining state information (Baron and Weil 1996).

Cookie files may someday enable users to prevent sites from tracking user activity over long periods, such as days and months, limiting them instead to tracking a single Internet session (Mills 1996). Privacy watchdog groups suggest that cookies transactions should be more transparent (Electronic Privacy Information Center 1997). There is no need to hide these virtual cookies in a cookie jar. In 1997 there was a general call to make cookies an opt-in technology, rather than an opt-out one, in the belief that users should be forced to consciously choose to allow cookies to enter their virtual lives and track their activity on the Web. In a letter to the IETF, both the Electronic Privacy Information Center and the American Civil Liberties Union asked for the development and adoption of new cookies standards that would prevent third parties, such as advertisers with banner ads on Web sites, from giving and receiving cookies (Kleiner 1997).

Bray (1997) reports that both Lou Montulli of Netscape Communications and David Kristol of Lucent Technologies have urged that the default setting for browser software should be to reject all cookies, unless and until the Web surfer specifies that the creation and use of cookies are acceptable. The use of cookies and the existence of virtual shopping baskets could have applications in the realm of scholarly information storage and retrieval. A virtual shopping basket could be filled with anything, from consumer electronics to preprints of scholarly publications.

It is curious that the diffusion of the use of cookies throughout the Web created a major uproar, while the use of Web server logs, which can monitor HCI in much the same way, receive scant attention. One explanation is that cookies involve the use of an individual's hard drive. Most people perceive this as an invasion of privacy, rather than as a form of personal empowerment and control.

The cookies controversies are particularly interesting in the broader context of the computer monitoring of HCI because they represent a direct clash and congruence of the gathering and use of both demographic and behavioral information. The demographic information is firmly rooted in the real world, while the behavioral information is being captured as people interact with computers in the spatial region known as cyberspace — the sense of which comes into existence through the process of people interacting with computers.

The development of persistent cookies resonates through the entire issue of privacy in cyberspace. Although the creation of a cookies file is considered by many people as an invasion of privacy, once the file is created and contains personal information, the file itself becomes a private space that must be protected either by the server that created the file, or by the Web surfer whose actions caused it to be created. Piven (1996) notes that, although cookies have many useful applications, they do fall into an ethical gray area — ripe for misuse and abuse by people so inclined.

Applets   One gap in Internet security and privacy is located in the browser software itself. Both the Netscape Navigator and Microsoft's Internet Explorer browsers contain tools that let Web sites access the hard disk of a user's PC and run programs. These applets (the best-known are Java and ActiveX) can customize visits to a Web site based on a user's previous activity (Rothfeder 1997). Todd Price from Netwalk, an ISP, says that Java makes it possible for a Web site owner to search a user's hard drive while the user runs an application (Claypoole 1996). Research studies that have used computerized monitoring to study the impact of applets have not been encouraging. Dreze and Zufryden (1997), for example, found that the use of JAVA applets significantly, adversely affected the effectiveness of a site.

JavaScripts   Although normal cookie files will store only information the server already has received from the client, JavaScripts incorporate more information, such as the user's e-mail address (Glass 1996). JavaScripts can be sent to a browser software program whenever a particular page is requested from a server. They can perform a range of tasks, from scrolling text to launching applets. Several webmasters have reported using JavaScripts to retrieve a user's real name, e-mail address, and recent activity from the cache file in Netscape. John Robert LoVerso, a researcher at the Open Software Foundation's Research Institute in Cambridge, Massachusetts, used JavaScript to create an agent capable of checking every second to see what page a user is on, then automatically forwarding the information to LoVerso's server. Although JavaScript code was not intended to remain at the client site after the user leaves the server site, this privacy and security measure was not activated in the final version of Netscape Navigator 2.0 (Staten 1996).

Scripts can be used as Web access counters. Perl, Java, or CGI scripts often are embedded into home pages to increment a counter in a single separate data file or in multiple data files every time the page is accessed (Nemzow 1997, 92). One major drawback of counters of this type is that they are not accurate. They will not count users retrieving pages with nongraphical browser software such as Lynx, with pages and graphics cached, with the graphics functionality turned off, or if the user clicks on the stop button before the HTML code for the counter is loaded (Nemzow 1997, 95). Aaron Weiss (1997) provides instructions on how to create nonintrusive Web-based cookies using JavaScript.

Shopping Baskets   Current shopping cart applications require state information about the human browsers and shoppers (Stout 1997, 98). Cookies serve as the basis of the shopping cart concept in virtual shopping, because they allow a shopper to leave a Web site and return later to find the originally selected items still in the shopping cart (Randall 1997b). Analysis of customer use of virtual shopping carts could become an interesting new branch of computerized monitoring of HCI. We could study, for example, how often shoppers remove items that were previously placed in their virtual shopping carts, then compare this analysis of shopping behavior in virtual environments with that in real environments.

13

Possible Futures for Computerized Monitoring

The future of using computers to monitor HCI appears to be healthy. Whether the future is bright or dark depends on one's evaluation of the entire amorphous movement. This chapter examines some possible future directions, characteristics, and issues for this project. For the first 30 years in its development, the general movement to use computers to monitor HCI has been a human project. Computers gained a toehold at the data collection stage, then moved into the data analysis stage. When they move into the interpretation and application stages, using computers to monitor HCI may cease to be a fundamentally human project.

Accurately Predicting HCI in Specific Instances The desire to use computerized monitoring to predict future human online behavior has been pursued for at least 25 years. Penniman (1975) was one of the first analysts to use the analytical tools of the stochastic process analysis, especially the Markov chain process, to develop a probability transition matrix for prediction. A probability transition matrix essentially indicates the probability of a user moving from one search state to another, from one moment to the next. One of the criticisms of computerized monitoring research has been that it can merely describe historical events — HCI interaction that already has occurred. The ability to consistently predict the future of HCI, at whatever level of specificity, seems to be too difficult in most instances. Despite the best prognostications of experts in the software industry, the emergence of a "killer app" fills us with an almost messianic wonder.

One of the enduring criticisms about computerized monitoring of HCI has been the general inability of these systems to predict future activity accurately, based on observations of past and current activity. While computerized monitoring systems may be able to do this at group or network levels, their inability to achieve success at the individual level has been lamentable. In the near future, however, accuracy of predicting HCI in specific instances may be achieved. If we know enough about the online environment and the person who soon will become an actor in that online environment, we should be able to predict resulting HCI. The power to predict with some accuracy is valuable because it opens up opportunities for persuasion and control.

One way computerized monitors will achieve this elusive predictive power is by altering the environment on the fly to match user behavior. The online environment is becoming more malleable than the people interacting with that environment. The entire process conjures up an image from a Saturday morning cartoon, in which the intelligent golfing green moves the cup after the golfer has swung the putting club, so that the ball in transit indeed falls into the cup. In essence, sophisticated computerized monitoring systems will be able to accurately predict future HCI at the level of individual users or individual search sessions because, to an increasing extent, the computerized monitoring system will control the environment.

That this accuracy will become technologically feasible seems certain. The value and worth of accuracy in this case, however, remains doubtful. Although people generally have valued the ability of others to predict the future, having computers be able to dumbly, consistently predict future human activities is not quite as appealing on its face. The question remains whether this can or should be done at the group and individual levels. The value of being able to predict group or individual HCI is undetermined.

Predictive power has many applications in the physical world. The ability to predict the weather accurately and consistently is one common example. "A society that can successfully predict the future history of the physical world is a much more efficient society" (Bailey 1996, 14). Although most of the social sciences place great value on the ability to predict future events, the traditional way of appreciating this ability probably will experience declining value in the realm of computerized monitoring. Perhaps another way of articulating the fundamental differences between the real world and cyberspace lies in the prospect that predictive powers will lose human value and appreciation as, first, human activity migrates to cyberspace, and, second, the honor or task of predicting the future passes from humans to computers. One reason for the declining value of the power of prediction is that the real power of computerized monitoring (once computers have taken over most or all of the processes involved in collecting and analyzing the data, then applying the results) lies in its ability, not to predict how people will act in a static environment, but to modify the environment to improve future HCI. As the colonization of cyberspace continues rapidly, another human task will be to rethink and reassess the power and use of the predictive sciences and arts. Madame Sosostris will lose her allure.

New Methods for Displaying, Visualizing, and Analyzing Computerized Monitoring Data   Computerized monitoring of HCI began as a data collection technique, then evolved into a full-blown behavioral analysis tool. Future development efforts in the field probably will concentrate on the analysis, display, and application components of the program, rather than on the collection of data. This has been one of the obvious lessons of the explosion of Web server log analysis software in the last few years. The methods for analyzing, displaying, and visualizing HCI are becoming quite vibrant and sophisticated. It should be possible to apply dynamic visualization techniques to the display and interpretation of computer monitoring data — to display multiple dimensions, to display transitions dynamically, or to play back full search sessions (Borgman, Hirsh, and Hiller 1996, 577).

We cannot forget, however, that the collection of data is the foundation for all other aspects of these monitoring projects. It is somewhat troubling to witness all of these fancy Web usage analysis tools that accept verbatim the data collected by the Web servers themselves. Data collection, like any form of human or machine perception, is limited. We need to choose our data collection methods, definitions, and techniques carefully and wisely. Just as there are colors and sounds beyond the range of normal human perception, we never get a complete record of HCI. Although computerized monitoring may overtake most or all aspects of the collection, analysis, and application of data, people will continue to control — at least temporarily — what data get collected in the first place. With that power comes the need for human responsibility and openness. At a fundamental level we need to think about data collection and cyberspace as an environment in computer terms, rather than in human terms. The challenge to humankind is daunting. It is like trying to prepare the real world for a control shift through which dogs will assume roles formerly held by people. For people to prepare for an orderly control shift, they need to be able to see, hear, smell, and think about the world as dogs do. How can they possibly do that? How can they possibly perceive the Web as a Web server does?

User Feedback in a Computerized Networked Environment   Computerized monitoring systems generally collect and analyze data about the interactions between humans and computers. After the data have been collected and analyzed, summary reports can be directed in three ways: to third party human beings (researchers, business managers, or Web masters), to the computer itself, or to the people originally involved in HCI. Redirecting the information to the human participants has not been seriously explored in this book. Rather, we have examined the history of the myriad ways third party human beings use this information, then explored the possibility that in the future the information will be plowed right back into the computer system, so that it can modify its software and the resultant virtual environment to better match or facilitate the observed human behavior.

Another potential future development for the computerized monitoring project in general is that soon it may be possible to provide users with histories of their searching in particular, and of general behavior of the virtual self in a computerized networked environment. To date most computerized monitoring of HCI has involved one or more people learning from the online behavior of *different* human beings. The user is often out of the loop — a mere actor beyond the realm of meaningful dialogue with the producer and director. Computerized monitoring has not been used as a tool for self-discovery and learning, even in the educational software sector that produces virtual learning environments. Future development of the amorphous movement could focus more on facilitating self-discovery about one's own style of interacting with computers. Computerized monitoring could also serve as a form of virtual memory, alerting users to bad habits and redundant behavior.

This potential development path either complements or competes with the general thesis of this book that, increasingly, computerized monitoring systems and virtual environments themselves will become the entities that learn most from HCI in cyberspace. Unless we can argue persuasively to the contrary, the need for people in online environments to learn from past experience almost certainly will diminish. Rather, the virtual environment in which they behave will learn from past experience, then modify its contours and characteristics to better match what it has observed.

If the human need to learn in this way will become less vital, what will people be asked to learn? Values, morals, and ethics will become increasingly important. Although computerized monitoring will be able to modify online environments to better match and facilitate behavior that occurs, it will be difficult or impossible for computerized monitoring systems to determine, especially a priori, what is good, true, and beautiful. Human learning may shift from "merely" learning how to cope and survive in real-world environments that are noticeably intractable to learning how to apply the best of all possible human values to very fluid online environments.

Real-time, Intrusive, Manipulative Monitoring of HCI   Most monitoring of HCI occurs after the fact. The data are collected as the behavior happens, and are analyzed later. The idea of real-time monitoring is not new. Sigfried Treu (1972) developed the idea of "transparent stimulation" in the early 1970s. Transparent stimulation was to identify and validate human behaviors in the context of HCI that should be encouraged and reinforced by the human-computer interface. Transparent stimulation is a method of unobtrusive, real-time observation of a search session that provides an opportunity for the normally unobtrusive observer to intrude into the search session and provide advice or ask questions (Treu 1973). Transparent stimulation could function as a virtual, invisible cattle prod, gently dissuading users from repeating behaviors that are considered suboptimal, ranging from poor spelling to e-mail flaming to visiting taboo Web sites.

Although the quest for real-time monitoring is at least as old as computerized monitoring itself, the idea lay dormant until the advent of Web server log analysis in the 1990s. Software improvements have increased the opportunities for sophis-ticated real-time monitoring. The Insight software from Accrue records site infor-mation and processes it instantly, enabling a human monitor to view the activity at a site in real time (Rich 1997a). Randall (1997c, 260) notes: "Live monitoring is obvi-ously a much more useful approach than log analysis from the standpoint of up-to-the-minute site analysis, which a growing number of organizations require." One could argue, however, that the fear of real-time, intrusive human monitoring and manipulation behind the guise of a computerized monitoring system — Oz behind the curtain, or your boss in a remote location spying on you while you work — misses the main point of the development of computerized monitoring systems in general. Real-time human intrusions into HCI are not the ultimate goal. It is difficult to imagine what long-term gain would be achieved from such an inefficient, sporadic practice; it would put people back into the loop at a very inopportune point.

Automatically Tailoring Systems to the Individual   The ability to sig-nificantly customize and personalize an online environments is another character-istic that distinguishes them from real ones. Personalization is expensive to realize in the real world (Wagner 1996e). Customizability is more useful than other soft-ware applications, such as Internet telephones, because it is both easier and less expensive to do online than offline (Wagner 1996e). Whether the customization is done intentionally (e.g., based on the user's intentional selection of environmental preferences) or unintentionally (e.g., based on interests and preferences inferred from a user's current and past behavior in an online environment), customization of online environments certainly is feasible, perhaps inevitable.

Customization or personalization of online experiences is being touted as a primary benefit of computerized monitoring and other potential threats to per-sonal privacy, particularly consumer privacy. Customization usually implies some level of conscious control by the user over the customization process, if not the parameters and range of options. Personalization, in this context, implies more provider or direct machine control over the individual-specific configuration of a malleable environment. Craig Donato from Excite, a Web directory company, differentiates between customization and personalization in this way: "Cus-tomization is when you remember something for the user — like his stocks. With personalization, we're taking information about our relationship and using that to deliver a better experience for the user" (quoted in Bayers 1998, 133). Personal-ization is more dynamic than customization, and based more on the history of pre-vious HCI between a specific individual and a specific online landscape. Megan Bowman, a government affairs manager at Microsoft, notes, "A lot of the promise of the Internet is in personalization. When people understand what value they get for providing information, and that that information is protected, they will feel quite comfortable providing it" (quoted in Blow 1998). Kirsner (1997b) predicts that content targeting based on a conversation between a Web site and visitors will soon be feasible. Conversational Web sites will not only respect users' privacy but also offer a dynamic experience with each visit.

In computer-augmented real-world environments, electronic systems are being merged with the physical world as experienced by human beings to provide computer functionality to everyday objects and environments, such as videoconference rooms (Cooperstock, Fels, Buxton, and Smith 1997). These real-world "ubiquitous computing environments" can be designed to adapt to the varying behavior of different users. The underlying assumption behind reactive real environments was that if one can infer a user's intentions based on the user's actions, so too should an appropriately designed computer system (Cooperstock, Fels, Buxton, and Smith 1997). It is possible to translate this concept from real to virtual realms. As adaptable computer systems can be interwoven into real-world environments, so too can computerized monitoring modules be used to create reactive online environments that adapt and learn based on the observed online behavior of both individuals and groups. As the computing cost of adapting to the online computing styles of individuals declines, there will be a declining incentive in the software industry to develop user interfaces whose one size fits nearly everyone — or no one in particular, depending on one's point of view.

In the past, if the results of computerized monitoring led to changes and improvements in a computer system, the results of individual HCI were aggregated and analyzed, patterns and problems were discerned, then the system was modified for all future human actors engaged in HCI within that system. Each individual human actor was treated as one small contributor to whole-group behavior. It was a very pure form of online communism. Individual needs, desires, and goals were sacrificed for the common good of the entire group. During the early years of the amorphous movement to use computers to monitor HCI, the intent of the analysis of computerized monitoring data was very utilitarian — to determine the single interface that would result in the greatest good for the greatest number of people. The goal was to find the sweet spot in the world of interface design. We all were guinea pigs in the grand pursuit of a generalized, one-size-fits-all interface. Once the general behavior of the entire group was known, the system was modified to respond in a better fashion to that normalized behavior. In fact, the interface itself encouraged normal behavior. In this sense, during the first 20 years of personal computing, online environments were as unforgiving as real environments. Neither Mother Nature nor Father Bill could be fooled. It is as if we all were living in a virtual commune, where the general good of the community far outweighed the needs and styles of specific individuals. Despite all of the color used with graphical user interfaces, behind it all was the notion of a drab gray unitog.

For the individual whose HCI is being monitored by computer, however, the tangible payoff for this subtle intrusion was slowly and massively delivered. Despite numerous transaction log analyses that have shown that, in general, persons searching online library catalogs tend to misspell and mistype with alarming frequency, it has taken years to incorporate spell-checkers and soundex mechanisms into online catalog interfaces and search engines. The net gain from the upsetting invasion of personal privacy in online environments was faint and vaguely communal.

The implicit social contract was that we all should be more than a little altruistic on this matter. Critics of computerized monitoring could (and did) argue that individual rights were being trampled in the name of either dubious social gains or to satisfy the idle curiosity of researchers and online marketers. Future developments in the ability to direct the outcomes of computerized monitoring of HCI back to the individual being monitored could change the focus and tenor of that debate.

The confluence of computerized monitoring and other factors has created realistic opportunities to make online environments truly personalized without relying on the conscious efforts of users to articulate and choose their personal preferences. Some prototypical aspects of this "automatic individualization" already are happening. Machine pacing in workplace environments, for example, may be a precursor of this form of automatic tailoring. Some of the machine pacing in the past, however, dictated by externally induced production quotas, rather than by any subtle analysis of the pace of particular HCI teams. In the formal learning domain, the STUDY software (Winne, Gupta, and Nesbit 1994) is an example of an adaptive system in that, during the course of an online tutorial session, data representing the learner's behavior can be operated on by programming rules that tailor and pace instructional events to better match the learner's prior and evolving knowledge, motivation, and strategies.

Web log analysis may lead the way toward mainstreaming this movement to automatically individualize virtual environments based on the outcomes of computerized monitoring. Already we have seen that Web log analysis is being used to customize online environmental conditions to correspond better with the online behavior of specific people. For better or worse, advertising is leading the way. The process whereby a Web server displays advertisements dynamically from a list is called a play list. By gathering and analyzing the click-through rates for each ad, the Web site designer can weed out the ineffective ads and replace them with new ones (Stout 1997, 208). Although it may be unfortunate and regrettable that the first customization activity has occurred in online advertising, the general drift of these developments may have long-term positive benefits for individuals. A regular play list for ads on a Web site does not take into account the characteristics or needs of the visitors to the site, but in the near future it will be possible to individualize the dynamism already developed.

The prospect of real-time (rather than delayed) individualized customization of online environments raises interesting possibilities. What if computerized monitoring could be used to individually modify the system on the fly (almost immediately) to match the idiosyncratic HCI styles of individual users? For such users of the system, the benefits of computerized monitoring would be much more self-evident and immediate. One challenge for designers of such a computerized monitoring system, however, would be to encourage to the utmost individual learning and self-realization. If this concept of real-time applications of computerized monitoring comes to broad fruition, there will be a fearful symmetry between the individual and the online environment that may leave little room for human learning as we know it. The real world often is described as the "School of Hard Knocks" because it is so unforgiving and difficult to change. After one gets knocked about for a bit, one modifies one's behavior to match the learned, enduring environmental conditions of the real world. The human learning that has proven effective in real-world environments may not be the optimal learning in online environments. Heretofore people have had little competition in learning. They are amazed when chimps learn to spell simple words. Smart, almost precocious online environments using computerized monitoring may provide people some stiff competition in learning and adaptability. Computerized monitoring may give the computer the upper hand in the online learning classroom.

After the emergence and diffusion of computerized monitoring and mutable online environments, the need to alter human behavior to exploit an essentially intractable real environment diminishes. This change may have profound effects on society, culture, systems of formal education, and other essential aspects of human being. Beyond the formation of young minds, other methods can help achieve the desired outcome of making people productive and useful in their environments.

The scenario being envisioned here, however, represents a completely different learning environment. The smart online environment would regulate and modify itself to match the observed behavior of the individual. The online world thus envisioned could be dubbed the "School of Soft (or No) Knocks." Although absolute environmental limits may continue to exist (based perhaps on a combination of technological limits, the limits of human perception and cognition, and universally recognized limits to human values, mores, and ethics), within the wide field defined by those limits the environment will present itself in unique ways to each human inhabitant of that environment. Vinge (1993) suggests that human-computer interfaces may become so intimate that users may be considered superhumanly intelligent. People become very intimate with their environments; the distinctions between information known to the human being and information suspended in the surrounding environment will fall away. The idea of a library without walls may be quickly surpassed by that of knowledge without cranial walls. If knowledge follows information and floats free from its human moorings, can wisdom be far behind?

If each individual's online environment becomes automatically customized, the social pressures and opportunities to establish and enforce behavioral norms will become becalmed. How would people act in the absence of any generally accepted idea of normal behavior? Will we all become self-actualized in a sense almost unimaginable in the real world, or will we all become outlandish and outrageous? If computers replace people as the major players in the analysis, interpretation, and application phases of using computers to analyze HCI, there may be little or no need to mark benches, establish norms, or look for recurring behavior among human groups. People are very good at pattern recognition, but it appears that the demand for the ability to recognize patterns in emerging online environments will not be great.

If and when all of this happens, we may experience a quick, irrevocable divergence between human intelligence and machine intelligence.

> Let an ultraintelligent machine be defined as a machine that can far surpass all the intellectual activities of any man however clever. Since the design of machines is one of these intellectual activities, an ultraintelligent machine could design even better machines; there would then unquestionably be an "intelligence explosion," and the intelligence of man would be left far behind. Thus the first ultraintelligent machine is the last invention that man need ever make, provided that the machine is docile enough to tell us how to keep it under control (Good 1965, quoted in Vinge 1993, 90).

The programming challenges behind this project to develop individualized, self-regulating online environments are not insignificant. Bailey (1996) explores the development of self-evolving computer programs and systems. A new breed of computers is emerging that uses parallel processing and new mathematics to continually change their own programs as they compute. The computers will emphasize emergent patterns. The new computers are being used to analyze the behavior of bird flocks and consumers, among other applications.

Dearnley and Smith (1995) also explore the possibilities for dynamic feedback as a self-correcting mechanism in knowledge-based management systems. Rather than have skilled system administrators conduct all monitoring of use, evaluation of use, and implementation of alternative physical designs within the system architecture, it would be more appropriate to embed the monitoring within the design of the system itself. This would allow a certain level of monitoring and environmental restructuring to be carried out routinely, without necessarily requiring the intervention of a skilled designer (Dearnley and Smith 1995, 660). In the late nineteenth and early twentieth centuries, the means of human production were routinized. In the late twentieth and early twenty-first centuries, the means of monitoring human behavior are being routinized. Computerized monitoring would become truly unobtrusive. Surveillance will become ubiquitous and mundane. In comparison, past state attempts to control human behavior have been cartoonish.

This prospect of self-evolving computer systems and self-correcting online environments can be seen as part of what James Bailey calls bit evolution. Bit evolution will join biological and cultural evolution as a third type of evolution on earth. "Just as cultural evolution learned to operate independently of biological evolution, so too will bit evolution become autonomous" (Bailey 1996, 6). Although cultural evolution has been the heyday of humanity for at least a few millennia, the prospects for humanity in the impending bit evolution remain cloudy.

Customization of a virtual environment can be undertaken deliberately by the user or automatically achieved by a computerized monitoring system. Deliberate overrides of automatic configurations and reconfigurations always could be possible. This may be the ultimate act of human control in cyberspace. Whereas in real-world environments often the struggle for control occurs between various groups of people, in online environments the struggle for control may pit humanity against the computerized environments themselves.

Several software developers appear to be pursuing this quest for a truly automatically customized online environment. Broadvision and Brightware are two software packages that have emerged as early entrants in the race to make the Web experience truly customizable. Broadvision's software program One-to-One Commerce seeks to individualize the online marketing experience (Wilder and Dalton 1997). The Brightware software is trying to tailor online customer service, rather than individualize ad content or the online environment in general (Wilder and Dalton 1997). Internet Profiles Inc. plans to be able to deliver demographic data in real time in the near future. This will mean that a Web site can be customized on the fly for a visitor, based on the visitor's identity (Buchanan and Lukaszewski 1997, 191). Software developers such as Brightware and Firefly Network have operational software that uses artificial intelligence, neural networks, and sophisticated statistical tools to analyze users' behavior and predict what each user would like to see, experience, and purchase in the future (Wagner 1996d).

Not all of the early attempts at customizing virtual environments are aimed at the consumer and end-user markets. The Illinois Chamber of Commerce, for example, spent $1.4 million on its Web site, according to Peter Creticos, assistant to the president. The bulk of that money was spent on custom programming and analyzing the kinds of skills a person needs to do a particular job (Wagner 1996d). The goal of this particular customization project was to better match employers with prospective employees.

An environment capable of modifying itself to match the observed proclivities of the human actor(s) is a strange notion, difficult to reconcile with our knowledge of the way the real world works. In the real world, the human body has a similar function. If, for example, one foolishly leaves one's jacket at home on a raw, windy, rainy day, one's body adjusts the best it can to compensate for the oversight. In a customized virtual reality, then, the lived environment will assume some of the functions of the body in the real world. Will cyberindividuals begin to understand this lived online environment as something akin to their real-world bodies?

For some people, perhaps most, the prospect of a sentient environment is not a major privacy concern, as long as people are kept out of the immediate loop. The idea that "it" knows what one is doing in an online environment is much less disturbing than the idea that another human being watches and knows all that one does. The recurring metaphor of prying human eyes in cyberspace — of human snoops inside the monitor — is a bridging mechanism from real-world privacy invasion to the new world of virtual intrusions of personal privacy that may not be of much use once we get both feet planted on the opposite shore. We need to both rethink and reimagine our concerns about human privacy in digital environments. The environments themselves, rather than other people (including corporate stooges and government goons), may become the major threat to a revamped understanding of individual human privacy. Perhaps it is part of the triumph and tragedy of human being that historically we have not displayed much interest in non-human forms of intelligence — higher, lower, or different.

Historically, the cost of customizing or individualizing something has been high. In a pure, real-world economy, a customized home, car, or hamburger all cost extra to build. Perhaps one of the differentiating characteristics of an online economy is that the cost of individualizing a good, service, or environment is dropping rapidly. The benefits of individualization always have been tantalizing. Witness all of the advertising slogans for real-world economic goods and services that attempt to create an illusion of individualization. In cyberspace, thanks in part to computerized monitoring, you may be able to truly have it your way — perhaps whether you want it your way or not. When online environments become a reflection of the individual, self-despair and loathing may set in, and psychoanalysis will become a growth industry.

One problem with the prospect of automatic customization of virtual environments is that it can (and probably will) happen without the direct knowledge, consent, and will of those to whom it is happening. The human will to control real environments can be amazing, sometimes frightening, and potentially destructive. Why should we assume that netizens will passively tolerate this fundamental, perhaps innate, manifestation of human will? Computerized monitoring and its applications need not be mandatory. The netizen could be allowed to choose a static, generic, dumb online environment, or a sentient, smart, automatically customizable one. Fink, Kobsa, and Schreck (1997) suggest that an optimal dialogue between person and computer could allow the user to choose between no user modeling, short-term modeling for the current session only, or long-term modeling. Envisioning this scenario from a marketing perspective, Hagel and Armstrong (1997) refer to individualized online environments as market segments of one. Now that the art of mass marketing in the real world has been refined and nearly perfected, the emergence of virtual economic environments opens a new challenge for marketers: mass customization (Hagel and Armstrong 1997). Personalized, individualized marketing has been a Holy Grail for some time. Computerized monitoring has put it within our grasp.

A good, enjoyable online environment would be the reward for certain behavior, based on an analysis, probably conducted by a computer, of computerized monitoring data. The threat posed by this scenario is that ultimately it is the programmers, or the employers of the programmers, who decide what behavior will "map to" or result in good, true, and beautiful online environments. Although the individual actor is the proximate cause of the good online environment, the individual is not the first cause. How does a group of netizens construct a good, just, virtual society from a series of monadic, personalized, online environments? Online environments are more like real-world suburbs in this regard than information superhighways or global marketplaces.

If the best-laid plans often go awry, the amazing lack of general awareness of the amorphous movement to use computers to monitor HCI could doom it to failure. The first 30 years of this movement have not been particularly auspicious, informed, and fruitful. Perhaps this daunting vision of an online environment perfectly suited to one's needs, as expressed through one's behavior, never will come to pass. The stumbling block is not a software problem, but rather a software developer problem. Will developers of computerized monitoring software have an interest in developing these absolutely individualized environments? In the last three years the power and influence of advertising on the development of Web software for computerized monitoring has been both astonishing and sobering. In three years within the realm of computerized monitoring the needs of that industry overtook the needs of the entire fields of education, librarianship, and human resource management. In the long term, however, advertisers do not want us to be perfectly happy, even though individual ads may implicitly promise this. As a lot, happy people do not need, do, and buy much. Advertisers want us to feel needs and deficiencies that compel us to buy and consume goods and services. In the mind of the advertiser (and perhaps also of the consumer) the pursuit of happiness is more beneficial than the happiness itself. The purpose of advertising, which is quickly gaining control of the major portion of the entire field of computerized monitoring, is not a perfect, virtual Shangri-La. Hunger, not satisfaction, is advertisers' desired state for us, and a personalized, customized online environment will not leave cyberindividuals chomping at the bit.

At least as a thought experiment, the stakes of this vision are high. Weber (1996) warns that privacy invasions of the type envisioned here could lead to subliminal behavior control. Santos (1995, 47) was part of a team of researchers at Georgia Tech University who worked to develop a fully automated system for the identification of user knowledge. To achieve full automation, the analysis of human behavior was based entirely on information that could be made known to the computer at the time of the interaction, without any external human intervention or analysis. They wanted to close the loop on the process of using computers to monitor HCI, so that the computer performed the data collection, analysis, interpretation, and application.

The challenge for people interacting with computer systems with embedded monitoring modules to create virtual environments will be to translate their innermost thoughts, desires, needs, and wants into appropriate action and behavior that leads to desired environmental changes — the ageless challenge for humanity, fundamentally unchanged from the time when we dwelled more often in the real world alone. Although computerized monitoring may help us bridge the gulf between action and environmental effect, the gulf between desire and action probably will remain as an essentially human problem.

The prospect of individualized online environments is both exhilarating and frightening. For marketers this environment represents the logical conclusion of all of their efforts. Finally they will be able to tailor their products and services to meet the individual needs of individual human beings. If this capability emerges and diffuses at roughly the same time as nanotechnology (a manufacturing technique for building things at the molecular level), a world of truly just-in-time personalized products and services will emerge. At the same time, there is something profoundly sad and disturbing about this prospect. The mystery of human dreams and desires may be discovered, revealing only their shabbiness. The commonality of certain hopes (e.g., a chicken in every pot) will be scattered by the winds of automatic online individualism.

Monitoring Human Movement Through a Process Space   Computerized monitoring technologies and techniques also could be used to monitor human movement through a process space. During the early years of computerized monitoring, human behavior during HCI was monitored rather passively and real-world behavior, much in the way that someone would watch with wonderment, amusement, or dismay a dog chasing its tail. Web site monitoring, on the other hand, tends to focus on human movement in a virtual correlate of real space. Individuals are monitored as they move from sector to sector within a site, or, less frequently, from site to site on the Web.

In the future, it may be more productive and useful to define process spaces, then use computerized monitoring to track human movement through these process spaces. All four of the principal human activities examined in this book — formal learning, working, information seeking, and shopping — involve processes that define spaces, complete with dead ends, grand hallways, harrowing gorges, and treeless plains. Despite the real-world, three-dimensional metaphors in the preceding sentence, it is important to remember that process spaces are radically different from real world or online environment dimensional spaces. Rather than use computerized monitoring to track human behavior and movement in some virtual space that mimics real space, as if people were little more than objects in a landscape, we could be using computerized monitoring to better understand how people create and participate in process spaces. Agre's (1994, 109) discussion of the grammars of action, which are essential to the capture model of privacy, intimates an emphasis on human creation of and movement through process spaces. It may be instructive to conceptualize a process space as a clearing that is also a maze.

Classification or Typing of Users   The need for pattern recognition and placing individuals into groups or categories may not be completely useless in these emerging online environments. Yan, Jacobsen, Garcia-Molina, and Dayal (1996) discuss the prospects for dynamic hypertext linking, based on the automatic classification of visitors to a Web site according to their access and usage. Based on the categories into which an individual user goes, the prototype system dynamically suggests hypertext links for the individual to navigate. The categorization of human beings into groups would be based on behavior, rather than on race, sex, religion, similarity of interests, and other more traditional classification schemes. The goal of dynamic hypertext linking is to match an active user's behavior with one or more of the categories discovered from the prior analysis of Web logs. Dynamic linking and automatic clustering may also lead to better server performance in that the server may be able to pre-fetch Web pages that the user is likely to request, based on what already has been accessed and the category into which the present user falls. This type of project involving Web log analysis raises some fundamental questions about the limits and ethics of social or behavioral engineering. By identifying categories of users in an online environment, then modifying the presentation of links and content to subsequent users who, based on their behavior exhibited early in a use session, appear to fall into a category, does the self-evolving environment subtly encourage subsequent users to behave in ways that mirror the behavior that led to the establishment of the category of users?

Environmentally Created Virtual Communities   As noted above, one of the shortcomings of the amorphous movement to use computers to monitor HCI is that much of the activity has focused on isolated individuals. The technique has not matured sufficiently to be able to study and understand the dynamic interactions of groups and communities. As the software becomes more sophisticated, and as human intermediaries are gradually removed from the process of collecting, analyzing, interpreting, and applying data about HCI at the group and community levels, it may be possible for the environment itself to create or foster virtual communities.

Of course, the notion of an environmentally created community may not be a unique new characteristic of cyberspace. In the real world, one could argue that many communities, from New York City to Oklahoma City, were created and maintained by a subtle, complex cluster of environmental factors. One sobering potential aspect of virtual communities in cyberspace is that they will be more homogeneous than most real communities. If the virtual communities created by people with similar interests, passions, or concerns are strikingly homogeneous, it is safe to assume that environmentally created virtual communities would be more so, unless the purpose behind the software that analyzes user behavior with an intent of creating virtual communities sees some benefit in having diversity. Even if that happens, we all will be token netizens of the virtual communities our benevolent computerized monitoring software encourages us to join.

From Databases to Knowledge Bases   Computerized monitoring may help online environments become more sophisticated and interesting. The environmental content itself, rather than merely the presentation of static content, will become malleable and capable of individualization. Databases may be evolving into more sophisticated knowledge bases. The environmental conditions of databases tended to be determined a priori, but the environmental conditions of knowledge bases may evolve on the fly as the online environment is used. Designers of knowledge bases will rely more heavily on usage information, and thus more on computerized monitoring.

> The need for usage information to guide the designer to an appropriate design is not peculiar to knowledge base systems. Similar information is needed in conventional database design, but there the applications supported often have few relations and well understood transaction types. By contrast, knowledge bases have many different data object types and are subject to a wider range of complex transactions, many of which may not be predicted when the initial design is being undertaken (Dearnley and Smith 1995, 660).

Another possible future outcome from the development of computerized monitoring systems is that design and use may become indistinguishable. In the early days of computers, first the system was designed, then it was used. If redesign occurred after use, it occurred outside the existing virtual environment, then appeared as an upgrade. In the near future, the use of the system may become crucial to its design in the sense that the system will not be designed until it is used. All users will become creators in their own ways of their virtual environments.

Path Analysis Through an Information Space   From the earliest stages of the era of computerized monitoring of HCI, the value of search path analysis has been known and appreciated. "Search path analysis allows us to examine intermediate search outcomes rather than the final search product alone. It also allows us to trace backward from outcomes and analyze the actions taken to reach that point" (Borgman, Hirsh, and Hiller 1996, 580).

As of late 1996 no Web site analysis software provided statistics on the top paths users take through a Web site (Stout 1997, 92). The situation, however, is changing rapidly. Graphical site analysis tools provide a visual representation of how a Web site is structured. Astra Site Manager from Mercury Interactive Corporation is an example of such software. When graphical site analysis software is combined with Web server log analysis software, it will be possible to visualize the traffic patterns through a Web site, represented as a three-dimensional information space (Rapoza 1997). Such path analysis in turn will bring to a head the question about the structure and nature of an information space freed from its earthly confines. We can begin to question whether three dimensions is the best way to visualize an information space.

Acceptance of Monitoring and Surveillance   Dwellers in any environment develop expectations about the nature of that environment. We expect real-world urban environments to be relatively noisy and scarce of vegetation. The extent of monitoring and surveillance activities on the Web may lead dwellers in cyberspace to accept and expect monitoring and surveillance as "normal" characteristics of that environment. Monitoring is becoming less clandestine and more mainstreamed. Monitoring is coming to be used more to understand the usual behavior of people in online environments, rather than to detect aberrant behavior. This acceptance by netizens of cyberspace as a monitored environment may have long-term effects on the feel of online environments.

Behavior Becomes Identification   A person's behavior in virtual environments (including purchasing and information seeking) may become as well known as one's or Social Security number. We still are not certain, however, that when analyzed in depth, an individual's behavior in virtual environments is truly unique to that individual. Poster's (1990) notion of a virtual self, leading a life somewhat parallel to the real self, is pertinent here. The rights and responsibilities of the virtual self may or may not coincide with the rights and responsibilities of the real self.

In the real world, a person's Social Security number (SSN) has become tender as well as a unique identifier. Gellman (1997) sees concerns about SSNs almost as a red herring that prevents us from sniffing other foul privacy practices in cyberspace. It is unfortunate that citizens often become concerned about loss of privacy only when SSNs become involved. In other situations, people reveal much personal data to America's vast marketing and information industries. It is as if neither the monitors nor the monitored really know what to make of these new data. Although advertising and marketing campaigns thrive on user feedback, when it comes to user behavior in online environments, advertisers want to use these data to infer real-world demographic information, rather than use the data for what they are.

Analysis of Thoughts and Emotions   Computerized monitoring currently uses HCI to infer people's thoughts, intentions, and emotions in the online environments created by these interactions. The inferential trip from observed behavior back to the thoughts, intentions, and emotions that caused or contributed to it remains very rocky and uncertain. The dark plain between behavior and intent remains even in vigorous computerized monitoring environments. Future developments in computerized monitoring modules may allow computers to monitor human thoughts and emotions more directly. "In the future, we may even have to confront questions about the right to control brainwaves and other biometric indicators thought to be relevant to work" (Marx and Sherizen 1989, 398). Botan (1996) briefly discusses the early developments in brain-wave monitoring. Even though thought may be the wellspring of action, computerized monitoring is allied first and foremost to action, not to thought. It is a method for analyzing online behavior. By thought alone we cannot modify a monitored online environment — at least not based on the current state of computerized monitoring technology. If computerized monitoring ever is able to tap human thought directly, so that our thoughts have a direct impact on the look and feel of an online environment, then the environment itself will become its own thought police. The environment itself will become Big Brother.

Computerized Monitoring in Real-World Ubiquitous Computing Environments   In the near future computerized monitoring could affect the ubiquitous computing, real-world environments being predicted by Mark Weiser and other researchers at Xerox PARC (Wasserman 1998). If this happens, computerized monitoring will have seriously invaded the real world. Computerized monitoring of motor vehicle location and movement may be a precursor of things to come. Computerized monitoring of HCI began in cyberspace, but human participation in online environments remains largely voluntary. To a certain extent, an individual can decline being in a monitored online environment (assuming that the individual is aware, or at least suspicious, that the online environment is heavily monitored). Human being in the real world is not voluntary. During the early years of the computer revolution, cyberspace and the real world have maintained relatively separate identities. If ubiquitous computing comes to pass, the real world and cyberspace will meld into one. A single experience or event will have both real-world and cyberspace perspectives and narratives. This condition exists now, but the real-world narrative of one's current cyberspace experiences (e.g., he sat, then sat some more, then concluded with some sitting, but his right index finger was preternaturally restless) might make for dull reading and disappointing sales.

What is the end or final cause of computerized monitoring of HCI? The general trend in computerized monitoring is to make collecting, analyzing, and applying data more computerized, with less human intervention. As Gary Marx notes (Westin, Marx, Zahorik, and Ware 1992), computerized monitoring is becoming less personal and less place-specific. What we may be witnessing is a kind of democratization of surveillance. The future of computerized monitoring should be user-centered rather than centered on a virtual site or on a primary human activity, such as learning, working, or shopping. The potential for creating new, valuable knowledge is much greater with the user-centered approach. Only connect.

14

Conclusion

That marketing effort [on the Web] may prove a harbinger of things to come, as the Internet moves closer to the television model and away from an esoteric academic stronghold (Wetli 1995).

The changes that are made possible by the computerized means of interaction are seemingly radical, but still far from complete (Rochlin 1997, 86).

The general thesis advanced in this book has been that the primary pure knowledge outcome from the amorphous movement to use computers to understand HCI has been to better understand how people act in online environments. The principal application of this movement is to create truly smart online environments by closing the loop of gathering, analyzing, and applying virtual behavioral data so that the computer performs all phases. If these dual theses are true, the movement to use computers to monitor HCI raises serious questions about the nature and future of human being in cyberspace, including questions about individual privacy in virtual environments and the role and value of human learning in forgiving, malleable environments.

As we enter the next decade, century, and millennium, participants in computerized monitoring projects find the field being driven primarily by the needs and investments of persons trying to make the Web a viable environment for commercial activity. Recent advances in the tools that support computerized monitoring have been impressive, in many ways outdistancing the development work of the previous three decades, particularly in the analysis, presentation, and application of information resulting from computerized monitoring activities. Collecting the data never has been much of a technical or economic problem, but more of a conceptual and moral problem. Although the development of computerized monitoring software in the last few years, driven primarily by commercial interests, has quickly outdistanced the previous 30 years of software development, driven primarily by academic interests, one could argue that the philosophical, theoretical, and moral foundations of the amorphous movement to use computers to monitor HCI have become less stable, and they never were firmly established. Computerized monitoring never has evolved into a discipline or community. Most of the parties interested in the subject do not express much sense of a comprehensive field. The reasons for this failure of insight probably are complex. Computerized monitoring began as a basal data collection technique created without a strong sense of purpose. It was not a "solution" that emerged deliberately in response to an articulated problem, but developed as a technique because technological developments suddenly enabled it to be done. It always has been a method in search of a purpose. The applications that have been identified and practiced, in formal learning, work, information seeking, and shopping environments, have been so diverse that practitioners often have seemed unaware of parallel developments in other fields. It is doubtful that many of the parties involved in Web log analysis realize the relatively rich tradition of computerized monitoring upon which they unwittingly draw.

When we began this examination of the use of computers to monitor HCI, the activities under study may have appeared to be too clear and self-evident to warrant lengthy attention. Despite all of the swirling moral and legal issues, at first glance the act of computerized monitoring itself seemed to be fairly cut-and-dried. Computers appear to capture irrefutable facts about the ways people use and interact with any computer system. Computers apply time stamps with the efficiency of a platonic pile-driver. The meaning and applications of computerized monitoring may not have been crystal clear, but at least the efficient gathering of raw data seemed to be straightforward.

Now everything seems to be all in a muddle — not only the ethical issues, but also the front-end issues (such as what data to collect) and the issues about the ultimate purpose and impact of computerized monitoring projects.

During its first 30 years, computerized monitoring essentially has been a human activity. People write the software that gathers (and occasionally analyzes) the data, decide on situations in which computerized monitoring will be used, interpret the results in human ways, and apply them in human ways, generally haphazardly and inefficiently, compared with the way a computer or computer system would apply them. Computerized monitoring of HCI could become a very liberating event for the individual, because it enables the tailoring of the online environment to fit the behavior, needs, and preferences of a specific person. The danger of this vision, however, is the prospect of an almost absolute solipsism. We should fear not Big Brother, but ourselves. How can we connect with others if the online environment we experience perfectly fits each of us as individuals? In this vision of the virtual world, there would be less incentive than in the real world to make friends, seek advice from others on how to think and act, disagree with others, or even fight. A radically self-correcting online environment may change the very nature of human being.

One counter-argument to the prediction of a future of extreme virtual solipsism, where the virtual environment resulting from a specific HCI is molded by the nature and progress of that interaction, is the simple phenomenological fact that nearly all HCI is experienced by the participating person as a transcendence, self-forgetfulness, or trance. Our own experiences with using computers does not seem to indicate that introspection is a major threat. When people interact with computers, they tend to forget about themselves, occasionally to the detriment of their bodies, minds, souls, and social lives.

This Town Isn't Big Enough It has become a truism that the current battle between media and computer giants is for control of eyes — at least those of persons of a particular socio-economic stratum. Stated differently and more blandly, despite the changing nature of human perceptions of time in cyberspace, there are only so many hours in the day (and, cumulatively, in a human lifetime), and one person can focus only on so many things. It remains to be seen whether the town of human cognition is big enough for two separate but equal realities — the real and the virtual. Rochlin (1997, 214), for one, thinks not, and fears that we are deconstructing the historically, socially constructed worlds of business, social institutions, and the military, transforming them into virtual spaces where integrated computerized monitoring systems interpret human behavior, wants, and needs and translate them into virtual reality with adaptable, automatic processes. Although we never really leave the real world, virtual worlds appear to be a threat to the real world we know. It is a threat not only in some zero-sum game between reality and virtuality, but also because cyberspace challenges all of our accepted ideas about ontology, perceptual psychology, and sociology. It seems to be developing into a world where observation and causation are perfectible. In the real world the saying is that a nation receives the government it deserves. It usually is invoked to explain governmental corruption or incompetence — in other words, when the system breaks down. In the virtual world, through the maturation and diffusion of computerized monitoring, each of us may get exactly (and nothing more than) what we deserve. Rather than embrace this as a perfect form of justice — perhaps analogous to Dante's schematic of hell — we seem to be collectively balking at it. We are reluctant to have virtual work environments where employees are reimbursed in a highly gradated meritocracy, based on computerized performance monitoring data. We do not want information environments where proficient seekers of information are rewarded not only with more pertinent information, but also with richer information environments. We seem to shy away from the prospect of advertisements that are so targeted to individuals that they cease to be annoying (or at least become significantly less annoying) and start to be welcomed information.

Ideal Penality and the Drive to Become Normal Foucault explored the ideal of observation and punishment in the real modern world. He extended the notion of surveillance and punishment in the modern era of the real world to its logical conclusion:

The ideal point of penality today would be an indefinite discipline: an interrogation without end, an investigation that would be extended without limit to a meticulous and ever more analytical observation, a judgment that would at the same time be the constitution of a file that was never closed, the calculated leniency of a penalty that would be interlaced with the ruthless curiosity of an examination, a procedure that would be at the same time the permanent measure of a gap in relation to an inaccessible norm and the asymptotic movement that strives to meet in infinity (Foucault 1977, 227).

The postmodern age may have found its own ideal of observation in computerized monitoring. It is an indefinite discipline and an interrogation without end, and computers are very meticulous and analytical observers. People, however, would be essentially removed from the process of observation and judgment. In my opinion, one of the grave errors of critics of computerized monitoring projects is their frequent assumption that individuals behind the scenes are intimately involved with each stage of the process: data collection, analysis, interpretation, and application. The development drive of computerized monitoring tools and techniques is to remove human intervention as much as possible from these projects. Big Brother is being replaced by a little chip. Finally, unlike the real modern world of surveillance explored by Foucault, the purpose of computerized judgment would not be to herd human behavior toward some inaccessible norm. With auto-individualized online environments, the importance of norms diminishes considerably. Compared with human beings, computers have very little use for behavioral norms, even from those involved in HCI.

What are the potential uses and environmental constraints that make the identification and differentiation of the normal and the abnormal worthwhile? With the emergence and refinement of online environments, we may be entering a realm where the impulse to normalize will not find much need for expression. If this impulse is thwarted because it suddenly becomes useless, what other behavioral channels will this impulse seek? When viewed as an essential, defining environmental factor, rather than as an assault on personal privacy, computerized monitoring can be viewed as the element that may shift attention from the behavior of the monitored to the behavior of those who monitor. To monitor is a form of human behavior, too, at least until the human monitor is taken completely out of the process.

Seeking Commonalities and Enduring Themes in Diverse Situations   A major challenge posed by HCI involves finding the common characteristics and fundamental themes in the diverse instances of computerized monitoring. What, if anything, do these different manifestations of computer monitoring have in common? By definition, all instances involve the use of computers to monitor HCI, but other commonalities have been difficult to detect. Although we have seen that the fundamental projects of these virtual environments (working, seeking information, learning, shopping) seem to have a major influence on how computerized monitoring manifests itself differently in these different environments, in the near future we may witness the emergence of virtual environments that lack a clearly distinguishable fundamental project for those who participate in these environments. Working, learning, seeking information, shopping, recreating and other fundamentally human pursuits may all become a blur in emerging online environments. The multifunctional aspects of many Web browsing sessions may be a faint harbinger of things to come. Time on task will become difficult to measure as well as meaningless. This same type of blurring of functional lines seems to be occurring in the postmodern real world. It is becoming increasingly difficult to tell when people are learning, working, relaxing, or domesticating. The real world, however, remains a largely intractable world. The nature of virtual environments is such that we can make them become anything we want or need them to be.

Is Control the Crux?   In the context of computerized monitoring, what is control? Bellotti and Sellen (1993) define control as "empowering people to stipulate what information they project and who can get hold of it" (quoted in Cavoukian and Tapscott 1995, 126).

The battle for control of cyberspace is shaping up to be a strange struggle — more fantastic than postmodern warfare in the real world, of which the Gulf War may have been a precursor. For beginners, we cannot be sure about the identities of the combatants. In the real world, we incline to struggles between two superpowers (e.g., the United States versus the Soviet Union) or between a David and Goliath (e.g., John Q. Public versus the multinational corporation). Rheingold (1993, 4–5) envisions virtuality as a leverage tool for ordinary citizens:

> The technology that makes virtual communities possible has the potential to bring enormous leverage to ordinary citizens at relatively little cost — intellectual leverage, social leverage, commercial leverage, and most important, political leverage.... The Net is still out of control in fundamental ways, but it might not stay that way for long. What we know and do now is important because it is still possible for people around the world to make sure this new sphere of vital human discourse remains open to the citizens of the planet before the political and economic big boys seize it, censor it, meter it, and sell it back to us.

Rheingold clearly sees the struggle for control of cyberspace as a struggle of the many little Davids versus a few big Goliaths, but his statement also contains a few interesting twists on this struggle for control. Rheingold seems to suggest that the only way ordinary "world citizens"* can maintain control over cyberspace is to maintain the fundamental uncontrolledness of the Internet. He also sees the struggle as not so much hand-to-hand combat, even in a metaphorical sense, but rather as a rush to inhabit, as if cybersquatters have inalienable rights and possession is more than nine-tenths of the law. Perhaps the primary struggle here is not for control of cyberspace, because it is not a tangible good or real estate, but rather a struggle for the control of the idea of cyberspace.

Bibliographic control usually entails both intellectual control over the content

---

* *This phrase clearly would have been an oxymoron to most people from the classical Athenians to the Victorians, but now is accepted as an apt description of denizens of the Web.*

of a book and physical control over the book itself as an object. Computerized monitoring of HCI may be aiming at a more pervasive environmental control over online environments. This struggle for virtual control seems to be closest to the surface in online work environments. Shaiken (1985), for example, asserts that the central issue behind technological development in the workplace is not increased productivity, but power and control, which has great impact on the character of society as a whole. Workers, who still retain an amazing amount of autonomy and anonymity in their productivity in real-world work environments, are understandably concerned that the use of computerized monitoring in virtual work environments will be deployed to such an extent that work organizations will become hyper-hierarchical, not organizationally and artificially, but based on performance and contributions toward the goals of the work organization as a social unit.

If the will to monitor exists as a particular manifestation of the will to power, perhaps the desire to control is the ultimate driving force behind computerized monitoring. But how does an analysis of data gathered with computerized monitoring result in heightened control, or at least a heightened sense of control, for the analysts or those who commissioned the analysis? If computerized monitoring of HCI is about power and control, who has gained and lost through the emergence and diffusion of this technique? And if the right to monitor virtual behavior eventually passes completely out of human hands and into computer chips, we cannot really assert that computers willed this power play. Agre (1994) suggests that the answer to these questions will be found in the roots of the ideals of the social culture of computing, rather than in any political or economic motives. Human beings are developing computerized monitoring systems at a rapid pace simply because it can be done. Such monitoring never really satisfied our innate snoopiness, and increasingly the application of the results of a computerized monitoring project are being applied without much human intervention.

The use of technology to achieve greater control in the workplace threatens to change fundamental relationships between employers and employees, making employees more dominated and powerless than ever before (Healy and Marshall 1987, 12, quoted in Baarda 1994, 24). The driving force behind CPM in workplace environments may be the competitive forces in today's economy that demand increased productivity, improved products, and higher service quality. The low cost of CPM also may have contributed to its rapid diffusion (Lund 1989, 14). Howard asserts that the "new model of the corporation, much like the old, is founded on the systematic denial of influence and control to the large majority of working Americans" (quoted in Weiss 1990, 4–5). The emphasis on organizational control from a focus on efficiency often is reformulated as a political fight (Kidwell and Kidwell 1996, 10).

Who controls the development and deployment of computerized monitoring software? Does anyone? Software that enables computerized monitoring has not been developed through massive, coordinated, heavily-funded development projects. Perhaps counterintuitively, parents and the police — two real-world bastions of social control — have not been in the vanguard of computerized monitoring. The emergence of the filtering controversy for underage netizens, a controversy that is only tangential to the topic of this book, indicates that parents are becoming more interested in monitoring online behavior. The CYBERSitter software from Solid-Oak advertises that it keeps a secret log of Web sites visited, thus making it easier for parents to monitor the online habits of their children (Winner 1997). Client-side monitoring appears to be of more interest and utility than server-side monitoring for both parents and employers.

Information is notoriously difficult to control. Our notion of personal privacy is based on the premise that information can be controlled by being withheld. Privacy can be understood as a special form of information control. "The reason privacy is an emotional issue is fear of loss of control. The fear is real. Philosophical, psychological and religious notions of the self will have to be rethought in the light of this loss" (Flood 1997).

Hagel and Armstrong (1997) speculate that the emergence of virtual communities probably will shift power from vendors to customers by reducing or eliminating the information advantages that vendors currently enjoy in real economic environments. The Internet promises to change the balance of power between consumers and marketers, because it can provide each individual the power and tools to bargain on one's own terms (Dyson 1997a).

Ironies of the Battle for Control   Computerized monitoring can become the opposite of an instrument of social control, if an instrument of social control is understood as something that somehow pulls individuals on the fringes of society, however the fringe is defined, back toward an immutable or slow-to-change social center. Computerized monitoring ultimately is a threat more to the future existence and configuration of a social center than to individuals on the fringe. This potentiality of computerized monitoring has been overlooked in the heated debates about personal privacy invasions in cyberspace. The true import of computerized monitoring may have been misplaced during the furor over cookies. Computerized monitoring does not curtail deviance. It enables it. The notion of social deviance will become more neutral or contradictory, because in cyberspace society's need for a strong social center may diminish.

Computerized monitoring could give inhabitants of a virtual environment complete control over that environment, in the sense that the software that creates the online environment would mold itself to fit the needs of the inhabitants as expressed through their behavior. It is ironic, therefore, that computerized monitoring has been perceived and denounced as a tool that enables increased authoritarian control — from bosses, advertisers, teachers, even librarians. If computerized monitoring software matures to the point that the user's online behavior becomes the primary "commands" to which the software responds (with the response a change in the online environment), the user will have gained more, albeit unusual, control. That newfound control, however, will have been wrested from, or abdicated by, the software designers and programmers, not from bosses, teachers, librarians, and other real-world figures of authority and control.

Is Trust the Crux?   In contrast to control, trust may be the crux of the amorphous movement to use computers to monitor HCI. People who wittingly or unwittingly are subjected to computerized monitoring need to be able to trust the gatherers and analysts that the data will be used only for socially beneficial purposes and that the data collected eventually will lead to improvements in online environments and experiences. Bayers (1998, 186) notes that the number-one issue on the minds of Web surfers, the issue that may be holding back the growth of one-to-one online relationships between individuals and corporate entities, either as providers of goods and services or as employers, is trust. "Unless government agencies, infrastructure suppliers, software wizards and producers of programming can guarantee privacy in the rapidly expanding web of cyberspace, it may be impossible for the trust upon which a virtual community depends to develop sufficiently to make the grand digital experiment a success" (Lang 1994, 65). If computerized monitoring is not entirely unobtrusive (i.e., if inhabitants of an online environment know or suspect that their behavior is being observed), it erodes the trust essential to the development of community. For years AT&T and General Magic have been working on the idea of trusted spaces in cyberspace (Lang 1994).

Information as Process, Not Commodity   People in the library and information science professions often speak and write about information as if it were a commodity. We talk about information storage and retrieval, data mining, and related concepts as if information were a pile of road salt, ready to be retrieved and applied when conditions warrant. What if we were to think about information as a process of human development, rather than as an externalized commodity? Information may be similar to other processes that change, and perhaps improve, human beings, such as acculturation, inspiration, and education.

Text, Location, and Availability   A basic assumption behind this research (Wyly 1996) is that the attempt to ascertain location and availability information about items described in bibliographic records indicates that the searcher has perceived an intimation of value in those items because of the description contained in the bibliographic records. If every search for information involves confirmation of the existence of needed or desired information, the location of that information, and its availability, is there any value in keeping those three "legs" of the search separate and distinct? Perhaps in the new online environments these three legs no longer are essential. Availability is essential knowledge for printed information, but has a different meaning for digital information. Location also takes on a different meaning and value as digital information becomes more commonplace. Furthermore, in virtual information environments, confirmation of the existence, location, and availability of a text is conflated.

Monadology   The emerging ability of computerized monitoring to create not designer virtual environments, but individualized environments that each of us deserves based on our behavior, could result in a virtual, yet absolute, solipsism.

We all will repair individually into our own Leibnitzian monadological environment. The ideal of widespread shared experiences, which reached its zenith in the last half of the twentieth century with the acceptance and diffusion of least-common-denominator radio, film, and television content, will quickly lose favor and die out. Eventually computerized monitoring may result in new relationships between the individual and the surrounding environment. Dumb real environments will be complemented (if not replaced) by sentient online environments. While a monadological existence in a dumb environment is very lonely and unappealing, it might be fundamentally different in a smart environment.

Perhaps one of the long-term weaknesses of the general movement to use computers to monitor HCI will not be the nefarious applications we all rightly fear, but rather the simple fact that computerized monitoring tends to focus on the behavior of individuals. Individually, we will be left with a denuded knowledge base on which to love and link with others.

> The puzzles of the world in which we live arise not only from individual behavior and capabilities, but from more complex, socially constructed webs of action, reaction, and interaction that make up the socio-political environment. What matters is not whether computers win, but how that will affect human perceptions of their role and place in the world (Rochlin 1997, 211).

Derek Foster (1997, 26) also worries that solipsism, the extreme preoccupation with and indulgence of one's own inclinations, is potentially engendered in the technology that supports computer-mediated communication. Group activities and individual consciousness and experience are becoming more closely intertwined. "Our useful artifacts reflect who we are, what we aspire to be. At the same time, we mirror the technologies that surround us; to an increasing extent, social activities and human consciousness are technically mediated" (Winner 1991, 18).

The Anxiety of Influence   If a cluster of online environments based on our behavior is the end of computerized monitoring — that toward which all this development activity tends — why are we fearful? Why is an aware online environment any more frightening than essentially intractable real environments, where environmental degradation is evidence of their intractability, or environmental conditions imposed by some human authority, including social mores? Computerized monitoring is an inner challenge. We must examine not only the human monitor to discern his motives in undertaking or setting into motion computerized monitoring tools and projects, but also look into the hearts of ourselves as beings who have willfully projected ourselves into self-created online environments. Although it is frightening to realize that we have been born unasked into the real world (no informed consent there), perhaps it is more challenging and frightening to realize that online environments are our own doing, freely chosen. Computerized monitoring projects force us as netizens to confront the fearful symmetry of these online environments where every action we make, and soon perhaps every thought we think and emotion we feel, somehow affects the environment. The anxiety of influence here is not about the influence of others who have come before us (*Ubi* *sunt qui ante nos fuerunt?*), but about our own influence over the experience of virtual environments. Cyberspace is not frightening like the coldness of real outer space, but rather like the warmth of the human heart. Virtual environments are human, and computerized monitoring makes them more so, directly so. The role played (at least in the imagination) by Big Brother in the modern real world is being replaced by the inner self in postmodern virtual worlds. This certainly is unsettling in many ways. The unsettlement manifests itself as a confusion about roles and responsibilities in these emerging, maturing online environments. Sometimes the confusion results in palaver about invasions of privacy and Big Brother in cyberspace.

Knowing People and Their Behavior   What does it mean to know a person and his or her behavior? Stated in a different way, what knowledge does computerized monitoring create? Through computerized monitoring it may be possible for the computer to "know" an individual without knowing the individual's name, and without creating a dossier containing that person's biogenetic traits, past actions, or official records. This amorphous movement to use computers to monitor HCI may raise some new epistemological questions about the nature of knowledge in cyberspace. We should not assume that the forms of knowledge people develop to survive and thrive in the real world will be the knowledge that will develop as cyberspace is colonized and matures. Through computerized monitoring online environments may be able to develop forms of knowledge about human beings that do not involve identifying specific individuals by name.

Monitoring software cannot know or discern one's attitude toward one's behavior. Attitude and behavior are not mutually exclusive. One must have an attitude toward one's behavior. For example, sometimes I get into a short-lived habit of mistyping a word. This behavior is very frustrating to me. The computerized monitoring module, however, senses only my repetitious typographical error, not my cognizance of and frustration with my own behavior. The module could conclude that, based only on my observable behavior, I am trying to change the spelling of that word.

The best computerized monitoring could become a truly mind-expanding psychoanalysis. The question concerning computerized monitoring is not whether or not we want another person to observe and know our indigenous online behavior, but whether or not we want to enter into this new relationship with online environments. The environment becomes an extension of the mind. Do we want to share our behavioral information with an active, sentient environment? No matter how much I walk upon the beach and shout at the waves, neither the beach nor the waves heed me. Online environments will heed us — not only our intentional becks and calls, but also our sub-reflective online behavior. Computerized monitoring could make both the workings and the outcomes of the human mind more interesting and vital, not less. Real environments share information with us as an other. We may learn that our immediate real environment is stressed, fecund, or healthy, independent of our own sense of being stressed, fecund, or healthy. In contrast, the online environment will be understood not as an other, but as a part of oneself. We will care for the environment in a new light.

Is Computerized Monitoring of HCI Good? One frustrating aspect of the amorphous movement to use computers to monitor HCI is the inability to determine if these activities are good or evil. Computerized monitoring is used in such a wide variety of situations that, by itself, it seems amoral. By their very nature, computerized monitoring systems are flexible. They can be designed to meet the demands of the environment, such as production demands in a workplace environment, without forcing the people in the system to act in potentially harmful ways (Miezio 1992, 108). For Lyon (1991a, 615), a radical critique of electronic surveillance in general would realistically recognize the need for, and benefits of, surveillance, but would advocate or judge them according to moral categories. Such a radical critique would entail an acute awareness of the inherent dangers of all surveillance techniques, including the panoptic and instrumental tendencies of electronic surveillance techniques in particular.

Two major problems are confronting the movement to use computers to monitor HCI. First, HCI is becoming much more complex and ubiquitous, and thus more difficult to describe and study. The good old days of a very limited set of alphanumeric commands are gone forever. Second, perhaps the fundamental criticism of computerized monitoring is that it misses the point of all this HCI. Computerized monitoring does not and cannot capture the essence of HCI, in the same way that a study of shifting weight load on a dance floor somehow misses the essence of the dance. A study of shifting weight loads may be of vital interest to architects and structural engineers, and in its way it contributes to a safe and successful dance, but it still misses the point of the dance as a lived, human experience.

When all of the computerized monitoring projects of the last 30 years are examined in toto, we must conclude we have little to show for all of the effort. The sense of a common field, full of possibilities for creative dialogue and cross-fertilization, has not fully emerged. Computerized monitoring of HCI is being used for very unimaginative, retrograde applications. We still assume that demographic information is vital, that the identity of the individual user is worth knowing, and that the knowledge gained by another human being is essential to a good and proper application of computerized monitoring of HCI.

An early working title of this book, *Inside the Monitor*, implied that there is someone inside the monitor watching the user. The imagined situation is similar to that in movie theaters originally designed and built to house live acts. People went behind the movie screen and unobtrusively watched people watching a movie. The audience could not detect the behind-screen observers, so it was possible to observe their unmitigated enthrallment with the movie — assuming they were truly absorbed in viewing the action on the screen.

The promise of computerized monitoring is not that our lives online will become transparent to all, but that they will rely less on volition. Good online environments will be inductive, based on lived experiences. Simply by being online we will be able to effect change, not only in ourselves but also in the virtual environments we create. Virtue truly will become its own reward. In online environments, living well will not be relegated to serve as the consolation prize to those who have done battle with the essentially intractable real world and lost. Living well could have a direct causal relationship to the good life. We cannot overlook the fact that the software development challenges necessary to realize the promise of computerized monitoring are enormous. Because good virtual environments will be the result of authentic existence, rather than the result of deliberate constructive actions, it will be difficult to convey blueprints for constructing good virtual environments. How will we (or our computer systems) teach our children to be good?

Appendix A

Standalone Commercial
Web Server Log
Analysis Software

These software packages enable on-site analysis and presentation of Web server log data. On-site analysis provides a higher level of interactivity (Robertson 1996).

Accrue Insight (Accrue Software, Inc.)

http://www.accrue.com

Accrue, headed by Simon Roy, is in Mountain View, California (Wagner 1997a). Niccolai (1997) also lists this price. Accrue was spun-off from Organic Online. CKS Group, a new media ad agency, is among its investors. Jonathan Nelson, founder of Organic Online, also serves as Accrue's chairman (Taylor 1996d). Accrue Insight is being used by Internet Services Group at Perot Systems Corporation (www.perotsystems.com) (Koprowski 1997).

Rather than rely entirely on data collected in the logs of a Web server, Accrue Insight gathers its own data at the network level (Taylor 1996). The software works on the level of the network protocols — the level where the HTTP protocol gets its data. The software can capture all attempts to access a Web site, both the successful and unsuccessful. It offers analyses of all network activity pertaining to the HTTP layer (Randall 1997c). It measures data delivery, download time, interrupted file transfers, and online speeds (Wagner 1997a). The software also can track multiple visits to a site by the same user (Busch 1997), and enables the site manager to view the site from the vantage point of the visitor. This enables the Web site manager to see how the site performs in real (yet virtual) situations (Fruth 1997).

The software runs on a Solaris server (Gage 1997), and uses client-side Java applets to generate performance and usage reports (Fruth 1997). Accrue Insight, a Java-based analysis tool, tracks Web site activity in real time and can report each visitor's experience in detailed session profiles (Bucholtz 1997). Simon Roy claims that Accrue Insight enables a webmaster or online marketer to understand what is driving the economics of an online purchase decision (Koprowski 1997).

Insight is unique in its network level residence, away from the single server. Because of this unique vantage point, the software can tell whether or not a page was delivered intact (Rich 1997a). Insight uses an embedded data collector in the Internet protocol switch processor to monitor site traffic and provide a complete view of how the site is being used (Bucholtz 1997). The software also notes how quickly pages were delivered. Insight is unusual because it offers a monitoring system that operates much lower in the network protocol chain than other Web analysis software tools (Randall 1997c). Insight also processes the data instantly, enabling "live" viewing of activity at a site. The software uses its own Java-based technique to monitor a user's click pattern in real time (Levy 1997).

Accrue is investigating the possibility of incorporating the principles of heuristics into future versions of the software. Heuristics is an analysis method that employs trial and error, rather than algorithms, to solve problems. Heuristics software examines a set of data repeatedly to find correlations and commonalities. Accrue also wants to leverage applications and wealth from recent developments in mathematics, such as clustering, which allows an analyzer to begin understanding behavior signs, users' intentions, and behavior (Koprowski 1997). More recently, Accrue has begun responding to the needs of publishers and advertisers by enabling third-party auditing of Web traffic information through Audit Bureau of Circulation Interactive (Walsh 1999b). First identified in Moeller (1996b). In 1997 the price of the software started at $15,000 (Wagner 1997a). See also Gage (1997).

AdCount (NetCount)

http://www.digiplanet.com

AdCount, released in the fall of 1996, recognizes any type of advertising file. Sites can accept animated ads, integrated advertising, and even beyond-the-banner ads that make it more difficult to tell if an ad is on the page. AdCount can track users' behavior, whether they simply viewed the ad on the page or clicked on it (Rich 1997a). NetCount also had early plans to be able to deliver demographic information about visitors to Web sites (Counting on the Web 1995). Paul Grand is the founder and chairman of NetCount LLC in Los Angeles, California (Cooper 1996a).

Aria (Andromedia)

http://www.andromedia.com

Andromedia was founded in May 1995 (Galenskas 1997). Andromedia, funded by Softbank, then partnered with K2 Design, Inc., a company based in New York City that develops corporate Web sites.

The Aria software avoids using Web server logs completely. It works with a server's API to monitor in real time all server activity (Randall 1997c). The software package contains three basic parts: the Reporter module, the Recorder module and the server-side Monitor module (Litras 1997). The system includes Aria monitor, which resides on the server as a linkable library that monitors the connection between the user and server. The server-side Monitor module, which works directly with the Netscape Commerce or Communications Server via the Netscape Server API, assumes the responsibility for logging hits, thus supplanting the server's own internal logging facilities (Litras 1997). After capturing information passed between the client and server, such as cookie profiles, data from form fields, and standard log file information, the monitor sends it to the Aria recorder module. Corporate clients access the recorder module and use a variety of navigation tools to devise a set of reports to better understand what is happening at their particular Web sites (Koprowski 1997).

Aria Recorder requires a Sun Solaris server (Busch 1997, 77). The Aria software is scalable, and it can reveal a user's navigational path through a Web site. Aria incorporates an ObjectStore database engine (Busch 1997, 82). The Aria suite of software products provides a framework for real-time data collection and decision-making. Aria tracks users and logs their actions to build user profiles and to generate dynamic, individualized content (Robertson 1997, 34).

Aria reports are created in HTML (Wagner 1997a). The reports are classified into four categories: Navigation, Content, Traffic and Visitor (Litras 1997). One of the most interesting and useful of these is Navigation, which provides "next click" analysis allowing the human analyst to see how users accessing the Web site navigate through it (Litras 1997). The Visitor report component tracks usage by visitors, instead of by systems. The computerized monitoring software accomplishes this by assigning a cookie to each new browser that accesses the system (Litras 1997).

Early in 1999 the company announced the availability of a new Aria eCommerce 3.0 product, which analyzes online shopping behavior (Walsh 1999a). Andromedia and BroadVision produced an integrated software package that enables Web retailers to watch in real time the online shopping behavior of individuals and groups (Dalton and Gallagher 1999). Andromedia has linked its Aria eCommerce 3.0 site analysis software tool to the Observer module in BroadVision's One-to-One commerce server, which lets companies see which items a potential customer inspects, puts in or removes from a shopping cart, and buys. When used together, the software products can alert a Web retailer to behavioral patterns as they develop (Dalton and Gallgher 1999).

First identified in Murphy (1996). See also Galenskas (1997).

Astra SiteManager (Mercury Interactive Corp.)

Developed by Mercury Interactive Corporation of Sunnyvale, California. Astra SiteManager is a management platform with link testing, site mapping, and an interface to other tools (Wagner 1997a). The software can scan an entire Web site and make a graphical map of the site (Mercury Interactive 1997). See also Bloomer (1997). List price is $495.

Bazaar Analyzer Pro (Aquas Inc.)

http://www.aquas.com

Nitin Komawar is the Chairman and CEO of Aquas (Adhikari 1996). The software was written entirely in the Java programming language and is accessible from any Java-compatible browser (Adhikari 1996). Because the browser software functions as the user interface, any authorized person can access the data and reports without loading special software (Busch 1997). Randall (1998a), however, notes that browser-based log analysis tools, such as NetTracker Pro, SurfReport, and Bazaar Analyzer Pro, often have problematic installation and setup, and weak export capabilities.

Reports can be produced on demand or on a specified schedule, accessed from remote locations, or e-mailed (Busch 1997). Because the analyzer software is Java-based, the log file does not need to be transferred to one's computer before it can be massaged (Randall 1997c). The software enables Web site managers to quickly gather and analyze information about user profiles, usage trends, and browser profiles. It tracks the number of visitors to a Web site, how long they spend on each page, the visitors' IP addresses, the external links used to get to the site, and how often each person visits the site (Adhikari 1996).

According to Nachiketa Lolla, an Aquas, Inc., spokesperson, Bazaar Analyzer can be used for real-time monitoring of a Web site (Balderston 1996). Alert mechanisms also can be installed to let the webmaster know when specific users are visiting the site (Busch 1997). One limitation of Bazaar Analyzer Pro is that it can handle only the common log format and the associated combined log format (Randall 1997c). The pathview feature of Bazaar Analyzer provides a graphical view of a visitor's path through a Web site (Borck 1998).

Version 2 of the software, launched in November 1996, was priced at $999 for a five-user license (Adhikari 1996). In 1997 the basic price for Bazaar Analyzer Pro was $599 (Randall 1997c).

Bolero (Everyware Development Corp.)

http://www.everyware.com

Dan McKenzie is president of EveryWare Development Corp. (Latest 1996). Bolero is a software application that intelligently captures log information from Web servers, enabling real-time analysis. Bolero is advertised as a complete package, containing capture, storage and report generation applications. It allows a Web site manager to speed up the Web server by turning off the server's own file-based logging and domain-name resolution. Bolero can simultaneously log multiple Web servers to a single database, and can calculate the number of both new and repeat users by the hour, day, week, and month. It can display the paths people make through a Web site, and can calculate average transfer rates. Version 1.0 of Bolero is compatible with Quarterdeck's WebSTAR, a popular Web server for the Macintosh.

Bolero logs user actions at a Web site into an SQL file that can be imported into a standard database, such as Butler SQL, Oracle, Informix, Sybase, or FoxPro. Although this approach to data capture makes data management more complex, it gives Bolero two important advantages over programs like WebThreads and Bien Logic's SurfReport, which log activities into a text file. First, the data is organized into hourly, daily, weekly, and monthly SQL records that can be searched, sorted, and reported in a variety of formats using the forms included in the package. Second, because the database includes the URL trail of everyone who accesses the site, the site manager can make frequent changes in the site's presentation details — such as frames, text elements, graphics, and JavaScript interactivity — to see how users respond (Seiter 1997).

Bolero logs the activity on a Web server in real-time, providing up-to-the-minute accuracy with no post processing required. Even hourly reports reflect the latest Web site activity with no lag time.

Version 1.1 of Bolero, released early in 1997, is available in three versions. The $4,995 Gold edition can store Web statistics in Oracle databases, the $1,795 Bolero Silver works with any number of StarNine WebStar servers, and the $995 Bolero Bronze supports a single server. Silver and Bronze versions store data in Butler, EveryWare's SQL database for the Macintosh (Pearlstein 1997).

See also EveryWare (1996) and Seiter (1997).

Clickshare (Newshare Corp.)

http://www.clickshare.com/clickshare/

The Clickshare system tracks movement and settles charges for multi-site information microtransactions by providing each user with a single, system-wide identification number. The service enables advertisers to track a user's movements across all Clickshare-affiliated servers (Conaghan 1995).

Clickshare software tracks a user's movements during a query, even between Web sites. Clickshare allows two different Web sites to exchange user behavioral information, and split a royalty on the information requested from each site (Fitzgerald 1996).

ClickTrack (eWorks!)

http://www.clicktrack.com

ClickTrack is an Internet monitoring and analysis service designed primarily for advertising and public relations managers who need non-technical views of site usage data. It also is a popular program for intranet site analysis. It runs in real time. It calculates session duration and the average number of pages viewed per session. ClickTrack reports only page views, not raw hits. It also records the most common entry pages — pages where visitors enter a Web site. This measure provides an indication of which pages are being book-marked. ClickTrack also measures the most common pages last viewed by users before they exit the site. First identified in Buchanan and Lukaszewski (1997). See also Agnvall (1997).

Cyber Patrol Corporate

http://www.cyberpatrol.com

The Cyber Patrol Corporate software program evolved from Microsystems Software's home product, designed to protect young children by blocking sites containing question-able content (Ginchereau 1997). The software logs activity to a standard .DBF database, but the log does not capture information about bandwidth usage (Ginchereau 1997).

See also Kathryn Munro (1998) and "Microsystems" (1997). Also mentioned in Gorman (1998).

Flashstats (Maximized Software)

http://www.maximized.com/products/flashstats/

Flashstats runs on a variety of operating systems, including Windows 95, Windows NT, Apple Mac OS, and Digital UNIX. This Web server log analysis software was first released in early 1997. It enables Internet service providers to allow secure access to real-time usage statistics for their clients, and enables the analysis of search phrases from the top 16 search engines. The list price since early 1997 has been $99 for up to 25 Web sites, with a $249 ISP version for an unlimited number of sites.

Funnel Web (Active Concepts)

http://www.activeconcepts.com

Funnel Web can read a variety of log file formats, including log files from popular Mac Web servers (Randall 1998). Funnel Web can report on the type of browser software and operating systems used by visitors to a Web site, but it cannot combine the two sets of stats (Heid 1998). The software can report the search keywords used by users to locate a site (Heid 1998). The software also enables the analyzer to track the behavior of individual vis-itors to a site, revealing how many pages they viewed and how much time they spent dur-ing site visits (Heid 1998). In early 1998 the list price for the basic software was $199, with the professional version retailing for $399 (Heid 1998).

Hit List (MarketWave LLC)

http://www.marketwave.com

Strom (1997b) indicates that there are three versions of this software: Standard, Profes-sional, and Enterprise, the high-end version both in functionality and price. By mid–1999 the MarketWave Web site was listing four different versions: Professional, Commerce, Enter-prise, and Live.

Both the standard and professional versions are Windows 95/NT applications. Hit List Pro also can trace which search engine was used to locate a site, including the keywords used in the search (Busch 1997).

Rather than rely on the Web server's log file, Hit List creates its own relational database

(Shankar 1998). A relational database enables the analyst to configure reports for specific time periods, for specific servers in a multi-server organization, or with other advanced queries and filters (Randall 1997c). The software can calculate the average number of pages that users coming from a certain site tend to view. It also offers extensive querying capabilities for click-through rates of specific online advertisements (Levy 1997). The software also can analyze the paths visitors take through a Web site, revealing common paths and trails (Shankar 1998).

Hit List Pro can track the advertising banner performance on a Web site. The software can exclude hits from the local domain (Strom 1997b). When version 3.5 of Hit List Enterprise was released in 1997, it contained a DataLink module which enabled Web marketers and webmasters to correlate Web traffic data with other data sources (Marketwave ships 1997). VBScript can be used to extend Hit List's functionality. For example, a particular customer can be identified by cookie or IP address. Then, whenever that customer visits the site, Hit List can be programmed to send an e-mail message with contact details from the customer database to a specific salesperson (Shankar 1998).

Version 3.5 of the software offers 27 standard reports and over 250 report elements (Randall 1997c). The reports generated by this software can include explanations of the results so that they are intelligible to untrained readers of the reports (Strom 1997b). The built-in reports, as well as the report creation capabilities, are very good. Another advantage of the software is that visitors can be monitored by name, rather than by IP address alone. The default output format for reports is HTML (Rapoza 1997). A particularly useful report allows the analyst to see the version and operating system of each browser that visits the Web site being monitored (Strom 1997b). The output options for reports include HTML, RTF, text files, or comma-separated files (Strom 1997b). Rapoza (1997a) concludes that Hit List Pro is easy to use and robust. Gerding (1997) opines that Hit List Standard cannot match the support provided by NetIntellect for BPA auditing.

Hit List Standard is free (but Busch 1997 lists a price of $345 for version 2.5), while Hit List Enterprise costs $2,995 (Wagner 1997a; also Strom 1997b). Both Rapoza (1997a) and Gerding (1997) list a price of $1,995 for Hit List Pro 3.0, which was released in April 1997.

iLux (Portfolio Technologies)

http://www.ilux.com/index.html

The iLux software can integrate data from the analyzed Web server log file and electronic commerce systems, so that site owners can create a combined analysis of the customer's virtual behavior, downloading activity, and purchasing behavior. Edge and Enterprise versions both include many basic features common to all log-analysis software tools: an array of reports, automatic DNS lookup service, and the analysis of current and historical data (Steiner 1999). The Enterprise edition of the iLux software includes the Automated Intelligent Marketing (AIM) feature. AIM enables the analyzer to identify individual shoppers online and cater to them, as a group or individually (Steiner 1999). Portfolio Technologies also markets a workflow software program called Office IQ.

Interlock (ANS)

http://www.ans.net/

Interlock is a proxy gateway that generates hourly reports on the top Internet users, the top sites visited, and the sites employees attempt to visit even though access has been denied (Maddox 1996). The software also can turn off applications, such as Java, that may be slowing down network traffic. The Kellogg Company in Battle Creek, Michigan, installed Interlock in December 1994. Kellogg has blocked access to approximately 170 Web sites, most of them pornographic. Kellogg is using the software to identify inappropriate surfing activity. If employees are caught attempting to access a smutty site, they are sent a warning via e-mail. Mike Moore, the project leader at Kellogg, reports that to date no employee has attempted to visit a restricted site after being warned once (Maddox 1996). Recently, ANS merged with UUNET Technologies, a MCI Worldcom affiliate.

Internet SnapShot (Tinwald Technologies)

Wilder (1996a) reported the release of Internet SnapShot from Tinwald Technologies, Inc., located in Mississauga, Ontario. Internet SnapShot specifically monitors Internet activity on a LAN. It examines all TCP/IP traffic and categorizes it by type and source. It can generate both graphical and tabular reports (Ferrill 1996). The software monitors and reports on use of the Internet by users of Windows-based local area networks. Internet SnapShot monitors Internet traffic on Ethernet, Fast Ethernet, and token-ring LANs. The software dissects Internet usage by function, such as Web browsing, FTP file transfers, remote logins, e-mail, Usenet newsgroup reading, and chat. The software also analyzes overall LAN traffic and reports what percentage is Internet-related. According to David Wright, executive vice president at Tinwald, Internet SnapShot provides company administrators with a view into their networks and into the way people acquire information (Wilder 1996, 34). According to Eric Hindin, program manager at the Yankee Group, a research firm in Boston, by monitoring Internet traffic on the LAN, network managers can facilitate better network design, undertake a chargeback program, or move heavy users to a different network segment to smooth out bandwidth requirements (Wilder 1996, 34, 36). The software can provide a network map of Internet activity at each workstation (Yasin 1996). One feature of Internet SnapShot is a topology map that provides a real-time view of the Internet users on a network (Maddox 1996). It also provides Internet activity summary that identifies the top Internet users and what they are doing, such as browsing or downloading files (Maddox 1996). Internet SnapShot is being used by Trails Communications, a network consultancy based in Walnut, California (Maddox 1996).

INTOUCH INSA (Touch Technologies)

http://www.ttinet.com/tti/nsa_www.html

INTOUCH INSA (formerly called Network Security Agency) is a powerful network monitoring software program capable of real-time surveillance of all network activity at the keystroke level. It can monitor both legitimate and illegitimate activity and behavior on a computer network. The software has received rave reviews from TheNet Digital Services, Inc., an Internet service provider in Miami, Florida (Babcock 1997).

Lilypad (Streams Online Media Development)

http://streams.com or http://www.lilypad.net/

Dominic Tassone is the general manager. Lilypad is a Unix-only software system with an interactive HTML interface for running reports, including comparative reports (Stout 1997, 131). The developers of Lilypad hope to differentiate their product from the rest of the field by focusing on how Web surfers found their way to a Web site, rather than on activity and behavior within the site itself. Lilypad ascertains whether visitors to a Web site arrived at their destination via a search engine or from a hyperlink paid for by the marketer (Jaffee 1996). See also Martin (1995).

LinkTrakker (GlobalMedia Design, Inc.)

http://www.radzone.org

LinkTrakker provides information about incoming hyperlinks that indicates how users are finding a Web site.

LinkView (Wavetek Wandel Goltermann)

http://www.linkview.com/

LinkView is a 32-bit LAN analyzer that gathers network information and presents it in graphical and tabular reports. The software also simulates network traffic (Ferrill 1996).

Log Analyzer (WebTrends) (formerly e.g. Software Inc.)

http://www.WebTrends.com

This is one of the dominant software programs in its class. Although the early official name of the software was Log Analyzer, it often is referred to simply as WebTrends. Early in 1998 *PC Magazine* honored Log Analyzer as the Editors' Choice for a midrange Web server log analysis software tool (Randall 1998).

Tabibian (1996a) provides a review and analysis of the software. One of the weaknesses of the software is its inability to create reports in standard formats, such as Microsoft Word. The software also has a difficult time handling large log files. Rapoza (1997a) reports that version 3.0 will not display Microsoft Word–formatted reports unless Word is present on the system. Tabibian (1996b) admits that version 2.0 of this software program is easier to use than version 2.07 of Market Focus, but it lacks a built-in database and real-time reporting. Rapoza (1997) concludes that WebTrends is easy to use and offers surprisingly strong capabilities for a low price. Its design, however, is relatively inflexible. Strom (1997c) concluded after testing that NetIntellect (see entry below) was less reliable than e.g. Software's WebTrends 2.0, and that WebTrends had a better interface. In an unusually critical review of the software, Szeto (1997) found discrepancies between compressed and uncompressed versions of the server log file.

The first version may have been released on February 5, 1996 (Raths 1996). Version 3.0 was released in March 1997 (Rapoza 1997). The company was founded in 1994, and Web-Trends is its fourth product (Raths 1996). WebTrends claims to have 20,000 corporate customers, including 3M, AT&T, and Siemens (Lamons 1997). The sellers claim that this software is compatible with log files created by any Web server. WebTrends Log Analyzer is a Windows-based application compatible with Microsoft Windows 3.1x, Windows 95, and Windows NT.

WebTrends analyzes logs created by the server software itself. It uses data compiled by a Web server's common log file, a database indicating the Internet Protocol addresses, domains, pages accessed, and which Web browser software was used (Wingfield 1996).

Reports can be generated as HTML files that can be viewed by any browser on a local system or remotely from anywhere on the Internet with any browser. WebTrends allegedly is designed to be equally useful to both the server administrator and the marketing department of the organization using the software. WebTrends includes a MegaViewer that will allow one to easily view, search and print log files. WebTrends has a built-in scheduler for automatic reporting, a color-coded viewer for working with large log files, a reverse DNS lookup for numeric IP addresses, the ability to filter in or out specific domains or pages, and allows one to select time ranges for reports, from minutes to years. The reports display usage according to numbers of hits, user sessions, percentage of total hits, or bytes transferred.

The WebTrends software also has an intranet management feature that lets administrators track site usage by groups, by individuals, or both, rather than by IP addresses and domain names alone (Rapoza 1997a). The software utilizes the cookies standard to record individual user sessions (Szeto 1997). WebTrends offers a real-time analysis capability (Rapoza 1997a).

WebTrends does not require a database to generate reports, although the software supports ODBC if an external database is desired (Szeto 1997). The software can automatically generate reports as often as every five minutes (Rapoza 1997a). The built-in database enables the analysis of historical trends over time (Rapoza 1997a).

The retail price was $299 (Stout 1997, 107; also Busch 1997, 83; also Rapoza 1997a).

LogDoor (Open Door Networks)

http://www.opendoor.com

LogDoor analyzes Web server logs in real time (Heid 1998). One of the strengths of this software is its ability to split a large server file into multiple logs, each tracking a specific folder or site (Heid 1998). Early in 1998 the list price was $249 (Heid 1998).

Log FM (Web Broadcasting)

http://www.macweb.com

Log FM analyzes web server logs in real time (Heid 1998). It stores log data in a database utilizing the FileMaker Pro format (Heid 1998). The software was released in November 1997. Early in 1998 the list price was $395 (Heid 1998).

net.Analysis (net.Genesis Corp.)

http://www.netgenesis.com

This software tracks Web use in real time, immediately displays the results in graphical form, and stores the data in an Informix database. The net.Analysis client queries the database and presents reports in a variety of two- and three-dimensional formats (Rodriguez 1996). Approximately 50 predefined reports are available with the software, including the number of visitors to the site per day, the top ten platforms and browser types used, and the most popular pages at a site (Niccolai 1997).

The net.Analysis Desktop software is a completely different product. Microsoft FoxPro is the database engine for the Desktop edition (Stout 1997, 125). The primary objective of the Desktop reports is to display them on the screen, rather than to create an HTML document with tables and graphs (Stout 1997, 127). The net.Analysis report writer filters and presents usage data as pie charts and comparative bar charts (Nemzow 1997, 97).

Two shortcomings of the software are the limited number of report templates and the limited support for log files. Analysis of large server log files can be very slow (Tabibian 1996c). The major difference between net.Analysis and Market Focus is that net.Analysis provides more onscreen, interactive reports, while Market Focus produces more static reports in Microsoft Word or HTML format (Buchanan and Lukaszewski 1997, 197).

Tabibian (1996c) reports that version 1.1 of net.Analysis Desktop sells for $495. The net.Analysis proper retailed for $2,995 (Stout 1997, 124) and net.Analysis Pro for Windows NT and Sun Solaris was priced at $4,495 (Niccolai 1997). First identified in Wagner (1996a). See also Stout (1997), Tabibian (1996c), Davis (1996a), Rodriguez (1996), and Curtis (1998).

NetIntellect (WebManage Technologies Inc.)

http://www.webmanage.com

   NetIntellect is similar to Web Trends in that they both use an internal, proprietary format to store the log files (Snyder 1998). This software tracks user information, such as names and e-mail addresses (Wagner 1997a). The program requires at least 100MB of Windows Virtual Memory, and it works best with at least 32MB of RAM on a 160MHz Pentium or faster system (Strom 1997c).

   One advantage of the NetIntellect software is that it enables the analyzer to process more than one log file at a time. It also provides a feature for comparing log files (Randall 1997c). A wide variety of reports can be produced by NetIntellect. The software comes with five major report types and a variety of built-in database queries (Randall 1997c). The reports can be output as HTML files, Microsoft Word files, spreadsheet files of various formats, and, when all else fails, as comma-separated text. Reports can be printed to paper, exported to disk files, or sent via Messaging API-enabled e-mail (Strom 1997c).

   Strom (1997c) concluded after testing that NetIntellect was less reliable than WebTrends 2.0, and that WebTrends had a better interface. Gerding (1997) thought that the geographical analysis provided by NetIntellect was useful. He also noted that NetIntellect comes with a preconfigured report that conforms to the BPA International Interactive Audit standard. Unfortunately, NetIntellect cannot track dynamically generated Web pages. In 1997 the retail price for version 2.1 was $199 (Busch 1997). In July 1999 the Web site quoted a price of $295 per copy. See also Wagner (1997a), Gerding (1997), Schwerin (1997), Rapoza (1997f), and Randall (1997c).

NetMinder (Neon Software)

http://www.neon.com/

   This software was designed for the Apple Macintosh system. It functions more as an analyzer of network traffic than as computerized monitoring per se. Like other network analyzers, NetMinder monitors network traffic by taking over an Ethernet interface in the computer, capturing and categorizing every packet. A set of five filters lets the analyst extract only packets of interest, and every protocol includes a decoder for viewing the contents of any packet (Beckman 1997). In late 1997 the retail price was $795 (Beckman 1997).

NetStats Pro (Insanely Great Software)

http://www.igsnet.com/netstats.html

   NetStats Pro works only with files in the common log format. The main strength of this software package is its ability to enable the creation of customized reports (Randall 1997c). The list price in mid–1997 was $129 (Randall 1997c). In July 1999 the site was still listed $129.

NetTracker (Sane Solutions LLC)

http://www.sane.com

   Jim Rose, Frank Faubert, and David Ceprano are the co-partners of Sane Solutions, which came into existence in September 1996 (Barmann 1997). The software was released in January 1997 (Barmann 1997).

   NetTracker is available for both Unix and Microsoft Windows NT Web servers (Masud 1997). The software resides on a Java-compliant server, and access to the data and the reports goes through a Java-enabled Web browser (Randall 1997c).

NetTracker tries to take the number of visits to a Web site and translate it into the number of actual visits to the site. Although the NetTracker software resides on the server, it can deliver textual and graphical summaries to remote locations, viewable with any Java-capable interface (Busch 1997). Jim Rose sees this ability to view traffic reports on a Web page from any Internet-connected computer as a strategic advantage over competing Web server log analysis software (Barmann 1997). Because no log files need to be downloaded to PCs, and because only browser software is required to use the analysis and reporting functions, this software is ideal as a tracking software package for Internet Service Providers who want to offer an analysis package to their subscription-based services to their customers (Randall 1997c).

The software also offers an analysis reminiscent of the early days of transaction log analysis of OPACs and other mainframe databases. The keyword summary report shows the keywords entered into search engines that generated referrals to the analyzed Web site (Randall 1997c). First identified in Busch (1997).

The retail price for the software for individual purchasers is $295. Sane Solutions has been giving away a copy of the NetTracker program to ISPs, asking them to offer their clients the ability to monitor their own sites with NetTrackers (Barmann 1997). The suggested retail price for the professional version is $495, and the enterprise version costs between $995 and $4,995 (Randall 1997c). In July 1999 the Web site listed prices for three versions: Professional ($495), Enterprise (starting at $995), and eBusiness (starting at $9,995). See also Masud (1997) and Rapoza (1997c).

Overdrive Logger (Navinet)

http://www.nvnt.com/

Tauscher and Greenberg (1997) report that the Overdrive Logger software module keeps a record of all URLs visiting by a human browser. A separate log file is created for each particular date during which online browsing behavior occurs.

PressVu (Academicus Press)

http://www.academicus.com

The software imports NCSA common and IIS standard log file data into an Xbase-compatible database (Randall 1998). Early in 1998 the list price was $55 (Randall 1998).

Prudence@Work (Blue Wolf Network)

http://www.bluewolfnet.com

This software is a Web monitoring system designed for networks in work environments. Like WinWhatWhere (see below), Prudence@Work keeps track of the files and applications opened by an employee or workgroup, the menu items selected, the history and bookmarks of the employee's browser, and keystroke sequences (Brandt 1999).

ServerStat Commercial (Kitchen Sink Software)

http://www.kitchen-sink.com

The software was written for the Macintosh operating system. ServerStat supports several server log formats: WebStar from StarNine Technologies, MacHTTP from Biap Systems, GopherSurfer from the University of Minnesota, and the Common Log Format. One limitation of ServerStat is that it generates a report as a single, dense HTML page, with no graphs (Heid 1998). Kitchen Sink allows free downloading of an earlier version of the software.

Early in 1998 the list price was $99.95 (Heid 1998). In July 1999 the Web site listed $99.95.

SiteScope (Freshwater Software)

http://www.freshtech.com

Released in April 1997, SiteScope is a Java-based software application that enables Web site administrators to monitor such functions as Web server performance, CPU usage, and Web access to external sites (Rapoza 1997a). A related SiteSeer service enables remote monitoring of a Web site's activity and performance.

SiteTrack (Group Cortex)

http://www.cortex.net or http://www.sitetrack.com

Cortex Group offers an advertising and general Web traffic tracking software application (Yesil 1996, 118). SiteTrack can track users and build a database of user activity (Strom 1996c). SiteTrack works only with a Netscape server running selected Unix operating systems (Stout 1997, 130). The developers of SiteTrack claim that the software works with every client browser in every conceivable situation, including across firewalls (Jaffee 1996).

SmartFilter (Secure Computing)

http://www.securecomputing.com/

The software, formerly called WebTrack from Webster Network Strategies, was being used by Salt River Project, a water and power utility located in Phoenix, Arizona (Maddox 1996). It is designed to run as a proxy server behind a corporate firewall, monitoring web browsing, file transfers, newsgroup postings, and other Internet activity. SmartFilter blocks access to over 40,000 sites in sixteen non-work-related categories, including sex, gambling, sports, and shopping. WebTrack monitors all outgoing Web, FTP, Gopher, and WAIS requests (Scott et al. 1996). In 1996 it cost $7,000 per license for an unlimited number of users. See also Wingfield (1995) and Dryden (1996b).

SNAG (Secure Net Access Guardian) (Chase Sales Development)

http://www.chasesales.com/

The program works at the network level to selectively monitor, log, and report on all Internet activities involving Telnet, FTP, Gopher, and WWW. Access profiles can be denied for each workstation. The monitoring component of the software logs the site name, the IP address, the date and time of the access, and the total number of accesses for each site visited. The log can be sorted by domain name, type of site (i.e., FTP, Gopher, Telnet, Web), the number of accesses, and time of day. The software also is capable of restricting access to unacceptable or unauthorized sites for all workstations on the LAN or WAN, including both Macs and PCs. When the SNAG software detects a user attempting to connect to a restricted or prohibited site, it truncates the attempt and reroutes the access attempt to a more appropriate site. The user experiences a common network error message. The software has been used since late 1995 at Sewickley Academy, a private K–12 institution in southwestern Pennsylvania (Software monitors 1996). Prior to receiving a computer account, all users are asked to read and sign an acceptable use policy. SNAG logs indicated that conformance with the acceptable use policy was very high. Several occurrences of access to unacceptable sites were detected coming from dial access users, generally during weekend hours. The SNAG software was expanded to include dial access use.

Statistics Server (MediaHouse)

http://www.mediahouse.com/

This software formerly was called IIS Assistant, and, as the name implied, it ran only on Microsoft's Internet Information Server (IIS) (Randall 1997c). Strom (1997d) reports that this software can create and analyze real-time reports about the usage of a Web site without relying on the server logs. The software collects its own data. Because this is an API analysis product, it links directly to the IIS API in order to intercept data at the HTTP level and compile statistics on the fly (Randall 1997c). The software does not access the log files at all (Randall 1997c).

Statistics Server provides real-time analyses of the corporate identities visitors to a Web site. The reports can be viewed with any browser software capable of handling frames. Early versions of the software package came only with seven pre-defined reports (Randall 1997c). Strom (1997d) suggests that the real strengths of IIS Assistant (now Statistics Server) are the real-time nature of the reports and the fact that it can consolidate statistics from multiple servers.

In July 1999 the corporate version (up to 50 Web sites) retailed for $395, and the ISP version (up to 500 Web sites) was $495.

StoryServer (Vignette Corp.)

http://www.vignette.com/

StoryServer customizes Web pages for individuals based on both clickstream information collected about them and demographic data provided voluntarily by them (Dalton and Gallagher 1999).

Surfcontrol Scout (JSB Computers System Ltd.)

http://www.surfcontrol.com

Surfcontrol offers a family of Internet usage monitoring and filtering software products, including Scout, ScoutPlus and SuperScout (Greenemeier 1998). This Web monitoring and control software was designed for use in work environments. It can prepare reports that differentiate business-related from recreational Web site access. It monitors various Internet protocols (e.g., HTTP, FTP, Telnet, etc.) as well as other ports (Munro, Jay 1998).The list price for Surfcontrol scout ranges from $49 for 20 users up to $949 for an unlimited number of users (Munro, Jay 1998). See also Schwerin (1998), Borg (1997), Rapoza (1996b), and Recipe (1996).

SurfReport (Netrics.com)

http://netrics.com/home.html

SurfReport, initially released by Bien Logic, is a CGI-based program written in PERL that runs on any Unix server and generates activity logs in the Common Log Format (Tiley 1996). It differentiates between raw hits, pages, and unique visits (Nemzow 1997, 100). In July 1999 the site listed $295 as a price for Linux and Windows NT operating systems, $695 for Unix servers. First identified in Tiley (1996).

Usage Analyst (formerly Market Focus from Interse) (Microsoft)

http://www.microsoft.com

This software, formerly called Market Focus and created by Interse, was released in December 1996. Market Focus 3.0 Developers Edition was awarded the Analyst's Choice Award by *PC Week* in the February 3, 1997, issue (Rapoza 1997). It visually maps site layouts and re-enacts users' traffic patterns through the site. The software also can integrate data from more than one source. For example, it could combine Web site information with psychographical Scarborough research. Also, Web site managers could merge information from the program with any site management tool used to serve up pages and banners (Rich 1997). In March 1997 Microsoft announced that it had acquired Interse in order to integrate the Market Focus 3 software into Microsoft's BackOffice family of software. Microsoft saw long-range possibilities in the integration of usage analysis data with the page generation process (Niccolai 1997). The purchase of Interse by Microsft raised fears in the site analysis software development community of a full-fledged incursion by the software giant into this small but rapidly growing software market (Nerney 1997b).

This log analysis was designed to run in Windows 95 or Windows NT. It was designed primarily to provide marketing information (Busch 1997). The software can follow a visitor's path through the site. It analyzes persistent cookie data, registered user names, and Internet host names to identify users and categorize them as first-time or repeat visitors. The software uses inference-based algorithms to reconstruct usage patterns (even across multiple Web sites) by estimating the amount of time users spend with each page (Tiley 1996).

First identified in Wingfield (1996). See also Strom (1997), World Wide Web (1995), and Busch (1997) for extended reviews.

WebReporter (Open Market Inc.)

http://www.openmarket.com/reporter/

WebReporter was released in May 1996. WebReporter took a different approach to server log analysis than most other commercial analysis software packages. WebReporter was a separate server installed on the system running the Web server (Stout 1997, 130).

WebReporter enabled Web server administrators to develop sophisticated demographic information about visitors to a Web site. It supported both the common log format and the extended log format (Tiley 1996). It allowed one to assign meaningful labels to cryptic URLs, host names, and other fields in the logs. It was possible to analyze multiple log files or a subset of a particular log file. Bivariate analysis allowed the manager to explore possible relationships within the data. A "visit analysis" feature allowed the site manager to determine the number of visits to the site, rather than simply the number of file requests sent to the site, followed by the number of bytes transmitted. When used in conjunction with Open Market's WebServer software, WebReporter enabled "anonymous ticketing," which permitted an analyzer to track users throughout their visits without requiring registration. WebReporter's "personal library" allowed users to create usage and activity report libraries. WebReporter's scalable architecture made it suitable for analyzing mirrored and distributed Web sites. It supported both common and extended log formats. Output could be specified in four formats: HTML, HTML 3.0 (with tables), plain ASCII text, and comma-separated plain text.

Web site managers can extend the functionality of WebReporter by adding their own C enhancements. In July 1999 the Open Market Web site contained an announcement that the company no longer supports WebReporter for standalone sale or distribution.

Web-Scope (TLC Systems)

http://www.tlc-systems.com

TLC Systems is a consulting firm specializing in systems architecture and design. Most of its clients are banking and brokerage firms. Web-Scope currently offers over 40 different reports covering many aspects of operating a Web server and developing a Web site. Web-Scope delivers Web statistics and performance monitoring in real time.

The Web-Scope package contains three parts: data capture, data analysis and report generation, and presentation. The data capture component creates additional logs to supplement the Web server's normal access log. The presentation portion can display the report in a Web browser, as a spreadsheet, as text that can be imported into other client-based applications, and as hard-copy printout.

Web-Scope can determine if users bookmark the site visited. It also can determine what other sites have links to the target Web site, as well as to what pages at the target site.

Web-scope is being offered as a service, rather than merely as a software package. TLC Systems installs, customizes, maintains, and modifies the service to meet the needs of individual Web sites. TLC handles all aspects of gathering, analyzing, and presenting the Web site usage data. The programs can run locally on the server site being studied, or they can run remotely on the server operated by TLC.

TLC spokesman Tony Karp contends that information about the use of a Web site will become an important corporate resource. The information will be used internally by the organization to plan and forecast, to get feedback from customers, to support customers and users, and to troubleshoot.

TLC Systems wants to be able to gather statistics about the next generation of Web sites: secure servers requiring authorization; sites that enable financial transactions; sites with attachments to other corporate resources; and sites where some of the processing is done on the Web server itself.

WebThreads (WebThreads)

http://www.webthreads.com

In 1996 WebThreads was spun off from Image Communications (Clark 1996). As of July 1999, new sales of WebThreads had been discontinued.

WebThreads was a program that tracked and reported on user activity at a Web site while enabling interactive customization in real time. The software helped to tailor a Web site's presentation based on a visitor's actions and choices while at the site (Murphy 1996). The reporting function did not rely on the log file. Rather, the software tracked visits to pages within the site on the basis of individual visitors. A number was assigned to each visitor, then the visitor's path through the site was tracked. The tracking reports indicated how many users visited the site during a specific period, which pages were seen by each user and when, and the most popular path through the site (Murphy 1996).

WebThreads software can be understood as a bridge between Web server log analysis, which is server-centric, and Web client log analysis, which is client-centric. Chris Stevens, an analyst for the Aberdeen Group in Boston, notes that WebThreads, like many other traffic analysis products, is limited by the inability to identify a user from one session to the next (Murphy 1996).

Banks appear to be very interested in Web site tracking software, so that they can tailor their virtual banking services to individual preferences (Clark 1996). According to Jeffrey Spillers, banks are looking to create a more personalized, interactive experience. For example, if the online banking customer initially balks at various offers, the system can be programmed to reduce interest rates gradually until the customer accepts, or until the profit margin becomes too narrow (Clark 1996). See also Easy (1997).

WebTrack (MarketArts)

A site-auditing program called WebTrack became available in May 1996. The program was used by Audit Bureau of Circulations (ABC) to offer a service — Interactive Audit Server — to provide an independent measure of traffic at a Web site. Some sites count each grab of each file at a Web site as a hit, even though several files must be grabbed to display one page to the visitor. ABC plans to track the length of time a user visits a web site, where the user went within the site, and where the user came from. WebTrack is expected to list advertising rates and provide demographic portraits of visitors to various Web sites (Strom 1996c).

Web Tracker (Cambridge Quality Management)

http://www.cqminc.com

According to the CQM Web site, Web Tracker is a graphical tool for analyzing Web server log files. The software uses patented sampling technology to rapidly extract information from the logs. The makers of this software package try to differentiate it from the field by focusing on exploratory analysis of the logs, rather than routine reports.

WebTrak and ServerTrak (Know-It)

http://www.know-it.com/webtrak.htm

WebTrak provides basic Web traffic analysis, while ServerTrak enables multiserver performance monitoring (Wagner 1997a). The software reads only common log file format. Early in 1998 the list price was $49 (Randall 1998). In July 1999 the price remained $49.

WebTraxPC (John C. Taylor)

http://www.jt.w1.com/webtrax

WebTraxPC is capable of keyword analysis. It ranks keyword phrases used by visitors who reached the analyzed site via a search engine. The software can handle only common log formats (Randall 1998). Early in 1998 the list price was $69.

WebWatch (Virtual Office, Inc.)

http://webwatch.com/

WebWatch can collect additional data via an extended log file (Tabibian 1996a). Virtual Office's promotional literature claims that access logs are necessary for Web site administrators to watch for signs of security breaches. Watchdog groups are calling for new ethics guidelines to prohibit the distribution of access logs to outsiders. WebWatch claims to protect user privacy by never requiring sites to expose their access logs.

WinWhatWhere (WinWhatWhere Corp.)

http://www.winwhatwhere.com

Richard Eaton is the president of WinWhatWhere (Lange 1996b). WinWhatWhere was created to facilitate work that involved billable hours spent in computer applications, such as word processing and computer-aided design. An allegedly unintentional outcome of the development of this software is its ability to enable network managers to record every keystroke and mouse click, every program run, and every Web site visited from a corporate computer (Wildstrom 1996). The software can be run in three different ways, resulting in three different levels of operator knowledge or intrusion: as a hidden program so that the persons being monitored do not know it is running; as a minimizable application that appears on each user's task bar; or as a hot-key-activated pop-up window for switching from project to project (Collora 1997).

WinWhatWhere 97 generates a detailed record of activity of one or multiple PCs on a network. It also can measure the distance a mouse has moved — a feature that may have some use in ergonomic studies. Although this computerized monitoring of time and usage may seem intrusive to some, WinWhatWhere can provide valuable productivity and ergonomic information (Rubenking 1997). The software runs in Windows 95 and Windows NT environments (Lange 1996b). In a networked environment, a detailed file of activity on each computer is sent to the central server every ten minutes (Collora 1997).

One negative aspect of WinWhatWhere is that, at least through release 97.1, if a person is working on multiple projects within a singular computer application, the person must remember to go into WinWhatWhere and notify the software each time the work changes from one project to another. Failure to do so results in one project being billed for time actually spent working on another project (Collora 1997). The software has been used by Environ Corporation of Portland, Oregon; 3Com Corporation, and the Florida Transportation Department (Lange 1996b).

By 1999 there were two strains of this software. According to WinWhatWhere's Web site, "Investigator's unique ability to invisibly monitor and record all computer activity along with keystroke logging make it ideally suited for the investigative needs of law enforcement, government, business, and private individuals." The Professional edition, on the other hand, "is ideally suited for capturing time that is to be billed to a Project or Customer."

In 1997 the retail price for a single-user workstation was $99, and a ten workstation license sold for $495 (Collora 1997). In July 1999 these prices still applied.

See also Lange (1996a) and Hogan (1997).

Appendix B

Third Party
Web Monitoring
Service Providers

Third party Web monitoring service providers also are known as Web traffic tracking services. They provide off-site analysis, and sometimes even off-site data collection, of the activity occuring on the Web site using the service.

ABC Interactive (Audit Bureau of Circulations)

http://www.accessabc.com

The Audit Bureau of Circulations (ABC), based in the U.S., is a member of the International Federation of Audit Bureaux of Circulations. It competes directly with the I/Audit service from Internet Profiles to supply independently audited Web site usage data analysis (Buchanan and Lukaszewski 1997, 193). Business Publications Audit and the Audit Bureau of Verification Services, which is part of the ABC, each have developed auditing services they hope will become standards against which Web sites using different server log analysis software can be compared (Keeping track of the traffic 1996). Early in 1996 the Audit Bureau launched its Web auditing service. The Audit Bureau's system measures the number and length of sessions, or visits, and "page impressions" — the number of pages requested and received by a user — during those sessions. The results can be reported as averages by day of the week and month. Reporting cycles can be monthly, quarterly or semiannually. The Audit Bureau also can provide advertiser-specific audits that will give the number of page impressions for the page containing their banner and the number of so-called "click-throughs" to an advertiser's site (Fitzgerald 1996). The electronic verification subsidiary of ABC, ABC Interactive, performed independent audits for 81 customers during late 1996 and early 1997, with prices starting at $400 for sites with fewer than 100 HTML pages and 50,000 page requests per month, and going up to $4,500 for complex sites with more than 1,500 HTML pages and 100 million or more page requests (Lamons 1997).

Accipiter (Ergage, a subsidiary of CMGI, Inc.)

http://www.accipiter.com

The merger mania involving Accipiter, Engage, I/PRO, and CMGI can be explained by quoting from the Web site (July 1999): "Engage has integrated product offerings with Accipiter, an industry leading online advertising management provider. The completed merger with Accipiter facilitated the integration of Engage Web Visitor Precision Profiling technology with Accipiter online advertising solutions. The integration of these two technologies enables advertisers and Web sites to leverage the next generation of online advertising: visitor-centric ad targeting. On April 7, 1999, CMGI acquired substantially all of the stock of I/PRO, a leader in World Wide Web traffic verification, analysis, and research. After completion of the transaction, I/PRO will become a wholly owned subsidiary of Engage. I/PRO analyzes and validates Web site activity, which enables marketers to understand their online business and improve the effectiveness of their site. I/PRO's services include Nielsen I/PRO I/AUDIT and Nielsen I/PRO NetLine."

AdForce (Imgis)

http://www.imgis.com

Prior to August 1998, the company name was Imgis (Mand 1998). AdForce is described as a centralized advertising management service for online publishers and advertisers.

BPA Interactive

http://www.bpai.com/interactive/index.html

BPA International has been auditing print publications for seven decades. In an effort to bring some consistency to the use of Web monitoring terminology, and to serve as a third-party check to Web traffic counting, in 1996 BPA launched BPA Interactive. A BPA audit electronically collects log file data from a Web site. Auditors check the data daily and are advised to watch for unusual fluctuations in traffic, which may be an indication that someone is tampering with the log file (Rich 1997a). BPA Interactive charges $900 for sites generating 3 million page requests or more (Lamons 1997). BPA claims to be the only not-for-profit Web auditing firm.

ClickOver

http://www.clickover.com

First identified in Williamson (1996c).

Cyber Dialogue

http://www.cyberdialogue.com

Mark Esiri is the CEO of Cyber Dialogue. Telescope and Microscope are their two tracking agents. Telescope asks users to indicate their media preferences, then places them in predefined psychographic profiles called "media communes." The Microscope tracking agent uses data mining technology and neural networks to recognize Telescope users based on their behavior patterns within a Web site environment (Carmichael 1996c). The Telescope service delivers information that is most relevant to each user's particular psychographic category. There are four psychographic categories (Hodges 1996). Microscope blends psychographic data with the user's behavior at the Web site. Microscope lets advertisers target their ads down to the individual level, even though the individual remains anonymous (Hodges 1996).

DoubleClick (Poppe Tyson)

http://www.doubleclick.net

DoubleClick is a media buying service launched in 1995 by Poppe Tyson. DoubleClick uses a software program capable of monitoring a user's activities on Web sites within the DoubleClick media network (Jones 1995). According to their own promotional Web site, their "revolutionary system provides you [i.e., the webmaster with something to sell] with the ability to conduct a highly targeted and cost effective Internet advertising campaign" (DoubleClick 1996). DoubleClick sells advertising through a variety of Web sites, including *USA Today Online*, Travelocity, Quicken (the financial software company), Virtual Comics, and Books That Work (a home and garden software publisher). When a user visits one of the 60 participating sites in the DoubleClick network, the Web server assigns the user an ID number. The information gathered from subsequent visits is stored in a cookie file created by the Web server and saved on the user's personal computer running the client software. The cookie file contains information on the customer's buying and browsing habits as well as the ID number (Moukheiber 1996). DoubleClick has been using Netscape cookies to collect and store demographic data about users without the users being aware that it is happening. The DoubleClick software uses the information from the cookie to decide which banner ad is most appropriate to display to that user (Foster 1996). This is an early development in what may be a long-term project to tailor a user's future online environment based on what the user currently is doing, including the user's past behavior.

The software works in real time. When a user visits a Web site in the DoubleClick stable, the DoubleClick database analyzes demographic and other information in the IP address and displays an advertising banner tailored specifically for that data profile (Jones 1995). DoubleClick matches each user's IP address against a database of 70,000 Internet domain names — a database that includes a line-of-business code (Moukheiber 1996). Basically, DoubleClick uses employer information inferred from domain names to target ads for potential buyers.

Kevin O'Connor is the CEO and president of DoubleClick. He claims that DoubleClick uses cookies files only to keep track of which ads have been displayed to an individual browser so that that person does not keep seeing the same one. Information about the user's geographical location and company affiliation is derived from the IP address, not the cookie file, and the user's browser identifies itself and the operating system it runs under. O'Connor admits that "The potential for abuse on the Web is great, because it is so powerful. But it really has little to do with cookies" (Foster 1996).

By tracking the behavior of Web surfers, including their Internet addresses, operating systems, browser client software, and Internet Service Providers, DoubleClick has amassed profiles of approximately 10 million anonymous visitors to DoubleClick's Web sites. Although DoubleClick remains a not-yet-profitable, private corporation, O'Connor claims it has already taken in approximately $10 million in revenue (Moukheiber 1996).

Roy Schwedelson, CEO of Worldata, a list firm in Boca Raton, Florida, considers DoubleClick's tracking methods to be an invasion of the Web user's privacy. Schwedelson contends that DoubleClick's data are not based on transactional or public information. They record every time a user looks in the store window (Jones 1995).

Firefly Network

http://www.firefly.com or www.firefly.net

Firefly Network has developed intelligent agent software that can watch users enter a Web site, see what pages they view, and then point users toward other areas of the site or deliver targeted ad banners (Carmichael 1996c). "The Firefly Suite of software tools is based on open industry standards and enables businesses to create trusted, high-value, personalized relationships with users, while building loyal communities around brands" (Netscape,

Firefly and VeriSign 1997). Firefly was the first Web site to employ a third party (Coopers & Lybrand) to audit its privacy policy (Sullivan 1997).

The concept behind the Firefly Network began in 1993 when six MIT researchers wrote a program that linked information about musical bands. The original intent of Firefly was to automate the word-of-mouth communication process. The technology now has a more highfalutin generic name, collaborative filtering (Weise 1997b). Firefly Networks, Inc., holds the license to a software technology with a goal of leveraging personal information from users of computer networks. The technology relies on consumer confidence in the privacy of data gathered and distributed over the Internet (Weise 1997b). The Web site operated by Barnes & Noble uses Firefly to link people with other like-minded souls (Weise 1997b).

Firefly has recently developed the Passport Web plug-in as the first client to comply with the Open Profiling Standard (Bayers 1998, 186). For this venture Firefly has placed confidence in user-articulated preferences. Firefly allows users to create profiles of their entertainment preferences, then allows vendors to use this information to sell products to the users (Hagel and Armstrong 1997b). In 1998 Firefly was acquired by Microsoft (Sacharow 1998).

Focalink (AdKnowledge)

http://www.focalink.com

Focalink was acquired in late 1997 by AdKnowledge. The Focalink branch tracked Web advertising activity from its own site, and provides Web advertising planning and buying tools. First identified in Stout (1997, 189).

Intermind

http://www.intermind.com

Intermind works as a collaboration between the Web marketer and the Web site manager. The marketer and the manager create hyperconnectors — sensitized areas where a user's behavior is monitored (Carmichael 1996c).

I/PRO and I/COUNT (Internet Profiles)

http://www.ipro.com/

I/PRO (Internet Profiles Corporation) is a San Francisco company that operates a service that tracks the number of visits a Web site receives (Wagner 1996a). Ariel Poler is the founder and president of Internet Profiles. The company emerged as the early market leader in the developing field of Web usage measurement, partially because of its partnership with the venerable Nielsen Media Research (Marx 1996a). I/PRO was founded in June 1994 and formed a strategic alliance with Nielsen Media Services in September 1995 (Lamons 1997). I/PRO the service was launched in May of 1995 (Wetli 1995).

Advertisers like the fact that the usage statistics are coming from a third party (Wagner 1996). The sellers of this software claim that sites using I/PRO obtain detailed demographic data while avoiding redundant site-specific registration that could affect site traffic.

I/COUNT is one of the core services of I/PRO. I/PRO and Nielsen Media Research (http://www.nielsenmedia.com/) have joined to create I/COUNT version 1.1. Among other things, I/COUNT analyzes site usage based on industry codes, number of employees, and corporate revenue. I/COUNT has been available since May 1995 (Bayne 1996). I/COUNT is aimed at Web site owners. The software distinguishes between hits and visitors, focusing on visitors, and can analyze Web site traffic by geographic region, average session length, and usage by day of the week (Wetli 1995).

I/COUNT provides details on how long users stay at a site, the number of visits to each page, and the clickstream (Rich 1997). Whereas NetCount provides grabs and analyzes log files on an hourly basis, I/COUNT retrieves the log file from a server only once per day (Stout 1997, 151).

The I/AUDIT service is a more sophisticated form of server log analysis. I/PRO runs additional software and algorithms against the server log data to reveal problem areas, such as days when the server may have been down or the Internet connection was broken (Stout

1997). According to the vice president of marketing at I/PRO, approximately 100 Web sites were using the I/AUDIT service early in 1997 (Rich 1997a). I/AUDIT provides independent, verified, and comparable reports of Web site usage. For Web sites with advertiser inserts or ad banners, I/AUDIT can report the number of adviews and adclicks per day, the adclick rate, and ad comparisons that do not compromise advertiser confidentiality (Buchanan and Lukaszewski 1997, 190). I/INDEX, a related service, is an attempt to measure overall Web activity, based on the number of visits to participating sites (Taylor, Cathy 1996a).

Late in 1996 I/PRO announced a new service, NetLine, which enables Web site administrators to track traffic graphically on their own Web pages (Angwin 1996). NetLine is described by I/PRO itself as "a data mining/reporting tool enabling a site to mine their usage data such as clickthroughs and referrals, time, etc." (quoted in Cohen 1997a). Unlike standalone Web log analysis software programs like WebTrends, NetLine is a fully outsourced service. I/PRO accesses the data, processes them, and creates reports as requested.

Modem Media (Poppe Tyson)

http://www.modemmedia.poppetyson.com/

Modem Media is located in Westport, Connecticut. It merged with Poppe Tyson in 1998. First identified in Marx (1996a).

NetBench (Delahaye Medialink)

http://www.delahaye.com/

NetBench was developed by the Delahaye Group in New Hampshire. Rather than simply report on the number of hits or accesses, NetBench can track how long a visitor stayed at a page and which areas of the site visitors found most useful (Bayne 1996). According to the information contained on its Web site, the Delahaye Medialink Internet analysis group sees indigenous online behavior as one big focus group: "The Internet revolution has provided us with the best source of perceptions — creating one giant focus group where all of your constituencies are collecting information as well as voicing and forming opinions."

NetCount (Digital Planet)

http://www.netcount.com/

NetCount is a tracking and auditing service from Digital Planet (http://www.digiplanet.com/) based in Culver City, California (Conaghan 1995). According to the advertisement in the back of Stout (1997), NetCount is now affiliated with Price Waterhouse. Paul Grand is the chairman of NetCount. He formed the company in 1995, after launching Digital Planet, a creator of content, with Josh Greer in 1994 (Rich 1997).

NetCount functions as a Nielsen rating for cyberspace advertising. It helps companies gauge the reach of their advertisements (Cohen 1995). NetCount focuses on the number of successful transfers, purported to be a more meaningful measure than the total number of hits. The number of successful transfers indicates how many users wait for all the data to appear on the screen before aborting to go to another URL (Jaffee 1996).

NetCount supports the common log format, the combined or extended log format, including referrer and user agent information, and the log files produced by the Microsoft Internet Information Server (Stout 1997, 135). Although NetCount produces daily and weekly reports, as of late 1996 they were not producing monthly summary reports (Stout 1997, 147).

NetCount distinguishes between a BIR (Browser Information Request) and a BIT (Browser Information Transfer). It also defines a PIR (Page Information Request) and a PIT (Page Information Transfer) (Stout 1997, 95). Note that patience, rather than persistence, has become a crucial characteristic for users in this environment.

NetCount does offer an upgraded service (HeadCount) that employs a more wholesome algorithm to determine human visitors, rather than DPOs (Distinct Points of Origin). A DPO is based solely on the user's hostname or IP address (Stout 1997, 144). HeadCount attempts to take into account factors like multiuser computer systems and cookies (Stout 1997, 137).

NetGravity

http://www.netgravity.com

Brad Husick, vice-president for marketing at NetGravity, admits that nearly all the ads they serve up on Web sites are bought based on the content environment, not the ability to target demographics (Williamson 1996c, 50).

One-to-One (BroadVision, Inc.)

Virgin Net uses software from BroadVision of Los Altos, California, to create rules for handling individual users. The software combines preferences indicated by users with data about their online behavior to create a customized virtual environment. The software tracks users' online behavior and reacts accordingly (Wagner 1996d). Evidently the software has been available since January 1996. Pricing for the software starts at $60,000. Average pricing is about $150,000 (Wagner 1997c). See also Wilder (1996b).

Open AdStream (Real Media)

http://www.realmedia.com

Open AdStream is Web server software that specializes in serving up advertisements, then tracking and measuring the effectiveness of the ads. First identified in Stout (1997, 283).

SelectCast (Aptex Software)

http://www.aptex.com/Products/index.htm

SelectCast is an advertising server software that promises to increase click-through rates and pinpoint receptive audiences so commercial messages reach the right audience (McNamara 1998). SelectCast is a neural-network-based software tool that constructs behaviorally based demographic profiles of Web users (Bayers 1998, 185). The Aptex Web site describes SelectCast as an "adaptive learning application that converts browsers to buyers by unobtrusively observing each client and offering him or her products catered to their specific needs." In 1998 the base price for access to SelectCast is $100,000 (Bayers 1998, 185).

TrueCount (MatchLogic)

http://www.matchlogic.com

MatchLogic sells marketers a service that centralizes the management of Web-based advertising banners and measures how often consumers see and click on those ads (Bayers 1998). TrueCount, an advertisement measuring system, was launched in October 1997 on the promise of overcoming the problem of undercounting page impressions (Taylor, Catharine 1997). The software has been endorsed by the Audit Bureau of Circulations (Schiesel 1997).

WebConnect (Worldata)

http://webconnect.net

Worldata and CMP Publications have a joint venture in WebConnect, a media placement service for the Internet (Internet a big hit 1997). According to information contained at the WebConnect site, the service enables Web advertisers to measure their Internet advertising (from page impression to click to sale) with WEBConnect's proprietary ICS tracking system.

WebCounter

http://www.digits.com

WebCounter was written by Gray Watson. It uses the GIF-manipulating GD library written by Tom Boutell. Both free and commercial services are available. The WebCounter Plus Service is a professional counting service with subscription fees based on average daily usage. For example, in July 1999 an owner of a Web site receiving less than 1,000 hits per day could expect to pay approximately $35 per year for the WebCounter service.

Appendix C

Web Server Log Analysis Freeware and Shareware

Most of the freeware that has been developed for computerized monitoring focuses on the analysis and presentation of Web server log data, rather than on collecting data itself. With the emergence of commercial Web server log analysis enterprises, freeware and shareware developers appear to have become discouraged. Many of them have mothballed their projects because they realize they cannot compete with the development efforts and resources of the commercial firms (Stout 1997, 156). C|Net's Shareware.com (www.shareware.com) contains a number of free log analysis software tools (Rahmel 1997).

AccessWatch (NetPresence)

http://netpresence.com/accesswatch

AccessWatch was written by Dave Maher, a student at Bucknell University, for UNIX-style Web servers. The output can be viewed with a Web browser. It counts the number of different browser software programs accessing the site, and it calculates the average number of pages viewed by each visitor. The software is free to academic, government, and other non-commercial sites, but for-profit sites must pay a nominal annual fee (Testerman, Kuegler, and Downling 1996, 410). First identified at www.hkstar.com/cwsapps/stat.html.

Analog

Developed by Stephen Turner at the Statistical Laboratory at Cambridge University. The program works in UNIX and DOS environments. Although the reports generated by Analog are not very different from those created by other log analysis software, Analog is easy to use, offers a wide variety of configuration options, and completes most analysis projects quickly (Musciano 1996a). Analog also is the name of the log analyzer software developed by Yan, Jacobsen, Garcia-Molina, and Dayal (1996).

BrowserCounter 1.0

http://www.netimages.com/showhare/utilities/browsercounter.html

First identified in Bayne (1996). BrowserCounter is a Perl language script that shows what browser software programs are used by each visitor to a site (Strom 1996c). It is a very specialized piece of software that captures and examines only one facet of HCI in a Web environment.

Bytecount

http://web-developer.com/management/management_log_analysis.html

Bytecount is a Perl script. "The Bytecount script accomplishes some very simple actions. It reads in a Web log file name, gunzips it if it's a gzip file, then analyzes the data stream by using the path. It grabs the first bounded directory — i.e., whatever it finds in /blah/ — and uses that to create an associative array where the transferred bytes are accumulated. When the file's done, it creates a short summary of the usage by top-level directory. The default cutoff point is 100 kilobytes" (Fleishman 1996).

Clark

Developed by David S. Carter at the University of Michigan. Clark is a Perl script that takes an access log from an HTTP server in common log format and transforms it into a transaction log, capable of being analyzed so that events are broken down by user.

Count WWWebula

http://www.edb.utexas.edu/greg/ftp/programming/counter/index.cgi

First identified in Nemzow (1997, 93). This hit counter was designed for the Apple Macintosh. Count WWWebula dynamically updates a GIF file and sends it back to the client application along with the HTML file.

CreateStats

http://wwwbprc.mps.ohio-state.edu/usage/CreateStats.html

CreateStats was designed as a front end to GetStats (see below) (Frentzen 1995a).

FTPWebLog

http://www.nihongo.org/snowhare/utilities/ftpweblog/

This is a freeware, integrated, WWW and FTP log reporting tool, developed by Benjamin Franz. It does not filter reports by date (Franz 1996).

GetStats

http://www.getstats.com

Developed by Kevin Hughes. GetStats takes the log file from a server and sorts the log data in a variety of ways, including monthly weekly, daily, and customized activity views (Frentzen 1995a). Because GetStats reports can be difficult to read, CreateStats was developed as a front end that puts the reports into an easier to understand HTML file (Frentzen 1995a).

Gwstat

http://dis.cs.umass.edu/stats/gwstat.html

Developed by Qiegang Long at the University of Massachusetts. The program takes output from wwwstat (see page 350) and generates graphs in GIF format. The emphasis of this software, then, is on the analysis and presentation of the data, rather than on collecting the data itself.

Inquisitor (RSPAC)

http://inquisitor.ivv.nasa.gov/

Designed and developed by RSPAC (Remote Sensing Public Access Center). Two of RSPAC's Web sites are The Observatorium and The Developers' Workshop. The Inquisitor is a highly configurable Web log analysis tool. It gathers usage information stored by the server and compiles it into an easy-to-use HTML format. The Inquisitor provides daily hit counts for the last three weeks plus the current week. Hits from specific groups (e.g., the internal development team) can be excluded. The hourly graph features shows the number of hits the server received during each hour of the previous day. The hits-per-page table shows the number of times each page was requested from the server.

By arranging hits on a site by IP number, the threads tool reveals how a visitor uses a site, in terms of the sequence with which an individual user hits your pages. A thread is a chronologically ordered listing of a user's site visit session. The threads tool also provides information on the number of pages the average user grabs, plus the average length of stay at the server site.

A referrer table shows the analyzer the last site each user visited before coming to your site. Finally, a browser graph creates a pie chart showing the percentage of each type of browser used to access the server site. Because different browsers have different capabilities, this information can be used when the Web pages are being redesigned or upgraded. The Inquisitor runs in the UNIX operating system, and requires several Perl applications.

LogAn

http://www.arlut.utexas.edu/csd/logAn/

LogAn is written in Perl 5, and it uses ACE/gr to generate graphs. Some portions of the code came from Gwstat (see above).

Meisters's Magic Counter

First identified at www.hkstar.com/cwsapps/stat.html. Meister's Magic Counter was written by Garrett Casey. This subscriptionware costs $16 per year.

MKStats

http://www.mkstats.com/

Developed by Mark Kruse. Buchanan and Lukaszewski (1997, 185) identify this as shareware. The software was written in Perl. MKStats supports only the common and combined log formats. This software package is used by Hiway Technologies, one of the largest Web hosting providers (Busch 1997). In November 1998 MKStats was acquired by WebTrends.

Pwebstats

http://www.unimelb.edu.au/pwebstats

Developed by Martin Gleeson at the University of Melbourne. Pwebstats can analyze server log files in common log format, including CERN proxy logs, or squid format, producing a variety of statistics output as a series of HTML pages and graphs.

Quickdirty

First identified in Fleishman (1996). Quickdirty is a Perl script that summarizes the number of times a browser or reference URL appears on the server log. It can measure the number of unique visits and visitors, successes and failures, the duration of the site visit, the pages visited, and the path through the pages.

Refstats

http://www.netimages.com/~snowhare/utilities/refstats.html

First identified in Testerman, Kuegler, and Dowling (1996, 409). The Refstats software program works with the NCSA and Apache Web server software. It produces a list of the URLs that referred users to the site under observation.

SingleStat

http://www.sprint.com.au/singlestat/

SingleStat was designed by Derek Moo in Australia. SingleStat is a software program that provides page-by-page statistics for sites served by O'Reilly's WebSite server, Microsoft's IIS server, and Netscape's FastTrack/Enterprise servers. Its primary purpose is to provide statistics for any single URL, IP address, user, or date (SingleStat homepage). The software can also analyze referring URL and browser agent information.

SpeedTracer (IBM)

http://www.alphaworks.ibm.com

The alpha version can be downloaded for free. SpeedTracer is a data mining tool that can analyze user-oriented online behavior from regular Web server log files without employing cookies or overt registration procedures (Wu, Yu, and Ballman 1998, 90). It tracks entry points, exit points, and link usage (Wagner 1997a). SpeedTracer uses the referrer page contained in the referrer log and the URL of the requested page as a traversal step to reconstruct users' traversal paths to identify discrete usage sessions. Once the user session has been identified, data mining techniques can be used to reveal the browsing patterns of users (Wu, Yu, and Ballman 1998, 91). Ultimately, SpeedTracer uses five data elements from Web server log files to identify user sessions: IP address, time stamp, URL, referrer, and agent (Wu, Yu, and Ballman 1998, 93). SpeedTracer seems to excel in the analysis and presentation of aggregated usage statistics.

Statbot

http://www.xmission.com/~dtubbs/

First identified at www.hkstar.com/cwsapps/stat.html.

3Dstats

http://www.netstore.de/Supply/index.html

3Dstats is a software program that takes a server log file and generates a three-dimensional VRML model of the load on the server. First identified in Stout (1997, 170).

VBStats

http://home.city.net/win-httpd

VBStats is a 16-bit Windows public domain software program initially written by Bob Denny. VBStats falls well short of wusage (see below) in flexibility and usefulness (Stout 1997, 167).

WebMiner

The WebMiner system, as described briefly in Cooley, Mobasher, and Srivastava (1997) and more fully in Mobasher, Jain, Han, and Srivastava (1996), is a software system that divides the process of mining Web server log data into two main activities. The first process transforms the Web server log data into a usable transaction format, and the second process applies generic data mining techniques (e.g., the discovery of association rules and sequential patterns) as part of the system's data mining engine.

WebTrac (Logical Design Solutions)

http://www.lds.com/

First identified in Tiley (1996). See also Tabibian (1996a; reviewed November 13, 1995), who confirms that this is freeware. The software was developed to enable phone companies to track communications services. It is donationware that runs under Windows 3.x. Weaknesses of the software: The command-line interface is difficult to use; there are not many ways to customize data collection and reports; it contains no documentation or online help; and it has limited export options (Tabibian 1996a).

wusage

http://www.boutell.com/wusage/

Developed by Thomas Boutell. The software is shareware, rather than freeware, which means that a registration donation of approximately $75 is requested. This statistics system is designed to provide valuable marketing information. It is a command-line program. By default, wusage runs statistics on all objects — pages, graphics, Java applets, etc. (Stout 1997, 162–163). The reports come in both tables and pie charts. One innovative feature of wusage is the "accesses by result code" table. The table shows the number of requests that resulted in each access code. Usually code 404 (not found) is the most common error code (Stout 1997, 165). The major shortcomings of wusage are its inability to identify and track visits, and the overall lack of detail in the reports (Stout 1997, 165).

wwwstat

http://www.ics.uci.edu/pub/websoft/wwwstat/

The wwwstat program was developed by Roy Fielding (fielding@ics.uci.edu) at the University of California at Irvine. It is a simple Perl program. One limitation of the software is that it can process only the single log file for which it is tailored (Stout 1997, 157). Udell (1996) describes the basic functionality of wwwstat, plus ways he has enhanced the software to meet his specific needs. It does not provide useful graphics, and wwwstat cannot provide an overall picture of true visitor movement to and through a Web site. It tracks every file access, including every GIF or other image file that has been downloaded, so it is difficult to construct a sense of page views (Bayne 1996). The program contains some design flaws that limit its usefulness for large server sites. It is difficult to reconfigure the reports. It does not handle well characters that should be escaped. It is difficult to make it support additional log formats, and it provides poor support for multiple servers (Franz 1996). As a tool for library and information science research, wwwstat has several shortcomings. The number of pages transferred probably would serve better as a basic unit of measurement than the number of requests made or the number of bytes sent. The number of bytes sent probably is of interest mainly to the site administrator. The program makes no attempt to count visits or points of origin, so it has no way to report the number of human visitors during a specific period, the average number of page views during a visit, or the average duration of a page view (Stout 1997, 159). The number of unresolved requests also can be frustrating to a server log analyzer. Although the software tracks usage by both reversed subdomain and the files transferred, it does not enable mapping specific file transfers to specific reversed subdomains. With a worldwide hypertext system, the local time when requests are made to the server is not particularly informative.

Appendix D

Web Client
Log Analysis Software

This software is also known as Internet access managers. It works at the client end of client-server computing either to monitor the activity on the client or to block incoming content from servers. Some Web client log analysis software performs both functions.

Packet-sniffing software works by monitoring the packets that serve as virtual ore carts as information moves around on the Internet or some other computerized information network. It focuses on packet origins, destinations, sizes, and movements. As such, packet-sniffing software is not directly related to HCI, nor is it particularly interested in the content of the packets. Several packet-sniffing software programs allow network managers to monitor network usage and size of downloads without knowing the content of the packets. Because the monitoring capabilities of packet-sniffing software such as LittleBrother and ON Guard are so good, many companies will be able to deter unauthorized or unacceptable use of Internet resources by informing employees of the company's Internet usage policy, and by letting employees know such software is monitoring net activity (Rapoza 1997b).

com.Policy (SilverStone Software)

http://www.silverstonesoftware.com/

The software takes random screen samples off employees' monitors (Gussow 1997).

CyberGuard (CyberGuard)

CyberGuard now incorporates WebTrack from Webster (Nunoo 1997). McClure (1998) notes that the logging capabilities of CyberGuard are weak and inflexible. The logs are reports statistically queried from the database.

CyberSentry (Microsystems Software Corp.)

http://www.microsys.com

CyberSentry logs all URLs requested by users, as well as the IP addresses of the requesting hosts. All URLs go to the server running CyberSentry, which looks for the URL on the banned site list. New, previously unknown URLs also are logged (Dutcher 1996).

CYBERSitter (SolidOak software)

http://www.solidoak.com

CYBERSitter was developed by SolidOak Software in close cooperation with Focus on the Family, a conservative organization. Winner (1997) argues that CYBERSitter contains an embedded political agenda (antifeminist and antigay), and it encourages parents to spy on their children.

See Nunoo (1997), Kathryn Munro (1998), CYBERSitter (1997), and Winner (1997) for more information.

Disk Tracy (Watchsoft)

http://www.watchsoft.com

Disk Tracy from Watchsoft is a new Web client logging software that produces reports on all Web sites visited by employees, including overt files downloaded (Gussow 1997).

Historian (FortresGrand Corp.)

http://www.fortres.com

This program records, audits, and reports computer use while being locally loaded on a Windows 95/98 workstation. The ergonomic function informs users who have been computing for too long to take a break (Avery 1998).

Instant Internet (Performance Technology)

Instant Internet controls access to specific news servers and newsgroups. It allows the LAN manager to control access for individual users or groups of users within an organization. The software can create an event log of destinations, activities, and session durations of individual users or groups (Internet control 1996).

Internet Manager (Elron)

http://www.on.com

ON Guard Internet Manager was re-released early in 1998 as Internet Manager from Elron Electronics Industries. It is a real-time monitor that uses a customizable dictionary of keywords to block access to Web sites. If the software detects a restricted keyword in a Web page title or URL, it then scans the entire site prior to confirming or denying access (Lindquist 1999).

Internet Resource Manager (Sequel Technology)

http://www.sequeltech.com

The software helps an information system manager control online activity and enforce a comprehensive intranet and Internet acceptable use policy (Coopee 1997a). Albert Behr, vice president of marketing, estimates that between 20 and 30 percent of corporate activity on the Internet is for non-business purposes (Enright 1997).

The software was originally designed to run on a dedicated server. It sits on a corporation's network server and monitors activity on the company's intranet, including outgoing and incoming traffic to and from the Internet (Eng 1997). An IP packet filter engine works at the operating system level, monitoring outbound requests and verifying inbound data packets arriving from the Web (Enright 1997). The software not only monitors HTTP,

FTP, NNTP, e-mail, and Telnet traffic by user or group, it also filters every IP packet leaving a network, thus allowing the network manager to restrict specific services or sites. The software also enables management to limit what types of files can be accessed (Spangler 1996). It can even monitor the use of push technology by employees (Coopee 1997).

The software monitors not only successful violations of a company's acceptable use policy, it also records every attempt to violate. Every time an employee tries to access a blocked Web site, it generates an entry of the attempt in a log file. The log files are used to produce a number of standard reports (Coopee 1997).

The software can link specific online activity with identified individual employees (Eng 1997). Reports also can be generated for groups of users (e.g., a department) or for an entire company (Coopee 1997). The software has been designed specifically to monitor employee use of the Internet, including the sending and receiving of e-mail. Shein (1996a) reports how the software was used by Mark Worsnop, the director of research and development at PSI International in Vacaville, California, to monitor the network activities of 500 Internet-using employees.

See also Fitzloff (1997), Davey (1997), Xenakis (1996), and Internet monitors (1996).

Keynote Perspective (Keynote Systems)

http://www.keynote.com

This software approaches the problem of user activity and response time from the user's perspective. It was designed as a quality-control tool for Internet service providers and Web sites.

LittleBrother Pro (Kansmen Corp.)

http://www.kansmen.com

In March 1997 the Kansmen Corporation, based in Milpitas, California, unveiled a new version of the LittleBrother software that monitors and selectively blocks employee use of the Internet and intranets (LittleBrother may be watching you 1997). The software can monitor many types of Internet activity, including Web surfing and Telnet sessions (Rapoza 1997b). The software allows managers of work environments to track which Web sites employees visit (Harmon 1997). One unusual feature of LittleBrother is that it can also monitor the amount of bandwidth used by a PC (Rigney 1997, NE6). The dynamically generated bar chart shows traffic analysis in terms of users or sites visited, time or volume of traffic, and the network protocol used or the site rating (productive, neutral or unproductive) (Hayes 1998). Little Brother Pro is capable of one type of intrusive, real-time monitoring in that it can automatically send an e-mail alert to an employee whose usage of packets exceeds an established threshold during a certain period (Rapoza 1997b).

LT Auditor+ (Blue Lance)

http://www.bluelance.com

The Blue Lance Web site describes this software as capable of doing for online environments what surveillance cameras do for the real world: "Just as surveillance cameras provide you with a record of who entered your premises and what they did while they were there, LT Auditor+ provides a record of who entered your network and what they did while they were on the network."

Media Metrix (formerly PC-Meter) (Media Metrix)

PC-Meter was developed by NPD Group, a major consumer research company. Catharine Taylor (1997) reported that the name of the company had changed to Media Metrix. In October 1998 Media Metrix and RelevantKnowledge (see page 357) announced that they would merge into one company, Media Metrix, capable of analyzing usage data from 15,000 Web sites (Thibodeau 1998). Media Metrix has been counting and analyzing Web traffic since January 1996 (Maddox 1997). PC-Meter enabled user-centric, informed, consensual computerized monitoring. The service monitored all computer activity in 5,000 U.S. homes in March 1996. By mid–1997 the monitoring software had been installed on 10,000 volunteer households in the U.S. (Kirsner 1997a). It provided detailed reports of consumer use of online services, including total connect time and a breakdown of activity into e-mail, chat groups, online shopping, and forums. Auer (1997) reported that PC-Meter found that home PCs often are not being used when they are turned on. Based on a usage analysis of approximately 10,000 households with computers, the average home PC is turned on 6.6 hours per day, yet is used for only 2.8 hours. The service also identified which Web sites have been visited by individuals in the participating households. The service could detect use of individual Web pages. This method of computerized monitoring has yielded information that no site-centric method can. For example, PC-Meter has been able to confirm that the average Web surfing session lasts approximately 30 minutes (Kirsner 1997a).

Net Access Manager (Sequel Technology)

http://www.sequeltech.com

Developed by Sequel Technology in Toronto, Canada, Net Access Manager helps an information system manager control online activity and enforce a comprehensive intranet and Internet acceptable use policy (Coopee 1997). Shein (1996) reports that the software is priced at $1,095. Albert Behr is the vice-president of marketing at Sequel Technology. He estimates that between 20 and 30 percent of corporate activity on the Internet is for non-business purposes (Enright 1997).

The software was originally designed to run on a dedicated server. It sits on a corporation's network server and monitors activity on the company's intranet, including outgoing and incoming traffic to and from the Internet (Eng 1997). An IP packet filter engine such as Net Access Manager works at the operating system level, monitoring outbound requests and verifying inbound data packets arriving from the World Wide Web (Enright 1997). The software not only monitors HTTP, FTP, NNTP, e-mail, and Telnet traffic by user or group, it also filters every IP packet leaving a network, thus allowing the network manager to restrict specific services or sites. The software also enables management to limit what types of files can be accessed (Spangler 1996). It can even monitor the use of push technology by employees (Coopee 1997).   .

Net Access Manager monitors not only successful violations of a company's acceptable use policy, it also records every attempt to violate. Every time an employee tries to access a blocked Web site, Net Access Manager generates an entry of the attempt in a log file. The log files are used to produce a number of standard reports (Coopee 1997).

The software can link specific online activity with identified individual employees (Eng 1997). Reports also can be generated for groups of users (e.g., a department) or for an entire company (Coopee 1997). The software has been designed specifically to monitor employee use of the Internet, including the sending and receiving of e-mail. Sequel Vice-President Tony Katz reported in May 1996 that 25 network administrators in government, university, and corporate organizations were already using Access Manager (Abate 1996). Shein (1996) reports how Access Manager was used by Mark Worsnop, the director of research and development at PSI International in Vacaville, California, to monitor the network activities of the 500 Internet-using employees. See also Fitzloff (1997), Davey (1997), Xenakis (1996), and Internet monitors (1996).

NetNanny

http://www.netnanny.com

NetNanny used lists of forbidden words, URLs, and phrases to filter out objectionable material (Ryan 1999).

NetRatings (NetRatings)

http://www.netratings.com/

NetRatings is a service that culls Internet audience data from a random sample of computer users. The service started in late 1997 (Taylor, Catharine 1997). The firm is located in Milpitas, California (Maddox 1997). The software creates detailed profiles of Internet users so that Web advertisers can better target their advertisements (Maddox 1997). The data are generated from both questionnaire responses and computerized monitoring.

NETScout Manager (NetScout Systems)

http://www.netscout.com

NETScout Manager monitors network traffic including percentage usage by Internet applications. The software gathers information through probes that sit on a network segment and monitor network traffic (Spangler 1996). See also Anderson (1996).

Optimal Internet Monitor (Optimal Networks)

http://www.optimal.com/

Optimal Internet Monitor was designed to enable administrators to measure the impact of Web activity on network bandwidth, and to provide both real-time and historical views of network traffic patterns. If the software is strategically placed between a Web server and the outside network, it can provide information about the users who connect to the Web server and the quality of service they receive (Wonnacott 1996).

The software parses major Internet protocols (e.g., HTTP, FTP, and NNTP), identifies the heaviest users of each protocol, records which Internet sites they are accessing, and sends alerts when a pre-set threshold has been exceeded (Spangler 1996).

Optimal's software tracks every Web site, newsgroup, and FTP location visited by the user. It records the size of every file that is downloaded. John Graham-Cumming from Optimal likens the data output to an itemized phone bill. He asserts that the software was developed not to monitor individual behavior, but to help network administrators spot anyone using unusual amounts of resources (Abate 1996).

The software cannot restrict end-user access to a specific Web site. The traffic map is perhaps the most informative output. The traffic matrix depicts where users on the local network were connected to each of the Web sites they visited in the specified period (Wonnacott 1996).

Graham-Cumming notes that except in cases in which data is encrypted, it is technically possible through the use of some monitoring software to see what the user is seeing. (This features harkens back to Sigfried Treu's notion of transparent stimulation.) Optimal decided not to include this capability in their software. The Optimal Internet Monitor software was developed to provide an overview of Internet use, not to be used as a tool for personal monitoring (Abate 1996).

Mike Elkins, the information systems director at V-Systems, a UNIX fax server manufacturer in San Juan Capistrano, California, began using Optimal Internet Monitor after an incident in which an information system employee violated company policy by finding certain information on a company-owned PC. Data gathered by the software revealed high incidences of flagrant policy violations, including extensive personal research being done on company time, moonlighting in Web administration during work hours, and visits to Web sites on recreational topics, such as music and swimming. After employees were notified that the software was being used, flagrant violations dropped almost to zero (Shein 1996a, 49).

Rod Trent, the LAN Administrator at Deloitte & Touche LLP's Cincinnati office, has been using the software to decrease network bottlenecks. Trent reports some limitations to the software. It does not enable him to see the TCP/IP address of the employee who is accessing the Internet, nor does it reveal the number of people going online simultaneously. Perhaps most importantly, the software monitors only use Netscape Navigator (Shein 1996). The software does not support other protocols, such as Telnet (Wonnacott 1996).

This software represents the convergence of several trends in the overall field of using computers to monitor HCI. The will to monitor employees and Web surfers is converging, as well as the dual paths of Web server monitoring and Web client monitoring. Wonnacott (1996) suggests that companies create formal Internet access policies, and inform their employees that their Internet activity is being monitored in an effort to gauge network performance, not to police the actions of individual employees. "The idea of monitoring people seems controversial," says Steve Holtzman, vice president of strategic marketing at Optimal Networks. "The goal is to improve Internet performance" (quoted in Cohen 1997a).

RelevantKnowledge

RelevantKnowledge was launched in June 1997 (Taylor, Catharine 1997). The company is based in Atlanta, Georgia (Maddox 1997). RelevantKnowledge claims it is able to project the number of unique visitors to a site using a system that tracks the real-time paths of specific users as they move through the Web. Software on the client desktop computer monitors their Net browsing. Users are selected to provide a good demographic cross section according to sex, age, income, real-world location, and frequency of use of the Net and the Web (Dunlop 1997).

SiteSpy (Reportech, Inc.)

http://www.reportech.com

SiteSpy extends the amount of information in the Web server common log format by including information gleaned from the client browser software. Output is sent to an SQL database. First identified in Rahmel (1997).

Smartfilter (Secure Computing Corp.)

http://www.securecomputing.com/P_Tool_SF_FRS.html

A report (censorware.org/reports/utah/) from a watchdog group called Censorware Project (CWP) criticized the SmartFilter blocking software's overreach on a statewide proxy server in Utah. SmartFilter blocked access for about 40 public school districts and at least eight public library systems to over 500,000 sites during a 30-day period (Goldberg 1998).

Sniffer Network Analyzer (Network General)

http://www.ngc.com

Whereas traditional network traffic analysis tools analyzed the transport layer, the newer software programs break down the application layer. The Sniffer Network Analyzer will monitor the percentage of the network used by Web requests and identify bandwidth abusers (Spangler 1996).Talley (1997) reports how he was able to monitor a specific user's session by first filtering the packet capture to the server and workstation and then using the database analyst function. Both successful sessions and failed sessions were easy to decipher.

SurfWatch

http://www.surfwatch.com

The software is designed strictly for online filtering. It can block Web, FTP, gopher, chat and newsgroup access (Munro, Kathryn 1998). It is possible with SurfWatch to block an entire domain, a directory within a domain, or a single page. The ChatBlock feature denies access to the IRC, Java, or HTML chat formats. In 1999 *PC Magazine* awarded Surf-Watch@Work, the workplace version of the software, an Editors' Choice award (Roberts-Witt 1999).

WebSense (NetPartners Internet Solutions)

http://www.websense.com

Of the six Internet-access manager software programs reviewed by *PC Magazine* in early 1997, WebSense received the Editors' Choice designation (Rigney 1997, NE14).

WebSense is a true proxy server that provides both Internet monitoring capabilities and content blocking for Internet and intranet HTTP and NNTP file transfers (Rigney 1997, NE14). WebSense generates reports that show which URLs users access and for how long (Hibbard 1996). WebSense logs all activity in the Windows NT Event Log (Rigney 1997, NE14).

Whereas most Internet-access manager programs block access only by domain name, WebSense can block sites by both IP address and domain name (Rigney 1997, NE14). If a user attempts to access a prohibited site, the user receives an "access denied" message and the software logs the attempt (Internet control 1996). A master database containing a collection of over 125,000 restricted Web sites in 29 categories is developed and maintained by professional Web surfers (Cohen 1998).

The WebSense software itself does not contain a report writer, but NetPartners offers a free piece of software (WebSense Reporter) that uses the event log to create graphical reports based on user specifications and needs (Rigney 1997, NE14).

Version 3.0 of the software does have some limitations. It is not capable of real-time monitoring, alerts, or usage reports by MAC address or machine name only (Rigney 1997, NE14).

Taylor (1996b) argues that products like WebSense are absolutely the wrong solution for a growing problem in virtual work environments. The troubling aspect of WebSense is that it monitors and logs all user activities, sending neat monthly reports to managers of not only where users spent their time on the Web and how long they were at those sites, but also employees' failed attempts to visit forbidden Web sites. In Taylor's mind, this is an entirely new version of thought control. Ironically, it is being touted as a solution to what is assumed to be an insidious problem in work environments.

The list price for version 3.0 of WebSense was free, but a subscription fee for unlimited users cost $6,995 (Rigney 1997, NE14). In early 1998 the suggested retail price for version 1.0 of WebSense Reporter Pro was $495 per workstation (Cohen 1998).

WinGuardian (Webroot Software)

http://www.webroot.com

WinGuardian was in beta testing late in 1997; it was designed to function as an alternative to filtering and blocking for schools, libraries, churches, and parents. WinGuardian is completely unobtrusive. It monitors almost everything a user dos on a networked computer: the programs a user runs, any text typed into a program, and all Web sites visited. It even captures screenshots at various specified intervals.

WinVista (WinVista)

http://www.winvista.com

WinVista is a monitoring software program for controlling the usage of other software applications (Luttjohann 1997). Winvista tracks not only Internet activity on an employee's PC, but also every file the person accesses from the hard drive. Every menu option selected by the user is recorded, as well as the start time and duration of every application (Xenakis 1998). First identified in Hutheesing (1997).

XNI (Fastlane Systems Ltd.)

http://www.xni.com

XNF displays network and Internet/intranet application traffic on both LANs and WANs, either in real time or after the fact (Garza 1998).

ZooWorks (Hitachi Software)

http://www.hitachisoftware.com/

ZooWorks' unique twist is that it appears to be designed for use as a memory extender for the actual Web surfer. It logs the address of every Web page the person hits with his browser, creating a database of URLs, page titles, and brief descriptions (Finnie 1997).

Appendix E

Cookie Control Software

Andy's Netscape HTTP Cookie Information

http://www.illuminatus.com/cookie.fcgi

This is not a software program, but a Web site resource for information about cookies, maintained by Andy Kington.

Anonymous Cookie (Luckman Interactive)

http://www.luckman.com/anoncookie/anoncookiebody.html

A free software utility program, Anonymous Cookie was released in June 1997. The program works by backing up, then deleting, the original cookie files. This allows the software user to then surf the Web in anonymous mode. When anonymous mode is deactivated, the backed up cookie files are restored (Anonymous Cookie 1997). Thus the software enables the individual to slip out of and back into one's virtual self.

Anti-Cookie

http://anticookie.home.ml.org

In early 1998 this software was $10 (Randall 1998b).

Buzof (Basta Computing)

http://www.basta.com

Buzof was designed to help the user avoid cookies, annoying messages, warnings, and confirmation prompts. In early 1998 this software was $15 (Randall 1998b).

Complete Cleanup (SoftDD)

http://members.aol.com/softdd

Complete Cleanup cleans up after other software programs, disposing of flotsam such as cookies, cache files, and history files. Because this program is a single executable file, there is no installation routine (Brown 1998). First identified in Randall (1997b). In early 1998 the software cost $30 (Randall 1998b).

Cookie Central

http://www.cookiecentral.com

This Web site informs people about cookies. Frentzen (1997) suggests that the Cookie Central Web site is the best site for investigating the pros and cons of persistent cookies.

Cookie Cruncher (Rendering Better Avenues Software)

http://home1.gte.net/dsavrnoc/cookie.htm

Cookie Cruncher is a free software program (Randall 1998b).

Cookie Crusher (The Limit Software)

http://www.thelimitsoft.com

Cookie Crusher automatically rejects incoming cookie files, saving the user from manually doing so. The software requires that the cookie notification feature of the browser software be turned on. The incoming cookies are accepted or rejected in real time based on the user's pre-stated preferences. Because the user can compile lists of Web sites that should or should not be allowed to set cookies, this software gives cookie-setting freedom to trusted sites while protecting the browsing privacy of the user (Desmarais 1998). First identified in Randall (1997b). In early 1998 this software was $15 (Randall 1998b).

Cookie Cutter (AyeCor Software)

http://www.ayecor.com

Steinberg (1997) describes Cookie Cutter as a technological solution to concerns about lack of informed consent regarding the use of cookies.

Cookie Jar (Eric Murray)

http://www.lne.com/ericm/cookie_jar/

Cookie Jar blocks all cookies coming from selected URLs while allowing others from other servers to be established. The software must be run under a UNIX machine and must use a browser that supports an HTTP proxy (Kalfatovic 1997).

Cookie Master (Barefoot Productions)

www.barefootinc.com

This free software program is available on ZDnet from Ziff-Davis, the computer magazine publisher. The program enables users to monitor cookie activity and to delete unwanted cookie files (Mosley-Matchett 1997). It shows the user the contents of all of the cookies on the user's hard drive (Machrone 1997). The software works with either Microsoft Internet Explorer or Netscape Navigator (Randall 1997b), and it provides access to each cookie from each Web site (Randall 1997b). Because the software does not work unobtrusively in the background, users need to spend time cleaning up the cookie crumbs (Brown 1998).

Cookie Monster (Nicolas Berloquin)

http://www.geocities.com/Paris/1778/monster.html

Cookie Monster is e-mailware that sniffs cookies files and erases them from the user's hard drive. Cookie Monster 1.5.1 runs on every type of Macintosh and is available as a Stuffit archive. There is no PC version of the Cookie Monster for either Windows or DOS.

Cookie Pal (Kookaburra Software)

http://www.kburra.com

Cookie Pal has two parts: The interactive monitor notifies the user when the user's browser software is asked to accept cookie information; the cookie management part enables the user to manage cookies that are already resident on the client computer (Randall 1997b). Cookie Pal uses a tabbed dialog box to show all cookies stored (Desmarais 1998). The use of wild-card preferences allows the user to accept or reject cookies from a group of Web sites from the same domain (Brown 1998). One potential drawback to Cookie Pal is that it must run in the background at all times to perform effectively; that might add to response time during a browsing session (Randall 1997b). In early 1998 this software was $15 (Randall 1998b).

Cookie-Server (Newfangled Software)

http://www.newfangled.san-jose.ca.us

This software tries to capitalize on cookies as a computer resource, rather than a persistent nuisance.

Cookie Web Kit

http://www.cookiecentral.com/files.htm

This free software handles both browser cache and history files (Randall 1998b).

Crumbler 97 (Scott McDaniel)

http://www.scscorp.com/personal/scottmac

The only function of Crumbler 97 is to sit in the background on the client computer and periodically erase cookies downloaded in Netscape Navigator (Randall 1997b). It revisits the cookies.txt file every 45 seconds and automatically deletes any cookies it finds (Desmarais 1998). In early 1998 version 4 cost $10 (Randall 1998b).

IEClean and NSClean Privacy Enhancement (Privacy Software Corp.)

http://www.wizvax.net/kevinmca/

This software won an Editor's Choice designation from *PC Magazine* (Randall 1998b). Kevin McAleavey has a family of IEClean (for Internet Explorer) and NSClean (for Netscape Navigator) Privacy Enhancement programs that help users know about, manage, and delete cookie information (Dern 1997). Although neither software program can monitor cookies from the background, each can erase newsgroup activity, clear out cache files and history databases, and other similar activities (Randall 1997b). These two programs work only on command, never automatically (Randall 1997b). Both software programs were designed under the premise that managing cookies is just one facet of the online privacy problem (Brown 1998). In early 1998 the software cost was $40.

Internet Fast Forward (PrivNet)

http://www.privnet.com

James Howard of Chapel Hill, North Carolina, is the founder of PrivNet, a company with a mission to develop privacy protecting software, such as Internet Fast Forward (IFF) (Weber 1996). IFF actively filters out cookies and advertising graphics (Berg 1996). It also prevents a Web site server log from figuring out the site previously visited by the user before coming to the site in question (Weber 1996).

Internet Junkbuster Proxy (Junkbusters)

http://www.junkbusters.com/ht/en/ijb.html

Internet Junkbuster Proxy is a free UNIX proxy server that can be used to control cookie access (Kalfatovic 1997). Junkbusters is a private company set up to promote privacy concerns (Murdoch 1997). To learn how to disable cookies, visit the junkbusters Web site (Web spies 1997). The software enables the user to selectively block offending commercial objects, such as cookies and ad banners, while viewing the remainder of the Web page (Brown 1998).

Malcolm's Guide to Persistent Cookies

http://fuev.adeit.uv.es/~mada/cookiesinfo.html

This brief introductory guide by Malcolm Humes, last updated in August 1996, still covers the basic concepts well.

Personalized Web Assistant (Lucent Technologies)

http://www.lpwa.com:8000/

Personalized Web Assistant automatically generates fake identities for Web surfers every time they log on to a new site. The software stores neither the user's real identity nor the computer-generated false identities, and it erases all of the personal information sent by default from the client software to the Web server (Freund 1998). The software acts as a middleman between a Web browser and Web servers. It was designed specifically to work with Web sites offering personalized information environments without sacrificing the user's privacy (Desmarais 1998).

PGPcookie.cutter (Pretty Good Privacy)

http://www.pgp.com

Phil Zimmerman has managed to anger and dismay both the U.S. federal government and the advertising industry with his software. His PGPcookie.cutter is a software program that lets one control which (if any) cookies are permitted to operate on one's system (Mann 1997, 48). The software filters cookies files, limits the kinds of information stored, and lists the companies that have stored cookies on a user's computer (Mosley-Matchett 1997). The success of PGPcookie.cutter at blocking cookies and the modifications of browsers to control cookies are indications of how detestable cookies are to many Web surfers (McMullen 1997).

The PGPcookie.cutter software program, which works with either Microsoft Internet

Explorer or Netscape Navigator, adds a tiny icon that looks like a gingerbread man to the title bar of the Web browser software. When the Web surfer clicks on this icon, a simple drop-down menu displays four options. After the Web surfer has initially configured the program to prevent Web servers from accessing the cookie file, the user can surf with peace of mind (Li-Ron 1997).

The software can be customized to limit or even prevent personal information from being transmitted via cookies files (Lee, Edmund 1996). PGPcookie.cutter does not prevent information from being written to the cookie file. Instead, the program lets the user control who can read the cookie information from the client PC's RAM or hard drive. The user simply types in the URLs of particular sites to whom he or she grants access — for example, personalized Web pages and service sites that deliver custom information based on individual tastes and past viewing habits (Li-Ron 1997).

This software program distinguishes between blocking and refusing cookies. If blocked, the cookie information is written to the hard drive on the client computer, so that the user can examine the information. Blocking, however, prevents the cookie information from being sent back to the depositing Web site. On the other hand, to refuse cookies means to prevent the initial acceptance of the information (Randall 1997b). The program also allows the user, rather than the webmaster, to control the expiration dates of cookies files. It tallies the number of cookies Web servers attempt to establish on one's hard drive (Eckhouse 1997). Overall, PGPcookie.cutter provides the end user more flexibility in accepting, declining, and managing cookies (Kalfatovic 1997).

PGPcookie.cutter, a $19.95 utility, prevents vendors or anyone with a Web server from viewing your browsing habits (Li-Ron 1997).

Robert Brooks' Cookie Taste Test

http://www.geocities.com/SoHo/4535/cookie.html

This site enables a Web surfer to browse a number of sites that use cookies for a variety of reasons (Pfaffenberger 1997, 79).

Bibliography

Abate, Marie A., James M. Shumway, Arthur I. Jacknowitz, and George Sinclair. 1989. Recording and evaluating end-user searches on a personal computer. *Bulletin of the Medical Library Association* 77(4): 381–383.

Abate, Tom. 1996. Someone could be watching.... *The San Francisco Examiner* (May 12): B1.

_____. 1997. These "cookies" don't taste so good. *Los Angeles Daily Journal* 110 (11) (January 16): S19.

Adams, Mignon. 1996. Assessment and academic libraries. *Library Issues* 16(5): 1–4.

Addressing the new hazards of the high technology workplace. 1991. *Harvard Law Review* 104(8): 1898–1916.

Adhikari, Richard. 1996. Tools track Web sites. *Informationweek* 606 (November 18): 82, 84.

Adler, Allan. 1993. Reintroduction of electronic monitoring legislation. *Telemarketing Magazine* 12(2): 16–17.

Agnvall, Elizabeth. 1997. eWorks keeps watch on Net for marketers. *Advertising Age's Business Marketing* 82(3): M1, M11.

Agre, Philip. 1997. Introduction. In *Technology and privacy: The new landscape*, edited by Philip Agre and Marc Rotenberg. Cambridge: MIT Press.

_____, and Marc Rotenberg, eds. 1997. *Technology and privacy: The new landscape.* Cambridge: MIT Press.

Agre, Philip E. 1994. Surveillance and capture: Two models of privacy. *The Information Society* 10: 101–127.

Aiello, John R. 1993. Computer-based work monitoring: Electronic surveillance and its effects. *Journal of Applied Social Psychology* 23(7): 499–507.

_____, A. S. Denisi, K. Kirkhoff, Y. Shao, M. A. Lund, and A. A. Chomiak. 1991. The impact of feedback and individual/group computer monitoring on work effort. Paper presented at the meeting of the American Psychological Society, Washington, D.C., June 1991.

_____, and Kathryn J. Kolb. 1995a. Electronic performance monitoring and social context: Impact on productivity and stress. *Journal of Applied Psychology* 80(3): 339–353.

_____, and Kathryn J. Kolb. 1995b. Electronic performance monitoring: A risk factor for workplace stress. In *Organizational risk factors for job stress*, edited by Steven L. Sauter and Lawrence R. Murphy. Washington, D.C.: American Psychological Association.

_____, and Y. Shao. 1993. Electronic performance monitoring and stress: The role of feedback and goal setting. In *Human computer interaction: proceedings of the Fifth International Conference on Human-Computer Interaction, (HCI International '93), Orlando, Florida, August 8–13, 1993,* edited by Gavriel Salvendy and Michael J. Smith. New York: Elsevier.

_____, and Carol M. Svec. 1993. Computer monitoring of work performance: Extending the social facilitation framework to electronic presence. *Journal of Applied Social Psychology* 23(7): 537–548.

Alexander, Steve. 1998. Web marketing gets personal. *InfoWorld* 20(2): 93–94.

Allen, Anita L. 1988. *Uneasy access: Privacy for women in a free society.* Totowa, N.J.: Rowman & Littlefield.

Allen, Jonathan P. 1994. Mutual control in the newly integrated work environments. *The Information Society* 10: 129–138.

Amend, Patricia. 1990. High-tech surveillance: The boss may be watching. *USA Today* (March 14): B11.

American Federation of Labor–Congress of Industrial Organizations. 1987. *Convention proceedings.*

Amick, B. C., and M. J. Smith. 1992. Stress, computer-based work monitoring and measurement systems: A conceptual overview. *Applied Ergonomics* 23(1): 6–16.

Anderson, Heidi. 1996. Eye on the Net: Monitoring Internet use within your company. *PC Today* 10(10): 96–98.

Anderson, Teresa. 1993. Is electronic monitoring getting the plug pulled? *Security Management* 37(10): 73–77.

_____. 1994. Privacy update laws on electronic monitoring of work areas. *Security Management* 38(4): 11–12.

Andrews, Whit. 1996. Sites dip into cookies to track user info. *Web Week* 2(7)(June 3): 20.

_____. 1997a. The cookie question: Blessing or curse. *Web Week* 3(14). Web document available at http://www.internet-world.com/print/wwback.html

_____. 1997b. Nifty tools, yes, but cookies don't appeal to all site builders. *Web Week* 3(14): 26–27.

_____. 1997c. Tracking users: alternative to cookies offered by vendors. *Web Week* 3(16). Web document available at http://www.internetworld.com/print/1997/06/02/news/ cookies.html

Angel, N. Faye. 1989. Evaluating employees by computer: Reasons to appraise employee performance electronically. *Personnel Administrator* 34(11): 67–72.

Angwin, Julia. 1996. I/PRO's web has begun to unravel. *San Francisco Chronicle* (December 11): D1–D2.

_____. 1997. Got cookies? *The San Francisco Chronicle* (March 11): C4.

Anonymous Cookie takes browser privacy further. 1997. *PC Week* 14(30): 26.

Anxiety over network privacy. 1995. *The Chronicle of Higher Education* 41(45): A17.

Association for Computing Machinery. 1993. ACM code of ethics and professional conduct. *Communications of the ACM* 36(2): 99–105.

Atkinson, Ross. 1996. Library functions, scholarly communication, and the foundation of the digital library: Laying claim to the control zone. *Library Quarterly* 66: 239–265.

Atlas, Michel C., Karen R. Little, and Michael O. Purcell. 1998. Flip charts at the OPAC: Using transaction log analysis to judge their effectiveness. *Reference & User Services Quarterly* 37(1): 63–69.

Attewell, Paul. 1987. Big Brother and the sweatshop: Computer surveillance in the automated office. *Sociological Theory* 5: 87–99.

_____, and James Rule. 1984. Computing and organizations: What we know and what we don't know. *Communications of the ACM* 27(12): 1184–1192.

Auer, Katherine. 1997. The home truth. *CIO* 10(20): 24.

Avery, Mike. 1998. Historian shelves valuable resource-usage statistics. *InfoWorld* 20(9): 74F.

Baarda, Carolyn W. 1994. Computerized performance monitoring: *Implications for employers, employees, and human resource management.* Kingston, Ont.: IRC Press, Industrial Relations Centre, Queen's University.

Babcock, Charles. 1997a. System brings surveillance into real time. *Computerworld* 31(8): 71, 73.

_____. 1997b. Sniffer tracks more than just Web hits. *Computerworld* 31(10): 63.

Backman, Dan, and Jeffrey Rubin. 1997. Web log analysis: Finding a recipe for success. *Network Computing* (8)11): 87.

Badre, Albert Nasib, and Paulo Alexandre Vieira Jacinto dos Santos. 1991a. *CHIME: A knowledge-based computer-human interaction monitoring engine.* Technical report no. GIT–GVU–91–06. Atlanta: Georgia Institute of Technology.

_____, and _____. 1991b. *A knowledge-based system for capturing human-computer interaction events: CHIME: Observations and issues.* Technical report no. GIT–GVU–91–21. Atlanta: Georgia Institute of Technology.

Bailey, James. 1996. *After thought: The computer challenge to human intelligence.* New York: Basic Books.

Baker, John, Janlori Goldman, Marc Rotenberg, Alan F. Westin, and Lance Hoffman. 1991. Personal information & privacy-I. In *The First Conference on Computers, Freedom and Privacy, held March 26–28, 1991, in Burlingame, California.* Los Alamitos, Calif.: IEEE Computer Society Press.

Balderston, Jim. 1996. Aquas dives in with Java-based Web tool. *InfoWorld* 18(28): 20.

Bangalore, Nirmala S. 1997. Re-engineering the OPAC using transaction logs. *Libri* 47: 67–76.

Barab, Sasha A., Bruce E. Bowdish, Michael F. Young, and Steven V. Owen. 1996. Understanding kiosk navigation: Using log files to capture hypermedia searches. *Instructional Science* 24(5): 377–395.

Barker, John C. 1992. Constitutional privacy rights in the private workplace under the federal and California constitutions. *Hastings Constitutional Law Quarterly* 19: 1107–1162.

Barmann, Timothy C. 1997. Rhode Island firm's NetTracker calculates Web sites' traffic. *Knight-Ridder/Tribune Business News* (April 10): 410B1091.

Barner, Robert. 1996. The new millennium workplace: Seven changes that will challenge managers — and workers. *Futurist* 30(2): 14–18.

Baron, Chris, and Bob Weil. 1996. Implementing a Web shopping cart: Online transactions in Perl. *Dr. Dobb's Journal* 21(9): 64–69.

Barr, Christopher. 1996. The truth about cookies. Web document located at http://www.cnet.com/Content/Voices/Barr/042996/, last visited on April 18, 1997.

Baudrillard, Jean. 1988. *Selected writings,* edited by Mark Poster. Stanford: Stanford University Press.

Bayers, Chip. 1998. The promise of one to one (a love story). *Wired* 6(5): 130–134, 184–187.

Bayne, Kim. 1996. Is your site a success? *American Demographics Marketing Tools* (March-April): 68–72.

Beatty, Sally Goll. 1996. Consumer privacy on the Internet goes public. *The Wall Street Journal* (February 12): B3.

Beckett, D. 1994. Combined log system. In *Proceedings of the Third International World Wide Web Conference, April 10–14, 1995, Darmstadt, Germany.* Web document available at http://igd.fhg.de/WWW/www95/Papers/46/comblog.html

Beckman, Mel. 1997. NetMinder 4.0. *MacWorld* 14(8): 78.

Beiser, Vince. 1997. The cyber snoops. *Maclean's* 110(25): 42.

Bellotti, Victoria. 1996. What you don't know can hurt you: Privacy in collaborative computing. In *People and computers XI: Proceedings of HCI '96,* edited by M. A. Sasse, R. J. Cunningham, and R. L. Winder. London: Springer.

_____, and Abigail Sellen. 1993. Design for privacy in ubiquitous computing environments. In *ECSCW '93: Proceedings of the Third European Conference on Computer-Supported Cooperative Work, 13–17 September 1993, Milan, Italy*, edited by Girogio De Michelis, Carla Simone, and Kjeld Schmidt, 77–93. Boston: Kluwer Academic Publishers.

Benedikt, Michael, ed. 1991. *Cyberspace: First steps*. Cambridge: MIT Press.

Beniger, James. 1991. *The control revolution: Technical and economic origins of the information society*. Boston: Harvard University Press.

Bennett, Colin, and Charles Raab. 1997. The adequacy of privacy: the European Union Data Protection Directive and the North American response. *The Information Society* 13(3): 245–263.

Bennett, Colin J. 1991. Computers, personal data and theories of technology: Comparative approaches to privacy protection in the 1990s. *Science, Technology and Human Values* 16(1): 51–69.

Bennett, Petra. 1994. *Private eye: Electronic monitoring systems within the workplace and their effect on employee stress*. Ottawa, Ont: National Library of Canada (Bibliothèque Nationale du Canada).

Bentham, Jeremy. 1838–1843. *The works of Jeremy Bentham*. 11 vols., edited by C. Bowring. Edinburgh: Tait.

Berg, Al. 1996. Cookies nibble at your disk drive. *LAN Times* (July 8): 85, 87.

Berger, Michael George. 1994. Information seeking in the online bibliographic system: An exploratory study. Ph.D. diss., University of California at Berkeley.

Bernstein, Nina. 1997. On frontier of cyberspace, data is money, and a threat. *The New York Times* (June 12): A1, A16, A17.

Berthon, Pierre, Leyland Pitt, and Gerard Prendergast. 1997. Visits, hits, caching and counting on the World Wide Web: Old wine in new bottles? *Internet Research: Electronic Networking Applications and Policy* 7(1): 5–8.

Berthon, Pierre, Leyland Pitt, and R. Watson. 1996. The World Wide Web as an advertising medium: Towards an understanding of conversion efficiency. *Journal of Advertising Research* 36(1): 43–54.

Bertot, John Carlo, Charles R. McClure, William E. Moen, and Jeffrey Rubin. 1997. Web usage statistics: Measurement issues and analytical techniques. *Government Information Quarterly* 14: 373–395.

Betts, Mitch. 1991. VDT monitoring under stress. *Computerworld* (January 21): 1, 14.

_____. 1995. Privacy fades for Web visitors. *Computerworld* 29(30): 162.

Bewayo, Edward. 1996. Electronic management: Its downside especially in small business. In *Social and ethical effects of the computer revolution*, edited by Joseph Migga Kizza. Jefferson, N.C.: McFarland.

Bickson, Tora K., and Constantijn W. A. Panis. 1997. Computers and connectivity: Current trends. In *Culture of the Internet*, edited by Sara Kiesler. Mahwah, N.J.: Lawrence Erlbaum Associates.

Bielski, Vince. 1997. Is eTRUST the answer? *The Village Voice* 42(13): 33.

Biocca, Frank. 1992. Communication within virtual reality: Creating a space for research. *Journal of Communication* 42(4): 5–22.

Blecic, Deborah D., Nirmala S. Bangalore, Josephine L. Dorsch, Cynthia L. Henderson, Melissa H. Koenig, and Ann C. Weller. 1998. Using transaction log analysis to improve OPAC retrieval results. *College & Research Libraries* 59(1): 39–50.

Bloom, Lisa A., Daniel Hursh, Wilfred D. Wienke, and Ronald K. Wolf. 1992. The effects of computer assisted data collection on student behavior. *Behavioral Assessment* 14(2): 173–190.

Bloomer, Lori L. 1997. Site management made easy. *Internet World* 8(9): 36.

Blow, Richard. 1998. Lock your windows. *Mother Jones* 23(1): 40–41.

Boehlefeld, Sharon Polancic. 1996. Doing the right thing: Ethical cyberspace research. *The Information Society* 12: 141–152.

Bok, S. 1983. *Secrets on the ethics of concealment and revelation*. New York: Random House.

Booth, William. 1987. Big Brother is counting your keystrokes. *Science* 238(October 2): 17.

Borck, James R. 1998. Aquas helps to provide I-commerce accountability. *InfoWorld* 20(10): 81.

Borg, Kim. 1997. On ramp closed ahead! *Computer Technology Review* 17(7): 1, 6+.

Borghuis, Marthyn G. M. 1997. User feedback from electronic subscriptions: The possibilities of logfile analysis. *Library Acquisitions: Practice and Theory* 21(3): 373–380.

Borgman, Christine L., Sandra G. Hirsh, and John Hiller. 1996. Rethinking online monitoring methods for information retrieval systems: From search product to search process. *Journal of the American Society for Information Science* 47(7): 568–583.

Bort, Julie. 1997. Web tracking tools chart Internet ROI. *Software Magazine* 17(8): 65–67.

Boss is watching. 1993. *Utne Reader* 57: 134–135.

Botan, Carl. 1996. Communication work and electronic surveillance: A model for predicting panoptic effects. *Communication Monographs* 63(4): 293–313.

_____, and M. H. McCreadie. 1989. Separating minds from hand? Information technology and policy in the work place. Paper presented at the annual conference of the American Society for Information Science, Washington, D.C., October 30–November 2.

Bott, Ed. 1997. C is for cookie. *PC/Computing* 10(7): 324.

Bradner, Scott. 1997. Death from a lack of privacy. *Network World* 14(36): 35.

Brandt, Andrew. 1999. Snoopware: For bosses who like to watch. *PC World* 17(7): 58.

Branscomb, Anne Wells. 1994. *Who owns information? From privacy to public access*. New York: Basic Books.

Braun, Hans-Werner, and Kimberly C. Claffy. 1994. Web traffic characterization: An assessment of the impact of caching documents from NCSA's web. In *Proceedings of the Second International World Wide Web Conference*, Chicago, Ill. Web document available at http://www.ncsa.uiuc.edu/SDG/IT94/Proceedings/Dday/claffy/main.html

Bray, Hiawatha. 1997. Relax and have a cookie. *The Boston Globe* (May 1): D1.

Bresnahan, Jennifer. 1997. Up close and personal. *CIO* 10(15): 62–74.

Brin, David. 1998. *The transparent society: Will technology force us to choose between privacy and freedom?* Reading, Mass.: Addison-Wesley.

Broder, John M. 1997a. F.T.C. opens hearings on computers' threat to the American's right to privacy. *The New York Times* (June 11): A20.

_____. 1997b. Making America safe for electronic commerce. *The New York Times* (June 22): D4.

Brodwin, David, Diarmuid O'Connell, and Marita Valdmanis. 1997. Mining the clickstream. *Upside* (Feb): 101–106.

Brook, James, and Iain A. Boal, eds. 1995. *Resisting the virtual life: The culture and politics of information*. San Francisco: City Lights.

Brown, Monique R. 1998. Tech issues: Revenge of the cookie monsters. *Black Enterprise* 28(10): 42–43.

Bruner, Rick E. 1997a. "Cookie" proposal could hinder online advertising. *Advertising Age* 68(13): 16.

_____. 1997b. Group offers solution to cacheing problem: Ad industry may get more accurate stats. *Advertising Age* 68(14): 34, 38.

_____. 1997c. Advertisers win one in debate over "cookies." *Advertising Age* 68(19): 62.

_____. 1997d. eTRUST pitches its seal of approval. *Advertising Age* 68(23): 36–38.

_____. 1997e. Personalizing content a priority for Net vendors. *Advertising Age* 68(45): S32, S33.

_____. 1997f. Companies back ad standard push. *Advertising Age* 68(14): 36.

_____. 1997g. MatchLogic service solves cache problem. *Advertising Age* 68(41): 34, 38.

Bruno [pseud.] 1996. The trouble with cookies. *NetGuide* 3(5): 24.

Bryant, Susan. 1995. Electronic surveillance in the workplace. *Canadian Journal of Communication* 20(4): 505–521.

Brzezinski, Zbigniew. 1971. Moving into a technetronic society. In *Information technology in a democracy*, edited by A. F. Westin. Cambridge: Harvard University Press.

Buchanan, Robert W., Jr., and Charles Lukaszewski. 1997. *Measuring the impact of your Web site*. New York: Wiley Computer Publishing.

Bucholtz, Chris. 1997. Whos, whats and wheres of the Web. *Telephony* 233(9): 38.

Burger, Katherine. 1995. Myths about monitoring. *Insurance & Technology* 20(5): 34–40.

Busch, David D. 1997. Count your blessings. *Internet World* 8(6): 74–83.

Bushey, Trudie. 1996. FTC & Internet privacy. *Credit World* 85(1): 7.

Byczkowski, John. 1996. "Cookies" track you on the Web. *The Cincinnati Enquirer* (March 3). Web document available at http://www.detnews.com/cyberia/daily/0303cookies.html

Bylinsky, Gene. 1991. How companies spy on employees. *Fortune* 124(11): 131–140.

Carayon, Pascale. 1993. Effect of electronic performance monitoring on job design and worker stress: Review of the literature and conceptual model. *Human Factors* 35(3): 385–395.

_____, Lim Soo-Yee, Yang Chien-Lin, Michael J. Smith, Katherine J. Sanders, and David Legrande. 1993. Recent research findings on stress and electronic performance monitoring. In *Advances in human factors/ergonomics* 19A: 1017–1022.

Carlberg, Conrad. 1996. "Cookies" gives WWW users "a trail of crumbs." *Denver Business Journal* 48(11): 2B.

Carmichael, Matt. 1996a. Puzzle fans play for online prizes. *Advertising Age* 67(33): 18.

_____. 1996b. Frames? Cookies? Good grief! *Advertising Age's Business Marketing* 81(7): M11.

_____. 1996c. Are cookies really monsters? *Advertising Age* 67(47): 50.

Carter, David S. 1995. Web server transaction logs. Web document located at http://www.sils.umich.edu/~superman/

Cate, Fred H. 1997. *Privacy in the information age*. Washington, D.C.: Brookings.

Catledge, Lara D., and James E. Pitkow. 1995. Characterizing browsing strategies in the World Wide Web. *Computer Networks and ISDN Systems* 27: 1065–1073.

Cavazos, Edward A., and Gavino Morin. 1996. A new legal paradigm from cyberspace: The effect of the information age on the law. *Technology in Society* 18(3): 357–371.

Cavoukian, Ann, and Don Tapscott. 1995. *Who knows: Safeguarding your privacy in a networked world*. New York: Random House.

Center for Democracy and Technology. 1996a. Web site at http://www.cdt.org/privacy/062096_Markey.html, last visited on April 18, 1997.

_____. 1996b. CDT press release regarding Rep. Markey legislation. Web site at http://www.cdt.org/privacy/062096_Markey_pr.html, last visited on April 18, 1997.

Chalykoff, John, and Thomas A. Kochan. 1989. Computer-aided monitoring: Its influence on employee job satisfaction and turnover. *Personnel Psychology* 42: 807–834.

Chandrasekaran, Rajiv. 1997a. It all ads up to who you know. *The Washington Post* (June 9): F15.

_____. 1997b. Database firms set privacy pact. *The Washington Post* (June 10): A1, A23.

Chapman, Fern Schumer. 1997. Web of deceit. *PC World* 15(8): 145–152.

Chen, Chaomei. 1996. Behavioural patterns of collaborative writing with Hypertext: A state transition approach. In *People and computers XI: Proceedings of HCI '96*, edited by M. A. Sasse, R. J. Cunningham, and R. L. Winder. London: Springer.

Chen, Ming-Syan, Jong Soo Park, and P. S. Yu. 1996. Data mining for path traversal patterns in a web environment. In *Proceedings of the 16th International Conference on Distributed Computing Systems, Hong Kong, May 27–30, 1996*, 385–392. Los Alamitos, Calif.: IEEE Computer Society Press.

Chen, Paul. 1997. Hit-or-miss measurement. *American Demographics. Tools supplement.* (March): 22–25.

Chen, Thomas M., Steve S. Liu, David Want, Vijay K. Samalam, Michael J. Procanik, and Dinyar Kavouspour. 1996. Monitoring and control of ATM networks using special cells. *IEEE Network* 10(5): 28–38.

Chisnell, Cheryl, Kathel Dunn, and Dean F. Sittig. 1994. A quantitative method for identifying specific educational needs among CD Plus Medline searchers: A pilot study. In *Transforming information, changing health care: Eighteenth Annual Symposium on Computer Applications in Medical Care: A conference of the American Medical Informatics Association, November 5–9, 1994, Washington, D.C.*, edited by Judy G. Ozbolt. Philadelphia: Hanley & Belfus.

Chlapowski, Francis S. 1991. The constitutional protection of informational privacy. *Boston University Law Review* 71: 133–160.

Chomiak, A. A., K. J. Kolb, and J. R. Aiello. 1993. Effect of computer monitoring and distraction on task performance. Paper presented at the meeting of the Eastern Psychological Association, Washington, D.C., April 1993.

Christenson, Eric Scott. 1988. A computer monitoring methodology. Master's thesis, Lehigh University.

Clark, Drew. 1996. Software for tailoring Web sales pitch to customers. *American Banker* 161(151): 18.

Clarke, Roger A. 1994. The digital persona and its application to data surveillance. *Information Society* 10(2): 77–92.

Claypoole, Ted. 1996. Privacy can be compromised through newer technology. *Business First–Columbus* 13(10): 15.

Cleland, Kim. 1997. New player joins fray of Web ad targeters. *Advertising Age* 68(8): 76.

Clement, Andrew. 1992. Electronic workplace surveillance: Sweatshops and fishbowls. *Canadian Journal of Information Science* 17(4): 15–45.

_____, and Patricia McDermott. 1991. Electronic monitoring: Worker reaction and design alternatives. In *Information system, work and organization design: Proceedings of the IFIP TC9/WG9.1 Working Conference on Information System, Work and Organization Design, Berlin, July 10–13, 1989*, 187–199, edited by Peter Van den Besselaar, Andrew Clement, and Pertti Jarvinen. Amsterdam: North-Holland.

Coates, James. 1997. Concern grows over computer data crumbs. *Chicago Tribune* (June 2): D1,D4.

Cockburn, A., and S. Jones. 1996. Which way now? Analysing and easing inadequacies in Web navigation. *International Journal of Human Computer Studies* 45(1): 105–129.

Cohen, Andy. 1995. The Nielsen of cyberspace? *Sales & Marketing Management* 147(9): 116.

Cohen, Emily. 1998. Watching your surfers. *PC Magazine* 17(3): 42.

Cohen, Jodi B. 1996a. Auditing the Web. *Editor & Publisher* 129(24): 88–89.

_____. 1996b. Measuring the Web audience. *Editor & Publisher* 129(26): 37.

_____. 1997a. Web audits: A complex art. *Editor & Publisher* 130(6): 241–261.

_____. 1997b. Too many hands in the cookie jar? *American Advertising* 13(2): 22.

Collora, Salvatore. 1997. Watching every move they make. *PC Week* 14(23): 59.

Comaford, Christine. 1996. Toward mutual electronic r-e-s-p-e-c-t. *PC Week* (July 15): 50.

Conaghan, Jim. 1995. Tracking Audiences on the Web: The Conaghan Report. (November 27, 1995). Web site located at http://www.naa.org/webcount.html

Cookies might hurt Web security. 1996. *Info World Canada* 21(12): 21.

Cooley, R., B. Mobasher, and J. Srivastava. 1997. Grouping Web page references into transactions for mining World Wide Web browsing patterns. In *Proceedings of the IEEE Knowledge and Data Engineering Exchange Workshop*, edited by X. Wu, J. Tsai, N. Pissinous, and K. Makki. Los Alamitos, Calif.: IEEE Computer Society Press.

Coopee, Todd. 1997. Net Access Manager monitors on-line use. *Info World Canada* 22(7): 28.

Cooper, Lane F. 1996a. More than just hits. *Informationweek* 608: 63–72.

_____. 1996b. The privacy issue is dormant — for now. *Informationweek* 608: 68.

Cooper, Michael D. 1998. Design considerations in instrumenting and monitoring Web-based information retrieval systems. *Journal of the American Society for Information Science* 49: 903–919.

Cooperstock, Jeremy R., Sindey S. Fels, William Buxton, and Kenneth C. Smith. 1997. Reactive environments. *Communications of the ACM* 40(9): 65–73.

Copeland, Ron. 1997. The individual's right to privacy vs. individualized offerings. *Communications Week* 647: 40.

Counting on the Web. 1995. *American Demographics (Marketing tools supplement)* (July): 27–28.

Cousineau, Laura, John Little, Derek Lane, and Jim Coble. 1997. Where our patrons go in cyberspace: Clickstream analysis in an academic research library. In *Digital collections: Implications for users, funders, developers and maintainers: Proceedings of the 60th ASIS annual meeting, Washington, D.C., November 1–6, 1997*, edited by Candy Schwartz and Mark Rorvig. Medford, N.J.: Information Today.

Crovella, Mark, and Azer Bestavros. 1996. Self-similarity in World Wide Web traffic: Evidence and causes. *Performance Evaluation Review* 24(1): 160–169.

Cummings, Joanne. 1997. Tools to tame by. *Network World* 14(7): S20.

Curbs on electronic monitoring of workers debated before Massachusetts labor panel. 1989. *Daily Labor Report* 49(March 15): A2–A4.

Curtis, Christine. 1998. It's not what you know, it's how you use what you know. *InternetWeek* (738): 51.

Curtis, Pavel. 1997. Mudding: Social phenomena in text-based virtual realities. In *Culture of the Internet*, edited by Sara Kiesler. Mahwah, N.J.: Lawrence Erlbaum Associates.

CYBERSitter provides IQS Limited in Japan its Internet filtering solution. 1997. *Business Wire* (April 22).

Dalton, Gregory. 1997. OPS: Answer to cookies? *Informationweek* 652: 62.

_____, and Sean Gallagher. 1999. Online data's fine line. *Informationweek* (727): 18–20.

Danann, Sharon. 1990. *Stories of mistrust and manipulation: The electronic monitoring of the American workforce*. Cleveland, Ohio: 9 to 5: Working Women Education Fund.

Davey, Tom. 1997. Monitor for the Net. *Informationweek* 617: 73–74.

Davies, Simon. 1992. *Big Brother: Australia's growing web of surveillance*. East Roseville, New South Wales: Simon & Schuster.

_____. 1996. *Big Brother: Britain's web of surveillance and the new technological order*. London: Pan.

Davis, Beth. 1996. Web services help measure site success. *Communications Week* 631: 1, 93.

Davis, Jessica. 1996. First Floor tools monitor Web site changes. *InfoWorld* 18(February 19): 51.

Dearnley, P. A., and D. J. Smith. 1995. On the use of dynamic feedback in knowledge base system design. *Information and Software Technology* 37: 659–664.

Debord, Guy. 1990 [1988]. *Comments on the society of the spectacle*. Translated by Malcom Imrie. New York: Verso.

DeCew, Judith Wagner. 1997. *In pursuit of privacy: Law, ethics, and the rise of technology*. Ithaca, N.Y.: Cornell University Press.

Demery, Paul. 1997. Keeping a reliable score of "hits." *The Practical Accountant* 30(3): 16.

Dern, Daniel P. 1997. Footprints and fingerprints in cyberspace: The trail you leave behind. *Online* 21(4): 44–48.

Desmarais, Norman. 1998. Innovations affecting us: The cookie monster: Personal privacy and the Internet. *Against the Grain* 9(6): 87–89.

DeTienne, Kristen Bell. 1993. Big Brother or friendly coach? Computer monitoring in the 21st century. *The Futurist* 27(5): 33–37.

_____. 1994. Big Brother is watching: Computer monitoring and communication. *IEEE Transactions on Professional Communication* 37(1): 5–10.

_____, and Nelson T. Abbott. 1993. Developing an employee-centered electronic monitoring system. *Journal of Systems and Management* 44(8): 12–16.

_____, and G. Stoney Alder. 1995. The Privacy for Consumers and Workers Act: Panacea or problem? *Managerial Law* 37(2/3): 1–32.

_____, and Richard D. Flint. 1996. The boss's eyes and ears: A case study of electronic employee monitoring and the Privacy for Consumers and Workers Act. *The Labor Lawyer* 12(1): 93–115.

Diffie, Whitfield, and Susan Landau. 1998. *Privacy on the line: The politics of wiretapping and encryption.* Cambridge: MIT Press.

DiTecco, D., and M. Andre. 1987. *Operator stress survey: Report to the Health and Safety Subcommittee on machine packing and remote electronic monitoring.* Montreal: Management Sciences Consulting, Bell Canada.

Doan, Amy. 1997. Web monitors, servers will debut at show. *InfoWorld* 19(10): 19.

Doherty, Brian. 1997. Tangled Web pages. *Reason* 19(6): 21.

Dorfman, Erik. 1996. How *not* to use HTTP log files. Web document located at http://selsvr.stx.com/~eryq/using-http-logs

Dorney, Maureen S. 1997. Privacy and the Internet. *Comm/Ent: Hastings Communications and Entertainment Law Journal* 19(3): 635–660.

DoubleClick. 1996. Web site located at http://www.doubleclick.net

Drabenstott, Karen M., and Marjorie S. Weller. 1996. Handling spelling errors in online catalog searches. *Library Resources & Technical Services* 40(2): 113–132.

Dreze, Xavier, and Fred Zufryden. 1997. Testing Web site design and promotional content. *Journal of Advertising Research* 37(2): 77–91.

Drucker, Mindy. 1990. On track with Eye-Trac research. *Target Marketing* 13(9): 57–58.

Dryden, Patrick. 1996a. Monitors emerge to diagnose backbones. *Computerworld* 30(4): 48.

_____. 1996b. Users go on bandwidth patrol. *Computerworld* 30(March 18): 61.

Dumais, Susan, Robert Kraut, and Susan Koch. 1988. Computers' impact on productivity and work life. *SIGOIS Bulletin* 9: 88–95.

Duncan, George T. 1996. Is my research ethical? *Communications of the ACM* 39(12): 6768.

Dunlop, Amy. 1997. Yahoo! wins in new ratings. *Internet World* 8(12): 24.

_____. 1998. Dealmakers. *Internet World* 9(2): 24.

Dunn, Kathel, Cheryl Chisnell, Suzanne Szak, and Dean F. Sittig. 1994. A quantitative method for measuring library user journal needs: A pilot study using CD Plus MEDLINE usage statistics. In *Transforming information, changing health care: Eighteenth annual Symposium on Computer Applications in Medical Care: A conference of the American Medical Informatics Association, November 5–9, 1994, Washington, D.C.*, edited by Judy G. Ozbolt. Philadelphia: Hanley & Belfus.

Dutcher, William. 1996. You can't get there from here. *PC Week* 13(17): N5.

Duvall-Early, K., and J. O. Benedict. 1992. The relationships between privacy and different components of job satisfaction. *Environment and Behavior* 24: 670–679.

Dyrli, Odvard Egli. 1997. Online privacy and the cookies controversy. *Technology & Learning* 17(6): 20.

Dyson, Esther. 1997a. Protect Internet privacy-privately. *The Wall Street Journal* (June 17): A18.

_____. 1997b. *Release 2.0: A design for living in the digital age.* New York: Broadway Books.

e.g. SOFTWARE WEBTRENDS 3.5 — Don't guess who's coming to dinner. Let this traffic analyzer show you exactly who visits your Web site. 1997. *LAN Times* 14(14): 46.

Earley, P. Christopher. 1988. Computer-generated performance feedback in the magazine-subscription industry. *Organizational Behavior and Human Decision Processes* 41(1): 50–64.

Easy market research from your Web site. 1997. *Datamation* 43(2): 72.

Eckhouse, John. 1997. Leaving tracks on the net. *HomePC* 4(4): 91–97.

Ehrlich, Scott C. 1993. *Electronic technology in the workplace.* Washington, D.C.: Employment Policy Foundation.

Eisenberg, Anne. 1996. Privacy and data collection on the Net. *Scientific American* 274(3): 120.

Eisenman, Elaine Judith Pivnick. 1986. Perceptions of supervisory behaviors under conditions of electronic monitoring. Ph.D. diss., New York University.

Eisman, Regina. 1991. Big Brother lives. *Incentive* 165(6): 21–27, 103.

Electronic Frontier Foundation. 1997. Legislation update on privacy. Web document located at http://www.eff.org/pub/Privacy/privacy_legislation.html, last visited on April 18, 1997.

Electronic Privacy Information Center. 1997. Surfer beware: Personal privacy and the Internet. Web document at http://www.epic.org, last visited on June 10, 1997.

Elliott, Elaine X. 1996. Measuring the Web's greatest hits: Independent audit software monitors site traffic for honest marketing. *Computer Shopper* 16(5): 514–515.

Eng, Paul M. 1997. Tracking the troops in cyberspace. *Business Week* 3515 (February 24): 122E.

Englander, Todd. 1987. How to use computer monitoring. *Incentive Marketing* 161(5): 88–89.

Enright, Gary. 1997. Workplace 'net abuse concerns arise. *Info World Canada* 22(1): 1, 10.

Ermann, M. David, Mary B. Williams, and Michele S. Shauf, eds. 1997. *Computers, ethics, and society.* 2d ed. New York: Oxford University Press.

Etra, Ian, and Paul Silverman. 1997. Get to know your Web site's visitors: WebTrends 2.1. *Windows Magazine* 8(3): 153.

Evans, James. 1998. City won't share cookies. *Internet World* 9(2): 22.

EveryWare. 1996. EveryWare announces Bolero Web site activity tracking tool. *Information Today* 13(5): 70.

Farnet. 1997. FTC holds hearing on privacy rights versus commercial use of information in cyberspace. *Farnet's Washington Update* (distributed as an e-mail message) (June 16).

Fenner, Deborah B., F. Javier Lerch, and Carol T. Kulik. 1993. The impact of computerized performance monitoring and prior performance knowledge on performance evaluation. *Journal of Applied Social Psychology* 23(7): 573–601.

Ferrill, Paul. 1996. Crystal Reports adds HTML output capability — Add-on tool creates various browser-formatted views at the click of a button. *InfoWorld* 18(22): IW3.

Fink, J., A. Kobsa, and J. Schreck. 1997. Personalized hypermedia information provision through adaptive and adaptable system features: User modelling, privacy and security issues. In *Intelligence in services and networks: Technology for cooperative competition. Fourth International Conference on Intelligence in Services and Networks, IS&N '97. Proceedings.* Berlin: Springer-Verlag.

Finnie, Scot. 1997. Trace your steps on the Web. *PC Computing* 10(2): 107.

Fitzgerald, Mark. 1996. Auditing the Web. *Editor & Publisher* 129(11): 26–27.

Fitzloff, Emily. 1997. Sequel to announce Net Access Manager 3.0. *InfoWorld* 19(45): 19.

Flaherty, David H. 1989. *Protecting privacy in surveillance societies: The Federal Republic of Germany, Sweden, France, Canada, and the United States.* Chapel Hill: University of North Carolina Press.

_____, Judith Krug, Gary Marx, Karen Nussbaum, and Susan Nycum. 1991. Computer-based surveillance of individuals. In *The First Conference on Computers, Freedom and Privacy, held March 26–28, 1991, in Burlingame, California.* Los Alamitos, Calif.: IEEE Computer Society Press.

Flaherty, Patricia. 1993. Transaction logging systems: A descriptive summary. *Library Hi Tech* 11(2): 67–78.

Fleishman, Glenn. 1996. Web log analysis: Who's doing what, when? *Web Developer* 2(2): 19–22.

Fleming, Heather. 1996. Consortium formed for 'Net privacy. *Broadcasting & Cable* 126(42): 87.

Flood, Barbara. 1997. The emotionality of privacy. *American Society for Information Science Bulletin* 23(3): 7–8.

Flores, Michele Matassa. 1996. Marketwave tracks Internet traffic. *The Seattle Times* (July 2): E1.

Fogel, Chuck. 1987. The electronic boss: How management is using the latest technology to control employees in the workplace. *Solidarity* 30(5): 11–14.

Foley, John. 1996. Data dilemma. *Informationweek* 583: 14–16.

Foster, Cormac. 1997. Slackers, beware! C|Net. Web document located at http://www.cnet.com/Content/Reviews/JustIn/Items/0,118,258,00.html, last visited on March 9, 1998.

Foster, Derek. 1997. Community and identity in the electronic village. In *Internet culture*, edited by David Porter. New York: Routledge.

Foster, Ed. 1996. Can mixing "cookies" with online marketing be a recipe for heartburn? *InfoWorld* 18(30): 54.

Foucault, Michel. 1979 [1977]. Discipline and punish: The birth of the prison. New York: Pantheon Books, 1977. Reprint, New York: Random House.

_____. 1980. *Power/knowledge: Selected interviews and other writings, 1972–1977.* New York: Pantheon Books.

Franz, Benjamin. 1996. FTPWebLog 1.0.1. Web document located at http://www.netimages.com

Frentzen, Jeff. 1995a. Log analyzers chart World Wide Web. *PC Week* 12(21): 14.

_____. 1995b. Net devices attract and track users. *PC Week* 12(38): 75.

_____. 1997. Are those "persistent cookies" good or evil? *PC Week* 14 (26): 177.

Freund, Jesse. 1998. Cookie crumbler. *Wired* 6(2): 108.

Friesen, Norman. 1997. Monitoring the Use of WWW-Pages. Web document located at http://www.ualberta.ca/~nfriesen/597/contents.html

Frisse, Mark E. 1996. What is the Internet learning about you while you are learning about the Internet? *Academic Medicine* 71(10): 1064–1067.

Fritz, Kentner V., and Lynn B. Levy. 1972. Introduction to computer managed instruction and the automated instructional management system. ERIC ED 069 757.

Fritz, Norma R. 1988. Big electronic brother is watching. *Personnel* 65(January): 4.

Frook, John. 1995a. New tracking tool. *Interactive Age* 2(13): 1+.

_____. 1995b. Virtual Office endorses in-house tracking. *Interactive Age* 2(22): 18+.

_____. 1995c. Tracking goes mainstream. *Communications Week* 575(September 18): 43–44.

_____. 1995d. Web-hit audit system called into question. *Communications Week* 589(December 18): 1+.

_____. 1996a. Net tracking on the PC. *Communications Week* 603(April 1): 1+.

_____. 1996b. NetCount readies AdCount service. *Communications Week* 612(May 27): 1+.

_____. 1996c. 'Net sites to get more personal. *Communications Week* 628(September 16): 63+.

Frook, John Evan, and David Joachim. 1997. Microsoft sweetens Web cookies. *Communications Week* 668(June 16): 1+.

Fruth, Pamela. 1997. Accrue Software Accrue Insight. *Network Computing* 8(2): 124.

Frye, Emily. 1997. Paying with personal information — yours. *Computerworld* 31(51): 29.

Fuchs, Lynn S., Douglas Fuchs, and Carol L. Hamlett. 1993. Technological advances linking the assessment of students' academic proficiency to instructional planning. *Journal of Special Education Technology* 12(1): 49–62.

Fuller, Rodney, and Johannes J. de Graaff. 1996. Measuring user motivation from server log files. Web document located at http://www.acm.org: 82/~fuller/www5/Overview.html

Gage, Deborah. 1997. Cruising through the Web. *Computer Reseller News* 737(May 26): 57, 62.

Galenskas, Stephanie Mariel. 1997. ARIA Recorder Reporter. *Direct Marketing* 60(2): 28–29.

Galkin, William S. 1996. Privacy issues in the digital age. *Maryland Bar Journal* 29(5): 46–51.

Gallant, John. 1997. The push and pull of privacy on the Web. *Network World* 14(16): 38.

Gallatin, Lisa. 1989. *Electronic monitoring in the workplace: Supervision or surveillance?* Boston: Center for New Office Technology.

Gandy, Oscar H., Jr. 1989. The surveillance society: Information technology and bureaucratic social control. *Journal of Communication* 39(3): 61–76.

_____. 1993. *The Panoptic sort: A political economy of personal information.* Boulder: Westview.

_____. 1995. It's discrimination, stupid! In *Resisting the virtual life: The culture and politics of information,* edited by James Brook and Iain A. Boal. San Francisco: City Lights.

Garber, Joseph R. 1997. The right to goof off. *Forbes* 160(9): 297.

Garber, Lee. 1997. eTRUST to launch Web security effort. *Computer* 30(3): 17.

Garfinkel, Simson. 1996. The persistence of cookies. Web document located at http://www.hotwired.com/packet/packet/garfinkel/96/50/index2a.html, last visited on July 15, 1997.

Garson, Barbara. 1988. *The electronic sweatshop: How computers are transforming the office of the future into the factory of the past.* New York: Simon & Schuster.

Garza, Victor. 1998. XNI nabs LAN/WAN usage hogs. *InfoWorld* 20(24): 76.

Gattiker, Urs E., Helen Kelley, Linda Janz, and Martina Schollmeyer. 1996. The Internet and privacy: Do you know who's watching? *Business Quarterly* 60(4): 79–84.

Gatusso, Greg. 1995. Web site "hits" viewed vague as measurement. *Direct Marketing* 58(4): 8–9.

Gaudet, Dean. 1997. Cookies, dialogues, and tracking. Web document located at http://www.arctic.org/~dgaudet/cookies, last visited on July 30, 1997.

Gellman, Robert. 1996. Action for privacy can force cookies to crumble. *Government Computer News* 15(11): 35.

_____. 1997. Battle for privacy has right fight, wrong focus. *Government Computer News* 16(21): 32.

George, Joey F. 1993. The multi-dimensionality of computer-based monitoring in the workplace. In *Proceedings of the 26th annual Hawaii International Conference on System Sciences* [January 5–8], vol. 3, 609–619. Los Alamitos, Calif.: IEEE Computer Society Press.

_____. 1996. Computer-based monitoring: Common perception and empirical results. *MIS Quarterly* 20(4): 459–480.

Gerding, David. 1997. Keep tabs on your Web traffic. *PC/Computing* 10(6): 168.

Gibbons, Andrew S., et al. 1993. The future of computer-managed instruction (CMI). *Educational Technology* 33(5): 7–11.

Gibbs, Mark. 1995. Electronic monitoring breeds employee mistrust. *Network World* 12(45): 62.

_____. 1996a. Fighting crime with IT: How safe do you want to be? *Network World* 13(April 1): 126.

_____. 1996b. The price of freedom (or: More on "How safe do you want to be?"). *Network World* 13(19): 66.

_____. 1996c. Web server viewmasters. *Network World* 13(49): 40–46.

_____. 1997. Cookies: Feeding session information from Web servers to clients, and back. *Network World* 14(3): S9–S10.

Gibbs, William J., and Virginia Baldwin. 1996. Evaluating users' interactions with WWW documents. Paper presented at the Centennial Conference of the Illinois Library Association, Chicago, Ill., 14–18 May 1996.

Gimien. Mark. 1995. One person's hit is another's glance. *Mediaweek* 5(21): 32.

Ginchereau, William. 1997. Cyber Patrol Corporate blocks inappropriate sites. *InfoWorld* 19(35): 100.

Giussani, Bruno. 1997. Proposed German statute would regulate content. *The New York Times CyberTimes* (January 11). Web document located at http://search/nytimes.com/web/docsroot/library/cyber/euro/011197euro.html

Glass, Brett. 1996. "Cookies" won't spoil your diet but might hurt Web security. *InfoWorld* 18(29): 54.

Gleick, James. 1996. Big brother is us: our privacy is disappearing, but not by force. We're selling it, even giving it away. *The New York Times Magazine* (September 29): 130–132.

Global privacy project focuses on credit card industry. 1996. *Credit World* 85: 30–31.

Godwin, Mike, and T. Smith, eds. 1998. *Cyber rights: Privacy and free speech in the digital age*. New York: Times Books.

Goldberg, Beverly. 1998. Internet watchdogs blast overreach of SmartFilter. *American Libraries* 30(5): 18–19.

Goldhaber, Michael H. 1997. Attention shoppers! *Wired* 5(12): 182–190.

Goldman, Janlori. 1991. Where the public draws the line. *Computerworld* (April 15): 25.

Gomes, Lee. 1996. Web "cookies" may be spying on you. *San Jose Mercury News* (February 13): 1C.

Good, Irving John. 1965. Speculations concerning the first ultraintelligent machine. In *Advances in computers*, vol. 6, edited by Franz L. Alt and Morris Rubinoff, 31–88. New York: Academic Press.

Gorman, John. 1998. Monitoring employee Internet usage. *Business Ethics: A European Review* 7(1): 21–24.

Graham, Bill. 1993. Privacy in the spotlight, again. CFO: *The Magazine for Senior Financial Executives* 9(5): 14.

Graham-Cumming, John. 1996. They spy while you surf. Go2: Guardian OnLine Internet. Web document located at http://go2.guardian.com/, last visited on July 1, 1996.

Grant, Rebecca A. 1989. Computerized performance monitoring and control systems impact on Canadian service sector workers. Ph.D. diss., University of Western Ontario.

_____. 1990. *Silicon supervisors: Computerized monitoring in the service sector*. Washington, D.C.: International Center for Information Technologies.

_____. 1991. Issues in conducting a field study of computerized work monitoring. *Computer Personnel* 13(2): 36–45.

_____. 1992. Work monitored electronically. *HR Magazine* 37(5): 81–86.

_____, and Chris A. Higgins. 1989. Monitoring service workers via computer: The effect on employees, productivity and service. *National Productivity Review* 8(2): 101–112.

_____, and Christopher A. Higgins. 1991a. The impact of computerized performance monitoring on service work: Testing a causal model. *Information Systems Research* 2: 116–142.

_____, and _____. 1991b. Computerized performance monitors: factors affecting acceptance. *IEEE Transactions on Engineering Management* 38(4): 306–315.

_____, and _____. 1996. Computerized performance monitors as multidimensional systems: Derivation and application. *ACM Transactions on Information Systems* 14(2): 212–235.

_____, and Richard H. Irving. 1988. Computerized performance monitors: Are they costing you customers? *Sloan Management Review* 29(3): 39–45.

Greenbaum, M. L., A. F. Westin, K. Nussbaum, and J. S. Petrie. 1988. Employee privacy, monitoring, and new technology. In *Arbitration 1988: Emerging issues for the 1990s, proceedings of the 41st annual meeting of the National Academy of Arbitrators*, edited by Gladys W. Gruenberg, pp. 63–96. Washington, D.C.: Bureau of National Affairs.

Greenberg, Saul. 1993. *The computer user as toolsmith: The use, reuse, and organization of computer-based tools*. New York: Cambridge University Press.

Greenemeier, Larry. 1998. Low tide for corporate Web surfing. *Midrange Systems* 11(18): 40.

Griffith, Terri L. 1993a. Monitoring and performance: A comparison of computer and supervisor monitoring. *Journal of Applied Social Psychology* 23(7): 549–572.

_____. 1993b. Teaching big brother to be a team player: Computer monitoring and quality. *Academy of Management Executive* 7(1): 73–80.

Gross, Hyman. 1971. Privacy and autonomy. In *Privacy*, edited by J. Roland Pennock and John W. Chapman. New York: Atherton Press.

Guglielmo, Connie. 1996. I/PRO vs. PC-Meter. *PC Week* 13(40): A5.

Gussow, Dave. 1997. Computer detective programs keep track of workers' work. *The St. Petersburg Times* (September 20).

Guzdial, Mark, Paulo Santos, Albert N. Badre, Scott Hudson, and Mark Gray. 1994. Analyzing and visualizing log files: A computational science of usability. Atlanta: Graphic, Visualization & Usability Center, Georgia Institute of Technology.

_____, Chris Walton, Michael Konemann, and Elliot Soloway. 1993. Characterizing process change using log file data. Atlanta: Graphic, Visualization & Usability Center, Georgia Institute of Technology.

Hagel, John, III. 1997. *Net Gain: Expanding markets through virtual communities.* Boston: Harvard Business School Press.

_____, and Arthur G. Armstrong. 1997. Net gain: Expanding markets through virtual communities. *McKinsey Quarterly* 1: 140–153.

_____, and Jeffrey F. Rayport. 1997a. The coming battle for customer information. *Harvard Business Review* 75(1): 53–55+.

_____, and _____. 1997b. Selling your privacy. *Futurist* 31(6): 15.

_____, and A. M. Sacconaghi, Jr. 1996. Who will benefit from virtual information? *McKinsey Quarterly* 3: 22–37.

Halpern, Sue. 1992. Big boss is watching you. *Details* (May): 18–23.

Hammontree, Monty L., Jeffrey J. Hendrickson, and Billy W. Hensley. 1992. Integrated data capture and analysis tools for research and testing on graphical user interface. In *CHI '92: Striking a balance: ACM Conference on Human Factors in Computing Systems, Monterey, California, May 3–7, 1992,* edited by Penny Bauersfeld, John Bennett, and Gene Lynch.

Hancock, Wayland. 1997. Cookies on your hard drive. *American Agent & Broker* 69(6): 8–10.

Hannaham, James. 1996. Microchips ahoy! *The Village Voice* 41(34): 20.

Harmon, Amy. 1997. On the office PC, bosses opt for all work, and no play. *The New York Times* (September 22): A1,C11.

_____. 1998. Technology to let engineers filter the Web and judge content. *The New York Times* (January 19): C1, C4.

Harris, Julian, and Hermann Maurer. 1994. HyperCard Monitor System. ERIC ED 388 251.

Hausman, Carl. 1994. Information age ethics: Privacy ground rules for navigating in cyberspace. *Journal of Mass Media Ethics* 9(3): 135–144. Reprinted in *Computers, ethics, and society,* 2nd edition, edited by M. David Ermann, Mary B. Williams, and Michele S. Shauf. New York: Oxford University Press, 1997.

Hawk, Stephen R. 1994. The effects of computerized performance monitoring: An ethical perspective. *Journal of Business Ethics* 13(12): 949–957.

Hayden Development Team. 1997. *Web designer's guide to cookies.* Indianapolis: Hayden Books.

Hayes, Frank. 1996. JavaScript can trace user tracks. *Computerworld* 30(12): 1, 113.

Hayes, Garrett Michael. 1998. Eye on 'Net users. *Network World* 15(21): I10–I11.

Healy, Dave. 1997. Cyberspace and place: The Internet as middle landscape on the electronic frontier. In *Internet Culture,* edited by David Porter. New York: Routledge.

Healy, Tim, and Peter Marshall. 1987. Workplace surveillance. *The Facts* 9(1): 9–12.

Heid, Jim. 1998. Log-analysis software. *Macworld* 15(7): 34.

Heidegger, Martin. 1977 [1954]. *The question concerning technology and other essays.* Translated by William Lovitt. New York: Harper Colophon Books.

Heller, Martin. 1996. Getting to know you. *Windows Magazine* 7(6): 226–228.

Hendricks, Evan. 1997. American [sic] Online snoops into subscriber's incomes, children. *Privacy Times* (May 30): 1–3.

Henkin, Louis. 1974. Privacy and autonomy. *Columbia Law Review* 74: 1410–1433.

Henriques, Vico E. 1986a. In defense of computer monitoring. *Training* (December): 120.

_____. 1986b. In defense of computer monitoring. *Industry Week* 230(July 7): 14.

_____. 1987a. Computer measurement: Capitalizing on U.S. values. *Manage* 39(1): 21–23, 35.

_____. 1987b. Hallmark of a computer's measurement is fairness. *The Office* (May): 40–44.

_____. 1987c. Positive monitoring: How employees benefit from computer measurement. *Management World* 16(4): 40.

Hertenstein, Edward. 1997. Electronic monitoring in the workplace: How arbitrators have ruled. *Dispute Resolution Journal* 52(4): 36–44.

Hertzoff, Ira. 1996. Cookies are not always a treat for Web users. *Network World* 13(48): 38.

Heubusch, Kevin. 1997. Big Brother and the Internet. *American Demographics* 19(2): 22.

Hibbard, Justin. 1996. Monitoring employee access to Web. *Computerworld* 30(50): 71+.

Highland, Harold Joseph. 1996. The cookie monster. *EDPACS* 24(6): 16–18.

Hightower, Christy, Julie Sih, and Adam Tilghman. 1998. Recommendations for benchmarking Web site usage among academic libraries. *College & Research Libraries* 59(1): 61–79.

Hildreth, Charles R. 1997. The use and understanding of keyword searching in a university online catalog. *Information Technology and Libraries* 16(2): 52–62.

Hinton, William Dean. 1997. Are cookies crumbling our privacy? *PC Novice* 8(45): 83–85.

Hirsh, Sandra G. 1996. The effect of domain knowledge on elementary school children's information retrieval behavior on an automated library catalog. Ph.D. diss., University of California at Los Angeles.

Historic judgement on electronic surveillance. 1992. *CAW Contact* (December 4).

Hodges, Jane. 1995. C|Net offers Web traffic tracking. *Advertising Age* 66(35): 15.

_____. 1996. Technology for targeting offers range of options. *Advertising Age* 67(47): 46.

Hodges, Mark. 1997. Building a bond of trust. *MIT's Technology Review* 100(6): 26–27.

Hogan, Mike. 1997. Control your Internet access. *PC Computing* 10(6): 172.

Holtsmark, Eva. [1996]. WWW Usage Statistics. Web document located at http://www.uiowa.edu/~libsci/studentalumni/asis/d-lib.htm

Horn, Stacy. 1998. *Cyberville: Clicks, culture, and the creation of an online town.* New York: Warner Books.

Howard, Dara Lee. 1991. What the eye sees while predicting a document's pertinence from its citation. In *Asis '91: Proceedings of the 54th ASIS annual meeting, Washington, D.C., October 27–31, 1991.* Medford, N.J.: Learned Information.

Hubbard, Joan C., Daphyne Saunders Thomas, and Ben E. Bauman. 1996. Who's watching us now: Monitoring employee's work. *The Journal of Computer Information Systems* 37(2): 41–43.

Huebert, Ronald. 1997. Privacy: The early social history of a word. *Sewanee Review* 105 (1): 21–38.

Huff, Thomas. 1980. Thinking clearly about privacy. *Washington Law Review* 55: 777–794.

Huston, T. L., D. F. Galletta, and J. L. Huston. 1993. The effects of computer monitoring on employee performance and stress: Results of two experimental studies. In *Proceedings of the twenty-sixth annual Hawaii International Conference on System Sciences,* vol. iv, 568–574, Wailee, Maui, Hawaii.

Hutheesing, Nikhil. 1997. What are you doing on that porn site? *Forbes* 160(10): 368–369.

Iadipaolo, Donna Marie. 1992. Monster or monitor? Have tracking systems gone mad? *Insurance & Technology* 17(6): 47–54.

Internet a big hit at Florida days. 1997. *Direct Marketing* 59(11): 10–11.

Internet control. 1996. *Communications News* 33(10): 66.

Internet firms whittling at user's privacy, survey says. 1997. *Chicago Tribune* (June 9): A9.

Internet monitors can aim at workers. 1996. *The New York Times* 145(May 13): C3.

Interse Market Focus 3. 1997. *Computer Reseller News* 724: 134.

Interse upgrades Web site analysis tool. 1996. *PC Week* 13(50): 57.

Irving, R. H., C. A. Higgins, and F. R. Safayeri. 1986. Computerized performance monitoring systems: Use and abuse. *Communications of the ACM* 29: 794–801.

Is your computer spying on you? 1997. *Consumer Reports* 62(5): 7.

Jaffee, Larry. 1996. Measuring Web site traffic. *CommunicationsWeek* 599: 8.

James, Frank. 1997a. On-line firms offer privacy guidelines. *Chicago Tribune* (June 11): A1, A24.

_____. 1997b. Microsoft, Netscape join push for privacy. *Chicago Tribune* (June 12): C3.

_____. 1998. FTC urges Internet privacy laws. *Chicago Tribune* (June 5): A3.

James-Catalano, Cynthia N. 1997. Fight for privacy. *Internet World* 8(1): 32, 34.

Jenero, Kenneth A., and Lynne D. Mapes-Riordan. 1992. Electronic monitoring of employees and the elusive "right to privacy." *Employee Relations Law Journal* 18(1): 71–102.

Johnson, Happy, A. Edward Blackhurst, Kelly Maley, Cheryl Bomba, Terry Cox-Cruey, and Amy Dell. 1995. Development of a computer-based system for the unobtrusive collection of direct observational data. *Journal of Special Education Technology* 12(4): 291–300.

Jones, Chris. 1996a. Vendors unveil Web-site monitoring solutions. *InfoWorld* 18(43): 39.

_____. 1996b. Net Access Manager monitors users' habits. *InfoWorld* 18(47): 58.

Jones, Lynn. 1995. DoubleClick: "We're no peeping toms": Privacy cops say new Poppe Tyson service is too nosy. Web page located at http://www.worldata.com/roy10.htm

Kalfatovic, Martin R. 1997. Cookies: Stating the not so obvious on the Web. *LITA Newsletter* 18(4): 22–23.

Kallman, Ernest. 1993. Electronic monitoring of employees: Issues and guidelines. *Journal of Systems Management* 44(6): 17–21.

Kanigel, Robert. 1997. *The one best way: Frederick Winslow Taylor and the enigma of efficiency.* New York: Viking.

Karpinski, Richard. 1997. Privacy solutions needed for 1: 1 Net marketing. *Advertising Age's Business Marketing* 82(6): 34.

Keeping track of the traffic. 1996. *MediaWeek* 6(44): IQ32–IQ33.

Keizer, Gregg. 1997. Private parts. *Computer Life* 4(10): 52–54.

Keller, M. 1997. Reading the reader: Privacy, magic cookies, and info tracking. Web document located at http://www.has.vcu.edueng/epiphany/cookie.htm

Kellner, Douglas. 1997. Computers, surveillance and privacy. *Contemporary Sociology* 26(3): 374–375.

Kelly, Kevin. 1997. It takes a village to make a mall. *Wired* 5(8): 84, 86.

Kelman, Herbert. 1977. Privacy and research with human beings. *Journal of Social Issues* 33(3): 169–195.

Kidwell, Linda Achey, and Kidwell, Roland E., Jr. 1997. Toward a multilevel framework for studying electronic control systems. *Journal of Accounting & Public Policy* 16(1): 89–109.

Kidwell, Roland E., Jr., and Nathan Bennett. 1994. Electronic surveillance as employee control: A procedural justice interpretation. *Journal of High Technology Management Research* 5(1): 39–57.

Kidwell, Roland E., and Linda Achey Kidwell. 1996. Evaluating research on electronic surveillance: A guide for managers of information technology. *Industrial Management and Data Systems* 96(1): 8–14.

Kiernan, Vincent. 1998. Use of "cookies" in research sparks a debate over privacy. *Chronicle of Higher Education* (September 25): A31–A32+.

Kiesler, Sara, ed. 1997. *Culture of the Internet.* Mahwah, N.J.: Lawrence Erlbaum Associates.

King, Nelson. 1997. OPS: A better recipe for cookies? *Internet World* 8(10): 13.

Kingston, Andy. 1996. Andy's Netscape HTTP cookie notes. Web document located at http://www.illuminatus.com/cookie.

Kipnis, David. 1990. *Technology and power.* New York: Springer-Verlag.

_____. 1991. The technological perspective. *Psychological Science* 2: 62–69.

Kirsner, Scott. 1997a. Web of confusion. *AJR: American Journalism Review* 19(6): 34–39.

_____. 1997b. Close encounters. *CIO* 11(1): 24–26.

Kleiman, Carol. 1989. Computer monitoring of work puts employees in the hot seat. *Chicago Tribune* (April 17): D7.

Kleiner, Kurt. 1997. How will the Net's cookies crumble [editorial]. *New Scientist* 154(2078): 12.

Klingler, Steven P. 1997. OPS keeps data private. *LAN Times* 14(18): 32.

Kolb, Kathryn J, and John R. Aiello. 1993. The effects of computer monitoring in a multiple task environment. Paper presented at the meeting of the Eastern Psychological Association, April 16–18, Arlington, Va.

_____, and _____. 1996. The effects of electronic performance monitoring on stress: Locus of control as a moderator variable. *Computers in Human Behavior* 12(3): 407–409.

_____, and _____. 1997. Computer-based performance monitoring and productivity in a multiple task environment. *Journal of Business and Psychology* 12(2): 189–204.

Koning, Dirk. 1996. Private eye, public thought. *Grand Rapids Magazine* 33(5): 11.

Koprowski, Gene. 1997. Portrait of a web surfer. *American Demographics. Marketing Tools Supplement.* May: 16–19.

Krantz, Michael. 1995a. Keeping an eye on I/Pro: New Internet-user tracking service draws competitors' suspicion. *Mediaweek* 5(15): 12.

_____. 1995b. Web feat: Site auditing. *Mediaweek* 5(34): 23.

_____. 1995c. Did Casie strike out? *Mediaweek* 5(38): 28+.

_____. 1995d. The medium is the measure. *Brandweek* 36(36): IQ20–IQ24.

Krick, John. 1997. A cookie for your thoughts: Cookies help webmasters harness user habits. *Computer Shopper* 17(7): 610.

Kurth, Martin. 1993. The limits and limitations of transaction log analysis. *Library Hi Tech* 11(2): 98–104.

_____, and Thomas A. Peters, compilers. 1995. *Browsing in information systems: An extensive annotated bibliography of the literature.* Ann Arbor: Pierian Press.

Kustis, Gary A. 1993. The short-term effects of computer monitoring on stress, performance, and satisfaction. Master's thesis, Cleveland State University.

Kvitka, Andrew. 1999. WebTrends strengthens feature-complete suite. *InfoWorld* 21(3): 50.

Laabs, Jennifer J. 1992. Surveillance: Tool or trap? *Personnel Journal* 71(6): 96–104.

Lakos, Amos. 1997. Identifying and assessing library clients in a networked environment: Issues and possibilities. Paper presented at the Second Northumbria Conference, Longhirst Hall, England, September 9, 1997.

Lam, Kwok-Yan, Lucas Hui, and Siu-Leung Chung. 1996. A data reduction method for intrusion detection. *Journal of Systems and Software* 33(1): 101–108.

Lamm, Stephen E., Daniel A. Reed, and Will H. Scullin. 1996. Real-time geographic visualization of World Wide Web traffic. *Computer Networks and ISDN System* 28(7–11): 1457–1468.

Lamons, Bob. 1997. Is your Web site living up to its potential? *Marketing News* 31(22): 8.

Lancaster, F. W., and Beth Sandore. 1997. *Technology and management in library and information services.* Champaign: University of Illinois Graduate School of Library and Information Science.

Lang, Curtis. 1994. Privacy in the digital age. *New Media* 4(4): 64–68.

Lange, Larry. 1996a. Big Brother is surfing the Net. *Electronic Engineering Times* 907 (June 24): 1, 22, 113.

_____. 1996b. Net monitoring tool fuels debate over privacy. *Electronic Engineering Times* 931 (December 9): 24.

Larsen, Valerie Ann. 1997. Exploring user behavior utilizing statistical analyses of WWW HTTPD access logs: An enquiry employing net-frog. Ph.D. diss., University of Virginia.

Larsson, Ingrid. 1997. *Monitoring an OPAC: A transaction log analysis at the Stockholm School of Economics.* Stockholm: BIBSAM.

Larter, George. 1984. Electronic monitoring causes VDT stress. *VDT Newsletter* 2(3): 2.

The latest in Web tracking. 1996. *Legal Assistant Today* 14(2): 76.

Laudon, Kenneth C. 1996. Markets and privacy. *Communications of the ACM* 39(9): 92–104.

Lee, Edmund. 1996. Mad ave versus the cookie monster. *The Village Voice* (December): 22.

Lee, Lydia. 1996. Beyond the hits: Mining Web sites for traffic data. *NewMedia* 6(15): 38.

Lee, S., and R. S. Heller. 1997. Use of a keystroke logfile to evaluate an interactive computer system in a museum setting. *Computers and Education* 29(2/3): 89–101.

Leibowitz, Wendy R. 1997a. Personal privacy and high tech: Little brothers are watching you. *The National Law Journal* 19(32): B16.

_____. 1997b. Spilling your cookies on the 'Net: A big, silly food fight on privacy. *The National Law Journal* 19(43): B7.

Lemmons, Phil. 1997. When the medium watches you. *PC World* 15(2): 17.

Levine, Shira. 1997. Privacy, please. *Telephony* 232(25): 28.

Levy, Josh. 1997. Policing Web site traffic. *PC Magazine* 16(4): 40.

Levy, Michael. 1993. Electronic monitoring in the workplace: Power through the panopticon. Document was located at http://www.sils.umich.edu/

_____. 1995. The electronic monitoring of workers: Privacy in the age of the electronic sweatshop. *Legal Reference Services Quarterly* 14(3): 5–56.

Lewis, Chris. 1997. Internet Rx. *Network Computing* 8(1): 94, 96.

Li, Tianzhu. 1994. An inquiry of users' mental models of the ERIC CD-ROM system and their search process. Ph.D. diss., University of Washington.

Lim, Peter C. H. 1993. *OLIVE: On-line interactive validation and evaluation maintainence* [sic] *and enhancements of the system.* London: City University, London.

Lindquist, Christopher. 1999. Be Big Brother. *PC/Computing* (August): 116.

Linowes, David R. 1993. Your personal information has gone public. *Illinois Quarterly* 6: 22–24.

Li-Ron, Yael, Yardena Arar, et al. 1997. PGP products protect you against Internet snoops. *PC World* 15(3): 78–79.

Litras, Steven W. 1997. Aria will have Webmasters singing its praises; Solid Web statistics, flexible reporting make this a comprehensive system. *InfoWorld* 19(14): 44.

LittleBrother may be watching you. 1997. *The Los Angeles Times* (March 25): Home Edition, Business Section, p. 2.

Lockard, Joseph. 1997. Progressive politics, electronic individualism and the myth of virtual community. In *Internet culture,* edited by David Porter. New York: Routledge.

Lohr, Linda, et al. 1996. Using a hypertext environment for teaching process writing: An evaluation study of three student groups. ERIC ED 397815.

Long, Richard. 1989. Human issues in the implementation of new office technology. In Computers in the human context: Information technology, productivity, and people. Edited by Fom Forester. Cambridge: MIT Press.

Lucas, Henry C., Jr. 1971. Performance evaluation and monitoring. *Computing Surveys* 3(3): 79–81.

Lund, John. 1989. Computerized work performance monitoring, office workers and industrial relations outcomes. Ph.D. diss., University of Wisconsin, Madison.

_____. 1991. Computerized work performance monitoring and production standards: A review of labor law issues. *Labor Law Journal*: 195–203.

_____. 1992. Electronic performance monitoring: A review of the research issues. *Applied Ergonomics* 23(1): 54–58.

Luttjohann, Sean. 1997. No more secret games of solitaire. *LANTimes Online* (December). Web document located at http://www.lantimes.com/lantimes/97/97dec/712b041a.html, last visited on March 9, 1998.

Lutz, W. E. 1997. Monitoring your movements. *American Society for Information Science Bulletin* 23(3): 8–10.

Lyman, Peter. 1996. What is a digital library? Technology, intellectual property, and the public interest. *Daedalus* 125(4): 1–33.

Lynch, Jaqueline A. 1997. Web site statistics for capacity planning. *Capacity Management Review* 25(9): 1–11.

Lyon, David. 1991a. Bentham's Panopticon: From moral architecture to electronic surveillance. *Queen's Quarterly* 98(3): 596–617.

_____. 1991b. *Citizenship and surveillance in the information age.* Studies in Communication and Information Technology Working Paper. Kingston, Canada: Queen's University.

_____. 1993. An electronic panopticon? A sociological critique of surveillance theory. *Sociological Review* 41(4): 653–678.

_____. 1994. *The electronic eye: The rise of surveillance society.* Minneapolis: University of Minnesota Press.

_____, and Elia Zureik, eds. 1996. *Computers, surveillance, and privacy.* Minneapolis: University of Minnesota Press.

Machlis, Sharon. 1997a. Security experts: Hacker detection is key. *Computerworld* 31(9): 59–60.

_____. 1997b. Want security? See what hacker does with a cookie. *Computerworld* 31(13): 69–70.

_____. 1997c. Gotcha! Monitoring tools track Web surfing at work. *Computerworld* 31(14): 1+.

_____. 1997d. Wrestling with Web privacy. *Computerworld* 31(25): 47–48.

Machrone, Bill. 1997. The cookie monsters are after our computers! *PC Week* 14(26): 89.

Maddox, Kate. 1996. Traffic cops for Web servers. *Informationweek* 597: 44–46.

_____. 1997. Web counting field crowds up with new player. *Advertising Age* 68(44): 56.

Magid, Lawrence. 1996a. Caring about online privacy. *Informationweek* 577: 94.

_____. 1996b. Protection or control? *Informationweek* 582: 126.

Magney, John. 1996. Computing and ethics: Control and surveillance versus cooperation and empowerment in the workplace. In *Social and ethical effects of the computer revolution,* edited by Joseph Migga Kizza. Jefferson, N.C.: McFarland.

Malcolm's Guide to Persistent Cookies Resources. 1996. Web document located at http://www.emf.net/mal/cookiesinfo.html

Mand, Adrienne. 1998. Imgis becomes AdForce: Receives financing from AOL. *Brandweek* 39(31): 38.

Mandese, Joe. 1995. "Clickstreams" in cyberspace. *Advertising Age* 66(12): 1.

Mann, Bill. 1997. Stopping you watching me. *Internet World* 8(4): 42–46.

Mannila, H. H. Toivonen, and A. I. Verkamo. 1995. Discovering frequent episodes in sequences. In *Proceedings of the First International Conference on Knowledge Discovery and Data Mining, Montreal, Quebec,* pp. 210–215.

Manning, Jane, William Scherlis, Sara Kiesler, Robert Kraut, and Tridas Mukhopadhyay. 1997. Erotica on the Internet: Early evidence from the HomeNet trial. In *Culture of the Internet,* edited by Sara Kiesler. Mahwah, N.J.: Lawrence Erlbaum Associates.

Marketwave ships Hit List with DataLink Technology. 1997. *PC Week* 14(37): 32.

Markey, Edward J. 1997. A privacy safety net. *MIT's Technology Review* 100(6): 29.

Markoff, John. 1997a. When Big Brother is a librarian. *The New York Times* (March 9): E3.

_____. 1997b. Guidelines don't end debate on Internet privacy. *The New York Times* (December 18): 24.

Martin, Ellen Rooney. 1995. Chicagoans' software lets shops track "hits" on Internet sites. *Adweek* (Midwest Edition) 36(37): 8.

Martin, James A. 1997. You are being watched. *PC World* (U.S. Edition) 15(11): 245–247, 250–251, 254, 256, 258.

Martin, Thomas H. 1977. Monitoring and individual rights. In *Information management in the 1980's: Proceedings of the American Society for Information Science Annual Meeting.* White Plains, N.Y.: Knowledge Industry Publications.

Marx, Gary. T. 1985. I'll be watching you: Reflections on the new surveillance. *Dissent* 32(Winter): 26–34.

_____. 1987. The company is watching you everywhere. *The New York Times* (February 15): E21.

_____. 1992. Let's eavesdrop on managers. *Computerworld* 26(16): 29.

_____, and Sanford Sherizen. 1986a. *Social aspects of changes in worker monitoring and com-puter/communications privacy and security practices.* Washington, D.C.: U.S. Government Printing Office.

_____, and _____. 1986b. Monitoring on the job: How to protect privacy as well as prop-erty. *Technology Review* 89(8): 62–72.

_____, and _____. 1987. Corporations that spy on their employees. *Business and Society Review* 60 (Winter): 32–37.

_____, and _____. 1989. Monitoring on the job. In *Computers in the human context: Infor-mation technology, productivity, and people,* edited by Tom Forester, 397–406. Cambridge: MIT Press.

Marx, Wendy. 1996a. "Light years ahead" but still confusing: Web measurement takes big steps forward. *Advertising Age* 67(9): S8.

_____. 1996b. How to make the most of traffic site reports. *Advertising Age's Business Mar-keting* 81(7): 3.

Masud, Sam. 1997. Web site analysis: NetTracker helps. *Computer Reseller News* 729: 53.

Mayer-Schonberger, Viktor. 1997. The Internet and privacy legislation: Cookies for a treat? Web document located at http://www.wvjolt.wvu.edu/issue1/articles/mayer/mayer.htm

McCarthy, Shawn P. 1997a. How to serve up "cookies" to your Web site visitors. *Logistics Management* 36(1): 70.

_____. 1997b. The Netscape biscuit company serves up a snack that knows you. *Govern-ment Computer News* 15(24): 55.

McClure, Stuart. 1998. CyberGuard offers hybrid defense, lacks refinement. *InfoWorld* 20(39): 40C.

McDermott, Patricia. 1987. The differential impact of computerization of office workers: A qualitative investigation of "screen based" and "screen assisted" VDT users. Report to Labour Canada's Technology Impact Research Fund. Ottawa: Labour Canada.

McGlamery, Thornton Patrick. 1997. MAGIC transaction logs as measures of access, use, and community. *Journal of Academic Librarianship* 23(6): 505–510.

McMullen, John. 1997. Technology and insidious threats to privacy. *Westchester County Business Journal* 36(February 17): 16.

McNamara, Paul. 1998. Aptex strikes gold on the Web. *Network World* 15(1): 15.

Meckbach, Greg. 1997. Using software to monitor corporate Internet use: Big Brother tac-tic or wise network management? *Computing Canada* 23(21): 45.

Meeks, Brock N. 1997. Privacy lost, anytime, anywhere. *Communications of the ACM* 40(8): 11–13.

Meister, David, and D. J. Sullivan. 1967. Evaluation of user reactions to a prototype on-line information retrieval system. Report to NASA by the Bunker-Ramo Corporation under Contract No. NASA-1369, Report No. NASA CR-918. ERIC ED 019 094.

Mendes, Meredith W. 1985. *Privacy and computer-based information systems.* Cambridge: Center for Information Policy Research.

Mercury Interactive Astra SiteManager. 1997. *Computer Reseller News* 724: 134.

Messmer, Ellen. 1997. Consortium takes a shot at sorting out Web user privacy and busi-ness marketing interests. *Network World* 14(27): 35, 40.

Metcalfe, Bob. 1997. TRUSTe uses consents and disclosures to protect privacy on the Inter-net. *InfoWorld* 19(45): 159.

Microsystems releases Cyber Patrol Corporate. 1997. *EDI Update International* 9(6): 10–11.

Miezio, Kathleen Rose. 1992. Computerized performance monitoring and job design: Impli-cations for worker health and well-being. Ph.D. diss., University of Wisconsin, Madison.

_____, M. J. Smith, and P. Carayon. 1987. Electronic performance monitoring: Behavioral and motivational issues. In *Trends in ergonomics/Human factors IV*, edited by S. S. Asfour. Amsterdam: Elsevier.

Miller, Arthur R. 1969. Personal privacy in the computer age: The challenge of new technology in an information-oriented society. *Michigan Law Review* 67: 1091, 1223–1226.

Miller, Naomi, Martha Kirby, and Etheldra Templeton. 1988. MEDLINE on CD-ROM: End user searching in a medical school library. *Medical Reference Services Quarterly* 7(3): 1–13.

Mills, Elinor. 1996. Navigator "cookies" files will monitor Web user activity. *Infoworld* 18(9): 51.

Mobasher, B., N. Jain, E. Han, and J. Srivastava. 1996. Web mining: Pattern discovery from world wide web transactions. Technical Report TR 96-050. Department of Computer Science, University of Minnesota, Minneapolis.

Moeller, Michael. 1996a. Bien Logic's SurfReport frees up Web traffic reports. *PC Week* 13(15): 57–58.

_____. 1996b. Accrue digs deep for real-time Web analysis. *PC Week* 13(40): 38.

Moen, William E., and Charles R. McClure. 1997. An evaluation of the federal government's implementation of the Government Information Locator Service (GILS). Internet Web document located at http://www.unt.edu/slis/research/gilseval/titpage.htm, last visited on November 5, 1997.

Moore, Steve. 1995. Let the browser beware. *Computerworld* 29(35): 59, 64.

Morris-Lee, James. 1996. Privacy: it's everyone's business now! *Direct Marketing* 58(12): 40–43.

Mosco, Vincent. 1989. *The pay-per society: Computers and communications in the information age*. Norwood, N.J.: Ablex.

Mosley-Matchett, J. D. 1997. Much ado about cookies. *Marketing News* 31(4): 14.

Moukheiber, Zina. 1996. DoubleClick is watching you. *Forbes* 158(11): 342–344.

Move toward global Web audits. 1996. *Editor & Publisher* 129(43): 28.

Munro, Jay 1998. Web time at work. *PC Magazine* 17(6): 42.

Munro, Kathryn. 1998. Monitor a child's access. *PC Magazine* 17(6): 185–194.

Munro, Neil. 1997. The magnetic poles of data collection. *Communications of the ACM* 40(6): 17–19.

Murdoch, Guy. 1997. Cookie trails on the Internet. *Consumers' Research Magazine* 80(5): 2.

Murphy, Ian P. 1996. On-line ads effective? Who knows for sure? *Marketing News* 30(20): 1–2.

Murphy, Kathleen. 1996a. Tracking tools follow visitors' footsteps. *Web Week* 2(11): 29, 33. Web document located at http://www.internetworld.com/print/1996/08/05/software/tracking.html

_____. 1996b. Tool tracks employee surfing. *Web Week* 2 (13). Web document located at http://www.internetworld.com/print/1996/09/09/news/tracks.html

Murphy, Samuel, and Michael Lynch. 1996. Are you being served?— Solutions for your Web Site. *NewMedia* 6(7): 35–40.

Musciano, Chuck. 1996a. Collecting and using server statistics. *SunWorld Online* (March 1996). Web document located at http://www.sun.com/sunworld/

_____. 1996b. Analyzing your referrer log. *SunWorld Online* (May 1996). Web document located at http://www.sun.com/sunworld/

_____. 1996c. Log analysis redux. *SunWorld Online* (June 1996). Web document located at http://www.sun.com/sunworld/

Nash, D., and J. Smith. 1981. *Interactive home media and privacy*. Washington, D.C.: Collingwood Associates.

Nebeker, Delbert M., and B. Charles Tatum. 1993. The effects of computer monitoring, standards, and rewards on work performance, job satisfaction, and stress. *Journal of Applied Social Psychology* 23(7): 508–536.

Neff, Raymond, K. 1997. A new consortial model for building digital libraries. Paper presented at the Scholarly Communication and Technology Conference organized by the Andrew W. Mellon Foundation at Emory University in Atlanta, Georgia, April 24–25, 1997. Web document located at http://arl.cni.org/scomm/scat/neff.html

Nemo [pseud.]. 1996. C is for cookie. Web document located at http://www.suck.com/daily/dynaframes/96/04/10/

Nemzow, Martin A. W. 1997. *Building cyberstores: Installation, transaction processing, and management.* New York: McGraw-Hill.

Nerney, Chris. 1997a. Are cookies bad for you? *Network World* 14(17): 1, 14.

_____. 1997b. Net.Genesis releases faster Web site analysis tool. *Network World* 14(26): 35.

Netscape Communications. 1996. Persistent Client State: HTTP Cookies. Web document located at http://home.netscape.com/newsref/std/cookie_spec.html

Netscape, Firefly and VeriSign propose Open Profiling Standard (OPS) to enable broad personalization of Internet services. 1997. Web document located at http://home.netscape.com/newsref/pr/newsrelease411.html, last visited on June 2, 1997.

New 'Net ratings system debuts. 1997. *Broadcasting* 127(38): 107.

Niccolai, James. 1997. Web analysis tools attempt to master measurement of site traffic. *InfoWorld Electric* (Posted March 21, 1997). Also printed in *InfoWorld* 19(14): 62.

Nicholas, David. 1996. An assessment of the online searching behaviour of practitioner end users. *Journal of Documentation* 52(3): 227–251.

Nideffer, Robert F. 1995. Review of Who owns information? From privacy to public access, by Anne Wells Branscomb. *Social Science Computer Review* 13(2): 282–285.

Nielsen, Inger Hoy, Ingar Lomheim, and Irma Pasanen-Tuomainen. 1992. *Monitoring online catalogues (OPACs) in the Nordic Technological University Libraries.* Esbo, Norway: NORDINFO.

Nietzsche, Friedrich. 1967 [1901]. *The will to power.* Translated by Walter Kaufmann and R. J. Hollingdale. Reprint, New York: Random House.

9 to 5: The National Association of Working Women. 1985. *Hidden victims: Clerical workers, automation, and the changing economy.* Cleveland, Ohio: 9 to 5: The National Association of Working Women.

_____. 1986. *Computer monitoring and other dirty tricks.* Cleveland, Ohio: The National Association of Working Women.

Noack, David. 1997. Publisher's lawsuit seeks "cookie" files. *Editor & Publisher* 130(45): 32–33.

Noonan, Dana. 1995. Making sense of Web usage statistics. Web document located at http://www.piperinfo.com/9512/usage.html, last visited on April 15, 1996.

Novak, Thomas P., and Donna L. Hoffman. 1996. New metrics for new media: Toward the development of Web measurement standards. Web document located at http://www2000.ogsm.vanderbilt. edu/novak/web.standards/webstand.html, last visited on January 8, 1998.

Nunoo, Mildred. 1997. Blocking the information superhighway: Employers are finding ways to monitor and restrict employee Web use. *Black Enterprise* 27(6): 33–34.

Nussbaum, Karen. 1984. *The 9 to 5 National Survey on Women and Stress: Office Automation Addendum.* Cleveland, Ohio: 9 to 5: The National Association of Working Women.

_____. 1989. Computer monitoring: A threat to the right to privacy? *The CPSR Newsletter* 7(4): 1–5.

_____. 1992. Workers under surveillance. *Computerworld* 26(1): 21.

_____, and Virginia duRivage. 1986. Computer monitoring: Mismanagement by remote control. *Business and Society Review* 56: 16–20.

Oberndorf, Shannon. 1996. Sleuthing through cyberdata. *Catalog Age* 13(10): 1, 28.

Ofeldt, Richard F. 1991. Electronic monitoring of employees: Issues and guidelines. Working paper WP-91-019. Waltham, Mass.: Institute for Research and Faculty Development, Bentley College.

Oldenberg, Ray. 1989. The great good place. New York: Paragon House.

Olson, Richard L. 1996. The right to privacy in an evolving electronic communications media environment. Master's thesis, Saint Mary's University of Minnesota.

O'Malley, Chris. 1997. Snoops: Welcome to a small town named Internet where everybody knows your business. *Popular Science* 250(1): 56–61.

Oravec, Jo Ann. 1996. *Virtual individuals, virtual groups: Human dimensions of groupware computer networking.* New York: Cambridge University Press.

Oreskovich, Carlie. 1985. Computer monitoring debate rages. *The Financial Post* (September 7): C14.

Organization for Economic Cooperation and Development. 1998. OECD tackles privacy on the net. Web document located at http://www.oecd/org/dsti/sti/it/secur/news/privacynews.htm, last visited on March 1, 1998.

Ottensmeyer, Edward J., and Mark A. Heroux. 1991. Ethics, public policy, and managing advanced technologies: The case of electronic surveillance. *Journal of Business Ethics* 10: 519–526.

Page, Bob. 1997. Network-based Web analysis tools help draw a detailed picture of site activities. *Network World* 14(38): 43.

Papp, Leslie. 1991. Working under the electronic eye: Is it Big Brother or a necessary management tool? *The Toronto Star* (July 27): D1, D5.

Parent, William. 1983a. A new definition of privacy for the law. *Law and Philosophy* 2: 305–338.

_____. 1983b. Privacy, morality and the law. *Philosophy and Public Affairs* 12: 269–288.

Parker, Edwin B., and William J. Paisley. 1966. Research for psychologists at the interface of the scientist and his information system. *American Psychologist* 21: 1061–1071.

Pasanen-Tuomainen, Irma. 1992. Monitoring online catalogues in the Nordic Technological University Libraries. In *8: de Nordiska Konferensen for Information och Documentation, May 19–21, 1992 i Helsingborg,* 199–201. Stockholm: Tekniska Litteratursallskapet.

Pearlstein, Joanna. 1997. Bolero revision links to Oracle. *MacWEEK* 11(16): 14–15.

Peek, Robin. 1998. Privacy, publishing, and self regulation. *Information Today* 15(2): 38–39.

Penniman, W. David. 1975. A stochastic process analysis of on-line user behavior. In *Proceedings of the annual meeting of the American Society for Information Science,* edited by Charles W. Husbands and Ruth L. Tighe, 147–148. Washington, D.C.: American Society for Information Science.

_____. 1981. *Modeling and evaluation of on-line user behavior.* Final report to the National Library of Medicine. Dublin, Ohio: OCLC Online Computer Library Center.

_____, and Wayne D. Dominick. 1980. Monitoring and evaluation of on-line information system usage. *Information Processing and Management* 16(1): 17–35.

Perrolle, Judith A. 1996. Privacy and surveillance in computer-supported cooperative work. In *Computers, surveillance, and privacy,* edited by David Lyon and Elia Zureik. Minneapolis: University of Minnesota Press.

Peschel, Joe. 1997. Guard Dog chases cookies before they reach you. *InfoWorld* 19(46): 110F.

Peters, Thomas A. 1993. The history and development of transaction log analysis. *Library Hi Tech* 11(2): 41–66.

_____. 1996. Using transaction log analysis for library management information. *Library Administration & Management* 10(1): 20–25.

_____, and Martin Kurth. 1991. Controlled and uncontrolled vocabulary subject searching in an academic library online catalog. *Information Technology and Libraries* 10: 201–211.

Pfaffenberger, Bryan. 1997. *Protect your privacy on the Internet.* New York: Wiley Computer.

Piller, Charles. 1993a. Privacy in peril: How computers are making private life a thing of the past. *MacWorld* 10(7): 124–130.

_____. 1993b. Bosses with x-ray eyes. *MacWorld* 10(7): 118–123.

_____. 1997. Net regulation: How much is enough? *PC World* 15(5): 60.

Pitkow, James. 1997a. In search of reliable usage data on the WWW. *Computer Networks and ISDN Systems* 29(8–13): 1343–1355.

_____. 1997b. In search of reliable usage data on the WWW. In *Sixth International World Wide Web Conference, Santa Clara, California*, pp. 451–463.

_____, and C. Kehoe. 1996. GVU's sixth WWW user survey. Web document located at http://www.ccc.gatech.edu/gvu/user_surveys/survye-10-1996

Pitkow, James E., and Krishna A. Bharat. 1994. *WebVis: A tool for World Wide Web access log analysis*. Atlanta: Graphics, Visualization & Usability Center, Georgia Institute of Technology.

Piven, Joshua. 1996. Outsmarting the cookie monster. *Computer Technology Review* 16(11): 4.

Porter, David, ed. 1997. *Internet culture*. New York: Routledge.

Poster, Mark. 1990. *The mode of information*. Chicago: University of Chicago Press.

_____. 1997. Cyberdemocracy: Internet and the public sphere. In *Internet culture*, edited by David Porter. New York: Routledge.

Postrel, Virginia. 1998. The politics of privacy. *Forbes ASAP* 161(11): 130.

Pounsett, Donald. 1989. Making monitoring work. *Computing Canada* 15(24): 26.

Privacy and the cookie pushers [editorial]. 1997. *The Washington Post* (May 29): A22.

Privacy fears and the Internet. 1997. *The Washington Post* (June 16): A20.

Privacy group urges FTC investigation. 1996. *Direct Marketing* 58(9): 6.

The privacy police. 1997. *PC Magazine* 16(4): 10.

Prosser, William L. 1960. Privacy. *California Law Review* 48: 383–423.

Qiu, Liwen. 1993. Markov models of search state patterns in a hypertext information retrieval system. *Journal of the American Society for Information Science* 44 (7): 413–427.

Quittner, Joshua. 1997a. No privacy on the Web: Snooping on your friends and neighbors has never been easier. *Time* 149(22): 64–65.

_____. 1997b. Invasion of privacy. *Time* 150 (8): 28–35.

Rachels, J. 1975. Why privacy is important. *Philosophy & Public Affairs* 4(4): 323–333. Reprinted in *Computers, ethics, and society*, 2nd edition. 1997. Edited by M. David Ermann, Mary B. Willliams, and Michele S. Shauf. New York: Oxford University Press.

Radcliff, Deborah. 1997. You've been warned. *Software Magazine* 17(1): 34.

Rahmel, Dan. 1997. Log analysis. Internet system. Web document at http://www.dbms-mag.com/9707i04.html, last visited on November 5, 1997.

Raisch, Robert. 1996. True names have power: User identity and the Web. Web document at http://netday.iworld.com/business/ad-mkt/am960723.html

Rampey, Jennifer. 1996. Cookies tell all. *Dallas Business Journal* 20(11): 26.

Randall, Neil. 1996. What happens when you click. *PC Magazine* 15(18): 245–246.

_____. 1997a. The new cookie monster. *PC Magazine* 16(8): 211–214.

_____. 1997b. Cookie managers. *PC Magazine* 16(15): 159, 162, 166, 168.

_____. 1997c. Who goes there? *PC Magazine* 16(17): 253–263.

_____. 1998a. Web site analysis tools: The results are in. *PC Magazine* 17(5): 188–210.

_____. 1998b. Cookie managers. *PC Magazine* 17(6): 182.

Rapoza, Jim. 1996. Package lets managers keep tight rein on Net use. *PC Week* 13(47): 70.

_____. 1997a. Tools access Web site visitor data: Hit List Pro 3.0 more robust, but WebTrends 3.0 more affordable. *PC Week* 14(18): 35.

_____. 1997b. Sniffing out Internet abuse. *PC Week* 14(23): 51.

_____. 1997c. Fast track for web site data. *PC Week* 14(33): 39.

_____. 1997d. Product sizes up where users go on busy Web sites. *PC Week* 14(5): 27, 32.

_____. 1997e. Aria gives real-time glimpse of Web site visitor activities. *PC Week* 14(9): 38.

Raskin, Robin. 1996. Double Click: Cyber eyes are watching. Don't look now, but your electronic footprints are showing. *FamilyPC* 3(3): 25–26.

Raths, David. 1996. Tracking Web demographics. *Business Journal Serving Greater Portland* 12(51): 8.

A recipe for profit or loss? 1996. *Accountancy* 118(1238): 56.

Reiman, Jeffrey. 1995. Driving to the Panopticon: A philosophical exploration of the risks of privacy posed by the highway technology of the future. *Santa Clara Computer and High Technology Law Journal* 11: 27–44.

Reynolds, Larry. 1991. Rights groups condemn eavesdropping supervisors. *Personnel* 64(4): 19.

Rheingold, Howard. 1993. *The virtual community: Homesteading on the electronic frontier.* Reading, Mass.: Addison-Wesley.

Rich, Laura. 1996. CASIE revises guidelines for Web measurements. *Adweek* 46(51): 51.

_____. 1997a. Count them in. *Mediaweek* 7(5): IQ24–IQ26+.

_____. 1997b. NetGravity proposal tries to untangle Web reporting. *Brandweek* 38(20): 57.

Rigdon, Joan. 1996. Internet users say they'd rather not share their cookies. *The Wall Street Journal* (February 14): B6.

Rigney, Steve. 1997. Surveying the wave. *PC Magazine* 16(9): NE1–NE14.

Riley, W. D. 1997. Want to play Internet cop? *Datamation* 43(1): 39

Roberts-Witt, Sarah L. 1999. Make Net work, not play. *PC Magazine* 18(9): 189–204.

Robertson, Niel. 1996. Stalking the elusive usage data. *Internet World* 7(4): 28–31.

_____. 1997. A personalized web. *Internet World* 8(4): 32–34.

Robertson, S. E., and Micheline Hancock-Beaulieu. 1992. On the evaluation of IR. *Information Processing and Management* 28(4): 457–466.

Rochlin, Gene I. 1997. *Trapped in the net: The unintended consequences of computerization.* Princeton: Princeton University Press.

Rodriguez, Karen. 1996. Net.Genesis Internet tool tracks usage. *CommunicationsWeek* 594: 12.

Rotenberg, Marc. 1993. Communications privacy: Implications for network design. *Communications of the ACM* (August): 61–68.

_____. 1994. Electronic privacy legislation in the United States. *Journal of Academic Librarianship* 20(4): 227–230.

Roth, Martin S. 1998. Customization and privacy. *Marketing Management* 6(4): 22.

Rothfeder, Jeffrey. 1997. No privacy on the Net. *PC World* 15(2): 223–229.

Rothwell, S. G. 1984. Supervisors and the new technology. *Employment Gazette* (January): 23.

Rubenking, Neil. 1997. Who's doing what when. *PC Magazine* 16(6): 76.

Rubin, Jeff. 1996. Log analysis: A brief overview. Web document located at http://headcase.syr.edu/text/logs.html

Rule, James, and Peter Brantley. 1992. Computerized surveillance in the workplace: Forms and distributions. *Sociological Forum* 7(3): 405–423.

_____, Douglas McAdam, Linda Stearns, and David Uglow. 1980. *The politics of privacy: Planning for personal data systems as powerful technologies.* New York: Elsevier.

Ryan, Michael E. 1999. Net guards. *PC Magazine* 18(9): 273–278.

Sabga, Patricia. 1998. Cutting out cookies. *Working Woman* (23)1: 18–20.

Sacharow, Anya. 1998. Create your own Internet. *Brandweek* 39(19): 42–44.

Safayeni, Frank, Ric Irving, Lyn Purdy, and Chris Higgins. 1992. Potential impacts of computerized performance monitoring systems: Eleven propositions. *Journal of Management Systems* 4(2): 73–84.

St. Laurent, Simon. 1998. *Cookies.* New York.: McGraw-Hill Professional.

Sajaniemi, Jorma, and Ismo Tossavainen. 1996. Session length and subjective satisfaction in information kiosk research. In *People and computers XI: Proceedings of HCI '96*, edited by M. A. Sasse, R. J. Cunningham, and R. L. Winder. London: Springer.

Sandore, Beth, Patricia Flaherty, Neal K. Kaske, Martin Kurth, and Thomas Peters. 1993.

A manifesto regarding the future of transaction log analysis. *Library Hi Tech* 11(2): 105–106.

Sangster, Don, ed. 1996. Measuring net worth: Marketing's first virtual roundtable tackles the thorny issue of developing standard measurement and audit tools for the Web. *Marketing 101* (December 16): 6–7.

Santos, Paulo Alexandre Vieira Jacinto dos. 1995. Automatic detection of user transitionality by analysis of interaction. Ph.D. diss., Georgia Institute of Technology.

Santos, Paulo J., and Albert N. Badre. 1994. *Automatic chunk detection in human-computer interaction.* Atlanta: Graphics, Visualization & Usability Center, Georgia Institute of Technology.

Scanlon, Thomas. 1975. Thomson on privacy. *Philosophy and Public Affairs* 4: 315–322.

Schiesel, Seth. 1997. Software to track business prospects by Web visits. *The New York Times* (October 6): 7.

Schleifer, Lawrence M. 1992. Electronic performance monitoring (EPM). *Applied Ergonomics* 23(1): 4–5.

_____, Traci L. Galinsky, and Christopher S. Pan. 1996. Mood disturbances and musculoskeletal discomfort: Effects of electronic performance monitoring under different levels of VDT data-entry performance. *International Journal of Human-Computer Interaction* 8: 369–384.

Schmetterer, Bob. 1997. Meeting the measurement challenge. *Mediaweek* 7(18): S72+.

Schofield, Janet W., Ann Davidson, Janet E. Stocks, and Gail Futoran. 1997. The Internet in school: A case study of educator demand and its precursors. In *Culture of the Internet,* edited by Sara Kiesler. Mahwah, N.J.: Lawrence Erlbaum Associates.

Schorr, Joseph. 1997. WebWatcher 4.1. *Macworld* 14(8): 72.

Schroeder, Elinor P. 1988. On beyond drug testing: Employer monitoring and the quest for the perfect work. *University of Kansas Law Review* 36: 869–898.

Schwartz, John. 1996. Trail of crumbs leads right to the cyber-cookie jar. *The Washington Post* (June 24): Business19.

Schweitzer, Kurt. 1996. Footprints on the World Wide Web. *Business Journal Serving Southern Tier, CNY, Mohawk Valley, Finger Lakes, North* 10(21): 14SB.

Schwerin, Rich. 1997. WebManage Technologies NetIntellect. *PC Computing* 10(2): 292.

_____. 1998. SurfControl Scout. *PC Computing* 11(1): 346.

Scott, Gini Graham. 1995. *Mind your own business: The battle for personal privacy.* New York: Plenum Press.

Scott, Karyl, John Foley, et al. 1996. Surf alert. *InformationWeek* 583(June 10): 10.

Seiter, Charles. 1997. Bolero. *Macworld* 14(4): 68.

Sellers, Len. 1997. Who's on line? *Brandweek* 38(6): 24+.

Sessler, Joshua B. 1997. Computer cookie control: Transaction generated information and privacy regulation on the Internet. *Journal of Law and Policy* 5(2): 627–677.

Sewell, Graham, and Barry Wilkinson. 1992. "Someone to watch over me": Surveillance, discipline and the just-in-time labour process. *Sociology* 26(2): 271–289.

Seymour, Jim. 1997. Whom can you trustmark? *PC Magazine* 16(12): 93–94.

Shafer, Dan. 1997. A persistent problem. C|Net. Web document located at http://www.cnet.com/Content/Voices/Shafer/063097/index.html

Shaiken, Harley. 1985. *Work transformed: Automation and labor in the computer age.* New York: Holt, Rinehart, and Winston.

Shankar, Gess. 1998. Hit List 4.0 strikes gold with impressive Web mining tools. *InfoWorld* 20(42): 62–64.

Sheets, Scott. 1998. Understanding WWW statistics. *Managing Office Technology* 43(1): 18–27.

Shein, Esther. 1996a. Big Brother? *PC Week* 13 (30): 43, 49.

_____. 1996b. You can eTRUST us. *PC Week* 13 (50): E1, E5.

Sherman, Barrie, and Phil Judkins. 1996. Licensed to work. London: Cassell.

Shi, Xirong. 1990. Usage of the online library catalogue at the University of Toronto: An analysis of computer monitoring data. Master's thesis, University of Toronto, 1990.

Shoeman, Ferdinand David. 1992. *Privacy and social freedom.* Cambridge: Cambridge University Press.

Shute, S. J., and P. J. Smith. 1993. Knowledge-based search tactics. *Information Processing & Management* 29(1): 29–45.

Silberger, K. 1990. The electronic snitch: The dark side. *The Village Voice* (September 18): 83.

Silverman, Marian K., and Carlla S. Smith. 1995. The effects of human versus computer monitoring of performance on physiological reactions and perceptions of stress. In *Organizational risk factors for job stress,* edited by Steven L. Sauter and Lawrence R. Murphy, 181–193. Washington, D.C.: American Psychological Association.

Simons, John. 1997. In cyberspace, nobody knows you're Ira. *U.S. News & World Report* 122(23): 50.

Siochi, Antonio C. 1989. Computer-based user interface evaluation by analysis of repeating usage patterns in transcripts of user sessions. Ph.D. diss., Virginia Polytechnic Institute and State University.

Sliwa, Carol. 1997. Netscape and friends look to personalize 'Net surfing. *Network World* 14(22): 42.

Smith, David Sumner. 1996. Calculating the Net response. *Marketing* (November 21): 27–30.

Smith, Mark, and Gerry Rowland. 1997. To boldly go: Searching for output measures for electronic services. *Public Libraries* 36(3): 168–172.

Smith, Michael J., P. Carayon, and Kathleen Miezio. 1986. Motivational, behavioral, and psychological implications of electronic monitoring of worker performance. In *The electronic supervisor: New technology, new tensions — contractor documents.* Vol. 2 (PB88-156369). Springfield, Va.: U.S. Department of Commerce, NTIS.

_____, K. J. Sanders, S.-Y. Lim, and D. LeGrande. 1992. Employee stress and health complaints in jobs with and without electronic performance monitoring. *Applied Ergonomics* 23(1): 17–28.

Snell, Jason. 1997. Big Brother meets the Cookie Monster. *MacUser* 13(7): 96.

Snyder, Joel. 1998. Know your audience. *Network World* 15(35): 17–18.

Software Monitors. 1996. Software monitors and provides Internet usage statistics. *T.H.E. Journal* 24 (1): 50.

Spangler, Todd. 1996. Is your company watching your Web usage? — New products let network managers see all. *PC Magazine* 15(11): 36.

Spinello, Richard A. 1995. Ethical aspects of information technology. Englewood Cliffs, N.J.: Prentice Hall.

_____. 1997. The end of privacy: companies that collect information for a specific purpose can resell or reuse it for other purposes with impunity. *America* 176(1): 9–13.

Sproull, Lee, and Samer Faraj. 1997. Atheism, sex, and databases: The net as a social technology. In *Culture of the Internet,* edited by Sara Kiesler. Mahwah, N.J.: Lawrence Erlbaum Associates.

Stabin, Tova, and Irene Owen. 1997. Gathering usage statistics at an environmental health library Web site. *Computers in Libraries* 17(3): 30–37.

Stahlman, Mark. 1996. Yes, it definitely could happen here. *Computer Reseller News* no. 689 (June 24): 14.

Stanton, Jeffrey Morgan. 1994. Relationships among personal control, satisfaction and performance in the use of computer performance monitoring. Master's thesis, University of Connecticut.

_____, and Janet L. Barnes-Farrell. 1996. Effects of electronic performance monitoring on personal control, task satisfaction, and task performance. *Journal of Applied Psychology* 81(6): 738–745.

Staten, James. 1996. Navigator tricks raise concerns. *Macweek* 10(11): 18–19.

Stehle, Tim. 1995. Getting real about usage statistics. Web document located at http://www. naa.org/marketscope/conaghan/stehle.html

Stein, Lincoln. 1996. CGI scripts and cookies. *The Perl Journal* 3 (Autumn): 13–16.

Steinberg, Steve G. 1996. "Cookies" baking up concerns of Web privacy. *The Boston Globe* (December 29): F4.

_____. 1997. New Web-based technologies tackle on-line privacy issues. *Inside Tucson Business* 6(41): 9–10.

Steiner, Jon. 1999. iLux sheds light on commerce statistics. *InfoWorld* 21(2): 63.

Step toward audit standards. 1997. *Editor & Publisher* 130(February 8): 27i.

Stout, Rick. 1996. Tracking down your Web site traffic. *NetGuide* 3(10): 135–141.

_____. 1997. *Web site stats: Tracking hits and analyzing traffic*. Berkeley, Calif.: Osborne McGraw-Hill.

Straeel, Holly. 1997. Farewell to privacy for the sake of electronic commerce. *American Banker* 162(109): 8.

Stratton, Jon. 1997. Cyberspace and the globalization of culture. In *Internet culture*, edited by David Porter. New York: Routledge.

Strom, David. 1996a. Digging for gold in your Web server logs. *Computerworld* 30(26): 1.

_____. 1996b. WebTrends reveals site traffic patterns. *InfoWorld* 18(36): IW2.

_____. 1996c. Your Web page: Get what you paid for. *Forbes* 157(7): S36+.

_____. 1997a. Market Focus 3: Power that comes with a price; Interse product still needs work. *InfoWorld* 18(7): IW3+.

_____. 1997b. Hit List Professional targets log-file information; Marketwave tool can generate reports, giving explanations for the results. *InfoWorld* 19(15): 72H.

_____. 1997c. NetIntellect's many options illuminate traffic patterns. *InfoWorld* 19(5): IW1–IW2.

_____. 1997d. Find out who came to call and where with IIS Assistant add-on. *InfoWorld* 19(23): 74A+.

Sullivan, Eamonn. 1996. Are Web-based cookies a treat or a recipe for trouble? *PC Week* 13(25): 75+.

_____. 1997. Invasion-of-privacy fears can be based on fiction, not fact. *PC Week* 14(23): 44.

Susser, Peter A. 1988. Electronic monitoring in the private sector: How closely should employers supervise their workers? *Employee Relations Law Journal* 13(4): 575–598.

Szeto, Lai-Han. 1997. WebTrends provides no-frills site traffic reporting. *InfoWorld* 19(30): 76F.

Tabbi, Joseph. 1997. Reading, writing, hypertext: Democratic politics in the virtual classroom. In *Internet culture*, edited by David Porter. New York: Routledge.

Tabibian, O. Ryan. 1995. Untangling a Web of information. *PC Week* 12(45): 137–138.

_____. 1996a. Look who's visiting your Web site now. *PCWeek Online* 13(9): [unpaginated].

_____. 1996b. Two Web server analysis tools are suited for different environments. *PC Week* 13(30): 50.

_____. 1996c. net.Analysis Desktop shines in ease of use — But Web server analysis tool provides only limited site-usage reporting capabilities. *PC Week* 13(30): 43, 50.

_____. 1996d. The trends of the site are in. *PC Magazine* 15(20): NE19–NE22.

Talley, Brooks. 1996. WebTrends cuts through log files fast. *InfoWorld* 18(16): I8.

_____. 1997. Sniffer adds database decoding for optical packet-capture analysis. *Infoworld* 19 (32): 56D.

Tan, Boon Hooi. 1990. The effects of computer performance monitoring, extent of VCT use, VCT work-related experience and user age on job satisfaction and occupational stress. Master's thesis, University of Wisconsin, Madison.

Tauscher, Laura, and Saul Greenberg. 1997. How people revisit Web pages: Empirical findings and implications for the design of history systems. *International Journal of Human-Computer Studies* 47(1): 97–137.

Taylor, Catharine P. 1997. But there's a cache. *Brandweek* 38(43): IQ46.

Taylor, Cathy. 1996a. I/PRO, the Internet-measurement and auditing services, is developing a Dow Jones–style index of activity on the World Wide Web. *Mediaweek* 6(17): 14.

_____. 1996b. Cache-flow problems: Web sites angle for data on uncounted visitors from online services. *Mediaweek* 6(23): 13–14.

_____. 1996c. The Internet ratings race. *Mediaweek* 6(24): 6+.

_____. 1996d. A closer look at Web traffic. *Mediaweek* 6(38): 3.

Taylor, Dave. 1996a. Web monitoring: Is it your business where users surf? *InfoWorld* 18(26): IW11.

_____. 1996b. Responsible users require your trust, not an overseer. *InfoWorld* 18(20): IW16.

_____. 1997. A solution in search of a problem: 'Net monitoring software. *InfoWorld* 19(19): 68H.

Taylor, Frederick W. 1911. *The principles of scientific management.* New York: Prentice Hall.

Teinowitz, Ira. 1997a. FTC expands probe of privacy issues. *Advertising Age* 68(10): 43.

_____. 1997b. DMA campaigns for privacy rules. *Advertising Age* 68(20): 81.

Teitelbaum, Sheldon. 1996. Privacy is history — Get over it — The issue isn't privacy, according to science fiction writer David Brin, it's equality of exposure. *Wired* 4(2): 125.

Ternipsede, Harriet. 1993. Is electronic workplace monitoring stressful to workers? *CQ Researcher* 3(43): 1025.

Terrell, Steve, and Paul Rendulic. 1996. Using computer-managed instructional software to increase motivation and achievement in elementary school children. *Journal of Research on Computing in Education* 26(3): 403–414.

Tesoro, Jose. 1996. Is the electronic eye watching you? *World Press Review* 43(10): 22–23.

Testerman, Joshua O., Thomas J. Kuegler, Jr., and Paul J. Dowling, Jr. 1996. *Web advertising and marketing.* Rocklin, Calif.: Prima Publishing.

Thibodoux, Patrick. 1998. Media Metrix, RelevantKnowledge merge. ComputerWorld Online. Web document located at http://www.computerworld.com/home/news.nsf/all/9810121web, last visited on October 13, 1998.

Thomson, Judith Jarvis. 1975. The right to privacy. *Philosophy and Public Affairs* 4: 295–289. Reprinted in *Philosophical dimension of privacy: An anthology.* 1984. Edited by Ferdinand David Shoeman. Cambridge: Cambridge University Press.

Tichenor, Charles B. 1997. Javascript cookies. *Dr. Dobb's Journal* 22(5): 42–45.

Tiley, Ed. 1996. Diving into your server logs. *NetGuide* 3(6): 91.

Titus, Jon. 1996. Keep secrets. *Test & Measurement World* 16(12): 5.

Tool gives view of Web users. 1996. *InfoWorld* 18(9): 3.

Treu, Siegfried. 1972. A computer terminal network for transparent stimulation of the user of an on-line retrieval system. Washington, D.C.: National Bureau of Standards, Center for Computer Sciences and Technology. ERIC ED 070 461.

_____. 1973. Techniques and tools for improving the interactive system interface. In *Interactive bibliographic systems: Proceedings of a forum held at Gaithersburg, Maryland, October 4–5, 1971.* Oak Ridge, Tenn: United States Atomic Energy Commission, Office of Information Services.

Trott, Bob. 1997a. Privacy issue unites rivals. *InfoWorld* 19(24): 10

_____. 1997b. Site Server more than the sum of its parts. *InfoWorld* 19(35): 64.

Tuan, Yi-Fu. 1977. Space and place: *The perspective of experience.* Minneapolis: University of Minnesota Press.

Tuerkheimer, Frank M. 1993. The underpinnings of privacy protection. *Communications of the ACM* 36(8): 69–73.

Turkle, Sherry. 1996. *Life on the screen: Identity in the age of the Internet.* London: Weidenfeld & Nicolson.

Udell, Jon. 1996. Damn lies. *Byte* 21(2): 137–138+.

United States. Congress. Office of Technology Assessment. 1987. *The electronic supervisor: New technology, new tensions.* OTA-CIT-333. Washington, D.C.: U.S. Government Printing Office.

_____. 1993. Protecting privacy in computerized medical information. OTA-TCT-576. Washington, D.C.: U.S. Government Printing Office.

_____. 1995. Electronic surveillance in a digital age. OTA-BP-ITC-149. Washington, D.C.: U.S. Government Printing Office.

Vandore, Simon. 1996. Netscape's cookies crumble. *Australian Personal Computer* 17(4): 208.

Varney, Christine A. 1998. You call this self-regulation? *Wired* 6(6): 107.

Vaughan-Nichols, Steven J. 1996. Classic hits: Hit counters are the newest Web craze: Which ones will rise to the top of the charts? *Web Developer* 2(5): 48–52.

Vinge, Vernor. 1993. Technological singularity. *Whole Earth Review* (Winter): 88–95.

Viveros, M.S., M. A. Wright, S. Elo-Dean, and S. S. Duri. 1997. Visitors' behavior: Mining Web servers. In *PADD97: Proceedings of the First International Conference on the Practical Application of Knowledge Discovery and Data Mining,* 301, 257–69. Blackpool, Eng.: Practical Application Company.

Von Keitz, Beate. 1988. Eye movement research: Do consumers use the information they are offered? *European Research* 16(4): 217–223.

Wacks, Raymond. 1980. *The protection of privacy.* London: Sweet & Maxwell.

Wagner, Mitch. 1996a. Custom software helps Web users follow "hit" parade. *Computerworld* 30(10): 63.

_____. 1996b. I/Pro to let users compare their Web site traffic with averages of other sites. *Computerworld* 30(18): 66.

_____. 1996c. There's a new traffic cop on the beat. *Computerworld* 30(7): 57.

_____. 1996d. Repeat traffic is goal of customized Web sites. *Computerworld* 30(48): 1+.

_____. 1996e. News for you. *Computerworld* 30(49): 71+.

_____. 1996f. Measure for measure. *Computerworld* 30(10): 63.

_____. 1997a. Tracking web users is getting easier. *Computerworld* 31(9): 59, 63.

_____. 1997b. Privacy standard draws ire. *Computerworld* 31(22): 6.

_____. 1997c. Firms offer up smart software for Web sites. *Computerworld* 31(15): 68.

Wallace, David. 1996. Web tracking software is misunderstood. *Philadelphia Business Journal* 15(22): 12.

Walsh, Jeff. 1999a. Andromedia pumps up Web marketing, measurement. *InfoWorld* 21(13): 56.

_____. 1999b. Tracking software zeroes in on customer traffic. *InfoWorld* 21(15): 16.

Waltner, Charles. 1997. Online audit sticking point for papers: Proponents split on importance for winning ad dollars to sites. *Advertising Age* 68(17): S8.

Walton, Richard E., and Wendy Vittori. 1983. New information technology: Organizational problem or opportunity? *Office: Technology and People* 1: 249–273.

Wang, Huaiqing, Matthew K. O. Lee, and Chen Wang. 1998. Consumer privacy concerns about Internet marketing. *Communications of the ACM* 41(3): 63–70.

Warren, Samuel D., and Louis D. Brandeis. 1890. The right to privacy. *Harvard Law Review* 4(5): 193–220.

Waskul, Dennis, and Mark Douglass. 1996. Considering the electronic participant: Some polemical observations on the ethics of on-line research. *Information Society* 12(2): 129–140.

Wasserman, Elizabeth. 1998. The next revolution in computers will be so big it'll fit in your pocket. *Chicago Tribune* (February 19): E1, E6.

Web spies. 1997. *Consumers' Research Magazine* 80(1): 7.

Web Statistics Task Force. 1998. Web Statistics Task Force establishes guidelines for electronic resources. Web document located at http://www.jstor.org/news/newsletter/taskforce. html, last visited on May 14, 1998.

Weber, Thomas. 1996. Browsers beware: The Web is watching. *The Wall Street Journal* (June 27): B8.

Weise, Elizabeth. 1997a. Net privacy standards rolled out for federal hearings. *The New York Times CyberTimes* (June 4).

_____. 1997b. Small company plays large role in Net privacy. *The New York Times Cyber-Times* (June 14).

Weiss, Aaron. 1997. Baking your own cookies. *Internet World* 8(7): 85–88.

Weiss, Carla M. 1990. *Electronic monitoring in the workplace: A selected bibliography*. Ithaca, N.Y.: ILR Press.

Wellman, Barry. 1997. An electronic group is virtually a social network. In *Culture of the Internet*, edited by Sara Kiesler. Mahwah, N.J.: Lawrence Erlbaum Associates.

Welz, Gary. 1997. Cookie fears half-baked, say AOP. *Internet World* 8(8): 22.

Westin, Alan F. 1967. *Privacy and freedom*. New York: Atheneum.

_____. 1984. The origins of modern claims to privacy. In *Philosophical Dimensions of Privacy: An Anthology*, edited by Ferdinand David Schoeman. Cambridge: Cambridge University Press.

_____. 1986. Privacy and quality of worklife issues in employee monitoring. Washington, D.C.: U.S. Congress, Office of Technology Assessment.

_____. 1988. Employee privacy, work monitoring and new office systems technology. In *Proceedings of the National Academy of Arbitrators* (41st). Washington, D.C.: Bureau of National Affairs.

_____. 1992. Two key factors that belong in a macroergonomic analysis of electronic monitoring: Employee perceptions of fairness and the climate of organizational trust or distrust. *Applied Ergonomics* 23: 35–42.

_____, Gary T. Marx, Kristina M. Zahorik, and Willis Ware. Computers in the workplace: Elysium or Panopticon? In *Conference on Computers, Freedom & Privacy* (2nd: 1992: Washington, D.C.) New York: ACM.

Wetli, Patty. 1995. Demand for accountability. *America's Network* 99(19): 22–23.

Wiberley, Stephen E., Jr., Robert Allen Daugherty, and James A. Danowski. 1995. User persistence in displaying online catalog postings: LUIS. *Library Resources & Technical Services* 39(3): 247–264.

Wicklein, John. 1981. *Electronic nightmare*. New York: Viking Press.

Wilbur, Shawn P. 1997. An archaeology of cyberspaces: Virtuality, community, identity. In *Internet culture*, edited by David Porter. New York: Routledge.

Wilder, Clinton. 1996a. Keeping an eye on net usage. *InformationWeek* 586(July 15): 34–35.

_____. 1996b. Easier Web apps. *InformationWeek* 604(November 4): 59.

_____, and Gregory Dalton. 1997. The world wide watch. *Informationweek* 652(October 13): 54–58.

Wildstrom, Stephen H. 1996a. They're watching you online. *Business Week* 3501(November 11): 19.

_____. 1996b. Privacy and the "cookie" monster. *Business Week* 3506(December 16): 22.

Williamson, Debra Aho. 1995a. Digital Planet's plan to track eyeballs: Web developer forms NetCount to track site traffic. *Advertising Age* 66(17): 14.

_____. 1995b. Inching toward Web measurement. *Advertising Age* 66(42): 48.

_____. 1995c. Web searching for a yardstick. *Advertising Age* 66(41): 21–22.

_____. 1996a. Web 21 ranks sites based on traffic. *Advertising Age* 67(26): 36.

_____. 1996b. I/PRO may link with ABC to audit Web site traffic. *Advertising Age* 67(46): 6.

_____. 1996c. Web advertising saunters toward personalization. *Advertising Age* 67(47): 44, 50.

_____. 1996d. Web ads mark 2nd birthday with decisive issues ahead: Standardization and measurement are just two hurdles to face. *Advertising Age* 67(43): 1+.

_____. 1996e. Smart agents build brains into Net ads: More companies tap technology to better target Web users who visit their sites. *Advertising Age* 67(15): 26.

_____. 1997a. PC Meter forms two units: Web media and technology. *Advertising Age* 68(8): 78.

_____. 1997b. Wanted: Info on you and your interests: MatchLogic to build giant data warehouse for targeted ads. *Advertising Age* 68(20): 60+.

Wilson, David L. 1995. The network has eyes: With computers tracking on-line activities, users' anxiety over privacy grows. *The Chronicle of Higher Education* 41(45): A17–A18.

Wingfield, Nick. 1995. WebTrack lets IS managers monitor corporate Web use. *InfoWorld* 17(28): 10.

_____. 1996. WebTrends Windows 3.1 application will chart World Wide Web site statistics. *Infoworld* 18(2): 48.

Winne, Philip H., Lorene Gupta, and John C. Nesbit. 1994. Exploring individual differences in studying strategies using graph theoretic statistics. *Alberta Journal of Educational Research* 40(2): 177–193.

Winner, Langdon. 1991. Artifact/ideas and political culture. *Whole Earth Review* 73(Winter): 18–24.

_____. 1997. Electronically implanted "values." *Technology Review* 100(2): 69.

Wonnacott, Laura. 1996. Build a little ROI by ensuring productive use of the 'net: Optimal Internet Monitor 1.1 provides real-time and historical views. *InfoWorld* 18(45): N4.

World Wide Web: Hits that rate attention. 1995. *Inc.* 17(September): 115.

Worsnop, Richard L. 1993. Privacy in the workplace: Does electronic monitoring violate workers' privacy? *Congressional Quarterly* 3(43): 1009–1032.

Wreden, Nick. 1997. Insight or intrusion? Data mining's effect on privacy. *CommunicationsWeek* 650(February 17): 44.

Wu, K.-L., P. S. Yu, and A. Ballman. 1998. SpeedTracer: A Web usage mining and analysis tool. *IBM Systems Journal* 37(1): 89–105.

Wyly, Brendan J. 1996. From access points to materials: A transaction log analysis of access point value for online catalog users. *Library Resources & Technical Services* 40(3): 211–236.

Xenakis, John J. 1996. How to prevent cyber-loafing. *CFO: The Magazine for Senior Financial Executives* 12(8): 17.

_____. 1998. Every move you make. *CFO: The Magazine for Senior Financial Executives* 14(6): 23.

Yakal, Kathy. 1997. Don't want a cookie? Web privacy software gives you cookie control. *Computer Shopper* 16(3): 98.

Yan, Tak Woon, Matthew Jacobsen, Hector Garcia-Molina, and Umeshwar Dayal. 1996. From user access patterns to dynamic hypertext linking. In *Fifth International World Wide Web Conference, May 6–10, 1996, Paris, France*. Web document located at http://www5conf.inria.fr/

Yasin, Rutrell. 1996. Taking a picture of Web usage. *Communications Week* 620(July 22): 41.

Yesil, Magdalena. 1996. *Creating the virtual store: Taking your Web site from browsing to buying*. New York: John Wiley & Sons.

Zuboff, Shoshana. 1988. *In the age of the smart machine: The future of work and power*. New York: Basic Books.

Index